D1175428

THE MARCOS DYNASTY

Other books by Sterling Seagrave

THE SOONG DYNASTY

YELLOW RAIN

SOLDIERS OF FORTUNE

The Marcos Dynasty

STERLING SEAGRAVE

MACMILLAN
LONDON

First published in the United States of America 1988 by
Harper & Row, Publishers, Inc., New York

First published in the United Kingdom 1989 by
MACMILLAN LONDON LIMITED
4 Little Essex Street London WC2R 3LF
and Basingstoke

Associated companies in Auckland, Delhi, Dublin, Gaborone,
Hamburg, Harare, Hong Kong, Johannesburg, Kuala Lumpur,
Lagos, Manzini, Melbourne, Mexico City, Nairobi, New York,
Singapore and Tokyo

ISBN 0-333-45721-8

A CIP catalogue record for this book is available from the
British Library.

Designer: Sidney Feinberg

Printed by Billing and Sons Limited, Worcester, England

For Dorothy and John Sawyer

CONTENTS

"History isn't through with me yet."

—FERDINAND MARCOS

"She is reputedly as crazy as a rat in a coffee can."

—P. J. O'ROURKE *on Imelda Marcos*

"In politics, while there is death, there is hope."

—HAROLD LASKI

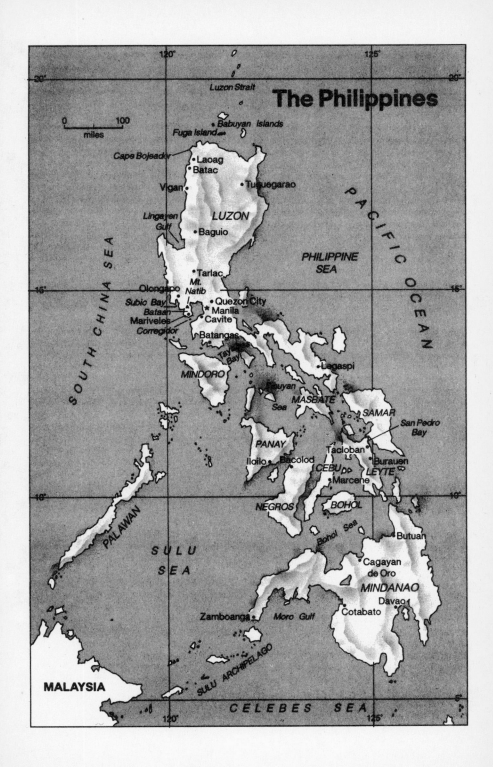

The Philippines

Prologue

A DISEASE OF THE HEART

BROKEN MASTS of sunken ships stuck up out of Manila Bay like a burned-out pine forest when I first arrived in the Philippines as a boy at the end of World War II. Ferdinand Marcos was then a young lawyer with a reassuring grin preparing to make his first run for Congress and his first million dollars, and Imelda Romualdez was a barefoot high school girl on the island of Leyte. Manila had been flattened by American artillery at the bitter end, but the fine old Manila Hotel on the bayfront seemed miraculously intact, some said because General Douglas MacArthur was a director of the hotel and had a penthouse on its roof; and over on the banks of the muddy Pasig River, where the bloated bodies of dogs drifted by on their way to the South China Sea, Malacanang Palace was unscathed, a sprawling Spanish colonial hacienda in the midst of its own walled park.

I made many other visits as a journalist over the years while Ferdinand and Imelda rose to power, secured the beginning of a dynasty, became arguably the richest couple on the planet, then in 1986 took what used to be called French leave, climbing tearfully aboard American helicopters with suitcases full of dollars in the time-honored tradition, heading—without yet realizing it—for exile in Honolulu, as mobs outside worked up the courage to storm the gates. The phenomenon of "People Power" took the overthrow of Ferdinand and Imelda out of the hands of ludicrously incompetent rival military factions; nuns stopped armored personnel carriers (everyone thought they were tanks) by kneeling in their path to say rosaries; and pretty girls blocked soldiers

1

in battledress to poke flowers down the muzzles of their assault rifles. There was a lot of weeping and singing, and in the midst of this great passion the knees of the renegade defense minister Juan Ponce Enrile were shaking so badly he could hardly stand up. Although he wore a flak jacket and carried an Uzi, and had a bodyguard of colonels and majors, when he passed through the crowds his real security was provided by a flock of nuns.

Under the Marcoses, Malacanang Palace had changed. Beneath its shady balconies there was now a "Black Room" where very special political prisoners were tortured. In addition to the three thousand pairs of shoes Imelda left behind, Filipinos searching the palace basement found her bulletproof brassiere, which could bring a tidy sum in auction at Christie's.

Manila also had changed. It was once a gracious city and may be again. But along the bayfront in the five-star tourist hotel district of Ermita facing the U.S. Embassy, little boys and girls age six or seven now plucked at the shirttails of tourists, offering to perform oral sex for a dollar. Among the most popular tours of the Marcos era were sex junkets for pederasts. As novelist P. F. Kluge observed, the Philippines had become "America's fellatrix."

From the heights of power—when they were fawned over by diplomats, bribed by an American president, paid off by the Pentagon, and indulged by the World Bank—Ferdinand and Imelda crashed into a public plight so demeaning it was pitiable. Under what amounted to modified house arrest in Honolulu, they appeared before television cameras like King Lear and his clown, wringing from the audience equal parts of sympathy and astonishment. In his humiliation, launching one desperate plot after another to regain the throne, only to have his most secret conversations taped and made public by men with fewer scruples than he, Marcos and his dynasty became a joke. Why, then, were we persuaded to take him seriously for more than twenty years? Was there some kind of game being played in which we ourselves were the unwitting fools? The answer, unfortunately, is yes.

Despite the blizzard of stories and TV interviews that followed the Marcos downfall, the public airing of Imelda's black lace underwear, and the revelations of grand larceny on both their parts, I found the Marcos saga deeply unsatisfying. What the Marcoses had done was clear—at least in broad outline—but not why they did it, what drove them to such extremes, and who helped them gain power and hold on to it so long. Among the press disclosures there were hints of Marcos' ties to underworld figures from America, Europe, Australia, China, and Japan; and there were reports that Ferdinand had been involved in peculiar gold bullion transactions with reputable bankers, statesmen, military men, and gold merchants. The sums mentioned totaled hundreds of tons of bullion, perhaps thousands of tons, far more than the Philippine gold reserves. Had Marcos actually found Yamashita's Gold, the legendary Japanese booty from World War II stolen from a dozen countries?

As I began to trace the secret bullion transactions, the real story of Yamashita's Gold unfolded in a totally unexpected manner. The facts and personalities were radically different from the legend and far more sinister, if that is an adequate word. Backtracking the trail of Ferdinand's involvement with the buried treasure, I was led eventually to a group of American generals, admirals, and former CIA officials operating as a shadow force of Paladins in world affairs—some of the same superpatriots identified with the Iran-Contra arms scandal, the Nugan-Hand Bank scandal, and other CIA misadventures. This tracing of Yamashita's Gold also led to a cabal of powerbrokers in Tokyo known as the *kuromaku,* the men behind the black curtain, whose wealth and leverage mysteriously survived Japan's defeat in World War II, emerging even stronger than before. These men—the Japanese *kuromaku,* the CIA Paladins, and Ferdinand Marcos—were all interlocked.

What puzzled me most about the Marcos story was the way Ferdinand was consistently portrayed as just another Third World politician, cleverer than most, who clawed his way up and then went bad—as if he suddenly appeared in the world at age forty-three. Everything before that was uncertain. Nobody knew much about Ferdinand Marcos—about his real origins, where his money came from, who his backers were, how he came to have an iron grip on America's only colony, and what made him so attractive to the White House, the Pentagon, and the CIA.

Over the years, Marcos avoided such questions and provided a self-flattering version of his life to biographers. They portrayed him as the superbright child of a poor but honest family in the north, a brilliant young lawyer who became the greatest Filipino resistance leader of World War II and the most decorated soldier in the U.S. armed forces, next to Audie Murphy. Unless you read several of these books about Marcos closely and noticed the discrepancies, there was no way to tell that his life was an ingenious work of fiction. To be sure, his campaign biographies were written by respectable journalists, including the Filipino editor and publisher Benjamin Gray, and the bestselling American author Hartzell Spence, who for many years had been the editor of the armed forces journal *Stars and Stripes* and was widely admired in the Pentagon.

It was Spence more than anyone else, with his military background, who gave the heroic Marcos legend a ring of validity when his biography *For Every Tear a Victory* was published in New York during the Philippine presidential campaign of 1964–65, which first carried Ferdinand and Imelda into Malacanang Palace. The Spence book was widely distributed to American newspapers and magazines, to embassies, and to U.S. government agencies. It was not clearly recognized that Marcos had tailored some information for the occasion. While some readers may have been suspicious, the mood in New York and Washington at the time was preconditioned to support Marcos, as the latest proxy brought forward in years of CIA manipulation in Manila, and as part of LBJ's desperate maneuvers to save face in Vietnam. Soon the most respected journals in America were repeating the gospel according to Spence, quoting long passages or summarizing his assertions as if they were palpable facts. After that, who was to challenge the authenticity of the Marcos legend?

Ferdinand learned a lot about presidential politics from Lyndon Johnson's example, as he had learned much from Douglas MacArthur about enhancing a military career. While MacArthur kept a public relations team busy full time identifying him as the hero of Bataan (to the private disgust of Dwight Eisenhower), President Johnson invented a grandfather who died heroically at the Alamo. Johnson then had no difficulty enlarging a minor incident in the Gulf of Tonkin into an excuse to escalate the Vietnam War. The same President Johnson had no problem praising President Marcos for faked heroics in Bataan, and did not hesitate to offer Marcos an open purse to back his Vietnam policy.

Many years later, several journalists finally gained access to long-hidden documents in the National Archives that exposed the fakery of the Marcos war record. They discovered that his claims had been investigated by the U.S. Army after World War II and were found to be false and "criminal." But these U.S. Army findings were tucked away for thirty-five years by the Pentagon, which resisted every effort to examine them, quite possibly with the approval of the White House or even at its instigation. Three presidents of the United States—Johnson, Nixon, and Reagan—publicly commended Marcos for wartime acts of valor that had been denounced repeatedly in the Philippine Congress over the years as sheer fabrication. The Marcos war hero fraud was ignoble enough, but Washington's apparent readiness to cover it up and capitalize on his vanity was far more cynical.

For these and many other reasons, the truth about Ferdinand Marcos is all the more interesting for what it reveals about others. It was easy to ridicule him after he fell from power, but he was really only a reflection; the insincere smile, the false heartiness, the watery mollusk eyes, the jaundice and puffiness of kidney decay, all looked disturbingly familiar. "While he lasted," a U.S. military attaché in Manila told me, "he was our boy. He was us. Maybe he still is."

Only after the fall was it generally agreed that there was something fishy about him all along.

The answers to Ferdinand Marcos are bound up in the secrets of his childhood.

There had always been rumors that he was illegitimate, but after centuries of Spanish colonial rule illegitimacy was not unusual among prominent people in the islands. The identity of Ferdinand's real father was well hidden and, in a place where tempers can be fatal, the persistent rumors were difficult and dangerous to verify. It was commonly accepted in Manila that his biological father was a wealthy judge in the province of Ilocos Norte, a man of Chinese descent who had paid the boy's way through law school, identified only as Ferdinand's godfather and friendly benefactor. Whenever Ferdinand mentioned such matters in his biographies, he assigned a name to his godfather that was completely misleading. Nobody realized that the identity of the judge was of special significance.

According to Ilocano sources close to the family, as well as respected journalists in Manila whom I have put to a lot of trouble, and several members of the old Marcos inner circle, Ferdinand's real father was not just a Chinese magistrate but a leading member of one of the six richest and most powerful clans in the islands, a billionaire clan involved in the daily financial, commercial, and political transactions that are the life-blood of the islands. Because of their clannishness and their control of the economy, Chinese in the Philippines are both despised and envied.

The leading clans (mostly natives of Fukien Province on the mainland opposite Taiwan) were traditional and conservative, and maintained close ties over the decades to the Chiang regime in Nanking and later in Taipei.

Once the stature of Ferdinand's father was confirmed, a number of other riddles were solved: How young Ferdinand eluded a murder conviction in his schooldays. How a place came to be waiting for him in a brotherhood Filipinos referred to as the Ilocano Mafia, whose pre-war enterprises were said to include smuggling, extortion, black marketeering, and murder-for-hire. And how, after the war, Ferdinand became a young congressman with extraordinary connections in the Chinese financial world, using his position in Congress to extort large sums from Chinese businessmen. The leverage of his father's clan enabled Ferdinand to ally himself secretly with agents of the Chiang regime, with Japanese underworld syndicates, and with some big-time American operators. His constituency soon floated like a huge jellyfish through the islands, trailing its tentacles everywhere.

Seen as a literary character rather than as a politician, Ferdinand Marcos occupies the rare and engaging role of the arch swindler, con man, survivor, and poseur, a role that has fascinated writers from Homer to Thomas Mann. For such men discovery is the unkindest cut, so some compassion is in order.

In Asia, lying to strangers bears none of the social stigma attached to it in the West. When Chinese are asked about their background, they usually invent one to suit the occasion. So do the Burmese, the Thais, and the Malays. It is a venerable tradition to lie to protect the truth, to protect one's ancestors, one's family, and one's fragile psyche, not to mention one's neck. It is not lying, but the creation of a fiction that will gratify the interrogator, which—on reflection—is really an act of courtesy.

Borrowing freely from others, the young Ferdinand Marcos created an entirely different identity for himself, a much happier one than his own, in which he was the hero, the boss, and the driving force. When he decided to go into politics, he went public with this fanciful legend, and used it to build a remarkable international career. In doing so, he was different from other charlatans only in the matter of degree. His success grew out of his resourcefulness, the gullibility of his audience, and the venality and opportunism of Washington.

When she married Ferdinand, Imelda did not suspect that she was tying herself to a consummate actor whose backstage life was drastically different. She did not know, for example, that he already had a common-law wife, and that he was already the father of three. A simple provincial naif, Imelda suffered at his hands a string of nervous breakdowns that transformed her into a relentless Filipina Medea, the enchantress who helped Jason gain the Golden Fleece but whose methods were frowned upon in polite society. Once Imelda grew used to the idea of falsification, she plunged vigorously into reconstructing both their histories. In his mother's hometown of Sarrat, Imelda rebuilt the Marcos "ancestral home" to create a museum. The original house was only a simple storefront. When she was finished, it was a fine hacienda complete with air conditioning and exhibit cases containing Ferdinand's shortpants from preschool days and assorted medals he never earned, including a U.S. Congressional Medal of Honor adorning a Marcos mannikin.

She did the same for herself, buying and remodeling one of the grandest houses in Manila, referring to it thereafter as her childhood home. In Tacloban, on the island of Leyte, she built a monument to herself, christening it the Santo Niño Shrine. Everyone in Tacloban called it "the Imelda Shrine." Set in a formal garden shaded by royal palms, the $30 million pink concrete palace looked like the box her shoes came in, furnished by someone who thought the Romanovs ordered Fabergé eggs by the dozen. The guest suites contained elaborate dioramas, crèche scenes depicting immortal moments in the First Lady's life: Imelda bestowing the wonders of modern technology on her "little brown people"; Imelda with Mao Tse-tung; Imelda with Muammar Khadafy. These miniatures were how she wanted to be remembered, not for three thousand pairs of size 8½ shoes, five hundred size 38 brassieres, and two hundred size 42 girdles.

On the second floor was a grand ballroom for imperial receptions. Silver his-and-her thrones sat before a faintly erotic floor-to-ceiling oil painting of Imelda rising from the sea like a Botticelli Venus. Beside the thrones stood the celebrated Santo Niño of Pandacan, a two-foot-tall ivory figure of Baby Jesus, dressed in the gold brocade damask cape and seven-league boots of a Spanish conquistador. On a more curious note, by the entrance to the throne room there was another shrine, tucked away in a corner, celebrating the mysterious origins of Ferdinand Marcos—a life-size statue of the Chinese pirate Li Ma-hong, who tried to establish his own dynasty in the Philippines in the sixteenth century. Ferdinand often hinted darkly that he was a direct descendant of Li Ma-hong. Since nobody knew he was 75 percent Chinese, they thought he was admitting to having the morality of a pirate.

To understand the peculiar grip Ferdinand had on the Philippines, it is first necessary to see why the Chinese occupy such an important position there. Chinese had been coming to the islands in small numbers since before the tenth century, while the Vikings were sacking monasteries in Europe. A few traders settled along the coast of Luzon, bringing with them silks, ceramics, metals, and mirrors to exchange for gold with the lowland Malays and mountain tribes like the terrace-farming Igorots. They maintained a modest trading link with Amoy, Canton, and Hainan, which were only a few days away by junk.

When Ferdinand Magellan anchored off Cebu in 1521, he found a scattered world of Malay stilt villages and fisherfolk living in aquarian harmony. Each community consisted of a few hundred people headed by a *datu,* or chief. Magellan was slain by warriors led by Datu Lapu-Lapu, and his crew completed the first circumnavigation of the world without him. It was not long before a flood of Spanish priests and conquistadors arrived in the islands to put matters right.

The Philippines grew rich on New World silver from Mexico. A small number of Spaniards in Manila (rarely more than a thousand) sent galleons filled with Chinese goods to Acapulco, where these luxuries were eagerly received, and the galleons returned to Manila laden with precious metals. After the Spanish traders in Manila took their cut, the rest of the silver and gold went to China to pay for its products, through Chinese middlemen in the islands. In this way, Manila became an important Chinese financial center as early as the sixteenth century. Around each Spanish settlement grew a support community of Chinese, who provided everything needed in the tropics, including energy. The way the Chinese handled their gold and silver and moved it around the Orient from Amoy to Hanoi and the Indies was never fully understood by the Spaniards, or any Westerner who has come to the islands since. But merchants were not the only Chinese attracted to the islands.

In 1574, three years after the Spanish moved their base from Cebu to Manila Bay, a squadron of Chinese corsairs—sixty-four war junks and three thousand men under Li Ma-hong—assaulted Manila and torched the town. Unable to drive the Spaniards out of their fortress, Li sailed north to Sual Bay, where he built a fort of his own and started a Chinese colony. A few months later, along came the Spaniards in what amounted in those days to hot pursuit. Three hundred angry conquistadors and twenty-five hundred easygoing Malays laid siege to Li Mahong's fort, burned his fleet of junks, and kept the Chinese bottled up for months till their provisions ran out. Li was no fool. He had his men dig a tunnel to the sea, and one moonless night he slipped away, leaving the islands to the Spaniards. Or so it seemed.

The Philippines, like other Spanish colonies, became a theocracy. Its administrators were less interested in heavenly estate than in real estate. As friars arrived and set about converting Malays, they acquired immense landholdings. In time, priests controlled twenty-one gigantic haciendas around Manila.

These Spaniards were fearful of the Chinese because of their incomprehensible language and customs, their greater numbers, their ambition, their financial acuity, their capacity to endure hardship, their secretiveness, and their clannishness. They put a ceiling on Chinese immigration, restricted their movement, confined them to Manila ghettoes, and barred them from citizenship or direct ownership of land. Periodically, Chinese were massacred.

Most Spaniards, like the Chinese, came to the islands without women and made temporary arrangements with Malay girls, producing prodigious numbers of illegitimate *mestizo* children. Fortunately, Chinese *mestizo* children were not considered Chinese. Raised as good Catholics by their Malay mothers, they could come and go at will, own land, and engage in business, more or less as Malay Filipinos did. However, since they had access to Chinese credit and often inherited their fathers' business sense, Chinese *mestizos* were in a much better position to buy property, and to act as middlemen or moneylenders, which gave them exceptional leverage.

Ordinary Malays foolishly but naturally tried to emulate their Spanish rulers by throwing pig roasts on feast days, christenings, confirmations, weddings, or any other occasion that came along. Without cash, in a rice and fish subsistence economy, they had to borrow money from the Chinese, using their traditional land as collateral. When the debt could not be paid, the land was forfeited. By this indirect form of extortion, more and more land came under the ownership of Chinese *mestizos*. The original Malay landowners became mere tenant farmers in their own country.

For Spanish *mestizos* there was a different path to wealth and power. Lacking the business sense, energy, and credit system of the Chinese, they turned to the professions, primarily to the law. Using the law, they enlarged their personal landholdings by entangling the original Malay owners in costly litigation. Any native Malays who had not already forfeited their land to the grasping Iberian friars were soon caught between the money squeezing of the Chinese *mestizos* and the legal squeezing of the Spanish *mestizos* and were turned gradually into a nation of serfs.

In 1896, the *mestizos* turned on their pure-bred Iberian masters and plotted revolution. The Spaniards responded by arresting and executing the wrong man—the celebrated poet and novelist José Rizal, who had remained aloof from the conspiracy. His barbaric execution drove the whole country into rebellion.

The rebel general Emilio Aguinaldo waged an effective military campaign against the Spaniards. Treachery always proving to be more effective than combat, the Spaniards offered Aguinaldo 800,000 pesos, to be paid in three installments, if he would leave the islands. Planning to trick the Spaniards and use the money to buy arms, Aguinaldo accepted the first installment and went off to Hong Kong, where the Americans found him the next year in somewhat shortened circumstances. He had spent all his money to buy weapons from a Japanese agent provocateur named Toyama Mitsuru, founder of the secret ultra-nationalist Black Ocean Society. After taking the money, Toyama claimed that the shipload of weapons from Japan had sunk.

The intervention of America at this point was less than praiseworthy. The United States now stretched from coast to coast, its frontiers were settled, a depression was eroding confidence, and politicians were looking for a diversion. A crusade against Spanish colonial oppression in Cuba and elsewhere seemed convenient. Chronic meddlers and robber barons went to work with the help of legions of Potomac jingoists. War became inevitable with the sinking of the battleship *Maine* in Havana in February 1898.

In Hong Kong, Yankee agents struck a secret deal with Aguinaldo, returned him to the islands, and supplied him with weapons. They carefully avoided putting any commitments in writing. While Aguinaldo resumed fighting the Spaniards, President McKinley sent Admiral George Dewey and the Pacific Fleet into Philippine waters, followed by a convoy with ten thousand Yankee soldiers. On May 1, 1898,

Dewey defeated the weak Spanish fleet in Manila Bay without the loss of a single man. Onshore, Aguinaldo's rebel forces gained control of all the countryside except Manila, and he declared independence on June 12, 1898. Filipinos became the first Asians to throw off European colonialism. It was instantly replaced by American colonialism.

Aguinaldo was tricked by the Americans into yielding his positions around Manila to Yankee soldiers. This enabled the Yanks to stage a sham battle with the Spaniards and to accept the surrender of the city for themselves, as an American war prize. Only then did Aguinaldo realize that the ten thousand Yankee soldiers offshore were not there to help him.

In Vice President Teddy Roosevelt's view, Manila would become an American Hong Kong. Others at home feared that Yankee blood would be mingled with that of "Malays and other unspeakable Asiatics." Admiral Dewey also advised keeping only Manila, and giving the rest back to Spain. But President McKinley insisted on having all the islands, describing his decision to Methodist churchmen:

> I got down on my knees and prayed to Almighty God for guidance. And one night late it came to me: we could not give [the Philippines] back to Spain— that would be cowardly and dishonorable; we could not turn them over to France or Germany . . . that would be bad business; we could not leave them to themselves—they were unfit for self-government. There was nothing left for us to do but to take them all . . . then I went to bed and slept soundly.

The successful Filipino revolution lay directly in the path of that irresistible American force called "benevolent assimilation," composed of equal parts Springfield rifle and apple pie. The Treaty of Paris ceded the entire archipelago to the United States. Although Washington claimed it had won the islands by conquest, no conquest had taken place and $20 million was paid to Spain as part of the Paris settlement. Independence had been sold out. Meanwhile, the U.S. Army was fighting Filipinos instead of Spaniards. Many American officers were veterans of the Civil War and the Indian Wars. To them Filipinos were "Niggers" or "Goo-Goos." By 1900, two thirds of the entire U.S. Army was tied down fighting in the Philippines.

The My Lai of this first U.S. guerrilla war in Asia occurred on Samar Island. Back home, President McKinley had just been assassinated and a company of U.S. soldiers in Samar was holding a memorial service when guerrillas disguised as women entered the church and attacked the Yanks with bolo knives, killing fifty-nine and wounding twenty-three. General Jacob Smith vowed to turn Samar into "a howling wilderness," and proceeded to do so. (It has never recovered.) Said he, "I want no prisoners. I wish you to kill and burn: the more you kill and burn the better you will please me." His men went on a rampage, with orders to "kill everyone over the age of ten," burning whole towns, torturing and slaughtering unarmed men, women, and children. Major General Adna Chaffee advised reporters not to be sentimental about the death of "a few Goo-Goos."

It was an ugly war and American soldiers wrote home about it:

> Last night one of our boys was found shot and his stomach cut open. Immediately orders were received from General Wheaton to burn the town and kill every native in sight, which was done to a finish. About one thousand men, women and children were reported killed. I am probably growing hard-hearted for I am in my glory when I can sight my gun on some darkskin and pull the trigger. . . . Tell all my friends that I am doing everything I can for Old Glory and for America I love so well.

. . . . . .

> As we approached the town the word passed along the line that there would be no prisoners taken. It meant we were to shoot every living thing in sight—man, woman or child. . . . Dum dum bullets were used in the massacre, but we were not told the name of the bullets. We didn't have to be told. We knew what they were.

On top of war, by 1902 the Philippines was crippled by famine. Wealthy landowners decided that some things were more important than independence, and threw their support to the Yankees. When America passed a law that any Filipino who continued to resist would be ineligible for a job in the colonial civil service, the middle class defected. Fighting ceased. Washington claimed victory and the American public put the whole unsavory affair out of mind. The war had lasted three years; only 883 Americans died in battle, 3,349 more of disease. Of the 1 million dead Filipinos (out of a population of 6 million), 16,000 were guerrillas, 984,000 civilians.

In place of Yankee soldiers came missionaries and teachers. Benevolent assimilation entered its apple-pie stage. William Howard Taft, weighing in at 300 pounds, was sent to head the first civil government in America's sole colony. This unique colonial experiment began with a declaration of principle, in language recalling the oratory of Tom Paine:

> . . . the Commission should bear in mind that the government which they are establishing is designed not for our satisfaction or for the expression of our theoretical views, but for the happiness, peace and prosperity of the people of the Philippine Islands . . . that the people of the Islands should be made plainly to understand, that there are certain great principles of government . . . essential to the rule of law and the maintenance of individual freedom . . . and that these principles and these rules of government must be established and maintained in their islands for the sake of their liberty and happiness, however much they may conflict with the customs or laws of procedure with which they are familiar.

Other great principles of government soon interfered, however. Taft was instructed to investigate the titles to large land tracts held by individuals or religious orders, and to correct any abuses. But the White House had to take into account the Vatican's influence on Catholic voters in America. Church lands in the islands were not seized after all. As a compromise, the Vatican agreed to substitute non-Spanish and Filipino priests for the hated Iberian friars, a rotation that posed only a minor inconvenience to the Church, and in return America purchased seventeen of the twenty-one friar haciendas around Manila from the Vatican for over $7 million. In a single grand public display intended to put the whole land reform issue to rest once and for all, these haciendas were sold in tiny parcels to former tenants, at a ruinous 8 percent interest rate far beyond their means. To meet interest payments, the Malay purchasers again had to borrow from Chinese moneylenders, soon forfeiting their land once more. Corrupt local officials helped divest unschooled farmers of their property, and by 1946, after half a century of enlightened and democratic American rule, the tenancy rate in the Philippines was actually higher than it had been under the feudal Spaniards. A Jesuit priest who spent thirteen years in the dehumanizing poverty of pre-revolutionary China came then to the island of Negros, the sugar capital of the Philippines, and was horrified to find it worse. "I never saw [in China] the exploitation of man by man," he said, "that I have seen in the Philippines."

The government in Manila became a genial collaboration between ambitious Americans and rich Filipino landowners. Four hundred millionaire families controlled 90 percent of the wealth. At their center were forty billionaire families who rivaled the great fortunes of Paris, London, and New York—the Rothschilds, the Mellons, the Rockefellers. Sugar generated many of these fortunes in a perverse way. Philippine sugar, so inefficiently produced that it could not compete on world markets, was allowed to enter the United States duty free. In return, Washington was guaranteed the support of a powerful political-economic bloc in Manila which mediated all issues with Filipino peasants and the middle class. Sugar barons held political power while Chinese clans controlled high finance. Of the top ten Chinese clans in this inner group of forty billionaire families, Ferdinand's clan ranked number six.

Outside Manila, provincial dynasties developed—such as the Laurels in Batangas, the Aquinos and Cojuangcos in Tarlac, the Quirinos and Crisologos in Ilocos Sur, the Lopezes in the Visayas—which formed temporary alliances to further their political ends. Unlike America, where the great industrial monopolies were broken up in the 1930s and "trust busting" has continued ever since, these corrective measures were never dispatched across the Pacific and implemented in America's colony. So the wealth of the Philippines remained in the tight grip of a few hundred families. In concept, this oligarchy was rigidly medieval in the Spanish model, but under America they became masters of insincerity. Democracy was only a well-oiled pretense. The most shopworn joke in Manila was that the Philippines had spent "three hundred years in a convent, fifty years in a brothel." The oligarchy kept the keys.

When asked about the enormous wealth that she and Ferdinand had amassed, Imelda once quipped, "Some are smarter than others." It was more than just a catch phrase. Ferdinand Marcos was beyond question a genius.

As a man who understood what Washington wanted, he and the White House had a courtship of favors. With America's blessing, Manila under the Marcoses became a center for money-laundering, arms trafficking, narcotics, amphetamines, gambling, white slavery, and the world center for child prostitution. The false specter of a Communist takeover, always made to seem imminent, and the exaggerated threat this posed to U.S. bases, were used to maintain a dictator who equally served American business and international organized crime. The Pentagon once added $300 million to its $500 million base rent merely to placate Imelda. The American general who negotiated this bloated deal then became the head of the Manila branch of the CIA-backed Australian bank where the Marcoses illegally deposited some of their money, including what may have been a sizable tranche of Yamashita's Gold.

Ferdinand Marcos may yet earn a place in history as an extraordinarily gifted politician who gave his countrymen what they really wanted in a leader, and still had the energy and the cunning left to swindle the people who helped put him there. If his kidneys had not failed him, the dynasty he founded might have become a permanent fixture.

What urge compelled him to keep accumulating wealth beyond any possible use for it? After $10 or $20 billion, what was the point? Unlike Imelda, who could always find some bibelot on which to lavish a few hundred million, Ferdinand seemed completely disinterested in spending it. He never missed a chance to extort a few million more, even from the transhipment of sardines that were well beyond their shelf life. Perhaps the act of getting away with it gratified some burning need to prove that he was a superman of Nietschean proportions. But was he the organ grinder or the organ grinder's monkey?

Hernan Cortés, in the midst of looting the Aztec civilization, melting down its marvelous objects in gold, burning its books, and demolishing its temples stone by stone, paused to offer Moctezuma a word of explanation. "I and my companions," he said, "have a disease of the heart which can be cured only by gold."

Perhaps Li Ma-hong could explain. His tunnel is still there, and it leads to strange discoveries.

One

MURDER MOST FOUL

FAR ABOVE MANILA in the northwest corner of Luzon is a dry, impoverished region called the Ilocos, a dusty yellow land with crumbling red brick churches. It bears more resemblance to Sicily or Sardinia than to visions of Pacific paradise. The small provinces called Ilocos Norte and Ilocos Sur are shielded from the rest of Luzon by a ridge of blue mountains inhabited by isolated hill tribes. Here life has never been easy. Survival was an act of desperation. The brown, weatherbeaten faces of the Ilocanos show grim self-reliance. According to tradition, they were forced out of Borneo long ago and settled here because these inhospitable valleys were only lightly inhabited. Nobody else wanted them. Adapting to the harsh landscape, the Ilocanos became more resourceful, more cunning, more clannish, and more vengeful than any other ethnic group in the archipelago.

The first European to arrive was a young Spanish nobleman, the conquistador Juan de Salcedo. In 1571, at the age of twenty-two, he sailed up from the original Spanish colony on Cebu to establish the new settlement of Manila, and then explored the coast of northern Luzon, founding many of the principal towns that remain today. He was appointed lieutenant-governor of the Ilocos, but died suddenly of fever at the age of twenty-seven.

The Spaniards had mixed opinions of the scantily clad Ilocanos. Some found them "more barbarous than the Tagalogs" to the south, while others considered them "a quiet and peaceful people, [who] dislike war, and are humble and well-disposed." It was the twofold

16

nature of Ilocanos to be very agreeable up to a point and then, when their sense of honor was disturbed, violent to a degree unusual even for the Malay archipelago, where the word *amok* originates. Pistols and rifles are common as toothpicks, and men boast of being crack shots, or black belts in karate. Boys carry butterfly knives, the Filipino switch-blade, flicking them open and closed with a wrist motion similar to twirling karate nunchuks. In more recent years, family and political grudges have been settled by burning down whole villages with flame-throwers.

Under Spanish rule, the Ilocanos grew cigar tobacco and rice, garlic and onions, and other vegetables; they harvested fish, salt, coconut, wove their own cloth, and smuggled goods the short distance from Hong Kong and Taiwan, only three days' sail.

Spaniards from sun-baked Grenada in particular felt at home here, and built most of the churches and haciendas. These friars were all Augustinians. They hired Chinese masons, who mixed sugarcane juice with coral limestone to produce bricks for the churches. Today there are primary schools in every town; literacy is high at 70 percent, but so is unemployment. There are only two roads out through the moun-tains, and a few bridges, which made it easy for local warlords to enforce control, to wage feuds and vendettas like the dons and capos of Sicily. It is an intensely parochial place.

Ilocano women are small, fine-boned, and pretty, but a hard life and family jealousies quickly take their toll. Ilocano men, although reaction-ary politically and thrifty by nature, spend like Beau Brummell on clothes and jewelry (for themselves) and like to prance and strut. Be-cause they are so poor, appearances mean a lot, especially in towns like Laoag, Sarrat, and Batac where people without money like to pretend that they have. In the absence of plumbing, villagers still wash their clothes, brush teeth, bathe, and defecate in the same muddy streams. There are several unattractive new towns with lights, toilets, TV, and paved streets, built by President Marcos as a birthday present to him-self. One is a village called Ferdinand, in a new community called Marcos.

The provincial capital of Ilocos Norte is Laoag, a stunted town which never grew into a city. It is built around a central market, and in addition to churches has a few very modest Chinese and Ilocano restau-rants, general stores, silversmiths, soap and candle makers, a town hall, a courthouse, and a jail. In the streets, besides ubiquitous Filipino jeepneys, some of them survivors of World War II, the favorite transportation for adults is the creaking, horse-drawn *banca,* or sway-backed Detroit dinosaurs with tail fins and musical horns playing the first bar of the Colonel Bogey March. Since cars are beyond the reach of most young Ilocanos, motorcycle gangs are everywhere, roaring through town like cowboys on payday.

Small, varicolored chickens patrol the country lanes, but there are few dogs to be seen, for good reason. On feast days they are eaten.

Here in the Ilocos, absolute loyalty to the family and the clan means resenting everybody else. Ilocanos make a fetish of traits that differentiate them from other Filipinos. Starting from the family cell and the blood clan, their tribal loyalties expand outward through a series of concentric circles by the practice of ritual kinship—friends who are not related are drawn into the clan by making them *compadres.* As in Chinese secret societies, this is a way to enlarge the only dependable support group (the family) into a much greater and more potent force. When the need arises, Ilocanos can extend *compadrazgo* to everyone in their home village, and ultimately to the entire ethnic bloc. So much superstition and magic are invoked that to be an Ilocano is like being born into the Rosicrucians, or some Satanic cult, and many Ilocano males act as if they were born with a forked penis. The typical adult boasts of having divine powers by implanting a tiny amulet, or *anting-anting,* beneath the skin, which can make him invisible, or bulletproof, or telepathic. Any small scar can be claimed as the site of a powerful *anting-anting.* The wonder is that they are believed.

Numerology is big and superstition strong, especially among the gangs and murder syndicates that thrive in Ilocano communities throughout the Philippines, particularly in Nueva Vizcaya, and in Pampanga just north of Manila. Former Labor Minister Blas Ople observed that, among Ilocanos, "Family feuds are passed on from generation to generation, and the dark instinctual drives sometimes shape the political alignments . . . even now the rule of the gun considerably modifies the rule of law in that province."

Political connections are vital to the gangs that dominate smuggling along the coast. Much of the smuggling comes in through a chain of small islands used as staging bases, the northernmost lying only 241 kilometers (150 miles) from Taiwan. The main smuggling stronghold is Fuga Island. From there, goods move around Cape Bojeador to Laoag, and on down the east and west coasts of Luzon to smuggling ports like

Cavite on Manila Bay, transhipped by the Ilocano underworld in league with shadowy Chinese syndicates that finance the black market throughout the archipelago. It is a rule of thumb that whoever bosses Ilocos Norte and Ilocos Sur also controls this flow of smuggled goods from the north, taking a percentage off the top. The bigger Ilocano clans—such as the one of warlord Floro Crisologo—have private armies of two hundred to three hundred paid thugs armed with Uzi machine guns, M-16s, and grenades, many of them sadists and professional killers. Their only distinction in life is the ease with which they can inflict spectacular cruelty, and Filipino newspapers are unique in Asia for their grisly homicides. With so many gangs smuggling everything from ginger fists and garlic cloves to television sets and computers, ambushes are common, and there are periodic executions and assassinations. In the Philippines, a slow ritual murder is preferred: the victim is given a *coup de grâce* with a bullet only after his eyeballs have been plucked from their sockets.

Young Ilocanos, as prisoners of this lingering medieval past, inevitably dream of escaping. Traditionally, they sought employment elsewhere in the islands as domestics and drivers. In recent decades, thousands emigrated to undeveloped Mindanao, to the Middle East, and to Hawaii, California, and British Columbia. In Honolulu, they became the largest single group of Filipinos and formed a potent voting bloc. In the Arabian Gulf, they earned fat salaries for contract labor, and sent most of it in remittances home. The government of the Philippines earned millions each year from taxes on the remittances. For an Ilocano, anything was possible. So there was always hope.

In the century before World War II, the Ilocos produced two famous personalities: the revolutionary bishop Gregorio Aglipay and a revolutionary general, Artemio Ricarte. Aglipay led the fight to expel the Iberian friars and Filipinize Catholic priests and properties, producing one of the few tangible successes of the revolution. General Ricarte refused to cave in to the Americans and continued to plot against them until he died during World War II. But each town has its local heroes, intellectuals who died protecting a village from warlord gangs, poets who became crusading newspaper editors in Manila, a guerrilla leader who fought the Americans or the Japanese or both, and students who resisted the encroachment of great logging companies or the insidious exploitations of multinational corporations.

During the Philippine-American War, all the able-bodied men in the farming town of Sarrat marched on Laoag to protest American rule. The Sarrat Heroes Monument was built to honor the leader of the march, the wealthy landowner Don Jose Ver, who in appreciation fathered a lot of local children in and out of wedlock.

In the same town of Sarrat on September 11, 1917, Ferdinand Emmanuel Edralin Marcos was born above the store owned by his maternal grandparents, followed over the years by his siblings Pacifico (1919), Elizabeth (1920), and Fortuna (1925).

When he grew up, Filipinos called him Ferdie, but among foreigners he referred to himself as Fred or Andy. As a child he was very poor and like his playmates ran around the dirt streets without pants. His mother, Josefa Edralin Marcos, was a hardworking grade-school teacher who doubled as a clerk in her parents' store. A tough, desperate, and resourceful young woman, she had to work hard because her husband Mariano Marcos was a spendthrift who was never at home and rarely had two pesos to rub together. When he did, they were spent on his cronies.

Josefa Edralin was part Chinese, part Ilocano. Her paternal ancestors were local Ilocano village chiefs who were permitted by the Spaniards to keep their landholdings in return for their loyalty and the loyalty of their followers. Josefa's father, Fructuoso Edralin, whose name must have taken some living up to, was a comparatively prosperous peasant. He owned 80 hectares of irrigated rice land and coffee plantation along the river in the barrio of Dingras near Sarrat, and another 50 hectares farther inland. By the time his grandson Ferdinand was born, Fructuoso was in the process of expanding his property by clearing 100 hectares of virgin forest at the foot of the mountains to grow more coffee. All forest land had once belonged to the Spanish Crown, but under American rule a public land law made it available in homesteads of up to 24 hectares. You could have nearly 100 hectares if you claimed homesteads for each of your children. Ownership of land was established simply by clearing it, and a diligent farmer and shopkeeper like Fructuoso could have this done for him. Chinese lumber mills would clear it in return for the wood.

Josefa's Chinese blood came from her mother's family, the Quetulios, wealthy Chinese *mestizo* merchants in Ilocos Sur who owned cigar tobacco plantations and big houses. This Chinese blood was thought to explain why the Quetulios were smarter and richer than their neighbors.

Thanks to his wife's Chinese connections, which allowed him to borrow money at good rates and to build upon his investments, Fructuoso Edralin was a respected man in Sarrat. The Edralin family lived in modest but comfortable quarters above their general store, which in the islands are called *sari-sari* stores. They sold rice, coffee, tobacco, hardware, and a variety of consumer goods such as mosquito nets, blankets, cooking pots, and iron works. It was a typical storefront. The downstairs—housing the shop, the rice granary, and the coffee beanery—was blank and featureless to discourage armed robbery, laid with brick and stone to discourage rats. Upstairs were big windows and cool porches with wide eaves to block out the sun. The living quarters had open wood siding that stopped short of the roof to let out heat and welcome stray breezes.

Fructuoso was big and blustery. He claimed to be the best of everything, including best pistol shot in the valley. His wife bore him no sons. Josefa had six sisters, but the gods must have favored her because one was stillborn and four died of dysentery from contaminated water. Only Encarnacion survived with Josefa into adulthood.

Once its colonial administration was in place, the United States launched a drive to educate "the little brown people." Between 1901 and 1902, a thousand American teachers arrived, known as "Thomasites" for the SS *Thomas,* which brought the original group. They fanned out across the archipelago. Enrollments mushroomed and within two decades there were more than a million students in elementary schools. Some Thomasites made their way to Laoag and other towns along the northwest coast. For the first time, basic education was available to everyone. Most families were so poor that their children were needed at home to help scratch a subsistence from the ground. The American educational system unconsciously favored those who were already doing well enough to part with their children for a few hours a day, Josefa among them. Although she was nine years old, she started in the first grade; when she began her senior year of high school in Laoag, in 1914, she was twenty-one. At the time, this was not unusual.

One of her fellow seniors was a handsome fourteen-year-old boy named Mariano Marcos, a streetwise young bravo. Mariano was from Batac, where he and his family were followers and distant relatives of the local hero, Bishop Aglipay. Mariano's grandfather had been the illegitimate son of a Spanish provincial judge, but the judge had allowed him to serve as his clerk, which gave him power in the community.

Because of this local influence, Mariano's father, Fabian Marcos, once served a brief term as mayor of Batac. After that, their fortunes declined. The Marcos home was like most others in the rural Philippines, a bamboo shack with a thatch and tin roof.

When the Thomasites arrived in Ilocos Norte, Mariano was only four years old, but in the rush to educate under the Americans he was given an early start. Everyone agreed that he was precocious. By age fourteen he was finishing high school in the same class as Josefa, who was seven years older, and had become pushy and aggressive. He exuded animal magnetism, dressed like a dandy, and had a reputation as a young ladykiller with a string of conquests.

As the Marcos myth has been contrived, Josefa fell under the spell of her attractive classmate and they were secretly married in 1916. Ferdinand arrived the next year. At three months the infant Ferdinand was said to have been baptized by Bishop Aglipay himself. When he was three years old, his mother, who was not a follower of Aglipay and had little patience with his cause, had the child baptized again in the Catholic church in Sarrat. Or so it has always been claimed, both his baptismal certificates apparently having vanished in blazes that consumed the two churches before he was born. There are many such inconsistencies in the family history. The more you look, the more you conclude that it must have happened quite differently.

The story—as it is told by well-informed Ilocanos and by knowledgeable journalists and members of the Chinese community in Manila—is that the heir of the wealthy Chua family in Batac, a young man named Ferdinand Chua, fell in love with Josefa. How it came about we don't know, although there were many young girls from Batac and Sarrat who were employed over the years as domestic servants in the Chua mansion, and Josefa might have been among them. They planned to be married, but Chua's parents intervened. "They were old-fashioned," explained Manila newspaper editor Max Soliven, "and the clan elders insisted that he follow tradition and return to Amoy for a proper Fukienese wife. As luck would have it, Josefa was already pregnant." A suitable husband had to be found, but in the meantime she was packed off to Manila where her condition would cause no loss of face. After what must have been considerable melodrama, Josefa agreed to a marriage of convenience to her young classmate Mariano Marcos, and an arrangement was made to Mariano's satisfaction. Josefa came back to Sarrat to have the baby at home.

If this version is accurate, and the essential details have been confirmed repeatedly by various independent sources, it would help to explain many peculiarities and inconsistencies in the official Marcos story. Such as the fact that Josefa was seven years older than Mariano, the fact that he spent little time with her and the children over the years, that he mistreated and abused Ferdinand as a boy, but was affectionate toward her second son Pacifico, and that Mariano's career advanced in ways that can only be explained by the intervention of a powerful but invisible patron. This would also explain why Ferdinand Marcos seriously considered himself to be a direct descendant of the Chinese pirate Li Ma-hong. There was no Chinese blood in Mariano's family, and only a little in Josefa's.

Josefa's choice of the name Ferdinand for her first son was attributed officially to Ferdinand Magellan and King Ferdinand of Spain, but—more important—it was also the name of Ferdinand Chua, although in a country fond of pet names he was usually called Fernando.

Chua was an urbane young law student at the University of the Philippines. He followed his family's wishes and brought back a proper Chinese wife from Amoy, and in due course became justice of the peace in Batac, then municipal judge in Laoag, which made him unusually powerful. For a Chinese in the Ilocos to enter the professions in those days was unheard of, rarer still to succeed, but Fernando Chua was an unusual man with extraordinary connections. Josefa only identified Judge Chua in public as little Ferdinand's godfather.

In official biographies, Ferdinand Marcos romanized his godfather's name as Quiaoit, which is all but impossible to pronounce. It comes out something like *Chwa-oy,* a combination of the family founder's Chinese surname and given name. The Chinese character for the surname normally is romanized as *Chua* by speakers of Hokkien, the dialect of Chinese from Fukien, while Mandarin speakers render it as *Ts'ai.*

The stream that flowed by the Marcos home in Batac was named after the Chuas. They were the wealthiest Chinese family in Ilocos Norte, part of the great Chua clan, the sixth richest and most powerful clan in the Philippines, numbering among its members many millionaires and several billionaires.

The Chuas established themselves in the islands early in the nineteenth century, some of them eventually becoming Filipino citizens, but they never gave up their links to their ancestral home. New generations continued to arrive from Amoy, and dispersed throughout the archipelago. The branch that settled in and around Laoag became the leaders of the Chinese community in the Ilocos.

To protect themselves, the Chuas and other leading Chinese families organized clan associations in Manila. Once or twice a year, all male members of the Chua families scattered around the islands gathered in Manila, ostensibly for ritual ancestor worship, but actually to assess family and business ventures and to review how one branch of the clan could assist another. It was absolutely essential for individual Chinese to maintain these ties because the clan association was the most important social organization in the islands. The Nationalist Chinese Embassy and many other political or business organizations would have nothing to do with a man who was not introduced by his clan association. He was considered a man without an identity. Eventually there were nearly fifty official clan groups, most of them registered with the Chinese Embassy and through it in close contact with the Kuomintang in Nanking.

The Chua clan was very active in the Chinese chambers of commerce, which provided leadership for the Chinese community as a whole. As Mao's forces gained momentum on the mainland, Chinese in the Philippines became the target of intense anti-Communist propaganda, which was bad for business. In the years following World War II, as Chiang Kai-shek's struggle with Mao reached a climax, a new Federation of Chinese Chambers of Commerce was formed by KMT loyalists in Manila, drawing its leadership exclusively from clans committed to support Chiang. The Chua clan was prominent among them. Two of its members served as presidents of the Federation.

What is significant, in the end, is not that Ferdinand was illegitimate—although that added to his personal burden—but that his real father had to remain invisible, while providing secret leverage and the temptation of access to a hidden world of limitless money and power.

As time passed, Judge Chua's hand could be seen as he intervened in the Marcos family's destinies.

The Americans had established a Normal College in Manila to train Filipino teachers, and Josefa applied for admission, determined to make a career in the school system. Mariano was immediately enrolled with her. Graduates received a certificate qualifying them to teach elementary school only. Two years later, their teaching certificates in hand, Josefa and Mariano came back to Ilocos Norte, where Mariano inexplicably got a choice job teaching at the Laoag High School where they had met, a job for which he was legally unqualified. Josefa was pregnant with Mariano's son Pacifico, and later with Elizabeth. Unable to teach, she lived with her parents above their store in Sarrat, and spent her days selling dry goods.

In 1924, she found a job at Shamrock Elementary in Laoag, housed in a row of wooden shacks. This enabled her to enroll Ferdinand for a negligible sum. In school, he was the smallest and the neatest, dressed in his first pair of short pants, hair parted in the middle and slicked down. His teachers noted that he was prone to quibble unnecessarily over words and meanings. He was a nervous, intense boy with a quick grin.

Education in the Philippines at the time turned entirely on rote memory, so Ferdinand did well in school. Nobody could memorize faster or recite better. His worst enemies concede that he was born a genius. He had total recall, one of the phenomenal memories that are the mark of *idiots savants,* people otherwise retarded, who cannot read or write, but who can hear a Mozart sonata only once and play it back immediately, or who can work out square roots to the fifth decimal place in seconds inside their heads. Ferdinand liked to show off this odd talent by quickly memorizing complicated texts and reciting them forward or backward. Later, one of his law professors recalled that as a student he was "the best [I] ever had, because he could recite the constitution backwards." When he became their commander-in-chief, military men were awed by the fact that he could recall every detail of tables of organization, and orders issued weeks earlier at which he had only glanced. As a politician, his ability to match the names and faces of thousands of constituents was a potent vote-getter.

If anything, he was too bright, and more than a little quirky. He had an overactive imagination, which he often confused with reality, and entertained his family at dinner with fantastic stories in which he insisted that he had played roles. To add to his awareness of being different, he was left-handed in an age when that was still considered freakish. Grandfather Edralin taught him to be ambidextrous with a pencil or a target pistol.

His early political education was administered by lashings of a leather belt in a manner typical of Mariano, who was a severe disciplinarian. Learning to adapt himself to Mariano's unpredictable moods, Ferdinand developed a range of instant personalities like a hall of mirrors. Later, in Congress or on political campaigns, he could stand in front of a crowd and change personalities as the occasion required.

He saw little of Mariano, which was fortunate, and grew up with an unusual attachment to his mother. Josefa was a handsome young woman, with tawny skin the color of hand-rubbed teak, and large, dark, fawnlike eyes. Disillusioned by love, she was tough and ambitious, and extremely protective of her favorite son. There is a striking resemblance between Josefa and the women who played major roles in Ferdinand's life. His wives and mistresses would all look remarkably like his mother.

Mariano's career, meanwhile, made unaccountable progress. After teaching high school for only three years in a post for which he was no more qualified than Josefa, he was appointed district school superintendent. In that capacity, he traveled around Ilocos Norte by pony, becoming a familiar sight. He drew the attention of Bishop Aglipay. By now Judge Chua had become president of the community, the most influential figure in the economic life of the region for many miles around Batac. But Bishop Aglipay—a pious figure with a moon face and prematurely white hair—was the town celebrity. The bishop came up with the idea that Mariano should study law and make a career in politics as a champion of the Aglipay movement. The Aglipays were locked in a losing struggle for power at the national level, and the bishop was rallying all the men he could muster to his cause.

With the bishop and Judge Chua as his sponsors, Mariano resigned the school superintendency in 1921 and went off to Manila with his wife and children, to enroll in pre-law at the University of the Philippines. It is claimed that he was a superior student, that he graduated in 1924 at the head of his class, and that the Aglipay faction immediately put him up for election as the congressman representing the second district of Ilocos Norte, which included Batac. This was an Aglipay stronghold. His victory was assured. But much of the story is hype. According to the official record of the Philippine National Assembly, Mariano spent his first term in Congress listed as "farmer," not "lawyer," suggesting that the law degree did not fall so quickly into his hands. Four more years passed before his official description was changed, as he finally passed the bar.

Now in his mid-twenties, Mariano seems to have swaggered out of an early Italian movie about the cruelties of life in the Sicilian Mafia.

Vain and egotistical, he had a voluptuous face, with cruel eyes and a pouting, sensual mouth set in a perpetual smirk. He was not without redeeming qualities—in private he was often gentle and affectionate toward his own son, Pacifico—but his public persona unnerved bystanders. Although there were long periods when he was too poor to own a horse, it was Mariano's custom at six each evening to put on a tan military uniform with a Sam Browne belt, holstered sidearm, riding breeches and boots, and strut around the village square cracking a riding crop on his thigh. People who watched his performance sniggered to each other that Mariano Marcos and his family were "different from you and me." It was this air of command that put people with less self-assurance completely under Mariano's spell. If he was a bully by nature, he was also devious and cunning. Mariano was not a man who looked you in the eye and then shot you in the back; he had somebody else shoot you in the back and then looked you in the eye.

In Manila, while Mariano attended to congressional matters, Josefa found a job teaching at Ermita Elementary School, where she could enroll Ferdinand and Pacifico on partial scholarships. Ferdinand remained in school there until he completed the seventh grade in 1930, interrupted by several periods of a month or two when there was absolutely no money. The Marcoses lived in a shabby rented house on Mabini Street, the first of many temporary accommodations. They moved every year, sometimes more often, as Josefa struggled to keep the family afloat on her meager earnings. The impression is that of a family constantly dogged by bill collectors and landlords, a family who wore out their welcome quickly. Josefa's salary was only 50 pesos a month, barely enough to buy food and shelter for such a large brood, and although her husband was now a member of Congress, he brought home nothing. It was rare that Mariano was even at home. He was always "engaged in politics." Or, as Josefa's official biographer put it, "The demands of politics kept Don Mariano broke most of the time."

He spent every penny on cronies, and on continual trips to Ilocos Norte "to rally support." On those rare occasions when he was home, he was a brooding, ill-tempered martinet. He had the reputation of picking on matters that were overlooked or forgiven by others. Punishment was inflicted by lashings, or by locking the boys in a closet the size of a coffin; once Ferdinand was locked in the closet for several days "to keep him from catching influenza." Pacifico said: "We were obedient, because my father was really a terrible disciplinarian. . . . We were born to strong-willed parents and it was this virtue of ramrod determination which surfaced in Andy whenever he was challenged. He would excel at anything he set his mind to." Pacifico always took a back seat. Mariano, he recalled, "was, however, a very loving and, at times, indulgent father. He praised us highly before visitors for good performance and gave us handsome rewards. He gave much of his time to teaching us the manly arts of boxing, fencing, shooting, horseback riding and many other sports before we fully understood their importance in our growth."

Sometimes he took the boys along on his political rounds, not so they might learn from observing the process, but so that he could pit them in the boxing ring against any challengers their own size, which was always an effective way to draw crowds. When he was in a mood to beat one of the boys, Josefa had to use extraordinary tact, as she put it, to win "clemency" for the child.

"Mommy attended to the finer things in life," Pacifico said. "She taught us to read and write before we entered school, led us to the many adventures of various heroes and great men, many of whom were models in make-believe plays, with either Andy or me as hero or villain and our playmates as followers or soldiers."

Thanks to his phenomenal memory, Ferdinand did brilliantly. When he graduated from elementary school, he missed being valedictorian only because he had skipped several months during his third year for lack of tuition money.

In 1928, again with the support of Bishop Aglipay and Judge Chua, Mariano was returned to Congress for a second term. The family finances did not improve.

To her children, Josefa explained that their grandparents on her side had big farms in Ilocos Sur, but the Marcos side had nothing. The official version is that Grandmother Edralin had to send money now and then, to tide them over. But Judge Chua, in his role as godfather, also sent money, possibly a good deal more than has ever been acknowledged. In 1929, Josefa was said to have sold a parcel of land that had been given to her as a birthright by her parents, and bought a house of her own at 1555 Calle Calixto, in Manila's working-class Paco district. There, she was able to ease the strain by taking in boarders, including Andres Chua, the nephew of the judge.

It was a square two-story house on a large plot of ground, with a porch overlooking a vacant lot where they planted vegetables. Most of the ground floor was occupied by a wide *sala,* or enclosed patio. There were four small rooms upstairs. Josefa had her own room, the two girls shared one, the two boys another, and the remaining room served as a dormitory for the boarders, never less than five at a time.

When her children could look after themselves, Josefa began night school and obtained a bachelor's degree that enabled her to earn more teaching high school.*

Judge Chua openly paid for most of Ferdinand's education, apparently having reached some understanding with the boy regarding their relationship. Ferdinand would return to Batac to see his godfather whenever he could. In 1930, he enrolled in a high school attached to the University of the Philippines, then began college on a two-year program for a liberal arts degree. With that in hand, he went on to law school, and joined the training program of the Philippine Constabulary. His main interest was the college pistol team, where he became a crack shot.

The world of politics that Mariano entered in Manila, and into which Ferdinand would soon be drawn, was a great game of pretense, manipulation, and patronage, in which egos were mashed and bruised, and murder was a viable option. It was murder that brought young Ferdinand into that world.

Under Spanish rule only wealthy, educated Filipinos were allowed to participate in politics, and then only at the local level to compete for appointment as mayor. Around the main market towns of each district, where the wealthy had their homes, leading families grouped themselves into factions to contend for this post. Politics was a family affair. There were no political parties, although in the last years of Spanish rule several revolutionary movements were organized.

When the Americans arrived, little changed. Governor-General Taft organized wealthy landowners into the first national political party, the

*In one of the more bizarre asides of the Marcos story, Y. S. Kwong, a Filipino millionaire who sold his businesses and resettled in Vancouver, British Columbia, asserted that Josefa Edralin was once arrested at Arellano High School in Manila, where she was a teacher and librarian, for having opium and heroin in her possession. Kwong was so certain of his facts that he gave the name of the arresting officer as Detective Telesforo Tenorio, who later became chief of police in Manila. Kwong claimed that the police believed Josefa was selling drugs to the students, but that she was able to bribe or cry her way out of the incident. There is no way to confirm Kwong's story, which was widely published. I repeat it only because it adds a curious touch to a family history sanitized by official propagandists.

Federalistas, who were committed to collaborating with the Americans against those who favored independence. Any party promoting independence was banned outright. Taft failed to take into account that once American soldiers had started shooting Filipinos, no political organization could survive if it failed to declare itself in favor of ultimate independence. Before the first national election in 1907, Taft was forced to acknowledge the importance of the issue by dropping the ban. Otherwise the elections would have been a joke with the Federalistas running alone. Immediately, a number of rival parties were started by young radicals who had fought the Yankees, including one called the Nacionalistas, which won overwhelmingly.

Despite American propaganda and self-congratulation, there was nothing democratic about the new government. Under the leadership of two men, Sergio Osmeña and Manuel Quezon, the Nacionalista party monopolized Philippine politics for the next forty years, until independence in 1946. While the Nacionalista platform called for immediate independence, Osmeña and Quezon had a secret understanding with Washington that they would block any attempt by the national assembly to legislate independence. Historian Ross Marley noted that "the trick employed so skillfully by Manuel Quezon fifty years ago [was to] play the nationalist fighting for the dignity and independence of the Philippines, knowing that the Americans will tolerate this from someone who protects American interests in the islands."

Powerful Americans wanted to hold on to the islands as long as possible until their economic interests were satisfied. While Dewey's fleet was still in Manila Bay, President McKinley was cabling the admiral for information on natural resources, mining, farming, and industry. An emissary of the secretary of state was sent out to prepare a catalogue for the economic exploitation of the colony. American companies were preempting the best land for their ventures. A subsidiary of the Del Monte Company, limited by law to no more than 1,024 hectares, appealed privately to the governor-general. He converted public lands into a U.S. Navy preserve and then had the navy sublease 20,000 hectares to Del Monte. This was done discreetly, out of public view, and was not unusual. In Hawaii, Sanford Dole of Dole Pineapple led a businessman's coup that toppled Queen Liliuokalani, and appealed for annexation, which President McKinley granted. Soldiers in the American expeditionary forces who could claim degrees in jurisprudence, like infantryman John Haussermann from Ohio, stayed in the Philippines to parlay their knowledge of American law into the control of key local industries. Haussermann and some clever law partners took over the struggling Benguet gold mine, which eventually grew into the second biggest in U.S. territory, and used it to build one of the great fortunes on the planet—a fortune that was later shared selectively with key political players such as General Douglas MacArthur.

Osmeña and Quezon recognized that this commercial audience was the dominant force behind the scenes in Washington, so they catered to it. In return, American officials looked the other way in Manila, making it possible for wealthy Filipinos to ignore basic questions of ethics and justice. This double standard had subtle, insidious, and long-lasting consequences. Its worst effect was to demoralize the great majority of Filipinos, who were poor and divested of their traditional lands, while permanently addicting the rich to massive doses of American favoritism.

Quezon was a flamboyant politician, whose magnetic personality and sheer exuberance disarmed U.S. officials and businessmen alike. They found it easier to work through Quezon and Osmeña than to deal with Filipinos directly. In return for guaranteeing the national assembly's approval of the governor-general's programs, Osmeña and Quezon were rewarded with patronage, which they could manipulate to keep their own factions in line.

Patronage, not democracy, was the most important force in the islands. Only part of the American system had been transplanted to Manila. Missing were the checks and balances so deliberately built into the original. In their place, Washington substituted the whims of its governor-general, and made all actions of the national assembly subject to veto by the U.S. Congress. With a broad wink from the governor-general and the White House, these vetoes were rarely exercised, and Osmeña and Quezon were given an open purse.

Manuel Quezon was from a well-educated Chinese *mestizo* family, schoolteachers of modest but adequate means, with good connections on the fringe of the oligarchy. He was a young man of such exceptional gifts at manipulation that as a schoolboy he was nicknamed *gularato*, the "bluffer." In his teens, he quarreled over a girl with a Spanish officer, beat him up, and was arrested and sentenced to prison. On his release, Quezon joined Aguinaldo's army to fight the Spaniards and ended up fighting Americans instead. Captured by the Yankees, he spent six months in jail. He then completed his law studies, and became a prosecuting attorney for the new colonial government. He was so gregarious and charming that Americans loved him. In 1906, with their encouragement, he ran successfully for governor of Tayabas Province. The following year, he was elected to the national assembly and became Osmeña's wily floor leader.

Osmeña may have lacked Quezon's charm, but he made up for it with exceptional organizational ability and command of detail. A college-educated journalist, he was the son of a *mestizo* shopkeeper on Cebu who had both Spanish and Chinese blood. With American support, Osmeña was elected governor. Cebu, as the second city of the Philippines, was in many ways its financial heart. Osmeña used his post to build a political machine representing the sugar bloc and other wealthy interests in the central islands. His machine evolved into the victorious Nacionalista party. At the age of twenty-nine, Osmeña was chosen to be the first national assembly speaker.

Before long, Quezon left Osmeña trailing far behind. He was a proud, vain, explosive personality, who knew how to appear to be everything Filipinos wanted. He had a keen understanding of his countrymen. Ordinary Filipinos were awed by his ability to mingle with world leaders, and admired his imperial style. He was a natural playboy, one of the world's best ballroom dancers, a celebrated drinker, a world-class poker player, and a peacock who designed his own clothes. His favorite attire was an informal uniform he designed himself with russet riding breeches, a soft white shirt, and a high-collared military tunic. Not so visible was the sly, shifting, ruthless side of his nature. He was a skillful liar, who coolly manipulated friends and enemies to gain his own ends, and a gifted actor, full of histrionics. Even in religion he was an opportunist. Born a Roman Catholic, he became a Freemason when he joined the anti-clerical revolution, then reconverted to Catholicism in 1928 to round out his image as national leader. While Osmeña was preoccupied running the party and the assembly, Quezon saw that real leverage was only to be found in Washington. He had Osmeña appoint him resident commissioner there, remaining in America from 1909 to 1916, and used the time well, making powerful friends in the Democratic party and the Anti-Imperialist League. During this period the U.S. Congress passed tariff acts providing free entry into the United States for all Philippine products. Unfortunately, the long-term result was to make the islands absolutely dependent on the U.S. market, and the wealthy producers addicted to the subsidy.

These ill-conceived tariff acts were followed in 1916 by the Jones Act, which promised that America would grant independence to the Philippines as soon as "a stable government" was established, but dodged the issue by setting no date. The act also created a Philippine Senate, but every law it passed could still be vetoed by the governor-general or the U.S. Congress. Claiming sole credit for these dubious achievements, Quezon returned to Manila in time for the 1916 elections. He led everyone to believe that he had struggled valiantly to win full independence, but that all he could pry out of Washington was an inexact promise. It was just smoke, but it made Quezon a hero and he rode a wave of popularity into the new upper chamber, where he was chosen Senate president. Osmeña continued to be speaker of the House of Representatives.

Quezon's plot to displace Osmeña as party leader moved ahead when President Harding appointed Leonard Wood as governor-general in 1921. His predecessors rarely used their veto, but General Wood was a tyrant, a military imperialist who believed that the withdrawal of America from the Philippines would be a disaster. He exercised his veto 126 times during six years in office. So unreasonable, overbearing, and contrary was he that the entire Filipino cabinet walked out. Quezon seized the opportunity, unfairly put the blame on Osmeña, and called passionately for a new national vision. Osmeña was upstaged and had to settle thereafter for second place. Quezon remained unchallenged as the autocratic ruler of the Philippines until World War II, providing an object lesson in politics for all to follow.

Quezon's domination did not mean his rivals retired from politics; they simply formed factions within factions. When ambitions conflicted, politicians jumped from one faction to another, or started a new faction.

Democracy became mere theater. Part of the show obliged politicians to reach out into the audience of the canefields and the barrios, seeking support from men able to purchase and deliver the bloc votes of whole communities, at 5 pesos a vote. The linchpins of this vote-buying system were local bosses or *caciques* (pronounced *"kah-seeks"*) who bartered money or favors for votes. On great estates the *cacique* was the landlord himself, or a member of his family, who kept tenant farmers under control by employing armies of thugs. The result was the beating and killing of upstarts who refused to play the game, the torment of their women and children, and the emergence of grass-roots warlords, who guaranteed with thugs and guns what could not be bought with gold. They shifted allegiance from one political faction to another according to who paid more.

In 1931, Mariano Marcos ran for a third term in Congress and was stunned when he was defeated by Emilio Medina of Dingras. Sourly, Mariano groused that he had been cheated by a stuffed ballot box in the town of San Nicolas. Voting in provincial districts could be decided by a few hundred ballots, most of them paid for well in advance, so a little cheating accomplished a lot. "I was never in a more intense campaign," Mariano said. "I spent my last centavo, forgetting that I had a wife and children."

In his hometown of Batac, where he had expected a landslide, a local tax official, a political novice named Julio Nalundasan, had decided to run for Congress. Nalundasan garnered only a few votes, but it was enough to split Batac, and to deny Mariano the comfortable margin he had counted on. Emilio Medina, the outsider, won the election, beating Mariano by a mere fifty-six votes.

Mariano never forgave Nalundasan. He took the defeat hard. He could not adjust to unemployment after six years as a public official. For a full year, he was emotionally crippled, unable to practice law, only to brood. He became a terrible burden to everyone. It is said in official histories of the Marcos era that strings were pulled and Senate President Quezon got Mariano out of everyone's hair by having him appointed governor of Davao, in remote Mindanao, a post that supposedly was reaffirmed two years later in 1933. Many other Marcos claims depend on whether this assertion was true.

Provincial documents for the period show that the governor of Davao in 1931 was not Mariano Marcos but Cayetano Bangoy, and the governor in 1932 was not Mariano Marcos but Juan Sarenas. Mariano was merely a clerk in the governor's office, at an annual salary of only 3,000 pesos, without an allowance for lodging or a horse. He was not a success, so the second year his pay was cut by 50 pesos. This was the same year that Ferdinand missed a month in school for lack of tuition fees. Hardly the plight of a governor's son.

In an effort to displace the Muslim Filipinos who lived along its coast, Mindanao was under intense development, and Filipino Christians were given incentives to move there. Mariano's job was to help these Christians get settled. He also found time to dispatch the occasional Muslim troublemaker.

During summer vacations in 1933 and 1934, Ferdinand said he visited his father in Davao, and had a number of memorable experiences. "In Mindanao," records one official biographer,

> Don Mariano showed his son the face of courage. . . . One day, a Muslim amok chanced upon the Marcoses' path. Andy looked at his father; he waited for his words. His father tapped his shoulder, then held his hand. Together, they stood their ground, watching the berserk. As the *huramentado* raised his kris, Don Mariano moved quickly. He drew his gun and blasted the culprit. The amok crumpled on the ground dead. Then they walked quietly away from the scene as if they were strolling toward the sunset. For Don Mariano, it was an ordinary feat. The savage was a poor tactician; his mind was crazed, indecisive. He did not fight to win; he took chances. For Don Mariano, it was different. He controlled the situation. He knew his ground, his strength. He knew he would win. He was prepared all the way. . . . Often he would tell Andy: "Don't start a fight until you know you can win."

According to official biographies, Mariano came into the ownership of a fine hacienda with many thousands of acres in the Padada Valley south of Davao, and stocked it with between two thousand and ten thousand head (the number varies) of expensive disease-resistant Nellore brahmin cattle from India. The story goes that Mariano transformed the Padada Valley from an unproductive wasteland to a bustling center of agriculture and commerce.

The facts are different. The wealthy American secretary of the interior, Dean Worcester, imported the first Nellore bulls to the Philippines. When he retired to the islands as general manager of the American-Philippine Company, Worcester established the Diklum Ranch, which maintained a Nellore herd of six thousand head. Worcester then set up his own Nellore Ranch near Mailag, and by 1940 this 7,000-hectare spread supported a herd of two thousand five hundred. All the other early Nellore cattlemen in the islands were American associates of Worcester.

It is difficult to believe that Mariano Marcos ever owned a ranch in Mindanao during the Great Depression with a big mansion and more than two thousand head of brahmins. In 1948, however, Ferdinand Marcos petitioned the U.S. government for half a million dollars in compensation for the theft of these cattle during World War II. The U.S.

government rejected his claim because there was no evidence that the herd had ever existed. Mariano and Ferdinand evidently had adopted the Diklum Ranch in fantasy.

While Mariano was busy shooting Muslims in Mindanao, the contest between Manuel Quezon and Sergio Osmeña was coming to a head in Manila and Washington, partly as a result of the Depression. From 1929 to 1933, Democratic party victories in America, the rise of Japanese militarism, growing opposition to the Philippines by U.S. labor and farm groups, and racial hostility toward Filipino immigrants all combined to make the U.S. Congress receptive to granting independence to the Asian colony.

Independence was the last thing the Nacionalistas really wanted. At least not until they had time to prepare. House Speaker Osmeña and his new floor leader, Manuel Roxas, hurried to Washington in 1933 to buy time, and secured the promise of independence only after ten years as a self-governing commonwealth. It was a decent compromise for which Osmeña deserved praise. Quezon could not afford to let his rival get that credit, so when the bill was passed by the U.S. Congress, it was blocked in Manila by Senate President Quezon. He argued that the bill did not offer genuine independence, since U.S. military bases in the islands would remain sovereign American territories. He persuaded the Philippine legislature to reject the offer, and headed for Washington himself.

Quezon thought he could get a better deal from his friend, the new Democratic president, Franklin D. Roosevelt, and from other old friends in Congress, notably Maryland Senator Millard Tydings. But horse trading with FDR was not as easy as Quezon expected. When Quezon pushed for better trade agreements, Roosevelt threatened him with independence in twenty-four hours. By gaining a few cosmetic changes, Quezon claimed that he had won better terms with "his" Tydings-McDuffie Act. There was little difference between the two bills, but it was a propaganda victory for Quezon. In reality, Quezon forfeited more than he gained. Under Tydings-McDuffie the common- wealth would have its own constitution and would be self-governing, but its foreign policy would still be determined by America, and laws affecting immigration, foreign trade, or currency had to be approved by Washington. Only fifty Filipino immigrants would be allowed into the United States each year, whereas American entry and residence in the islands would be unrestricted. Philippine goods could enter the United States free for five years, followed by five years of gradually steepening tariffs, reaching 100 percent in 1946, while during the same period American goods could enter the islands unrestricted and duty free.

A bitter fight ensued in Manila over these unequal terms, which caused the Nacionalistas to split finally into two parties. Osmeña and Roxas, and their contingent, broke off to start the Liberal party. But the "great split" was only a family spat. The two parties were like Tweedledum and Tweedledee. Politicians changed from one to the other indiscriminately.

There was no question who would be president of the new commonwealth. Quezon, the poker player, held all the cards. Osmeña decided to be content once more with second place, and ran as Quezon's vice-presidential candidate.

Not everyone was happy with this one-sided deal with America. A new movement was launched called the Sakdal party (the word *sakdal* means "to accuse"). Some two hundred thousand Filipinos rushed to join Sakdal ranks, revealing for the first time the persisting hostility toward America and toward Quezon. Sakdalistas campaigned for complete independence by the end of 1935, redistribution of land, and an end to *caciquism,* winning a number of seats in the legislature. When Quezon prevented them from taking these seats, the Sakdalistas took up guns, but their revolt was put down by the American-trained Constabulary. Echoing Mussolini, Quezon declared: "The good of the state, not the good of the individual, must prevail."

In 1935, Mariano Marcos returned to Batac from Mindanao to run again for the national assembly.

Four years earlier, when he had lost to Emilio Medina of Dingras, he had blamed the defeat on his neighbor, Julio Nalundasan. This time, Medina decided not to run. The election pitted Mariano directly against Nalundasan.

Nalundasan was on Quezon's Nacionalista ticket. Bishop Aglipay was running for president at the head of his own Republican party, formed for the purpose, and Mariano was the Republican party candidate for Congress in the second district of Ilocos Norte. Their prospects were not good. Aglipay was now seventy-five and his popularity had greatly subsided.

Every dirty trick was employed. Quezon's machine was better oiled and Nalundasan defeated Mariano easily. Mariano groused blackly that his opponent had taken advantage of his position as an official with the Bureau of Internal Revenue to extort votes. It was typhoon season, and tempers were hot. One of the other disappointed presidential contenders, General Aguinaldo, plotted a coup, and Quezon became so concerned about assassination that he slept in a different house every night. (Under pressure from the American governor-general, Aguinaldo finally abandoned his plot.)

To rub Mariano's nose in failure, Nalundasan's supporters borrowed a coffin and lashed it to the rumble seat of a car. Two men sprawled in the casket facing each other, one labeled Aglipay, the other Marcos, both politically dead. They roared up and down the dirt streets of district villages, finally reaching Batac, where they made several noisy, horn-blowing circuits of the town and then buzzed the Marcos home, stopping in front to hoot and razz, then drove away, leaving a cloud of dust and a deafening silence.

Ferdinand was in Batac and saw it all. His academic standing, by the end of his first college semester in 1935, had dropped below the level required to maintain his scholarship. He had been spending too much time on the .22-caliber pistol team, and hanging around with friends. Years later, he boasted that he had been the national pistol champion, but this was not true; he was just another team member. To raise the 200 pesos he needed to see him through the rest of the school year, he went to Sarrat and Batac to ask Grandmother Edralin and Judge Chua for further loans.

Three nights after the election, on September 20, 1935, a heavy tropical downpour drove everyone off the streets. In Nalundasan's house, the victorious candidate enjoyed a late supper with family and friends. A few minutes after 10:00 P.M., he got up from the table and crossed the porch to a wash basin by the railing to brush his teeth. The rain had stopped but the banana plants in the yard still dripped. Nalundasan was clearly silhouetted by the porch lantern. Among the waxy leaves there was a loud pop. A .22-caliber bullet entered Nalundasan's back, piercing his heart and lung. He gasped, *"Jesus, María y José! Me pegaron una tira!"* ("I've been shot!") and collapsed. Minutes later he was dead.

Early the following morning, Ferdinand was among the curious crowd milling around the town hall to view the corpse of Congressman-elect Nalundasan, while an autopsy was performed. The next afternoon, his pocket stuffed with 200 pesos for tuition, Ferdinand left for Manila in a borrowed car with two other men and his uncle Quirino Lizardo, who was married to one of Mariano's sisters.

Suspicions were immediately directed at Mariano Marcos and his family and friends, but on the afternoon of the murder Mariano had made a public display of leaving Batac for Laoag. Everyone knew Mariano was miles away when the murder occurred. One of Mariano's relatives and campaign workers, a Batac villager named Nicasio Layaoen, was accused of the murder. Mariano rushed back to Batac to organize Layaoen's legal defense with his brother Pio Marcos, who was also a lawyer. The trial was staged in the provincial capital. The case against Layaoen was thin and circumstantial from the beginning. He was promptly acquitted on insufficient evidence. Nobody was satisfied, especially Nalundasan's friends and relatives. It was suspected that the case against Layaoen had been deliberately contrived as a red herring, to throw everyone off the trail of the real killer. After all, was it not true that Mariano's son boasted of being the best .22-caliber marksman on his college pistol team? After the trial, Mariano prudently packed up and moved to Manila to live with his wife and children for the first time in many years. Pio remained in Laoag to keep their dingy law office open.

There the matter would have rested—as so many unsolved murders rested in the Ilocos over the years—had it not been that the chief investigating officer, Constabulary Major Jose P. Guido, felt he had been made to look a fool. Quezon himself had ordered him to find Congressman Nalundasan's killer, and that he was going to do.

In 1936, entering the college of law, Ferdinand was commissioned a third lieutenant in the reserves of the Philippine Constabulary. Among his fellow cadets were Primitivo San Augustin, Saturnino and Leonilo Ocampo, and Roberto Benedicto, clever young men who would play important roles later in his life. They hung around together after classes each night, and took an oath to come to each other's aid no matter what.

Just before Christmas 1938—three years after the Nalundasan murder—Constabulary soldiers burst into Ferdinand's room and arrested him on the charge of being the triggerman. Also charged were his uncles Pio Marcos and Quirino Lizardo. The next day in Laoag, Mariano was in court where he too was arrested.

Quezon sent a special legal team headed by the celebrated Manila attorney Higinio Macadaeg to handle the prosecution. The trial was presided over by Judge Roman Cruz. Another acclaimed lawyer, Vicente Francisco, headed the defense panel. After preliminary investigation, Ferdinand was held at the Ilocos Norte provincial jail in Laoag.

He was five months shy of graduating with honors from law school. From his cell, he petitioned the Philippine Supreme Court for release on bail. He may have had some discreet assistance from Judge Chua and the Chua clan, for in a precedent-setting decision the high court ruled that Ferdinand was entitled to bail, "unless the prosecution could show a strong evidence of guilt." Prosecutor Macadaeg, not wishing to reveal his evidence prematurely, declined to argue the case at bar. All the accused were therefore granted bail. For many months thereafter, every time the case was calendared, the hearing had to be postponed. By coincidence or otherwise, defense attorney Francisco always had other hearings elsewhere. After many delays the case was finally postponed to September 1939.

Out on bail, Ferdinand hied to Manila to get his degree. He found himself a celebrity. It was not that everyone thought he was innocent, no matter how often in later years this assertion would be repeated in his biographies. It was just that no senior in law school had ever been charged with murder on the eve of graduation. A great rhubarb. During the graduation exercises, when Ferdinand was called to receive his diploma from President Quezon, students and audience exploded into deafening applause. Quezon was startled by the unexpected ovation.

On September 9, Josefa was beside her son when he was finally brought to trial. One embarrassing family secret revealed in court was that there had been bad blood between the Marcoses and Lizardo, which had climaxed in the filing of a criminal complaint against Lizardo for attempted homicide in which the offended party was Mariano's mother.

The government case against Ferdinand rested on the testimony of one Calixto Aguinaldo, a dark little man, only four feet tall, unusually gentle in speech and manner. He was from Tarlac, a province just outside Manila, and spoke a number of dialects including Tagalog, Ilocano, and Pampangan. Although he had dropped out at the beginning of high school, his gift for dialects and his subservient manner had enabled him to earn a modest living running errands for lawyers and helping them as a clerk and interpreter. Calixto Aguinaldo was accustomed to being bullied, so he had developed the peculiar strength of the meek. On the witness stand, he told his story simply and convincingly, and could not be shaken no matter how the defense tried to intimidate or confuse him.

Calixto was forty-seven years old, married, and a small property owner. He knew Quirino Lizardo because he had worked for him when Lizardo once served as a public defender. Since Lizardo was married to one of the Marcos sisters, Calixto knew the whole family, and that was how he came to be at the scene of the crime. Lizardo was a grossly overweight man who sweated a lot and always shouted, especially when he was angry, which was most of the time. His poor wife had shriveled up into a frail, birdlike creature, dying slowly of tuberculosis.

Calixto testified that just before election day, Lizardo decided to help his brother-in-law as a poll watcher. Calixto obligingly borrowed a car from his nephew, Francisco Aguinaldo, who came along as driver. Calixto himself accompanied Lizardo to Ilocos Norte as a bodyguard. Although fat Lizardo boasted that he knew jiu-jitsu, he liked to take the precaution of having tiny Calixto walk around two paces behind him, to cover his back. You could never be too careful.

They arrived two days before the election, bringing along Lizardo's consumptive wife and her youngest child, a frail girl of three. The Marcos home in Batac was now owned by Mariano's other sister, Antonia Marcos Rubio, and was under renovation. The original house of bamboo and tin roof was still used as kitchen and dormitory while a new house was being built in front. The unfinished structure was covered temporarily by corrugated zinc to serve as Mariano's campaign headquarters. The Lizardos were given the use of a bamboo shack in the yard, while Calixto bunked on the upstairs floor of the new house, and his nephew, the driver, slept in the car.

Calixto was introduced to Mariano, and Lizardo emphasized that he had complete trust in his small bodyguard. Accordingly, Calixto was accepted around the house and in the meetings of political henchmen as if he were a fly on the wall.

All the men gathered in the unfinished upstairs area of the new house, sitting on bare planks, to discuss the prospects. Included were Lizardo, Calixto, Pio, and Mariano, and young Ferdinand, the law student. Mariano told them it was going to be difficult for him to win because of the fading appeal of Bishop Aglipay. Fat Lizardo butted in immediately and said, "If we are defeated in the election, we can win in another matter and that is to kill Nalundasan." Calixto testified that it was not the first time Lizardo had offered that solution. Twice he had suggested liquidating Nalundasan, when Pio Marcos had visited him in August.

Calixto testified that Mariano replied, "Think it over if it is convenient that we do that." (They were speaking Ilocano.)

On election day, Calixto served as poll watcher, driving around the district with Lizardo and sometimes Mariano. After his defeat was certain, Calixto was in the Marcos house when Nalundasan's followers roared up in the jalopy with the coffin and effigies. The next morning there was another conference with Mariano, Pio, Ferdinand, Lizardo, and Calixto, in the unfinished room upstairs.

They felt humiliated and resentful. Calixto said Lizardo asked if they were going to get revenge. Everybody agreed they should. Lizardo said, "Who is going to kill Nalundasan?" After a pause, he said, "If no one of you dares to shoot him, I will do it."

Ferdinand Marcos spoke up: "It is better that I do it because I am a better shot than you." Calixto testified that Ferdinand switched suddenly to English and added, "You might miss him."

Since Mariano would be the prime suspect, they would make sure everybody saw him leave town immediately for Laoag.

That night it rained hard. When it was time, Lizardo got out a .32-caliber police positive, while Ferdinand prepared his .22 target pistol, which had a small handle and a very long barrel. Lizardo asked Calixto to come along to stand watch. It was pitch black. Calixto testified that they picked their way carefully to the narrow alley leading to Nalundasan's house.

Ferdinand and Lizardo posted Calixto at a corner, then the two of them entered a rice shed at the back of Nalundasan's property, and passed through it into a small orchard where they could stand among the dripping banana plants and fruit trees, and see the victorious candidate eating dinner with his family by lantern light on the open porch.

Calixto was frightened and lost his nerve. He retreated up the dark alley toward the Marcos house, hearing a shot behind him. Hurrying on, he climbed into the car where his nephew was sleeping.

Three minutes later, Ferdinand and Lizardo returned. Peeking out,

Calixto saw Ferdinand go directly upstairs. Lizardo stopped at the car, stuck his head in, and said, "Go to sleep, Nalundasan is already dead." When Lizardo went inside, Calixto heard his wife cry out, "How cruel you are! At last you have killed him."

Calixto said the murder weapon was buried by a coconut palm in the yard. Two days later they drove back to Manila, as they had come, but this time young Ferdinand accompanied them because he had to return to law school. Eventually, Major Jose Guido of the Department of Investigation had tracked down the car, found that it belonged to Francisco Aguinaldo, and that led him to Calixto. The prosecution brought in witnesses who corroborated various elements of Calixto's testimony.

Under cross-examination, defense attorney Francisco was unable to shake Calixto or to alter his testimony. Francisco brought to the stand various members of the Marcos family who testified that Calixto was not at the Marcos house in Batac during the time of the election and murder, and that they did not even know him. Antonia Rubio, elder sister of Mariano and Pio, who had been rebuilding the Marcos house in Batac, testified that Calixto Aguinaldo was never in the house and that she saw him for the first time in court.

Finally the four accused were presented as witnesses in their own defense. Pio Marcos testified that he spent the whole day on his small farm, going home at six o'clock. He said he went to bed after supper and was awakened at midnight and told that Lieutenants Lasola and Villanueva of the Constabulary were in the house. It was only then, he said, that he heard of Nalundasan's murder. The two officers asked for his gun, and Pio gave it to them without hesitation. It was returned to him the following day by Lieutenant Villanueva, who said the gun had not been used for a long time as evidenced by its rust. Pio declared that he and Nalundasan were friends.

Mariano told the court that he did not mind the Nalundasan victory parade.

"I also celebrated my triumph when I was elected representative of the second district of Ilocos Norte in 1925 and 1928," he declared, "but of course it was not like that of Nalundasan which, frankly, was in bad taste." Concerning Ferdinand, he said: "Ferdinand never meddled in politics. He did not grow up in Batac, and was not familiar with the town. Ferdinand did not conspire against Nalundasan nor would I have allowed him to do that. What reason would he have to conspire? I am not a mad or unnatural father to have my son commit a crime for which he would have to pay with his life. I am not a coward, your honor." Then it was his son's turn.

"On the night of the 20th," Ferdinand testified, "I went to our house after supper to ask my uncle Quirino when he was going back to Manila. My father had advised me to go with my uncle because I was carrying money. My aunt informed me that my uncle was out because he had cabled his mother in Manila for some money as they were short of cash, and stated that as soon as the money arrived they would leave for Manila. I told my aunt that my father had advised me to go with them, and that I hoped to leave as soon as possible so as not to miss classes and so I could prepare for my semestral examinations scheduled on the first week of October. The conversation with my aunt lasted around ten minutes, after I went back to the Verano house and began studying for the semestral exams, as I had taken my books along with me. After two hours of study, I went to bed. My roommate, Efrain, was still reading when I fell asleep.

"It was probably past six o'clock in the morning of the 21st when I woke up. I learned of Nalundasan's death from a personal attendant of the town president's niece, Miss Aurora Chua, who also lived in the house. As I was curious, I asked her when the murder was committed, what weapon was used, if the murderer had been caught, and who the suspects were. At past eight that morning, Efrain and I went to the town hall to get more news about the death of Nalundasan."

On December 1, 1939, the Laoag Court of First Instance found Ferdinand Marcos guilty beyond any reasonable doubt. Because of his youth, he was given ten years minimum to seventeen years and four months maximum. Lizardo was sentenced to life imprisonment. Mariano and Pio were acquitted. Ferdinand asked to be set free on bail pending an appeal. The request was denied. A few days later, Judge Cruz called Ferdinand to his private chamber. He told Ferdinand that President Quezon was ready to pardon him. This was a surprising and peculiar development. It was never explained beyond the assertion that Ferdinand had become a national celebrity, which is a great exaggeration. A more likely explanation is that Quezon had long since been advised of the special relationship that existed between Ferdinand and Judge Chua, and that a deal had been cut. Quezon's term as president ended in 1941, at which time he would be running for re-election. The Chua clan's support could make a big difference. Ferdinand realized that he was now in a rare position. The advantage was his.

He turned down Quezon's pardon and returned to Laoag jail. News of the pardon offer, and his refusal, spread quickly. Before he could get to his cell he was called to the mayor's office. Roque Ablan, the young mayor who had been elected with Chua support, greeted him warmly. They had been acquainted for years, but now that Ferdinand was his guest, the mayor could not do enough. Ablan had a Ping-Pong table set up in the jail courtyard, and made it clear that Ferdinand only had to ask. Ablan also sent him a set of law books so that the convicted murderer had at his disposal a complete law library. Ferdinand remained in Laoag jail for six months while he wrote his appeal brief for the Supreme Court; the finished brief was 830 pages long. It was submitted in May 1940. He was then moved to Bilibad Prison in Manila for another six months while the Supreme Court deliberated on whether to hear his appeal.

In the meantime, Ferdinand took the bar examinations and, in spite of being in jail, or perhaps because of it, topped the results. His score of 98.01 on the bar exam was so high that he was accused of cheating. He insisted on being re-examined, and was taken by the dean of law to a confrontation with justices of the Supreme Court, who administered the exam orally. Ferdinand challenged them to ask any question on criminal law, legal ethics, civil law, commercial law, procedural law, or political law. His replies showed that he had committed to rote memory entire sections of the textbooks. He passed this expanded test with a score of 92.35. (A few years later, Jovito Salonga bested this with a score of 95.3.) The justices then asked if newspaper reports were true, that Ferdinand could recite the constitution backwards. In reply, he gave a demonstration. It was a tour de force. The day was his.

The Supreme Court scheduled oral arguments on Ferdinand's appeal for Saturday, October 12, 1940. For the occasion, he wore a white shark-skin suit to symbolize his innocence. His uncles, Pio Marcos and Quirino Lizardo, arrived early. Mariano was conspicuously absent. Perhaps Judge Chua warned him that he had caused Ferdinand enough trouble.

The celebrated orator Leon Maria Guerrero presented the government's case. Presiding for the high court was its most controversial figure, Associate Justice Jose B. Laurel.

Laurel was an extraordinary character. He first came to public attention in 1909 at the age of eighteen when he stabbed a man in a fight over a girl. Convicted of murder, he defended himself successfully in an appeal before the Supreme Court, which agreed that he had acted in self-defense. This victory marked him as a brilliant young comer. He attended Yale, where he felt he was treated badly by Americans, and in 1923 became secretary of the interior at age thirty-two. In that post, he was involved in the cabinet showdown with Governor-General Leonard Wood. It was Laurel who led the celebrated cabinet revolt and walkout which failed when Quezon used it to upstage Osmeña. The cabinet drifted back into office without Laurel. He was embittered by the way his contemporaries turned their backs on principle to advance their careers with the Americans. His own political career never fully recovered. He was a successful attorney, and continued to be a leading opponent of American rule—not only because of his treatment by Leonard Wood, and at Yale, but because his father had been tortured by American soldiers in a concentration camp in 1901. Quezon eventually appointed Laurel to the Supreme Court to sidetrack him. There Laurel displayed an unusual interest in the Marcos case and preempted his colleagues by announcing that he would pen the majority decision himself. According to one source, Laurel went individually to all the members of the Supreme Court and pleaded emotionally for the acquittal of young Ferdinand.

Why Laurel should become so exercised has never been satisfactorily explained. The entire future of Ferdinand Marcos turned on the intervention of Laurel at this point. The way in which Laurel resolved the case legally was so discordant that it adds to the mystery. To be sure, the murder trial had been heavily covered in the press. But efforts to explain Laurel's intervention as an act of compassion, based on his own experience as a law student accused of murder, are unconvincing. So are arguments that the young defendant had to be saved for society because he was so brilliant. It is only with the discovery of the identity of Ferdinand's father that the Laurel mystery begins to resolve.

Laurel was a man of all-consuming ambition, a nationalist visionary who believed that the Philippines had to be rescued from American domination at all cost. The effort to expel Western imperialism was a major force at that time in India, Burma, Indonesia, Indochina, revolutionary China—and in the emergence of Japan as a military power with international designs. Laurel was trying to rebuild his political fortunes, to enlarge his constituency, and to gain the discreet backing of financiers who had no reason to love America. His aim was ultimately to wrest the presidency from Quezon. A presidential election was scheduled for 1941, to determine who would preside over the last term before independence. There was an eight-year limit on how long any president could serve. Quezon would have to step aside eventually.

In addition to seeking the support of disgruntled Filipino oligarchs, Laurel turned to Japanese industries that were investing heavily in the islands, becoming their legal consultant. He also courted the Chinese. The Chuas were pilot fish for the entire Chinese community; their support could shift Chinese banking and commercial interests in Laurel's favor.

The most likely explanation for what happened is that Judge Chua appealed to Justice Laurel privately, in the manner of such things, and Laurel was happy to respond. The two men were contemporaries in the legal profession, and it was a small favor, in a country where such favors are a part of life. As Joseph Lelyveld once commented in *The New York Times*, "To be convicted of a crime in the Philippines is almost to be convicted of lacking influence."

When the high court convened to hear the oral arguments, Laurel obviously had his mind made up in advance. He listened impatiently while Guerrero, the famous prosecutor, summarized the testimony of the star witness, Calixto Aguinaldo—testimony that had been remarkably persuasive up to this point and that remains persuasive reviewing the court records half a century later. Suddenly, Laurel interrupted the prosecutor and announced that he simply did not believe Aguinaldo.

In his decision, Laurel wrote: "By and large, we find the testimony of Calixto Aguinaldo to be inherently improbable and full of contradictions in important details. For this reason, we decline to give him any credit. In view of this conclusion, we find it neither necessary nor profitable to examine the corroborative evidence presented by the prosecution. Where the principal and basic evidence upon which the prosecution rests its case fails, all evidence intended to support or corroborate it must likewise fail."

Before he had heard the case through, Laurel simply dismissed all arguments with a wave of his hand and the matter was closed.

Ferdinand was free—along with his astonished uncle, Lizardo. By his own account, Ferdinand went directly to the post office to wire the good news to his father (we are not certain whether he meant Mariano or Judge Chua, or both). Then he rushed home, where he had a joyful and tearful reunion with his mother.

The following morning, he returned to the Supreme Court, where

Laurel administered his oath as a lawyer while Chief Justice Avancena handed him his certificate.

Some people remained unimpressed, among them Cesar Nalundasan, son of the murder victim, who said: "I personally believe that Mr. Ferdinand Marcos killed my father."

Years later, when Ferdinand was looking for backing to run for president, two of his oldest and closest friends from law school, Roberto Benedicto and Claudio Teehankee, discussed the prospects and rejected the idea of him as president because of the Nalundasan case. According to one source, the two lawyers concluded: "No, Marcos killed Nalundasan. People are convinced about that. . . . We should not have a murderer in Malacanang."

The question was also raised by Ferdinand's own son. "Little boys have amazing minds," Marcos told *Time* correspondent Arthur Zich. "Just the other day our nine year old, Bong-Bong, came to me and said: 'Hey, Dad, what's this about you having murdered a man once?' And I said: 'Well, if that had been so, I wouldn't be standing here with you now, would I?' Bong-Bong said: 'O.K., who did kill him, then?' We just left it there."

Perhaps the final word on the matter comes from Imelda's family. In the course of a number of lengthy interviews, Imelda's cousin Loreto confided that one of the Romualdez family once asked Ferdinand privately whether he really had shot Nalundasan. Ferdinand brushed the question aside with the remark, "That was just kid stuff."

Two

THE ROSE OF TACLOBAN

THE ROMUALDEZ FAMILY, like so many other prominent Filipino families, prided itself on being started by the illegitimate children of a Spanish priest. They were *mestizo anak para,* "friar mixtures." These were the hybrids who—benefiting from Spanish blood, European education, and social prestige—turned on their Spanish masters and began the movement for independence. With their eyes always on the main chance, they were also the first to turn against independence and welcome American rule, becoming its handmaidens. For the Romualdez family, such clever foresight brought power and glory to spare. But it was a string of family tragedies that produced Imelda's branch, the dark side.

Her grandmother, Trinidad Lopez y Crisostomo Talentin (called simply "Tidad"), was one of eight children sired out of wedlock by a Franciscan priest. A native of Grenada, Francisco Lopez was sent to the islands in 1838 to be the spiritual leader of Basey parish on the island of Samar. He was forty years old, a skilled silversmith, and a man of great energy. The love of his life was Concepcion Talentin, a child of the parish fathered by one of his predecessors. She lived in sin with Father Lopez for thirty-four years. After the birth of Tidad, their first child, in April 1853, the padre was transferred to Burauen, a village on the neighboring island of Leyte, remaining there nearly two decades. As the years passed, he built a church, a courthouse, and a school, and Burauen grew into a small town.

When he was in his sixties, Father Lopez was again transferred, far away to the dusty parish of Pandacan on the outskirts of Manila. He left Concepcion behind but took his children for schooling. At nineteen, Tidad was a solidly built young woman with a deep contempt for men. She wanted to be a nun but was barred because she was illegitimate. She earned her keep sweeping the parish church, where one day her confessor suggested an alternative: She could marry somebody about to die and make the poor fellow happy, then she would be a widow, which was more acceptable socially than being an illegitimate child. The confessor had in mind poor, sickly Daniel Romualdez, an unemployed schoolteacher of twenty-one who was dying of tuberculosis. His family were also *mestizos,* parish folk of similar origin. Daniel was educated and had been a leader of the village, but resigned his teaching post when he found he was dying, and had come to pray for a miracle. The miracle he had in mind was that the girl sweeping the floor would marry him. So he spoke to the priest, and the miracle was arranged.

Daniel Romualdez was lucky to be taken in tow by a woman of great fortitude. To cure his illness, Tidad took him to Leyte, to live with her mother. When he failed to die, and lived to a ripe old age, making her pregnant repeatedly in the process, Tidad concluded that it was all part of the male conspiracy.

"He would curse her right and left," complained his granddaughter Loreto, the family historian, who began to talk openly about such things only after her cousin, the First Lady, had gone into exile far away. "Many of her relatives were resentful of him. When he was weak, there was Trinidad taking care of him; now he's fine, look at him."

Ever after, Doña Tidad grumbled to her granddaughters, "Don't get married, men are liars. Why don't you become nuns, enter the convent? I want you to have peace of mind. If you get married, you don't know to what kind of a man, so you don't know what's going to happen." Good advice ignored.

Thanks to the many years Father Lopez had invested in Burauen, Tidad and her husband were well received in Leyte. In no time at all, the sickly unemployed teacher from Manila was Capitán Daniel, the town boss.

Compared to Luzon, Leyte is a peaceful place, its low green hills overgrown with banana plants, and hot plains along the coast growing rice, sisal, sugarcane, and coconuts, the main industry. Typhoons blacken the sky in autumn, flattening buildings and leveling crops. The population is peaceful, overwhelmingly Catholic, and there is little cash in circulation. What there is stays in the tight fists of local gentry, who are rarely seen except as election time nears, when they distribute 10-peso notes. By pooling these pesos with *compadres,* a poor man can buy a squealing ridgeback hog with a string through its nose, for a feast or *merienda* where the *lechon,* the best pieces of golden brown skin, dripping fat, go to the elders.

As the local teachers, Capitán Daniel and Tidad were respected but poor. After five years, they moved up the dirt road to Dagami, and finally to Tolosa on San Pedro Bay, where they lived in the schoolhouse, a nipa hut divided in the middle by a tiny kitchen. Tolosa's main attraction was a sandstone spire that stuck up out of the beach 1,000 feet, resembling Corcovado above Rio. (Like Corcovado, on its summit now is a concrete Christ, a gift of the Romualdez family.) In time, Capitán Daniel became mayor and acquired coconut groves. Half a century later the family owned the whole town. The Romualdez name is on its schools, markets, civic buildings, utilities, and churches.

Daniel Romualdez matured into a giant, with a large head, a barrel chest, and a vast belly. At one sitting, he could tuck away an entire goat. Every five years, he stopped cursing Tidad long enough to get her pregnant. Their first son, Norberto, was born in Burauen in June 1875; a second, Miguel, at Dagami in September 1880. By the time their third son arrived in Tolosa, Tidad was feeling the strain of living with a tyrant and had a nervous breakdown. Filipinos point out darkly that the child delivered on July 3, 1885, named Vicente Orestes, was the product of a woman in mental collapse.

He was a runt, a dainty boy with effeminate features. Tidad sighed, "He is the tenderest, the weakest, my youngest boy Vicente Orestes." She fawned over him, and he became the family toy. "Orestes will have to be looked after," she said. "He does not have his brothers' vigor and ambition." By his teens, Orestes had become a village idler who spent his time playing dominoes or a guitar. Because he spoke little, people took his silence to be profound. Copying his eldest brother, he carried around a book of poems to stare at vacantly. Strangers believed him to be a man of exquisite sensibilities.

The eldest brother, Norberto, was just the opposite, a dynamic young man educated by Jesuits in Manila, gifted in music, scholarship, business, and politics. He married well at twenty-one and started a local college for Filipinos. The success of the Romualdez family over the years was largely Norberto's doing.

The middle brother, Miguel, was a man of action and a natural politician. He went off young to fight the Spaniards in 1898, then turned his back on independence and joined the Yankee cause. English-speaking natives were needed to help administer the islands, so the entire Romualdez family moved 20 kilometers to Tacloban, where Norberto was appointed clerk of the court. Under the Americans, practicing law replaced the priesthood as the path to power and glory. Norberto earned a law degree and in 1906 was appointed the prosecuting attorney for Leyte. As legal fees, he accepted some of the best property, and bought a mansion on Gran Capitan, the main street of Tacloban. He published poetry, wrote articles on Filipino etymology, composed a popular song entitled "My Nipa Hut," and was elected a member of the Society of International Law in Washington, D.C., the kind of accolade that Americans arranged for promising Filipinos. Appointed a judge in the booming sugar capital of Bacolod, he gained influence with the sugar barons and developed political clout throughout the central Visayan Islands. In 1919 he moved to Manila, bought a mansion on the bayfront, and started the law firm of Romualdez & Romualdez with his brother Miguel. Two years later, the Americans appointed Norberto to the Philippine Supreme Court. Until 1916, all the justices were Americans, so Norberto's appointment was quite a plum.

Brother Miguel became a favorite of Governor-General Leonard Wood, who ruled the islands as a petty despot. Deliberately going against the wishes of Manuel Quezon, Wood in 1925 appointed Miguel to be mayor of Manila, where the perks and patronage soon made him the richest Romualdez.

Life moved at a slower pace for Vicente Orestes. He held down a job briefly for the Tacloban weather bureau, reading the barometer. He attended Norberto's Colegio de San Jose, where the family name guaranteed passing grades. Norberto found him a place in law school, and eased his way toward a degree. In 1908 Orestes eloped with a Tolosa farm girl, Juanita Acereda, who bore him five children in rapid succession.

By the 1920s, all three brothers were settled in Manila, with Orestes being swept along in his brothers' wake. Once on the Supreme Court, Norberto had to withdraw from private law practice. Miguel ran the firm. The only obligation on Orestes was to be physically present to receive inquiries from his brothers' clients. Surrounded by such prosperity and power, he became reckless. Using borrowed money, he bought property on a tree-shaded street called Calle Solano near Malacanang Palace. With family funds, he built a typical Manila house with high ceilings and elaborate grillwork. He had a garage built onto the house and bought a shiny black Berlina limousine. In August 1926, just three months after they moved into the new house, Orestes's wife— who had never been sick a day in her life—astonished everyone by dying suddenly of what was uncertainly described as "blood poisoning."

The family matriarch, Doña Tidad, immediately began to fret about her youngest son. He was, as a family biographer put it delicately, "emotionally burdened."

Doña Tidad was now a formidable old woman. For years Norberto had been putting money at her disposal, so that his mother could make generous gifts to convents she admired. He conveyed to her all his properties in Leyte, to distribute as she wished among members of the family. She decided that the best property, a 10-hectare lot on Calle Real in Tacloban, should go to Orestes, to "guarantee his future." But all her efforts to insulate Orestes and give him the trappings of a normal life were to no avail. No sooner was his dead wife in her tomb than he was carrying on with a married woman. Doña Tidad decided to find him a proper wife.

It would have been better for everyone if she had not interfered. Orestes already had more children than he could manage: Lourdes, Vicente Junior, Dulce, Victoria, and Francisco. In addition to paying installments on his lot and car, the cost of feeding and educating his children was leaving a hole in his pocket. If he remained single, the children would soon grow up, and Orestes could go back to Leyte, as he dreamed of doing, to become a gentleman beachcomber surviving on the rental of his Tacloban property. For once, Tidad meddled too much.

In her opinion, the best women were nuns, so the best wife for Orestes would be like a nun. The Asilo de San Vicente de Paul in Manila was a shelter for orphaned or indigent girls who sought a basic education and vocational training. Many became nuns, but from time to time one would be taken away by a wealthy family to provide an obedient wife for an errant son. For a roof overhead and food to eat, such a girl could endure almost anything.

The Asilo was one of the charities Doña Tidad had been supporting. As mother of the mayor and a Supreme Court justice, she could expect cooperation. One day in 1927, Tidad appeared at the Asilo and broached her matter forthrightly to the mother superior. Without hesitation, Sister Modesta assured her that there were several young women in her care who might be suitable, particularly a charming young *mestiza* named Alice Burcher, and a quiet, serious girl from Baliuag, just north of Manila, named Remedios Trinidad. Excuses were devised to bring each young woman into the mother superior's reception room. Doña Tidad approved them both.

The next Sunday, a *merienda* was thrown at the Romualdez mansion, to which everyone in the family was invited. As her part in the plot, Sister Modesta sent Alice Burcher and Remedios Trinidad from the Asilo bearing an envelope containing blank stationery. The unsuspecting girls, carefully scrubbed and primped for Sunday Mass, appeared at the mansion and were drawn into the feast, unaware that they were under scrutiny like vegetables being fondled or meat being pinched. When the time came for music, they were asked to contribute a song. To everyone's horror, pretty Alice Burcher confessed that she did not know how to sing, a devastating admission for a Filipina. Not only did everyone sing, everyone sang all the time, in private, in public, in churches, latrines, brothels, political campaigns—especially in public. It did not matter if you were good or bad, on key or off, so long as you were open about it. In the Philippines, singing was like a grin or a handshake, something you did to let the tribe know you were not carrying a weapon. The only time you did not sing was when you were about to kill somebody. Silence was a danger signal.

The party was rescued by Remedios Trinidad. Shyly, the quiet girl from the Asilo stepped forward, and gave a performance of the Tagalog love song *"Ako'y Ibong Sawi"* that brought down the roof.

Medy, as she was called, was an attractive young woman whose appeal was completely obscured by a somber nature. The daughter of an itinerant peddlar of costume jewelry, she had been placed in an orphanage at an early age. Making her way to the University of the Philippines, she took a degree in music before she was ruined by a love affair. She had fallen in love with a young engineer, but his wealthy family frowned on a match with a penniless orphan. They sent him off to America to finish his training. Soon his letters stopped. Heartbroken, Medy fled to the Asilo, where she taught piano, a stricken look never far from her face. She was twenty-seven when Orestes saw her pouring her grief into her song.

He was utterly smitten. He visited the Asilo daily, bringing her flowers and candy. For Medy it was a losing battle. Everybody went to work on her. The bishop, the mother superior, her confessor, all tried to convince her that Orestes and his children were a cross she should take up on the path to salvation. It took a year.

They were married on May 21, 1928, at three-thirty in the morning. The early hour was necessary because everyone was frightened. Threats had been made by Orestes's jilted lover. The day before the wedding, a taxi had drawn up to his house, and a wild-eyed woman screamed: "Orestes, if I cannot have you, nobody will!" In a panic the ceremony was rescheduled. Nobody explained to Medy why this was necessary, nor why the doors and windows of the church remained bolted. Nor why the groom's children were not in attendance.

Orestes had not told his children that he was getting remarried. The first they knew was when he brought Medy home. Not surprisingly, they refused to accept her, and the eldest girl, Lourdes, who ruled the house and her father with an iron hand, declared open warfare. The house was filthy, with dirty dishes everywhere and trash under the beds. Medy started putting things in order, which provoked a violent reaction from Lourdes.

"Who does she think she is?" Lourdes raged. "This isn't her house. My father bought this house for my real mother."

Orestes lacked the strength of character to be firm with his children, except when it came to the subject of sex, and then he overdid it. He was so determined not to let his daughters be victimized by men that he poisoned their imaginations. They had no male friends of any kind. Medy's attempts to introduce them to people their own age were rejected. Orestes's influence was lasting.

Dulce, after studying to become a teacher, withdrew to a convent before she was twenty, eventually becoming mother superior of Holy Ghost College in Manila. Victoria, the family beauty, had a nervous breakdown when she passed through puberty and ran through the streets of San Miguel nearly naked. Surviving this sensation, she became an accomplished violinist and doctor of law, but rejected all suitors and fled the islands to be a spinster professor of languages in Spain.

At seventeen, Lourdes had made herself into a caricature of a Spanish noblewoman, arrogant and high-strung. As she saw it, her father had brought home a woman who was little more than a servant, and she was luring him into the bedroom and debasing him. When the children saw that their father was not defending his new wife, they grew more aggressive.

"Remedios would leave the house when she couldn't stand it any longer," Loreto explained, "and she would go to our house and spend one or two days with us, crying over my mother's shoulder until my father would send her home."

She gave birth to Imelda on July 2, 1929, followed the next year by Benjamin, who was given the pet name "Kokoy." Each time Medy became pregnant, Orestes lost interest till the child was born, then he would follow her to bed while Lourdes sat in the living room wringing a hanky.

There were two servants in the house, seventeen-year-old Marcelo Carpio Cinco, or "Siloy," and Estrella Cumpas, both brought from Leyte by Norberto to take care of Orestes and his children. During the days the servants observed Medy scrubbing, ironing, and putting away the girls' clothing. At night, they overheard shrieking attacks by Lourdes, after which Medy would retreat weeping to sleep in the garage.

For years, Orestes had enjoyed the illusion of prosperity with Norberto on the Supreme Court and Miguel as mayor. Unexpectedly, in 1930–31 the family fortunes plummeted. One of Miguel's daughters, Estela, was studying law, and Miguel got her a job as private secretary to Justice Norberto. Estela knew Norberto was chairman of the bar exams, and had copies in his office. She gave a set to a boyfriend. He was caught, and there was a scandal. Political opponents seized the opportunity. The trial dragged on two years and was heavily covered in the press.

"It made us shrink this small," said Loreto. "My father thought it his moral duty to resign, at the height of his career." He still controlled the southern districts of the Visayas, including Leyte, Samar, and neighboring islands, in alliance with political leader Tomas Oppus. Norberto represented Leyte in the national assembly, and served as dean of various law schools, but from then on he exercised leverage behind the scenes. It was said that he could commit a million provincial votes this way or that. Estela's indiscretion also cost Miguel his career as mayor of Manila, which ended with the one term. By then enough money had been salted away, and enough property had been acquired, so that the Romualdez family remained powerful, in Manila and in the Visayas. But the free ride for Orestes was over. He became short-tempered with Medy and arguments over money grew violent. One night the servants heard Medy being beaten. The next day, she packed up Imelda and Kokoy and took them away for three months, living in a gazebo on Norberto's property. Family pressure forced her to return.

All this was too much for Doña Tidad. At the height of the scandal in 1932, the old woman, bedridden for months, called out the names of her three sons and died.

Orestes was desperate. His Manila lot had been purchased on install-ments, which he could no longer afford. The house, built with family funds, was now mortgaged for 6,000 pesos, which dribbled away. Late in 1931, Medy moved out completely, taking her infants and the maid Estrella with her. They spent nine months crammed in a cheap room. Medy supported them by making spicy *chorizo* sausages to sell, and embroidering baby dresses that brought a dollar apiece. She opened a bank account and gradually built up her savings.

In 1932, Orestes attempted a reconciliation. He was desperately short of cash—his electricity and water had been turned off, and Nor-berto and Miguel refused to help until he made peace with his wife. When Medy resisted, he wheedled. Finally, she said, "Look, Orestes, I will go with you because I am your wife, and you don't like me living away from your house because the Romualdez name will be smeared, so I will live in the same compound, but do not force me to live in the house. I will live in the garage."

The moment she got home, Medy's frugal savings were spent by Orestes to pay his bills and school fees for the children of his first wife.

The garage was a shanty, a roof extending out from the main struc-ture, to which some flimsy walls had been added to shelter crates and trash discarded there. The back end was a makeshift servants' quarters for Siloy and Estrella, who worked without pay. Imelda and Kokoy slept with Estrella on planks laid across packing crates at one end, Medy on a long table opposite. At night, while the children slept, Orestes would come out to talk with Medy, and force himself on her. In the gloom afterwards, Estrella could hear her sobbing. She gave birth to Alita on January 3, 1933, to Alfredo on July 16, 1935, and to Armando—eight months later—on March 6, 1936.

Without telling anyone, Orestes stopped paying installments on the house. The Franciscan order which held the mortgage threatened to foreclose. The land Doña Tidad had left him in Leyte was also in jeopardy. The 10-hectare property in Tacloban consisted of a number of lots, ranging from ordinary wooden houses down to rickety nipa huts. Occupants paid a few pesos ground rent each month; when these small sums were put together, it was more than enough to cover the mortgage for the whole parcel. But the woman in charge of collecting ground rent was pocketing the money. The mortgage had gone unpaid long enough to bring threats of foreclosure.

Again, Orestes begged Medy's savings to make a token payment on the Manila house, and sent her off to Tacloban to collect the ground rent and resume payments. She took Imelda, Kokoy, and her three babies with her, shepherded by Estrella. While the property quarrel was settled, they lived in a hut Estrella described as being fit only for birds. Finally, Medy received assurances that the property would not be foreclosed, and they returned early in 1937 to Manila.

She retreated to the garage, which she shared with the prized Berlina. Orestes refused to forfeit the car. He sold its tires, mechanical parts, chrome bumpers, and ornaments. Beside the Berlina one night, her last child, Conchita, was conceived. A change had come over Medy. She was gloomy and defeated. Estrella watched her grow sickly. When the pregnancy was nearing full term, Medy had a visitor. Her long-lost love, the engineer who had gone to America and stopped writing, returned. He came to visit Orestes and asked permission to see Medy and her children. The meeting was subdued and Medy humiliated. After introducing her children, she withdrew meekly to the garage. Within hours, contractions began. She fled across Manila to a rented room in Ermita. Estrella bundled up the children and followed.

Medy, virtually penniless, then checked into the hospital. When Imelda was born, Orestes had booked Medy into a private room. This time it was different. The discovery that one of the family had given birth in a charity ward scandalized the Romualdezes. Orestes was ordered to act urgently to protect their reputation. He went to Medy in the hospital, and told her simply, "We are going home." She was too weak to argue. It was the end of December 1937, and Estrella and Siloy could sense the defeat. Medy had always been a lonely woman. Now, her spirit was broken. Four months later, in April 1938, she curled up in the dark on her table in the garage and wept. Touching her forehead, Estrella found her running a high fever. They rushed her to a clinic, where she lapsed into a coma and died. The diagnosis was pneumonia.

"Remedios was a saint," Loreto concluded. "Many people malign her. They say she lost her mind, that she was crazy. Poor woman, she suffered a lot."

The Romualdez family packed Orestes and both sets of children off to Leyte, out of sight and mind.

Seven months later the house at 278 Calle Solano was for sale, with 8,000 pesos still owed on the mortgage. The sellers were listed as Vicente Orestes Romualdez and his children: Vicente Junior, Lourdes, Dulce, Victoria, and Francisco. No mention was made of Imelda or the others.

When she became First Lady, Imelda had the house on Calle Solano torn down. She bought the once-magnificent Goldberg Mansion nearby and had it renovated by the leading architect in the Philippines, filling it with fine antiques. There she entertained foreign guests, referring to it as "my childhood home."

When the steamer from Manila docked at Tacloban in December 1938, a troupe of five children was herded down the gangplank by a nine-year-old girl. Imelda Remedios Visitacion Romualdez was a tall, bony child with soulful eyes, long straight black hair hanging down to her waist. She wore her mother's white dress, several sizes too big, reaching to her ankles.

The ship was met by Lourdes and Victoria, who had come ahead to make preparations. Lourdes was now twenty-six, a doctor employed in Tacloban as a government health officer. She was also a surrogate mother. The small children—Imelda's brothers and sisters—were too young to be aware of tragedy. For many years, Conchita believed that Lourdes was her real mother, an impression her father did nothing to correct.

Orestes was looking forward to a quiet life. Norberto's original Spanish mansion on Gran Capitan had been replaced in 1935 by a fine new two-bedroom villa. They could live there rent-free. By carefully collecting ground rents on his property, Orestes could maintain title to the land and earn enough from its coconut groves to pay for food. There was a little cash left from the sale of his Manila house. As insurance, he had a secret stash—a moneybelt stuffed with diamonds dug out of jewelry Doña Tidad had left him when she died.

The first two years in Leyte went smoothly. The girls attended a Benedictine convent school, and kept to themselves. Imelda and Kokoy collected the ground rent, earning a tiny commission.

In 1941, news came that Norberto, politicking on neighboring

Samar, had suffered a heart attack and died. Their protector was gone. Pearl Harbor followed, the Japanese invaded, and Orestes took his family to stay with cousins in Guinarona, a rural barrio near Dagami, where the girls in particular would attract less attention. By June 1942, the Japanese had settled down to stay, and Orestes felt safe returning to Tacloban.

The occupiers had commandeered Norberto's villa, so Orestes had no choice but to take his children to a rickety two-story wooden house on his own property at Calle Real. That autumn it blew down in the first typhoon. Nearby was a derelict shack with sagging wood walls and a thatch roof, no better than the Manila garage in which Remedios had lived and died. Orestes remained in the hut for many years. It seemed to suit him.

Under the Japanese, occupation pesos became worthless, dollars were confiscated, and military scrip was printed at whim by local commanders. Most Leyteños survived as they always had, growing their own fruit and vegetables, fishing, bartering, and scrounging. Not Orestes. Although he had no visible means of support, when nobody was looking he dug into his moneybelt for a diamond to live on for the next few months.

While others were scrounging, he amassed a collection of old *Reader's Digest*s in Spanish. This reinforced his reputation as a scholar. He spent days reading the *Digest,* pausing to pontificate to his children, or whiled away the hours playing dominoes with parish priests. For him the war was a time of peace.

His indolence bothered others who were having a difficult time, but the name Romualdez still carried weight. Because of his name, and the fact that he was said to be a lawyer by training, Orestes was made honorary head of a neighborhood association that rationed rice, sugar, and salt among its members. When there were leftovers, Orestes pleaded to have them for his large family.

The children depended upon Lourdes. However poorly she had treated Imelda's mother in the past, she proved to be a woman of courage and determination in caring for the children now. As a doctor she earned what she could, handled family finances, and doled out food at meals. Breakfast was black coffee and one piece of bread each.

In 1944, Leyte was thrown into confusion by the American invasion. Tacloban was the first town in the Philippines to be liberated. The departure of the Japanese left Norberto's villa vacant, and Orestes hurriedly moved his brood back in before the idea occurred to anyone else.

Lourdes opened a clinic. Imelda sang songs to the GIs. In the general exhilaration, it seemed natural to give Orestes Romualdez (a friend of the church whose name was famous in legal circles, and who owned a grand piece of Tacloban property) the post as dean of the law faculty at the newly reopened St. Paul's College. The title of dean was deceptive because there were very few law students. The figurehead post was created for Orestes as a gesture to his late brother, and obliged him only to teach occasional classes in legal history and legal bibliography, which the professor with the oddly vacant expression insisted on teaching in Spanish, to the bewilderment of his students. His salary was 100 pesos a month, which paid his bills.

But the family's euphoria did not last. Norberto's villa had been willed to his son, Norberto Junior, and in 1946 he decided to return to Leyte to build a political career there. Norberto's heaviest hints were lost on Orestes, and both families ended up jammed into the house, which became impossible. Imelda's branch had no choice but to move out, back to the thatch shack on Calle Real. Orestes never told his children that Norberto Junior was the proper owner of the villa, so they bore their cousin a heavy grudge that would have ugly consequences years later.

With liberation, Imelda was able to enter high school. She became a familiar sight in her usual white dress, black hair straight to her hips. She was not a brilliant student, but managed to pass. Her brothers and sisters were so sensitive about their poverty that they found ways to slip in and out of classes unobtrusively, avoiding after-school activities where they might be embarrassed for lack of pocket money. This made ordinary friendships impossible. On weekends the family went to the beach, which was free, and there was a great deal of singing. Still there was always something furtive about them. Their school fees were always tardy, and the girls were chagrined to find their names always on the delinquent list, posted in the school hall. Once when Imelda's sister Alita was absent from school for a week, a nun came to see if she was ill and was astounded to discover the kind of place in which this branch of the famous Romualdez family lived. She was not invited in.

Following this discovery, Imelda was offered a job in the school canteen for 15 pesos a month. She seemed listless and dreamy, and found the work too demanding, so she was moved to the library to dust books and file cards.

At sixteen she was filling out, a striking beauty with an innocent face and huge limpid eyes. Everybody called her Meldy. She acted or sang in school programs with a big, booming mezzo-soprano (her favorite song was "You Belong to My Heart"). She dreamed of being in opera, on the stage, or in movies. Desperate for recognition, when important people came to town she was always among the local belles distributing leis. In a parade celebrating the second anniversary of Tacloban's liberation, she rode on a float as the local Miss Philippines.

Orestes restrained her as best he could. She was forbidden to go to dances, but was grudgingly permitted to attend certain very proper parties, if she came home early. He frowned on any extravagance, limiting her to two new dresses a year and one pair of shoes.

In 1948, about to turn nineteen, she graduated from high school, then hurried across town to Leyte High to watch the graduation of some friends. A young lawyer, Ferdinand Marcos, who was running for Congress from Ilocos Norte, delivered the commencement address. Then, at the flower festival that year, Imelda had her big moment when she was chosen "Rose of Tacloban."

In the postwar flush, the new generation of the Romualdez family was rapidly recovering its wealth and high estate. They had a game plan. While Norberto Junior re-established his father's political base in the Visayas and ran for governor of Leyte, Miguel's son Daniel became a congressman in Manila, where the family still owned choice property. Daniel's brother Eduardo became a leading banker, chairman of the Rehabilitation Finance Corporation (RFC) set up to funnel American aid into projects to rebuild the shattered economy. As chairman, Eduardo became a powerful figure behind the scenes. In time, the RFC was renamed the Development Bank of the Philippines and remains today the chief instrument for granting long-term government loans.

Following their game plan, Daniel, Eduardo, and Norberto Junior set up a political tripod with one foot in the Visayas, one foot in Congress, and one foot in the government bank, restoring all the leverage lost in the previous generation.

Whenever politics came to Tacloban, as it did in a big way during the 1949 campaign, family grievances were temporarily forgotten as the Romualdez rich hobnobbed briefly with the Romualdez poor. Imelda was essential decoration at every banquet Norberto Junior threw for visiting politicians, or when Congressman Daniel came to campaign. Naturally, Imelda's father would be included in his role as Dean Orestes of the law faculty.

Imelda was becoming a political commodity very much appreciated

everywhere, a pretty girl with an engaging manner, a voluptuous singing voice, and powerful relatives. Because of the sheltered life she had
led up to this point, ashamed of her poverty and guarded obsessively
by her father, her personality and character were largely undeveloped.
To sophisticates from Manila, she was only a provincial naif. But thanks
to her Romualdez ties and her high visibility, she had many unsuccess-
ful suitors—sons of politicians, a young widowed congressman, an ambitious attorney. Orestes found them all unsuitable. That same year, when
President Elpidio Quirino came to town, recently widowed, Imelda
sang for him in a school concert and the old rogue charmed her by
saying he wished he could carry her off, but he would lose as many votes
as he would gain. During the same campaign, presidential candidate
Jose Laurel was wined and dined at Norberto's house and Imelda
caught his eye. Years later, his son Salvador "Doy" Laurel recalled, "I
remember coming home late one night in 1949 and hearing Papa
saying: 'You know, Mama, in Tacloban there's a good-looking girl, the
daughter of Romualdez. She is not only a good singer, she is a real
beauty.' Papa may have hoped that, by overhearing what he said, my
curiosity would be aroused." It was not.

Obediently, Imelda spent the next four years at St. Paul's pursuing
a degree in education, majoring in English and history. Her mother
only a dim memory, she became attached to Lourdes. Barred by poverty from ordinary wholesome outlets, she passed long hours posing
before her mirror, practicing facial expressions and gestures while she
sang.

In 1951, Lourdes and Orestes decided that Imelda was old enough
to go to dances. As a symbol of her own liberation, she styled her hair
in a chignon and immediately fell in love with Victoriano Chan, the heir
of a wealthy Chinese family that owned the Tacloban Electric Plant. His
parents considered her ineligible, and ended the romance abruptly.

Imelda recovered quickly. Before the year was out, she fell in love
with a young medical student, Justo Zibala, from the island of Negros.
He had dark good looks, deep-set eyes, and a promising future, but he
was a Protestant. Orestes asked the Bishop of Palo to intercede, but the
bishop's efforts were fruitless and the two grew inseparable. Orestes
became alarmed.

For a long time, people had been telling him that Imelda was wast-
ing her talents in Leyte. She ought to go to Manila. Congressman Daniel
was now speaker *pro tem*, and he and his wife had left a standing

invitation for Imelda to stay with them. Daniel assured Orestes that he would find Imelda suitable employment. He was acutely conscious of her political value in campaigning and lobbying, and he had in mind making use of her as a hostess. Another recent visitor to Tacloban, Imelda's cousin Loreto, promised that she would get her a scholarship to study voice.

For Orestes, the idea was repugnant. Manila meant nothing but grief. Still, Imelda had become a serious problem, ever more deeply involved with "that wretched fellow" Justo Zibala, the Protestant. Another suitor that Imelda had spurned—rich, intense Dominador Pacho, who owned the Dagami Saw Mills and had a reputation for getting what he wanted—had been hanging around looking dangerous. Imelda was worried that he was going to "try something." That dissolved Orestes's remaining will. When Congressman Daniel agreed to pay her travel expenses, Orestes sent his daughter off to the big town with 5 pesos in her purse.

Imelda arrived in Manila at age twenty-two with a head full of cravings. She moved in with her rich cousins and found a job as a shopgirl selling sheet music. When her father objected, cousin Eduardo the banker found her a more respectable job as a clerk in the Central Bank. Cousin Loreto, true to her word, arranged for voice lessons from a teacher at Philippine Women's University (Loreto footing the bill).

One day the editor of a Sunday supplement, *This Week,* discovered Imelda at work in the bank. She personified innocence, so he photographed her for his Valentine's Day cover. Distributed to a large readership, her cover attracted the attention of Manila's polo pony set. The name Romualdez had instant recognition. They all knew where to find her.

Congressman Daniel's home was a center of political activity for the Nacionalistas. Frequent parties and open houses brought clouds of political mosquitoes, and, as Daniel had anticipated, they swarmed around Imelda. Many were members of the oligarchy, some the sons of billionaires, their lawyers, their generals or colonels, with a sprinkling around the edges of lower castes, people who knew how to do things with their own hands—doctors, architects, and columnists. Of the four hundred families who owned everything in the islands, many were represented here, self-important men in embroidered *barongs* open at the throat, sipping cocktails while their heavily armed chauffeurs and bodyguards sweated in the tropical night outside, grinding out cigarette butts with their steel-tipped stomping shoes. Among so many admirers, there was no question that Imelda could have found someone to marry with money, looks, haciendas, yachts, planes, offshore portfolios, and a few Arabians for breeding purposes.

But she was very young, and did not comprehend the value system of the oligarchy. Manila matriarchs and debutantes sniggered when Imelda rushed about at parties, fetching chairs or canapes. In her anxiety to please, she was acting like a servant.

Perhaps the difference was insurmountable. Imelda's hopes for fame and glory were secretly fixed on winning the Miss Manila beauty contest. In the past, poor but beautiful Filipinas had made the leap from oblivion to the gentry by winning beauty titles. For the first time since the war, the contest of 1953 would be linked to international pageants. Whoever was chosen Miss Manila would make public appearances throughout the islands, have a chance to become Miss Philippines, then compete overseas. The idea was pushed by Imelda's music teacher Adoracion Reyes, and her husband Ricardo, a member of the original Bayanihan Dance Company. Through friends at City Hall, Reyes bypassed normal channels and submitted an application and a photograph of Imelda in a polka-dot dress directly to Manila's mayor, Arsenio Lacson, the main man in the competition.

Congressman Daniel was furious. He thought the whole idea demeaning. Here was Imelda surrounded by wealthy suitors, and she wanted to run for a beauty title. Cousins Loreto and Eduardo were equally dismayed. It was universally assumed in Manila that girls did not win beauty contests without granting sexual favors to the mayor or some other political figure. Although Mayor Lacson was married and a potential presidential candidate, he was a celebrated playboy. It was his custom to spend every afternoon between three and four at the Hotel Filipinas, where he had "Chinese tea"—an hour in bed with one or more Chinese girls provided by his constituents. (He later died of a heart attack during one of these tea parties.)

Imelda's photograph had the desired effect on Lacson. Friends at City Hall said she had a good chance of winning; others were not certain. At the conservatory, fellow students wondered at the fuss. Imelda was attractive, but immature. Her manners were low class, her taste in clothes was "corny," and her idea of great literature was *Reader's Digest.* All she ever talked about was romance and the social prestige of the Romualdezes. One girl defended her, arguing that Imelda was just a repressed and lonely girl trying too hard to dazzle people and to be glamorous.

The Reyes were willing to do all the legwork and promotion to hustle votes for the contest, and Philippine Women's University agreed to be Imelda's official sponsor. But when the votes were canvassed, the Miss Manila title went to twenty-year-old Norma Jimenez from Pangasinan Province.

Imelda was stunned. Ricardo Reyes filed a protest on a technicality, arguing that no representative of the mayor had been present when the votes were tallied. Imelda went alone to see Mayor Lacson in private. By her own account, she broke down in his office and sobbed uncontrollably. When their meeting ended, the mayor astounded everyone by rejecting the decision of the pageant judges. Newspapers reported: "Mayor Lacson yesterday disowned the choice of the International Fair Board and named Imelda Romualdez of Philippine Women's University as Manila's official candidate for Miss Philippines."

Immediately, rumors spread that Imelda was Lacson's newest conquest, and that only in this way could she have made it worth his while to provoke such an uproar. The mayor charged that the judges had broken the rules, so he was personally choosing Miss Manila. The judges were stubborn. When the night came to present all the candidates for Miss Philippines, both Mayor Lacson's candidate and the Fair's candidate were present. Norma Jimenez appeared as Miss Manila, Imelda Romualdez as Muse of Manila, a title Lacson concocted. The scandal did little to help either girl—the Miss Philippines title went to someone else.

Imelda was convinced that she had won fair and square. Throughout her life, publicists and admirers persisted in asserting that she was once Miss Manila. Eventually, most people forgot the real story. It mattered only to Imelda.

On the heels of the scandal, she became involved with one of Manila's wealthiest young men. Ariston Nakpil had just finished his architectural studies at Harvard University, Cranbrook Academy, and the Fontainebleau School of Fine Arts in France. He was tall, dashing, articulate, belonged to one of Manila's oldest families, and would have been considered an excellent catch but for one small problem. He was already married. It was a teenage marriage that failed immediately, and the family claimed to be seeking an annulment, a lengthy process in the

Catholic Philippines. Imelda spent weekends with Nakpil at his family farm in Batangas and went with him on her first trip to the mountain resort of Baguio in the summer of 1953.

When Orestes learned of Nakpil's courtship and his previous marriage, he flew to Manila to confront Imelda. Even with an annulment, he insisted that she would never be more than a mistress to Nakpil. To Orestes and many other old-fashioned Filipinos, a Catholic marriage was a marriage even if it was annulled. Whatever followed was sequential polygamy.

Orestes forced her to return with him to Tacloban to get some distance from Nakpil. When she returned to Manila in mid-December 1953, she was still torn between her feelings for Nakpil and her obligation to her father. It was at this difficult moment that she met Ferdinand Marcos.

Three

THE LOST COMMAND

AFTER THE NALUNDASAN MURDER conviction was over-
turned in 1940, the Marcos family was deeply in debt to Jose Laurel.
Such a debt could work both ways.

They were now penniless, unable to pay their legal fees to defense
attorney Francisco. Ferdinand, Mariano, and Uncle Pio set up a one-
room law practice in Manila, a bolthole typical of 1930s detective novels
in the Heacock Building on the Escolta, the main street of the financial
district. Hanging your shingle on the Escolta signified that you were on
your way, or at least that you had bought a ticket, even if you could only
afford third class. Several of Ferdinand's old prisonmates at Bilibad
asked him to represent them on appeal, which gave him his first work
as a defense attorney, and did his reputation no harm in the Manila
underworld.

They tried to capitalize on their endless Ilocano friends and relatives, and the promising new Laurel connection. Like most strong leaders, Laurel had a lot of followers; Ferdinand was not the first in line. But
in law and politics there was always somebody's dirty work to be done.
Nearby were the law offices of the most powerful Ilocano politician of
the 1930s, President Quezon's valued and ambitious ally Elpidio
Quirino, still only a congressman, and his brother, Tony "the Fixer."
The political boss of Ilocos Sur, Quirino was a lawyer and a legislator
who had served at various times as secretary of finance, interior, and
foreign affairs and would eventually become president. He neatly

dodged charges of corruption by delegating the nightwork to his two brothers. In addition to being the reigning Ilocano warlord, Quirino had married into one of the top Chinese clans, the Syquias, and he was reputed to be the boss of the northern Luzon smuggling networks in partnership with Fukienese triads. The Marcoses became Quirino men.

One of Ferdinand's uncles was Congressman Narciso Ramos from Pangasinan Province, north of the city, another powerful man in Ilocano circles who had found jobs for hundreds of his followers in the civil service and in all ranks of the Constabulary, which had become almost a Ramos preserve. There were many transplanted Ilocanos in Pangasinan and in neighboring Tarlac Province who had fled the waste-land of the Ilocos for the farmlands of central Luzon, not to be farmers but to find jobs as chauffeurs or enforcers with the landlords. Many of them became members of Ilocano black-market syndicates operating in and around Manila. They were in competition with similar syndicates run by other tribal groups based in Batangas or in Cavite, or in China-town, all of them providing the grease for Manila's gears. Through Ramos, Laurel, and Quirino, the Marcoses stood a fair chance of becom-ing part of these mutual aid societies, and rescuing themselves from poverty.

But they had little time to cultivate these connections. On the eve of World War II, Manila was tense. Centerstage was taken up entirely by President Quezon's new field marshal, Douglas MacArthur.

Back in the autumn of 1934, worried about Japan's long-range plans, Quezon had gone to Washington to ask for the services of General MacArthur, who was about to be retired after serving as U.S. Army chief of staff. President Roosevelt, the New Deal Democrat, was only too glad to be rid of MacArthur, a saber-rattling Republican with monumental ambitions. For Douglas MacArthur, Manila was a tempting post: his father, General Arthur MacArthur, had been the military governor of the Philippines at the turn of the century. As a young officer, Douglas had served in the islands, and he had returned as a general to command the U.S. Army garrison in Manila, becoming an admirer of Quezon. In Washington as chief of staff, MacArthur had found his ambitions thwarted by growing ranks of adversaries. He was anxious to get away from the poisonous atmosphere of Washington and to make the Philip-pines his base for a new career, one that might lead eventually to the White House.

As a West Point graduate and a patrician, MacArthur identified with the Filipino oligarchy, shared their prejudices, and was determined to become one of them. He saw himself as America's proconsul in the islands, which was a decided improvement over the obscurity of retirement in the United States.

The current governor-general was Frank Murphy, a liberal and a pacifist. MacArthur despised liberals, pacifists, and Murphy in particular. He wanted the post of governor-general for himself. When Roosevelt refused to oblige, MacArthur persuaded Quezon to create the title of field marshal of the Philippines. At Quezon's urging he designed his own uniform—black trousers, white tunic, and a braided cap, the whole costume spangled with medals, stars, and gold cord like a matador's suit-of-lights. At ceremonies in Malacanang Palace, First Lady Aurora Quezon presented him, appropriately, with a proconsul's gold baton. On top of his ongoing U.S. salary as a major general, MacArthur was to receive $33,000 a year from the commonwealth, plus lavish imperial perks. Through Quezon's initiative, he was inducted into Manila's most exclusive clubs, including the president's own coven of the Freemasons, became a director of the resplendent Manila Hotel, one of the all-time great watering holes, and was given opportunities to acquire shares in gold mines and valuable property along Manila Bay. Since Governor-General Murphy, the pacifist, occupied Malacanang Palace, Quezon built his field marshal a luxurious penthouse atop the Manila Hotel, overlooking the swimming pool and the magnificent bay, with its lush sunsets over Bataan. MacArthur conducted much of his business on its terrace. When Mrs. MacArthur gave birth to their only child, a son, the godparents were Manuel and Aurora Quezon, which made the field marshal and the president *compadres.*

MacArthur's theatrical posturing impressed many Filipinos. He looked like the doorman to Quezon's New Age. As MacArthur became increasingly absorbed with the better things in life, defense was neglected. MacArthur's twenty-two thousand American soldiers had begun to go soft, and his commonwealth army of eight thousand Filipinos received only cursory training. Morale was low; Filipino soldiers were paid $7 a month compared to $30 for Americans. Preparedness was solely MacArthur's responsibility, although Washington was also to blame; much of the ammunition provided by the United States were duds. Admiral Tom Hart, MacArthur's naval counterpart, commanded an outmoded force of only three cruisers, thirteen destroyers, eighteen submarines, and half a dozen PT boats. The air corps was in worse shape. In the six years prior to Pearl Harbor, little was done to improve the situation.

While Quezon courted Americans, Tokyo wooed Filipinos. Japanese diplomats and businessmen spent large sums on gifts and entertainment, and created dummy corporations to be headed by famous Filipinos. Ferdinand's patron, Jose Laurel, was only one of many retained to lobby for Japanese interests.

By midsummer 1941, war with Japan was inevitable. Roosevelt had blocked Tokyo from access to oil in the Dutch East Indies, and on July 26 he ordered all Japanese assets in the United States frozen and the Panama Canal closed to Japanese shipping. At the same time, American and Filipino forces were merged, making Filipino soldiers members of the U.S. Army, which theoretically entitled them all to GI benefits and U.S. citizenship. MacArthur was reappointed a U.S. Army general. He shed the field marshal's uniform, but kept its gold-encrusted hat, which became—along with his corncob pipe and aviator's sunglasses—part of his carefully considered wartime image. It was time to dust off Plan Orange, America's defense strategy for the Philippines.

The dust was thick. Plan Orange was first drawn up during the Russo-Japanese War in 1904. It called for American and Filipino soldiers to fight a holding action on Bataan Peninsula till the Great White Fleet arrived with reinforcements and fresh supplies. But Plan Orange was designed for a war between America and Japan, not a global conflict. Now Europe was already at war, and London was more important than Manila. A new British-American strategy called Rainbow Five was drafted secretly in the fall of 1940. If America came into the war against the Axis, the Allies agreed to attend to Europe first. Asia would be limited to delaying actions. Not until October 1941, two months before Pearl Harbor, did Washington realize that MacArthur had never seen Rainbow Five.

The Allies were confident that Japan would not attack before spring 1942. Plan Orange was reviewed, but left basically unchanged. When the Japanese invaded, MacArthur was to block them on the beach or withdraw to Bataan to await reinforcement. MacArthur was supremely confident that he could stop them at the beach. When the invasion came on December 22, 1941, two weeks after Pearl Harbor, nobody was prepared, or alert. While MacArthur brooded about what to do, his air force was caught on the ground and destroyed. From a beachhead on Lingayen Gulf, General Homma Masaharu pushed quickly south toward Manila. Major General Jonathan Wainwright's forces were all that stood in the way. Unable to operate their old Enfield rifles properly, his men broke and ran, leaving their artillery unprotected. Wainwright asked MacArthur for permission to withdraw toward Bataan. Everything was going according to Plan Orange, but no comfort was to be gained from that. MacArthur had made no serious preparations in Bataan. Under his own plan to block the Japanese at the beaches, supplies and equipment were moved to forward areas facing the beaches instead of to Bataan as specified by Plan Orange. Most of these supplies were lost. By the end of their first week in Bataan, the defenders were already on half rations. The 26th Cavalry eventually had to shoot and eat their horses.

As darkness fell on Christmas Eve 1941, the general and his staff escaped from Manila by boat to the fortified island of Corregidor at the mouth of the bay. Nine days later the Japanese Army entered the city.

There was never any question that Ferdinand Marcos served on the U.S. side in the early days of the war, but after that his tales of heroic exploits as a guerrilla leader were completely at odds with the facts. Many people suspected this over the years, but his war records vanished mysteriously from the U.S. archives sometime during the 1950s. Thirty years later, in 1985, they reappeared, revealing bits and pieces of a surprisingly different story—one with large gaps and question marks.

A month before Pearl Harbor, as a Reserve Officers' Training Corps graduate, Ferdinand was called into the army as a third lieutenant. When the Japanese invaded, he was assigned to General Mateo Capinpin's 21st Philippine Division, one of the elements pushed back into Bataan where it was to support General Wainwright's main force.

By pulling strings while everything still looked easy, Ferdinand and some college friends, including Primitivo San Augustin, wangled vague assignments in "intelligence" under General Capinpin's G-2. As defenses collapsed, telegraph lines were down and communication became difficult. Ferdinand was the only subordinate on the G-2 staff who had a car handy, a battered Oldsmobile sedan. He volunteered to "reconnoiter Japanese progress," got back into civilian clothes; and drove around Pangasinan and Tarlac provinces with some Ilocano pals. There was chaos as people fled. Finding stores deserted or unguarded, they loaded the Olds with canned goods, rice, sugar, and clothing, making repeated trips. Pangasinan was the constituency of his uncle, Congressman Ramos, so these operations may have been more methodical than Ferdinand let on. They were, in short, looting. It might be argued that if they did not loot, the Japanese would, and meantime General Capinpin could get along without him.

The invasion had panicked shopkeepers, and liberated a lot of suppressed bitterness, greed, and vengeance. Most of the businesses and homes looted at the end of December and the beginning of January belonged to Chinese, who controlled 80 percent of trade in the islands, which galled many ethnic Filipinos. Ferdinand was always ambivalent about his Chinese ties; if they were not Chuas, it was open season. Even certain Chuas were fair game. Next, the Chinese had to face the Kempeitei. Japan and China had been at war since 1933, and once in Manila the secret police wasted no time rounding up and executing Chiang Kai-shek's consul general, his staff, and other prominent members of the Chinese community who were active supporters of the Kuomintang. Supporters of Mao Tse-tung were also arrested and executed. With the help of wealthy Chinese collaborators, a new pro-Japanese chamber of commerce was set up.

The brutality of the Japanese Imperial Army was to be expected, but Filipinos were killing each other instead of Japanese. Murders were committed to settle old scores, or as part of rape or armed robbery. While Ferdinand and his friends were "engaged in a delaying action" in Tarlac, they snared Calixto Aguinaldo, the chief witness against him in the Nalundasan case. They claimed they caught the meek little man looting a bank. Calixto's prospects at that point were not worth a bent centavo, but Ferdinand insisted that he spared Aguinaldo's life and that he was slain by guerrillas on some other occasion for having dealings with the enemy. Applying the Marcos Axiom—everything said is the opposite of the facts—one wonders.

One day early in January, while they were still driving around "reconnoitering Japanese progress," Ferdinand said he and his six pals were captured and put to work as handymen and houseboys for the Japanese. (There are some clues later that the Japanese in question were senior officers in the Kempeitei, and that Ferdinand's presence may not have been entirely innocent.) He and two others then escaped, but the other four were killed. In a different version of the same episode, Ferdinand said he "volunteered to be captured by the Japs, posing as a houseboy, then made his escape back to our lines with information as to the enemy's number and location"!

Back again with Capinpin's division in Bataan, Ferdinand's idea of "good intelligence work," according to what he told biographer Spence, "was to find a weakness in his own lines and then personally to organize a defense, holding the position himself. . . . His patrols functioned as miniature armies. . . ."

So here we have the two contradictory versions: Marcos as one-man army, and Marcos as looter and scrounger (and possible double agent). The version related to Spence—Marcos as one-man army—was accepted by many as fact.

"Marcos required only a few weeks to become a hero," *Time* Magazine reported in a 1966 cover story relying on the Spence book.

> His idea of intelligence duty was to prowl behind the Japanese lines often in his personal Oldsmobile sedan probing for weak spots. He found one on Bataan's Mount Natib, a Japanese military battery that was lobbing 70 mm shells into U.S. General Jonathan Wainwright's beleaguered defenders. Marcos and three privates scouted the battery, trailing two near dead Japanese artillerymen to it, then cut loose. They killed more than 50 Japanese, spiked the guns and escaped with only one casualty. Marcos won the first of a brace of Silver Stars for the operation, and a few weeks later was recommended for the U.S. Medal of Honor for his part in the Defense of the Salian River. But the recommendation was never filed with Washington, and Marcos failed in becoming the only Filipino to win America's highest military award.

Ferdinand's war stories should never have been taken seriously. Some are just yarn spinning of the Colonel Blimp tradition, some are militarily illogical, while others collapse on close scrutiny—the dates are wrong, he really was not there at the time, some other person did it, or eyewitnesses say nothing of the sort happened. The more people believed him, the wilder his inventions became. Eventually, he was able to claim that because of these many feats he was one of the most heavily decorated heroes of World War II. Going unchallenged, the assertion gained a life of its own and crossed the fine line between hyperbole and methodical fraud. Long after the war was over, this legend drew international attention to him, attracted sensational press coverage, and snowballed into popular American support.

On Bataan, most people were too busy fighting for their lives to notice the glaring inconsistencies that would emerge twenty years later. Consider just the high points of January 1942 alone: After the better part of a week liberating other people's property, then escaping from work as a Japanese houseboy, Ferdinand had scarcely returned to duty with General Capinpin when, "patrolling several miles behind Japanese lines," he was hit by sniper fire in the hip. Unable to move, he ordered his men to return without him. "He then tried to crawl," says Spence, "but when he did so he felt the bullet grating on his hip bone. With the Japanese only five hundred yards away, he cut out the bullet with his knife, then dragged, weak and bleeding, several miles to his own lines."

Although this painful wound had prevented him from walking, Ferdinand gamely went back on patrol several days later, on January 16, this time a few miles behind his own lines. According to a postwar affidavit supporting the award of a U.S. Silver Star, he earned the medal in action that day at Guitol, in Bataan. "[Marcos] with three men attacked and dislodged a greatly superior enemy force which had captured the outpost and machine gun emplacements of the 21st Division." (The history of the 21st Division states that Lieutenant Marcos was nowhere near Guitol that day because he was assigned elsewhere to guide a regiment to the front. It says nothing about Marcos earning a Silver Star.)

Two days later, eight miles west, he supposedly stormed the Japanese heavy mortars on Mount Natib, earning him the U.S. Distinguished Service Cross and the eventual approbation of *Time*. According to Spence, at 25 yards Marcos "knocked off its commander with a rifle shot." When two Japanese with machine guns appeared, "Ferdinand destroyed them." He then finished off the ammunition carriers. His patrol killed more than fifty men, including eight officers, and pushed the mortars off the cliff.

Unaccustomed to idleness, that same afternoon Ferdinand and his patrol set out again. But they were tired and grew careless, so they were captured, taken to a Japanese command post, and tortured. "Finally," says Spence, "exhausted from torture, they were tied and left on the ground with a guard of two soldiers. In the night, Ferdinand chafed free from his bonds, slit the throats of the guards, released his companions, and led them to safety. . . ." These repeated escapes from the Japanese are extraordinary, one might even say peculiar, and the stuff of which legends are made. They all happened during the first few days of the war.

On January 20, Ferdinand carried out the operation that supposedly inspired General Capinpin to recommend him for the U.S. Congressional Medal of Honor. He rallied a group of one hundred stragglers to block a Japanese offensive, enabling U.S. forces to withdraw to a new defensive line. His daring included "a suicidal charge against overwhelming enemy forces" at the junction of the Salian and Abo Abo rivers. No other soldier was doing anything comparable. Like the Scarlet Pimpernel, Ferdinand was everywhere at once.

Spence quotes General MacArthur as saying that "without Ferdinand's exploits, Bataan would have fallen three months earlier." Unfortunately, this quote cannot be authenticated. Neither in MacArthur's *Reminiscences* nor in William Manchester's biography is there any mention of Ferdinand Marcos. In the official history, *Fall of the Philippines,* no acknowledgment is made of Ferdinand's exploits delaying the fall of Bataan by even an hour.

Nevertheless, Spence and other Marcos biographers claim that General Capinpin spoke to General Wainwright, who immediately promoted Marcos three grades to captain by telephone from Corregidor, and directed that papers be prepared recommending him for the Medal of Honor. A postwar Filipino chronicler explained that due to confusion during the fall of Bataan, the papers prepared by Capinpin were lost. It is only a very small point that Wainwright did not move to Corregidor for another month or that a member of the decorations board appointed by Wainwright, Colonel John Vance, later said: "We never saw anything about Marcos."

After the war, General Capinpin's missing recommendation was reconstructed by a former member of his headquarter's staff, Colonel Aurelio Lucero, at the specific request of Ferdinand Marcos, by then a powerful politician. Lucero stated that everything happened exactly as Marcos said. It is puzzling why an affidavit was not obtained directly from General Capinpin or General Wainwright, who were both still around. Only in October 1958, when both Capinpin and Wainwright were dead, did the Philippine Army award Ferdinand the Philippine Medal of Valor in place of the U.S. Medal of Honor. By then, he was a leading senator with influence over the military budget and his eyes on Malacanang Palace. (When Imelda had the Marcos birthplace in Sarrat rebuilt as a museum for his memorabilia, the centerpiece was a figure of Ferdinand in uniform wearing a chestful of Filipino and American medals. An observant journalist attending the opening noticed that around the neck of the mannikin was the U.S. Medal of Honor with its conspicuous blue ribbon, and turned to ask President Marcos if indeed that had been among his awards. The president scowled angrily and ordered an aide to remove the medal immediately.)

As the situation in Bataan grew desperate, the convoy of U.S. troop reinforcements and relief supplies called for in Plan Orange crawled slowly across the Pacific, only to be recalled by Roosevelt. The men and materiel were more urgently needed in Europe. President Quezon complained bitterly to MacArthur's aide, Charles Willoughby, that "America writhes in anguish at the fate of a distant cousin, Europe, while a daughter, the Philippines, is being raped in the back room." Quezon cabled Roosevelt that "after nine weeks of fighting not even a small amount of aid has reached us from the United States. . . . While perfectly safe itself, the United States has practically doomed the Philippines to almost total extinction to secure a breathing space." While this was starkly apparent to Quezon in Corregidor, it was not evident to Filipinos in general or to Wainwright's doomed men.

During the entire struggle on Bataan, MacArthur never went anywhere near the front, relying on staff officers to keep him informed. On January 9, 1942, he boarded a PT boat in Corregidor and made his first and only visit to the peninsula, remaining as far as possible from the enemy.

It would have been a demoralizing situation for any commander. MacArthur had allowed his air force to be crippled on the first day of the war. His grandiose defense plan had resulted in near disaster and the starvation of the Bataan forces. His grandiloquent pronouncements and his refusal to visit the front demoralized his men, who made up a contemptuous ditty:

Dugout Doug's not timid, he's just cautious, not afraid;
He's protecting carefully the stars that Franklin made.

That February, Corregidor's defenders were treated to some curious sights. The gold reserves of the Philippine treasury had been transferred hastily to the island fortress, accompanied by all the gold bullion stockpiled against market fluctuations by the Benguet mines, the second-largest gold producer in U.S. territory, of which MacArthur was a prominent stockholder. President Quezon then issued an executive order commending General MacArthur and his staff for "their magnificent defense" of the islands and giving them "recompense and reward" of $500,000 to MacArthur and separate gifts of less than $100,000 to each of three aides—totalling $640,000 in American currency. MacArthur and his aides, curiously, were given Philippine currency to hold until the American currency could be transferred into their bank accounts from the Philippine government account in the United States. (This extraordinary reward, which President Roosevelt knew about, and apparently chose not to block, was successfully kept secret till it was discovered in 1979 by historian Carol Petillo.) No explanation was offered, but some historians including Petillo have since speculated that MacArthur had lost his nerve, or was in danger of losing it, and Quezon chose this method to restore his resolve. More than one scholar has labeled this an outright bribe; but at the very least, MacArthur violated U.S. military regulations by accepting it.

Dwight Eisenhower, who had worked closely with MacArthur in the Philippines in the 1930s, wrote in his diary in January 1942 that MacArthur was "as big a baby as ever. But we've got to keep him fighting." On February 3, 1942, Eisenhower wrote again that it "looks like MacArthur is losing his nerve."

Historian Ronald Spector concluded, "At this point, MacArthur might justifiably have been relieved." Australian historian Gavin Long observed, "MacArthur's leadership in the Philippines had fallen short of what might have been expected from a soldier of such wide experience."

Instead of being relieved, MacArthur became a hero and a legend in America. Fed concoctions by MacArthur's clever public relations staff, the U.S. press published breathless accounts of the exploits of "The Lion of Luzon." Walter Lippmann wrote of his "vast and profound conceptions." He was named "Number One Father of 1942." President Roosevelt awarded him the Congressional Medal of Honor for "the heroic conduct of defensive and offensive operations on the Bataan Peninsula." Of the 142 communiqués released by his headquarters in the first months of the war, 109 mentioned only one individual, MacArthur, while omitting the names of combat units, commanders, and individuals who had performed exceptional exploits. Eisenhower observed, "The public has built itself a hero out of its own imagination." Roosevelt needed a hero. It was General Marshall and FDR who conceived the scheme to award MacArthur the Medal of Honor, and to rescue the false hero from his doomed command and have him take charge of a new American force in Australia.

At MacArthur's orders, a U.S. submarine was then loaded with 20 tons of gold "as ballast" and sailed for Australia. It has never been clear whether this was Filipino government gold or private stock, but it matters little. Manuel Roxas, the wealthy brahmin MacArthur and Quezon were grooming to succeed Quezon one day as president, was left in charge of sinking the remaining gold reserves in Manila Bay to keep them from falling into Japanese hands, before making his own escape from the Rock. On March 11, MacArthur and his inner circle left Corregidor by PT boat for the Del Monte pineapple plantation in Mindanao, and from its airstrip flew on to Australia. With him went the ailing Quezon and Vice-President Osmeña. Roosevelt was determined to maintain them as the legitimate Philippine government-in-exile.

For the American and Filipino soldiers remaining in Bataan, food rather than gold became an obsession. Front-line troops received only a third of a ration a day and were starving. In Bataan, the exhausted Americans and Filipinos grumbled bitterly. General William Brougher, commanding the 11th Division, wrote, "Who had the right to say that 20,000 Americans should be sentenced without their consent and for no fault of their own to an enterprise that would involve for them endless suffering, cruel handicap, death or a hopeless future? A foul trick of deception has been played by a commander in chief and small staff who are now eating steak and eggs in Australia. God damn them!"

"Corregidor surrendered last night," Eisenhower recorded in his diary. "Poor Wainwright! He did the fighting in the Philippine Islands. Another got such glory as the public could find in the operation." At the end of the war, Harold Ickes concluded, "Blame is due to Roosevelt. . . . [He] should have left MacArthur to clean up his own mess and taken Wainwright out. Truman agreed, saying that Wainwright was a better soldier. He knows, as do others, that the Philippine campaign under MacArthur was a fiasco."

Tokyo was not happy that General Homma had allowed the defenders to retreat to Bataan. A special task force headed by the ruthless Colonel Tsuji Masanobu flew down to take matters into their own hands. Estimating that he would capture twenty-five thousand men in Bataan, General Homma turned over all logistics to his transportation officer, Major General Kawane Yoshikata. Homma was so preoccupied mounting his assault on Corregidor that it was two months before he learned that more Filipinos and Americans had died on their way to the POW camps than on the battlefield. As many as ten thousand perished during the Death March to Camp O'Donnell, from malaria, starvation, beatings, or execution. Two thousand were Americans, the great majority Filipinos.

Ferdinand was somewhere among these POWs, although he gave conflicting explanations of how he got to Camp O'Donnell. By one account, he and three companions fled to the north but were captured. In another version, he was wounded by shrapnel and rifle fire, was unable to flee north, and began the Death March "half dead already."

While he was at Camp O'Donnell he ran into his old school chum, Primitivo San Augustin. San Augustin and some comrades planned to escape, make their way to a fishing schooner moored in Tayabas Bay southeast of Manila, and sail to Australia to join MacArthur. Sure enough, a few days later San Augustin made good his escape and headed for the wilds of Mount Banahaw, overlooking Tayabas Bay, where he found other men hiding. Instead of leaving for Australia, he and a comrade-in-arms, Vicente Umali, organized these men into a guerrilla force named President Quezon's Own Guerrillas (PQOG).

Ferdinand did not take part in this escape. His situation at Camp O'Donnell, and his relationship with the Japanese, had become too complex.

Once fighting in Bataan ended in the summer of 1942, the Japanese began freeing Filipino prisoners with severe health problems and those whose families cooperated. The names of sick prisoners were published as they were released. Ferdinand was not among those named. According to him, he was released on August 4, 1942. He said his mother bribed the Japanese and he was summoned to camp headquarters. There an officer in civilian clothes who spoke idiomatic English with an American accent told him, "There are no strings. You may go home if you wish." Josefa met him inside the gate with clean clothing, and they were given railway tickets to Manila. Since he was not among the ill, could he, perhaps, have been among those who cooperated?

Josefa told him that Mariano was under house arrest in Batac "for refusal to join the Japanese civilian government in Ilocos Norte." According to a U.S. intelligence report, Mariano Marcos was not under house arrest. In fact, he had taken part in a welcoming ceremony for the Japanese in Laoag early in 1942, long before Ferdinand was captured. Then—while Ferdinand was in Camp O'Donnell—Mariano spoke at a pro-Japanese rally in Batac. After being unemployed for nearly a decade, Mariano had finally found a full-time job. For the rest of the war, he was a propagandist for the Japanese in northern Luzon, making speeches from village to village, protected at all times by a bodyguard of Japanese soldiers. Near the end of the war, Mariano himself admitted that "he had been recommended to the Japanese . . . by his son," Ferdinand. (Although the dates are not certain, it appears that Ferdinand made this recommendation in January 1942 when he said he was a houseboy for Japanese officers.)

No sooner did Ferdinand arrive at Josefa's house than the smooth-talking Japanese agent sent a car to take him to Fort Santiago, Manila headquarters of the Kempeitei. The urbane Japanese was a colonel in the secret police. There, at Fort Santiago, Ferdinand claimed he was "subjected for eight days to the most incredible forms of human torture" to make him reveal what he knew about the plans of "some guerrillas" to flee by boat to join MacArthur in Australia. He said he was given the dreaded water torture, in which water was forced down his throat and the Japanese jumped on his bloated stomach. He was, he said, bludgeoned in the face repeatedly with a rifle butt—blows that ordinarily fracture cheekbones, split skin, and remove front teeth. Ferdinand survived without a trace. People who saw him several days later remarked only that he was down with a fever and fatigue.

According to a secret report prepared for MacArthur by one of his top agents, Jesus de Villamor, "It is a known fact that almost every person who has been confined in Fort Santiago has been asked by the Japanese to act as informers for them. Acceptance of the offer means release from confinement; refusal represents prolonged confinement, torture or death. It is obvious that the majority will accept the offer."

Men who were prisoners at Fort Santiago insist that Ferdinand was never jailed there. After the war they refused to give him membership in their veterans association. Official Japanese records do not list him as a prisoner in Fort Santiago. It is probable, then, that he was not taken there as a prisoner.

After this extraordinary torture, Ferdinand said he agreed to guide the Kempeitei to San Augustin's escape boat. He then led truckloads of Japanese troops to the base of Mount Banahaw, where they were ambushed by the PQOG. Ferdinand said the ambush was set up "by prior arrangement," although how this could have been done while he was a guest of the Kempeitei is unclear. He said he saved himself by shouting in Tagalog that he was a friend. This would hardly have been necessary if the guerrillas had been expecting them.

San Augustin took Ferdinand to his guerrilla camp, where he was bedridden with a mysterious fever and stomach pains for five months, until December 1942. "The torture had almost killed him," says Spence, "and he mended slowly." It is likely that these symptoms and his other long periods of illness during the war were not caused by malaria or torture, but signaled the onset of lupus, the degenerative disease that ultimately broke his health. Lupus often strikes people first in their twenties and then goes into remission for long periods, making it difficult to diagnose. Its symptoms can be confused with other ailments, such as Blackwater fever, and it can respond superficially to the same treatments given for malaria.

At a moment when everyone around him on Mount Banahaw was engaged in high adventure, plotting ambushes, assassinations, secret missions, and intrigue, cleaning rifles and machine guns, and sharing in the camaraderie of a resistance movement, Ferdinand once again was unable to participate. Lying on his pallet, his imagination working overtime, he invented a starring role for himself. Later he insisted that San Augustin begged him "to guide both staff and combat echelons [of the PQOG], and [he] was offered the rank of general, which he refused."

This moment was a major turning point for Ferdinand Marcos. In childhood and adolescence he had merely exaggerated, boasting of being the class valedictorian and the best marksman, claiming that Mariano was a provincial governor and a rich man with a great hacienda and thousands of special cattle. He changed reality into something more glamorous. His life had been deformed by the circumstances of his birth. His real father was an elusive and remote figure; a potent and successful man, but whose power and influence were discreetly hidden. Compared with Judge Chua, Mariano Marcos was a failure. This created a situation common in folk tales the world over, from Snorri Sturlason to the Brothers Grimm, from the operas of Wagner to the operas of Peking: the legend of the dark prince born in a stable whose real father is a great god or a mighty emperor. Unable to disclose the identity of his true father, Ferdinand boasted of being a direct descendant of the pirate Li Ma-hong. He was intensely superstitious. The movie he commissioned before running for president the first time in 1965 was titled *Marked by Fate,* and the campaign biography written by Benjamin Gray for his second presidential campaign in 1969 was called *Rendezvous with Destiny,* both revealing his preoccupation with supernatural origins. He had Imelda commission ornate doors in Malacanang Palace depicting the legendary first Filipino man and woman: Malakas (strong) and Maganda (beautiful) who both emerged like sperm from a bamboo stalk.

Although the life Ferdinand invented was full of heroic deeds, he was not audacious or physically brave, but furtive and indirect, the result not of cowardice but of cunning. (There are certain episodes that demonstrate fatalism rather than personal courage, particularly the final moments in Malacanang before his downfall.) In Asia, cunning is valued infinitely more than courage, and confrontation is positively discouraged. The sages contend that bravery is the height of folly if it results in failure or the destruction of family, community, or nation.

Investigators who studied Ferdinand's claims and affidavits in detail were uncertain where he found his inspiration, especially for the wartime heroics. Ferdinand himself would never discuss the subject except to condemn anyone who challenged his version of events.

The inspiration was Primitivo San Augustin. He was the unwitting prototype for the legend that paved Ferdinand's path to power. Ferdinand idolized him. In college and afterwards, he dogged his hero's heels. San Augustin was one of those fortunate souls who do everything well, and never hesitate. He had longstanding ties to the Quezons and was linked romantically to the president's daughter, Baby Quezon. (Ferdinand ungallantly claimed years later that it was he who had been her favorite.) San Augustin seemed destined for greatness until his fantastic luck ended suddenly one day after the war, on a car trip with Aurora and Baby Quezon. Driving along a lonely road, they were all slain in an ambush. The ambush was attributed as a matter of course to the Communists, often a dead giveaway that the victim was done in by political rivals. Once Ferdinand's role model was dead, he helped himself unabashedly to whole segments of San Augustin's history.

The parallels are instructive. San Augustin had been a legitimate war hero in Bataan. His field promotion to major had come honorably. He had escaped dramatically from POW camp, started his own guerrilla force, and organized a network of spies and saboteurs that ranged all over central and southern Luzon (exactly what Ferdinand would later claim). He was one of only a bare handful of Filipinos in the resistance who were eventually considered so important as secret agents that they were given codenames by MacArthur's command. Why, then, did he not take Ferdinand as a senior partner in his guerrilla unit, his corps of spies, and later his direct pipeline to MacArthur? Why did Ferdinand find it necessary to invent his own identical secret organization and pretend to be all the things San Augustin was? The answer appears to be inescapable: San Augustin, who knew him well, did not trust him. Ferdinand did not completely invent his own secret command; he merely created a more glamorous identity for an organization already in existence. This was the Ilocano black market syndicate identified on the eve of the war with the powerful Quirino brothers, a fraternity of political operators, shady entrepreneurs, and Constabulary officers on the fringe of the Manila underworld, typical of cities everywhere, which the French in Marseilles call "the milieu." In the 1930s, Ferdinand's father and uncle had been vaguely associated with this syndicate as legal functionaries doing errands for the Quirinos, and Ferdinand had come to be associated with it since he was freed from his murder conviction by Justice Laurel. What it needed was a romantic name and a proud commission. During his months of recuperation on Mount Banahaw, and with a little inspiration from the example of San Augustin and the PQOG, Ferdinand dreamed up both.

When he recovered enough to return to Manila, early in 1943, Ferdinand decided to call "his" secret organization *Ang Mga Maharlika* (Noble Studs). Even the name was second-hand. The original Maharlika had been organized by one of his friends, Cipriano Alles, in August 1942, the month Ferdinand was freed from POW camp, said he was tortured, and fell among the PQOG on Mount Banahaw. Cipriano's Maharlika was briefly given official U.S. recognition as an intelligence-gathering unit. But early in 1943 Alles was captured and his unit fell apart.

Ferdinand claimed to have enlisted spies, saboteurs, and assassins throughout Manila and across several provinces, especially in his old haunt of Pangasinan. In fact, documents show that many of the men closely identified with Ferdinand and his Maharlika were forgers, pick-pockets, gunmen, and racketeers. Others were part of an Ilocano black-market syndicate engaging in extortion, theft, smuggling, profiteering, and occasional atrocities. There has never been any concrete evidence that these men were united in anything but a common interest in the black market. So, instead of being a new secret organization, Maharlika was simply a name Ferdinand gave to a loosely strung network of his friends and relatives that was already in existence before the war.

In a perverse way, it was a stroke of genius. Although Ferdinand was never able to gain official U.S. military recognition for his Maharlika, by giving them a name and an identity he transformed these shadowy syndicates into the beginnings of a consolidated political machine. Before the war was over, the struggle to gain control of Ilocos Norte, Ilocos Sur, Pangasinan, and vital parts of the economy in central and northern Luzon was being waged not by gangs of faceless cutthroats but by an integrated organization with a glamorous identity. When the war ended, it was only a matter of the right public relations to turn the Maharlika into a political vehicle, one that Ferdinand could ride into Congress, even into Malacanang.

He did not have to look far for his constituency. In time, the Philippine resistance movement would become, like its counterparts in Greece and Yugoslavia, one of the big romantic themes of World War II; when the Allies returned in force in October 1944, they would be supported by 250,000 guerrillas. In the north, around the Ilocos and in the mountain provinces, a large guerrilla force developed known as the U.S. Army Forces in the Philippines, Northern Luzon (USAFIP, NL), organized by Colonel Russell W. Volckmann, a U.S. Army regular who disobeyed MacArthur's orders to surrender and took to the hills. Volckmann's USAFIP grew to five infantry regiments. In central Luzon, where landlords traditionally employed mercenary armies to keep tenant farmers in line, angry peasants formed the Communist Hukbalahap, an anti-Japanese guerrilla army that also assassinated landlords who collaborated with the Japanese. While most guerrillas avoided contact with the enemy, following MacArthur's orders to await his return, the Huks sought out the Japanese and their Filipino supporters at every opportunity. They were so effective that they took control of the central provinces, introducing reforms that farmers had been seeking fruitlessly for decades.

But there were other groups that had no interest in fighting or reform. The situation in Luzon was ripe for exploitation. The economy was in shambles, crops were seized, and starvation confronted everyone. Gangs calling themselves guerrillas terrorized the countryside. Old feuds between rival clans and political factions were settled at gunpoint. Currency became useless, homes, factories, and warehouses were abandoned, and desperate civilians bought food and commodities on the black market with payment in gemstones and scraps of gold. Gangs who had something to sell to the occupation forces made fortunes. The Japanese needed steel cables and copper wiring, which could be stolen. These gangs looted buildings, expropriated food, destroyed property, and bullied whoever got in their way. Some of them were called "Escolta Guerrillas" because they were led by shady lawyers with offices on the Escolta, who claimed to be members of the resistance, but sought only to make fortunes on the black market.

When Cipriano Alles was released from prison during the general amnesty of October 1943, he joined Ferdinand's Maharlika, and the two worked together for the rest of the war. Cipriano had hardened in prison and now was considered "the worst perpetrator of scrap metal deals in the black market." (Whether this was bad or good depended on your station in life: Sergio Osmeña, Jr., the son of the vice-president-in-exile, also was said to have made a fortune selling scrap metal to the Japanese, but the charge had little impact on his political career.) Cipriano's black-market broker was identified in intelligence reports as none other than Ferdinand Marcos. U.S. Army investigators after the war found evidence that "the other Maharlika [Ferdinand's] was a buy and sell organization," not a fighting unit. Legitimate guerrillas reported hearing that Alles and Marcos were "engaged in buy-and-sell activities . . . in the province of Pangasinan." It was a question of survival. According to a Chinese businessman acquainted with the Marcos family, they were so poor and their situation so desperate that Ferdinand "sold anything he could lay his hands on."

According to Ferdinand, it was not like that at all. The main objective of the Maharlika, he said, was espionage. He claimed that plans for the Japanese defense of Manila were filched from the pocket of an officer by one of the Maharlika's professional pickpockets. It was a family affair. According to Ferdinand's official unit history, his executive officer was his uncle, Narciso Ramos, the prewar congressman from Pangasinan, which was probably why their activities outside Manila were concentrated in that province. Headquarters was in a storefront on Leroy Street, near Josefa's house. Narciso (the father of General Fidel Ramos) ran the headquarters with the assistance of Ferdinand's brother Pacifico, who had just returned from Sulu in August 1943, after being interned there briefly by the Japanese.

As a front for their buy-and-sell operations, the Maharlika started a trading company called The Ex-Servicemen's Corporation (TESCO). According to Ferdinand, TESCO manufactured items such as toothbrushes. Its office was in the Regina Building, one of the buildings "most frequented by Jap spies and collaborators," teeming with Kempeitei

agents, stated an intelligence report. Mariano Marcos, the full-time
Japanese propagandist, was listed as chairman of the board of TESCO.

Another of Ferdinand's many Ilocano uncles, Simeon Valdez, who
had connections in Chinese financial circles, ran TESCO on a daily
basis, and supervised its finances. Tony Quirino was the Maharlika's
liaison with various Luzon guerrilla groups, and coordinated intelligence activities with Simeon Valdez. The Maharlika also had a "smuggler's ring" along the coast, Ferdinand said. All supplies needed by the
Maharlika were either bought in the black market or stolen from the
Japanese. Profits were used to buy firearms and ammunition, automobile spare parts, medicines, clothing, and foodstuffs, which were distributed to members of the Maharlika. Its "sabotage section" stole
enemy communication wires, food, medicines, clothing, firearms, and
ammunition. They had a delivery truck with double walls specially
designed for smuggling weapons. Maharlika even published a mimeo-
graphed underground newspaper. Unfortunately, all supporting evidence of these activities, Ferdinand said, was "lost due to continuous
searches by the Japanese."

The Battle of the Coral Sea, followed by the American victory at
Guadalcanal in February 1943, began to blunt the Japanese advance in
the Pacific. American and Filipino agents started to trickle back by
submarine, to make contact with the resistance. That February, MacArthur's favorite secret agent, former Manila businessman Chick Parsons,
left Australia aboard the submarine *Trout* to contact a guerrilla command in Mindanao headed by the flamboyant American Wendell Fertig.

Rumors soon spread in Manila about the operation of wireless trans-
mitters in Mindanao, Panay, and the Visayas. These were the first indications Ferdinand and others in Luzon had that guerrilla groups on
other islands were in radio contact with MacArthur.

Primitivo San Augustin, who never got around to making his voyage
to Australia, decided to go to Mindanao instead to see Fertig and
through him establish communications with MacArthur's headquarters.
With Japanese patrol boats everywhere it was a dangerous trip, but any
smuggler could slip easily from island to island at night in a *banca*
outrigger.

Ferdinand first claimed that he and San Augustin made the whole
trip together, joined by their old school chums Leonilo Ocampo and

Vicente "Banjo" Raval. There were, in fact, two trips. Ferdinand accompanied San Augustin the first time, in March 1943, only as far as Leyte. San Augustin then proceeded to Mindanao alone, while Ferdinand ran into peculiar delays and turned back. The likely explanation is that he undertook the trip with an ulterior motive on instructions from his benefactor Jose Laurel, and was sidetracked.

Besides his Maharlika dealings in the black market, the evidence suggests that Ferdinand was working part time for Jose Laurel, who in turn was working closely with the Kempeitei. The first puppet administration set up by the Japanese was an executive commission under Jose Vargas, Manuel Roxas, and Jose Laurel. Vargas had been President Quezon's executive secretary, left behind as mayor of Greater Manila to keep the city going. In this commission, Laurel was essentially minister of the interior, with responsibilities for internal security, supervision of the puppet Constabulary and its intelligence divisions, and the suppression of anti-Japanese guerrillas. Laurel undertook the job vigorously, remarking that Japan had done enough in fighting for "all the races of Asia."

The Japanese did not have enough troops in the islands to suppress the guerrillas in any case. They leaned on Laurel, who actively used secret agents, informers, and the Constabulary to track down, ambush, or betray guerrillas. Periodically, leading guerrilla commanders—Filipinos and Americans—were snared and beheaded. These traps depended on intelligence reports from spies, infiltrators, or collaborators. In his secret report to MacArthur after a wartime visit to Manila, Villamor said these spies were

> drawn from among the scum of the community. Swindlers, pimps, whores, racketeers, crooks, ex-convicts and the like constitute this group which, from all reports, appears to be a large one. They are normally headed by notorious characters, often by ex-secret service men of bad record and reputation. They are dangerous because they seem to be very well paid, are very active and have no scruples in the methods they use to accomplish their purpose. Many succeed in joining anti-Japanese organizations, take active part in their doings and thus are able to turn over complete information on them.

A number of Ferdinand's Ilocano friends and relatives (former lawyer and newspaperman Venancio Duque, for example) were officers in Laurel's puppet Constabulary and were simultaneously members of well-known anti-Japanese guerrilla units. Thus they were in a position to be double agents serving either side.

As a patriot and a nationalist, Laurel had long been opposed to America's economic domination of the Philippines. He genuinely admired Japan and what it had accomplished. After attending Yale, he had obtained a doctorate of jurisprudence in Tokyo in 1938, and sent one of his sons there for military training. Everyone clinging to Laurel's coattails in Manila was careful to share his attitudes.

"The Tragedy of Bataan," Laurel said, taught "the bitter lesson that the United States used the lives of the Filipinos to defend purely American interests." Filipinos, he believed, were sacrificed ruthlessly in a delaying action that had no purpose because no American reinforcements were ever sent, and in fact none were intended to be sent. Laurel hated colonialism, and condemned its legacy: "We are weary with the pretensions of the white man's burden, which more often than not has only served to cloak the exploitation of weaker peoples."

Laurel's values were not typical of the easygoing Philippines. As an authoritarian, he admired Japan's code of social responsibility and self-sacrifice, virtues he thought his own society lacked. He believed that the Philippines needed constitutional dictatorship and that totalitarianism would eventually replace democracy throughout the world.

Some investigators who have studied the long-missing Marcos wartime archives, including John Sharkey of *The Washington Post*, suspected that Ferdinand may also have done occasional odd jobs directly for Colonel Nakahama Akira, the urbane and ruthless chief of the Kempeitei in Manila who had released him from Camp O'Donnell, played host to him at Fort Santiago, and probably made the decision to hire Mariano Marcos as a propagandist. I suspect that Ferdinand met Nakahama even before the Bataan campaign, while claiming he was forced to work as a houseboy in January 1942. An open letter published in the Maharlika newspaper and attributed to Ferdinand was written in reply to Colonel Nakahama's offer of amnesty to all guerrillas. In it, Ferdinand wrote passionately of his great regard for Nakahama's sincerity, and said the offer of amnesty "has wrung from my men and myself tears of regret that we should face gentlemen of honor and chivalry, bearing the Oriental strain of which we are inordinately proud." He assured Nakahama that the Maharlika believed in the "Oriental Sphere of Co-Prosperity." Sounding like Laurel, he denounced Americans as "transgressors," who "robbed our country of its independence." He wrote that he "is still groping for the true meaning of Japanese intervention in his native land. . . . But it is the beginning of [my] conversion into the new way of life of Greater East Asia."

Elsewhere in his Maharlika documents, Ferdinand noted that orders were issued for several of its officers to seek employment with the Kempeitei, with the puppet Constabulary, and with the puppet government. He does not give names, but various clues suggest that he and his brother Pacifico were among them. He boasted that during the war he was under Laurel's care and protection, and at one point he openly used a Japanese staff car, while wearing the full uniform of the Constabulary, passing unchallenged through Japanese checkpoints. He busied himself throughout the war trying to locate all the guerrilla forces operating in the area north and east of Manila. It would have been easier, he once said, if the guerrillas had not considered him a Japanese spy, or at least an unwelcome busybody. He said he was a marked man to three guerrilla leaders near Manila, who warned him not to set foot in their territories, issuing orders to shoot him on sight.

Ferdinand claimed that he was simply "establishing contact" with guerrilla commanders because he wanted to "forge links" for his own Maharlika. He claimed that MacArthur himself had given him the mandate to coordinate all guerrilla groups under a unified command. This is incorrect. On the other hand, Jose Laurel certainly wanted this information, as did the Kempeitei. From Laurel's viewpoint, these guerrilla groups were outlaws, troublemakers, and profiteers. In Leyte, for example, Marcial Santos owned a small fleet of *bancas* that would set sail each night to ambush Japanese supply barges making deliveries between islands. Santos sold the captured supplies on the black market and made himself a fortune. Other renegade guerrillas terrorized Leyte villages, demanding rice and girls. When Laurel and the Japanese decided to crack down on Leyte's guerrillas, their sweep across the island coincided exactly with the period Ferdinand spent there after getting separated from Primitivo San Augustin. His presence in Leyte may have been more than coincidental.

Ferdinand claimed that when he got to Leyte, his journey on to Mindanao was delayed six months because Japanese patrols were so thick. He might have been delayed six months, but he did not spend them all on Leyte. That June, he came back to Manila requiring urgent hospitalization for the same symptoms that had made him an invalid on Mount Banahaw the previous autumn.

Angered by the Japanese sweeps, the guerrillas struck back by murdering key collaborators among the Filipino elite. If they murdered a Japanese officer, there was always a savage reprisal, so instead they murdered members of the puppet regime. Tee Han Kee, vice-president of the Japanese-sponsored Chinese Association, Jose de Jesus of the finance ministry, and Andong Roces of the Manila *Tribune* were all murdered. Then, on June 6, 1943, the guerrillas shot down Jose Laurel while he was playing golf. Laurel was critically wounded, one .45-caliber slug just missing his heart, another missing the liver, one hitting his collarbone and another—as his son put it—"just under the balls." For seven weeks he was confined to a bed in the Manila General Hospital, which had been taken over by the Japanese Army as a high-security military hospital for their own officers. Specialists were flown in from Tokyo.

Laurel's narrow escape from death made him extremely popular with the Japanese. They had found Jose Vargas pliant as head of the puppet regime, but realized that the only way to win widespread Filipino support was to grant independence, before America did, and install as president the most popular Filipino available. Even before Bataan fell, Premier Tojo had promised independence in 1943.

There were only three Filipinos of Quezon's stature: Benigno Aquino, the head of the Kalibapi, a political party set up to support the Japanese; Jose Laurel; and Manuel Roxas, who had escaped Corregidor only to be captured in Mindanao. The Japanese had permitted him to return to Manila. They wanted Roxas, the youngest, most charismatic of the prewar elite, to be the first president of the independent Philippines. But Roxas alleged that he had a coronary condition. The Japanese then shifted their attention to the second choice, Jose Laurel, and the attempted assassination of Laurel convinced them that he was their man. After his release from the hospital, Laurel was inaugurated as the first and only president of the Japanese-sponsored republic. Ferdinand's patron achieved under the Japanese what had always eluded him under the Americans.

Who should go into the same Japanese military hospital with Laurel after the golf course shooting that June but Ferdinand Marcos, suffering what his brother Pacifico (a doctor) diagnosed as Blackwater fever and a gastric ulcer. Ferdinand said he was disguised as a patient in the cancer ward. Early in August 1943, when Laurel came out of the hospital, Ferdinand came out also, ready to resume his trip to Mindanao. This time, the odyssey took nine months.

As the story goes, he and his friends caught a ride south to Lucena City, then walked to Pagbilao on Tayabas Bay, where Ferdinand had shown the Japanese San Augustin's fishing schooner the previous August. There they hired a sailing *banca* from a smuggler who had twenty *bancas* operating in the islands. They sailed south to Bohol, near Leyte, and were immediately arrested by guerrillas who thought they were spies. Ferdinand talked the Bohol guerrilla chief, Major Ismael Ingeneiro, into releasing them by claiming that he was the leader of a big guerrilla force on Luzon called Maharlika, *and* also the leader of the famous 14th Infantry based in Mountain Province, part of Volckmann's USAFIP, NL command. Ferdinand knew that the original leaders of the 14th Infantry (Guillermo Nakar and Manuel Enriquez) had been captured and executed. Command of their unit was assumed by its executive officer, Major Romulo Manriquez, a graduate of the Philippine Military Academy. But Ferdinand claimed that he, not Manriquez, was its commander. This caused quite a stir. A coded message to MacArthur by Lieutenant Colonel Edwin Andrews from his station in Negros, dated November 19, 1943, said that according to his "Bohol man" (Ingeneiro), "MARCOS WAS CLAIMING TO BE IN CHARGE OF FORMER NAKAR AND ENRIQUEZ UNITS SINCE THE CAPTURE OF THE LAST TWO." The message added that Marcos was on his way to see Fertig "TO ARRANGE FOR THE RECOGNITION OF HIS UNIT BY . . . HIGHER AUTHORITY."

None of these guerrillas had ever heard of Ferdinand Marcos, but he was a convincing talker and they decided to believe him. When they let him go, Ferdinand and his comrades returned to the smugglers' haven on Bohol. They rented a 43-foot *banca,* hired a Cebuan fisherman as skipper, and set sail for Mindanao, 75 miles to the south. They reached the big island in November 1943, but landed at Oroquieta in the northwest only to learn that Fertig was at the opposite end. After more wandering, they arrived at Fertig's camp late in December. By then, San Augustin had long since come and gone.

When he heard that Ferdinand had sailed all the way from Manila, Fertig was suspicious, but Ferdinand produced documents which were intended to show that he had vital information.

The documents portrayed him as a tough young guerrilla with excellent connections, contacts with guerrilla units in every province of

Luzon, and spies even in Kempeitei headquarters. In short, a man cut from the same cloth as San Augustin. There was a handwritten note to President Quezon saying the Maharlika "greets your Excellency with a pledge of loyalty and fealty. We await orders from Your Excellency and General Douglas MacArthur." A letter to MacArthur said: "Your old men from Bataan and Corregidor . . . await your orders and return." In the meantime, he added, please send money. There was a roster of Maharlika's general staff and district commanders, with Mariano Marcos as "inspector general." There was also an intelligence report listing the number of troops at each Japanese camp on Luzon, plus the number of trucks, tanks, artillery pieces, and other materiel. It stated that the Japanese had 142,000 men on Luzon alone in October 1943. (At the time, Japanese strength in all the Philippines was less than 60,000.) If anything, this exaggeration would tend to discourage a U.S. invasion, which (assuming the figures were provided to him by Laurel or by Nakahama) may have been the motive. Another document called "Memorandum on Political Developments" portrayed Laurel as a patriotic stand-in for Quezon.

Marcos said he supplied Fertig with information on every guerrilla force encountered in his journey from Luzon to Mindanao. Biographer Spence claims that Fertig gratefully relayed all this intelligence to MacArthur. "General MacArthur responded quickly," Spence says. "His headquarters promoted Captain Marcos to major and directed the officer to establish contact with as many guerrillas as possible and to convince them of the need for united action."

Official records show otherwise. Fertig never mentioned Ferdinand Marcos in any of his messages to MacArthur. A "P. V. Marcos" is mentioned in a message sent seven months earlier, in April 1943, listing men who had joined the puppet Constabulary. This probably referred to Ferdinand's brother Pacifico, who was interned in Sulu (off Mindanao) just long enough to become fluent in the Japanese language, then was released to return to Luzon. Fertig sent only one terse, unfavorable message about Maharlika: "ANG MGA MAHARLIKA GUERRILLA ORGANIZATION IN ILOCOS SUR AND MOUNTAIN PROVINCE WHO CLAIM TO BE UNDER MY COMMAND. NEVER AUTHORIZED BUT CAN DO NOTHING ABOUT IT NOW."

It was not Ferdinand but his role model Primitivo San Augustin who featured prominently in Fertig's messages to MacArthur. San Augustin had reached Fertig's camp many months earlier and, unlike Ferdinand, supplied him with solid intelligence on the guerrillas and Japanese forces in Luzon. And it was to San Augustin, not to Ferdinand Marcos, that MacArthur sent a message on September 6, 1943 (months before Ferdinand arrived): "I have instructed Col. Fertig to extend to you every possible facility and assistance and relay on to me such information as your group may obtain and believe needs to be brought to my attention until such time as some direct means of communication are established."

MacArthur had decided not to have anyone coordinate the scattered guerrilla groups at this stage. It was better to compare their separate reports "without it being known that this procedure is followed. . . ." Control would be exercised directly by MacArthur's headquarters. Meantime, the senior espionage assets in Luzon would be Colonel Narciso Manzano, Primitivo San Augustin, Chick Parsons, and Jose Osamiz.

Ferdinand left Mindanao in late January or February 1944, and headed back toward Manila. It was a successful trip, Spence declares, because he had "established a complete chain of communication linking Colonel Fertig to Manila, and shortly he extended this to contact with Colonel Volckmann in the northern mountains. . . ."

In April 1944, he staggered into his mother's house in Manila and collapsed, violently ill. Once more, Pacifico diagnosed his brother's condition as Blackwater fever, and took Ferdinand to the same Japanese military hospital where he had been treated the previous summer. According to Spence, this time Ferdinand was hidden behind bookshelves in the hospital library. While he recuperated over the next four months, he said he was able to receive a long string of high-level visitors, including Manuel Roxas, General Capinpin, and General Vicente Lim, and managed to make his way freely through the hospital corridors unsuspected by Japanese guards posted everywhere. President Laurel and other officials of the puppet government were all said to be aware of his hiding place, and to have conspired to keep it secret. Ferdinand quotes General Capinpin, who was then Laurel's military adviser, as saying that Laurel knew he was in the hospital: "Otherwise you'd have been routed out within a week." Altogether, Ferdinand spent a total of eight months of the war receiving treatment in a Japanese high-security military hospital, which is only plausible if he had the protection of Laurel or the Kempeitei.

He was definitely in the hospital, because one visitor he did have was Amparo Males, a woman active in the resistance and an agent for

Colonel B. L. Anderson's guerrilla unit who was visiting the hospital posing as a relative. Her intelligence report is in the U.S. archives:

> During our brief meeting he [Marcos] told me of his outfit in . . . Manila. That he had a radio receiver operating. . . . That he had boys doing intelligence work. That he had trigger boys . . . in charge of eliminating persons loyal to the enemies. . . . He said he had different groups of men assigned to each branch of work, but did not specify to me how many men in each group. No intelligence report was submitted to me whatsoever. On my way back to our headquarters, two of his men came with me to contact our commanding officer Lieutenant Colonel B. L. Anderson. These two boys went as far as Captain A. C. Bello's post at Piyapi. After a brief stay in the said camp these boys left for Manila. That was the last time I heard of this unit.

"These boys" did send a written message from Ferdinand to Colonel Anderson. In it, he again claimed falsely that the Maharlika had been given Fertig's blessing. Anderson was suspicious and asked MacArthur's headquarters for instructions: "LIEUTENANT FERDINAND E. MARCOS CONTACTED UNDERSIGNED WITH REQUEST THAT HE AND HIS UNIT (AS HE SAYS IS AUTHORIZED BY COLONEL FERTIG) COME UNDER THIS COMMAND. HE ALSO REQUESTED FUNDS AND OTHER AID. REQUEST AUTHENTICATION AND VERIFICATION."

Since Bataan, Ferdinand had been passing himself off first as a captain, then as a major. In his letter to Colonel Anderson he referred to himself prudently as a lieutenant.

That August, Ferdinand said he was forced to flee for his life because his mother came to visit him in the hospital and the Kempeitei followed her. He said he hid in the office of the hospital secretary until they gave up their search, then made a harrowing escape, crawling under barbed wire and into the night, his pockets bulging with vitamin pills. When he reached Josefa's house, a new identification card was awaiting him with the name Pascual Esguerra (literally a nom de guerre), a lieutenant in the puppet Constabulary. Also waiting was a bodyguard named Inigo Ventura. Putting on a full Constabulary uniform, Ferdinand got into a Japanese staff car with Narciso Ramos, Ventura, a PC colonel, and a captain, and they all drove to a Constabulary barracks in Malolos, Bulacan. They were stopped at two Japanese checkpoints along the way but passed through without difficulty. In Malolos they were warmly received because the two PC officers in the car were Colonel Fidel Cruz, commander of the barracks, and Captain Alfredo Santos, senior inspector for the province of Bulacan. A few days later, an old car with a converted charcoal-fed engine picked up Ferdinand, this time clad inconspicuously in a *gris* peasant shirt with baggy pants and bare feet.

He claimed that he was on a secret mission to clear a small airstrip so that Manuel Roxas could be spirited out of the country to join MacArthur; but the autumn passed with no airstrip being started. Instead, he was observed trying to organize bands of armed men, villagers, and country folk in the manner of a political agent. Other officers of Maharlika were similarly engaged in provinces farther north. Mariano Marcos was busy around Ilocos Sur, Simeon Valdez of TESCO in Ilocos Norte, assisted by Juan Crisologo, another commander of Laurel's Constabulary. At that same time, President Laurel appointed another Maharlika/ TESCO officer, a jai alai sports promoter named Modesto Farolan, to be the new governor of Ilocos Norte. The appointment is just one of many indications that Laurel was well acquainted with key people in Maharlika and made use of them.

An American invasion was expected at any time somewhere in the Philippines. It appears that Jose Laurel was taking whatever steps he could to prepare for it by dispatching agents throughout Luzon. As a far-sighted man, he was certainly looking beyond the immediate threat to his presidency, and laying the groundwork for what might follow. If the Allies were successful in recapturing the Philippines, it would spell the end to his Japanese-backed regime, but he was a man accustomed to setting long-range objectives and working his way through the political labyrinth to attain them. It was known that the exiled President Quezon was near death from tuberculosis, which meant that a scramble for power would soon be under way in any event. Laurel had to believe he would survive whatever reprisals he suffered at American hands, to resume his political career eventually. Meanwhile, there was time to get his followers into positions of leverage in key constituencies, time for them to enlist their own followers and to prepare for the political struggle ahead. The Laurel family stronghold of Batangas was not in question, but other power centers in northern Luzon needed to be secured while there was still time. Control of the Ilocano constituency, scattered throughout the central and mountain provinces, had fragmented under the intense pressures of the occupation. The Ilocano officers of Maharlika, all identified with Laurel and the Quirinos, evidently were given the job of rallying and reorganizing in the north.

This sudden outburst of political activity angered the American guerrilla officers under Colonel Volckmann's command, who were busy tightening their own ranks in preparation for MacArthur's invasion. Volckmann's men were under orders to crack down on any suspicious undertakings. On the list were spies, racketeers, men who changed sides too often, men promoting spurious schemes, and men attempting to organize new guerrilla bands, private armies, or political movements.

One of the first to be captured in Ilocos Norte was Ferdinand's uncle, Simeon Valdez. He was arrested by Captain John P. O'Day.

"The rivalry between the guerrilla groups," Governor Farolan reported, "had broken into open warfare...." There were killings on both sides. Down at the southern end of the Ilocos, near the border of La Union, another Volckmann guerrilla force under Major George Barnett arrested Mariano Marcos. His days as a Japanese propagandist were over. Barnett's unit included a number of friends and relatives of the late Julio Nalundasan, bent on revenge.

In East Pangasinan, Ferdinand's Maharlika comrades were locked in direct combat with guerrillas under Major R. B. Lapham and Captain Ray Hunt, two of Volckmann's commanders. On October 9, 1944, Captain Hunt issued orders for the arrest of Ferdinand Marcos himself. The order read: "I want you to arrest every organizer operating in Pangasinan without the authority of this office and turn said individuals over to this H.Q. I want Ferdinand Marcos specially...."

Captain Hunt met Ferdinand only once, when he was arrested and brought to his headquarters. "He was barefoot, unarmed," Hunt recalled. "We talked for 15 or 20 minutes about this or that. He was never identified to me as a guerrilla, and we didn't talk about guerrilla activities. I had no further contact with him." Major Lapham later filed a brief report stating that Captain Hunt placed Ferdinand under arrest for collecting money under false pretenses. He added, "It is quite obvious that Marcos did not exercise any control over a guerrilla organization prior to liberation."

When word of his arrest was passed up the line to Volckmann's headquarters, a radio message came back from Volckmann's G-2, Lieutenant Colonel Arthur Murphy: "EXECUTE FERDINAND MARCOS AND REPORT COMPLIANCE WITHOUT DELAY."

Four

YAMASHITA'S GOLD

IT WAS APPARENT to Tokyo by the summer of 1944 that an Allied invasion of the Philippines or Formosa was imminent. At Hollandia in New Guinea, a great fleet of American ships was assembling. To prepare for it, General Kuroda Shigenori was relieved of his command in the Philippines and replaced by the "Tiger of Malaya," General Yamashita Tomoyuki (pronounced Ya-MASH-ta). He was a big man, heavyset, with a bull neck and a large, close-cropped head. A product of the Prussian-oriented military tradition in Japan, his face was kept expressionless and he appeared to be brutal and insensitive, but he was actually a moderate who had resisted the explosive growth of the Imperial Army, and the growing fanaticism of its officer corps. The son of a mild-mannered country doctor, Yamashita had not chosen a military career; it was his father's idea. "I was big and healthy," he said, "and my mother did not seriously object because she believed that I would never pass the highly competitive entrance examination." He proved to be a brilliant commander, but his resistance to the ultranationalism of his fellow officers caused him serious trouble. In 1929 he supported an unpopular plan to reduce the size of the army by several divisions. As a consequence, he felt that his promotion to lieutenant general had been delayed for years. Yamashita resented the fanatical clique that had gathered around Tojo, and he was almost paranoid in his suspicion of their motives. And rightly so. Tojo had given him the difficult job of conquering the supposedly impregnable British bastion of Singapore, and if that did not destroy him, planned to have him assassinated as soon as Singapore surrendered. As it turned out, Singapore fell with catastrophic suddenness, and Yamashita's lightning campaign and humiliation of the British raj made him a national hero. Instead of having him murdered, Tojo put him on ice, dispatching him to Manchuria to train troops. By calling out the Tiger of Malaya to defend the Philippines, Tokyo gave Yamashita the burden of what many suspected would be an exhaustive delaying action and ultimately a losing battle.

Yamashita arrived in the Philippines only on October 6, 1944, too late to alter the equation significantly. At almost the same moment, the vast Allied armada in New Guinea sailed for Leyte, manned by fifty thousand sailors. MacArthur was still smarting from the way in which he had been surprised, cut off at the knees, and unceremoniously booted out of the islands at the start of the war. This time, he was taking no chances. He had a quarter of a million soldiers and marines with him, many of them battle-hardened, while most of the twenty thousand Japanese troops garrisoned on Leyte had never before seen combat.

The Battle of Leyte Gulf, the biggest sea battle in history to that point, resulted in disastrous Japanese naval losses. The outcome was decided not by superior force or ingenuity but, as is often the case, by miscalculations and luck. Both sides blundered ludicrously. Outnumbering the Japanese by nearly ten to one, MacArthur was ultimately victorious ashore. As 1944 drew to a close, he prepared to invade Luzon.

It was impossible to defend Manila, Yamashita realized, so to spare it from pointless destruction he declared it an open city and withdrew his command to the mountains in the north, leaving only 3,750 security troops to maintain order in the city. Without consulting or informing Yamashita, Rear Admiral Iwabuchi Sanji, the commander of the Japanese naval district, then reoccupied Manila with 16,000 marines and sailors. He had orders from Vice Admiral Okochi Denshichi to destroy all port facilities and naval storehouses, but Admiral Iwabuchi also had his own urgent and sinister reason for taking matters into his own hands.

With the Japanese conquest of East and Southeast Asia had come loot beyond dreams. Gold and gems were confiscated from private citizens, churches, temples, monasteries, banks, corporations, and fallen governments—and from the gangster syndicates and black-money economies of each nation. After Korea and Manchuria, loot came from China, Indochina, Thailand, Burma, Malaya, Borneo, Singapore, the Philippines, and the Dutch East Indies; a vast hoard of jewelry, gems, gold Buddhas, bullion, public and personal treasure. Speculation over the years on the total worth of this war loot ranged up to 3 billion 1940s dollars—the equivalent of over $100 billion today. According to various postwar estimates, the amount of gold bullion alone was between 4,000 and 6,000 tons. These estimates were probably far too conservative, made at a time in the late 1940s when little was known and much was being covered up. We might arrive at a more accurate total if 6,000 tons was considered to be only the amount stolen or seized from legitimate sources including banks, adding to it a bigger sum in illicit or black gold, perhaps two or three times as much. What few people in the West grasped in the late 1940s was the amount of illicit funds, unreported assets, illegal earnings, criminal profits, black market proceeds, secret hoards of gems and precious metals, and other forms of black money that existed in Asia. After 1942, comparatively little of this loot actually reached Tokyo, perhaps less than a third. Most of it was thought to have gone no farther than the transshipment point of Manila, where its journey was interrupted by the war's changing fortunes, and had to be hidden.

Since the war, it has all come to be known (inaccurately) as Yamashita's Gold.

Although he seems to have had no direct knowledge of the great hoard, Yamashita was hardly an innocent. There were instances early in the war where he was involved indirectly in extorting large sums from vanquished populations. In Malaya, the Kempeitei preyed on the overseas Chinese community. Its leading members, including wealthy Lim Boon Keng and the Shaw Brothers, the motion picture producers, were coerced into setting up an Overseas Chinese Association, then forced to raise 50 million Malay dollars as a "gift" to Yamashita to atone for supporting China's anti-Japanese efforts in the 1930s. Yamashita officially accepted their offering on June 25, 1942, in the name of the emperor. Soon afterward, he was reassigned to Manchuria.

Another documented example of how the Kempeitei helped itself was the seizure of 780 million piastres from the Indonesia Bank of Indochina in March 1945. To provide a sense of scale, it would have taken a middle-class bureaucrat in Saigon a million years to earn such a sum.

While the Kempeitei took over the Asian opium and heroin trade, the Imperial Army set up gambling establishments and lotteries throughout the conquered countries, and encouraged wealthy collaborators to lose fortunes. Because of the traditional contempt for paper money in the Orient, Japanese officers personally required payment in precious metals and gems.

Part of the treasure was Philippine government bullion. Manuel Roxas had been left in charge of sinking the government reserves, but apparently was not successful in keeping the locations secret.

Officially acknowledged war prizes and booty had to be shipped back to the Home Islands by sea along the route of conquest; they could not be sent by land because Japan did not control an overland route through China to Southeast Asia until mid-1944. Theoretically, these shipments eventually would reach Tokyo, to sweeten and replenish the Imperial treasury. However, there were two good reasons why little booty reached Japan. One was the American submarine campaign, armed with effective new torpedoes, which cut the sealanes abruptly before the end of 1943. Despite this, the Japanese used every opportunity and subterfuge to get the loot to Japan. Even at the end of the war they were still resorting to deception to ship home treasure rather than abandon it. Under Allied guarantees, the cargo vessel *Awa Maru* made three mercy missions to Southeast Asia at the end of the war to pick up Japanese war prisoners, before it was accidentally torpedoed by the U.S. submarine *Queen Fish*, on April 1, 1945. The *Awa Maru* went to the bottom of Formosa Strait, 14 miles off the Chinese mainland with 2,007 souls and at least $500 million worth of war loot hidden aboard.

The other reason the treasure failed to reach home was the Japanese criminal underworld, and the immensely clever and powerful people who were its patrons. Although small portions of the treasure may have been hidden in each of the conquered countries by the field commanders who seized it, or by rogue agents of the Kempeitei, the great bulk of it appears eventually to have come under the control of senior Imperial Navy officers and was conveyed by them to Manila by sea. Keeping it secret was easy. The navy, the air force, the army, and the Kempeitei were full of factions, personality cults, and cells of secret societies readymade for such conspiracies. The most powerful of these were the ultra-right Black Dragon Society, the Cherry Blossom Society, and their underworld equivalent, the Yakuza (pronounced YAK-cuz-ah).

In the late nineteenth century, when ultranationalism first swept Japan, a man named Toyama Mitsuru took part in uprisings against the new Meiji government and was jailed. On his release, he founded the paramilitary Dark Ocean Society (a name with profound Zen mystical connotations), pledged to revere the emperor, love and respect the nation, and defend the people's rights. Through blackmail, extortion, terror, and assassination, the Dark Ocean Society gained extraordinary influence over the army and bureaucracy. It provided bodyguards for officials, thugs for political bosses, zealots for the armed forces, and spies for foreign subversion. Its members practiced the martial arts, and the most adept became ninja assassins. The Dark Ocean Society and its successor, the Black Dragon Society, provided the core of Japan's pre–World War II secret service, who were sent abroad to prepare the way for the conquest of Korea, Manchuria, and northern China. The ultranationalism of Toyama and his followers became the driving force in Japanese politics and conspiracy their way of life. He inspired the growth of hundreds of other secret societies with names like Loyalist Sincerity Group, Blood Pledge Corps, and Association for Heavenly Action, supported by wealthy patrons and financing operations through gambling, prostitution, protection rackets, blackmail, extortion, strike-breaking, and labor control, activities that brought them into close contact and partnership with the Yakuza.

The word *yakuza* refers to the lowest score in a card game. Yakuza see themselves as society's losers—gamblers, thieves, outcasts, and petty criminals. During the civil wars of the seventeenth century, when unemployed Samurai called *ronin* terrorized the peasantry, they were driven off by local toughs in the manner immortalized by the Kurosawa film *Seven Samurai* and its Western version, *The Magnificent Seven.* The modern Yakuza like to trace their origins to these roots, although the connection is fanciful. Like the Corsican and Sicilian underworlds, the Yakuza began as families involved in criminal activities. They expanded gradually through adoption, in a manner similar to the triads of China and the *compadre* system of the Philippines. Some Yakuza are conspicuous because their rituals include slicing off the top joint of the little finger in penitence and covering the body with tattoos. Just as Lucky Luciano brought the New York waterfront under Mafia control in the 1930s and played bash-the-Bolshies for the FBI on the eve of World War II, along Japanese docks the Yakuza organized longshoremen for grand larceny and far-right politics, and went into partnership with navy commanders and the secret service. Kobe's longshoremen became the biggest Yakuza syndicate in Japan, the Yamaguchi Gumi.

Just before World War II, Toyama's lieutenant Uchida Ryohei founded the Black Dragon Society, the offspring of the Dark Ocean, which dominated the Kempeitei during the war and led the struggle to expel Bolshevism, democracy, capitalism, and Westerners from Asia. The looting of East and Southeast Asia brought the Black Dragons and the Yakuza together. The interests of the political right and the underworld fused.

Most of the Yakuza's wealthy patrons were more interested in money than in politics—militant Fascism was a natural ally of extortion. From 1931 to 1945, they made huge fortunes trading in the black market, which they secured in diamonds, gold, and platinum. As the Kempeitei and the Imperial Army took over the opium trade in Manchuria in the 1930s, a drug cartel was established in collaboration with the Shanghai Green Gang and other Chinese underworld syndicates tied to the regime of Generalissimo Chiang. The Japanese Army, aided by this underworld cartel, made $300 million a year in the Manchurian drug trade alone; over a decade, this came to $3 billion (1940 dollars), most of it secured in gold. This was an amount equal, in other words, to the early estimates of the size of Yamashita's Gold, and demonstrates how much black money really was in circulation.

In Asia, gold smuggling and narcotics have been the foundation of wealth for centuries. During the Pacific War, although thousands were starving, foods, medicines, and most luxury items could be purchased readily on the black market, if you could pay in gold. A flourishing trade in precious metals continued throughout the war, run by Chinese syndicates under Japanese control.

Yamashita's Gold was not merely the military's booty; it was the accumulated overseas loot for more than a decade of conquest of the entire Japanese establishment. As the war reached a climax, hiding this huge treasure became a matter of urgency to senior Japanese navy officers in Manila who were responsible for its security and its shipment homeward. Beginning in late 1943, some of the loot apparently was taken in truck convoys to the mountains, near the Benguet mines in Baguio, where it was hidden in tunnels or caves and sealed with concrete, and to other areas outside Manila, where it was buried in deep pits. Other quantities were sunk on coral reefs blasted open for that purpose, and then corked with coral and concrete. There were grisly stories about Allied prisoners—mostly Britons, Australians, Americans, and Filipinos—being forced to dig these pits and tunnels during 1943 and 1944, only to be buried alive. They would never reveal the location, and their spirits would guard the treasure. Not to leave matters to chance, Japanese engineers rigged elaborate booby traps at each site, including fully armed 1,000- and 2,000-pound bombs, so that safe access to the treasure could be gained only if an excavator followed precise technical instructions described on secret maps. As a final precaution, the maps were inscribed in an ancient and esoteric Japanese script.

Most people assumed all this was just legend, but certain elements of the legend were bizarre enough to be persuasive, such as the deliberate sinking of various ships loaded with treasure, including the Japanese cruiser *Nachi*, sunk in Manila Bay. The story goes that late in 1944 the *Nachi* was loaded with 100 tons of bullion and prepared to sail home. Before she got out of Manila Bay, a Japanese submarine lying in wait sank her in a previously calculated spot. Nearly a thousand Japanese sailors went down with the *Nachi*. Those who came to the surface were said to have been machine-gunned by sailors on the sub so that no witnesses would survive.

As the story came out of Manila many years after the war, this sinking of the *Nachi* and others, and many of the treasure burials, *were* in fact witnessed by two young men of dual Japanese-Filipino nationality—Leopoldo "Paul" Jiga and Benjamin Balmores. Paul said he was twenty-three when the war started, born in Manila, the son of a Japanese father and Filipino mother. When the Imperial Army occupied the Philippines, he said his father was pressed to work as an aide and translator to a Japanese general (sometimes he said admiral). Paul became the general's houseboy, valet, and interpreter. This particular general, he said, was the senior officer in charge of burying the war treasure. Because of his job waiting on the general hand and foot, Paul said he was personally present when the treasure was buried at a number of sites, onshore and offshore. From what he observed, the treasure was buried under Japanese Army supervision by teams of POWs, all of whom were then shot or buried alive in the pits and tunnels. At offshore sites, their bodies were dumped in the water for disposal by sharks. Paul said he was an eyewitness when the *Nachi* was sunk.

Ben Balmores told a similar story. He also was a dual national. Employed as an interpreter, spy, and scout, he had observed the Japanese beheading or burying alive thousands of prisoners of war, atrocities that he said nauseated him when he thought about it. The Japanese had used the Spanish dungeon at Fort Santiago to contain prisoners, and these prisoners were forced to dig miles of tunnels beneath the grounds of the fort. When part of the treasure was hidden there, he said, the POWs were sealed inside, dying either of starvation or suffocation. At the town of Teresa outside Manila there were two treasure chambers deep underground where Paul and Ben said they had witnessed twelve hundred Australians and Americans buried alive. The secret treasure maps, they said, were kept in the headquarters of the Japanese high command in Manila until Yamashita pulled out of the city.

Since mid-December 1944, when his puppet government moved to the mountains, Jose Laurel and his colleagues had been operating from General Yamashita's new headquarters at Baguio.

Yamashita had 170,000 troops on Luzon, many of them seasoned. Most withdrew with him to the north, but other units took up positions in the mountains to the city's east, northeast, and northwest. Yamashita's job was to delay MacArthur, to deny his use of airfields in northern Luzon in support of a forthcoming U.S. attack on Okinawa, and to kill as many Americans as possible.

When MacArthur invaded Luzon in January 1945, on the Lingayen Gulf north of Manila, the same landing point that the Japanese had chosen three years earlier, he had the option of bypassing Manila, leaving it an open city as Yamashita had chosen to do, and concentrating his attack on Yamashita's army in the mountains. Tragically, MacArthur insisted upon advancing directly on Manila. Although General Willoughby had grossly underestimated the strength of the Japanese, MacArthur imagined that Yamashita's abandonment of Manila gave him a golden opportunity to seize it quickly and stage a triumphal entry like de Gaulle in Paris. He directed the XIV Corps to drive on to Manila immediately. General Walter Krueger figured that MacArthur wanted to be in Manila by his birthday, January 26. MacArthur's move blocked the withdrawal from Manila of Admiral Iwabuchi's sixteen thousand sailors and marines. Cut off and stranded without ships, they were unable to escape either by sea or overland. Given the Japanese abhorrence of surrender, they had no choice but to stage a suicidal fight. Against Yamashita's specific order, they panicked and turned Manila into a battlefield, fighting house-to-house, committing atrocities on the city's inhabitants that rank among the great crimes of the war. One hundred thousand Filipinos, sixteen thousand Japanese, and one thousand Americans died in the carnage. Manila was 80 percent destroyed.

Only Warsaw suffered more. Of the one hundred thousand Filipinos murdered, many of the women were first raped, pregnant women disemboweled, the men sexually mutilated, and infants had their eyes gouged out and their brains dashed against walls.

Even before this slaughter ended, MacArthur celebrated his triumph at a gathering in Malacanang Palace on February 27. Manuel Quezon had died of tuberculosis in America. While fighting continued in other parts of the city, MacArthur conveyed to the new president, Sergio Osmeña, the formal responsibility for governing the restored commonwealth. MacArthur pronounced that Manila, "cruelly punished though it be, has regained its rightful place—Citadel of Democracy in the East."

William Manchester characterized MacArthur's campaign on Luzon as "the achievements of a great strategist," and speculated about "what would have happened had MacArthur, not Mark Clark, been the U.S. commander in Italy." It is not a happy thought.

While fighting continued in Manila, MacArthur ordered General Eichelberger's Eighth Army to begin the liberation of all the remaining islands of the archipelago. Seizure of these islands was of little importance for the defeat of Japan. Military historians regard it as a pointless campaign. MacArthur assigned five full divisions to do the job, leaving Krueger's Sixth Army badly depleted as it confronted Yamashita's main force in the mountains. However, MacArthur wished to be remembered as the liberator of all the islands, and his employment of the Eighth Army, the Eleventh Air Force, and much of the Seventh Fleet in the southern archipelago kept these valuable assets under his command. His vanity played into Yamashita's hands.

At first Yamashita planned to hold the airfields in the Cagayan Valley, and to retain the northern port of Aparri, through which he hoped to be relieved by the arrival of additional Japanese forces, although the hope was remote.

He held out in Baguio as long as he could. Then he led sixty-five thousand troops into the mountainous area between Routes 4 and 11, a last-ditch redoubt that became known as the Kiangan Pocket. Just before Yamashita's staff left Baguio, the trusted houseboys Paul and Ben said they walked into headquarters (where they always had the run of the place) and stole the master treasure maps. They said they did not have any definite plan to recover the gold themselves because the Japanese had made each site too intricate with booby traps for casual retrieval. It would take teams of men and equipment, not to mention lots of money and engineering skill, to circumvent the booby traps and to find the precise locations. But somehow the maps would be valuable.

Captain Ray Hunt was unable to keep prisoners in the forward area. The options were to send Ferdinand Marcos up the line to the 14th Infantry under Major Manriquez, in Mountain Province, or in the other direction to the 121st Infantry under Major Barnett, on the far side of Baguio. Ferdinand had friends in the 14th, among them a former law school classmate, Captain Lino Patajo, who warned him not to fall into the hands of the 121st, because Major Barnett had arrested Mariano Marcos, and the unit included many friends and relatives of Nalundasan. These Nalundasan partisans, he said, were itching to get their hands on Ferdinand as well. Accordingly, Ferdinand asked to be sent up the line to the regimental headquarters of the 14th. Ironically this was the very unit Ferdinand once pretended to command, when he was arrested by guerrillas on the island of Bohol in 1943, on his way to Mindanao. He was going to the 14th now as a prisoner, not a commander.

Soon after he arrived at 14th HQ, orders came in by radio from Volckmann's G-2 to execute him as a spy. The G-2, Lieutenant Colonel Murphy, knew that Captain O'Day had arrested Simeon Valdez and other Maharlika recruiters in Ilocos Norte, and that Major Barnett had arrested Mariano Marcos. Under interrogation, Mariano had identified Ferdinand as the person who had recommended him to the Kempeitei at the start of the war. So, when word came that Ferdinand had been arrested by Captain Hunt, Murphy may well have felt justified in ordering his execution.

Uncertain what to do, the commander of the 14th HQ battalion, Captain Saturnino Dumlao, sought the advice of one of his relatives in the battalion, Ferdinand's friend Venancio Duque. Venancio Duque was one of the men who had picked up Ferdinand in the old charcoal-fired car at the PC barracks in Malolos three months before he was arrested. His name does not appear on any list of officers in the 14th, because he was an intelligence agent who slipped back and forth from side to side. Like Ferdinand, his real allegiance was probably to Jose Laurel and the Quirino brothers.

In a panic, Duque rushed to Major Manriquez and protested. The major gave him two days to prove that the execution order was in error.

Duque rushed around, obtaining affidavits from various friends. Manriquez radioed the gist of the affidavits to Volckmann's G-2, but Lieutenant Colonel Murphy radioed back: "RECEIVED AFFIDAVITS IN RE MARCOS. CARRY OUT PREVIOUS ORDER AND REPORT COMPLIANCE." In desperation, Duque radioed his uncle, Colonel Calixto Duque, a senior Ilocano staff officer in charge of training at Volckmann's headquarters, and one of the top Quirino men in the guerrilla command. Colonel Duque immediately intervened, ordering Lieutenant Colonel Murphy to cancel the execution.

By early January 1945, Yamashita's troops were beginning to move up toward the 14th Infantry, blocking all routes south. Ferdinand was no longer a prisoner, but he was unable to leave. He was reinstated on U.S. Army roles as a third lieutenant, and Major Manriquez assigned him to a clerical job as S-5 in charge of civil affairs. From December 1944 till mid-April 1945, when Ferdinand requested transfer for personal reasons to Volckmann's headquarters at Luna, La Union, Manriquez insisted that Marcos was only a clerk and was never involved on patrol or in combat operations, which was confirmed by Captain Vicente Rivera of the 14th. Yet many years after the war, when Ferdinand was a politician angling for the presidency, he was awarded a number of medals for awesome and virtually single-handed combat exploits in the closing months of the war. During state visits to America as president of the Philippines, he was commended for these phony exploits by three presidents of the United States and was given a specially mounted display of his undeserved U.S. medals by Secretary of Defense Caspar Weinberger. All three presidents and Weinberger had knowledge that the truth of Marcos's heroic war record was widely questioned. Their decision to endorse his fraud makes it important to give Ferdinand's final wartime adventures a brief summary. It was also during this period that he showed his first interest in Yamashita's Gold.

On March 19, Tokyo ordered that President Laurel be flown to Japan to establish a government-in-exile. Three days later, Laurel and other leading collaborators, among them Benigno Aquino of the Kalibapi party, left Baguio secretly. The rest of the puppet government, including Manuel Roxas, remained behind.

Ferdinand's biographers all assert that he led an assault and demolition team to an unguarded section of road near Baguio, and mined it for half a mile. A dozen cars came down the road, one carrying President Laurel. Through binoculars, Ferdinand recognized Laurel and General Capinpin. He waited till their car passed, then fired his charges. All the Japanese in the convoy were killed.

As it actually happened, "Doy" Laurel was with his father on the journey. According to him, it was a tiresome and uneventful trip until the afternoon of March 28. Then, with the Japanese airfield at Tuguergarao only 27 kilometers away, their trucks (not cars) were set upon by guerrillas. "Behind us, we heard the burst of machine-gun fire. . . . We ducked, seeking hollows in the ground. . . . Taking the offensive, our escorts finally drove away the attackers with a continuous barrage of machine-gun fire. Ten minutes later we were told to go back to our trucks." (Tuguergarao is over 100 kilometers from the area where Marcos said the incident took place.)

The next weeks were very busy. Ferdinand met an American demolition expert, Captain Donald Jamison, who was landed by submarine. They became close friends, and in later years Jamison filed numerous affidavits describing Ferdinand's heroic missions: "From January to early March, 1945, under Major Marcos' leadership and personal direction, we discharged our mission of demolishing bridges, roads and other man-made obstacles." (Ferdinand's rank was still third lieutenant.) Sergeant Larry Guzman, an American who accompanied Jamison, said that in the middle of March 1945 the command post of the 14th HQ came under siege. "Marcos, though ill at the infirmary, left his sick bed and engaged the enemy in a running gun battle." Among several decorations for this action, Ferdinand received the Distinguished Conduct Star, for courage and gallantry in single-handedly holding at bay and later pursuing an enemy patrol.

A different story is told by Captain Rivera, who was the officer in charge of security at 14th HQ on March 17. Ferdinand was Officer of the Day, which involved checking guards posted around the camp. That evening, before he left for duty around the perimeter, he asked for food. Sergeant Sofronio La Rosa killed a small chicken, roasted it, and gave him half. At three in the morning, the camp was awakened by bursts of gunfire from a Thompson submachine gun. Everyone took cover in a nearby creek while the executive officer went to investigate. On his return, the exec reported that Marcos had fired at rustling leaves thinking Japanese snipers were lurking behind them. The only other time Ferdinand fired a gun, Rivera recalled, was when he was issued the Thompson and fired to test it. Verdict: Indigestion.

Three weeks after this "Battle of the Drumstick," Yamashita abandoned Baguio and led his army to the Kiangan Pocket for the showdown. Okinawa had been lost, so there was no point in continuing to hold airfields or ports. On April 5, Ferdinand claimed that he and an enlisted man were patrolling an area near 14th HQ when he saw camouflaged enemy trucks approaching with a large body of hostile troops. He sent the enlisted man back to report while he posted himself at a vantage point. When the enemy vanguard came within 15 yards, Ferdinand opened fire with his Thompson and inflicted heavy casualties, forcing the Japanese to withdraw. He was wounded in the thigh, he said, and had to cut the bullet out. Then he pursued the Japanese two kilometers down the trail before reinforcements caught up. For this remarkable action, Ferdinand claimed he was awarded a second U.S. Silver Star.

On another occasion, he literally tumbled onto some of Yamashita's Gold. Ferdinand claimed he was leading a patrol in Kayapa, a mountainous district of Nueva Vizcaya. There he encountered a Japanese patrol of twenty men. Following them, he was led north toward the Ifugao rice terraces. One Japanese soldier was lagging because his pack was too heavy. Ferdinand raised his rifle and picked off the straggler. As he went forward to reach for the dead man's pack, a bullet struck him in the back, and he pitched down the mountain clinging to the pack. The wound was superficial, but the pack contained three gold bars.

There is no evidence that Ferdinand was anywhere near the rice terraces in the closing months of the war, but there is lots of evidence that he found some of Yamashita's Gold.

In mid-April, Ferdinand learned that his father Mariano Marcos, after months as a prisoner of Major Barnett, had been tried for war crimes and executed. It was not a simple execution. Barnett's guerrillas—friends of Nalundasan—after interrogating Mariano and confirming that he had worked for the Japanese throughout the war, executed him by tying him to four carabao water buffaloes, which tore him limb from limb. They hung the pieces in a tree.

Burdened by this news, Ferdinand requested transfer to Volckmann's headquarters in La Union at the end of April 1945. He said he went looking for Mariano's remains but did not find them. He always told people that his father had been executed by the Japanese.

General Yamashita remained in the Kiangan Pocket for months, fighting an impressive and ultimately futile rearguard action. No force was sent to relieve him. Kiangan itself was captured in July 1945, after some of the harshest mountain fighting ever. During the last month, the Americans advanced only three miles. Yamashita was neither captured nor defeated. On August 15, 1945, after Japan itself surrendered, Yamashita surrendered. Ferdinand always claimed that he was the one who accepted Yamashita's surrender. In a way he did. Years after the war, a friend offered him as a gift a photostatic reproduction of the original surrender document, and he accepted it.

Five

UNNATURAL ACTS

AT THE END of the Pacific War, life in the Philippines did not return to normal but took on a surreal, nightmarish quality as America refused to leave.

Throughout the Far East, Washington was attempting to install right-wing governments as a first line of defense against communism, and its success depended heavily on two dubious allies, Generalissimo Chiang Kai-shek's notoriously corrupt KMT and the Japanese underworld. Because of the nature of things in Asia, conservative political movements derived their power from the muscle of the underworld, which could be paid to knock heads and counted on to resist reform of any variety. In Korea and China, as well as in Japan and the Philippines, MacArthur's G-2, General Willoughby, was purging radicals with the single-mindedness of Torquemada and the help of the underworld. In Washington, Senator McCarthy and the China Lobby were coming into full cry. Although one day McCarthy and the China Lobby would be discredited, by then MacArthur, Willoughby, and the CIA had mid-wifed a string of bone-crushing regimes calling themselves the Iron Triangle. One leg of this tripod was the Chiang regime, transposed to Taiwan and protected by the U.S. Seventh Fleet. Generalissimo Chiang was anxious to influence the politics of wealthy overseas Chinese and maintained an undercover army of political agents throughout the Far East. This provided an ideal funnel for the CIA's anti-Communist funds and a ready-made vehicle for U.S. covert operations. The Philippines became a staging area for intervention in the affairs of Indonesia, Indo-

112

china, Thailand, Vietnam, Malaya, and Burma. America's huge air and naval bases in the Philippines provided jumping-off points. Controlling politics in the archipelago became more important after America allowed the Philippines to become independent in 1946. For its part, the KMT became more obsessed than ever with destroying leftist and liberal elements in the Philippines and with dominating its Chinese community. A secret war got underway in which ordinary Filipinos became the enemy.

On the very eve of independence, Washington began to intervene once again in favor of those members of the oligarchy prepared to engage in unnatural acts. The rule of law was to be honored in the breach, appearance was to count instead of reality, and the whole charade was to be mimed with a bogus air of piety. The scene was set for a new generation of corruption and malfeasance on a monumental scale, a large standing army would be engaged full time only in protecting vested interests, all democratic protest in the islands would be labeled subversive or Communist-inspired, and opportunities for bribery to achieve short range goals would prove irresistible even for the White House. Again it was Douglas MacArthur who set the standard.

As the U.S. Army advanced into the mountains around Baguio in April 1945, remaining members of the Laurel government began to slip away from the Japanese. Manuel Roxas, three other cabinet ministers, and the chief justice reached American lines. MacArthur sent a plane for Roxas, but had the other men detained, and ordered the *Free Philippines,* a newspaper of the Office of War Information, to run a trumped-up story: "ROXAS IS AMONG LIBERATED, 4 CABINET AIDES CAUGHT." MacArthur thus set his protégé Roxas apart, distorting postwar politics in the islands and turning ethics on their head. Manuel Roxas was freed, restored to his rank of general, and given MacArthur's special pardon. The rest of the wartime puppets, most of them MacArthur's personal adversaries, or rivals of MacArthur's business associates in Manila, were interned.

"MacArthur could be wildly inconsistent when the oppressors were friends of his," conceded biographer William Manchester. Locked away in the files of U.S. Attorney General Tom Clark was a secret report identifying Roxas as one of the leading Filipino collaborators; this document (still classified decades later) contained hard evidence that members of the senate, cabinet, and Roxas himself had helped the Japanese wipe out Filipino and American guerrillas, seize food from poor farmers to feed Japanese troops, and draft the Laurel government's declaration of war against the United States.

Despite this evidence, at MacArthur's urging President Truman abandoned Roosevelt's policy that there must be an American-enforced purge of collaborators. Truman's decision was influenced by America's growing obsession with communism, a fear being fanned energetically by the Republican party in its effort to recapture the White House from the Democrats. In Manila the excitement of independence gave way to the jingoism of the McCarthy era. General MacArthur and High Commissioner Paul McNutt, nicknamed the "Hoosier Hitler" by his Filipino opponents, urged vigorous support for the oligarchy as the only way to restore "law and order," to fight communism, and to assure pro-American leadership in the future. That was true so far as it went. The oligarchy had the most to lose if reforms of any kind occurred and was accustomed to keeping order, although its methods were brutally undemocratic. So many of them had been collaborators that the issue had to be buried quickly, except where MacArthur himself had other reasons to fear or hate the men in question.

As America's supreme commander in the Far East, MacArthur was based in Tokyo rather than Manila, but he was up to the same mischief in both places. His treatment of senior Japanese military officers was vengeful and hypocritical. Generals Homma and Yamashita were railroaded by courts in Manila at MacArthur's instigation. When Filipino collaborators were tried, there had to be at least two eyewitnesses for every charge; in the trials of Homma and Yamashita the wildest hearsay was admissible. Yamashita, who was arguably the most capable Japanese commander the Allies faced during the war, was deliberately and unscrupulously maligned. MacArthur hurried their trials so the verdicts could be announced on the fourth anniversary of Pearl Harbor. Twelve journalists who sat through all the Yamashita testimony found for the defendant, 12 to 0. Homma, an amateur playwright, had been unable to control the cruelty of his men, but there was no evidence at all connecting him to the Death March. However, both men were sentenced to death. U.S. Supreme Court Justice Wiley Rutledge condemned the proceedings, quoting Tom Paine: "He that would make his own liberty secure must guard even his enemy from oppression; for if he violates this duty he establishes a precedent that will reach himself."

MacArthur relished the hanging of Yamashita, ordering that he be "stripped of uniform, decorations and other appurtenances signifying membership in the military profession." Homma was shot by a firing squad. MacArthur wanted them executed because they had humiliated him professionally, not because they were Fascist war criminals. This is revealed by what he was doing meanwhile in Tokyo.

In 1945, billionaires Kodama Yoshio and Sasakawa Ryoichi were among those locked up as "Class A war criminals" in Sugamo Prison to await trial. Kodama, a lifelong member of the Yakuza underworld, and its most brilliant patron, had made more than $200 million during the war just selling stolen goods to the Japanese Navy, a small part of his wartime activities. Sasakawa was one of Kodama's cleverest associates. Both men had served prison terms in the 1930s, Kodama for plotting to murder government officials who were not far enough to the right, Sasakawa for repeatedly threatening people with violence to extort money from them. Both energetically supported the Tojo regime. U.S. intelligence described Sasakawa as "potentially dangerous to Japan's political future." Of Kodama: "His long and fanatic involvement in ultra-nationalistic activities, violence included, and his skill in appealing to youth make him a grave security risk." On the day Tojo was hanged, MacArthur quietly had Kodama and Sasakawa released along with fifty-two of their politically powerful cellmates. He needed them to suppress Japan's postwar radicals and to impose a malleable right-wing regime. With his blessing, Kodama and Sasakawa became key organizers and financial backers of the Liberal Democratic party, which has dominated Japanese politics ever since. But there is much more to this intrigue than a simple case of political horse trading.

Sasakawa was born the son of a village sake brewer near Osaka in 1899. In 1927, after compulsory military service, he started his own ultra-rightist society, entered politics, and amassed a fortune which he attributed blandly to speculating in rice futures. In 1931, as the Imperial Army seized Manchuria, Japan was swept by a wave of nationalistic fervour and Sasakawa joined a young Yakuza terrorist named Kodama Yoshio in founding a nationwide organization, the Patriotic People's Mass Party, or *Kokosui Taishuto* (KT).

Members of the KT dressed in black shirts like the Fascists of Mussolini, who was one of Sasakawa's heroes. The KT specialized in blackmailing or extorting money from businessmen, politicians, and bureaucrats by threatening to denounce them as unpatriotic. Sasakawa was said to have made huge sums out of the general fear in Japan at the time of "intimations of disloyalty"—a situation not unlike the McCarthy hysteria in postwar America. In 1934 Sasakawa was jailed for threatening people who refused to comply with his demands. When he was released from prison in the late 1930s, he had his KT membership build a big airfield in Osaka that he donated grandly to the army. Soon he had put together a private fleet of twenty planes to form a volunteer air force, and in 1939 he flew off to visit his idol Mussolini in Rome. In 1942 he was elected to the Diet as a backer of Tojo's scheme to expand Japanese conquest in Southeast Asia.

Despite its political party trappings of twenty-three chapters and thousands of members, the KT was different from other patriotic groups because its main function was to collect unwilling donations. While Sasakawa concentrated on directing the party's domestic strongarm fund-raising activities, cultivating the army and air force in the process, his partner Kodama devoted his attention to the navy and the secret service and to collecting donations overseas.

Kodama was twelve years younger than Sasakawa, the fifth son of a broken gentleman in Nihonmatsu City. At age eight, he was dumped on relatives in Korea who put him to work as a child laborer. He was "adopted" by Yakuza gangsters and in his teens became an organizer for ultranationalist groups, showing a real genius for violence. He became, in effect, a professional terrorist, apprenticing himself to Toyama Mitsuru of the Dark Ocean Society. In the early 1930s, he and Sasakawa launched their *Kokosui Taishuto* "people's party" with the primary purpose of using extreme patriotism to bully money. In 1934 Kodama participated in an abortive attempt to assassinate cabinet members, including Prime Minister Admiral Saito. Sentenced to prison, he had time to brood, and when he was released in 1937 he embarked on an extraordinary new career. Joining the army, he became a staff officer at headquarters, and was posted to the Foreign Ministry's information bureau as a secret agent.

Kodama was no longer an ordinary gangster or terrorist. He had matured into a high-level "fixer," a master of conspiracy, and a trusted ally and close friend of many senior Japanese ultranationalists. Among them were the Imperial Army's Lieutenant Colonel Tsuji, the "God of Operations," who later designed Yamashita's assault on Singapore; Vice Admiral Onishi, who planned the assault on Pearl Harbor and created the kamikaze corps; General Ishihara, who developed Japan's scheme for the conquest of Manchuria; and a prince of the royal blood who was the overlord of the secret service. When Colonel Tsuji discovered that

Prime Minister Konoye was trying to avert war with the United States by reaching a compromise with Roosevelt, he asked Kodama to assassinate the prime minister by blowing up his train. The attempt at peace failed, so the murder was not carried out.

Long before Pearl Harbor, Kodama accompanied the Japanese expeditionary force to North China and Manchuria where he showed himself to be an arch criminal organizer. Kodama was one of those in charge of looting Manchuria and portions of North China as they came under Japanese military control. He put the Yakuza to work in concert with the army and the Kempeitei to bleed the country dry, using kidnapping and extortion on an unprecedented scale and setting up monopolies under Japanese protection. Kodama's agents looted hundreds of millions of dollars worth of gems and precious metals from Manchuria and North China while plundering them of strategic materials. The opium monopoly he helped set up in Manchuria generated $300 million a year in profits for the Imperial Army.

For a time, Kodama was in Nanking where he posed as a bodyguard for the puppet prime minister, Wang Ching-wei. At the time of Pearl Harbor, he was in Shanghai smuggling in heroin from Manchuria disguised as war materiel, and marketing it in collaboration with the Green Gang.

The day after Pearl Harbor, Kodama set up the Kodama Agency in Shanghai with an exclusive contract from the Imperial Navy Air Force to supply it with strategic materiel. This meant armed robbery and grand larceny on a monumental scale, and put Kodama in a rare position to strike bargains and make deals with the biggest criminal organizations in China. He dealt directly with Nationalist China's underworld boss, Tu Yueh-sheng (known as "Big-eared Tu"), and with the dreaded Ku brothers, one the Green Gang ruler of the Shanghai waterfront, the other a top KMT general soon to become chief-of-staff of Chiang Kai-shek's army. The Shanghai-based Green Gang became one of the means by which the Kempeitei and the KMT arranged mutually beneficial wartime deals throughout the Yangtze River valley, including the sale to Japanese agents of warehouses full of American Lend-Lease supplies, all with the cooperation and active participation of Generalissimo Chiang's inner circle. In the process, Kodama established a lasting bond with Chiang.

Through the Kodama Agency, he created his own secret service combining members of the *Kokosui Taishuto* with Yakuza gangsters and members of the Kempeitei, the army, and the navy. Although he had been an army officer, Kodama now was made a rear admiral, enjoying extraordinary influence in the naval hierarchy, with direct connections to the Imperial family.

Kodama's main preoccupation was the systematic looting of the conquered nations and (theoretically, at least) the transportation of that loot back to the emperor. As Japan consolidated its conquest of Southeast Asia, Kodama made his way from China down through the Co-Prosperity Sphere to Vietnam, Thailand, Burma, Malaya, Singapore, and the East Indies, working in each country with Colonel Tsuji and others to strip them and their populations of their wealth and strategic materials. Eventually, he made his way back up the coast of Borneo through Brunei to the Philippines, shepherding masses of war loot in naval vessels ahead of him under the watchful eye of naval officers seconded to him.

In Manila, the treasure was assembled for onward shipment to Tokyo, and was stored meanwhile in the labyrinth of tunnels that had existed since Spanish days beneath Fort Bonifacio, Fort Santiago, and the old walled city of Intramuros, and also in the tunnels at Corregidor. The Japanese were continually enlarging these tunnels under Intramuros and Corregidor by slave labor, using teams of Allied POWs who were literally worked to death below ground. It was estimated that they dug some 35 miles of tunnels in all beneath Intramuros, many of the passages designed specifically for storage of the treasure.

The shogun of this extraordinary and very secret operation was not Kodama but the man he worked for, the overlord of the Japanese secret service. This man was said to be an exceptionally urbane aristocrat, a prince and a cousin of Emperor Hirohito, who spoke flawless English and who regarded these treasures as a natural entitlement, no different from the loot that England, France, and other colonial powers had traditionally removed from Asia. Privately after the war he was said to have put an estimated value of $50 billion on the treasure left behind and hidden in the Philippines, and he conjectured that it would take a hundred years to recover it all.

By the end of 1943 American submarines posed such a hazard that it was increasingly risky to send shipments of the treasure home. Six months later, as the Americans massed to invade, so many ships had been lost that the Japanese in Manila found themselves sitting on top of a great hoard of loot in a country other than their own. Priority had to be given to burying it right where it was, disguising its locations, and booby trapping all possible approaches. For security reasons, all the POWs involved at each site had to be buried alive with the treasure, or machine-gunned.

It is likely that Kodama never intended to send all of the loot back to the Imperial Treasury. There was so much of it that from the beginning the temptation was irresistible to bury portions of it for recovery later. Kodama had always kept the platinum and diamonds for himself, as a "finder's fee." Nobody ever calculated how much he had in gems alone. He was proficient at seeing to it that freighters and warships carrying treasure were "sunk" on their way home, and that trucks filled with gold never reached their destinations. Fifty- or one-hundred-ton shipments of bullion were not that big and could be "lost" in creative ways. (Thirty thousand tons of gold bullion sounds like it would take up a football field, but gold is so dense that this amount would all fit into a single-family dwelling. This shows how easy it would be to hide large quantities; this of course is one of the reasons for gold's appeal throughout history.) By early 1944, the war was reaching its turning point, and Kodama knew what was in the divine wind. He began making preparations accordingly, and by the start of 1945, he was already back in Tokyo setting the stage for a new career.

After Hiroshima and Nagasaki, with defeat at hand, Tokyo became a dangerous place as political leaders and military officers committed ritual suicide, while others carried out assassinations of government officials they blamed for the defeat. To keep a lid on things during the transition, and to rescue as many chestnuts as possible, Prince Higashikuni Toshihiko became the interim prime minister. The thirty-four-year-old Rear Admiral Kodama, perhaps the master thief and master fixer of all time, was one of his advisers.

Early in 1946, Sasakawa and Kodama were rounded up by the Occupation forces and detained in Sugamo Prison for three years. According to Sasakawa, "Life in prison was a vacation given me by God." The time he spent in Sugamo, he said, was the key to his political education. With his politically powerful cellmates Kishi Nobusuke (later prime minister), Kaya Okinori, Kodama Yoshio, and others, Sasakawa joined in planning the resurrection of Japan. This time their energies and genius would be devoted to economic rather than military imperialism. The wealth that Sasakawa had accumulated, and the loot that Kodama had amassed all over Asia, would provide the financial foundation for the political organization that would lead the way, the Liberal Democratic party.

The liberation from Sugamo and the emergence of Kodama and

Sasakawa as two of the leading power brokers in East Asia was part of a package deal they made with Generalissimo Chiang and MacArthur's G-2, General Willoughby. Facing a showdown with the forces of Mao Tse-tung, the Generalissimo was seeking help urgently anywhere he could find it. Kodama knew where all the skeletons in China were hidden. As part of the deal, Kodama turned over half of what was then considered to be his immediate personal fortune of $200 million (obviously only a fragment of the whole) to the American Counter-Intelligence Corps to be split with Chiang Kai-shek. How much Kodama's wealthy cellmates like Sasakawa contributed to the deal has never been disclosed. Willoughby's part in this intrigue becomes understandable when seen in light of the fact that after his retirement from the U.S. Army he became the chief American adviser to Generalissimo Franco in Madrid. It was Sasakawa himself who revealed Chiang's role when he blurted out to an interviewer, "I was one of the 54 'war criminals' released by Chiang. . . . Chiang pardoned us all. People don't realize this point."

The deal made Sasakawa and Kodama the *kuromaku* ("the men behind the black curtain"), the fixers of Japan's biggest postwar political and commercial deals. In 1975, *The Guardian* said the two men could pull "enough strings to run a kind of shadow government in Japan." Privately the Japanese called Kodama "the Monster." He and Sasakawa became secretly active in sponsoring right-wing elements in the countries Japan had briefly conquered. Men in Bangkok, Jakarta, and Saigon who had collaborated with the Kempeitei were soon back at work for the KMT and the CIA.

After Japan's defeat in the Pacific war, Sasakawa's real interests revolved around rebuilding Tokyo's economic penetration of Southeast Asia and gaining new leverage for Japan in the Middle East. His boast that his time in prison had been a God-given opportunity was no idle statement, for he and his cellmates emerged with a grand strategy. Sugamo cellmate Kishi Nobusuke became Japan's prime minister, and Tokyo launched a campaign to rebuild its damaged ties with Jakarta and Manila, offering stepped-up war reparations accompanied by a strong commercial thrust. Sasakawa became president of a new Japan-Philippines Association and a Japan-Indonesia Association, followed by other friendship societies in neighboring countries.

Although Kodama was tight-lipped about his part in all this, Sasakawa was a vain man who occasionally revealed glimpses of his secret world. In his advancing years he suffered from chronic media lip-flap. He was Kodama's geisha, plucking the koto and stroking the shakuhachi for foreigners who had a taste for green-tea fascism. It was Sasakawa who volunteered that the special relationship between Ferdinand Marcos and the Japanese *kuromaku* grew out of a long-standing friendship. "I was very close to Marcos long before he became president," Sasakawa once admitted.

It is likely that they became acquainted during the Quirino presidency at the end of the 1940s when Marcos and other Quirino lieutenants were busy trying to discover where Yamashita's Gold was hidden, and Fukumitsu was interviewing Japanese government figures and military officers in their behalf. However they first met, by the late 1950s Marcos and Sasakawa were collaborating energetically. Officially, they were brought together by the CIA in the secret supply of arms and consumer goods during the CIA's anti-Sukarno rebellion. (Sasakawa told an interviewer, "I was taking charge of [supplying] materials to the anti-Sukarno camp.")

This was one of the first examples of the new CIA bringing in foreign proxies and cutouts to supply sterilized weapons for a secret war. Before the rebellion collapsed, the Agency trained forty-two thousand Indonesian dissidents and mercenaries at bases in the Philippines. The sheer numbers involved offer a clue to the scale of the operation, and to the number of people who were required to keep it all going at the quartermaster level. Air attacks by CIA mercenaries on shipping in Indonesian waters forced up insurance rates, and brought commercial navigation to a halt, enabling Kodama, Sasakawa, Marcos, and his friend Lino Bocalan, the Cavite warlord, to make millions smuggling goods to Indonesian islands cut off from normal supplies.

Although the attempt to topple Sukarno failed, Sasakawa was not discouraged. His methods proved much more effective than those of the CIA. He himself recounted how, during a state visit the Indonesian leader made to Tokyo, he made a present to Sukarno of a beautiful young Japanese girl named Dewi, who became one of Sukarno's wives. In return, Sasakawa was said to have become the agent for all trade between the two nations, which over the years involved billions of dollars.

Never one to be sentimental, Sasakawa also boasted that he played a decisive part in the September 30, 1965, coup d'état that marked the end of Sukarno's reign.

Many of MacArthur's friends in Manila were bound to him by a common commitment to big money and fascism. In the islands, priority was given to defending billionaire landowners from peasant farmers who earned less than a dollar a day, forfeited half their harvest, and could only make ends meet by borrowing from the landlord at 500 percent interest. (The situation was getting worse, not better. In 1969, when a typical tenant farmer in Tarlac Province still was lucky to make $200 the entire year, wealthy young Benigno Aquino, Jr., remarked that his wife Cory's big landowning family—the Cojuangcos—had a $500 million turnover.) Decade after decade, American officials studiously ignored the grievances of these rural poor, who along with the urban poor in Metro-Manila totaled 70 percent of the population.

Back in 1935 when MacArthur first became Quezon's field marshal, a peasant rebellion had been in progress in the countryside for many years. As the Spanish Civil War raged in Europe, MacArthur's sponsors, among them Franco's wealthy consul in Manila, Andres Soriano, persuaded him that Filipino farmers were led by Communist cadres plotting a Marxist regime. Eventually, this became a self-fulfilling prophecy, but it was not true in the early decades. Even Luis Taruc, the leader of the peasant rebellion, did not join the Communist party until four years after MacArthur became field marshal. As were many others, he was driven to it. Most Filipinos started out as grievance guerrillas, not as Marxists, and surprisingly few ever became ideological converts. But that mattered not at all.

During the Japanese occupation, this unequal conflict between landlords and farmers intensified. Big landowners supported the Japanese because the Japanese protected their property. Tenant farmers were brutally treated and their produce confiscated. To fight back, many joined Taruc's Hukbalahap, the People's Anti-Japanese Army, which soon numbered thirty thousand men. Unfortunately, the Huk leaders offended American guerrilla officers by refusing to put themselves under American command. The Americans retaliated by issuing a general order that all anti-Japanese guerrillas who were not members of USAFFE were *enemies of the American government.* Thereafter, USAFFE guerrillas did everything they could to discredit the Huks, reporting to MacArthur (inaccurately) that they were a "subversive . . . radical organization. . . . Its operations [of] carnage, revenge, banditry and highjacking . . . never [have been] equalled in any page of history of the Philippines." After fighting the Japanese so energetically, the Huks hoped to have American support to resolve their grievances, but were treated as enemies instead of allies. MacArthur arrested Luis Taruc. When the Huks turned over their wartime rosters to the U.S. Army as a gesture of good faith, the lists were used to identify, arrest, or kill Huk veterans, or were circulated among landlords and employers who turned down Huks for jobs and evicted them as undesirable tenants. The worst incident was the massacre of 109 Huk guerrillas at Malolos in Bulacan, the town where Ferdinand Marcos had been the guest of friends running the Constabulary. Huk Squadron 77 was walking home to Pampanga in early February 1945, passing through Malolos. American and Filipino soldiers surrounded the Huks, disarmed them, and took them before a USAFFE colonel named Adonias Maclang. He accused them of looting the town. Without a trial, Maclang forced the Huks to dig a mass grave, then had his soldiers shoot them all. Those only wounded were clubbed to death with their shovels. American counterintelligence officers were present the entire time. They later picked Maclang to be mayor of Malolos.

In 1946, the Huk army disbanded as its leaders shifted to political campaigning in an effort to win legislative representation in Congress by accepted channels. The democratic approach proved impossible, however. Landowners paid vigilante groups to beat up anyone campaigning for land reform. A U.S. official explained: "Only if U.S. security were [directly] threatened would we assist in realizing land reform in the Philippines. It would be difficult, but we could pull it off. If the Huks had been perceived as more of a threat, we would have done what we did in Japan, Korea, and Taiwan." In all three countries, the United States forced through draconian land reform measures. But in the Philippines, Washington chose not to follow the same policy. Thus the Huk threat really was not grave, and was purposely distorted for purely political ends. Long after granting independence to the Philippines, America would continue to use the same Huk bogeyman to justify political manipulations in Manila and its military presence in the islands. Looking back at it now, American posturing in those days had the demented quality in paintings by Hieronymous Bosch; like a man with a violin sticking out of his ass.

Many of these perverse developments and petty interferences were kept secret or were disguised by rhetoric or by propaganda. So it is only after the passage of many years that the real pattern becomes apparent. It would be wrong to suggest that there was a single grand design, rather that a number of influences were at work that converged and built upon each other. Consider only a few:

Sergio Osmeña was now president of the commonwealth. MacArthur disliked Osmeña and dismissed him as "incapable of meeting the situation." Long ago, MacArthur had chosen Roxas as the man to do his bidding. Roxas's great appeal lay in the elasticity of his convictions. He was MacArthur's *doppelgänger*. Families sent petitions to Roxas asking for the release from detention of Laurel and his colleagues. Roxas did nothing. MacArthur had ordained that Laurel and the others would remain confined in Japan's Sugamo Prison until Roxas had displaced Osmeña as president.

To prepare for independence on his terms, MacArthur wanted the prewar Congress recalled, but so many of its members were collaborators that a quorum was impossible. President Osmeña wanted to wait until the accused among them had been tried; otherwise, legislative immunity would make a mockery of the issue. Roxas countered that they could personally determine who was guilty or innocent. MacArthur agreed, Osmeña capitulated, and the old Congress reconvened in June 1945. Roxas was elected president of the Senate—a position of power second only to that of Osmeña. With MacArthur's help, Roxas was now in a position to undermine President Osmeña politically.

As the first election of the new republic approached in 1946, MacArthur arbitrarily withheld American reconstruction aid, preventing President Osmeña from taking credit, or from using it for campaign patronage. Roxas had to be elected president before MacArthur would release the funds.

With the general's blessing, Roxas started his own Liberal party to split Osmeña's Nacionalistas. He then made a deal with Elpidio Quirino to trade the vice presidency for the bloc vote of northern Luzon. It was a terrible mistake. This was the deal the boss of the Ilocano political machine had been waiting for. The historical consequences of Quirino's vice presidency far outweigh those of Roxas's presidency. Although an international publicity campaign made Roxas out to be the founding father of a new nation, in retrospect he emerges as little more than MacArthur's pawn, the author of the U.S. Military Bases Agreements and preferential treatment for American business. Quirino, on the other hand, was a fat sturgeon pregnant with intrigue, and before he was finished he would spawn a generation of conspirators. Roxas needed him, but it was a ruinous price to pay. Provincial leaders were again ready to deliver large blocs of votes in exchange for virtual warlord status. Floro Crisologo, a relative of Ferdinand Marcos, ran Ilocos Sur for Quirino with a gang of 125 full-time thugs and "reserves" of 300 who terrorized villages and assassinated political opponents. When one village voted for a rival candidate, Crisologo had his troopers burn it down with flamethrowers. He was elected to Congress, his wife became governor, and his son took over command of their private army. The brutality and corruption of Quirino's followers became so notorious that politicians who rode to power on his coattails (like Ferdinand Marcos) later found it prudent to identify their early success with Roxas.

Roxas and Quirino waged an effective election campaign against Osmeña by promising economic stability and prosperity through their connections with MacArthur. Their campaign was paid for by MacArthur's friends, including the Elizalde family, and the Sorianos.

Fatalistically, Osmeña refused to campaign and his chances steadily worsened. He seemed weary and old. Because of his prior commitment to Roosevelt's policy of prosecuting collaborators, he had picked a cabinet from those free of taint; this limited his choice of talent and offended old friends among the sugar barons who wanted the posts for their men. Deprived of sugar backing, Osmeña reluctantly formed an alliance with the Huk candidates and other reformers out on the fringe. This alienated middle-class Filipinos, and Osmeña was doomed.

Because Osmeña promised a new law giving tenants 60 percent of their harvest rather than the customary 50 percent, in central Luzon peasant farmers turned out heavily, electing six Huk-backed congressmen. Nationwide, three reform senators were elected, including the well-known non-Communist Jose Diokno.

Roxas himself won handily, but his men gained only thirteen of the twenty-three Senate seats—too narrow an edge to control the legislature. Without a quorum, and in violation of the constitution, they declared the six Huk congressional victories invalid, and refused to seat the three reform senators, including Diokno. Among the new congressmen expelled was Luis Taruc, leader of the Huks.

In all of this, there was an ulterior motive. All nine expelled legislators had campaigned on a platform opposing an important treaty pending between the United States and the Philippines. The Bell Trade Act would open Philippine markets to a duty-free flow of American products, and grant Americans equal rights with Filipinos to exploit the country's natural resources—but not the other way around. Further-more, Washington would only release postwar reconstruction money to the Philippines once the Bell Act was approved. "A more brazen at-tempt at blackmail could hardly be conceived," commented *The Nation*. Roxas won approval of the act by a single vote. If the nine expelled legislators had been present, the Bell Act would have been blocked. The islands became a dumping ground for duty-free American com-modities—a classic replay of sixteenth-century colonialism. As presi-dent, Roxas went on to negotiate other one-sided treaties with Washing-ton—the Mutual Defense Treaty and the Military Bases Agreements.

With Roxas securely in power, MacArthur decided that the time had come to put the collaboration issue to rest. The leading collaborators were let out of Sugamo and brought back from Japan for trial with Jose Laurel's case as the centerpiece. Under pressure from President Roxas, the courts evolved a peculiar theory that a public official was not re-sponsible for his public behavior if a disclaimer was expressed after the fact. The wartime elite claimed that they had been motivated only by patriotism and therefore were innocent—the courts upheld this de-fense. After years of being kept incommunicado by MacArthur, Laurel finally was released. As he was freed, he observed trenchantly that all Filipinos were collaborators. Thanks to his foresight, Laurel's political power was intact. In May 1947 he was nominated for the Senate, and by October he was being talked up for the presidency.

Now that everything was rigged in its favor, Washington opened its purse, giving Roxas and Quirino $539 million to pay for war damage to private property and to rebuild government facilities and services. Other grants, loans, and credits brought the total package to nearly $1 billion. Indirect assistance—including redemption of guerrilla currency and back pay for soldiers, plus military payments for services and con-struction—came to an additional $1 billion. Most of this money never got beyond Roxas and Quirino, and their friends. The $2 billion aid package was fought over and devoured by politicians, by rich MacAr-thur partisans, and by packs of bureaucrats. Instead of revitalizing the economy, much of it ($150 million by one estimate) went to rehabilitate a few privileged American-owned businesses and import-export com-panies. Six million dollars went to rehabilitate the fabulously rich Ben-guet goldmines, in which MacArthur held stock. (Its owners were reluc-tant to foot the bill themselves.) Beer baron Andres Soriano, MacArthur's wartime aide-de-camp, was a Spanish citizen, but quickly took Philippine citizenship as the war approached. Then, one day after Pearl Harbor, MacArthur made him a colonel in the U.S. Army and arranged to get him instant American citizenship. In 1946, when Soriano's San Miguel Brewery urgently needed bottle caps, MacArthur had the War Department fly 20 tons of caps across the Pacific. So things were.

Everybody was on the make. Millions of dollars worth of consumer goods flowed into Manila just for the maintenance of the U.S. Army. One quarter of these goods ended up on the black market. GIs working with civilians sidetracked trucks, powdered milk, pistols, stockings, typewriters, and cigarettes. Two months after Yamashita's surrender, over $1 million in U.S. government-owned goods were seized when police broke up a Manila ring. After that it became serious.

"It may well be," journalist Robert Shaplen observed, "that in no other city in the world was there as much graft and conniving after the war." The Surplus Property Commission, intended to dispose of excess U.S. military property, became the preserve of Roxas backers. Washington industrial lobbyists contrived to make it illegal to bring surplus war goods home. Thousands of jeeps, tanks, planes, and munitions went on the market in every former combat zone. President Roxas offered Washington 1 peso for 90,000 tons of surplus ammunition stored on Luzon. The State Department fumed, but turned the munitions over. Tons of U.S. Army scrap metal in the Philippines were sold to an American concern through various fronts for a mere $335,000. The deal was arranged by MacArthur's associate, former High Commissioner Paul McNutt, whom Filipinos called the "Hoosier Hitler."

While politicians and businessmen grew wealthy, Manila's balance-of-payments deficit with the United States jumped to over $1 billion. "The future of the islands is not bright," commented an American magazine. "The United States is responsible for the situation and should do what it can to rectify it."

From the turn of the century, America's involvement with its Pacific colony had been composed of halfway measures—grand designs without adequate follow-through, democratic institutions without checks and balances, permissiveness without restraint, financial aid without accountability, cunning manipulation masked by expressions of virtue—all engineered with the help of agreeable men lacking in principle. America sought out and encouraged a tiny group of leaders who were servile toward their masters, ruthless among their own kind, and contemptuous of all those beneath them. The colonial experiment was doomed by its own hand, a form of suicidal opportunism. After setting such an example for half a century—"fifty years in a brothel"—it is no wonder that corruption had eager understudies waiting in the wings. One of them now took over. MacArthur's conspiracy to put Roxas in power had been fulfilled only by an accommodation with Quirino. In poetic justice, this arrangement now flip-flopped with appalling consequences.

On April 15, 1948, President Roxas died of a heart attack at Clark Air Force Base after straining to deliver yet another speech pledging Philippine loyalty to America in the event of another war. Quirino succeeded to the presidency and the Philippines entered a dark period climaxed by the notorious elections of 1949, a neap tide which washed Ferdinand Marcos into Congress.

A few months after the death of Manuel Roxas, President Quirino went to the polls to win a full term and take proper advantage of Malacanang Palace. He was determined that whatever it took he would win by a landslide. His vice president was to be sugar baron Fernando Lopez, of Iloilo. Fernando and his brother Eugenio were the most powerful men in the Visayas; owned Manila utilities, newspapers, and broadcasting; and had hundreds of millions of dollars invested in the United States, including Filipino-American newspapers in San Francisco and Chicago. During the war, according to charges brought against him by his own employees, Fernando had worked closely with the Japanese, published a Japanese-sponsored newspaper, and operated a chain of illegal gambling casinos with Japanese protection that contributed to the undoing and impoverishment of his own sugar workers. Now he brought all the Lopez clout to bear in getting the Quirino slate elected.

Quirino did not need Lopez funds—he had the government purse to pick through. Public funds flowed like wine. From one social relief program, Quirino spent 4 million pesos buying votes.

Opposing Quirino was his old friend Jose Laurel, now back as leader of the Nacionalista party. Going instinctively for the groin, Quirino campaigned almost exclusively on the collaboration issue. Wartime newsreels of Laurel consorting with the Japanese were distributed by Lopez media. Forgotten were Lopez's own record as a collaborator, and Quirino's involvement with the black market, the Maharlika, and Laurel. Quirino claimed that if Laurel was elected, American aid would be cut off. Scurrilous though this might seem, there was truth behind it. In Tokyo, MacArthur was determined to prevent Laurel, a man he loathed, from regaining power. The general bluntly told roving ambassador Manuel Gallego that he wanted Quirino re-elected "or else" he would personally guarantee that all U.S. aid and loans would be canceled. Gallego was astounded. When word got back to the State Department, President Truman was asked to order MacArthur to apologize for interfering in the internal affairs of the Philippines. But Truman was not yet ready for his showdown.

MacArthur then sent another emissary. Generalissimo Chiang Kai-shek called on President Quirino in Baguio in July 1949. Quirino and his wife, Alicia Syquia, of the billionaire Syquia clan, entertained the generalissimo at the Syquia family mansion in Vigan, Ilocos Sur. At the end of their meetings, the two statesmen issued a joint declaration against communism. Chiang was urgently preparing the way for his escape from the mainland to Taiwan. Five months later, he fled to Taipei. By then Quirino had secured his presidency, aided by millions of pesos donated grudgingly by Chinese businessmen under pressure from the KMT-controlled Chinese chambers of commerce in Manila.

After Chiang's 1949 summit with Quirino, the Philippines became the only Asian nation that permitted the KMT to operate openly as a political party. As one Filipino Chinese businessman summed it up: "The Kuomintang is what you call a kingmaker here. They're the power behind the throne and while they don't always run things directly, they have a great deal to say about who will."

Quirino's 1949 election was the most corrupt in the history of the Philippines up to that point. Gangs of thugs assaulted rival candidates and intimidated voters. That much was normal, but Quirino also pardoned convicted murderers who went to work under the direction of his brother, Judge Tony. Scores of people were brutally, even hideously murdered. To have shock value during a Philippine election, a murder must have garish qualities, conspicuous evidence of sadistic torture beforehand. All these qualities were on display for the education of the voting public. Quirino was accused of bribery, extortion, and tampering with ballots: results were declared even before ballots were counted, and the total tally exceeded the population. Despite all this, his victory margin was narrow.

During this campaign, the Huks and other radicals had no choice but to endorse Laurel for president, a self-proclaimed Fascist, but the lesser of two evils. Their endorsement gave Quirino an excuse to use police and soldiers even against Laurel's right-wing backers, declaring that certain Fascists were subversive because they were allied to leftists.

As the absurd returns came in, Filipinos howled for revolution. All those excluded from power—right, center, or left—began plotting. Laurel had pledged that his Nacionalista party would stage an armed uprising if Quirino cheated him out of victory. In his home district of Batangas, Laurel supporters broke out weapons. Fighting raged there for days, but Laurel finally backed down under direct threat of intervention from the U.S. Embassy, which was preparing to call in the Seventh Fleet in the interests of democracy. However, he refused to concede the election, and referred to President Quirino thereafter as "the squatter in Malacanang."

This was the second time since Philippine independence that America had intervened to guarantee the election of its candidate. Roxas was one kind of man, Quirino another. He intended to punish those who had opposed him, particularly Colonel Napoleon Valeriano, a Filipino Constabulary officer and arch rightist who had urged Laurel to fight. Valeriano found himself facing court-martial on charges of sedition and treason. It was an unusual case.

Valeriano was a high school classmate of Ferdinand Marcos and a graduate of the Philippine Military Academy. After fighting in Bataan, he escaped from concentration camp, was picked up by an American sub, and reached Australia where he joined MacArthur's command. MacArthur sent him to America with secret agent Jesus Villamor, where they toured aboard a "Freedom Train" selling War Bonds.

Valeriano's father, Benito, a Constabulary colonel, was murdered meanwhile by guerrillas on the island of Negros who decided he was helping the Japanese. Valeriano believed that the assassins were Communists led by a member of the Manila Politburo. Encouraged by Willoughby and MacArthur's virulent anti-communism, he conceived a lifelong hatred of all leftists, into which he lumped everyone who was not a member of the armed forces or an executive in big business.

Valeriano's whole life was then dedicated to killing radicals of any type. His Constabulary units, called Nenita, or "skull squadrons," were death squads famous for their efficiency. His men wore skull-and-crossbones patches and carried flags with the same emblem, a Filipino version of Hitler's SS. For Valeriano, every night was *Kristalnacht*. In order to avoid public accountability, his Nenita were administered by the intelligence branch of the Constabulary. They terrorized farmers in central Luzon and were dispatched on bloody missions to other islands until the mere mention of the name "Nenita" terrified villagers. There was good reason for dread: the Nenita bludgeoned its victims to death, or shot them repeatedly in the legs before delivering a coup de grâce, then hacked off their heads to put on display. One Nenita tactic was to cordon off an area where Huks were rumored to be operating; everyone caught inside was killed. Inevitably many victims were innocent. When the Nenita operated in Pampanga, there were corpses floating in the river nearly every day. By 1949, Valeriano was a senior strategist in the campaign against Huks and peasants.

He found himself in strange company when the Nacionalistas struck their alliance with the Huks during the 1949 elections. Valeriano suspended his anti-peasant activities for the duration and concentrated on helping the Nacionalistas win on the island of Negros. There, Governor Rafael Lacson's private army of "special policemen" was terrorizing voters to guarantee a landslide for the Lopez-Quirino slate, which meant defeat for the Nacionalistas. To neutralize Lacson's thugs, Valeriano dispatched a Nenita squad under Captain Diosdado Junsay, a handpicked detachment of twenty Huk killers. Their cover story was that they were investigating the circumstances surrounding the death of Valeriano's father during the war.

On October 21, 1949, shortly after midnight, Captain Junsay's squad arrived for a meeting at the sugar plantation of ex-Senator Pedro Hernaez, an opponent of President Quirino and Governor Lacson. Expecting no trouble, the Nenita were only lightly armed, but Governor Lacson had been tipped off. His police caught the Nenita offguard. Junsay had both kneecaps and ankles broken, and two ribs kicked in. His men were so battered that they were only partly conscious when they signed confessions to plotting a coup. To support the charge, Lacson's police "discovered" a big stash of weapons in a nearby canefield.

As their commanding officer, Valeriano was charged with thirteen counts of sedition. Acting on instruction from Nacionalista party chief Jose Laurel, he asked Ferdinand Marcos to defend him. The old fox was calling in the debt from the Nalundasan case.

To backtrack a bit, Ferdinand had spent the last few months of his hitch with the U.S. Army as a deputy to the judge advocate general in northern Luzon, involved with many others in the tedious job of re-establishing civil government in those nine provinces. Among other things, this entailed choosing people to fill countless minor civil service jobs, which gave him a chance to do favors for friends and relatives, a golden opportunity to build a constituency.

Through his patron, then Vice President Quirino, Ferdinand wangled a position on a team sent to Washington by the Philippine Veterans Commission to negotiate for $160 million in military back pay and benefits. The trip accomplished little, but it did produce a memorable anecdote. Hartzell Spence recounted that Ferdinand bumped into General Omar Bradley on a busy Washington street. When Bradley "saw Ferdinand's six rows of ribbons headed by twenty-two valor medals including the Distinguished Service Cross, the four-star general saluted Marcos." It was only in 1963—sixteen years later—that Ferdinand arranged to be given twenty different Philippine medals, so the comic-book encounter with General Bradley is a concoction from a later period. Photos of Ferdinand in uniform during the trip to Washington in May 1947 show him wearing no medals at all.

Back in Manila, veterans became an industry in themselves. The U.S. Congress passed bills providing back pay and benefits, but all applicants had to produce documentary evidence or affidavits to back up claims of service, a situation ripe for exploitation. Ferdinand made money contriving affidavits to support hundreds of claims, some legitimate, many not.

The success he had with the claims of others emboldened him to try a big one for himself. It was at this point that he brought all Mariano's phantom cattle back to life. He presented to Washington a claim that the 101st Division, USAFFE, had commandeered 2,366 head of Nellore brahmin cattle from the imaginary Marcos hacienda in Mindanao. Ferdinand wanted $594,900 in damages. After a thorough review of the evidence, Washington concluded that the cattle had never existed. Representing the United States in the matter was Attorney Warren Burger, future justice of the Supreme Court, which led to the Filipino gag: "The beef was imaginary, but the Burger was real." The U.S. government also was not amused by Ferdinand's efforts to prove that he had headed a guerrilla force bigger even than Colonel Volckmann's. His Maharlika roster (now inflated to over nine thousand men) was another attempt to gain recognition and benefits for a ghost army. "The Ang Mga Maharlika Unit under the alleged command of Ferdinand Marcos is fraudulent," investigators for the U.S. Army concluded. "The insertion of his name on a roster other than [the 14th Infantry under Major Manriquez] . . . was a malicious criminal act."

Criminal acts are not necessarily an impediment to a political career anywhere in the world, so Ferdinand decided to apply his talents where they would be more appreciated. In Ilocos Norte, he began his campaign for Congress with image building. One day in December 1948, writer Teofilo Agcaoili phoned Benjamin Gray, the editor of a Tagalog weekly magazine called *Bannawag,* and invited Gray to lunch to meet Ferdinand Marcos. Table talk centered on Ferdinand's extraordinary World War II exploits. Two months later, Gray ran four articles based on the history of the Maharlika. In Washington, the U.S. Army had just concluded that the Maharlika was a fraud.

Ferdinand established residence in Batac at his aunt's house, which he purchased and enlarged. This put him in Mariano's old congressional district, dominated by Judge Chua. The judge was now even more popular and powerful than before the war, having spent part of his personal fortune generously helping people in his community get back on their feet. Opening a law office in Laoag, Ferdinand began to campaign intensively in the barrios. Veterans' benefits and claims were a major issue in 1949 because the deadline for claims imposed by the U.S. government had already passed. Attempting to force Washington to reopen the issue, President Quirino's brother, Judge Tony, promised publicly to get benefits for two million Filipinos who (he said) had not been properly recognized. He might as well have promised free lunches. Defense Minister Mercario Peralta, the former guerrilla leader, called the figure of two million absurd. Ferdinand also campaigned on the platform of benefits. "Look," he said, "I have a lot of money because I got all my war benefits. If you want to receive your own benefits, vote for me." He won by a landslide, with 70 percent of the vote.

Once he was in the legislature, there was so much public outrage over Quirino that it became important for Ferdinand to distance himself from his own peers. When Jose Laurel asked him to defend Napoleon Valeriano it was the perfect marriage of mischief and theater. Nothing would help Valeriano so much in the press as to be defended against Quirino's charges by a member of Quirino's own Liberal party.

By claiming publicly to defend Valeriano out of concern for human rights and ethical principle, Ferdinand could distance himself from Quirino without defying him directly. The Liberals were incensed by Ferdinand's ploy, but there was not much they could do about it.

In Congress, Ferdinand delivered a privileged speech that the court-martial of Valeriano was unconstitutional. During the trial, he brought members of the Nenita to the stand, still showing the effects of their beating six months earlier. Some wept openly in court. All swore that their confessions had been forced by the sadistic punishment.

Blithely, Quirino's prosecutor claimed that Governor Lacson was merely taking steps to ensure an honest election. However, when the press took up Valeriano's cause, the government dropped its case, and the defendants were freed. Ferdinand, the freshman congressman, became the celebrity of the moment.

While this mummery was going on before the public eye, Ferdinand was busy engineering some of the biggest money-making ventures of the postwar period, with the help of an American GI named Harry Stonehill and a KMT legman named Peter Lim.

Ferdinand had been appointed by Quirino to a lucrative post on the Rehabilitation Finance Corporation (RFC), headed by Eduardo Romualdez, which was supposed to extend credit facilities to projects that would diversify the Philippine economy, revive existing industries, and repair public facilities damaged by the war. In practice these loans were granted only to parties well connected to RFC executives. When the United States sent an economic mission to survey undeveloped Philippine resources, Ferdinand and his friends made a valuable discovery. The Ilocano provinces were the only part of the archipelago that had no major cash crop, but Virginia cigarette tobacco was ideal for the area. Ferdinand decided to pursue the idea with the help of Stonehill and Lim.

The Ilocos traditionally produced a rich cigar tobacco that had been elbowed out of American markets by superior Cuban leaf. Ferdinand pushed through legislation to turn Ilocano tobacco-growing areas over to Virginia leaf, to produce Philippine cigarettes able to compete with imported American brands. As an Ilocano, Quirino loved the idea, and agreed that the government would subsidize the purchase of the tobacco grown to the tune of 70 million pesos a year, then about $35 million. Enter Harry Stonehill. He had arrived in Manila as a young lieutenant in 1945, working in the U.S. Army real estate section, where he arranged the resale of fifty surplus army trucks for his own benefit. Following his discharge he returned to Chicago, dumped his American wife and child, and came back to Manila alone. He and Ferdinand became silent partners. Stonehill's job was to introduce bright-leaf tobacco cultivation to the Ilocos. A tobacco boom began. Farmers who once earned $100 for a hectare of rice now made four times that on bright-leaf subsidized by the government.

In 1950, Stonehill took on as another partner Peter Lim, a leading member of the KMT and the Chinese chambers of commerce. Within a short time, Stonehill and Lim controlled half the bright-leaf business in the Philippines. Stonehill bought cheap, inferior tobacco and sold it to the government at the subsidized bright-leaf price. The government tobacco monopoly soon found itself burdened with huge quantities of high-priced trash, and half the cigarette manufacturers in the Philippines closed down. Stonehill's profits were smuggled out through Chinese black-money channels to accounts in Switzerland.

With the money he made, Stonehill diversified into glass; cotton; oil; insurance; newspaper publishing; cement; housing; real estate; land reclamation, resulting in a multi-million-dollar conglomerate with property in eight countries; and a personal fortune of $50 million.

Ferdinand and his associates—Stonehill, Lim, and others—were not content simply to prosper from the bright-leaf subsidies. They also reorganized cigarette smuggling on a monumental scale. The government was already losing 100 million pesos a year because of the smuggling of duty-free American cigarettes from Taiwan and Hong Kong. The cost of producing cigarettes in the Philippines was much lower, but the evasion of taxes made smuggled American cigarettes competitive. Senator Benigno Aquino, Jr., charged that in order to distribute smuggled cigarettes openly, Ferdinand had fake cigarette-package revenue stamps printed.

In all these undertakings, Ferdinand showed a double standard. He made a great deal of money through entrepreneurs such as Peter Lim. But in his dealings with Chinese who were not connected with the Chuas or with the Chiang regime, he demonstrated a predatory aggressiveness, using his congressional position to extort commissions and percentages in return for import licenses, foreign exchange credits, and residency permits.

All Filipino politicians realized the vulnerability of the Chinese.

Campaign expenses were extorted from Chinese businessmen, who were expected to pay a regular retainer to a politician's law firm as cumshaw or risk losing their import licenses or their residency permits. A routine technique was to introduce blackmail bills that penalized particular industries or firms. A congressman introducing anti-Chinese legislation approached the Chinese business community and hinted that he would drop the bill if a certian amount were paid.

After World War II, the first legislation to be considered by the infant republic was designed to restrict Chinese ownership of businesses. One way to get around this was to become a Filipino citizen. The nominal cost of citizenship was 250 pesos, but legal fees and bribes brought the total to 10,000 pesos. With the Communist victory in China, many refugees were seeking entry to the Philippines and were ready for fleecing. An immigration racket came into existence, controlled by Ferdinand, in which government officials were alloted a "quota" of fifty Chinese each who would pay up to 10,000 pesos under the table for entry permits. Both retail licenses and import permits were authorized by the Committee of Commerce and Industry, which in turn was dominated by Ferdinand. His longtime adviser, Jaime Ferrer, told us in an interview that "when Marcos was a young congressman, he picked commerce and industry as his area. He had import controls at the time. And he became a fixer. A friend of mine had to pay Ferdinand specific sums of money [for his permits]." The minimum fee he demanded for an import license was 10,000 pesos. He had full-time staffs at his office and at his home to process, follow up, and receive donations from grateful businessmen.

Chinese merchants also needed permits to get foreign exchange, so they could pay dollars for their imports. Ferdinand traded foreign exchange credits for political contributions. Complained banker Martin Tinio, "We had to pay 10 percent in kickbacks—apart from interest. Credit is chokingly tight and politicians control the funds, so we all have to pay and pay." Washington Sycip, head of Manila's largest accounting firm, recalled in an interview how Ferdinand "was often seen roaming through the Central Bank of the Philippines after completing his deals. Ironically it was during this time that [he] was cited for his fiery oratory and economic expertise. His Central Bank forays, however, gave him more than the coveted access to foreign exchange. He also used his visits to eye the young clerks processing the cumbersome paperwork.

One of those clerks was a young woman from the island of Leyte, Imelda Romualdez."

As Ferdinand began to make serious money, he had to salt it away, invest it abroad, and hide his ownership. Jose Campos, a Chinese businessman, began working for him in 1949, putting together forty companies. Campos described how: "Following his directive, I instructed my lawyers and requested the assistance of my other business associates and officers . . . to organize, establish and manage these business ventures for and on behalf of [Marcos.]" In each case, a deed of trust was executed with "an unnamed beneficiary" listed and the deed was then delivered to Ferdinand, who could fill in any name he wished when it suited him. In effect, Campos wrote him blank checks. The dummy corporations included two Panama companies, two in Hong Kong, and one that controlled Texas real estate.

Self-interest in Filipino politics was openly celebrated. Clan leaders like the Quirinos of Ilocos Sur, Lopezes of Iloilo, and Laurels of Batangas ran machines that aspiring politicians were frantic to join. Election codes forbade a candidate from spending more than a year's salary on his campaign. He was prohibited from buying votes, giving gifts, or providing free food and drink. This was all ignored. A congressman earning 7,500 pesos a year would spend 700,000 to get re-elected. Once in the national assembly, an energetic congressman could get half a million pesos in public funds for civic improvements in his bailiwick, to guarantee his popularity. Every budget was larded with pork-barrel projects that never went through legislative hearings but mysteriously appeared in the printed budget by a technique called "smuggling." One-time Senate President Jose Avelino who made $500,000 during his first congressional term summed up the golden rule this way: "We are not angels! What are we in power for? When Jesus Christ died on the Cross, He made the distinction between a good crook and the bad crooks. We can prepare to be good crooks."

By the end of his first term in Congress, Ferdinand was a millionaire. He bought a Cadillac convertible to celebrate. But he was soon confiding to friends that not all the money came from fleecing Chinese. He hinted that he was onto Yamashita's Gold.

Immediately after the war, a number of Japanese syndicates mounted salvage operations in the Philippines, claiming that they were seeking to recover steel from sunken ships, but concentrating only on particular wrecks. Other small groups of Japanese returned to Luzon to carry out discreet excavations at remote locations. They had come for Yamashita's Gold. Ferdinand said he became involved in the early 1950s, when he was a congressman still maintaining law offices in Ilocos Norte and Baguio, for the contact it gave him with constituents. One day, two Filipino laborers came in to ask for his help in a labor dispute with two Japanese. The laborers said they had been hired by two Imperial Army veterans to dig a deep pit. But once the pit was dug, exposing a stash of gold bars, the Japanese became so inflamed with greed that they refused to pay for the digging. According to Ferdinand, he looked into the matter and discovered that the laborers had told the truth. He quickly paid them off and struck his own deal with the Japanese. What kind of deal was never explained, but he implied that he ended up with most of the gold bars, which started him on a thirty-year quest for the remainder.

The next arrival was Fukumitsu Minoru, an American-born Japanese working as a war crimes investigator. The Nisei had little money because they were crippled financially when they were interned in America during the war. But few Americans or Filipinos were fluent in Japanese, which put Fukumitsu in an unusual position. He arrived in Manila for the first time in 1953 to negotiate the release of two hundred Japanese prisoners of war facing death sentences or life imprisonment, some of them suspected of having buried part of Yamashita's Gold. He said he was able to persuade President Quirino to free all these men in return for a pledge that Fukumitsu himself would look into the legend and get to the bottom of it.

Quirino was a man of unusual cunning, who numbered among his lieutenants many avaricious characters eager to learn about the treasure and where to find it. To assist Fukumitsu and keep an eye on him, Quirino assigned none other than Venancio Duque, the Ilocano intelligence officer who was involved with Ferdinand at the time of his arrest by Captain Hunt during the war, and who won Ferdinand a reprieve from his death sentence. (They were so close that Duque later became Ferdinand's appointments secretary in Malacanang Palace.)

From March to November 1953, with Venancio Duque always hovering nearby, Fukumitsu said he interviewed more than three hundred witnesses, including members of Yamashita's staff still living in Tokyo. With the cooperation of the Japanese government, he claimed he was given access to secret documents. His search took him also to the National Archives in Washington. He came up with a map and, in November 1953, began digging.

Fukumitsu said he made excavations at various points along Yamashita's route of withdrawal from Baguio to Kiangan, found nothing, packed up, and went home.

Critics said that if he had found portions of the treasure, he and his sponsors—Quirino, Duque, Marcos, and others in Manila, and nobody knew who in Tokyo—would hardly have admitted it. They charged that he deliberately looked in the wrong places, because the idea that the Japanese had buried the loot only during their final retreat to Kiangan was absurd. At that point they were in a hurry, and it was unlikely that there was much treasure left to worry about. It was well known that Yamashita had few trucks and was unable to take even enough food and equipment with him, let alone gold bullion. Most of the loot, they said, certainly was buried before Yamashita was even assigned to the Philippines.

Whatever the truth, Fukumitsu made a lot of powerful friends in Manila and Tokyo, and was able to resign his job as a war crimes investigator and set himself up as a businessman in Tokyo, commuting regularly to the Philippines, where he became a prosperous fixture. (He made six hundred trips to the Philippines between 1951 and 1988 but was unable to explain why.) In Manila, meanwhile, Ferdinand Marcos began preparing excavations of his own, far away from the Kiangan escape route.

Six

COWBOYS IN THE PALACE

IT WAS A BIT LATE in the day when President Truman received the following top-secret report from his National Security Council:

> Failure of the Philippines to maintain independence would discredit the U.S. in the eyes of the world and seriously decrease U.S. influence, particularly in Asia. . . . Although on the basis of military factors alone the Huks lack the capability to acquire control . . . their continued existence, growth, and activities reflect the ineffectiveness of the Philippine armed forces and the generally unsatisfactory social, economic, and political situation in the Philippines. . . . Denial of the Philippines to communist control depends not only upon military measures but even more upon prompt vigorous political and economic action. . . . Inequalities in the Philippines, always large, have become greater during the past few years while the standard of living of the mass of people has not reached the pre-war level. The profits of businessmen and the incomes of large land owners have risen considerably. The deterioration of the economic system has caused a widespread feeling of disillusionment. . . . The communist-led Huk movement has taken advantage of the deteriorating economic situation and exploited the antagonistic attitudes of the people toward the government in order to incite lawlessness and disorder. . . . The extent and manner in which the necessary influence is brought to bear on the Philippine Government to accomplish essential reforms presents to the U.S. Government a most difficult and delicate problem. Extreme care must therefore be exercised in the methods used to persuade the Philippine Government to take the necessary action, to do nothing would result in disaster.

This refreshingly candid report acknowledged that half a century of American colonial rule had resulted in dismal failure. Living conditions were much worse for the majority of Filipinos, while the handful of rich had become very much richer, encouraged by MacArthur's postwar favoritism. The economy was being abused and exploited by those MacArthur had put in power, and most Filipinos had lost any hope of reform. Misery, desperation, and antagonism were creating a dangerous situation, which was being exploited by the Communist leadership of the Huks. The Huks were *not* a serious danger, the report noted emphatically, because they were in no position to seize power. But the Philippine Army was incompetent, the government was corrupt, and the country could simply fall apart. If something was not done soon, Washington would be embarrassed.

This warning was sounded in 1950, but it could just as well have been the 1980s. All Washington's efforts during the intervening decades were expensive failures. Disinformation campaigns portrayed the crisis as a bold struggle against communism, which it never was. No matter how many crash efforts were mounted, they failed for the same reason. Under U.S. colonial rule, expediency always overruled principle—a lesson not lost on Filipinos, who demonstrated an uncanny knack for caricature.

The cure recommended by the NSC report was to introduce "essential reforms." Instead, expediency triumphed again. To rescue a thoroughly corrupt regime of its own invention, and to protect privileged U.S. investment, America returned to Manila clandestinely. The CIA and the Pentagon stepped into the breach and once again made a fool of Tom Paine.

World War II had been America's first heady experience in large-scale covert operations. When the war ended, Truman disbanded the OSS on the grounds that paramilitary operations, psychological warfare, and political manipulation were not acceptable in peacetime, in a nation nourished on the premise that principle was important. However, Truman accepted the need for a permanent organization to coordinate intelligence gathering. In 1947, he created the Central Intelligence Agency. Despite his efforts to prohibit the CIA from undertaking covert operations, there was already a covert action cell within the State Department, jealously guarded by the old OSS fraternity. A rush of anti-Communist anxiety overcame Truman's restraint. This existing covert action cell was grafted on as a clandestine part of the new CIA, with a secret charter based on National Security Council directives and presidential executive orders.

It was all done surreptitiously because everyone involved recognized that conducting foreign affairs without the awareness of Congress and the American people was at odds with the intent of the Constitution. This lack of accountability set the covert professionals apart, as a priesthood, and gave them a sense of something bordering on supernatural power. There were those who were covert, and then there was everybody else. As their numbers multiplied, simply being in the covert club encouraged an explosive growth of amorality.

"In a government of laws," Justice Louis Brandeis observed, "the existence of the government will be imperiled if it fails to observe the law scrupulously. . . . If government becomes a lawbreaker it breeds contempt for law: it invites every man to become a law unto himself."

It is the nature of covert action to be beyond the law, so it requires extraordinary restraint. Too often, the end justifies any means. Since the private lives of agents also must remain covert, it takes abnormal restraint for them to avoid enriching themselves. During the period from 1950 to 1988, the Philippines provided classic examples of both—one in the form of a CIA officer who became carried away by his own omnipotence, the other in the form of a secret team of senior American officers who became entangled with Ferdinand Marcos and Yamashita's Gold.

America's new proconsul in the Philippines was Edward G. Lansdale, the Walt Disney of covert action. Lansdale was a peculiarly American mixture of naivete and aggressiveness; some thought him a dangerous adolescent (Graham Greene characterized him as such in his Saigon novel, *The Quiet American*). Lansdale was the first in a long line of postwar secret agents totally dedicated to apple pie laced with blowfish toxin. He was a pleasant, warm, good-natured man, with a sincerity that disarmed all but his most determined critics. A former advertising executive, Lansdale had the spontaneous imagination of a copy writer, an instinctive grasp of modern psychology, behavior modification, and psychological warfare. Many of his ideas now seem harebrained, but on unsophisticated people they sometimes had surprising effect. The age of media mystification made him a guru to those looking for a quick fix overseas. His techniques were so admired in the CIA and the Pentagon that they became routine procedure a decade later in the Vietnam War. He tried them out first in the Philippines. There was a straight line leading from Lansdale's persecution of the Huks in the 1950s to William Colby's Operation Phoenix in Vietnam, which resulted in assassinating perhaps as many as forty thousand civilians.

Lansdale had found a niche in psychological warfare with the OSS during World War II as an intelligence officer on MacArthur's staff, working for General Willoughby. By the war's end he was their chief of intelligence in the Philippines. During this period Willoughby was seeing Bolsheviks under every bed, and the men working for him did their best to prove that it was not hallucination. Lansdale left the islands in 1948, ostensibly to be an instructor at the Air Force Strategic Intelligence School in Denver, but he was actually in Washington being considered for a role in the CIA. He was put to work setting up a Philippines desk for the new agency.

Lansdale understood very clearly the temper of his times and the anxieties of his new clients, the generals and bureaucrats of the McCarthy era. While President Truman was being told that the Huks posed no real military threat to the Philippines, Lansdale was doing everything he could to make the Huks look like a large and extremely dangerous guerrilla army personally guided by secret agents of Stalin and Mao.

Much of Lansdale's strategy was built around the promotion of a bearlike Filipino congressman named Ramon Magsaysay, destined to be America's new hero in Manila. At the time, Magsaysay was in Washington "conferring with the U.S. Congress about Filipino veterans' benefits." But he found time to join CIA planning sessions in which Lansdale argued that the Philippines was about to go Communist like Yugoslavia, Albania, and the rest of Eastern Europe.

"Mindful of the part played by Americans in the recent Greek struggle against Communist guerrillas," Lansdale wrote years later in the oily language of Foggy Bottom, "I talked to United States leaders about giving similar help to the Philippines. . . . It was suggested that I draw up a modest plan for simple measures that could be added to the United States' military and economic assistance already being given. . . . I went to work on a plan for . . . less conventional actions against the political-military tactics of the Huks." As the first step in the CIA program, President Quirino was pressed by the U.S. Embassy to name a new defense minister, Lansdale's friend Magsaysay.

Ramon Magsaysay was an uncomplicated man of great energy—high-strung, restless, and brusque. For the islands he was a big man, at five feet eleven inches, and hefty. He did not gamble, drink, or smoke. Magsaysay liked to claim that he was a man of the people, with a humble background; he said his father was a poor carpenter in Zambales Province, 85 miles northwest of Manila, his mother an Ilocano woman who had to struggle to make ends meet. The truth was that his family owned a general store and several farms, one of over 1,000 acres, and employed tenant farmers to work their fields. In 1927 he entered the University of the Philippines, but dropped out to go to work for a bus company. As a guerrilla during the war, Magsaysay became very popular with his American advisers, and at war's end was rewarded with an appointment as military governor of his native province. This encouraged him to run for Congress and, with a bit of nudging from Lansdale, he was soon listening to the CIA's long-range plans for his career.

Once he was in position as defense minister, Magsaysay and Lansdale set about purging top echelons of the Filipino military establishment. With the discreet backing of the U.S. ambassador and the chief of JUSMAG (the Joint U.S. Military Assistance Advisory Group), Magsaysay pressed President Quirino to get rid of the politicking army chief of staff, General Mariano Castaneda, and the corrupt boss of the Constabulary, Brigadier General Alberto Ramos, who were both cronies of the president.

"Each night we sat up late discussing the current situation," Lansdale recalled. "Magsaysay would air his views. Afterwards, I would sort them out aloud for him while underscoring the principles or strategy or tactics involved. It helped him select or discard courses of action."

Magsaysay was not interested in the world at large, nor was he especially concerned about due process of law. Thanks to Lansdale, he had a tight focus on what needed to be done each day. At his urging, reinforced by the U.S. Embassy, President Quirino suspended the writ of habeas corpus to enable the arrest and imprisonment of anyone remotely suspected of communism, Hukism—or simply being stubborn, and therefore subversive. Suspending the writ was essential for the CIA program to succeed. Providing evidence was time-consuming or impossible, so Magsaysay had to be free to arrest, imprison, and interrogate suspects without evidence. The writ was restored in 1953, but only as a legal pretense that could be dropped again momentarily. Once dishonored, it is a difficult legal tradition to re-establish.

Lansdale then set up a psychological warfare unit euphemistically christened the Civil Affairs Office. His enemies were the poor, so for inspiration Lansdale studied peasant superstitions. One result was the "eye of god."

"The idea," he wrote, "was to get exact information about the enemy and then broadcast it through loudspeakers in combat situations, making individual enemy soldiers feel that they couldn't hide from an all-seeing eye." In areas where villagers were thought to be helping the Huks, a psy-war team crept in at night and painted an Egyptian-style evil eye on a wall facing the house of each suspect. The mysterious appearance of the evil eyes (Lansdale claimed) had a sobering effect. Another operation played upon peasant dread of the *asuang* or vampire. In an area thought to be harboring a team of Huk guerrillas, Lansdale's ambushers snatched a peasant one night, punctured his neck with two holes, vampire-fashion, hung the body by the ankles to drain it of blood, then put the corpse back on the trail. When the peasants found the toothmarked bloodless corpse, the entire Huk unit moved away. The novelty of these games amused Lansdale, who slyly passed them on as combat anecdotes to his superiors in Washington, disguised in his unctuous prose, enchanting his CIA superiors. This was a period when the CIA was busy engineering cobra-venom dart guns and building cigarette lighters with cyanide jets. The very real grievances of Filipino farmers were forgotten. Lansdale's experiments were given top priority.

The anti-Huk campaign was fought mostly on that old agrarian reform battleground, the rice bowl outside Manila. At Lansdale's urging, Magsaysay politicized his job by roaming the provinces in car or jeep, often with Lansdale beside him, visiting troops and talking with farmers and villagers, a burly man always in an aloha shirt. Poor people liked him because he made personal contact and because he corrected some of the worst abuses of the army and Constabulary: rapes, theft, and bullying. These minor reforms were promised everywhere, but implemented selectively. They were window-dressing, as part of Lansdale's scheme to build Magsaysay up for the presidency.

Success was measured by the attention given Magsaysay by American journalists. Lansdale knew that few correspondents were in a position to check the facts, or had the patience to do so in the stultifying heat. One story given wide publicity then (and repeated many years later in praise of Magsaysay) was that he had arranged for thousands of safe-conduct passes to be dropped to the Huks by plane over the islands.

These passes supposedly meant any Huk could come in and surrender without fear of being killed. This made persuasive copy for feature writers in New York. The catch was that passes were dropped only in areas where the Huks were not operating. Meanwhile, the real scoops of Magsaysay's war against the Huks were kept hidden from the press. Magsaysay offered "cash incentives" or bounties for Huk bodies—preferably identifiable Huks, but any peasant would do. The "incentive" of 5,000 pesos represented ten years' wages for a Filipino farm worker. A bounty of 100,000 pesos was offered for the body of a Huk leader, the money apparently coming partly from the CIA and partly from a 1 million peso "Peace Fund" raised from big landowners by Vice President Fernando Lopez.

Although it became customary in the American press to refer to Magsaysay with the veneration reserved for heroes, and to take Lansdale seriously as a cold warrior, some of their antics were comic. To create the impression that his man was personally brave, Lansdale had soldiers dress up as Huks, so that Magsaysay could safely lead government troops to victory. CIA technicians forged Huk documents for Magsaysay to capture, while false reports were planted in the press that repression of peasant farmers in the Philippines was coming to an end. These tricks, orchestrated as part of a slick promotional campaign, had an impact on individual members of the Huk rebellion. Many Huks stopped fighting because they wanted to believe what they heard. Few of them cared anything one way or the other about Marxism, so they were not ideologically committed enough to stay in the movement as things actually grew worse militarily.

To increase military pressure, Lansdale and Magsaysay announced that they were making the Constabulary part of the armed forces. It would be more accurate to put it the other way around: they began turning the army into a police force, something that the CIA would eventually make part of its Third World doctrine. Despite the talk of Stalin and Mao, the Philippines were not threatened by foreign enemies, only by internal misery. The main job of the armed forces was not national defense but population control. Combining the Constabulary with the army brought total strength up to fifty thousand men, and permitted the deployment of troops in larger units under a single command. The old Nenita death squads became death battalions, consisting of three infantry companies, 110 men each, a heavy weapons company, a reconnaissance company with armored cars, a headquarters and service company, and a battery of artillery. When its training by JUSMAG was complete, each Nenita battalion was made responsible for part of a province, creating much larger free fire zones where they were licensed to kill anything that moved.

Colonel Valeriano, the inventor of the Nenita, became Lansdale's chief peasant killer, now assisted by tactical fighter support and napalm. Local oligarchs participated enthusiastically in his campaigns, as if they were fox-hunting to hounds, and posed for commemorative photographs beside dead peasants. On one killing spree, Valeriano's men murdered eight farmers who were attending a funeral and displayed their corpses beside a highway with crudely painted signs reading "HUK." By summer 1951, Lansdale noted with satisfaction that the Huks were showing the strain of being under constant attack. So, for that matter, were *all* the impoverished farmers in the rice bowl around Manila. It was open season on peasants.

Other CIA operatives were busy arranging the 1951 Philippine congressional elections. Internationally, these elections had to be seen as exceptionally honest, in order to inspire the right press coverage, to undercut peasant grievances further. A secret State Department memo to Truman summed it up: "Our Embassy at Manila is seeking to convey indirectly the intense interest of the U.S. in fair and honest elections. A repetition of the intimidation and fraud of 1949 would provide great impetus to the Huk movement and would add even more to the Filipinos' already cynical attitude about the type of democracy they now have."

Onto the scene came Lansdale's alter ego, Gabe Kaplan, New York lawyer, politician, and public relations man, who understood the many levers of a political campaign and how to pull them. Kaplan's first operational cover was the Asia Foundation, later the Committee for Free Asia, and then the Catherwood Foundation of Bryn Mawr, Pennsylvania. He had a knack for dealing with civic groups, chambers of commerce, Rotary Clubs, and veterans' organizations. With a team of eager and well-paid young Filipino CIA employees, Kaplan persuaded these middle-class organizations to support a nationwide effort to "educate" the public about the importance of free and honest elections. Kaplan's umbrella was the National Movement for Free Elections (NAMFREL), which Lansdale and the CIA set up with the help of some Filipino friends—Terry Adevoso, Jaime Ferrer, and Frisco Johnny San

Juan, all former guerrillas and national commanders of the politically powerful Veterans Legion.

President Quirino was conveniently out of the country for medical reasons while these CIA maneuvers were set into motion on the political front. The U.S. Embassy had generously offered to arrange for Quirino to have an operation at Johns Hopkins Hospital in Baltimore, after which he was encouraged to take a long vacation in Spain. By the time he got back to Manila, the stage was set.

The action phase started with a formal request by the Commission on Elections (COMELEC) to Secretary of Defense Magsaysay asking for the assistance of the military in policing the polls. NAMFREL and "a group of public-spirited citizens" (plus some publishers friendly to the U.S. Embassy) encouraged citizens to get out and vote, while Magsaysay's army transported and guarded ballot boxes until the final official count was completed. The declared objective was to prevent cheating by anyone. The biggest cheating in the previous election had been carried on by President Quirino's supporters, so he returned from Spain to find the dice loaded against him.

Lansdale meant business. Colonel Valeriano headed one of the poll-watching units. As balloting closed at each precinct, radio reporters obtained the unofficial tally and relayed the numbers immediately to Manila, where friendly newspapers and radio stations announced the results to the public, forestalling the manipulation of ballots. As Lansdale put it: "The honesty of the election was attested to by the fact that most of the candidates who were elected belonged to [our side]." From America's viewpoint, the "clean" election of 1951 served notice to the world that genuine democracy was restored in the Philippines, that there was no need for anyone to join the Huks. Because it had all been done so cleverly, many Filipinos were persuaded that it was true. Good had beaten evil. Sympathy for the Huks had been growing not only on the left but in the political center. But the "clean" election so impressed the Filipino middle class that middle-of-the-road support for the Huks dwindled to a trickle.

Following the election, Magsaysay's popularity grew enormously. He acquired the reputation of being the one honest man in the Manila government. American magazine readers were told again and again that he had all the makings of a presidential candidate who could restore confidence and, more important, would not hesitate to cooperate with American interests in the islands. In Washington, the formal decision was made to remove Quirino like a bad tooth and to put Magsaysay in his place.

A high-powered international media campaign was launched. In New York, Lansdale and Kaplan's associates held meetings with publishers, editors, and journalists. Soon Magsaysay was on the cover of *Time* and other magazines as "the man who broke the back of the communist rebellion in the Philippines." If you have imaginary enemies, it is possible to have imaginary victories.

It was necessary to project Magsaysay not only as a great anti-Communist fighter but as a man of large ideas capable of leading a nation. Here his image makers had a problem, for he was not articulate, and most of his ideas came from Lansdale. In mid-1953, an invitation was arranged for him to deliver the keynote address at the world conference of the Junior Chamber of Commerce in Mexico City, with controlled press coverage. For many days beforehand, Lansdale had Magsaysay locked with a language instructor in a hotel room in Los Angeles, learning to read a speech in Spanish. His performance was a resounding success. Whatever his delivery lacked in eloquence could be attributed to the language problem.

Before Magsaysay could be run for president, he had to be eased out of Quirino's cabinet and set up with a rival political machine. An oust-Quirino pact was negotiated by the CIA with the aging bosses of the Nacionalista party—Jose Laurel and Claro Recto—and with Lorenzo Tanada of the idealistic Citizens party. All were eager to tar-and-feather the Quirino brothers right out of Malacanang Palace, eager enough even to strike a bargain with Washington, which all three detested. Accordingly, the Citizens party temporarily merged with the Nacionalistas, Magsaysay resigned from Quirino's cabinet and from the Liberal party, and became the presidential candidate of the Nacionalista/Citizens alliance.

For years, Washington had been keeping Laurel and Recto out of Malacanang by regurgitating the issue of their wartime collaboration, a tiresome device but one that inevitably worked on a population with bitter memories. Both Recto and Laurel were gentlemen of extraordinary guile, for whom one need not feel pity, only compassion. They thought they were taking this opportunity to lay the collaborator issue to rest by joining forces temporarily with the CIA. Years later Recto told a CIA agent, "I thought it amusing to arrange a deal with the American military who spent most of their time unjustly defaming me. As for Ramon [Magsaysay], he was so dumb I knew I could handle him."

The Philippine presidential election campaign that followed was incongruously American. Filipinos were coaxed by slick radio jingles, children sang "Magsaysay is my Guy," and couples danced to the "Magsaysay Mambo." Planted news photos showed the overweight candidate sharing humble meals with peasants and workers. Lapel pins, wall posters, and bumper stickers appeared everywhere. Nobody thought to ask where Magsaysay had gotten all the dough.

The volatile Manila press, tired of the monotonously single-minded Quirino brothers and their legions of thugs and triads, universally favored Magsaysay, especially the American-owned Manila *Daily Bulletin* and the Manila *Times*. With CIA assistance, newsman Teddy de Los Santos and his staff generated pro-Magsaysay articles for newspapers all over the archipelago. The CIA unabashedly published and distributed a monthly "Digest of the Provincial Press," featuring articles that it wanted to emphasize as the dominant views in the provinces, all favorable to Magsaysay.

Lansdale and Kaplan were pouring millions of dollars and pesos into the campaign, buying the archipelago back from the forces of darkness, but Magsaysay resolutely denied that he ever received a single contribution from any foreigner, insisting that his campaign was financed entirely with voluntary and unsolicited contributions. In his memoirs, Lansdale remained as pious as ever: "I was surprised to hear my name included in the rumors as having given Magsaysay three million dollars for his campaign. The rumormongers certainly didn't know the tiny budget of government and personal funds on which I was operating."

Outwardly, the Magsaysay-for-President Movement was billed as an independent political group. But the organization, headed by Lansdale protégé Colonel Terry Adevoso, had a more sinister role. If Quirino's Liberals, to ensure his re-election, again resorted to cheating and murder on the scale of 1949, Adevoso's team was to take over radio stations and military installations throughout the country. Secret planning sessions were held at the Del Monte pineapple plantation, MacArthur's old haunt, and at the homes and estates of landed gentry. One of the CIA's favorite estates was the Cojuangcos' Hacienda Luisita in Tarlac, which provided the Agency with facilities to train agents for conspiracies throughout Southeast Asia. Some Filipino elite were offended by the suggestion that they should participate with the CIA in a military conspiracy. In deference to their sensibilities, Lansdale was careful not to be present at any of the secret briefings.

To prevent any possible "misuse" of the Philippine Army and Constabulary during the election, JUSMAG's General Robert Cannon sent American military officers on inspection rounds of all Philippine Army units in areas of potential trouble. Several days before the election, a flotilla of American destroyers and a light aircraft carrier appeared in Manila Bay, seeming to confirm rumors leaked slyly by the Magsaysay camp that a U.S.-backed coup was in the works in the event of "large-scale fraud and coercion of voters." The naval exercise was stage-managed by the CIA's Far East Division to frighten Quirino. When polling began, Magsaysay and the Nacionalista party bosses were guarded at the U.S. Navy's Subic Bay base.

With so much backstage help, Magsaysay won by the biggest landslide in the nation's history, taking 68.9 percent of the vote. At noon on November 12, 1953, Quirino conceded defeat and went home to count his bank balance. Everybody at the U.S. Embassy and at JUSMAG felt that it was a memorable day for democracy.

One of the CIA's post-election contributions to the democratic process was the passage of President Magsaysay's new Anti-Subversion Act, under which many Filipinos were stripped of jobs and reputations, or sentenced to prison. McCarthyism suffocated dissent in the islands; subversion thereafter became whatever Malacanang Palace wanted it to be. Lansdale's many Filipino protégés remained politically powerful behind the scenes; anyone running for office for the next thirty years had to take them into consideration. Whenever a leading leftist was murdered, the running gag of the Lansdale gang was that he had been executed by his own supporters to create ill-feeling against the entrenched right.

One of the persistent myths about Magsaysay was that he was an enlightened man who brought the Huk movement to an end by making genuine concessions to the embittered rebels, offering them land and a chance to start a new life, trading plowshares for rifles. It was Lansdale, not Magsaysay, who created the land resettlement program, as a media device to impress journalists. The first farm showplace was established on 4,000 acres in Mindanao. There, nine hundred fifty families were resettled, but less than two hundred fifty had any remote connection with the Huk peasant movement. The Magsaysay government hoped that few Huks would accept this offer of land, because only a little land was available—why waste it on Communists? The gentry could not be persuaded to part with more, and except in the most extreme cases Washington considered land redistribution a dangerous manifestation of Marxism. Jose Crisol, principal Filipino architect of Magsaysay's "agrarian programs," candidly described these efforts as "psych-war aimed at the soft core of the Huk movement." Crisol was not an expert on agrarian policy but a secret policeman.

The Magsaysay gambit was such a success that the CIA was encouraged to try the same thing elsewhere—in Indonesia, where President Eisenhower was anxious to end the flamboyant career of Bung Sukarno, in Cuba, in Chile, and in Vietnam. The same Americans and Filipinos who created Magsaysay created the Diem regime, tried unsuccessfully to remove Fidel Castro, and succeeded in removing Salvador Allende.

Edward Lansdale arrived in Saigon in June 1954 to set up the Saigon Military Mission after the French defeat at Dienbienphu.

"I talked to Magsaysay," he said, "about the conditions under which Prime Minister Diem was working, particularly the inadequacies of the military guard. Magsaysay agreed that, if Diem desired it, Colonel Napoleon Valeriano might be spared to advise on ways to improve security for the prime minister." Soon after Valeriano came to Saigon, opponents of Diem began to experience fatal accidents. It was the start of an impressive international career for the Huk killer. Through Lansdale, Valeriano became a favorite of CIA covert operations specialists William Colby and Theodore Shackley, moved on from Saigon to train Shackley's Cuban Brigade for the Bay of Pigs, then back to Indochina as chief "gook-zapper" in Colby's Operation Phoenix. In Washington, D.C., where he made his new home, he was something of a hero. When he died years later, apparently of natural causes, his *Washington Post* obituary portraying him as a national patriot of the Philippines was read into the Congressional Record.

As for Lansdale, he was so much in demand in the cause of freedom elsewhere that he was not in the Philippines when, shortly after midnight one Saturday in March 1957, Ramon Magsaysay's presidential plane, *Mt. Pinatubo,* crashed into a mountainside near Cebu City, killing all but one of the twenty-seven aboard. The lone survivor was Nestor Mata, a reporter for the *Philippine Herald.* The *Mt. Pinatubo* was an old C-47 given to Magsaysay by the CIA. Despite its age, it was in excellent condition. Magsaysay's pilot had more hours than any other Philippine aviator. The crash was said to have been caused by failure of the electrical system—power failure.

Back in 1953, when it was arranged for Magsaysay to be nominated for president by the Nacionalistas, the CIA had agreed as a trade-off to run crusty Carlos Garcia for vice president. Garcia was a lawyer who had been in politics since the 1920s as a congressman, a governor, and a senator, and he owed everything to party bosses Laurel and Recto. The CIA considered him a meaningless cipher. Magsaysay's men warned that Garcia was "a crook like Quirino." But the Agency never anticipated a fatal plane crash. With Magsaysay's death, Garcia automatically became president and the Nacionalista old guard had no difficulty getting him elected to a full term in 1957. Once Magsaysay was gone, the intricate electrical circuits set up by Lansdale shorted out quickly.

Magsaysay's popularity with ordinary Filipinos had been great, but Recto and Laurel had reason to regret their pact with Lansdale. They found it was really the CIA that had taken over Malacanang. There were cowboys in the palace. Claro Recto became the leader of an anti-Magsaysay (anti-CIA) faction among the Nacionalistas. The Agency chose to interpret his opposition as an obstacle to its sincere activities throughout Asia. When he ran for president with Lorenzo Tanada under the Citizens party banner in 1957, Recto was smeared by the Agency for his role as Laurel's foreign secretary during the war—in support of fascism—and was simultaneously labeled a Communist. At one point, CIA station chief General Ralph Lovett and U.S. Ambassador Raymond Spruance considered poisoning him. Lovett later revealed that they decided not to do it for practical reasons rather than moral scruples. When CIA agent Joseph Burkholder Smith was assigned to the Manila Station, he discovered envelopes containing defective condoms bearing the inscription "Compliments of Claro M. Recto, the People's Friend."

Looking back, former President Truman mused:

> For some time I have been disturbed by the way [the] CIA has been diverted from its original assignment. It has become an operational arm and at times a policy-making arm of the Government. This has led to trouble and may have compounded our difficulties in several explosive areas.
>
> I never had any thought when I set up the CIA that it would be injected into peacetime cloak and dagger operations.

. . . the last thing we needed was for the CIA to be seized upon as something akin to a subverting influence in the affairs of other people. . . .

. . . I, therefore, would like to see the CIA be restored to its original assignment as the intelligence arm of the President, and whatever else it can properly perform in that special field, and that its operational duties be terminated or properly used elsewhere.

We have grown up as a nation, respected for our free institutions and for our ability to maintain a free and open society. There is something about the way the CIA has been functioning that is casting a shadow over our historical position, and I feel that we need to correct it.

Seven

A MESS OF POTAGE

IT WAS ONE OF THOSE soggy Aprils when the heat hangs over Manila like a wet diaper, the air is foul, pedestrians move slowly, and storm clouds obscure the mountains across the bay.

Mrs. Daniel Romualdez had gone to Congress to fetch her husband, the speaker *pro tempore*, and had taken Imelda along for the ride. Intending to wait in the car, Imelda had not bothered to dress up and was wearing slippers. After a while there were so many mosquitoes she fled inside.

When Ferdinand Marcos saw her in the Visitors' Gallery, he put aside everything and pursued. He had seen her before, often, in the clerical section of the Central Bank, when he was there as a congressman pressing bureaucrats for foreign exchange and import permits. Someone had told him she was the country cousin of the banker Eduardo Romualdez and the speaker *pro tempore*. But the opportunity to introduce himself had not arisen.

From the gallery, the two women went to the office of the congressional secretary, where there was an ice-cream party. Ferdinand entered and approached various people in the room, but they all refused to make the introductions. "Don't you monkey with that girl," one of them said. Finally he forced Congressman Jacobo Gonzales to present him, although Gonzales did not know her, either. When the formalities were finished, Imelda said, "And who are you?"

Since his first campaign for Congress after the war, Ferdinand had learned to get his way by direct assault, taking people off guard and

155

exploiting the initiative. Within minutes over their ice cream he told Imelda that he was in love with her, that he was going to marry her, win the presidency, and lay the world at her feet.

It was rude and awkward, but Imelda was ready for something outlandish. She had suffered a long string of petty humiliations since leaving Leyte. The controversy over her campaign for Miss Manila, and her romance with Ariston Nakpil, had left her frustrated. She was powerless. Even her provincial title, Rose of Tacloban, had been awarded primarily because she was a Romualdez. She had used family connections to obtain a screen test for a Manila producer, a test she had been told was successful, but the Romualdez clan was scandalized at the prospect and her father was mustered out of his drowsy existence in Leyte to declare himself flatly against the idea. After that, Imelda did not even bother to see the test. She could not face turning down a movie contract, for whatever reasons it was offered.

Her face had appeared on a magazine cover, but her wealthy suitors were not interested in marriage. Nakpil's family was still trying to have his teenage marriage annulled. During their year-long affair, she was unable to exact a commitment even for some future date. Her father had intervened, forcing her to return to Leyte. She had been back in Manila only a few weeks when she was rushed by Ferdinand Marcos.

After the ice-cream party he pestered her with calls, flowers, and visits. To escape his relentless attentions, she took the Romualdez children to Baguio for Holy Week, accompanied by three girlfriends as chaperons. Ferdinand followed. He told her he had a marriage contract in his pocket, ready to be signed. He even brought a justice of the peace in tow, to perform a civil ceremony as soon as she capitulated. Doggedly paying court to her day and night, he pressed her repeatedly to sign, promising that with his money and bright future everything she wanted could be hers. At Mass each morning, he sat beside her.

"He would read my missal and afterward he knew the whole Mass by memory," Imelda told friends. "I don't know how he did it. He was terrific, his memory was impressive. I would test him the next day. He would be beside me again, in church reading from my missal. It was a different Mass, but again he memorized the whole Mass!"

On the way to a restaurant, he took Imelda and her three friends to his bank. Leading them into the vault, he unlocked a large safe-deposit drawer and revealed a portion of his treasure—stacks upon stacks of cash. After lunch, Imelda phoned a cousin in Manila, described the money, and gave the dimensions of the drawer in length, width, and height. By her calculation, the drawer held several million pesos, the better part of a million dollars in cash. Here was clear evidence, if evidence was needed, that the young congressman could do what he promised.

At 2:00 A.M. on Maundy Thursday, Imelda made a desperate call to Ariston Nakpil in Manila, trying to elicit some encouragement. Nakpil brushed her off. Impetuously, on Good Friday, Imelda took the first independent action of her life. Without consulting anyone, family or friends, she signed Ferdinand's marriage license. The siege had taken exactly eleven days. On Holy Saturday they formalized the marriage before the justice of the peace. Ferdinand presented her with a wedding band of white gold set with eleven diamonds, one for each day of the courtship.

Imelda remarked to friends, "Even I am surprised at the suddenness of our civil wedding. I found I could not say no to him. . . . I did not know anything about him except that he was a brilliant congressman. . . . But then, that is how marriage is, sometimes. It comes like death, sudden and unexpected."

She wired Orestes in Tacloban, then rushed back to Manila. "My father knew about Ferdinand only when I was already married to him." A few days later, she took him to Leyte. It was a delicate task. Her father was ill, later to find he was dying of cancer. He was a staunch Nacionalista, and because of President Quirino the Liberals had a bad image. Unexpectedly, he took a liking to Ferdinand.

Next came a gala church wedding. At the last minute, Ferdinand could not produce a baptismal certificate. He had himself baptized hurriedly at Lourdes Catholic Church in Quezon City. Their church wedding at San Miguel Pro-Cathedral in Manila, on May 1, 1954, was a glittering society affair with President Magsaysay serving as sponsor. (The same year, Magsaysay served as sponsor when Benigno Aquino, Jr., married Corazon Cojuangco.) Imelda's gown, designed by Manila couturier Ramon Valera, was made of nylon tulle and white satin, the skirt covered with leaves of sequins, seed pearls, and rhinestones. Her branch of the Romualdez family stayed in the background, unaccustomed to all the glamor; her sister Conchita conceded that "it was a political wedding." Many senators and congressmen were present, and there was a reception afterward at Malacanang Park across the Pasig River from the palace, attended by three thousand guests. The cake was a replica of Congress.

Ferdinand wasted no time hurrying Imelda out of town for a short honeymoon in Baguio. A public honeymoon applied the ultimate seal.

There was a good reason: Imelda knew Ferdinand's reputation as a lady's man, but she did not know he already had a wife and three children—two boys and a girl. Carmen Ortega was only his wife by common law, but she was the woman his mother, Doña Josefa, had wanted him to marry. In fact, his cronies claimed among themselves that Josefa considered her son properly married to Carmen Ortega and regarded Imelda only as a political mistress.

Pretty Carmen Ortega had met Ferdinand four years earlier, in 1950. She was an Ilocano, a poor girl from the country, and he offered to sponsor her in a contest for Miss Press Photography. She became his full-time mistress and moved into the house he shared with his mother. Around town, Carmen was known as Mrs. Marcos. Once, Ferdinand withdrew $50,000 from his Manila bank to take Carmen on a spree to America. He introduced her to the bank officers as his wife. Imelda's cousin Loreto was in the bank at the time, and witnessed the interchange, but the name Ferdinand Marcos meant nothing to her then. An announcement of his forthcoming marriage to Carmen had appeared in the Manila press, but neither a civil nor a church wedding seems ever to have taken place. Carmen was not politically valuable as a wife. Her family had some political clout, but only around their home in La Union, where Ferdinand already had a solid base. On the other hand, the Romualdez family were an invaluable asset politically and financially. In the central Visayan Islands, they controlled at least a million votes; their name had national recognition. Ferdinand was planning to run for the Senate. Unlike congressmen, senators were national representatives, obliged to campaign throughout the islands. Equally important, Eduardo Romualdez was chairman of the Reconstruction Finance Corporation on which Ferdinand had served; Eduardo controlled access to millions of dollars in foreign exchange credits. Imelda did not realize it, but she was worth a great deal to her new husband.

While they honeymooned in Baguio, Carmen Ortega and her children were moved out of Josefa's house to a mansion in the suburb of Green Hills. Once the coast was clear, Imelda was brought back and installed as Mrs. Marcos, in Carmen's place. When gossip caught up, she discovered that she was not the only Mrs. Marcos, simply the newest. To her dismay, the Marcos home was on Ortega Street—the name of her rival. She wanted to sell it immediately and move elsewhere, but Josefa and Ferdinand refused. Worse yet, Imelda learned that he was still visiting Carmen on the sly. Mustering her courage, she went to Green Hills and asked Ortega to stop "entertaining" Ferdinand—it was breaking up the marriage and destroying her happiness. Carmen's response was devastating: Imelda was destroying *her* happiness. Furthermore, Carmen had just become pregnant with Ferdinand's fourth child; conception had taken place since Imelda's church wedding. Carmen had no intention of letting go.

It was impossible to walk out and be done with it. They had been married under false pretenses, but in a rigidly Catholic country after the public honeymoon Imelda was damaged goods. To walk out would consign her to limbo for the rest of her life. She could not expect an annulment. Divorce was not possible. Nor could she stop him from seeing Carmen.

Imelda was sometimes known to remark wistfully, "My only dream in life is to have an average home by the sea, perhaps in Tolosa . . . I don't care about riches and jewels . . . just give me that home by the sea and I will ask nothing more." That would change.

The Carmen Ortega dilemma drove her to the edge. Anxious about her mental state, Ferdinand flew her to America, where she spent three months under psychiatric care at the Presbyterian Hospital in New York City. An announcement was made in Manila that the newlyweds had gone abroad on a second honeymoon.

As she later told Loreto, the New York psychiatrist helped her see that the choice was simple: leave her husband or stick it out—but if she stuck, she had to make the best of it. From New York she flew to Portugal on a pilgrimage to the shrine of Our Lady of Fatima. If she was going to see it through, she had to find ways to secure her position. She prayed for children. Then she flew home to Manila.

In November 1955 the first of three children, Imee, was born. Imelda's eldest half sister, Lourdes, whose own marriage had not been a success, returned from the United States to help look after the child, along with Imelda's youngest sister, Conchita. But a baby was not the end of the problem. There was the continual, twenty-four-hour invasion of her home, even her bedroom, by campaign workers and constituents, all wanting to touch her and receive handouts. Imelda was unaccustomed to attention and exposure. She needed privacy, and was still shy. She was under pressure to perform around the clock, the household became campaign headquarters, and as each campaign intensified, she suffered a crisis.

In the early stages of Ferdinand's third race for Congress, Imelda had another breakdown, remaining in bed for days. She sought refuge in migraine headaches and there was speculation that she took an overdose of medication. Her brother "Kokoy," now Ferdinand's political valet, saw Imelda lying on her bed cold, pale, motionless, hardly breathing, and thought she was dying. She told friends, "I came to a point when I felt I couldn't go on. I had a nervous breakdown. I had to have medical treatment."

Each time there was a crisis, Ferdinand became attentive and showered her with gifts and affection. Early in January 1957, while she was stricken with migraines, they made up and she became pregnant, giving birth in September to Ferdinand Junior, nicknamed Bong-Bong. During the pregnancy, there was no time for psychiatrists; Ferdinand continued his campaigning and Imelda endured the invasions of her privacy. According to Loreto, Imelda's doctors made no progress until they convinced her to accept her lot. Then the headaches stopped. A different woman emerged, one tougher and more calculating.

The next crisis at the end of 1959, when Ferdinand ran for the Senate, brought their third child, Irene, in September 1960. Between pregnancies, romance was on ice. Ferdinand was said to have confided to his extramarital conquests that Imelda was frigid, that he had become impotent with her. Once he blurted out in public that she had "virginitis."

If domestic bliss was elusive, political success was not. By 1957 Ferdinand had become the leader of the Liberal party in the House of Representatives—a powerful position for patronage and the ideal jumping-off point for the Senate in 1959. President Garcia, the Nacionalista machine politician who had moved into Malacanang on the death of Ramon Magsaysay, was elected to a full term in 1957 with a Liberal, Diosdado Macapagal, as vice president. In the Philippines, it was possible for a split ticket to win the top two posts. Macapagal was destined to be Ferdinand's main rival for power. Like Ferdinand, he had entered

Congress after the war as part of the Quirino brothers' machine. He was from a poor family, but again like Ferdinand a local philanthropist had underwritten his education—a law degree and later a doctorate in economics. Careful to be friendly toward the United States, Macapagal had been secretly feeding the CIA political information for years. In return, the Agency helped his vice presidential campaign, as a way to balance the uncooperative Garcia.

Garcia refused to give Macapagal a cabinet post, leaving the vice president to his own devices. It was a mistake. With little to do, and lots of encouragement from the CIA station, Macapagal emulated Magsaysay and spent the next four years visiting barrios, talking to people in isolated districts, promising to correct economic ills and to combat corruption. He began to look like a new, more intellectual Magsaysay.

Garcia's administration was openly corrupt. Unlike Quirino, who looked like the Chinese kitchen god, Garcia was a pleasant-looking fellow—a bit jowly perhaps, but not the sort who would leave a ring around the tub. Looks can be deceiving. His wife, Leonila, brokered the biggest deals.

A big-time operator under Garcia was the American gambler Ted Lewin. During the war, Lewin had been interned by the Japanese at Capas concentration camp, where he ran a floating crap game and made a bundle from everyone including Japanese guards and officers. When peace came, Lewin opened a bistro in Manila catering to GIs with a casino in the back frequented by high government officials. Technically, gambling was illegal, but through his powerful clientele, Lewin bought protection from the police. He also ran a black-market operation. American GIs and Filipinos with American PX privileges (acquired as part of their veterans benefits) bought large quantities of duty-free U.S. cigarettes, soda pop, and other luxury items, which Lewin then resold to local retailers for big profits. He modeled himself on the film roles of Humphrey Bogart and George Raft, and provided special services to high rollers among the oligarchs such as sugar baron Fernando Lopez, who had operated casinos on Negros under the Japanese. When a Lopez daughter-in-law left her husband and took their child to America, Lewin reportedly arranged through friends in the American Mafia to have the boy kidnapped and returned to Manila. Apparently he also provided the CIA with inside information on the gambling debts and peccadilloes of government officials and legislators.

At this time, the CIA was making secret tape recordings in the love nest of the same Senator Fernando Lopez while he carried on an extramarital affair.

As Garcia began replacing Magsaysay men holding key positions in the bureaucracy, the CIA drew the line. It had gone to a lot of trouble to put those assets into position. Working with tame Filipino Army officers, the Agency began plotting a coup. The plot was discovered and the affair had to be hushed up by President Eisenhower to avoid embarrassment in the United States.

After tempers calmed, the CIA tried a milder approach, putting together a Magsaysay-style coalition joining Vice President Macapagal and other Liberals friendly to the Agency—among them Ferdinand—with a CIA-backed splinter party called the Progressives, made up of "clean" politicians who were outspokenly pro-American. A "Grand Alliance" was proclaimed. The Alliance drew up a slate of senatorial candidates to oppose President Garcia's men in the 1959 congressional elections. If the incumbent president's party was trounced in congressional elections, Garcia himself would lose when the next presidential election came around—the same approach Lansdale had taken in 1951 to set the stage for Magsaysay's presidential victory in 1953.

This Alliance proved less than grand. There was too much bickering over whether Ferdinand Marcos should be allowed to run for the Senate. Nobody trusted him. Leaders of the Progressive party were afraid of him, convinced he was the most dangerous man in the legislature. Among his peers he had a reputation for cutthroat tactics that frightened even the corrupt old lions in Congress. On one occasion when an official of the Central Bank refused to authorize an import permit for a well-heeled Chinese businessman, Ferdinand burst into his office waving a revolver and pointed the muzzle at his head till the documents were signed and turned over to him. The bank official was so shaken that he resigned his job the same day and shortly afterward emigrated with his entire family to the United States. This was not an unusual incident. Dealing with Ferdinand was never easy, according to one of the technocrats at the Development Bank of the Philippines. "It's rough," he said. "You risk losing not only your reputation but also your life." Some of his victims said he had their wives kidnapped and held in solitary confinement until their husbands met his demands. These reports were not discussed openly because the victims were afraid to complain (it was safer to emigrate), but within Congress there was enough anxious gossip to create fear of what would happen if Ferdinand became any more powerful.

It was widely believed among his congressional peers that he had ties to an Ilocano murder syndicate that included senior officers in the Constabulary, gangsters, smugglers, triads, and teams of professional hitmen. He was linked, as Quirino had been, to Congressman Floro Crisologo, the warlord of Ilocos Sur, whose private army used flame-throwers to settle arguments. He was also close to the warlord of Cavite, smuggler Lino Bocalan, the principal southern outlet for the Ilocano/ Chinese syndicates bringing goods in from Taiwan and Hong Kong. Nobody dared to accuse Ferdinand directly. To do so, it was believed, would invite reprisals against your family.

Imelda's accounts of life with Ferdinand always glossed over this sinister side of his character—she apparently never discussed Carmen Ortega and Carmen's children outside the Romualdez family. How much she knew remains a mystery. As his wife, such unwholesome discoveries may have contributed more to her nervous breakdowns than just the pressures of public life. She was always coy about such things. At one point, a reporter asked her what she thought about the allegation that her husband had murdered Julio Nalundasan, and she responded: "Do you think I could have married a man who was guilty of such things?" Her former boyfriend, architect Ariston Nakpil, did not escape attention. Ferdinand was infuriated when a Filipino biography of Imelda was published alleging that she had spent weekends with Nakpil at his country estate; according to the biographer, Carmen Pedrosa, Ferdinand sent men to demand that Nakpil refute the allegations. They implied that if he failed to do so, Nakpil's children would be in danger. Nakpil rightly said these matters were too well known for the denials to have any meaning.

Since 1949, Ferdinand had boasted openly of his intention to become president, and the logical path was to move from the House of Representatives to the Senate, to become Senate president, there to use the patronage and leverage of the position to become president of the republic. He was now about to make the jump from House to Senate. If he was to be blocked, it had to be done immediately.

Vice President Macapagal was playing a dangerous game. He was promoting Ferdinand for the Senate in 1959 as part of a package deal to take turns backing each other on the way to Malacanang. Macapagal needed Ferdinand's support to become president, and seemed willing to promise anything in return. Apparently he thought that once he was in the palace there would be time enough to destroy Ferdinand's career, by exposing his ties to Lino Bocalan, Harry Stonehill, Ted Lewin, and others. When their relationship did eventually sour, Macapagal declared: "Marcos is a murderer, a thief, a swindler, a forger and a threat to the country. He is a dangerous man addicted to violence."

To which Ferdinand replied: "The only true thing Macapagal says is that I have killed people. I killed lots of Japanese soldiers during the war, and that's all."

The CIA also had its misgivings.

On the way to a 1959 strategy meeting of the Grand Alliance, CIA agent Joseph Burkholder Smith was given a lift by Ferdinand in his Cadillac, who took the opportunity to deride Macapagal's presidential ambitions. He told Smith, "[Macapagal] has an exaggerated opinion of himself and his own importance. . . . We don't necessarily think Macapagal must be the presidential candidate in 1961. Only he does." Smith concluded, "Marcos was terribly inscrutable . . . I could not really tell whose side he was on. I trusted [him] even less than [the others]. . . . [He] wouldn't make his position clear."

When Smith remarked that Macapagal had also promised to support another politician, Ambrosio Padilla, as his successor, Ferdinand replied, "Ha, he said the same thing to me, too. God knows how many others he's said it to. . . . He'll do anything, absolutely anything, to get his own way."

When election day came in November 1959, the CIA's Grand Alliance slate failed miserably. In the nationwide race for the Senate, Ferdinand was its only victor. He beat all other contenders, suspiciously receiving three hundred thousand votes more than the second-place winner, the Nacionalista party's Genaro Magsaysay, brother of the late president. Sugar magnate Fernando Lopez came in third.

This failure of the CIA and the Grand Alliance to steal the initiative from President Garcia led to two more years of jockeying for the covert American endorsement. The Agency desperately wanted to replace Garcia with another Magsaysay. But no single individual possessed the necessary qualities. Some were clean but ineffective, others were effective but not clean. Technically, Ferdinand could not be Macapagal's running mate, because both men came from northern Luzon, and traditionally the ticket had to be split geographically. The Agency was not unreservedly happy about backing Macapagal, but a compromise was finally arranged in which he agreed to take as running mate a CIA favorite—"clean" Emmanuel Pelaez of the Progressive party. Pelaez had a reputation as a man who was tediously honest, whose honesty prevented him from making headway.

As the 1961 presidential election approached, Garcia tried to improve his chances by choosing as running mate Jose Laurel's eldest son, Jose Junior. The sugar bloc backed them lavishly, but Macapagal's early lead was solidified when a sudden and very suspicious rice shortage pushed up food prices and made the incumbent Garcia look bad. Voters flocked to Macapagal and Pelaez, who won handily. They failed, however, to win control of both houses of Congress, which put Ferdinand in a crucial bargaining position. He persuaded twenty-nine Nacionalistas to jump to the Liberal party. Most of them were his confederates, or owed him favors that he was able to call in.

Once in the palace, President Macapagal introduced far-reaching agrarian reforms with a new leasehold system, which would eventually make tenant farmers the owners of the land they cultivated. Critics pointed out that it would have taken five thousand years for the program to achieve its ultimate goals. There were rude suggestions that the plan was devised with no intent of paying off. Gradual reform programs were always doomed by the disinterest of the next faction in Malacanang. Everybody acknowledged that when it came to land reform only draconian measures would be effective, as the Huks always argued.

The alternative was for Macapagal to serve a second term to carry out his programs. Although Quirino and Garcia had each served one and a half terms because of the death in office of their predecessors, no president since independence had won a second full term. The only way to do this was to neutralize the leading rivals—the Lopez-Laurel coalition in the Nacionalista party, and the Marcos cabal in the Liberal party.

Macapagal first attacked Eugenio and Fernando Lopez, the biggest bankrollers of the Nacionalista party. Fernando, who had been Quirino's vice president, was now aspiring to the presidency for himself in 1965. The Lopez family had persistently attacked Macapagal in its newspaper, the Manila *Chronicle*. Macapagal tried to wound them politically by charging that they used their wealth to buy politicians, and then used the politicians to obtain giant loans from the government. The Lopez brothers blandly replied that Macapagal's idea of reform was to reform only his political enemies. As if to demonstrate that they were not afraid of Malacanang Palace, they announced the purchase of Manila's giant Meralco electric company from its American owner, Alfred Tegen. The transfer of such a major industry to Filipino hands made the Lopez brothers look very good indeed, so Macapagal was obliged to back off his attack and approve their transaction. Rather lamely, he cautioned that "we will prevent this group from continuing their harmful activities to exploit political power for personal profit." The best he could do was to scold them. As one government official put it: "Don't forget the oligarchs have survived here, not through confrontation with either the Americans or the Japanese or their local successors. Their technique is to give an opponent enough rope to hang himself—and their opponents so far have usually done so."

Frustrated in his efforts to neutralize the sugar bloc, Macapagal turned on his more dangerous adversary, Ferdinand Marcos. A frontal assault was not prudent, but Ferdinand might be vulnerable to flanking maneuvers—a public-spirited crusade against the tobacco bloc and Harry Stonehill. It was not difficult to find others eager to use Stonehill to bring down Marcos.

More and more smuggled U.S. cigarettes were appearing on the streets, costing the government 100 million pesos a year in lost revenues. It was suspected that Stonehill, Lim, Marcos, Ver, Crisologo, and Bocalan were all tied in to this smuggling, but nobody was yet rash enough to try to prove it.

Harry Stonehill had been busy over the years, since he made his first million taking advantage of the government's bright-leaf tobacco subsidy. To protect the infant bright-leaf industry, it was made illegal to import American tobacco in bulk. After sabotaging their rivals, Stonehill and his friends still needed bright-leaf to manufacture palatable cigarettes themselves. Ferdinand announced that he had a "new" idea for saving the native cigarette industry and at the same time eliminating cigarette smuggling, by making Filipino cigarettes of equal quality. It was double talk but it worked. He pushed through legislation allowing the import of 10 million pounds of Virginia tobacco each year for blending. Harry Stonehill received from a committee under Ferdinand Marcos the *only* permit to handle Virginia bright-leaf imports. At the time, journalists had no conception of the magnitude of bribes involved. Legal records in the Stonehill case show that Stonehill paid a lump sum of $5 million to "high Philippine officials" for the exclusive permit. This

$5 million payoff was made on the eve of Garcia and Macapagal's inauguration.

The permit gave Stonehill and his secret partners another monopoly. Because of tight currency controls, they could only spend $4.9 million each year, or 49 cents a pound, for what they needed, and Virginia tobacco was selling for 75 cents a pound. The extra dollars were obtained by illegally moving pesos to Hong Kong where they were exchanged for U.S. currency at better rates on the black-money market. The dollars then were transferred to America through numbered accounts in Switzerland.

All arrangements were made through Universal New York (UNY), Stonehill's personal import-export firm, run by his stateside partner Ira Blaustein and his Manila partner Robert Brooks. The Virginia tobacco imported to the islands by Stonehill was then sold exclusively to his own cigarette company. Before he got this import permit, Harry controlled only 4 percent of the Philippine cigarette market; fifteen months later his share was 58 percent.

To increase profit margins, Stonehill purchased revenue stamps from the same printer who supplied them to the government. According to Senator Benigno Aquino, Jr., this crooked tax stamp deal was arranged personally by Ferdinand Marcos. Stonehill then pocketed his normal profit from each pack of cigarettes sold, plus the cut that would ordinarily have gone to the government in taxes.

Bank accounts were opened in Switzerland, and offshore corporations were set up in Liechtenstein, Guernsey, and the Bahamas. Nine million dollars flowed into these secret accounts and $4 million more were funneled into American real estate and U.S. government securities.

By 1962, Stonehill controlled an empire of sixteen corporations, among them the Manila *Evening News*—anybody who mattered in Manila owned part of a newspaper. He got all the government contracts he wanted, plus import licenses, loans, tax write-offs, and other facilities, by the wholesale bribery of hundreds of politicians. Stonehill boasted to friends that he had the entire administration in his pocket. Like gambler Ted Lewin, Stonehill apparently did favors for the CIA, gaining in return a certain immunity from Filipino criminal investigators.

His empire came unglued when Meinhart Spielman, a European refugee hired as general manager of Stonehill's U.S. Tobacco Company, turned evidence over to the National Bureau of Investigation in Manila

that Stonehill had illegally imported millions of dollars' worth of cigarette paper under false customs declarations. Harry reacted quickly.
Spielman said he was then beaten senseless in a Manila apartment by
Stonehill and Brooks. Stonehill had a reputation for violence; he was
once prosecuted for attempting to strangle a newspaper photographer.

In March 1962, Stonehill, Brooks, Ferdinand's millionaire KMT connection Peter Lim, and two others were charged with corrupting government officials, defrauding the government by violation of monetary,
internal revenue, and customs laws, economic conspiracy, and attempting to influence decisions of the Supreme Court. (Ferdinand's name was
not mentioned in any of the charges.) They were accused of spending
millions of dollars' on payoffs to politicians of all parties, to obtain favors
or to ensure their loyalty. Government agents confiscated Stonehill's
records, including a "blue book" listing politicians who received contributions from him. While Stonehill and Brooks were under arrest in
April 1962, Meinhart Spielman disappeared, reportedly murdered
while trying to escape from the Philippines by crossing the Sulu Sea in
a smuggler's motorboat.

Secretary of Justice Jose Diokno, always a political maverick, said he
would disclose the names of all officials on Stonehill's payroll. Somebody—possibly Marcos himself—pointed out discreetly to Macapagal
that if Diokno made the names public, it would embarrass the Liberal
party as much as the Nacionalistas, and might even bring his government down. The staggering $5 million bribe might come out as well,
and it would be difficult to convince the public that Malacanang Palace
did not receive the lion's share.

Macapagal immediately fired Diokno, claiming that the justice secretary was tainted by once having served as a lawyer for co-defendant
Peter Lim. The identities of officials linked to Stonehill were withheld,
only fifteen officials were exposed, and when the "blue book" of bribes
was made public, sixteen pages were missing.

Criminal proceedings began against Stonehill and his co-defendants,
but after Spielman's ominous disappearance President Macapagal—in
what he described as "an act of self-preservation on a national scale"—
ordered Stonehill and Brooks deported immediately, without further
prosecution. To permit these men to remain in the Philippines, he said,
would jeopardize the welfare of the country. Peter Lim, the KMT
frontman, was in Taiwan at the time, and Macapagal barred him from
returning. Lim had major investments in Taipei and intricate ties to the

Chiang regime, so this was no special hardship. Other defendants were put on probation. The U.S. Embassy advised Washington that it was imperative for American interests in the Philippines to get Stonehill out.

Was Stonehill working all along for the CIA? For fifteen years he had been in an extraordinary position to serve as a commercial cutout in the Philippines, with lines into every branch of the bureaucracy.

Stonehill traveled to Mexico, where he was arrested. But he was then allowed out on bail and disappeared. If the U.S. Embassy was so anxious to get him out of Manila, why was he permitted to vanish when the U.S. Internal Revenue Service had a $25 million lawsuit for tax evasion facing him in California? The IRS struck back by attaching a multi-million-dollar trust fund that Stonehill had set up for his children, and the case remained unresolved at the end of 1987. Overnight, Stonehill's Philippine assets dwindled magically to less than a million pesos.

After a few years, most of the key people in the scandal, including Brooks (now a citizen of Canada), returned to Manila and picked up where they had left off. The empire did not collapse, its components were just moved around like walnuts in a shell game. According to the Philippine press, Stonehill continued to control his Philippine operations from South America through middlemen.

Despite the best efforts of Macapagal, Ferdinand avoided being smeared by the Stonehill scandal. In April 1963, he pulled off a political coup and was elected president of the Senate. A long-standing 12 to 12 deadlock had existed in that chamber between the Nacionalistas and the Liberals. This was broken suddenly when Ferdinand's old friend Nacionalista Senator Alejandro Almendras defied his party and cast the tie-breaking vote in favor of Marcos. It was an old debt. When Almendras was governor of Davao, Ferdinand had helped him get U.S. aid money to build a north-south motor road across Mindanao. This opened virgin wilderness to colonization and started a land rush; coconut, palm oil, and coffee plantations were built, and Almendras became the most powerful politician on the island. Eight years later, he repaid Ferdinand with his tie-breaking vote in the Senate.

This victory in the Senate brought a fresh spasm of accusations. President Macapagal publicly charged Senate President Marcos of taking bribes from Stonehill, and produced a receipt showing that he had accepted money from Stonehill's New York partner, Ira Blaustein. Ferdinand denounced it as a forgery and produced another receipt showing that anyway he had given the money back. But which receipt, his enemies asked, was the work of a local master forger known as "the Man with a Golden Arm"?

The lines were now drawn between Ferdinand and those trying urgently to block his move toward Malacanang. Hoping to catch him in a different net, President Macapagal launched a new investigation, this time into the biggest smuggling ring in the islands.

Lino Bocalan was a Cavite fisherman who made millions smuggling and gunrunning. Until 1957, he called himself a poor man. That year, the CIA began backing rebel colonels in an effort to topple Indonesia's Bung Sukarno. All went well until the spring of 1958 when a CIA pilot, Allen Lawrence Pope, was shot down over Amboina Island and the resulting international scandal forced President Eisenhower to call the operation off. Ferdinand boasted to Benigno Aquino, Jr., that he had friends running guns to the Indonesian rebels. (He explained his role more discreetly to U.S. Embassy officials who reported, "[Marcos] said that he had been a very strong supporter of the Indonesian independence movement, that he had very close friends who were killed or arrested for gunrunning in that cause.") He was evidently referring to Bocalan's ring.

Bocalan was making serious money from both the CIA and the KMT, shipping weapons, ammunition, and gunpowder from Taiwan through the Philippines to anti-Communist organizations in Malaysia, Burma, and Indonesia in trade for contraband goods. Bocalan's main base was Cavite, south of Manila. Two hundred carbines and Garand rifles, a million rounds of ammunition, and 2,000 kilos of gunpowder were shipped out of Cavite to Borneo each week. His syndicate spent 70,000 pesos a month buying tax-free cigarettes, perfumes, and cosmetics abroad, netting a profit of 1.8 million pesos per month, a tidy sum in 1957. The contraband was carried by inter-island vessels, fishing boats, and Moro sailing *vintas*. Upon reaching Cavite, these goods were loaded in trucks and escorted by the Constabulary itself to their destination. According to charges leveled by President Macapagal, two top government officials, three mayors, a Constabulary commander, and all the policemen in Cavite were members of the ring. "Everybody's on Lino Bocalan's payroll," marveled a customs commissioner. The Constabulary commander in Cavite was Ferdinand's childhood friend and alleged half brother, Fabian Ver.

Ver was gradually assuming a more significant role in Ferdinand's life. When Stonehill and his associates were expelled from the country, their interests in the tobacco scam apparently were shared out by Ferdinand to Ver and to Congressman Crisologo, boss of Ilocos Sur. Crisologo reportedly ran the tobacco monopoly with his private army while Ferdinand and Fabian Ver remained as silent partners. Ver's role always seems to have been as an enforcer, keeping an eye on things in Cavite, using his position as chief of the Constabulary there to police Lino Bocalan's distribution of smuggled cigarettes and other goods and to make sure that Ferdinand got his proper cut.

When President Macapagal launched his attack on the Bocalan ring and its high-level patrons, he was evidently trying to get at Ferdinand through Fabian Ver. He underestimated Ferdinand's speed and resourcefulness, if not his cunning. Using his clout in the Senate, Ferdinand had the Constabulary transfer Ver to America for training by the U.S. Secret Service and the police academies in Los Angeles and Louisville, remaining in the United States until the scandal subsided. On his return, Ver became Ferdinand's security chief, bodyguard, and chauffeur.

As Senate president, Ferdinand was extremely powerful. Among other things, he controlled the military budget. It was at this point that he arranged, as public relations for the presidential race, to have twenty medals awarded to him. Nine were given to him on a single day. Overnight he became the most decorated Filipino war hero. To justify the awards, there was a flurry of affidavits. Officers in the armed forces fell over each other to fawn on him. Careers were advanced. Ilocano officers rose fast in the army, and the Constabulary.

It was apparent to everyone after the Stonehill and Bocalan scandals that there was bad blood between Marcos and Macapagal. As 1964 approached, Macapagal let it be known that he planned to seek a second term. Marcos told everyone he had been betrayed.

The Liberal party split into three factions: the first supporting Macapagal, the second supporting Ferdinand, the third supporting a new "Grand Alliance" of Emmanuel Pelaez and Senator Raul Manglapus—Washington's team of choice. It had been CIA policy to hedge all bets by giving a little money to every candidate. Ferdinand had been on sufficiently intimate terms with the Agency to drive its senior agents back and forth to secret strategy meetings with party leaders. Macapagal had also been backed at times by the Agency. This put the CIA in the curious position of having been in bed with all three factions contending for the palace.

In a last effort to neutralize Ferdinand, Macapagal tried to oust him from the leadership of the Liberal party. But in a stunning reversal, Ferdinand jumped parties, joining the Nacionalistas and taking the Senate presidency with him. His move suddenly gave the Nacionalistas control of the Senate. All he asked in return was to be the Nacionalista candidate for president.

Eight

THE HIDDEN AGENDA

THE MARCOS CAMPAIGN for the Nacionalista presidential nomination brought Imelda into her own. She threw herself with a vengeance into the job of getting her husband the nomination.

Imelda's favorite clothes in shades of blue were packed away during the eighteen months of campaigning, and she wore chartreuse, neon pink, and canary yellow. "I wanted people to spot me in a room," she said.

She staged tea parties, and fed campaign workers and constituents at least sixty breakfasts, two hundred and fifty lunches, and thirty dinners each day. On Ferdinand's birthday she produced ninety-eight roast pigs and three hundred and fifty birthday cakes. She also took charge of handling the mysterious cloth bags of money that men kept bringing to the house. She told Loreto, "I am tired of counting money, I don't know how much we have. It comes in sacks." Ferdinand, she explained, "has a lot of businesses." Hitting the campaign trail, sometimes with her husband, sometimes on her own, she became the star of mini-carnivals throughout the islands, making speeches and singing love songs to dazzled peasants. The frustrated performer had found her stage. No political wife had ever made such a display of herself, and it brought out the country folk, who were impressed that the pretty wife of Senator Marcos cared enough to mingle with poor people. Working from intelligence reports on each local leader and his private life, Imelda visited every delegate to the forthcoming Nacionalista convention three times. The first time, she introduced herself, was charming, and asked the delegate to vote for her husband. She took note of something she could bring as a "gift" the next time—say, a new swivel chair. On the second trip, she brought the gift, refused any payment, and urged the delegate again to come to the convention. On the third visit, she reminded him to vote for Ferdinand.

By the terms of Filipino hospitality she was obliged to eat every meal put in front of her, if it meant ten meals a day. Ferdinand normally watched her food intake carefully, weighing her portions on a scale at the table, promising her any dress she wanted so long as it was size ten. She came back from the campaign looking like a suckling pig.

Her energy was limitless. During a sweep through Zambales, Imelda visited fifteen out of eighteen towns in three days. The towns she bypassed felt slighted. She apologized, canceled other commitments, and drove back.

The message was that Imelda and Ferdinand really cared. They cared so much that reporters covering the campaign were given gifts of cash every time a picture of Ferdinand was printed in their newspapers.

Just before the convention, Richard Usher, chief of the political section at the U.S. Embassy, filed a classified report to Washington on a conversation with Ferdinand, which noted Marcos's "obviously high intelligence and superior qualities of leadership, and determination to achieve his goal." Senator Marcos

spoke with . . . intensity of the manner in which Macapagal had "betrayed" and "humiliated" him. In 1961, he said, Macapagal had told the Ilocanos during speeches . . . that Marcos would, on Macapagal's word of honor, be the LP Presidential nominee in the next election. . . . Since that time Macapagal had subjected Marcos to many harassments. . . . He had tapped his telephone lines, had had him trailed, and there had been an "ambuscade" which had not succeeded. Marcos likened this treatment to that he had received during the Bataan death march. . . .

Marcos added that he had many personal issues against Macapagal, but that he would not use them during the campaign. He did not wish to incite anyone . . . since if Macapagal did get shot, he, Marcos, would get the blame. . . . Marcos expressed full confidence that he would win the election by a landslide. . . .

At the convention, the Marcos camp had two huge balloons overhead, a party boat chugging back and forth in front of the Manila Hotel seawall, and scores of secret agents mingling with the delegates. Fabian Ver had returned from his U.S. police training courses to be on hand as chief of security.

Ferdinand's rival for the Nacionalista nomination was Vice President Emmanuel Pelaez, who had resigned from the Macapagal cabinet in disgust during the Stonehill scandal, and like Ferdinand had jumped parties to the Nacionalistas. An outspoken supporter of the United States, and a favorite of the U.S. Embassy, Pelaez made such a poor showing on the first ballot that Jaime Ferrer, Lansdale's protégé who engineered Magsaysay's victory, threw his support to Marcos.

Ferdinand won on the second ballot with 777 votes to 444 for Pelaez. As a superstitious man and numerologist, Ferdinand read significance into the numbers—others found them very suspicious.

There was now an unexpected problem: nobody wanted to run with him. Imelda came to the rescue. With tears and sobs, she persuaded Fernando Lopez to put his clan behind Marcos. Although Lopez had failed to get the presidential nomination for himself, the leverage he could enjoy as vice president was not to be discounted. He could extract elaborate concessions from Marcos, including a ceiling on fuel-oil prices, which affected profits from the Lopez utility company, Meralco. When he finally consented, Imelda whipped out a document for him to sign on the spot and then flashed her biggest smile. He must have regretted his decision immediately for he refused to share the same campaign headquarters with Marcos.

On the day newspapers printed Ferdinand's acceptance speech, the Malacanang press office released an ominous statement from Defense Secretary Peralta, the wartime guerrilla leader on Panay Island: "Knowing [Marcos] well, I can also say he does not possess the maturity, integrity, and moral rectitude required of a good President. Because of his known record of ruthlessness and unscrupulousness, I would be recreant to my duties, if I did not express my concern over [President Macapagal's] personal safety."

The Marcos campaign took off at high velocity. Many on the campaign team were old Lansdale men. One of them, Jose Aspiras, an Ilocano from La Union and former president of the National Press Club, headed the Marcos press campaign. Rafael Salas, a professorial-looking bachelor of thirty-seven, one-time head of the National Economic Council, served as the campaign coordinator and legal counsel. He had been president of Lansdale's National Student Movement when it launched Magsaysay's presidential bid in 1953. Blas Ople, Ferdinand's propaganda chief, was a former newspaperman and assistant to Magsaysay. Jose Crisol was a CIA-trained secret policeman who joined the Marcos team to gather political intelligence. He had been chief of Magsaysay's bogus land reform program intended to undercut the Huks. The Agency's fingerprints were everywhere.

Imelda had her own group of twenty-five young women from wealthy families dressed in blue who became known first as the Friends of Imelda and then as the "Blue Ladies." The big Tuesday and Friday political teas at the Marcos home became their responsibility. They were also assigned to pay special attention to foreign journalists. It was during this presidential campaign, under the direction of Ople, Crisol, and Aspiras, that Ferdinand finally capitalized on the myth building he had been doing since World War II—the unearned medals, the fake heroism—and it was at this time that his wartime records were tucked out of sight in a government warehouse in St. Louis, Missouri. The biography *For Every Tear a Victory*, written by Hartzell Spence, appeared, along with a movie on his exploits with the "Maharlika Division"—it had now become an entire army division. The movie was made by the family of Ernesto Maceda, one of Ferdinand's chief political operators.

Ferdinand always maintained that he had nothing to do with either the book or the movie. He told the U.S. Embassy that he "wished he had been given the opportunity to look at the text of . . . Spence's . . . book on him before it had been published, as he would have made a number of changes."

The film was called *Iginuhit Ng Tadhana—Marked by Fate*. It was a production of a new film company called 777 (the magic number that won the presidential nomination). In the film, there were short scenes of Nalundasan's murder while he was brushing his teeth, longer scenes of Ferdinand defending himself before the Supreme Court, war scenes of Ferdinand shooting Japanese soldiers and shoving a mortar down the cliff of Mount Natib, diverting scenes of Ferdinand persuading Imelda to sign their marriage certificate, followed by footage from their society wedding, and sentimental scenes between Ferdinand and his mother played to the last teardrop.

Thus inspired, Macapagal commissioned a biography called *Macapagal the Incorruptible*. But the original author, Quentin Reynolds, died suddenly in the Italian villa where he was working, apparently from a faulty gas valve. The book was finished by Geoffrey Bocca. While the Marcos movie soundtrack was in Tagalog, both biographies were written in English and intended primarily to influence a small but important group of American journalists and government officials. Thousands of copies of the Spence biography were distributed to American newspapers and magazines and to members of the U.S. Congress.

Naturally, Ferdinand was taken to be America's anointed one. Since so many of his team were identified with Lansdale and Hartzell Spence was an old Pentagon hand, it was only natural for the word to get around Manila that the CIA—having given up on the candidacy of Emmanuel Pelaez—was doing everything it could to boost Marcos. Those who presume to know how the CIA operates cite the lavish positive coverage by the major U.S. media as one of the indicators, and point for comparison to the treatment given to Air Marshal Nguyen Kao Ky before he became premier of South Vietnam, to Indonesia's Suharto, and to Magsaysay. Certainly Ferdinand received a buildup that no Philippine presidential candidate hitherto had enjoyed, even Magsaysay. American journalists visiting Manila were told by U.S. Embassy officials, off the record, that Macapagal had become corrupt and that Marcos was "the new Magsaysay." In cover stories and feature articles he was portrayed as an authentič war hero, recipient of the U.S. Medal of Honor, and one whom America could depend upon to preserve democracy with his very life. The articles were almost without exception uncritical.

Macapagal's team was not above its own dirty tricks. During the campaign, a nude photograph of Imelda was circulated, and it was put about that the snapshot had been filched from Ferdinand's private collection. Imelda went into a state of shock. The photo was denounced by Marcos intelligence chief Jose Crisol as a clever composite, Imelda's head superimposed on another woman's body. Then Nalundasan's son appeared on television to discuss the murder of his father: he said he still believed Ferdinand had fired the fatal shot. Macapagal's campaign distributed black toothbrushes.

While Imelda and the Blue Ladies made the barrio rounds by car and bus, Ferdinand flew around the islands in his private Cessna. He claimed that he piloted the plane himself, although the flying was actually done by a former Philippine Airlines pilot with Senator Almendras as co-pilot.

Cable traffic was thick and fast between Manila and Washington, as America monitored campaign progress. One cable reported that "A late development of some importance involved the reported withdrawal of Iglesia ni Kristo [Church of Christ] support from Marcos because of the unauthorized duty-free importation of campaign materials by the Marcos camp in the name of the religious sect." Several times, the U.S. Embassy reminded the State Department that there were certain negative aspects to Ferdinand's career:

Marcos . . . [is] under heavy fire from the Liberals who are striving hard to demonstrate to the public his alleged unfitness for the Presidency by suggesting that he is guilty of everything from accepting a bribe to murder. . . . Liberal propaganda described Marcos as ruthless, venal, unprincipled, and given to violence. . . . Among the more important charges . . . are that he accepted a bribe from Harry Stonehill, that he was involved in some questionable land dealings that . . . dispossessed a number of small farmers . . . more effective is the whispered warning . . . that "Marcos is a killer," a reference to . . . the . . . Nalundasan murder.

Washington was watching closely because of growing desperation within the Johnson administration over America's entanglement in Vietnam. The White House wanted the Philippines to play a public relations role in beefing up Johnson's image in time for the upcoming U.S. congressional campaign. Assistant Secretary of State William Bundy took the pragmatic point of view that Marcos posed a bit of a problem and that the whole Philippine election was significant only because of Vietnam, as apparent in this classified memo to Secretary of State Dean Rusk:

If Macapagal is re-elected, we can expect him promptly to call a special congressional session to enact the bill to send an engineer task force . . . to Vietnam. We can also expect . . . expanded use of U.S. bases and facilities in support of the Vietnam war effort. . . . We are rapidly building up an important U.S. Air Force facility at Mactan Island, Cebu. . . .

If Marcos wins the Presidency, we will first of all have a difficult lame-duck period of some two months before his inauguration. . . . It is unlikely that we could make much progress on aid to Vietnam during that period, although it could be used to bring Marcos . . . more fully aboard . . . on this question. Nationalist elements around Marcos . . . are likely to make a strong bid for influence in the event of his victory. We might therefore have more difficulties than we would with Macapagal on foreign policy. On the other hand, Marcos . . . might be more dynamic and effective in moving the country forward internally.

Eighteen months of campaigning, a movie, a biography, a Cessna, and countless free meals all cost a great deal of money. The Marcos propaganda budget alone was 3 million pesos, nearly $1 million. One of the most important sources of funds for any candidate was the Chinese business community, as represented by the KMT-dominated Federation of Chinese Chambers of Commerce, set up in 1954 with the help of the CIA's Lansdale and Taiwan-backed businessmen like Peter Lim. Through his secret Chua clan connections, Ferdinand was in an unusual position to tap into the Federation, headed by a Chua—Santos Chua Haw-ko. But, instead, there was a clash of wills. Santos Chua Haw-ko was a *compadre* of Macapagal, which put him in a dilemma. He pointed out to Ferdinand that it was well-established precedent for the Federation to support the incumbent president. If the Federation did not support the incumbent, Macapagal could cause serious trouble for the Chinese community while he was still in Malacanang. However, there was a way to get around this and not cause embarrassment to the Federation. Ferdinand could get money from members of the chamber before they put it into the campaign chest.

Ferdinand immediately went to one of his *compadres,* Ralph Nubla, president of the Chinese Tobacco Association. He could expect cooperation. It was through bills he had authored that fortunes had been made in the tobacco business, both by Stonehill's associates and by a number of Chinese entrepreneurs loyal to Marcos. Ralph Nubla agreed, and was able to divert to him all the money that the Tobacco Association normally would have subscribed to the Federation's campaign fund. Nubla went even further by interceding with the Chinese Textile Association to switch its contribution directly to Ferdinand. In return, Ferdinand reportedly saw to it that the Tobacco Association was given a 5 percent cut off import duties on Virginia leaf and, reportedly, that the Textile Association was allowed to import Japanese textiles in violation of tariff restrictions.

The Federation, realizing its mistake in opposing Ferdinand, hastily replaced Santos Chua Haw-ko with Ralph Nubla as president. Thereafter, the presidency rotated between Nubla and members of the Chua clan who were more cooperative toward Ferdinand. Nubla became one of Ferdinand's most valuable allies. In addition to running the Federation, he became the head of the Philippine Bank of Communications, a branch of Taiwan's Bank of Communications, which had been under the control of Chiang Kai-shek's in-laws, the Soongs and Kungs, since the mid-1930s. When Antonio Roxas-Chua wanted to succeed Nubla as president of the Federation, he took the precaution of going up to Ilocos Norte to see Judge Chua in Batac to gain his blessing and intercession with Ferdinand.

Ferdinand also was reported to have received large secret campaign contributions directly from Taiwan and Japan. One of Imelda's Blue Ladies, Presy Lopez Psinakis, whose uncle was the vice presidential running mate, told of "suitcases full of cash" being delivered to the Marcos home by Chinese businessmen. In Japan, powerful lobbies existed that were tied closely to the anti-Communist regimes of Taiwan, South Korea, South Vietnam, and the Philippines. Sasakawa Ryoichi, the multimillionaire "Class A war criminal" and patron of the Yakuza, headed one of the most dynamic lobbies, anxious to help elect anti-Communists everywhere. Sasakawa was working with the Reverend Sun Myung Moon's Unification Church to set up the Tokyo chapter of the World Anti-Communist League as a funnel for funds. Ferdinand told the U.S. Embassy before the presidential election campaign began that he had just made a "secret trip to Tokyo," but he did not reveal what business he had transacted. He and Sasakawa boasted of their close friendship over the years and had a number of joint business deals in the works. Just as General MacArthur was able to channel U.S. war reparation funds to his political favorites, Tokyo used its own war reparations to reopen contacts with powerful wartime collaborators in Korea, Taiwan, the Philippines, Thailand, Malaysia, and Indonesia. When Manila began negotiations with Tokyo for reparations, Jose Laurel headed the team.

Thanks to his seemingly bottomless resources, Ferdinand won the 1965 presidential campaign by 670,000 votes. The Marcoses entered Malacanang Palace on December 30, 1965, settling in for twenty years. The next morning, before the inauguration ceremonies, there was a private Mass for the family. In his homily, the priest chose as his text the story of a king being told, as the crown was lowered onto his head, that "he had been told the truth for the last time." It was also the last time the king's subjects ever heard the truth.

In the inauguration parade, the CIA's Napoleon Valeriano rode horseback. Vice President Hubert Humphrey represented the White House.

The Kennedy era was over in America, but through the Doppler effect it was just beginning in the Philippines. Ferdinand and Imelda did everything they could to make it seem that Camelot was now theirs.

In September 1966, nine months after his inauguration, Ferdinand flew to Washington with Imelda to see President Johnson. In return for promising to back LBJ's stand in Vietnam, they received millions of dollars in cash from "unvouchered funds." More important than the cash were credits Johnson made available to them through the State Department, the Pentagon, the International Monetary Fund, and the World Bank.

Americans were already familiar with Ferdinand through the press buildup before his election. One of the first post-election image builders appeared in *The New York Times* on November 13, 1965, under the headline: "Philippine 'No. 1' Ferdinand Edralin Marcos." The story said that Ferdinand

> was "No. 1" to his countrymen long before they voted him into the highest ... office. . . . His father, Mariano Marcos, was a well-to-do teacher, lawyer and politician. . . .
>
> As a law student at the University of the Philippines, he won a series of scholarships, debated, became the national small-bore rifle champion and was a member of the boxing, wrestling and swimming teams. In September, 1935 . . . he became implicated in a murder case that made him a national public figure. . . .
>
> Convicted in a trial that became an issue in national politics, he refused a proffered presidential pardon, scored the top grade on his bar examination while out on bail, and then was acquitted by the Supreme Court after arguing his own appeal before the bench.
>
> When the Japanese invaded . . . Marcos fought as a guerrilla officer beside American soldiers. He was wounded five times, won 22 American and Philippine medals, was captured and tortured by the Japanese and was commended by Gen. MacArthur for his exploits in the defense of Bataan.
>
> The war cost Lt. Marcos his father, who was bayoneted by the Japanese.

Since *The New York Times* sets the lead for most North American newspapers, this article was taken as confirmation of these biographical details.

Not all appraisals were so flattering. The November 26, 1965, *Life,* waxing sweet and sour, said that Marcos "had a kind of all-Filipino-boy air about him, as well as a gorgeous wife who had been Miss Manila of 1954. . . . Marcos . . . has a reputation of being both unscrupulous and exceptionally ruthless, and there are those who predict that he will do absolutely nothing about corruption. He is perhaps the only president-elect anywhere to have been convicted of murder. . . ." Then *Life* went on to repeat the usual record: "When Japan invaded the Philippines, Marcos joined the U.S. Army as a lieutenant, was captured at Bataan, survived the Death March, escaped and then fought the Japanese as a guerrilla until the end of the war. He emerged as a colonel with 27 decorations, including the U.S. Silver Star and the Distinguished Service Cross, five wounds and the most heroic record of any Filipino fighter."

Ferdinand's visit to Washington was of major political value to President Johnson on the eve of the 1966 congressional elections in the United States. Americans were asking why their sons had to die in South Vietnam while few of America's allies and aid beneficiaries gave more than token support to the war. Johnson wanted to present Ferdinand as a staunch ally from the area of conflict. Filipino officials returned from Washington with glowing reports that development loans from the United States had been "approved in principle," subject only to President Johnson's signature.

While the public relations puffery was going on in the American press, there was a hidden agenda for the Philippines. "To LBJ from David Bell, Department of State":

> . . . the Government of the Philippines has developed, in consultation with JUSMAG . . . a proposal to provide special military forces to Vietnam. These forces would consist of a 34-man medical and civic action team and a 2,300-man task force composed of an engineering battalion together with security and support units. [But] the Philippine Government cannot provide funds to cover all the costs of these forces for Vietnam. In addition, because these forces are a significant portion of the Philippine armed services, it will be necessary to train and equip replacements for the contingent going to Vietnam: . . . It is highly desirable that the U.S. financial support not be apparent, to avoid . . . accusations that the . . . personnel are U.S. "mercenaries," . . . to effectively conceal the U.S. payment. . . . The use of unvouchered funds is considered necessary. . . . The amount involved for Fiscal year 1965 is $4.5 million.

And in a letter dated April 9, 1965, Bell wrote to Kermit Gordon, director, Bureau of Budget:

> Attached is a memo . . . to the President requesting confirmation that he has already approved the use of unvouchered AID funds to meet costs of a Philippine International Military Assistance Force . . . for Vietnam. . . . In accordance with the sensitivity involved . . . I can assure you that we have taken appropriate security measures to restrict to as limited a group as possible knowledge of U.S. funding of these particular IMAF costs.

Macapagal had intended to send an engineering battalion of two thousand men to Vietnam to accommodate Johnson. Ferdinand had opposed the idea during the campaign, arguing that the battles Filipinos needed to win were in the Philippines, implying that Macapagal was influenced improperly by American pressure, always an effective charge. After only six weeks in office he reversed himself and dispatched the battalion, alienating Filipino intellectuals who had supported him. As they saw it, their country's greatest need was a new definition of its Asian identity, yet here was another president catering to a former colonial power. Ferdinand then backpedaled furiously, saying he wanted to rekindle the anti-Communist fervor of his people and to show potential foreign investors that the Philippines was not "turning down a path of sterile nationalism."

In advance of the Marcos state visit, presidential adviser Walt Rostow gave Johnson the following summary:

> Marcos Objectives: To highlight his support for our policies in Southeast Asia and to obtain tangible evidence of American support for his leadership and for rapid improvement in the Philippine economy . . . to advance his country and to overcome criticism of his strongly pro-American leads. . . . To use the Army in rural development projects as the most effective means of . . . coping with rising popular dissatisfactions . . . to hold his critics at bay he needs . . . to bring home some concrete achievements on the veterans' benefits and claims problem (a hot political issue in Manila). . . .
>
> Our Objectives: Keep Marcos on our side and help him silence his critics. Keep him and the Philippines cooperative regarding the use of our bases in the Philippines, especially as regards logistic support for Vietnam. . . . Continue and possibly expand Philippine engagement in Vietnam. . . .

As the Marcos visit to Washington approached, the skids were greased with gifts. Imelda's brother Kokoy, named special envoy to coordinate the visit, arranged to see LBJ to present him with the head of a wild water buffalo, supposedly shot by Ferdinand himself. Wags in the State Department christened the beast "Nalundasan." In Manila, other gifts were boxed for shipping: three Philippine hardwood tables, three swivel chairs, and a cabinet. The University of Michigan announced that it was going to give Ferdinand an honorary degree in civil law.

No fewer than ten diplomatic cables dealt with the question of what official gift Johnson should "properly" give Marcos, finally settling on a desk set, a silver cigar box, and a silver picture frame. Then there was the problem of what to inscribe on the cigar box. Researchers came up with the peroration from Ferdinand's inaugural address: "Come then, let us march together toward the dream of greatness." The U.S. Embassy nervously cabled: "Possible problem arises from fact that phrase . . . might well be construed to mean 'Let the U.S. and the Philippines march together.' " LBJ decided to throw in a set of golf clubs, so the Department of State cabled Manila urgently: "We need President Marcos' swing weight, flexibility of shaft, height, age, handicap and whether he is right- or left-handed." Finally, State advised its embassy that the Pentagon was

> ready and willing to go ahead with presentation Distinguished Service Cross and Silver Star medals on basis that Marcos' U.S. Army records do not . . . show he ever received them. However . . . biographic booklet in official [Philippine] press kit for visit contains picture of Marcos' medals, including DSC and Silver Star, with the following explanation . . . QUOTE *Leading critical patrol and combat missions in such famed battle areas as Mt. Natib, Mt. Samat and Salian River, he (Marcos) won many citations, including Silver Star medal and U.S. Distinguished Service Cross, which General Douglas MacArthur himself pinned on.* UNQUOTE . . . Spence biography jacket shows Marcos wearing Silver Star, but not, apparently, DSC.
>
> . . . You should ask Marcos soonest whether or not he ever received medals and, if not, ascertain his reaction to idea of low key White House presentation on September 14 during afternoon meeting with President Johnson.

Enough questions had been raised in the Philippine press regarding Ferdinand's war record and his dubious medals during the recent election campaign that no American diplomat or intelligence analyst responsible for the Philippines could claim genuine ignorance. It was a scandal in Manila. The U.S. Embassy reported in June of 1965 that Marcos had been publicly denounced as "ignoble and dangerous," his "fraudulent war-damage claims" being but one example. Obviously, Ferdinand would deeply appreciate LBJ's gesture on more than one level.

It was known that President Marcos planned to visit former presidents Truman and Eisenhower, the son of Douglas MacArthur, and other prominent Americans in hope of getting them to express support for his claims for veterans' benefits, and the State Department decided to speak to each of these people ahead of time to "forestall [the] possibility [of] their making statements which he might later use in support of Philippine case on such claims." This proposed Filipino vet benefits package would cost the United States about $17 million a year. In a memorandum to President Johnson from his adviser Walt Rostow marked "SECRET," Rostow reminded LBJ about the veterans' claims issue and remarked, "You are familiar with this one," indicating that there had already been some internal discussion of the sensitivities involved. Nevertheless, Johnson needed Marcos's support on Vietnam so badly that any doubts about the legitimacy of his personal claims were set aside.

As the two presidents exchanged greetings on September 14, 1966, Johnson said warmly: "More than anyone here today, Mr. President, you know the price of freedom. You were wounded five times in freedom's cause; you survived the Bataan Death March and for 2 years led a force of guerrillas with great and legendary courage. You wear two Silver Stars. And you carry the Distinguished Service Cross—one of the highest awards a grateful United States can give its heroes."

After twenty years of trying and being rebuffed, Ferdinand had finally succeeded in having no less than an American president confirm war claims that U.S. Army investigators had considered "malicious and criminal." A priceless opportunity existed to capitalize further when he addressed a joint session of the U.S. Congress the next day, ending his speech with the following:

I have been hounded by the loud persistent criticisms that I am much too pro-American in my policies. Perhaps I am—emotionally so. For I was one of the many who gambled everything—life, dreams, and honor—on a faith and the vision of America, when all was lost as the Stars and Stripes for the first time in history was trodden to the ground in Asia. . . .

There is no price tag for faith except justice . . . even the veterans scoff at our own scars in battle. One of these scars I received in trying to save an American comrade. . . .

Yes, my American comrade died in my arms. We were surrounded and we had to break out. He fell and, as he tried to crawl to safety, I returned to him, to fall at his side—Filipino and American blood commingling in Philippine soil.

As I cradled him in my arms to a foxhole, he died with the words: "Tell them back home, you who will live, my only regret in dying is that America has failed us."

I, the Filipino, assured the American, as if this would assuage his dying, "No, America does not forget and will not fail us."

With the applause of Congress still ringing happily in their ears, the Marcoses went off to a presidential reception where Imelda, dressed in Texas yellow, fixed LBJ with a starry-eyed gaze, and sang "Because of You" in Tagalog.

Ferdinand went home with more than a new set of golf clubs. Secretary of State Dean Rusk and Philippine Secretary of Foreign Affairs Narciso Ramos (executive director and chief-of-staff of the Maharlika) exchanged diplomatic notes dealing with U.S. bases in the Philippines. Washington agreed to shorten its lease on the bases from the original period of ninety-nine years to twenty-five years. President Johnson signed two bills liberalizing and extending Filipino vet benefits, one providing additional funds for health and education of dependents, another increasing benefit payments to $25 million a year for the next two years. Marcos also received $20 million to equip five new construction battalions to replace the engineers he would send to Vietnam. Another $45 million was committed for programs such as irrigation, rice production, rural electrification, and feeder-road construction; plus additional funds for surveys, feasibility studies, training, and research. The World Bank approved new credit lines to the Philippines. The wishes of Lyndon Johnson heavily influenced the Bank's decision. Summing up, Finance Secretary Eduardo Romualdez (Imelda's cousin) said the Philippines could expect $125 million from the United States spread over the next two and a half years.

In return, Ferdinand agreed to push through the bill sending Philippine combat engineers to South Vietnam. The troops, he said, were going in support of a principle. He did not explain what principle, but he added that no price was too high to pay for freedom.

Johnson also persuaded Ferdinand to play host just before the U.S. congressional elections to a Vietnam summit meeting in Manila, including the heads of the seven Pacific nations contributing in one way or the other to the war. Johnson wanted to get away from Washington during the campaign rather than perform the obligatory whistle-stop tours in support of Democratic candidates. With Vietnam an important campaign issue, what better than a "surprise" presidential visit to the troops? But to fly 24,000 miles for two hours on the ground in Vietnam (all that security would permit) was stretching credibility. There had to be some compelling reason to take him across the Pacific so that an "unscheduled" side trip to Cam Ranh Bay would seem natural. Johnson hit on what looked like the perfect maneuver: a visit to the boys in Vietnam, and a summit conference on peace in Manila.

To prepare, Ferdinand released $190,000 to patch Manila's potholed roads. Hotels and nightclubs indulged in hasty face-lifting. Johnson's press secretary, Bill Moyers, bustled from airport to embassy to Malacanang Palace making arrangements for everything from protocol dinners to a Lyndon–and–Lady Bird tour of Corregidor. Marcos aides wrote position papers, while Imelda supervised a renovation of the palace. Manila's pickpockets were rounded up by the police and kept aboard a ship offshore for the duration of the summit.

The Manila Summit was convened for all the wrong reasons, so anything useful coming out of it was bound to be accidental. In the end, the only agreement reached was that all six Pacific nations backing Saigon—America, Australia, New Zealand, Philippines, Thailand, and South Korea—would pull out of South Vietnam six months after peace, whenever that occurred. This gave Johnson a piece of paper he could take home with the signatures of his allies, which he could wave and say: "We have a policy. Here it is. We have unity and understanding and a sense of direction for the future. We have reviewed the war and prepared for peace." The only sour note was that South Korea's President Park Chung Hee was outraged at the choice of Manila for the meeting, since six months earlier he had suggested such a conference in Seoul.

While the men talked business, Imelda entertained the ladies. They visited two barrios in Cavite, then toured Taal Volcano. At an old church, she offered Lady Bird a skull and suggested that she might take it home with her.

The last night, Imelda threw a small party at the palace. Three thousand guests saw a procession of decorated barges float along the Pasig River, watched native dances, and wandered under palms and banyan trees illuminated with paper lanterns. President Johnson and all but one of the other leaders appeared in slacks and embroidered white barongs. President Park was alone in wearing a dark business suit.

The heavily publicized Marcos-Johnson rapport of the Washington state visit and the Manila Summit did not last long. It was broken one year later, in December 1967, when the two leaders met again in Australia at the funeral of Prime Minister Harold Holt. By then, LBJ had found Ferdinand too expensive. He sent Filipino troops to Vietnam in a noncombat role, but once Johnson had made his secret bargain and paid his bribe from unvouchered funds, there was no end to the demands Ferdinand made. It was simple extortion. Ferdinand sought— and received—more and more aid under the table, some of which he and Imelda deposited discreetly in Swiss banks, some of which lined the pockets of his friends and cronies, and some of which was used to turn the Philippines into a police state. With Johnson's help, Ferdinand was able to transform the Philippine armed forces, the Constabulary, the police forces, and the intelligence services into a new centralized command under his personal control. No other Filipino president since Quezon had been able to bring all the security services under his personal authority and simultaneously purge them of factions loyal to other power centers. Johnson made it possible for Ferdinand to remain in Malacanang forever, if he wished.

Even that was not enough. At the Holt funeral, according to William Bundy, President Marcos presented President Johnson with a new shopping list. Johnson hit the roof and warned Bundy: "If you ever bring that son of a bitch within fifty miles of me again, I'll have your job."

Nine

LADY BOUNTIFUL

UPON BECOMING FIRST LADY, Imelda Marcos did something no other Filipino First Lady had ever done—she became actively involved in national affairs. With what seemed to be a free hand from Ferdinand, she embarked upon a visionary building program of Olympic proportions. She began restoring Manila's old walled city of Intramuros as a tourist attraction, and started filling in waterfront on Manila Bay to build a sprawling Cultural Center that would be the Acropolis of a new Athens in the Pacific. This was followed by a film center modeled on the Parthenon, where she could stage film festivals, Miss Universe contests, and professional boxing matches between such reigning champions as Joe Frazier and Mohammed Ali.

"She would sow beauty where she could," said one of her official biographers, Kerima Polotan. At Luneta Park and around historic cemeteries, she sponsored tree planting, and beautification and cleanliness drives. She held a yearly nationwide contest for the most beautiful town, barrio, and schoolhouse. If Filipinos could have order and cleanliness around them, she believed, they would be clean and orderly.

"Yes," Imelda said, "the Filipinos are living in slums and hovels. But what counts is the human spirit, and the Filipinos are smiling. They smile because they are a little healthy, a little educated, and a little loved. And for me the real index of this country is the smiles of the people, not the economic index." Another time she remarked, "It is to the psychology of poverty that our education must address itself. But it is not merely material poverty that we speak of. We must begin with

189

spiritual and moral poverty. We gain nothing if in the achievement of material goals, we sacrifice the integrity of our heritage, our minds and the nobility of our spirit."

Her social welfare program included Christmas bags, home gardens, disaster relief, and a project called Save-a-Life-in-Every-Barrio. "Culture and art and a taste for the beautiful," she lectured, "must lead to goodness."

There were moments when people wondered if such noble sentiments were entirely sincere. In an interview, Jaime Ferrer confirmed that evidence of corruption came in the very first year under the Marcoses. "Imelda had a Christmas drive for the poor, which was the traditional job for the First Lady. But all the checks were made out to her, and were deposited in her name. They were not used for the poor. Word got around. What I remember is that the following year, San Miguel Corporation did not send checks again. They sent goods." When there were calamities, earthquakes, typhoons, and eruptions of volcanoes, foreign embassies donated emergency food. A U.S. Embassy official recalled, "We naturally checked to see if Imelda's people were following through, and discovered that she was withholding our food bags for a day or two till they could each be tagged 'A Gift from the First Lady.'"

The Philippine-American Cultural Foundation had raised 90,000 pesos to build a modest Cultural Center, and Imelda adopted both the fund and the project. "She was familiar with the pain of abortive talent," wrote Polotan, "and knew that many a Filipino artist died unheard because he had none to hear him, and nowhere to be heard." Imelda declared that it was all to be done without government involvement. However, Ferdinand contributed a stretch of government-owned waterfront on Roxas Boulevard, a dramatic site looking across the water to the mountains of Bataan. Imelda commissioned a land reclamation project to expand the waterfront site far out into the bay (the idea had originated with Harry Stonehill). In a matter of months she had raised 35 million pesos. Some came from a benefit show of the musical *Flower Drum Song*—one night for the wealthy Chinese community, another night for non-Chinese. Caltex and San Miguel beer underwrote the production. Other contributions were collected by personal letter, a call, or supper at the palace. The Liberal opposition called her style "indirect coercion, indirect bribery, sophisticated extortion."

"I'm like Robin Hood," Imelda would say, with a twinkle in her eye,

"I rob the rich . . . it's done with a smile. It's the rich you can terrorize. The poor have nothing to lose." On her birthday and Ferdinand's, or their wedding anniversary, Imelda asked the rich to give donations to the Center. When wealthy foreigners arrived, she met them at the airport, to lunch with them and get donations. In exchange for cutting ribbons and attending inaugurations, she demanded donations in kind: cement, tiles, fixtures, drapery, and carpets. The Eltra Corporation of New York donated a printing press; the Rockefeller Foundation gave fellowships; a New York businessman gave a Steinway concert grand.

"My projects run into the billions," Imelda said, referring to pesos. "But many of these projects are built with money from the private sector, from friends here and abroad. It's so funny. I just invite them to a fund-raising lunch and in one hour I get twelve million or thirteen million pesos. That's why they kid that there are two bureaus of internal revenue here. The official one and Mrs. Marcos." San Miguel Corporation chairman Andres Soriano, Jr., said, "We don't say 'no.' But we're free to discuss the amount."

The Cultural Center was planned in four parts—a library, a museum, an amphitheater, and a theater seating seven thousand. The centerpiece and first to be built was the theater, a monumental white slab set off by wide reflecting pools, containing a large auditorium for performances of opera, ballet, and symphony. Imelda was determined to have perfect acoustics, and a stage deep enough for grand opera, broad enough for a troop of horses. It was originally planned to cost 15 million pesos, and to be finished in two years. Polotan wrote that "by Christmas of 1968, it had run through 48 million pesos with but three fourths of the work done. The principal cause was the variable cost of material. . . . In just two years, prices rose by 30 to 40 percent, and these included elevators, escalators, lighting, and other electronic equipment." While Polotan said costs had gone up 40 percent, expenditures were in fact 300 percent more than first estimated.

After a year, the Center was broke. Imelda seemed stymied by the continual escalation in costs, but it was a problem of her own making. Around her had begun to gather like schools of shrimp a great following of lickspittles, votaries, intriguers, and opportunists. Everybody got a piece of the action. A Manila architect described how it happened: "Several key men in the construction industry decided, just for fun, to work out the percentage of project cost that went to kickbacks. The process started at the top when a senior official demands 20 percent.

. . . As the inflated bid works its way down the system from general contractor, to subcontractor, to supplier—each adding . . . 10 percent for himself—the total for kickbacks grows as high as 80 percent of overall contract costs." The people Imelda liked most were put in charge of her projects and became instant millionaires. In the Philippines, in polite company they are called *tutas* (lapdogs), in not-so-polite company *sip-sips* (cocksuckers). They provided her with the beginnings of her own espionage network; what the husbands told Ferdinand, the wives and their lovers told Imelda. These courtiers and courtesans needed nourishment. Culture had become Imelda's own personal pork barrel, as patron of the arts.

In a sense the Cultural Center was a monument to Lyndon Johnson, a Texas-sized white elephant. For it was Johnson's generosity that helped to make Imelda independently wealthy, and caused this first display of what Filipinos called her "edifice complex." Imelda had received a direct infusion from Johnson, a $3.5 million slice from the Philippine veterans' "special" educational funds. When Johnson first learned during their Washington trip that Imelda wanted to build a Cultural Center, he proposed that she use part of the new package of veterans' benefits he was wrapping up at Congress as a $50 million *cadeau* for President Marcos. However, this was Ferdinand's personal preserve, so Imelda wisely demurred. Johnson then came up with a Philippine claim that nobody had heard of in years, a claim for veterans' educational benefits of $28 million that Congress had not acted upon before. Johnson said he would approve the bill and see it through Congress if Imelda promised to use a big piece of it for her Cultural Center. After discussing LBJ's proposition with her husband, she agreed, but insisted that she would take only $3.5 million of it for the Center, instead of the whole $28 million. Johnson asked Montana's Senator Mike Mansfield for a helping hand and Mansfield graciously saw Imelda's bill through. (Her $3.5 million slice supposedly was set aside as a trust fund to maintain the project. But within months, the Center was flat broke and unfinished.)

As Finance Secretary Romualdez calculated, the public proceeds from the Marcos state visit to Washington came to $125 million counting only grants from the U.S. Congress, State Department, and Pentagon. The Romualdez total is the sum of the following amounts: U.S. Congress $50 million in increased vet benefits, State Department general civic aid programs at $45 million plus $10 million for surveys and research, and from the Pentagon $20 million to create a new construction battalion to replace the group sent to Vietnam.

In addition to this, however, LBJ personally authorized $38.8 million in secret Pentagon military funds, with no insistence on accountability, over and above the regular $61.6 million given to the Philippines as normal military aid during the period from 1966 to 1971. Because of its secret nature, this $38.8 million was in effect a gift to Ferdinand for him to use as he wished. Adding on the $28 million in "special" educational funds for veterans' dependents and the $3.6 million paid to the Marcoses from AID unvouchered funds bumped the grand total to $195.4 million. (This does not include the open-ended new credits from the IMF and World Bank that became ongoing programs, and eventually ran into the billions.)

What happened to all this money when it got to Manila? Little of it seems to have reached its intended destination. Eventually, enough questions were raised about Johnson's grants that a secret investigation was conducted by the U.S. Government Accounting Office and a congressional committee, producing some surprising details.

The cash grant of $3.6 million in unvouchered funds supposedly was made to help pay the expenses of the Philippine Civic Action Group (PHILCAG) sent to Vietnam. This money was delivered by State Department courier to Manila in quarterly installments between October 1966 and October 1969, in the form of U.S. Treasury checks of approximately $500,000 each. The Johnson administration did not impose any conditions on the use of the funds. The checks were endorsed and cashed by Defense Secretary Ernesto Mata and were deposited in the Philippine Veterans Bank in an account set aside as a "special intelligence fund" for the personal use of Ferdinand Marcos. The Philippine Military and Veterans Bank had been set up in 1963 with a U.S. grant of $25 million. Ferdinand held in trust over half of its shares, so the bank was entirely under his control. (By 1984, the bank was saddled with $64.9 million in bad debts in the form of loans made to Marcos cronies during the time that secret police chief Fabian Ver was the bank's chairman.)

Although the United States had already paid secretly to have the PHILCAG unit sent to Vietnam, and to cover its expenses in the field, Ferdinand proceeded to move a bill in his own Congress to pay for the mission again, in effect double billing, to the tune of 35 million pesos. This would have been blatantly obvious to those at the U.S. Embassy, the State Department, the Pentagon, and the White House, who were aware that PHILCAG had already been paid for, but their lips were sealed.

Some Filipino legislators, not realizing that they were being asked to pay a double bill, fought its passage on the basis that the Philippines should not be participating in the Vietnam War to begin with. Later, when the U.S. Congress began investigating the PHILCAG payments, the implication was that the Philippine government as a whole had misappropriated the funds. "Unfortunately for the Philippines," said a columnist in the Manila *Evening News*, "the implication of the rhubarb is that the Philippine government was paid a 'handsome fee' for sending a contingent to South Vietnam and that this country misused that money. Either the Americans are telling a lie or there is too much corruption in the government." In Washington, Senator Stuart Symington said, "It is a pretty shoddy story." He then explained that the Nixon administration insisted on keeping the matter secret, so he could not discuss it further. (Today, the investigation is still secret.)

The Marcoses were able to be poor in Manila and rich overseas by salting—stashing all their hard currency in secret bank accounts in Europe, North America, and the Caribbean. The Marcos income tax returns declared a gross income of only $17,000 in 1960, rising to $60,000 in 1961, and to $69,300 in 1966, when he ran for president. In that same year, Ferdinand listed his total assets at only $30,000. Such modesty was becoming for a presidential candidate running on a law-and-order, anti-corruption platform. In truth, Ferdinand was already a millionaire many times over, with safe-deposit drawers crammed with dollars, offshore corporations all over the world, and large bags of money arriving at their home so frequently that Imelda had given up counting the contents. Such modesty might be necessary in Manila, but the Marcos family could afford to be more extravagant on foreign trips where nobody was watching. When Imelda took her eldest daughter Imee on a shopping spree to the United States in June 1968, when the Cultural Center was still broke, the two ladies spent a total of $3.3 million in only eight weeks, or just under $100,000 each shopping day, in fashionable boutiques from coast to coast. This was nearly the amount LBJ had given her from the vets' special educational fund—$3.5 million—which shows that he was an uncanny judge of what a First Lady needed for pocket money.

In March 1968, Imelda and Ferdinand opened their first separate numbered accounts at Crédit Suisse in Zurich, providing the bank managers with their real names and the aliases William Saunders and Jane Ryan. In all, documents reveal that they eventually opened more than half a dozen secret accounts in Switzerland alone, mostly in Crédit Suisse and the Swiss Bank Corporation, and deposited in them over the years more than $1.5 billion, some think as much as $5 billion. In addition to using aliases, the Marcoses gave their Swiss bankers an elaborate code to authenticate all messages they sent from Manila, a code that varied according to the month of the year. Ferdinand's magic "7" appeared repeatedly in his account numbers.

Other large sums were salted in offshore accounts through corporations based in Hong Kong, the Netherlands Antilles, the Bahamas, and the Cayman Islands, set up by Jose Campos and managed by cronies Roberto Benedicto and Antonio Floirendo, a Filipino businessman who was especially close to Imelda and often fronted for her overseas.

Aside from putting more than $1 billion in their secret Swiss accounts, documents also show that the Marcoses salted more than $200 million in banks in other countries, including Chase Manhattan Bank and First National City Bank (Citibank) in New York. They also set up a Liechtenstein account, called the Sandy Foundation, and instructed its trustee Markus Geel in Zurich that when either Imelda or Ferdinand wanted to withdraw cash, they would send him a cable wishing him "Happy Birthday." When he received the cable, Geel was to contact his associate in Hong Kong, Ralph Klein, who would then fly to Manila to get their instructions personally. This was only one of eighteen overseas foundations the Marcoses set up whose assets eventually totaled at least $183 million.

If Ferdinand and Imelda declared a net worth of only $30,000 in 1966, where did all these hundreds of millions come from—besides that given them by President Johnson? The evidence indicates that a lot of the money came from war reparations paid to the Philippines by the United States and Japan, from the Philippine Treasury, from veterans' benefits and other grants deposited in the Marcos "special intelligence fund," from credits given to the Philippines under various World Bank projects, and from the seizure of more than 215 Philippine firms belonging to other people. (In 1986, for example, the U.S. government reported that over $226 million in Economic Support Funds provided to the Marcos administration could not be accounted for.) These diversions of money by Ferdinand and Imelda have since been labeled racketeering, mail fraud, wire fraud, extortion, embezzlement, theft, transportation of stolen property, and illegal laundering of funds.

Some U.S. government officials were aware of what the Marcoses were doing at the time. This is apparent from various clues. An undersecretary of state cautioned Ferdinand in March 1968 (three months after the sour LBJ confrontation in Australia) that he should not request any more American aid "when so many wealthy Filipinos were not keeping their money in the country." The following year, 1969, a secret CIA report on Ferdinand stated that he had already stolen at least several hundred million dollars. Naturally this report was top secret, only for circulation within a small circle in Washington, but this circle included top officials of the White House, the State Department, and the intelligence community. One of those who read it was an officer of the Intelligence & Research Bureau at the State Department, named John Marks. His boss at I&R (or INR, as it is sometimes called) was Ray Cline, previously CIA station chief in Taiwan from 1958 to 1962, who had been such a great success in East Asia that he had become the CIA's deputy director for intelligence, before moving to the State Department. Marks later left the government and collaborated with former CIA official Joseph Marchetti on the book *The CIA and the Cult of Intelligence.* On May 11, 1975, Marks astonished an audience of scholars attending a seminar at Chicago's Lutheran School of Theology with the revelation that the CIA knew as far back as 1969 that Ferdinand and Imelda had already "stolen funds ranging from not lower than several hundred million U.S. dollars to two billion U.S. dollars." The CIA was in a position to know. Over the years, CIA agents actively helped Marcos salt money in America, especially in Hawaii. This became abundantly clear during the fraud trial of Ronald Rewald in Hawaii in 1983–85 when it came out that Rewald's investment firm, Bishop, Baldwin, Rewald, Dillingham & Wong, had been set up as a conduit for CIA funds, and as a way of helping Ferdinand Marcos and a variety of Filipino oligarchs to salt black money in America. The CIA had also been funneling Marcos black money out via Australia and Hong Kong through the Nugan-Hand Bank in Australia, which had branches in Manila, Hong Kong, Singapore, and elsewhere till it collapsed in scandal in 1980. (Both the Rewald and Nugan-Hand affairs are dealt with in a later chapter.)

Ferdinand had been playing games with black money ever since he became a congressman in 1949. But high finance and international intrigue were new to Imelda as an impoverished provincial girl from Leyte, and must have required a period of adjustment. Once she got the hang of it, though, Imelda cut out middlemen and sent couriers with suitcases of money directly to her numbered account at Crédit Suisse in Zurich—so many suitcases that, according to international banking sources, "the bank managers eventually had to ask her to stop."

Imelda wanted to set some money aside for her own use while shopping, so she kept petty cash accounts in America and Europe, and funneled hundreds of thousands of dollars to them. This enabled her to make purchases and investments without having people associate her name with them. At the time she went on her $3.3 million shopping spree with Imee in 1968, she opened an account at Citibank through two close friends, Dr. Daniel Vazquez and his wife, Maria Lusia. Dr. Vazquez ran a clinic in Manila, and Maria Luisa, the daughter of the wealthy Madrigal family, was one of Imelda's Blue Ladies. She often accompanied the First Lady on overseas trips. In the beginning, Mrs. Vazquez personally paid Imelda's bills, apparently with funds provided beforehand by Malacanang Palace. During the June 1968 spree with Imee, Mrs. Vazquez paid for purchases at exclusive boutiques such as Giorgio's in Beverly Hills, using checks drawn on Citibank account number 05069031, which she held jointly with her husband. This was a clumsy arrangement unless Mrs. Vazquez was to accompany Imelda overseas all the time. So in November 1968, the month before the Cultural Center went belly up, Citibank was asked by Dr. and Mrs. Vazquez to add the name "Fernanda Vazquez" to their joint savings account; this was accompanied by a deposit of just under a quarter of a million dollars. Subsequently, all but Fernanda's name were removed from the account and it became hers alone. Fernanda Vazquez and Imelda Marcos were, of course, one and the same. In addition to other evidence, there are pieces of stationery from Malacanang Palace that bear notations in Imelda's handwriting about the balances in the Citibank account of Fernanda Vazquez.

With so much on her mind, Imelda could be forgiven for letting the Cultural Center get a bit out of hand. True, she could easily have paid for the Center any time out of her own purse, but it was a matter of some pride to her that it be built by, as she said, "robbing from the rich."

In February 1969, as a new presidential election campaign got under way, the opposition Liberals tried to discredit her by mounting a concerted attack on her spending. To complete the Center, Imelda had obtained a 20-million-peso foreign loan and had the loan guaranteed by the government's National Investment Development Corporation (NIDC). Since the Cultural Center was Imelda's private pet project, the Liberals wanted to know how a government agency could properly guarantee such a loan. From Imelda's viewpoint, the gadfly in her soup was young Senator Benigno "Ninoy" Aquino. Ninoy was the heir to the vast Aquino holdings in Tarlac, with a family tradition of involvement in politics at the highest level. His father had headed the wartime pro-Japanese Kalibapi party. As a youth, Ninoy had been one of the wealthy playboys who ebbed and flowed around Imelda when she first came to Manila. Their dislike of each other is said to have originated in those days. Apparently he took an interest in her at first, then snubbed her. People said Imelda fixed upon Aquino as a personification of the elite that had always rejected her, and Ninoy had continually aggravated matters by being abrasive and cutting whenever they came into each other's orbits. In his youth, Aquino was also ostentatiously self-centered, a flamboyant young political showman, and he attacked Imelda not only to get under her skin but to get at Ferdinand. In due course, the Marcoses would take their revenge in a variety of ways, putting Aquino through a crucible that matured him into a far more noble figure. But at the time, he was their brashest critic, the sharpest tongue, and their most dangerous rival for the presidency. To make matters worse, Aquino was clean, which made it difficult for them to retaliate with ordinary mud slinging.

In the Senate, where Aquino was doing some empire building of his own, he condemned Imelda's handling of the Center, and asked why it had been undertaken at a time when so many Filipinos were starving or barely subsisting in squalid poverty, tens of thousands in Manila alone living in packing crates and garbage dumps. Imelda's projects, he declared, were necessary only for her vanity. For example, Imelda was ordering statues of the president and herself to be put in the Center. He pointed out that the administration was suddenly full not only of Ilocanos related to Ferdinand, but of people named Romualdez. He said Imelda reminded him of Eva Perón.

When she heard all this, Imelda dissolved in tears of rage, and Ferdinand issued an angry statement: "Those who want to destroy me should fight like men and leave the women and children out of it." On this signal from "the boss" (as he was known within his own circle), Ferdinand's supporters everywhere chivalrously protested that it was un-manly to drag a woman into the political mud. The Cultural Center's wealthy donors threatened to withdraw. Imelda spent a week begging them not to. When the controversy subsided, biographer Polotan wrote, "There was still the Center to finish, and the Liberals still had offered not one helpful suggestion. Instead, they continued to harp on the Center. As for the charge of nepotism, Imelda herself would gladly step aside, but she wished to make certain that politics would not kill the Center, as it had killed a lot of other things in the country." This was the beginning of an intense public rivalry between Imelda and Ninoy, which would lead ultimately to his undoing—and to hers.

When the Cultural Center was finished at last, Imelda wanted the hall inaugurated in a manner emphasizing Philippine roots. The result was a pageant-drama involving an orchestra of native instruments, dance, solo and choral singing, pantomime, to a story in an ancient form of Tagalog, which not even the Tagalog speakers in the audience could understand. *The Golden Salakot* was based on a Philippine legend of the hero Puti, who sets sail with his followers from Borneo, lands on the island of Panay, and cons the local ruler out of his property by giving him a golden salakot, a traditional piece of Filipino headgear. Roughly equivalent to pulling the wool over everybody's eyes.

The Marcoses attempted to get President Richard Nixon to attend the gala opening, or at least Julie and David Eisenhower, but Nixon sent California's Governor Ronald Reagan. The gala was an opportunity to show Manila that Imelda and Ferdinand had international celebrities on their side. When she learned that Reagan was coming on Air Force One, Imelda tried to get free seats on the plane for a mob of Hollywood friends; the White House firmly refused.

No detail of protocol was overlooked. Governor Reagan's office in Sacramento was informed that he would be in Manila on the fifty-second birthday of President Marcos. He took a gift, and Nancy Reagan thoughtfully brought a gift for Imelda as well, a jade tree she herself had designed. Reagan was advised by the Department of State that he had to be prepared to wear a formal barong buttoned at the neck without a tie (the Spaniards did not permit Filipinos to wear ties), tuxedo trousers to be worn with a belt, not suspenders, and a white, round-neck T-shirt under the barong. The Reagans were perfect guests of Malaca-nang, and Embassy Manila soberly advised Washington that everyone was impressed by "the Governor's good-humored and effective performance." It was the beginning of a warm and lasting friendship between the Reagans and the Marcoses.

Not all celebrities were so eager to get an invitation to Malacanang. When they came to Manila to do a show in the course of a world tour, the Beatles received an invitation to perform in private for Ferdinand and Imelda before they left. It was hot and they were tired, so the Beatles gave it a miss. Imelda was sorely miffed. Security was withdrawn from the Beatles' entourage, private exits at Manila International Airport were blocked, the escalator was shut off, and a 100,000-peso tax assessment was slapped on the Beatles' manager. As the group tried to board their plane, a mob surged forward, shoved the singers, kicked and slugged a member of their party, and shouted unprintables. The Beatles vowed never to return to Manila without an H-bomb. Said son Bong-Bong irritably: "I prefer the Rolling Stones anyway."

While Imelda was busy with the Cultural Center, Ferdinand was using his new presidential powers to shut down the private armies, smuggling strongholds, and warlord sanctuaries of all his rivals. During his first month in office he sent paratroopers jumping into the smugglers' island of Semirara, between Mindoro and Panay, and sent marines wading ashore at the village of Capipisa on Luzon's south coast. A private aviation company was shut down for the same reason. He reshuffled the Constabulary to bring it entirely under his control, putting his own men in command, appointed a new chief of customs, and replaced the director of prisons. (The man he put in charge of the prison system was Vicente "Banjo" Raval, the friend who had accompanied him to Mindanao to see Wendell Fertig during World War II. Raval was eventually promoted to brigadier general and became chief of the Constabulary.)

To casual onlookers this appeared to be a new broom sweeping clean, a serious law-and-order administration taking a firm grip on corruption. But before long, the real purpose began to dawn. The price of a pack of smuggled U.S. cigarettes jumped in one month by 30 percent. While most people thought this was because Ferdinand had blocked the pipeline, others guessed that the new president was taking an extra cut off the top to pay his bills. They pointed out that while Marcos was cracking down on some smugglers, he was helping others. When Macapagal had tried to expose Ferdinand's involvement in the Bocalan ring smuggling U.S. cigarettes into the islands, by getting at him through Fabian Ver, Marcos simply had Ver transferred to his personal staff and sent to America for special police training. Lino Bocalan had been denounced and arrested, but now that Ferdinand was president, Bocalan was liberated and permitted to go off for a world tour. On his return, Ferdinand helped get him elected governor of Cavite, where he was able to resume smuggling without further interference. If Bocalan now felt like charging 30 percent more per pack, there was not much doubt where the extra revenue was going.

Similar strange things were happening in the tobacco bloc. After Stonehill, Brooks, and Lim were all expelled or barred from the Philippines, their tobacco interests were turned over to Congressman Floro Crisologo. Peasant growers got their credit from the Crisologo bank, cured their leaves in Crisologo sheds, and sold their leaf to Crisologo. When farmers attempted to get around him, Crisologo created a tobacco blockade. On the only highway to Manila, his troopers set up a roadblock and collected $500 on every truckload of tobacco leaving the province. According to Primitivo Mijares, a palace insider who later defected, Ferdinand ran "a triangular tobacco monopoly" in which Crisologo looked after day-by-day operations, secret policeman Fabian Ver oversaw Bocalan's smuggling of foreign brands into Cavite, and Ferdinand served as their mastermind. Crisologo was not happy. "Floro berated both Marcos and Ver for grabbing the lion's share of the proceeds of the tobacco monopoly," Mijares said. "Crisologo even threatened to expose the entire operation." Apparently he also had learned that Stonehill cronies Brooks and Lim were coming back to Manila, and this threatened his part in the monopoly. He did not have to wait long for an answer. While kneeling in prayer at Sunday Mass, two assassins stepped out of a confessional booth and shot him in the head. His murder remained unsolved, although locals maintained that the murderers were felons facing capital punishment who agreed to do the job in return for knowing that their families would never want for anything again. Mijares discussed the killing with members of Ver's presidential security command at Malacanang Palace and was told that the killers were " 'silenced' while trying to collect [the] fee."

After ten months of "all-out war" on smuggling, not one boss or financier of a smuggling syndicate had been prosecuted or imprisoned. The biggest protection racket of all was being run by Marcos himself. He put on the squeeze by sending in the marines, then let the culprits go free, in a variation of carrot-and-stick. In this version, Marcos hit them with a stick till they gave him their carrots.

His "crackdown" had impact as far away as Zamboanga. Traditionally, smuggling in the Sulu Sea was portrayed as a Muslim enterprise, with Moro smugglers owing their loyalty to the sultans. In reality, most Moro smugglers were fronting for Chinese financiers in Zamboanga; since World War II, these Chinese owed their fealty to the KMT in Taiwan, through the Federation of Chinese Chambers in Manila. In what was portrayed as an attempt to control Muslim smuggling, Ferdinand introduced a barter trade market for the Sulu Sea, to cut off the flow of pesos used to purchase smuggled goods. Its real purpose was to bring pressure on the existing Chinese syndicates until they manifested a new loyalty directly to Ferdinand and then to Taiwan. Once they met his requirements, he returned the favor by having Constabulary soldiers escort smugglers to provide safe conduct. The navy thereafter was regarded as the main supplier of diesel fuel and protection for Sulu smugglers, while Ferdinand's army controlled the biggest marijuana plantations in the Sulu archipelago.

Another type of smuggling also took up much of Ferdinand's time— technical smuggling. Unlike the kind of smuggling Bocalan was doing in fast boats at night, technical smuggling went on in broad daylight on Manila's docks. Cargo was unloaded in the normal manner, but documents were falsified—either by undervaluing the cost of the goods being imported and thus paying a fraction of actual duties, or by misdeclaring the contents of shipments altogether and importing goods that competed with struggling native industry—through the connivance of importers, customs officers, and President Marcos himself. The scam worked because customs officials earned only 360 pesos (about $93) a month. Industrial losses due to technical smuggling were estimated at $350 million a year, plus $85 million in lost tax revenue. By allowing foreign goods to be smuggled in this way, infant local industries had their tariff protection undercut. So while one part of the government was attempting to build up local industry by providing loans for new equipment and expanded facilities, another part of the government was sabotaging the effort by permitting technical smuggling in return for kickbacks. This was essentially what Ferdinand had arranged with Harry Stonehill fifteen years earlier when he pushed through legislation to build up the bright-leaf tobacco industry with one hand while enabling Stonehill to rip off the infant industry with the other. Ferdinand got kickbacks building the industry, and more kickbacks tearing it down.

Hardest hit were embroidery processors. The Philippines is a world center for embroidery, supplying a major share of the market in fine lingerie for Europe and North America. Because of the detailed needlework involved, the world's leading brassiere manufacturers are based in Manila. In a typical scam, a firm posing as an embroidery factory, but with capitalization of only $2,000, was able to bring in tax-free fabrics worth over $1 million. These textiles were supposed to be under consignment from famous labels in the United States and Japan, to be embroidered and then re-exported. But no major brand in New York or Tokyo would trust valuable materials to a firm with such measly capitalization.

An embittered ex-crony whose properties were given to a Marcos military ally in the 1970s put it this way: "As far back as the 1960s, when Marcos was a congressman, he was known as a 10 percenter. Business people wanting favors turned over 10 percent of their shares to him—and they got their favors."

Ferdinand took a special interest in customs procedures on the humblest transactions, even taking a percentage off the top of shipments of canned sardines. Documents found in Malacanang Palace show that importers routinely paid him a "donation" of 15 pesos for every carton of canned fish brought into the country, in one instance paying him 4.5 million pesos to import three hundred thousand cartons. Another importer offered to make a special deal if Ferdinand would allow 15 million cartons of canned sardines from Japan to be "transshipped" through Manila supposedly on their way to the Middle East. Philippine laws permitted foreign goods to be transshipped so long as none were diverted into the local economy—a restriction easily bypassed. In this case, the Japanese sardines were obtained at a "special" price (possibly because they were contaminated or past their shelf life), brought to Manila for transshipment, and ended up in Philippine food markets. The difference between the "special" price and the market value enriched everyone from Ferdinand on down. As World Health Organization investigators discovered, similar deals were struck for foreign drugs past their shelf life. These were dumped in the Philippines, and ended up on shelves in *sari-sari* stores.

One of the best examples of Ferdinand's stick-and-carrot game at work was his appointment of Colonel Jacinto Gavino, a retired army officer, as customs commissioner. Gavino had an unparalleled reputation for honesty and efficiency, the perfect appointee to convince people that the Marcos administration was serious about ending corruption. To put a stop to technical smuggling, Gavino invited trade groups such as the Textile Mills Association, the Pulp and Paper Manufacturers, and the Association of Drug Manufacturers to provide advisers at the docks to see that competing importers paid full duty. They also kept a sharp eye on customs officials. Gavino awarded new contracts to supervise the unloading of cargoes and the collection of fees. Manila was infamous for pilferage and diversion; cargo bound for the port carried the world's highest insurance rates. Thanks to Gavino, customs collections rose dramatically, and Ferdinand was able to claim after only a few months that he had cut smuggling there by 40 percent.

But before the end of 1966, Gavino had been fired. As the editor of Manila's magazine *Graphic* put it back in 1967 before Ferdinand closed the publication down, "Because of such splendid work, and for stepping on the toes of big shots who have had to reduce their 'business' at customs, Gavino found himself out . . .by presidential edict. Without much ado and . . . [not] a single sentence of explanation to the public . . . Gavino was relieved of his duties as customs boss." He was replaced by Ferdinand's lawyer, Juan Ponce Enrile. Ferdinand regularly used Enrile as a surgical glove. As customs boss, undersecretary of finance, and insurance commissioner, Enrile was able to "speed up" paperwork from customs to finance and back. "This saves a lot of time and effort," the editors of *Graphic* commented sarcastically.

The moment he took over from Gavino, Enrile announced that he would never be able to bring smuggling and corruption under control, and that it would be best if Congress spent a few years studying the issue. The fact that Gavino had already solved the problem was conveniently forgotten. He had done his job too well.

What he was doing to the economy, Ferdinand was also doing to public security and law enforcement—turning them into his own fiefdom. In the old system, municipal police forces came under the authority of mayors; provincial Constabulary were controlled by governors and congressmen. This made regional warlords possible, but in an archipelago bosses or warlords on each island are inevitable. To "reform" this system, Ferdinand rammed through legislation to put all local police under a central administration; because he himself appointed the central administration, this put all police under his direct command.

What Filipinos were witnessing was a consolidation of power in the hands of one man—the creation of a police state and the birth of a dictatorship. President Johnson secretly authorized a multi-million-dollar plan to reorganize, retrain, and re-equip the entire Philippine police establishment from top to bottom as a computerized paramilitary force under the control of President Marcos, to suppress any form of protest against his continued rule. It was an extraordinary gift.

The second step was to change the armed forces into a super-police force, by turning its mission from external defense to internal population control. The Philippines had no external enemies, and in any case its defense was guaranteed by the United States. The remodeling of the police and army was directed toward one end: suppressing internal dissent, including whatever Ferdinand chose to identify as subversive. Peculiar to the Philippine constitution was the power granted the president to make a personal determination of "imminent" subversion, to suspend the writ of habeas corpus, and to declare martial law whenever he personally determined that there was a danger of "imminent" subversion.

Ferdinand intended to suppress any and all resistance to his personal rule, whether it arose from political activity by rivals, criticism by journalists, protests by students, demonstrations by labor, or armed resistance by farmers. He understood that American officials were impatient with complex ideas, preferring labels, so the most powerful and flexible word in Washington's vocabulary was "subversive." Ferdinand held long talks with the U.S. Embassy in which he pushed the idea that his dearest purpose in life was to suppress Communists and other subversives. On December 15, 1966, three months after he returned from his state visit to President Johnson, a "Survey of Philippine Law Enforcement" was begun under the USAID Office of Public Safety (AID/OPS). Heading the survey was Frank Walton. Between them, Marcos and Walton instituted radical and ominous changes in the training, organization, and management of the Philippine police and armed forces.

Walton had just reorganized the police of South Vietnam into a paramilitary force for counterinsurgency and urban population control. After he was finished in Manila, Walton would move on to Iran, where he reorganized the Shah's police into a paramilitary force and remodeled the secret police, SAVAK, into the terror organization the world has since come to know and love. In all three cases, the excesses made possible by Walton's extreme security systems eventually contributed to the downfall of the regimes in question.

Under Walton's guidance, America provided counterinsurgency training for hundreds of Filipino police and army officers at military schools like Fort Bragg and Fort Benning, the U.S. Army Intelligence School, the International Police Academy in Washington, the FBI National Academy, and the Border Patrol training center in Los Fresnos, Texas. In the Philippines, academies were established at Baguio, Fort Bonifacio, Legaspi City, Bacolod City, Cebu, Tacloban, Cagayan de Oro, Zamboanga, and at the Constabulary's Special Warfare Training Center at Laur, Nueva Escija. These centers later were turned into detention camps for political prisoners.

Mobile U.S. training teams directed by the CIA, the FBI, the Secret Service, and the Border Patrol came to the Philippines to teach army and police agents the latest techniques of torture, surveillance, explosives, and terrorism. The Agency for International Development's Office of Public Safety (OPS) had parallel programs under way in South Vietnam and the Philippines, designed, as Filipino sociologist Walden Bello put it, "to institutionalize the most advanced techniques of information and confession-extraction from psychological torture, and selective beatings—methods remarkably similar to those employed in Brazil, Korea, Vietnam, Iran and Uruguay, all of which have received significant amounts of OPS assistance and training." OPS eventually became so notorious that the U.S. Congress phased out the program. The 1974 Foreign Assistance Act prohibited further use of foreign aid funds for the training and financial support of foreign police forces. This was intended to bring USAID's involvement in these programs to an end. But the White House got around this by continuing police training under the International Narcotics Control Program run jointly by USAID and the Drug Enforcement Agency.

U.S. investigators, including former Attorney General Ramsey Clark, found a Filipino officer commanding a compound of tortured political prisoners who had received his training at Fort Bragg and Fort Benning. One of Clark's aides stated that "we found . . . evidence of torture, approximately eight 14-inch reinforcing rods next to a single-burner electric plate." Also in a small back room were a number of auto batteries attached to a recharging device.

Some men were trained in Taiwan at a special school Ray Cline had set up with the agreement of Chiang Ching-kuo. The Political Warfare Cadres Academy is at Peitou, outside Taipei. Since 1959, the Academy has offered two-month training courses in "psychological warfare and techniques of interrogation." Graduates are very circumspect but admit: "We were taught that to defeat communism, we had to be cruel; you have to be as cruel as the enemy." Cline arranged for American military personnel, drawn from the Military Assistance Advisory Group stationed on Taiwan, to conduct the classes. In twenty-eight years, the Academy has graduated thousands of Taiwanese, Filipinos, and leaders of death squads in El Salvador, Paraguay, Argentina, Guatemala, and Honduras. The Academy often recruits its students during meetings of the Asian People's Anti-Communist League and the World Anti-Communist League. Taiwan customarily offered to pay all the "students'" expenses.

Walton had the enthusiastic help of Filipino intelligence officers who had been trained by Lansdale and the CIA under President Magsaysay, and who had then moved on with Napoleon Valeriano to become advisers in Indochina. As many as ten thousand counterinsurgency jobs in Indochina were filled by Filipinos, in CIA-financed fronts such as Operation Brotherhood, Eastern Construction, Vinnel Corporation, International Volunteer Services, Air America, and Bird & Sons. They brought these skills back to Manila and applied them on their own countrymen under Walton's guidance. Methods first tested on the Viet Cong and Pathet Lao in a state of war were turned on Filipinos in a state of peace.

Walton expanded and modernized police communication networks, improved record systems and internal security. For the first time, tight coordination was introduced between the national police, municipal police, and Constabulary, locking their command structure to that of the National Bureau of Investigation (NBI) and the Armed Forces of the Philippines, all under the personal control of President Marcos.

By the middle of 1970, more than 10,500 policemen had been trained, more than 2,000 specialists in police communications, and 50 senior police officials had attended the Police Academy in Washington. The greatest emphasis was placed on the control of urban protest, which at this time consisted of student demonstrations against further rule by Ferdinand and Imelda.

One result was the creation of the Metropolitan Command (METROCOM) in July 1967, with jurisdiction over all riot control and internal security operations for Greater Manila. To make its job easier, USAID supplied METROCOM with computerized identification systems.

The whole idea, as U.S. Ambassador Henry Byroade put it, in a masterpiece of doublespeak, was to make the police under Marcos more efficient "so that the safety of the public can be improved and maintained." This included giving the NBI a computerized intelligence network and data-processing system at Camp Aguinaldo, hooked to an Inter-Police Coordinating Center in Camp Crame in Manila containing lists of thousands of Filipino citizens considered "political activists" to be arrested during any police sweep. This marvel of American security technology was vested in the new secret police chief of the Philippines, Ferdinand's most loyal follower, Fabian Ver. At this point Ver became one of the most dangerous men in the archipelago.

Fabian Ver was born in Sarrat on January 20, 1920, and used his mother's maiden name. He was said to be an illegitimate half brother of Ferdinand Marcos, having the same father, which could be taken various ways. Imelda had the original Ver home in Sarrat rebuilt and turned into a museum, giving the impression that he came from landed gentry. Aided by a benefactor, Ver became a pre-law student at the University of the Philippines and joined the Constabulary. He spent the war in Ilocos Norte, apparently working with the Japanese in Sarrat, and was listed as a member of the Maharlika.

Ver was a policeman all his life. He served in the PC's criminal records service and its intelligence branch and did a stretch as a prison warden. A colorless man, devoid of humor, he won promotions very slowly; second lieutenant in 1946, first lieutenant in 1953, captain in 1955. In the late 1950s, he was the commander of the Constabulary at Cavite on Manila Bay. During the same period, he was linked to Marcos, Crisologo, and Stonehill in the complicated workings of their tobacco scam. When the Bocalan smuggling scandal burst in 1963, Ver was rescued by Ferdinand and sent to America for training at the Police Chiefs Academy in Washington, at the VIP Protection School run by the U.S. Secret Service, a drug enforcement program at the Treasury Department, and the Police Administration School at the University of Louisville. He also received police training in Hawaii and Los Angeles. (The Secret Service insists it has "no record" of training Ver.)

When Ferdinand became president, Ver was promoted to colonel, chief of the Presidential Guard Battalion, and chief of the civilian Presidential Security Unit, or secret service. During Walton's reorganization of the police establishment, Ver was given a new Presidential Security Agency, with twelve hundred men, computers, telecommunications with scramblers, armored cars, helicopters, and navy patrol vessels. He was also charged with the use of the "black room" at Malacanang Palace where special political prisoners were entertained, and never came out.

Ver apparently enriched himself by kickbacks on the sale of espionage and internal security equipment through the Amworld Corporation, and other kickbacks on high-tech telecommunication systems. In 1984, an American grand jury began probing U.S. defense contracts in the Philippines. Defense Department auditors examined three California companies that won contracts to supply communications equipment to the Philippine armed forces, contracts financed by the Pentagon's foreign military sales program. The companies—Amworld, Telecom Satellites of America, and Digital Contractors—were all set up in 1981 by Ver's friend Raymond Moreno. Amworld purchased $17 million worth of U.S. military communications equipment for the Philippines as part of a $100 million U.S. aid package in 1983. Payments to the company were halted by the Pentagon when evidence surfaced that some of the money may have been diverted to Ver through overpricing.

Ver also apparently received hefty commissions from contracts with local weapons firms that short-changed or overbilled the Philippine military. On behalf of U.S.-based arms traders, Ver awarded secret contracts to companies in the Philippines to produce the weapons. Among the firms was Avacorp, partly owned by Edna Camcam. Ver was married to Aida Petel, with five children, but for many years his mistress and business partner was Edna Camcam. These firms delivered only a fraction of the arms paid for by the armed forces. The rest were diverted to Iran and sold at inflated prices.

As the recipient of these kickbacks, Ver probably had as much on the U.S. agencies and individuals involved as they had on him, which could explain why he was always able to travel freely in and out of the United States. Ver was given so much latitude by Washington that he could support both his wife and his mistress in lavish style, maintaining two families openly, one in the Philippines and one in America.

The development of a police state under Marcos and Ver was recognized as an ominous development from the beginning. As early as 1968, Ninoy Aquino denounced the "menace of militarism," and Manila periodicals drew attention to the way security operations in urban and rural areas were being integrated under a unified command. But few grasped its full significance.

While Fabian Ver served as secret police chief, the top civilian intelligence officials in the Marcos regime were Rafael Salas and Ernesto Maceda. Salas and Maceda handled political espionage through the early years of the Marcos regime. Salas once said of Ferdinand, "He knows the average Filipino: to what degree [he] can be scared, what are the limits before he becomes violent. Within these limits, he will apply any sort of artifice." The way they worked is revealed by a story of how Ferdinand tried to bully Salvador "Doy" Laurel out of running for the Senate in 1967. A few weeks before the Nacionalista nominating convention, Ferdinand ordered Maceda and Salas to do a head-count of delegates. This showed that Laurel would get a place on the Senate ticket, knocking out a Marcos man. Doy's older brothers, called "Pito" (Jose S.) and "Pepito" (Jose B.), were already major figures in the Nacionalista party—Pepito as speaker of the House and Pito as a leading senator. Doy was a dove on the Vietnam issue, and Ferdinand was determined to keep him out of the Senate. The night before the convention, the Laurels threw a house party for the delegates. Ferdinand heard about it, and swung into action.

He arrived at the party with Maceda and Salas. With false conviviality, he said to Doy, "Oh, brod, you're the one I have to talk to." (As old fraternity brothers, they still used this form of address.) They went into the library.

"Brod," said Ferdinand, "I'd like to ask you to withdraw. . . . I'd like to appoint you secretary of justice tonight. Instead of running this year, I'd like you to run for the Senate in 1969."

Doy said he knew he would lose if Ferdinand did not support him, but he would rather lose than withdraw. Ferdinand looked stunned. "Where's Pepito?" he asked. Doy took him to his brother. In private, Ferdinand repeated his offer. Pepito said, "I'm afraid that's completely up to Doy. He makes his own decisions."

Ferdinand looked grim, then smiled and put his arms around Doy like a Mafia don. "In that case, brod, forget that I ever asked you to withdraw." And left.

Only then did Doy discover what had happened. While Ferdinand had the Laurels secluded, Salas and Maceda had moved like eels through the partying delegates and told them that the president had convinced Doy to withdraw from the Senate race in return for a cabinet post. Astounded at this apparent sellout, most of the delegates left. The few that remained told Doy that Salas and Maceda had given each delegate a typed list of the eight candidates Marcos wanted. Doy's name was not on it.

The Laurels struck back. Using a similar typewriter, they prepared a new "Marcos list" of candidates with Doy's name included. Calling in a hundred campaign workers, they stayed up all night and by six o'clock the next morning all delegates had the doctored lists. Each was convinced that the new list was genuine, because he was dragged out of bed to get it. At the convention that day, Doy won his nomination, and went on to win the Senate race.

It was rare that anyone succeeded in outmaneuvering Ferdinand, but his first use of the reorganized police apparatus made 1967 the bloodiest election in Philippine history. There were at least 117 politically motivated killings, most attributed to his U.S.-trained paramilitary and police agents. In the last thirty-six hours, thirty-seven people were killed.

Imelda was also cracking a whip and settling old scores. As the election approached, she invited her cousins, the sisters of Norberto Romualdez, Jr., to lunch at Malacanang. There she let them know that her brother Kokoy was going to run for governor of Leyte, on the Nacionalista ticket, so it would be necessary for Norberto, the Liberal incumbent of twenty years standing, to step down. It was Norberto who had inherited the Romualdez villa in Tacloban and moved into it in 1946 so that he could run for governor of Leyte—obliging Imelda and her family to move back into their shack. The time had come for revenge.

"It will be useless for him to fight Kokoy," Imelda said. "He will have the money and the entire machinery of the party in power. How can Norberto fight that? Fetch him. Tomorrow I'll dispatch a plane for your use just to fetch him."

On the plane coming back to Manila, Norberto told his sisters that he refused to go to Malacanang to see Imelda. If she wanted to persuade him not to run, let her come see him. Imelda arrived with an entourage of security men and screaming sirens.

"She talked tough," cousin Loreto recalled. "Imelda said in no uncertain terms that if Norberto Junior ran for re-election, he would suffer a devastating defeat." According to Loreto, Imelda threatened him:

"I'll use every available means to ensure Kokoy's victory. The whole weight of Malacanang will bear down on your shoulders."

Norberto replied, "I will still run." Imelda left in a huff. The following week, she changed her approach. This time she went to Norberto with tears in her eyes. "I come not as First Lady," she said, "but as a humble cousin. Please try to understand why I am doing this." Norberto capitulated. Kokoy became governor of Leyte, and began seizing Norberto's properties.

Deprived of the governorship, and soon divested by Imelda's brothers of most of his real estate, Norberto took refuge in Manila where he found employment as a clerk, and then fell ill with a brain tumor. He died impoverished in 1972, requesting only that he be buried back in Tacloban. His widow could not pay his medical bills, so she went to the First Lady to ask for money, and for help getting the body to Leyte. Imelda turned her down. Ninoy Aquino paid the bills and took the body on his private plane. In Tacloban, Governor Kokoy had false timetables broadcast for the funeral. Norberto's branch of the clan, he said, "must suffer the way we suffered."

Ten

THE CASTING COUCH

As PUBLIC RELATIONS for his re-election in 1969, Ferdinand wanted a new biography written and a new movie made about the Maharlika. This time the book, *Rendezvous with Destiny,* was to be done by the Ilocano journalist Benjamin Gray, who had helped Ferdinand get elected the first time in 1949 by writing articles on his heroism in the magazine *Bannawag.* Unlike the first Maharlika movie—*Marked by Fate*—the new movie was not to be a documentary but a full-scale jungle epic along the lines of *Bridge on the River Kwai,* with Hollywood stars. Ferdinand turned the project over to a group of cronies: businessman Potenciano Ilusorio, manager Diosdado Bote of the Wack Wack Golf and Country Club, and Manuel Nieto, president of Philippine Overseas Communications.

So long as they were casting actresses, the cronies decided to pick girls who would appeal to Ferdinand. Somebody had to play the role of his wartime sweetheart. (Ferdinand claimed that she was a Filipino-American guerrilla named Evelyn who saved his life by "stopping a Japanese bullet" meant for him.)

At the time, President Marcos was showing great interest in Gretchen Cojuangco, the pretty wife of his wealthy friend Eduardo Cojuangco, of the billionaire Tarlac sugar clan. She was one of Imelda's Blue Ladies, and Imelda was furious, but Cojuangco support had been crucial in Ferdinand's political career. Instead of confronting Gretchen Cojuangco directly, as she had Carmen Ortega so many years ago, Imelda dispatched another Blue Lady with a message. Whatever the message said, Ferdinand later told a mutual friend, Gretchen "will no longer stop weeping." Eduardo Cojuangco, her husband, tried a more diplomatic approach. He knew people in Hollywood who had worked on films in the Philippines, including Paul Mason, a minor producer at Universal Studios. At Cojuangco's suggestion, Ilusorio approached Mason, and asked him to arrange for the audition in Manila of several actresses who might fit the type Ferdinand associated with "Evelyn." Mason came up with two, Joyce Reese and Dovie Beams. The two women were flown to Manila in December 1968. Dovie Beams suspected the whole thing was just a set-up. She had heard that American girls were brought to the Philippines to "audition" for movie parts, then were drugged and passed around.

Dovie and Joyce were checked into a Manila hotel and invited to a party that night at a house in the posh Greenhills suburb. Oddly, the house was under reconstruction, with makeshift furniture and a big hole in the yard for a new swimming pool. They were taken upstairs, where drinks and snacks were set out on a picnic table in a room with a large bed. Ferdinand arrived a few minutes later. He was introduced as "Fred," but Joyce told Dovie later that she recognized him immediately. They talked about movies, and Dovie sang "I Want to Be Bad." As the party wore on, Ferdinand said something to the other men in Tagalog, and they drifted out of the room, taking Joyce Reese with them.

He talked with Dovie for several more hours. At one point she asked if he was a lawyer. "I have something to do with the legal profession," he said. "I am the president of the Philippines." Then, according to Dovie, he stood up to leave, shook her hand, gave her a light kiss on the back of her neck, and said, "I'm in love with you." The next day he returned and they became lovers, an affair that lasted nearly two years. Dovie got the role of Evelyn.

Dovie Beams was born Dovie Osborne in Nashville on August 5, 1932. She was thirty-six years old, but she looked much younger and claimed to be twenty-three. In Tennessee, she was briefly married to Edward Boehms, and had a daughter. When they were divorced, she moved to Hollywood, keeping his name but changing the spelling to Beams. Over the years, she supported herself in various ways, eventually getting small roles in television soap operas. She said she was the occasional houseguest of Mr. and Mrs. William Randolph Hearst, Jr., at their home in Palm Springs. When Paul Mason sent her to Manila, she had a mortgage on a small house in Beverly Hills.

Ferdinand installed his new mistress in the unfinished Greenhills house, with a staff of servants, bodyguards, and a social secretary named Vicky Abalos. In the early days of their liaison, he told Dovie that he was impotent with Imelda and that they had been sexually estranged for many years. They remained together, he explained, because it served a purpose, but each lived a separate life. Dovie also discovered about Carmen Ortega, and learned from Ferdinand that his mother still considered him married to Ortega. Once they had a quarrel, and Ferdinand went off to find consolation with Ortega. According to Dovie, during this visit Ortega became pregnant again.

After a few weeks of bliss, Ferdinand gave Dovie a trip to Hong Kong to buy jewelry, and a holiday in the Bahamas, where he wanted her to deposit some black money, including $10,000 he gave her "tax free." She took her daughter Dena with her. Among her other acquisitions in Hong Kong, Dovie purchased a small cassette tape recorder, so "Fred" could teach her words and phrases in Tagalog and Spanish for the movie. He was writing new lines for her in the script. Sometimes they would interrupt these language lessons to make love while the tape recorder continued running. Once Ferdinand turned it on to sing his favorite Ilocano love song, *"Pamulinawen,"* and other love songs in Spanish. Soon Dovie had a collection of incriminating tapes.

Whenever Imelda was out of the country, Ferdinand spent all his time in Greenhills, or brought Dovie to Malacanang Palace. After he had fallen asleep, she would look through the papers on his desk in the palace study and select particular documents to tuck away for a rainy day. On one occasion, he flew her mother and daughter to Manila and gave them a tour of the palace. If Imelda was in town, Dovie sometimes met him at a cottage on the palace golf course, which Ferdinand used for assignations.

The movie proceeded slowly because Ilusorio had invested all the production money in Benguet mining stocks, and the price had temporarily plunged. Ferdinand was angry, but he put up more money and eventually shooting started with actor Paul Burke playing him and Farley Granger playing his faithful American sidekick (apparently modeled on Captain Jamison). As Evelyn, the female lead, Dovie became a Manila celebrity. To provide her with a public residence, Ferdinand made available a house on Princeton Street near the Wack Wack Country Club. It was there that she gave interviews to the press, although she continued to live at their love nest in Greenhills.

Whenever Ferdinand was around, Colonel Ver was always nearby, on an eternal vigil for the First Lady and her spies. When the president went to Baguio for a break, Ver smuggled Dovie in and out of the presidential retreat on the floor of his sedan.

Ilusorio was afraid that if Imelda found out about the love affair, and that it was he who had brought Dovie to the Philippines, she might have him shot. He had good reason to be worried. A member of Ver's palace security guard said in an interview, "Whenever Imelda became suspicious, she ordered us to drive her around Manila searching for her husband or his car. We always knew where the president was, so we always drove her somewhere else." Some people in the palace, he said, thought Imelda was having a wholesome relationship with her husband because she got up in the mornings looking radiant, but the truth was that she kept an oxygen tank beside her bed and spent a few minutes each morning doing breathing exercises, which made her feel vigorous, and brought a flush to her cheeks.

Once Dovie read a Hong Kong magazine article saying that Ferdinand was the richest man in Asia. She asked him about it. He replied, "Well, Imelda has more money than I do." Dovie told him frankly that she herself had only one purpose in life, to make a lot of money. He answered that he was grateful to her because she had saved him from having a nervous breakdown. Because of that, he had made financial arrangements that would take care of her for life, apparently through banker Roberto Benedicto, who managed a number of his offshore companies. (Marcos and Benedicto owned a bank in Beverly Hills.) He told her that he and Ilusorio had done some smuggling together during the war. He talked about how the Japanese had killed his father, and bragged that he had found some of Yamashita's Gold, which he had hidden and used after the war. He also confided that he carried a poison pill: if his enemies captured him, he would take the pill to avoid being tortured. It was then April 1969, and his campaign for re-election was under way. He told Dovie that no president had ever won a full second term before, but that he was going to win the election by any means, fair or foul, and if necessary he was prepared to use the Communists as an excuse to declare martial law.

As they lay in bed together, Ferdinand told Dovie that he had tricked the Liberals into selecting Sergio Osmeña, Jr., as their candidate, because Osmeña would be easier to beat. He was even going to defeat Osmeña in his home province, because it had never been done before. How many votes did Dovie think he should beat Osmeña by—

two million? The way he had things planned, he told Dovie, it made no earthly difference if everyone in the islands voted against him, he would win the election anyway.

While Ferdinand was reinflating his own war hero image with the Gray biography and the new Maharlika movie, he publicly denounced Osmeña as a traitor for collaborating with the Japanese during the war. Just because Osmeña had been given amnesty along with all the other collaborators, he said, did not mean he was not guilty of treason. Both Osmeña and his vice presidential running mate, Genaro Magsaysay, portrayed themselves as strongly pro-American. So, for good measure, Marcos labeled Magsaysay as a CIA candidate. The Osmeña camp struck back, circulating black toothbrushes to remind voters that their president had been convicted for shooting a man in the back while the victim was brushing his teeth.

Five months before the November polls, President Nixon came to Manila. Ferdinand was threatening to turn against America unless he was given visible support. Nixon understood the ramifications, and decided to pay a visit to America's staunch ally. To offset the impression that he was there exclusively to help President Marcos, Nixon met leaders of the opposition, and expressed concern about the pressure he was under in America to accelerate troop withdrawal in Vietnam. The Marcoses gave up their master bed for him, a large bed with a purple velvet headboard which they apparently had never slept in together. Mrs. Nixon occupied her own suite in the guest wing.

One day Diosdado Bote arrived at Dovie's love nest in a sweat and said, "You've got to call the palace! My son has been shot." Bote assumed that Dovie knew all about what was going on in the campaign, so he was indiscreet and babbled about Ferdinand's election methods. As the campaign proceeded, he said, there were ambushes, and people on both sides were being murdered. It was worse than Bote said. Seventeen out of sixty-six provinces were bloody. "Terrorists" in Constabulary uniforms took over polling places in province after province; warlords in nineteen provinces used private armies to force the voting; houses and whole villages were burned to the ground. On Batanes, an armed band known as the Suzuki Boys took over the entire island, murdering the local public prosecutor, closing the airport, occupying the radio and telegraph offices, as well as the polling stations. Special Constabulary murder squads known as "the Monkees" were intended to achieve what the military called "a balance of terror" in central

Luzon. Congressman Jose Cojuangco (brother-in-law of Ninoy Aquino) pointed out that there were at least six teams of Monkees in his area of Tarlac. Another group of thugs, the Barracudas, guarded Marcos candidates in Lanao del Norte. Constabulary soldiers in Agusan Sur shot up a schoolhouse polling station, killing four, wounding five, taking ten hostages. Brigadier General Vicente "Banjo" Raval, the Constabulary chief fresh back from training in Washington, was accused of partisanship and his men of terrorism. On election day his Special Forces terrorized the provinces of Marinduque, Cagayan, Ilocos Sur, and Batanes, including forty-six killings. Ballot boxes were burned, and replaced by stuffed boxes stored for the purpose in Philippine army safe houses, all handled by specially trained "fraud" teams of the air force and navy. In southern Cebu, the Liberals controlled one polling station, the Nacionalistas the other; the Liberals announced that every single one of the 9,400 voters registered in the area had chosen Osmeña, but Ferdinand won with a vote 2,000 greater than the registered total.

On paper, the Marcos slate won seven of the eight senatorial seats, and all but 24 of the 110 races for the House. This was so improbable that it made the fraud embarrassingly obvious. As he met supporters in Malacanang Palace to declare his victory, Ferdinand was leading in every single province. It was a landslide, on a scale surpassing even Magsaysay's 1953 win backed by the Seventh Fleet. He claimed a margin of 1.7 million votes, or 74 percent of the votes cast, just shy of the 2 million he had promised Dovie.

It cost Ferdinand $168 million to be re-elected. Back in 1946, national parties and presidential candidates had spent $1.5 million; by 1961, the cost jumped to $30 million. By 1969, Ferdinand had expanded patronage to such an extent that the election crippled all but his richest opponents. The Marcos political machine was heavily oiled down to the barrio level by Executive Secretary Ernesto Maceda, known to foreign correspondents as Oil-can Ernie.

Ferdinand paid for his campaign in several ways—one was by printing more money and causing runaway inflation. The Philippines' foreign exchange reserves were completely exhausted and short-term loans were falling due. Embarrassingly, he had to press Washington for a $100 million advance on base rents. He was now president of a bankrupt country, forced to seek IMF assistance to stabilize his currency with a special loan of $27 million, and he had to roll over $275 million dollars worth of short-term indebtedness to American and European banking groups. Despite these emergency measures, Ferdinand was forced to adopt austerity measures and devalue the peso by 50 percent. The 70 percent of Filipinos living on less than $200 a year had their buying power cut in half.

Eduardo Lachica of the *Philippines Herald* said, "The Liberals were outspent, outshouted, and outgunned." Osmeña charged that "democracy was raped" and refused to concede.

Dovie had missed all the fun. Since "Fred" was busy, she had gone off on a holiday just before the election. When she left, he had seemed exhilarated. When she came back, he was morose, withdrawn. She did not understand the change until Colonel Ver came in for a talk one day and explained what had happened. Despite everything, Ver told her, "the boss" had lost. Despite all the money, all the killings, all the manipulation. She said Ver talked about it at great length.

Ferdinand could falsify the ballots, but he could not change the realization that he had really lost. As it had done for Mariano Marcos in 1931, this came as a terrible blow to his ego. "It was devastating," Dovie said. From then on, everything was different.

So obvious was the election fraud that Ferdinand became a target of unprecedented contempt from students and opposition. He had stolen the presidency, and found himself nearly in the state of siege that he had prepared for so deliberately with U.S. help.

Charges of corruption, fraud, and hidden wealth became the basis for impeachment proceedings. To avoid impeachment, he announced that he was giving away everything he owned. Later, he disclosed that he was giving it all to something called the Marcos Foundation. Then he amended his announcement to say he would give away only what he could legally dispose of—excluding the holdings of his wife and children.

When Ferdinand took his oath of office on December 30, 1969, tight security had to be imposed. Machine guns were mounted on the grandstand, a helicopter hovered over Luneta Park, and navy gunboats patrolled Manila Bay. In his inaugural address, Ferdinand portrayed himself as a champion of the underdog, determined to tame the oligarchy. "The decade of the seventies," he said, "cannot be for the faint of heart and men of little faith. It is not for the whiners, nor for the timid. It is not a decade for the time-wasters and the fault-finders. . . . Our society must chastise the profligate rich who waste the nation's substance including its foreign exchange reserves in personal comforts and luxuries." Alluding to influence peddlers, he warned that no man who claims to be a friend, relative, or ally should try to take advantage—"if he offends the New Society, he shall be punished like the rest." Nobody took him seriously. Who could rule without the support of the Lopezes, Ayalas, Elizaldes, Ongpins, and Chuas? Meanwhile, in the streets of Manila fifty thousand demonstrators denounced his victory as a joke. The demonstrations went on for days. The first big success of the new U.S. trained METROCOM paramilitary security force was the bloody suppression of these demonstrations. The demonstrators were protesting that they had been swindled out of the one thing America always boasted it gave the Philippines—democracy. But times had changed. What America was now giving the Philippines was dictatorship.

Several weeks later, on January 26, 1970, Ferdinand made his state of the nation address at the Legislative Building. As he and Imelda listened to an invocation by Father Pacifico Ortiz, president of Ateneo de Manila University, Ferdinand grew rigid and the First Lady's cheeks flushed with fury. The priest spoke of "the growing fears, the dying hopes, the perished longings and expectations of a people who have lost their political innocence; a people . . . who now know that salvation, political or economic, does not come from above, from any one man or party or foreign ally; that in the last analysis, salvation can only come from below—from the people themselves, firmly united . . . to stand for their rights whether at the polls, in the market place or at the barricades."

Outside the Legislative Building there was a demonstration by twenty thousand students, workers, and farmers. One of the organizers was Edgar Jopson, president of the National Union of Students. The demonstrators were parading a cardboard coffin containing a stuffed crocodile with a mouthful of money. As the president and First Lady emerged, they were greeted with a shower of bottles, sticks, and placards. There was a scuffle and Colonel Ver thrust Ferdinand into the car, bumping his head on the door. Imelda was several meters behind in the melee. No security man dared to grab her. Ferdinand climbed out, took her wrist, and dragged her into the car, spraining his ankle. Both were badly shaken. As army and police moved in, what had begun as a peaceful protest turned into the bloodiest confrontation in a decade.

Four days later, a group of student leaders was summoned to a meeting at Malacanang, watched by reporters. Again the students were led by Edgar Jopson. The son of a middle-class grocer who had introduced the first American-style self-service supermarket to Manila after the war, Jopson at age twenty-one had been named the outstanding young man in the Philippines by the Junior Chamber of Commerce. He was studying business management and planned to go to law school. Jopson summarized the issues that had led to their protest rally, but their dialogue with Ferdinand quickly turned sour. When he asked the president to guarantee that he would not seek a third term, Ferdinand blandly replied that he was barred from doing so by the constitution. Jopson persisted, demanding that Marcos put the promise in writing. Infuriated, Ferdinand exclaimed, "You are only the son of a grocer!"

When news that the meeting had collapsed reached a crowd of four thousand students waiting outside the palace, they commandeered a fire truck and rammed it through the gate, storming in. Six students were killed and hundreds injured as the riot raged on for eight hours, from Malacanang Palace down the street to Mendiola Bridge. The riot of Bloody Friday was the first of its kind in contemporary Philippine history. The brutal military suppression that followed drove the student movement sharply to the left. It did not help that the students killed in the riots were killed by squads specially trained and supplied by the U.S. government.

Ferdinand holed up in Malacanang for weeks, turning it into an Alamo. Workmen welded the palace gates shut. Armed guards patrolled the riverfront. Under the banyan trees loitered soldiers and plainclothesmen. A large air force helicopter made a test landing in the palace garden. When its rotor blades grazed branches, a general ordered a dozen trees cut down. The regular palace helipad was across the river, but a river crossing in an emergency was considered too risky.

Ferdinand was rattled by the violence of the demonstrations against him, and he seemed incoherent—or at least illogical—in his interpretation of the episode. At first, he blamed "non-student provocateurs" for the riots, then inflated the protest to "an insurrection" by Maoists. A soothsayer chose this moment to predict that the president would be assassinated before April by a "light-skinned man wearing a suit." Ferdinand then complained that the CIA was sponsoring a right-wing coup plot against him. He was habitually frightened by the specter of his rich rivals hiring Mafia hitmen to rub him out. Later, he claimed there were eight such attempts in 1972 alone.

One day Dovie returned to Greenhills to discover that their love nest was being packed up. Ferdinand explained that spies were watching the house, making it too risky to continue using it. Dovie agreed to move to her public residence, near Wack Wack. Afterwards she learned that it was all a lie and Carmen Ortega had moved into the Greenhills house. The renovation and the swimming pool had been for Carmen all along.

In this atmosphere of growing tension between them Dovie made two new tapes, on January 17 and 22, of President Marcos making love with all the bells and whistles. She added these to a small hoard of documents, tapes, and articles of his clothing that she had thoughtfully sent to America for safe keeping.

One night, Ferdinand took Polaroid shots of Dovie in the nude, in startling poses on the bed and in the bathroom, and asked her for a lock of pubic hair. Dovie agreed, but only in trade for a lock of his. It was a disastrous mistake. To Filipinos, Dovie might look twenty-three and vulnerable, but she was turning forty and no fool. She had to protect herself. Ferdinand was losing interest in her—he was withdrawn, distracted. Everything he said had a hostile undercurrent; he was not the same person. Quarrels were more frequent. It was only a matter of time before she was dumped.

A few days later, just before Black Friday and the siege of Malacanang, she came home one morning furious. The Maharlika movie was in rough cut, but Marcos would not allow it to be shown; he said it was not good and was miscast. Dovie swore revenge. She packed her bags and returned to Los Angeles. Seven months later, in August, she came back with a full quiver of threats against Ferdinand and demands upon the production house USV Arts. She was either being very bold or very rash, encouraged by a number of people, apparently including billionaire Eugenio Lopez, whose feud with Ferdinand was now near the breaking point. A showdown with Dovie Beams could only embarrass the Marcos administration. It has been alleged also that Dovie was a CIA plant all along, that there were factions in the Agency determined to ruin Ferdinand by making a fool of him.

In public statements, Dovie claimed that she had come back to produce a travelogue in which President Marcos would be featured. At USV Arts, Diosdado Bote complained that Dovie insisted on being paid "fantastic" amounts in U.S. dollars. His attorney said that she threatened to "involve Mr. Bote and other directors of the corporation in a scandal which she said she would create should her demands not be met." Bote said he finally gave her $10,000 and nothing more, just to silence her. However, Dovie now had a letter dated September 25, 1970, in which Bote acknowledged that she was due more than $100,-000. When Dovie increased her demand to $150,000, Potenciano Ilusorio refused and Bote filed a complaint against her with the National Bureau of Investigation.

That night, Dovie was picked up by secret police chief Ver and taken to a safe house for a showdown with Ferdinand in front of his cronies. Face to face, she lost her temper and yelled, "You're a goddamned liar!" They had a terrible row while Ver, Bote, and Ilusorio looked on wide-eyed. It ended, she said, with Ferdinand trying to make up. He wanted to kiss her. She refused, and was driven by Fabian Ver to Malacanang, where she was kept until 5:30 A.M., talking to Ver.

"He's a murderer," she said.

"But, Ma'am, you loved him," Ver said, denying nothing.

"Well . . ."

"Ma'am, you called him a goddamned liar, and you know, no one talks to him like that, not even his Cabinet."

From the palace, Dovie claimed that Ilusorio, Bote, and others took her to a room at the Savoy Hotel on Roxas Boulevard (now the Hyatt Regency) where the men assaulted her and tortured her. After some time, they let her go to the bathroom. It was the only thing she could think of to get away from them for a few minutes. In the bathroom she discovered a telephone that the men did not know was there. She decided to take the chance and called her friend and onetime social secretary, Vicky Abalos.

Before leaving California, Dovie had set up a code by which she could call for help in an emergency. Among her anxious friends, she claimed, were Mr. and Mrs. William Randolph Hearst, Jr., the publishers, who were friends of Governor and Mrs. Reagan. Whispering over the phone to Vicky Abalos, Dovie asked her to send a telegram to the Hearsts in Palm Springs: "Happy birthday on this your special day."

Dovie's tormentors then took her back to her own room at the Manila Hilton. She was in pain and went immediately to bed. Shortly, she said, a telegram arrived from the Hearsts in California. According to Dovie, they had contacted Senator Alan Cranston of California and Senator Howard Baker of Tennessee, Dovie's home state. In their telegram, she said they told her to go straight to the U.S. Embassy and see Ambassador Byroade. By then, she had begun to hemorrhage, and left the hotel to check into the Manila Medical Center under a false name.

Her disappearance caused speculation in the press, and Manila buzzed with rumors about the president's torrid affair with Dovie Beams. Was she kidnapped? Was she killed? Or was she hidden at Clark Air Base? From the papers, Imelda learned everything and was said to be livid with rage. It was rumored that the First Lady's agents were searching for Dovie everywhere.

Dovie phoned the U.S. Embassy and was immediately visited by Consul Lawrence Harris, who told her that he was speaking for Ambassador Byroade. According to Dovie, Harris and Byroade initially tried to help the First Lady buy her off, offering her $100,000 directly from the palace if she agreed to keep quiet—and hinting that they might be able to get her double that amount. She was given to understand that the offer came directly from Imelda. "Think about it—it's tax free," she was told.

When she was strong enough to leave the hospital, Dovie was taken to the embassy for a conference with Ambassador Byroade, during which she said the $100,000 bribe was again proffered. She was warned that if she did not accept the bribe, Imelda might have her killed. Apparently Harris and Byroade were not yet aware that Dovie had assembled a great deal of incriminating evidence to support her claim.

Dovie now realized that she was putting herself in grave danger by keeping her mouth shut. When she told Ambassador Byroade and Consul Harris what she had collected as insurance, their whole attitude changed. They booked her into the Bay View Hotel across Roxas Boulevard, where embassy security men could keep a close watch on her. There, she called a press conference.

She was careful to refer to Ferdinand only as "Fred"—which made it possible for reporters to print her allegations freely without being vulnerable to charges of libeling the president of the republic. During the press conference Dovie played one of her tapes complete with moans, murmurs, creaking bed, and an Ilocano love song, which every Filipino knew to be a Marcos favorite. His voice and that of Dovie were clearly recognizable. While she was talking with one reporter, two others were busy at a table patching their tape recorder to hers and making a duplicate. She put a stop to it midway, but made no effort to recover what they already had transcribed. (Copies of the tape were then made available to a number of people, including Ninoy Aquino, who is said to have paid $500 for his.)

Student protestors at the University of the Philippines commandeered the campus radio station and broadcast a looped tape; soon the entire nation was listening in astonishment to President Marcos begging Dovie Beams to perform oral sex. For over a week, the president's hoarse injunctions boomed out over university loudspeakers. Special forces troopers sent to recapture the radio station crumpled with laughter. Barely able to keep a straight face, Ninoy Aquino called for a Senate investigation.

As the scandal raged to new levels of intensity, Ambassador Byroade's aides escorted Dovie to the airport. Manila International was swarming with Marcos aides, Imelda's spies, immigration officers, and U.S. Embassy people as Dovie boarded Philippine Airlines Flight 396 for Hong Kong. Ferdinand did not attempt to stop her; he was too busy trying to outmaneuver the First Lady's secret agents. It became a contest between those sent to protect Dovie and those sent to kill her. Lurking in the background was a very competent bodyguard Ferdinand had long ago assigned to look after her. Imelda dispatched forty-three-year-old professional killer Delfin Cueto. Although the U.S. Embassy had secured seats around Dovie for her loyal Filipino servants, Imelda had an airlines official oust them to other seats across the aisle and put Cueto next to her. The First Lady also sent to Hong Kong a ten-man flying squad of her own thugs in a Philippine Air Force C-130.

At Kai Tak airport in the Crown Colony, Dovie's bodyguard and Delphin Cueto had a grim confrontation, after which Cueto went his own way, to strike again elsewhere.

A few days later, when Dovie came out of hiding and tried to leave Hong Kong for Los Angeles, Imelda's pursuers were waiting to pounce. As she walked toward the Pan American departure ramp, Philippine Consul General Rafael Gonzales popped out of nowhere and blocked her. British police in plainclothes moved in and stopped the altercation. Dovie went back into protective custody for five days, this time courtesy of MI5. At last she was put aboard a plane with three new bodyguards. The moment she left, Hong Kong police captured Cueto, disarmed him, and deported him to Manila. Cueto told reporters that *his* name was Fred and it was he who had been keeping Dovie Beams as *his* mistress. A Presidential Security guard at Malacanang said during an interview that Ferdinand had even asked him to claim that he was Fred. "Marcos always had plenty of girlfriends," he said. "Marcos even wanted me to take the heat for Dovie."

Ever since 1954, when Imelda had discovered the existence of Carmen Ortega and her children, she had been forced to stifle her fury at Ferdinand's betrayal. Now the shoe was on the other foot. Imelda was embarrassed, but Ferdinand was humiliated. As the palace security man put it, "Imelda went crazy over the Dovie Beams affair."

Once safe in Los Angeles, Dovie produced mounds of the president's clothing, additional tape cassettes, secret documents from Malacanang Palace, and a tuft of pubic hair that she threatened to turn over to a laboratory for identification. Her charges were all published in great detail in the Manila journal *Graphic*, earning its editors the eternal enmity of President Marcos and the First Lady. Their publishing days were numbered.

In the years to come, Imelda's emissaries came to Los Angeles to see Dovie periodically with inducements to turn over her treasured mementoes. She was told that if she did not cooperate, the scandal would spoil the First Lady's chances of becoming president herself. To which Dovie replied: "Good! Then I'll be doing the Filipino people a favor." (This neatly paraphrased what Imelda and Carmen Ortega said to each other nearly twenty years earlier.)

For life insurance, Dovie stashed multiple copies of everything with attorneys and friends. She told her story to a Filipino-American journalist, Hermie Rotea, who produced a small book titled *Marcos' Lovie Dovie*. The moment the book appeared, it magically disappeared, snapped up by Imelda's agents. Copies were stealthily removed from libraries across America, and from the Library of Congress. Rotea's book was a bit too frank, clearly favoring Dovie but also including the celebrated nude photos and a summary of Imelda's counter charges, alleging that Dovie was a professional. Dovie was not happy with Rotea's book, and went on to write her own, as yet unpublished, copies of which she kept in different vaults in case anything odd happened to her.

The Dovie Beams affair was neither the first nor the last Marcos sex scandal. Among U.S. diplomatic dispatches from Manila, there is a secret message, stamped "No Forn" to bar it from foreign eyes, which describes Marcos as "a ladies' man." The message was intended for the edification of Governor Reagan during his visit to Manila for the gala opening of Imelda's Cultural Center in 1969, giving him discreet background on Filipino problems. One of the most delicate problems, according to the message, was President Marcos's backstairs romance with the wife of a U.S. Navy officer. The embassy was deathly afraid that the First Lady would find out and kick up a fuss, to the detriment of Filipino-American relations.

Filipino singer Carmen Soriano was another celebrated romance. The First Lady sought out the singer in San Francisco in 1970, going to her apartment accompanied by her financial adviser, Ernesto Villatuya. Imelda demanded that Soriano sign a prepared statement that she and the president had never gone to bed together. When Carmen told Imelda to go to hell, the First Lady took a roundhouse swing at Soriano—which she ducked—and the blow landed on Villatuya, knocking him flat. In consolation, Imelda saw to it that Villatuya became president of the Philippine National Bank, a position he held until 1972.

The movie *Maharlika* was banned in the Philippines because it starred Dovie Beams. Producer Luis Nepomuceno said Imelda railed at him for six hours and finally had government banks foreclose on his production company. "What really bothered her," added Nepomuceno, "was that Dovie said Imelda was no longer attractive to her husband."

Imelda would extract a heavy price from Ferdinand for his philandering—from shares in gold mines to unbridled political power. Sighed a former family friend, "In the Philippines, a philandering husband has to pay for the rest of his life. Marcos just used our taxes."

Eleven

IRON BUTTERFLY

THE EMBARRASSMENT CAUSED to her by the Dovie Beams affair gave Imelda a weapon to extract unprecedented concessions from her husband. One of Ferdinand's biggest plums had to be given away. Her branch of the Romualdez family suddenly gained control of the Benguet gold and copper mines, which Ferdinand had been painstakingly acquiring for himself. It is known from the accounts of Dovie Beams that early in the affair—early in Ferdinand's first term in office—he was involved in an elaborate intrigue with Potenciano Ilusorio to gain control of Benguet, the biggest mining company in the Philippines and the second-richest gold mine in U.S. hands. For many years the majority ownership was held by New York's Charles and Herbert Allen. Over the years, Ferdinand gained majority ownership, but after the Dovie scandal, his interest in Benguet fell into the hands of a company fronting for Imelda and Kokoy.

Prior to the broadcast of Dovie's tapes, Imelda had no choice but to ignore Ferdinand's philandering. Infidelity is one of the realities of a marriage in a country where divorce is not possible. But there were certain rules. One was that the philandering man had to seem detached and in control. Ferdinand's detachment was destroyed when the tapes were broadcast. Imelda's fury demonstrated itself in several strange ways. Over the years, she would pull out nude pictures of Dovie and show these angrily to startled friends. She also kept in her bedroom a detailed dossier which claimed that Dovie's amorous adventures were

In happier days, the Marcos dynasty assembled for the classic family portrait beneath the presidential seal, the men in *barongs*, the ladies wearing *ternos*, the puff-sleeved national dress. In front of Bong-Bong and Ferdinand, left to right, are Irene, Imelda, and Imee; in the foreground is little Aimee. (*Courtesy Joe Cantrell/ Black Star*)

Frugging the night away, the First Lady shows her appreciation for the stellar qualities of actor George Hamilton at one of her Manila film festivals. (*Courtesy AP/Wide World*)

At the height of their power, Ferdinand and Imelda shared their thrones with the ever-charming Juan Ponce Enrile (seated right), the wealthy defense minister who served them for twenty years, then turned on them and tried to seize power for himself. Behind are a slew of Malacanang Palace intriguers. (*Courtesy Reuters/ Bettmann Newsphotos*)

Imelda on the day she graduated from high school in 1948, and as she appeared five years later at a Manila fashion show. (*Courtesy Loreto Romualdez Ramos*)

Ferdinand Marcos: The War Hero.
(*Courtesy Raya Books*)

Captain Daniel Romualdez and his family. His wife, Doña Tidad, and son Norberto are seated to his right. (*Courtesy Loreto Romualdez Ramos*)

Remedios Trinidad, Imelda's mother. (*Courtesy Loreto Romualdez Ramos*)

Vincente Orestes Romualdez with Imelda and Kokoy. (*Courtesy Loreto Romualdez Ramos*)

The Marcoses in the late 1920s: (left to right) Pacifico, Josefa, Elizabeth, Mariano, and Ferdinand. Youngest daughter, Fortuna, is not present. (*Courtesy Raya Books*)

Mariano Marcos: The Educator. (*Courtesy Raya Books*)

Roxas. (*Courtesy AP/Wide World*)

Quirino. (*Courtesy AP/Wide World*)

Magsaysay. (*Courtesy AP/Wide World*)

Garcia. (*Courtesy AP/Wide World*)

Macapagal. (*Courtesy Reuters/Bettmann Newsphotos*)

While preparing to campaign for the presidency in the early 1960s, the Marcoses posed for thousands of pictures, making the most of their handsome features. Ferdinand always appeared fresh-scrubbed, pomaded, bright-eyed, and bushy-tailed. Imelda was at the peak of her natural beauty, hiding well the shock and tragedy of her marriage. Journalists were paid a thousand dollars each time a photo made their papers. (*Courtesy AP/Wide World*)

A costly indiscretion: Dovie Beams after the scandal. (*Courtesy Wide World*)

FEUDING AQUINOS AND COJUANGCOS

President Corazon "Cory" Aquino. (*Courtesy AP/Wide World*)

Benigno Aquino photographed in San Francisco a few years before his assassination on his return to Manila. (*Courtesy UPI/Bettmann Newsphotos*)

Jose "Peping" Cojuangco, brother of President Corazon Aquino. (*Courtesy AP/Wide World*)

"*Let no youth in Tarlac say that he was a failure because he was not given the opportunity to study.*"

Eduardo "Cujo" Cojuangco, first cousin of President Aquino. (*Courtesy Presidential Commission on Good Government*)

Major General Edward G. Lansdale, who played an important role behind the scenes in the 1950s. (*Courtesy W. W. McNamee*)

Major General John Singlaub. (*Courtesy AP/ Wide World*)

Armed Forces Chief General Fidel Ramos. (*Courtesy Reuters/Bettmann Newsphotos*)

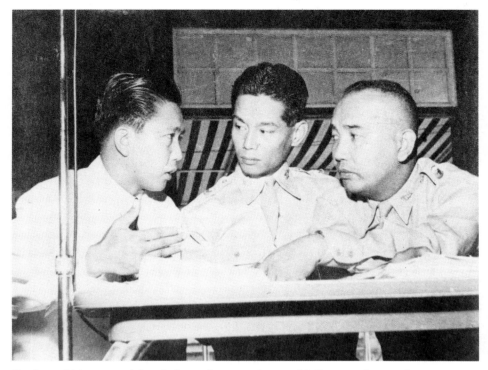

Ferdinand Marcos with his dashing client, professional killer Napoleon Valeriano (center). Valeriano was later a top gun for the CIA in Vietnam and Central America. (*Courtesy Raya Books*)

Benjamin "Kokoy" Romualdez, Imelda's brother and in 1965 the president's special emissary, greeting U.S. Secretary of State Dean Rusk. (*Courtesy AP/Wide World*)

Great friends to the bitter end, President Marcos and President Reagan perform the ritual salute of democracy with somewhat different effect. Sincerity was one of the qualities that most Americans never doubted in Ronald Reagan, whatever their political views, but Ferdinand's hand hid more than his heart. (*Courtesy Penelope Breese/Gamma-Liaison*)

"mere hallucinations." She still had the dossier with her sixteen years later when she landed in Honolulu exile in 1986.

Gossip had it that after Dovie there was no question who was boss in Malacanang. Filipinos joked: "What happens if death takes the chief from our midst? Then the president would have to run the whole thing himself." In other ways, Dovie liberated Imelda. She gained a free hand in pushing her pet projects in the Philippines. She began globetrotting as the Philippines' new ambassador extraordinaire. Her foreign policy statements were short on substance, but were loudly acclaimed by the pro-Imelda media, creating the impression that Philippine foreign policy was no longer following the American lead. Others in Manila did not take her seriously. Cracked one editor, had "Mrs. Marcos gone to Disneyland to explore the possibilities of diplomatic relations with Donald Duck . . . people would not have been surprised."

When Imelda visited China in September 1974, with Bong-Bong in tow, Mao greeted her by saying, "My dear little girl, I like you because you get such bad press from the Western journalists." Her only achievement during the trip was to drag the ailing Mao before Filipino news cameras, revealing how feeble he had become, which had been kept carefully hidden until then. Imelda said it was Madame Mao, Chiang Ching, who made her visit a success. The two ladies had so much in common, Imelda said. "First ladies are very lonely."

"Orientals are more total beings," she added, and their encounter had been between two "total persons." She was very impressed with Chiang Ching's China: "So dedicated. So one-track mind." At such moments there was a disarming freshness and vivacity about her, as if she had never grown up.

In Moscow, she was entertained by the Politburo, chatted with Premier Kosygin, and visited Lenin's tomb. The she was off to see Pope Paul VI in Rome. The Philippine Senate asked if next time the First Lady would mind getting congressional approval before negotiating with Communist states.

These Socialist flirtations were all part of a bluff to cause members of the U.S. Congress to pony up more aid money. The CIA observed that her trips to Cuba and the Middle East were noteworthy only for publicity. They were portrayed in the press as negotiating efforts to ensure oil supplies to Manila and to relieve Arab concerns about the fate of

Philippine Muslims. "Such tangible results as these visits produced," said a CIA analyst, "were usually negotiated in advance by the responsible government agencies, leaving the publicity for her. . . . Her enthusiasm for third world and communist causes can be explained by the fact that the relationships are new and she does not have to share the spotlight. These enthusiasms also fit well with her growing anti-American bias." Imelda's own recollections of the trips seem to reinforce this. In a debriefing for the CIA after her trip to Libya, she was asked if Khadafy had made a pass at her, and she implied, coyly, that she *had* had an affair with him. However, to friends, she confided that Khadafy was gay, saying, "All you have to do is rub his leg."

The social event of the 1970s was the Shah of Iran's party in the ancient ruins of Persepolis, to celebrate the 2,500th anniversary of the founding of the Persian Empire. The guest list included all manner of royalty along with the rich and famous. It was the kind of party Imelda dreamed of throwing after the Marcos dynasty was firmly established. As she descended from her aircraft, her military aide raised a dainty cream lace parasol. She and fifteen-year-old daughter Imee were met by the Shah's younger brother, who escorted them to a carpeted platform with gold pillars at the corners, then down a red carpet to a black Cadillac and off through the desert to pavilions where the Shah and his empress awaited surrounded by six hundred members of the Imperial Guard. It was between lashings of Caspian caviar that Imelda became intimate friends with the Italian socialite Cristina Ford, wife of Henry Ford II. They seemed inseparable, and shared the same tent throughout. Rumors about a torrid lesbian affair began to circulate in the jetset.

Next came the coronation and wedding of Nepal's King Birendra. Imelda commandeered four PAL airliners and took Cristina Ford and six hairdressers. When all Katmandu had to offer was Indian food, Imelda sent a plane back to Manila to bring delicacies more to her liking. King Birendra was upstaged by the spectacle of Imelda Marcos finding ways at every function to place herself next to Prince Charles. Other guests included the Duke and Duchess of Windsor, Lord Mountbatten, and the Crown Princes of Japan and Laos. To accommodate her new friend Cristina, Imelda ordered a member of her Filipino entourage to move out of their hotel, the Soaltee Oberoi. Then the two ladies made the rounds of all the best parties.

Henry Ford II, by then involved with a new woman, Kathy Du Ross, had been encouraging Cristina to make as many foreign excursions as she wished, much as Ferdinand encouraged Imelda. But as this Ford marriage came to the breaking point, he apparently began to resent the amount of time she was spending with Imelda. He began to suspect that they *were* lesbians. Cristina denied the charge, but rumors continued to circulate. After the divorce, the ladies got their revenge, after a fashion.

Ford Motor Company stockholders brought suit against Henry Ford, charging him with taking a $2 million bribe from the Marcoses in return for building a sheet-metal stamping plant on property owned by the Romualdez family in Bataan. The Ford plant was in Mariveles, across the bay from Manila, where Ferdinand had created an "Export Processing Zone" on a Taiwanese model. By 1980, the Bataan EPZ had attracted fifty-seven foreign enterprises, many of them runaways from the rising cost of labor in South Korea, Hong Kong, and Taiwan. In court papers filed in Manhattan, the dissidents claimed that Imelda gave $2 million personally to Ford in return for his agreement to set up the plant. Cristina denied reports that she was helping Roy Cohn, lawyer for the dissident shareholders. Eventually the suit was dropped when Ford settled out of court.

It was many years before Imelda herself finally addressed the lesbian rumors in public. During an interview with a Manila paper, she said: "When Cristina Ford used to come here, everybody would say I was a lesbian. . . . One time, we were with Placido Domingo, the singer, and there were about 12 women at one round table, and all of them did not want to touch me with a ten-foot pole because I was such a queen of lesbians." Despite her denials, there was still speculation in 1986 when the magazine *Vanity Fair* headlined part of an interview: "Rumors persist about Mrs. Marcos' supposed romantic attachment to a member of the Ford clan."

Filipinos had their own doubts about the First Lady's private life, which contributed to the rumors. The well-publicized love affairs of President Marcos indicated that all was not well in Malacanang Palace. Palace security men said the First Lady led her own life, but could not have had love affairs with outsiders (meaning men) because she was always under their close scrutiny. On the other hand, she was spending a great deal of time and money on beauty contestants, taking groups of them for holidays at her beach house in Leyte or to the presidential beach retreat facing Corregidor in Bataan. She spared nothing to make them happy; once she sent two Philippine Air Force C-130 aircraft to Australia to bring back cargoes of clean white sand to dress the beach up for a bevy of beauty queens, and had Australian seashells sprinkled around for them to find.

The government-controlled press could only report that the First Lady was dining and dancing the night away with various androgynous celebrities. Next to Cristina, her dearest friend was the actor George Hamilton. Hamilton bought Charlie Chaplin's old mansion in Beverly Hills in 1982 with $1.2 million said to have been provided by Imelda. The house, an ersatz Tuscan villa built in 1923, was refurbished at Imelda's request by a Filipino architect. Hamilton subsequently used the house as collateral for a five-year $4 million loan from a Netherlands Antilles offshore company, Calno Holdings, presumed to be one of the Marcos offshore companies. The loan was negotiated by an assistant of crony Antonio Floirendo who often fronted for Imelda. Eventually Hamilton sold the house to the daughter of another Marcos ally, Saudi Arabian arms merchant Adnan Khashoggi, for $6 million. Inevitably, onlookers speculated that with so much money changing hands there might be more to the Hamilton friendship.

San Francisco *Examiner* correspondent Phil Bronstein was the closest there was available to an expert source. He bore a strong resemblance to Imelda's old flame, the dark and swarthy medical student Justo Zibala. "Imelda was more interested in the way you looked than who you were," Bronstein confided. She seemed interested in younger men, and Bronstein was young enough to be her son. "After a year of trying," he said, "Marcos finally gave me an interview [and] portions of it were shown on television." Imelda saw it and liked the way Bronstein looked. She asked for her own interview with him, but would not allow his cameraman to attend. "That interview lasted from 11:00 A.M. to 8:00 P.M.," recalled Bronstein. "The next day, Imelda invited me to a dedication ceremony . . . and then I was taken on a guided limo tour around Manila." A week later, one of her aides called him to set up a dinner date with the First Lady. Again, he asked if his cameraman could come along. Absolutely not.

Imelda had an elegant Manila restaurant closed on a busy Saturday night. Besides waiters, the only other man present was her favorite piano player. The lights were low. They talked about the gossip of the day (Khadafy was gay, so was the Shah, the antic sex lives of various Philippine cabinet members). Trying to get something out of the interview, Bronstein asked about her wealth. She opened her purse and showed him it was empty. As the hour grew late, she asked the pianist to play a song she had just written for Bronstein. Looking longingly into his eyes, she sang, "I love you beyond reason . . ." Bronstein decided it was time to cut off the budding relationship.

Despite the rumors, there was no real evidence that Imelda was ever seriously interested in anyone but herself. She needed constant reassurance. She was obsessed by a need for recognition, for the stage, modeling, movies, and beauty contests. Once in the palace, she was constantly being painted, photographed, sculpted, in exotic costumes and settings ranging from da Vinci Madonna to Botticelli Venus. She was surrounded by sycophants.

A prime example of one of her courtiers was Roman "Jun" Cruz. His entry into her charmed circle was described in detail by his companion of nearly a decade, Barbara Gonzalez. "I watched Jun [pronounced "June"] turn from a bright, ambitious, brilliant man of integrity into a universally touted Imelda protégé," said Gonzalez. "It was like watching a prince turn into a frog." Palace spokesman Primitivo Mijares said Cruz became the "principal tong collector [bagman] of the First Lady."

Jun was the son of the judge who had found Ferdinand guilty of the Nalundasan murder. His older brother, J. V. Cruz, had been Magsaysay's press secretary and a Lansdale boy. J. V. caught Imelda's fancy and became a frequent guest at her parties. This close association gave him access to privileged information, and he occasionally picked up stock tips that he passed on to his brother. One time J. V. passed on a tip advising Jun to sell short, but a last-minute move by a Marcos crony reversed the situation and Jun was suddenly $500,000 in debt. Feeling responsible, J. V. got his kid brother a post in the Ministry of Finance, where a few under-the-table deals soon solved his financial problems.

In 1971, Jun was appointed general manager of the Government Service Insurance System (GSIS), one of the biggest financial institutions in the Philippines, with funds derived from the pension payments of all government employees. The GSIS also is a major lending institution. Imelda had visited the Houston Medical Center and wanted one just like it. To build it she turned to the GSIS for loans. "Jun," said Gonzalez "[made] possible everything she wanted." The original Heart Center budget was $5 million; the finished project cost $50 million. "Our telephones rang incessantly from the day Imelda gave her go signal for the Heart Center construction," Gonzalez said. "Her private secretary wanted to make sure a personal friend got the plumbing contract. . . . Every relative . . . wanted a piece of the action. We were wooed by contractors, interior decorators, hospital-equipment manufacturers.

"By the end of the Heart Center project we had built a palatial home on a country property and we had three more Mercedes-Benzes in our garage—a red one from the contractor, a green one that we picked out in Germany from the hospital equipment suppliers, and a white one from Jun's stockbroker. Now there was no turning back. Jun had become a full-fledged protégé. There was nothing on his horizon but wealth and power, the achievement of everything he suddenly realized he wanted."

Imelda eventually gave Cruz control of the lucrative renovation of the Manila Hotel. In return he helped Imelda wrest the ownership of Philippine Air Lines from Benigno Toda. For years, Imelda had freely commandeered aircraft from Philippine Air Lines, sometimes taking an extra jumbo jet just for her luggage. Later, to ease the strain of globe-trotting, she ordered her own plane, complete with built-in shower and gold bathroom fixtures. Unwisely, Toda had sent a bill of several million dollars to Malacanang for Imelda's international junkets. Imelda responded by seizing his company. Cruz was set to become the director of the airline. He and Barbara Gonzales began appearing at hotel openings, on television shows and magazine covers. Imelda apparently became jealous when she discovered that his girlfriend was very pretty and cultivated. Gonzalez told the story this way: "Very early [one] morning Jun was asked to meet the First Lady on the presidential yacht. . . . Imelda took him to task [about openly keeping a mistress]. She claimed that the president was not only displeased, he was aghast." Imelda insinuated that Cruz might not get the Philippine Air Lines job because of his involvement with another woman. The Cruz-Gonzalez relationship broke under the strain. Gonzalez left the country and Cruz became the head of the airline.

In the jetset, it became chic to pop in on Imelda at Malacanang Palace. It was said that if she liked you, she showered you with pearls, and you could keep everything in the closets. Among her favorites was the pianist Van Cliburn, with whom she had hour-long international phone conversations. She bought three grand pianos for him to play at her townhouse in New York. In 1977, Van Cliburn, Margot Fonteyn, and Rudolf Nureyev were flown to Manila to perform for delegates to "Human Rights Week."

Imelda threw parties that were legendary for their tackiness, and preserved them all on videotape. On a typical night in New York, in a black-lit disco in her own building, the First Lady crooned "If You Loved Me" to the rotund arms merchant Khashoggi, and boogied the night away. Bong-Bong led the clan in stirring renditions of "We Are the World." During one party, Imelda played a piano duet with Richard Nixon.

Her private discos were littered with gaudy pillows embroidered with slogans such as "Good Girls Go to Heaven, Bad Girls Go Everywhere," "Nouveau Riche Is Better Than No Riche at All," "You're Twisted, Warped, Depraved, Wicked, Perverted, Sick, and Rotten to the Core—I Like That in a Person," and "To Be Rich Is No Longer a Sin—It's a Miracle."

Her spending habits caused a sensation. She became a collector—of houses, apartments, buildings, jewelry, lingerie, paintings, and whatever else caught her eye. Among her friends in the art world was Armand Hammer, chairman of Occidental Petroleum and Hammer Galleries on New York's East Side. He came to her rescue in October 1976 when she desperately needed art to fill a new museum in Manila in time for an international conference. In appreciation, Imelda spent $4.61 million on seventy-seven paintings from Hammer's gallery.

She always insisted on a discount so some galleries automatically raised their prices 25 percent when they learned she was coming and then gave a discount of 15 percent. In all she spent $40 million in art galleries, a lot of it on worthless items or fakes. Gallery owners said she could have had it all for just $20 million if she had been well advised.

Between 1975 and 1981 she was the most influential jewelry buyer in the world. A night person by nature, she asked jewelry store managers to open for showings at 4:00 A.M. Her bodyguards paid for the gems with thousand-dollar bills they pulled out of paper bags. Her retinue would return from these 4:00 A.M. shopping sprees to a brunch of filet mignon, fresh vegetables, Dom Pérignon, strawberries, Courvoisier, and Godiva chocolates. Imelda would entertain lady friends by dumping the contents of large jewelry boxes on the floor, beaming happily while her guests tried them on. When she was bored with the latest offerings of Bulgari, Bucellati, and Harry Winston, she bought "historical" pieces, paying Harry Winston $5.5 million for the "Idol's Eye"—a gem that supposedly inspired Steven Spielberg's movie *Indiana Jones and the Temple of Doom*.

When she visited New York, Mayor Koch sent her roses and she was photographed bussing U.N. Secretary General Kurt Waldheim. It was suspected that Imelda was the mystery donor of Waldheim's official residence. She often stayed at the Waldorf Towers (for $1,700 a night), tipped bellboys $100, and ordered $1,000 worth of flowers a day. In Rome she stayed at the Excelsior or the Grand, at $1,400 a night for her suite; her entourage required another twenty-five rooms. She was hard to dodge. After the 1980 U.S. presidential election, she bribed a hotel elevator operator to arrange a "chance" meeting with Nancy and Ronald Reagan, who had been ducking her.

Ferdinand eventually gave Imelda her own account at the Veterans' Bank, "Intelligence Account Number Two," and primed it with $1.5 million from government funds to pay for her junkets to New York, Kenya, Iraq, and Cancun.

Correspondents visiting Manila began to joke about the lunacies of Caligula and Messalina, or Adolf Hitler and Cinderella. The circus was in town to stay.

Take Imelda's 1982 International Film Festival. When it came to a diamond-studded end after twelve days of relentless triviality, it was estimated that $100 million had been spent, much of it on a huge Parthenon-style film center. Early in the construction, while Imelda was out of town, Ferdinand ordered work halted. When she returned, he backed down. The idea had come to her in a mystical vision in June 1980, to create an Asian answer to Cannes, next door to her Cultural Center. So much of the construction money was siphoned off by her claque that structural engineering was neglected. Two months before the festival was to open, two floors of the center collapsed, taking a number of workers with it. Officially, eight laborers died—the real figure was said to be over thirty. Not to delay construction, it was alleged that the bodies were left in situ and concrete was poured over them. This distressed the superstitious, so Imelda reportedly had the center exorcised.

Many of the stars she invited did not show up. Those who did included George Hamilton, Sylvester Stallone, Jeremy Irons, Brooke Shields, Peter O'Toole, and Franco Nero. Brooke Shields stayed with her mother in the Tagalog suite of the Coconut Palace, a guest mansion Imelda built entirely out of coconut products where Cristina Ford was often in residence. (Imelda wanted Pope John Paul II to stay there during his 1981 visit to Manila, but he refused and she had to be content with Brooke Shields and Van Cliburn.) In her visionary fashion, Imelda projected that the film festival would attract 4,500 celebrities, and would earn $52 million. In the end the Central Bank had to cough up $4 million just for operating expenses. The highlight of the gala came when everyone was invited to a party at old Fort Santiago, where they washed down lechon with Dom Pérignon, while Ferdinand and Imelda presided from their throne-chairs.

The Second International Film Festival was a bigger fiasco. This time Imelda underwrote festival costs by showing pornographic movies. Strict government censorship laws were relaxed temporarily to allow thirteen X-rated films to be shown at local theaters. Crowds of the faithful turned out to watch explicit scenes of fornication on the giant screen culminating in simultaneous orgasm.

When the cardinal of Manila, Jaime Sin, attacked the showing of the sex films, Imelda responded enigmatically: "Truly, pornography is all in the mind and the heart." Sin had the last word, remarking that one of the fringe benefits of being a priest was that "one does not have to argue with a woman [wife]." Asked what would he think if Imelda were to succeed her husband as president, Sin groaned, "Where will this country go with this kind of leader?"

Imelda and Ferdinand were becoming objects of public ridicule at a time when he was trying hard to win the press to his side. It was not only students and radicals who were after them.

Following the student siege, Ferdinand invited Manila publishers to lunch and asked for their cooperation and support. With his track record, few were prepared to cooperate. But he saw himself as the injured party. At a National Press Club dinner, he complained bitterly, "You elect a president, award him the mantle of authority, make him the symbol of sovereignty of the people, and after that you shoot him down with every weapon you have." This completely ignored the fact that most members of the Press Club thought he had stolen his re-election.

The Manila press was often described as the freest in Asia; certainly it was the most unruly. Traditionally, Filipino politicians felt it necessary to own, or influence, at least one major news outlet, while attacking the journals of rivals as irresponsible. Ferdinand had only a few allies in the press and no newspaper of his own.

In March 1970 the regime made its own publishing debut with *Government Report*, a weekly distributed free by the Office of the President. Its first issue carried the headline: "Can Publishers Foment

Disorders?" and went on to say that "the national press can no longer be trusted," and therefore, the government had to tell its own story.

When he tried to silence the Lopez clan, which controlled the Manila *Chronicle* and a multimedia network through the ABS-CBN Broadcasting Corporation, they declared war. The *Chronicle* labeled Ferdinand's New Society a system that enabled the rich and poor "to seek their livelihood from garbage piles." Days later, Vice President Fernando Lopez resigned from his cabinet post as secretary of agriculture and natural resources. President Marcos accepted the resignation with a letter denouncing the Lopez family as "a pressure group intent upon the destruction of my development program."

The Lopez-Marcos feud had many roots, not least among them the widespread assumption that the vice president's brother, Eugenio, was secretly encouraging Dovie Beams. Few people felt any sympathy with the Lopez side of the quarrel. During the years 1950–86, some $30 billion was taken out of the Philippines, only part of it by the Marcoses; the Lopezes were credited with inspiring this flight of capital. They set the standards by which the elite did such things. Concluded journalist Tom Buckley, "No one much likes the Lopezes."

When Fernando Lopez agreed to be Ferdinand's vice president, his clan expected concessions and put forward proposals for a lubricating-oil factory, a petrochemical complex, the purchase of Caltex Philippines, and the use of reclaimed areas of Laguna Bay for an industrial complex. Whatever Imelda had promised Lopez, Ferdinand turned down the projects on the grounds that they would concentrate too much power in Lopez hands. He gave the Manila Electric Company, the largest user of fuel oil in the country, a smaller rate increase than the Lopezes expected, and increased fuel prices. Jeepney drivers were worst hit and went on strike. Ferdinand sent in troops who killed three people and hurt scores of others.

The Lopezes struck back when Ferdinand was about to make a televised speech backing down from his fuel price increases. A total blackout struck the Manila area and adjacent provinces, delaying his speech two hours. Electricity for the TV station was being supplied by Meralco. Ferdinand raged, but the Lopezes shrugged that it was all because a truck had run into a power line somewhere.

The Lopez media said Ferdinand had brought the country to a point where people thought only of "revolt or revolution, of assassination as a solution, of large-scale arson as a warning of things to come, of violent mass action." The Lopezes charged that "the development [of the Philippines] to an industrial and self-sufficient society can never be accomplished . . . by cronies," that the impoverishment of the islands was due to the "insatiable appetite of gangs of high officials who have been rendered sleepless by their greed." This was cutting close to the bone, and people wondered how long Ferdinand would take it.

The *Chronicle* published cartoons in which a teacher asked his class, "Who is the richest man in Asia today?" "Who gets all those kickbacks from government loans?" Others accused Ferdinand of having a vast collection of diamonds; of being the biggest shadow stockholder in various corporations; of acquiring landholding around the country and lavish estates all over the world; and of having "by conservative estimate," $160 million in Swiss banks.

As if to make up for all the bad blood, the Lopezes invited the First Lady to a grand party at a hacienda in Mindanao. It was all a cruel trick. Many of her enemies were also present. During the party, the owner of the hacienda invited a group of male guests to a back room. There they discovered to their immense delight that he had installed a one-way mirror just for the occasion, which allowed them to see into the ladies' room. A camera was ready. They were barely able to contain themselves when who should appear in the ladies' room but First Lady Imelda Marcos, who proceeded to take a pee in front of them all. The camera clicked away, and prints were made for all the men present. (One print was treasured by Ninoy Aquino and kept in his wallet until just before the day he died.)

Imelda was informed immediately by one of the ladies, and was speechless with rage. There are those who attribute the fall of the Lopezes to this one sophomoric prank. Fernando Lopez was Imelda's chief political rival at this point, and the time for a showdown had come.

President Marcos was nearing the end of his second term. He could not run for another unless the constitution was amended. When Vice President Lopez announced his intention to run for president in 1973, the big question was whether Ferdinand planned to rig things so he could have a third term. A Constitutional Convention was about to begin, and everyone was anxious to see whether he would attempt to manipulate its outcome. One alternative, to keep power in the family, was to have Imelda run for president in his place as the new champion of the Nacionalista party. As early as 1971, *Time* magazine noted that "Imelda is being built up as a possible candidate to succeed him." The

Far Eastern Economic Review went even further, declaring: "If Mrs. Marcos wants the job . . . no one can beat her." The convention was to consider whether to maintain the presidential system, which would permit him to become prime minister with Imelda or someone else as a figurehead president. It was known that the First Lady favored continuing the presidential system, so that she could be more than just a figurehead.

It was not certain that Ferdinand wanted Imelda in either role. One minute he announced: "I have no intention of allowing her to enter politics." The next he told correspondent Henry Kamm of *The New York Times* that he was thinking of fielding Imelda against Ninoy Aquino, whom he called a "Communist supporter." Ferdinand said, "If all else fails, then probably the First Lady would have to come in." Observed a Manila journalist, "Anybody in possession of his wits can see the grand scheme of deception that has been foisted on the Filipino people. . . . Even Miss Imee Marcos contributed to the denial farce thus: 'That's a mad rumor [her mother's candidacy]. One politician in the family is enough.' " The Philippines, added *Graphic* magazine, "might yet see the likes of a Marcos dynasty."

Efforts to intimidate delegates began. On August 16, 1971, a bomb exploded in a men's room at the Constitutional Convention. Less than a week later, on August 21, two grenades were thrown at a Liberal party rally of ten thousand people in Manila's Plaza Miranda. Ten were killed and sixty-six wounded. Among the wounded were all eight of the party's senatorial candidates—Senator Sergio Osmeña, Jr.; his nephew, Representative John Osmeña; Senator Genaro Magsaysay, brother of the late president; Senator Gerardo Roxas, son of President Roxas; and Senator Jovito Salonga. The only member of the Liberal leadership who escaped injury, because he arrived late, was Senator Aquino.

Blaming the attack on Communist terrorists, President Marcos suspended the writ of habeas corpus and jailed a number of leftists. Senator Jose Diokno charged that "the military or men trained by the military, threw [the] hand grenades." Palace insiders eventually confirmed it was all a set-up, carried out by Ver's agents. According to Primitivo Mijares, chief press spokesman for Marcos at the time, orders for the bombing came from the Presidential Security Command, which made all the arrangements with the grenade throwers, including the payoff. Mijares discussed the bombing immediately afterward with members of the Command, and was told that the men who threw the grenades were murdered when they tried to collect their fee, apparently standard procedure for Ver.

Public sympathy for the wounded Liberals was so widespread that they won an overwhelming victory in the November 1971 congressional elections, taking six of the eight senatorial seats contested. Encouraged by the Liberal victory, delegates at the Constitutional Convention bravely put forth a proposal to ban Ferdinand Marcos and all members of his family from ever holding the position of head of state, no matter what form of administration was finally chosen. Ferdinand and Imelda were not pleased. To make sure the measure was defeated, delegate Eduardo Quintero of Leyte, a former ambassador to Japan, was called to Malacanang Palace and presented by Imelda with eighteen envelopes containing a total of 400,000 pesos. The envelopes were distributed to key convention delegates on the understanding that they would vote against the Ban Marcos clause. Quintero then suffered a twinge of conscience and revealed to the press his role in the bribes. In reprisal, his home was raided by the National Bureau of Investigation and he was charged with perjury, graft, and corrupt practices—for daring to link the First Lady to bribery. The Ban Marcos clause was defeated. (Quintero took up voluntary exile in the United States, where he died shortly before Imelda and Ferdinand departed Malacanang Palace for the last time.)

In what many observers concluded was nothing more than a callous appeal for public sympathy, Malacanang suddenly announced that the First Lady was pregnant and in danger of a miscarriage. Blame was laid on "increasing innuendoes unflattering to the president and Mrs. Marcos in connection with the payola scandal." Malacanang then announced that the baby had been lost. Critics groused that the only miscarriage had been of justice. The palace struck back with a heavily photographed funeral for the "lost child," in the Romualdez family plot in Leyte. There Ferdinand and Imelda buried a white box tied in ribbon under a slab marked: "To our unborn child, with whom so many of our dreams died—Ferdinand and Imelda."

The bereaved parents once more denied any political ambitions. "I have no intention of running in 1973," swore Ferdinand. "The First Lady, too, has no intention of running in 1973." Two weeks later Imelda resumed her high-speed existence, roaring out to visit her mother's hometown in Bulacan, preceded by twenty-four army trucks loaded with rice and medicine. Said her ardent supporter, Immigration Commissioner Reyes: "Some day, historians [will] record this occasion as the day that launched Mrs. Marcos's candidacy for president."

A rash of new explosions rocked Manila. President Marcos and his new defense minister, his personal lawyer Juan Ponce Enrile, blamed "subversives," and the Constabulary claimed it had obtained a copy of a "blueprint for revolution" by the Communist party. However, American intelligence officials observed that the bombings were actually the work of the regime's paramilitary unit, "the Monkees."

Ferdinand soon proved that when his enemies closed in on him he was a close student of Lyndon Johnson's Tonkin Gulf maneuver. That summer of 1972, the fishing trawler M/V *Karagatan* went aground off the northeast coast of Luzon and was boarded by the military, who reported to headquarters that they found nothing suspicious, only some food supplies. The crew had vanished. Ferdinand made a great issue over the *Karagatan,* claiming it was running guns to the Communists. He sent troops to scour the jungles, and planes to strafe deserted hilltops. According to Malacanang, the trawler had aboard 3,500 M-15 rifles, 30 rocket launchers, and 160,000 rounds of ammunition—completely contradicting the original military report. The palace claimed that the boat was a "foreign vessel," which had sailed from Japan on its sinister mission. A guerrilla force known as the New People's Army (NPA), modeled on Maoist dogma, was operating in the countryside. The palace initially had said the NPA consisted of only one hundred men. A few days after the *Karagatan* flap began, the Constabulary inflated the number ten times to get two hundred NPA regulars and eight hundred part-time guerrillas.

Journalists confirmed that the gunrunning shipment was a sham. The real owner of the trawler was the Karagatan Fishing Corporation, with offices in Manila. Before running aground, the trawler had stopped at ports in Ilocos Sur, Ilocos Norte, and Fuga Island—the smuggling haven where the Marcoses frequently vacationed—and apparently had been engaged in nothing more sinister than cigarette smuggling for an Ilocano syndicate.

Senator Aquino disclosed that President Marcos had secretly purchased three thousand guns from Eastern Europe with the apparent intention of planting them where they could be discovered by the Constabulary as NPA "caches."

The NPA was hardly a serious threat. In a nation of 50 million people, even a thousand full-time guerrillas, backed by ten thousand part-time supporters, were scarcely a grave danger. In secret intelligence reports, the CIA concluded year after year that the NPA was not a formidable threat and had received little, if any, foreign assistance.

But if Ferdinand needed a Communist menace, he could manufacture it. Martial law was on its way. To foment hysteria, Ferdinand was telling people that the defense establishment needed more authority to meet the "imminent danger" of Communist subversion. On September 13, 1972, Senator Aquino revealed that President Marcos had prepared Plan Sagittarius to put Greater Manila and most of central Luzon under military control. The palace denounced Aquino's account as sheer fabrication.

Ferdinand was meeting regularly with twelve top military advisers (eventually known as the "Rolex 12" because he gave each of them a gold Rolex wristwatch). There were two civilians in the group: Defense Minister Enrile and Tarlac governor Eduardo Cojuangco, Jr. This Cojuangco was continually at war with the rest of his clan and despised his cousin Cory's husband, Senator Aquino. He was temporarily in uniform as a colonel in a special unit of the Constabulary reported to be directing the bomb attacks of the paramilitary Monkees. The regular military men among the "Rolex 12" were chief-of-staff General Romeo Espino, General Rafael Zagala, and General Ignacio Paz, all army; General Fidel Ramos, General Tomas Diaz, and Colonel Romeo Gatan of the Constabulary; General Jose Rancudo of the air force, Admiral Hilario Ruiz of the navy, General Fabian Ver of NISA, and General Alfredo Montoya of METROCOM.

What really alarmed Ferdinand was information that his harshest critic, Senator Aquino, had met secretly with NPA leader Jose Maria Sison, alias Amado Guerrero, or at least with one of Sison's top lieutenants, Julius Fortuna. The meeting was by all accounts inconclusive and harmless, but the very fact that it had happened provided Ferdinand an excuse to charge that the opposition was considering an alliance with Communists. Although he did not accuse Aquino of treason, Ferdinand did accuse him of consorting with enemies of the state. (During the same period, Imelda was conferring with both Chinese and Russian politburos, without authorization of the Philippine legislature.) The same day, September 17, Ferdinand signed a martial law decree. He waited a few days to issue it because, as he later put it, "I wanted time to commune with God and await His signal."

The U.S. government knew martial law was going to be declared in the Philippines long before it happened, and that Marcos was creating a false crisis in order to void the constitution and seize dictatorial power. President Nixon, Henry Kissinger, and Ambassador Byroade all gave their explicit approval. Ferdinand held a number of meetings with U.S. Embassy officials, and saw Ambassador Byroade for two hours. He then telephoned the White House, and President Nixon gave "his personal blessing." Primitivo Mijares revealed as early as 1976 that he was told by Imelda Marcos Ferdinand made an overseas call to President Nixon a few days before he declared martial law; Imelda said Nixon told Marcos to "go ahead with his plans." Mijares said Byroade and Kissinger actually had copies of the full martial law declaration days before it was promulgated. In his conversations with Nixon and Byroade, Ferdinand apparently agreed that in return for America's support, he would not let anything interfere with U.S. investments. Mijares made these revelations at a time when attacking Ferdinand Marcos was not fashionable in America, and they were soon forgotten.

Apparently one of the conditions for U.S. support was that Ferdinand had to give prominent leaders of the opposition a chance to leave the country first. A messenger from Malacanang went to each of them on September 18. While Senator Aquino felt it necessary to remain behind, other politicians took the tip and left Manila hurriedly. Sergio Osmeña, Jr., went to America, as did Eugenio Lopez, brother of the vice president. Raul Manglapus suddenly departed for a U.S. "speaking tour" on September 21.

The following day, bombs exploded in Quezon City Hall where the Constitutional Convention was still meeting. Somebody blew up a police car while the policemen were off having lunch. Bombs exploded in department stores, city halls, and schools, at night when the buildings were empty. It was like Chinese New Year with loud fireworks and paper dragons. There was a rash of kidnappings of the families of wealthy Chinese, including the wife and son of Antonio Roxas-Chua. The victims were released after large ransoms were paid. The kidnappings, like the bombings, were blamed on subversives and the New People's Army. However there were no arrests and there was no flurry of activity on the part of the police or the Defense Ministry. There seemed to be a deliberate campaign to spread hysteria and to prime the population for drastic government action to restore public order.

On Friday night, "Communist terrorists" swooped down on the two-car convoy of Defense Minister Enrile, riddled one car with thirty rounds, and sped away. Enrile was riding in the escort car and escaped without a scratch, as did everyone else in his party. (Enrile later admitted that the ambush was staged.) Ferdinand announced that this "Communist" attack on his defense minister was the last straw. At 9:00 P.M. he issued an executive order implementing martial law for the first time in Philippine history:

> WHEREAS, the rebellion and armed action undertaken by these lawless elements of the communist and other armed aggrupations organized to overthrow the Republic of the Philippines by armed violence and force have assumed the magnitude of an actual state of war against our people and the Republic of the Philippines;
>
> NOW, THEREFORE, I, FERDINAND E. MARCOS, President of the Philippines . . . do hereby place the entire Philippines . . . under martial law and, in my capacity as their commander-in-chief, do hereby command the armed forces of the Philippines, to maintain law and order . . . prevent or suppress all forms of lawless violence as well as any act of insurrection or rebellion and to enforce obedience to all the laws and decrees, orders and regulations promulgated by me personally or upon my direction.

In pre-dawn raids, government troops seized control of all communications and public utilities, closed schools, and arrested more than forty opposition politicians and newsmen charged with plotting to overthrow the government by violence and subversion.

The military arrested members of Congress, governors, student and labor activists, and rounded up miscellaneous criminals. Some thirty thousand people were put in concentration camps. Among the first to be arrested were Senator Aquino and Senator Jose Diokno.

Newspapers and broadcast facilities were taken over and later transferred to Marcos cronies. One television network and one newspaper, the *Daily Express* (both owned by crony Roberto Benedicto with Imelda's cousin Enrique Romualdez), and the government radio station resumed operations after the coup.

Few Filipinos were distressed by these arrests and takeovers. Under Marcos, the legislature had lost whatever effectiveness it had and became only a rubber stamp. So when Congress was abolished and many of its members were arrested, Filipinos shrugged and were ready to give Ferdinand and his "technocrats" a chance to show what they could do.

Media control was essential to promote two myths: That crime had been eliminated, and that there was no longer any such thing as corruption. After the coup, crime stories were rarely reported. The public awareness of crime went down sharply and Ferdinand was credited by many, including American businessmen, with instituting law and order. It became illegal to wear a sidearm on the street in Manila unless you were an official. Spreading rumors became subversive, and punishable by death. At the end of November 1972, Ferdinand claimed that the Communist menace had been eradicated. A lot of people were impressed.

The first fatality of martial law was General Marcos Soliman, the U.S.-trained chief of the National Intelligence Coordinating Agency. General Soliman had leaked the martial law plans too far in advance to the CIA and to Senator Aquino. Within a week of the coup the palace announced that he had died of a heart attack. His family said he was shot by Marcos agents.

Twelve

SALVAGING DEMOCRACY

THE MAIN CONCERN of a bad government, as everyone knows, is to protect itself from its own subjects. Under martial law, the Philippines entered a grim period of human rights abuses. A new term, "salvaging," came into use to cover the torture, disappearance, and death of ordinary citizens. The army and Constabulary set out to discipline the population by creating an atmosphere of terror. Here and there a few good officers tried to win the support of the local population, and punished troops who abused civilians. But they were rare exceptions.

Many of the horror stories were independently corroborated by diplomats, journalists, priests, scholars, and international organizations such as Amnesty International. They are a litany of sadism, of dead rats being stuffed in mouths, of electric cattle prods jammed into vaginas, of mashed testicles, and prisoners being forced to eat their own ears. These atrocities were often performed by, or supervised by, men trained and employed in various ways by the U.S. military and intelligence services. These were the people produced by the Colonel Lansdale and Frank Walton programs, and trained at various police and security academies in America and Taiwan. They were the new combined military-police establishment provided to Ferdinand Marcos as part of his deal with Lyndon Johnson. With their help, Ferdinand was able first to force his own re-election, then to declare martial law and make it stick. Now they were the instrument by which he would suppress all dissent and retain power for himself and his family as long as he wished. The U.S. Embassy was not ignorant of these practices. Official protests were not made under Presidents Nixon, Ford, and Reagan—only during the presidency of Jimmy Carter—but the Carter administration did not follow through by halting over $500 million in military aid from going to the Philippines.

Under the Marcoses, the army, Constabulary, Civilian Home Defense Corps, and intelligence agencies employed such methods as "submarine," where your head was submerged in a toilet or bucket of water; "zap-zap," where electric shocks were applied to your genitals or nipples; "water-cure," where gallons of water were poured up your nose till you almost drowned; "baggy," where a plastic bag was placed over your head till you nearly suffocated; "buttstroking," where you were beaten on the back with a rifle; "telephone," where your eardrums were popped from behind with the flats of the hand; "Saigon roulette," where the torturer loaded all but one round in a revolver and fired at your legs. And, of course, "San Juanico Bridge," where you were forced to lie with your feet on one bed and your head on a second, and were beaten and kicked whenever you let your body sag—named after the new bridge connecting Samar to Leyte, built as a wedding anniversary present to Imelda from Ferdinand. The Marcoses called it the "bridge of love."

These human rights abuses came from both ends of the military ladder: provincial bullies, and high-ranking sadists at headquarters in Manila. Of the bullies, the archetype was Constabulary Sergeant George Presquito on Negros Island, a sweaty man with a big stomach, scraggly beard, and a drunken manner, even when he was sober, which was rare.

Presquito was famous for shooting people who had already surrendered, even when their offenses were minor. He was said to have murdered forty-two people personally. The government and military never interfered. He liked to undress and sexually abuse women in front of their husbands or their families, which he found produced quick results. He led his men on sprees where they beat and robbed villagers. He devoted himself to tormenting political activists and union organizers.

It was Presquito and his men who one morning in July 1977 picked up Vilma Riopay, a twenty-one-year-old catechist at the Magballo church, and brutally tormented her until she was turned into a mental and physical invalid. The case was so shocking that it appeared in newspapers and publications around the world. She had been taken to a safe house where she underwent an interrogation that included the "zap-zap," the "water-cure," denial of sleep, and beating on her genitals. After the government received thousands of petitions from villagers in Negros, Presquito was finally called into Constabulary headquarters at Camp Crame in Manila. Despite all the evidence and witnesses, a military court exonerated him. Presquito, the court decided, was just doing his duty.

Inside one of the buildings of Camp Crame was the headquarters of the dreaded 5th CSU (Constabulary Security Unit). The 5th CSU created many martyrs, but few as celebrated as Edgar Jopson, the student leader who had asked President Marcos to sign a pledge that he would not violate the constitution and seek a third term. His confrontation with Ferdinand had climaxed in the student siege of Malacanang Palace, after which Jopson was forced to flee for his life. He went underground as one of a growing number of grievance guerrillas. He had never been a Communist or a radical but had been the "man of the year" of the middle-class Jaycees. Eventually, he joined the Communist-led NPA, becoming one of its commanders. Jopson was captured on June 14, 1979, and underwent torture at the 5th CSU for many months.

Using money given him on visiting day by his father, Jopson "befriended" a guard and escaped. He was recaptured in Mindanao in the summer of 1982, shot three times, and then later six times more to finish him off. His bloated and bullet-ridden body was turned over to his father by the Constabulary. The slaying caused an outcry in Manila, particularly at his alma mater, the elite Jesuit-run Ateneo, where a memorial service was scheduled. It was called off at first when threats were received from the army, but was held anyway after a storm of protest from its affluent alumni, which included Ninoy Aquino.

The man accused by human rights groups of being "the top torturer" at the 5th CSU, one of those said to have tormented Edgar Jopson, was Captain Rodolfo Aguinaldo. According to his accusers, Aguinaldo was a legend in his own time, feared throughout the archipelago: a man whose talents left detainees permanently disabled or mentally crippled. Aguinaldo was a Marcos favorite, a fellow Ilocano from Laoag. He graduated second in his class at the Philippine Military Academy in the late 1960s and immediately joined the 5th CSU. He received special training from American army and CIA instructors in the fine art of extracting information. After proving himself to be unusually gifted, he was sent to the CIA/KMT Political Warfare Cadres

Academy in Taiwan, where he received additional training from the past-masters of the Chiang dictatorship. Aguinaldo was a trim and muscular athlete, who favored jogging suits with a Belgian 9mm Browning tucked in the waistband. He liked to swim and skydive, one of the favorite sports of his ultimate boss, Constabulary chief General Fidel Ramos. According to a study of human rights abuses in the Philippines published by the Catholic Church, the sport Aguinaldo enjoyed most was having sex with the wives, sisters, or daughters of his prisoners. None of these charges had any effect on his career.

The head of 5th CSU was another Ilocano, Colonel Ishmael Rodrigo, whose parents came from the Marcos hometown, Batac. He served with Fidel Ramos in the Filipino contingent during the Korean War, became one of Lansdale's top Huk killers, and worked for the CIA in Manila and Saigon. In time he transferred directly to the U.S. Army Green Berets as an intelligence officer with the rank of colonel. In Vietnam, Rodrigo became friends with William Colby, and was sent to CIA headquarters in Langley, Virginia, to study tradecraft. After the declaration of martial law, the CIA sent Rodrigo back to Manila, where General Ramos gave him the job of running 5th CSU. Thus the man heading the most notorious torture unit in the Marcos dictatorship was a long-time CIA agent and Green Beret. It was Colonel Rodrigo who applied brainwashing techniques to young Edgar Jopson, then turned him over to Captain Aguinaldo's men for physical abuse.

Aguinaldo was assisted in his efforts by Major Cesar Garcia and Colonel Miguel Aure, both rabid anti-Communists. Colonel Aure had directed the 1977 torture, rape, and murder of Purificacion Pedro, a twenty-eight-year-old graduate of the University of the Philippines arrested on suspicion of being a member of the NPA. She was shot in the shoulder during the arrest and beaten with rifle butts. Then she was taken to a Bataan hospital, where she was gang-raped and hung by her neck with her brassiere. As the troopers left her room, the colonel reportedly growled at her relatives waiting outside: "Remember the name Aure."

There were many opponents of the Marcos regime who drew attention to what was happening in the Philippines, but so long as Nixon and Kissinger remained in control, Washington was firmly on the side of the dictatorship. Nothing was done to assist political prisoners, and a great deal was done to intimidate anti-Marcos exiles living in America.

Senator Aquino had been arrested in the early hours of September 23, 1972, in his suite in the Manila Hilton. Two days later he petitioned the Supreme Court from his cell for a writ of habeas corpus, challenging the validity of martial law, his arrest, and detention. The petition was denied.

A year later he was charged with murder, subversion, and illegal possession of firearms. The murder charge related to the death of a barrio captain in Tarlac in 1967. The subversion and illegal possession of firearms charges involved accusations that Ninoy supplied arms to Communist terrorists to overthrow the Marcos regime. Before a military court, Aquino responded that Marcos had simply framed him, and he accused Juan Ponce Enrile directly of trumping up the charges. He refused to defend himself, saying he would rather "accept a tyrant's revenge." The government-controlled press did not carry any portion of Aquino's statement, but a videotape was made and kept by Imelda, and she was said to review it from time to time when she felt the need to refresh her sentiments.

Early in 1975, Aquino went on a hunger strike. At the end of the thirty-first day, he was rushed to a hospital, down to 124 pounds from his original 191. His legs no longer supported him and he had difficulty focusing his eyes. His prolonged fast produced a profound religious experience, from which he emerged and slowly regained some of his health.

In late June 1977, he was granted a two-and-a-half-hour interview with Ferdinand. As old fraternity brothers, they still addressed each other as "brod," although by this point the effect must have been surreal. Ferdinand said: "Do you remember that I sent a message to you two days before the declaration of martial law that I will declare martial law? Well, I really wanted you to run away." Aquino replied, "I told the messenger that I am a senator of the republic and I will stick by my position—and I was arrested." Aquino asked that his case be transferred to a civilian court, but Ferdinand turned him down.

On November 25, a military tribunal found Aquino guilty and pronounced his sentence—"death by firing squad." Because of the recent election of President Carter, the sentence was not carried out. Carter made repeated representations to Manila through emissaries.

In June 1978, an agreement was reached with Cory Aquino that her husband would apply for amnesty and write a letter expressing his desire to live outside the country, promising that while abroad he would not "take any action that would affect the image and security of the country." This was done, but action was delayed on various excuses, reportedly because of pressure from the vengeful First Lady.

While Aquino was being neutralized in this manner, others were beginning to strike back. During the summer and fall of 1979, a number of government and commercial buildings in Manila were put to the torch, including a floating casino moored at the bayfront which was owned and operated under martial law protection by Imelda's brothers Kokoy and Alfredo. The fires were the work of a group calling itself the Light-a-Fire Movement.

Fabian Ver's security forces seemed helpless to stop the arson. But that December they arrested an American citizen, Ben Lim, at Manila International Airport and charged him with attempting to smuggle explosives into the country. Lim had a weak heart and when his pills were withheld during his confinement, he died. His interrogation led to the arrest of fifteen other "terrorists," reportedly all members of the Light-a-Fire Movement, headed by a Harvard-educated business executive, Eduardo Olaguer. A raid on Olaguer's home produced explosives and instruction manuals with CIA markings. It was alleged that the explosives were sent from San Francisco by lawyer Steve Psinakis, son-in-law of Eugenio Lopez. Psinakis had been a thorn in the side of Ferdinand and Imelda since the Lopez showdown. He published frequent attacks on the regime in books, pamphlets, and newspapers, and kept up a steady barrage of the U.S. Congress protesting the illegal seizure of Lopez family assets in the Philippines. In 1977, Psinakis helped organize and carry out a daring jail break at Fort Bonifacio to spring his brother-in-law, Eugenio Lopez, Jr., and fellow prisoner Sergio Osmeña III. Since then, Psinakis had been active in the Movement for a Free Philippines headed by Raul Manglapus. He was now accused of being behind the Light-a-Fire Movement.

By the end of December 1979, more than two hundred men and women had been arrested as "potential sources of information." All those arrested were told they could go free if they signed statements that Psinakis was guilty. Those who did not accept the offer were tortured until they signed anyway. But soon afterward, Ferdinand announced that the Light-a-Fire Movement had been extinguished and Aquino was free to go.

The senator's long imprisonment had taken a toll on his heart. Doctors said he needed bypass surgery. This could have been done at Imelda's luxurious Heart Center, but nobody in Manila had the bad taste to suggest it. He and his family were suddenly, with only a few hours' notice, put aboard a plane to the United States.

Imelda, the target of Aquino's often satirical criticism, personally brought him the word that he was free to leave. Then, in his presence, she gaily telephoned key men at the foreign ministry, U.S. Ambassador Richard Murphy, and Philippine Air Lines to arrange his hasty departure.

After undergoing a triple bypass operation, Aquino settled with his family in Boston on a grant from Harvard University. He then formally broke the vow extracted from him in Manila that he would refrain from making political statements. Attacking the agreement as "a pact with the devil," he warned President Marcos of a "gathering storm." Idealistic groups of Filipinos were preparing to strike at the dictatorship with "bombings, assassinations and kidnappings of public officials and military officers . . . to bring the Marcos regime to its knees."

Less than three weeks later, the attacks began. Bombs exploded simultaneously in nine buildings after the occupants had been warned to evacuate. No one was hurt but international press coverage was heavy. In October 1980, the group struck again as delegates gathered in Manila for a convention of the American Society of Travel Agents. The setting was Imelda's $150 million Convention Center. A bomb exploded only fifty feet from Ferdinand Marcos. He was not injured but twenty others were, and the convention was canceled in panic. Manila's luxury hotels emptied and stayed empty. American tourism had been bringing the regime $400 million a year. Malacanang Palace issued thirty arrest warrants, including one for Aquino. There was no extradition agreement between the United States and the Philippines, so Aquino was safe for the time being.

Asked what the U.S. government would do about the warrants, an official of the Carter administration said, "Nothing—[Washington] would not bend the law to suit Manila." That stand was reversed a few months later when Ronald Reagan became president.

The turnabout under Reagan began with the arrest in Manila of a U.S. citizen accused of being involved in the Light-a-Fire Movement. Victor Burns Lovely was a fifty-eight-year-old Filipino-American businessman from Los Angeles. He arrived in Manila with a bomb in his luggage, checked into a hotel, and when he unpacked the bomb exploded, blowing off his right forearm and blinding one eye. Lovely was taken to a military hospital and interrogated. Ver's agents told him he was on the seventh floor and anyone falling from that height would not survive. Lovely signed a confession. President Marcos showed up for the occasion and was photographed waving the confession over Lovely.

In the confession, Lovely said his trip had been planned and bankrolled by Aquino and Psinakis. He claimed Psinakis had sent him to a secret camp in Arizona where he was instructed in the use of bombs by the American-based Movement for a Free Philippines.

The FBI became involved because Lovely was an American citizen. The FBI had not shown similar interest earlier with Ben Lim. The reason was simple—a policy decision had since been made by the Reagan administration to help the Marcoses by interfering with the exile movement. FBI agents were sent to Manila to question Lovely about Aquino and Psinakis. Secretary of State Alexander Haig met privately with President Marcos and promised him that the Reagan administration would help "fight terrorism" by vigorously prosecuting U.S.-based Filipino activists.

Soon after Reagan became president, Ferdinand Marcos began lobbying hard for an extradition treaty so that he could get his hands on some of his enemies in exile. He could then frame criminal charges against anyone he wished. Such a treaty was proposed in the U.S. Congress but was defeated despite the best efforts of the Reagan administration to push it through. The main reason for its defeat was the concern of Congress to distinguish between political opponents of a foreign government and common criminals—a distinction that many foresaw would be blurred deliberately by the Marcos regime. Unable to make use of extradition, the Reagan administration turned next to the Neutrality Act, which prohibits Americans from engaging in conspiracy to overthrow friendly governments. By Reagan's estimation, the Marcos regime was friendly, no matter what its record of human rights abuses.

After being terrorized by Ver's thugs, Victor Lovely was understandably anxious to go back to America under any circumstance, even as a federal witness. He was returned to the United States in September 1981. According to FBI affidavits, Lovely repeated his charges before a grand jury that Psinakis organized the Manila bombings. Although grand jury proceedings are supposed to be secret, Lovely's testimony was turned over by the FBI to Malacanang. FBI agents questioned Aquino and Manglapus closely. Aquino had been under intensive FBI surveillance since he arrived in the United States and his house in Boston was raided.

FBI agents also raided the Psinakis home in San Francisco on December 17, 1981. Twenty agents appeared at midnight accompanied by San Francisco police and sheriff's deputies. Psinakis and his family were locked in the kitchen while agents thumbed through his files, slit open vacuum cleaner bags, unwrapped Christmas presents, and searched every room with dogs trained to sniff out explosives. The FBI claimed that a "confidential source" (evidently posing as a baglady) had poked through Psinakis trash barrels that morning and found 600 feet of detonating cord, an empty battery package, a box for a Westclox pocketwatch, and a pair of orange rubber gloves. But no evidence of bomb-making was found that night nor when a second search was made in January.

During these raids the FBI removed a number of documents from Psinakis's files, including a coded list of underground anti-Marcos operatives in the Philippines. These were turned over by the FBI to General Ver, who had those named arrested, interrogated, and tortured. One of those arrested was Doris Nueval, who was interrogated in the Philippines not only by Ver's agents but by the FBI and the CIA as well. Two of those arrested and interrogated vanished without a trace.

Ferdinand had become paranoid about his critics in America. He and Imelda evidently discussed the matter repeatedly with their friends the Reagans in long-distance phone calls with the White House—personal contact that they kept up throughout the Reagan presidency. Department of State reports on Filipino dissidents were routinely sent to the embassy in Manila, to be shared with Marcos and Ver.*

While Washington hounded Ferdinand's enemies, nothing was done to prevent Ver's secret agents from striking at enemies inside the United States. The FBI, Justice Department, and State Department said that the presence in America of intelligence agents of such "friendly" countries as the Philippines, Chile, and Iran did not present a danger. According to a secret U.S. Senate report, the Justice Department did not consider national security to be threatened if agents of friendly countries—Ver's NISA or the Shah's SAVAK—came to America to threaten and harass dissidents in order to curtail their political activities. Officials did admit that the activities of Ver's agents included the "possibility of violence." But any "complaints" would have to be handled on a case-by-case basis.

According to one FBI agent, it was a very simple application of

*I have documents obtained under the Freedom of Information Act showing that U.S. counterintelligence surveillance reports of Filipino dissidents in America were regularly passed to the Philippine Constabulary.

"white hat–black hat" criteria. Since the Philippines was not Communist—a black hat—it was good and wore a "white hat." No concern was expressed over extraordinary evidence of Marcos involvement in corruption, embezzlement, extortion, theft, torture, murder, and organized crime.

The CIA routinely informed both the FBI and the State Department when it learned that NISA agents had entered the United States. The CIA reported that Ver sent nineteen NISA agents to the United States in May 1973 as "bodyguards" for Imee Marcos, when she attended Princeton. In just one of many cases, in February 1974, the FBI learned that six NISA agents had been sent to Los Angeles to watch Sergio Osmeña, Jr., who had run against Ferdinand in the 1969 presidential race. It was also known that a military attaché at the Philippine Embassy in Washington was involved full time in surveillance of exile leaders, and that a NISA agent was based in Chicago where one of his duties was to maintain liaison with Tony Accardo, chairman of the board of the mob. According to exiled leader Raul Manglapus, General Ver once traveled to Chicago to arrange his murder. Manglapus said Ver approached a Filipino exile and told him that President Marcos would drop all charges against him if he agreed to assassinate Manglapus. Instead, the Filipino got word to Manglapus that Ver had made this offer and that he had turned it down.

In June 1981 in Seattle two Filipino-American labor leaders, Gene Viernes and Silme Domingo, who were trying to organize opposition to Marcos in the labor movement, were shot to death. Their families charged that the murders were carried out by NISA agents on orders from President Marcos and Fabian Ver. Three members of a U.S.-based pro-Marcos gang were convicted and sentenced to life; a fourth member of the gang was murdered just before he was to give testimony against Anthony Baruso, owner of the murder weapon, implicating him in the conspiracy. Baruso was an Ilocano and an intimate of Ferdinand and Imelda, who was on a first-name basis with Ver's guards at Malacanang Palace. The families of Viernes and Domingo charged that U.S. intelligence agencies were aware that the murder was being planned, and that Baruso was never indicted because he was being protected by the CIA and FBI at the request of General Ver.

Ferdinand was initially named as a defendent along with his government in the 1982 lawsuit, but this was dropped at the request of the U.S. State Department. Under the "Head-of-State Doctrine," the leader of a foreign nation cannot be prosecuted for acts undertaken while he was head of state. The lawyer for Domingo and Viernes argued that Marcos, although immune under the doctrine, should still be required to testify. The real purpose of the "Head-of-State Doctrine" is to prevent embarrassment to the U.S. government.

To what extent were American officials aware of what Ferdinand and Imelda were doing? The CIA was demonstrably aware that the Marcoses were looting the Philippines and embezzling hundreds of millions. The CIA was intimately acquainted with the nature and extent of torture and political murder under way in the Philippines because many of those involved were men trained by the CIA, and in some cases were still on the payroll providing the Agency with inside intelligence.

Through access I was given to twelve thousand pages of top-secret CIA documents covering an entire year of intelligence summaries to the White House, it is possible to say that very little of the dark side of the Marcos regime was conveyed directly to the president of the United States during that period. This was probably due to the manipulations of the director of central intelligence, the secretary of state, and members of the National Security Council, all of whom would have had reason to modify what the president was told. But it is wrong to assume the president would act differently. President Johnson knew that the Marcos war record was a total sham, but endorsed it publicly to gain support for his Vietnam policy. President Nixon and Secretary of State Kissinger were comfortable with President Marcos, as they were with President Pinochet, and they gave him the nod to usurp power. The human rights initiatives of President Carter were reversed the moment Reagan gained office. These men and their policies were not inspired by better intelligence reporting.

When Imelda was confronted by a group of U.S. congressmen in 1978 with questions about her hidden wealth and documented cases of beatings, water torture, and electric shock treatments being administered to enemies of the regime, she shrugged it all off. "The stories have . . . been made up," she said.

Thirteen

FILIPINO ROULETTE

ONE OF THE BUILT-IN disadvantages of a dictatorship is that the moment conspiracy is institutionalized, others in the regime begin conspiring over the succession. The one-man rule of Ferdinand Marcos was no exception. Rival factions, cliques, and personality cults had been building from the beginning, and were clearly identifiable by 1972. But it was not until September 1975 that the struggle for power in Malacanang broke into the open with a confrontation between Imelda Marcos, Defense Minister Juan Ponce Enrile, and Executive Secretary Alejandro Melchor.

A big amiable Teddy bear of a man, and a graduate of the U.S. Naval Academy, Alex Melchor was a technocrat who was completely sold on the idea that President Marcos was a reformer correcting long-standing abuses of power. Although there were many curious things going on, which would tend to arouse suspicion, there were a number of men in the government who were not fully aware of the degree of corruption, but who were prepared to accept that in politics there would always be some. Imelda's extravagance was conspicuous, yet few people were aware of the extent of fiscal irregularity involved, and they were inclined to write her off as an eccentric. As for President Marcos, he gave every appearance of being what he claimed to be. Ferdinand, like any gifted leader, was deft at convincing people that he was sincere and that they should work for him. Only those who worked closely with him, or ran afoul of him, were aware of the darker side of his nature and were sensitized to some of the more sinister undercurrents of his administration. Many technocrats came on board with the conviction that they were going to help Marcos straighten out the mess. The process of their disenchantment could take months or years, depending on how observant they were, or how soon they became tangled in the conspiracies of their associates. At that point, many were entrapped by their own appetites, as in the case of the Cruz brothers, while others dropped out to resume private lives or to go abroad.

After three years of martial law, Alex Melchor saw disturbing signs that political factions within the regime were subverting the entire effort. He never thought to blame Marcos himself. He went to the president to complain. Ferdinand instructed him to draw up a list of the backsliders so they could be summarily fired.

Melchor went to every department head and gathered the names of the worst offenders, compiling a master list of 2,664 officials wrecking government operations through personal corruption. True to his word, Ferdinand began firing from the top of the list, only to be halted abruptly by the First Lady and Juan Ponce Enrile. Most of the backsliders were her personal appointments, the rest were Enrile's. Imelda was so furious that she demanded entirely new concessions. Less than two months after he drew up the master list, Melchor lost his job.

Ferdinand pacified Imelda by appointing her governor of the new province of Metro-Manila. Imelda thought she needed to demonstrate her administrative talents in order to be taken seriously as a presidential contender. Too many people were deriding her frivolous lifestyle and shallow preoccupation with celebrities. As governor, she headed the consolidated administration of four cities, thirteen municipalities, and a combined population of five million—one tenth of the total population of the Philippines. People began referring to her as the "de facto vice president." She started to drop in on cabinet meetings, and was abuzz with glamorous ideas for a new airport, reclaiming 12,000 acres in Manila Bay, setting up a nuclear power plant and a thermal power plant, and a recycling plant to turn Manila garbage into fertilizer. These were all things the Philippines could ill afford. Unwilling to tap into her own hidden assets, she flew off to see Robert McNamara, head of the World Bank.

Increased centralization of power in Ferdinand's hands made it possible for Imelda to turn her mob of courtiers into a political base, so she could take over the presidency in the event of her husband's sudden departure. She was emerging from her cocoon as an iron butterfly. In a top-secret paper drafted in December 1975, a CIA analyst reviewed her situation and concluded that

> Mrs. Marcos is ambitious and ruthless. . . . She has a thirst for wealth, power and public acclaim and her boundless ego makes her easy prey for flatterers. Although she has had little formal education, she is cunning. . . . Her political organization is largely made up of media people . . . plus a scattering of politicians and a few military men. Most are sycophants seeking protection. . . . Her political advancement has been handled largely by her brother, Benjamin Romualdez. . . . Much of her power is based on her husband's authority and on the belief among both foreigners and Filipinos that she is able to influence his decisions. . . . The Marcos marriage is essentially a business and political partnership, but no one is sure just how close this working relationship is. At times, the two clearly compete with one another, at others, the President will give in to her unless he believes a vital interest is at stake. . . .
>
> Many Filipinos believe that Marcos has left a political will naming his wife his successor. She does not yet have the stature, however, to make a serious bid for the presidency. . . . [She] is now trying to strengthen her political position at home.
>
> Mrs. Marcos regards Defense Secretary Enrile . . . as the principal threat to her ambitions. . . .
>
> . . . Mrs. Marcos will have her work cut out for her. . . . She has a short attention span and it is possible that she will not have the administrative follow-through to accomplish much. . . .
>
> In the event of President Marcos' death, his wife would doubtless make a bid to replace him. In the political confusion, she might succeed; but if she is ever to rule as well as reign she will need the support of the military, and she is not well-regarded by senior officers.
>
> . . . There is already a group of senior military officers who are reportedly engaged in contingency planning for a post-Marcos government that would exclude his wife.
>
> Mrs. Marcos may not be aware of the group's existence, but she realizes that many of her husband's most loyal military supporters do not like her. She has been trying to develop a military following of her own by courting the officers and by working through their wives.

That December, Marcos did draw up a political will naming Imelda as his successor. The CIA did not know this at the time, but had heard rumors. The analyst commented that "She does not yet have the stature

. . . to make a serious bid for the presidency." But she was gradually strengthening her position.

From the early days of martial law, Juan Ponce Enrile was considered the most obvious successor. As there was a long-standing antagonism between them, an Imelda-Enrile alliance was out of the question. They did not like each other, and it soon hardened into mutual loathing. Imelda was far too erratic, irrational, hysterical, and vengeful to appeal to Enrile, who was intensely wary of her and kept his distance. Having tried and failed to lure him into her orbit in the late 1960s, Imelda never trusted Enrile thereafter, fearing him as a rival for the throne. Instead, she tried to undercut his credibility with Marcos, to cripple him as a competitor. By the mid-1970s, Imelda and Enrile were waging a cold war.

He was a cagey adversary.

Juan Ponce Enrile was born in northeastern Luzon, in the sleepy town of Gonzaga, Cagayan Province, on Valentine's Day, 1924. Because he was illegitimate, he was baptized Juanito Furruganan by his mother, Petra Furruganan, a peasant woman. Like Ferdinand Marcos, his real father was a man of exceptional power and wealth. But Juanito was not acknowledged, and grew up impoverished and barefoot. He attended high school, where he was good at math and wanted to be a scientist. He earned extra money tutoring the daughter of one of the richest men in town. One day when he was seventeen, four bullies jumped him. He was stabbed three times, in the arm, stomach, and throat, and nearly died. When he recovered, he complained to the local authorities, but they told him to forget it or leave town. He set out for Manila to confront his father. Along the way, he worked for months here and there as a fisherman and road laborer, arriving in Manila at age nineteen.

His father was Alfonso Ponce Enrile, an Ilocano and one of Manila's leading corporate lawyers, a partner in the law firm of DeWitt, Perkins & Enrile, which handled the affairs of General MacArthur and of leading firms such as Benguet Mines. Don Alfonso decided to recognize his son, and underwrote his education. Juanito Furruganan became Juan Ponce Enrile. He attended the Jesuit-run Ateneo, graduated at the top of his class in law at the University of the Philippines in 1953, and took a master's in law at Harvard in 1955. Returning to Manila, he became a partner in his father's law firm and matured into one of the cleverest corporate lawyers in the islands, with Dole Pineapple as one of his clients. He taught law at Far Eastern University from 1955 to 1962, and was recruited by Ferdinand in 1964 to handle his personal legal affairs—a tricky assignment but a profitable one.

After Ferdinand was elected president, he named Enrile to a series of posts including commissioner of customs, minister of justice, and finally minister of defense. Enrile's influence was considerable. Often, he was given the job of working out on paper the legalities of questionable moves Ferdinand wanted to make. Better informed than most officials, he knew more than any other crony with the possible exception of Roberto Benedicto. Many considered Enrile to be the real architect of martial law. He was also the chief martial law administrator, bearing much of the responsibility for its fakery and excesses. He eventually admitted to having set up the attack on his own motorcade that was the final excuse for martial law. During Senator Aquino's long imprisonment, it was Enrile who served as turnkey, personally approving any visitors to Aquino's cell.

As Ferdinand's legal counsel, Enrile benefited lavishly. He was a primary figure in the takeover of the coconut industry. His closest associate after the president was Eduardo Cojuangco. It is significant that Enrile was ranked after Marcos and Cojuangco as the third-richest man in the Philippines, well ahead of billionaires Andres Soriano of San Miguel and financier Enrique Zobel.

He lived in one of Manila's most luxurious houses, had sprawling landholdings in the Cagayan Valley, and owned eight logging companies that provided raw material for his Pan Oriental and Eurasian match companies. He served on the National Security Council, on a number of corporate boards, and was chairman of the Philippine National Bank and other banks and exchanges. In reply to charges of corruption, Enrile once said, "If you can find my name on a single deed, you can have it." Just to be safe, he added that he would have his detractors "eat the [false] documents."

Enrile married a striking woman, Cristina Castaner, by whom he had two children, Jackie and Katrina. When the Enriles bought a home in California valued at $1.8 million, it was acquired in the name of "Renatsac," the backward spelling of his wife's maiden name. They also had a company called "Jaka" from a combination of the names of their children.

As a top official of the Marcos regime, Enrile was by nature abrasive, short-tempered, and ruthless, but this was sweetened by a beatific smile. He was both intelligent and charming. On his bookshelves he kept Toynbee, Clausewitz, *Mein Kampf,* and *Das Kapital* prominently displayed, but he surrounded himself with a flying squad of machos once described as "a lobotomized brain-trust." He displayed a genius for malapropisms—"Hurry up man and step on the brakes."

Manila journalists claimed that Enrile had a large collection of the dried ears of dead Muslim rebels. But a lot of this was simply showmanship and flash. Those who knew him well said he was strictly a Latin lover, a political jellyfish who lacked the spine to stand up to Ferdinand, to Cojuangco, to Ver, and certainly to Imelda. He enjoyed conspiracy, but preferred to have it executed by others while he remained a spectator. For Ferdinand, that was an advantage: Enrile posed no serious danger to him.

In the event of Ferdinand's death, the CIA concluded, Imelda would definitely make a bid for the throne. But there was already a group of senior military men plotting to exclude her from any post-Marcos government. The key figure was Lieutenant General Fidel Ramos, head of the paramilitary Constabulary and the Integrated National Police, and also vice chief-of-staff of the armed forces. Ramos was the son of Narciso Ramos, Ferdinand's uncle, who had been executive officer of the Maharlika and later foreign minister at the time of the deal with Lyndon Johnson. There the similarities ended. Fidel Ramos was a graduate of West Point, who went on to earn a master's degree in civil engineering from the University of Illinois, then served in the Korean and Vietnam wars as a young officer. He chose to live a spartan life, was an ardent skydiver and weight lifter, and jogged every day at 5:00 A.M. In the ranks he was highly respected, particularly for his self-restraint. He lived modestly, within his meager army salary, and was sometimes said to be one of the few senior officers who were totally clean. Around him over the years gathered a hard core of younger officers who followed the same code.

Ramos was not normally aggressive, not a risk taker. He would be a tough adversary in a confrontation, but he lacked charisma and was not as forceful as he might be. Already his rigid ethics were causing him to lose out to secret police boss Ver in the contest for leadership of the armed forces.

Long-range strategies were developed by the CIA and the Pentagon to increase the visibility of Ramos, to build his reputation as an honest commander. Other strategies were developed to cultivate Enrile and

to encourage him to take a stand. If events could be engineered so that
Enrile acted in harness with Ramos, Ramos could provide the spine
while Enrile provided the flash.

The succession issue was becoming a hot topic by the winter of
1975–76. In any scenario, the role of the military was key, so one burning question was whether General Ver or General Ramos would become the next chief-of-staff on the retirement of General Romeo
Espino. The CIA was listening intently. It had sources within each
camp. In March 1976, these sources began to buzz and the Manila
Station filed a top-secret report on what they were saying. This report
is raw intelligence from field officers; it is not the kind of predigested
analysis that eventually makes its way up the pecking order to the
National Security Council and the president. So it is an unusual example
of actual CIA reporting, evaluating, and disseminating—a jewel in the
rough. In Manila, it had been shown only to very senior officers of the
U.S. Embassy and the CIA station. In Washington, its distribution was
tightly restricted to protect sensitive intelligence sources and methods
involved. (I have deleted the identification of sources except in a general way.)

> Undersecretary of Defense Carmelo Barbero told Brigadier General Tomas
> P. Diaz, the recently appointed deputy Chief Philippine Constabulary, that
> President Marcos will, in time, appoint Major General Fidel Ramos . . . to
> the Post of Chief of Staff of the Armed Forces. Barbero said that Marcos
> decided against retiring the Chief of Staff, General Romeo Espino, now
> because of the rivalry that has developed between Ramos and National
> Security Advisor, Ver. Marcos, Barbero said, felt that this is not the propi-
> tious time to make this important change. . . . On whether Ver or Ramos
> would make better chief of staff, Diaz replied: "Both generals are loyal to
> Marcos and, while they have had different kinds of experience in their
> military careers, they would both serve Marcos well in this position. The
> more important question is which has the highest number of the best caliber
> officers supporting him? This is the General who should be chosen." . . . Diaz
> noted . . . that loyalty is a trait which is hard to evaluate . . . as Filipinos
> generally tend to shift their loyalty to whomever seems to have power at
> the moment. Nonetheless, he speculated that Ramos has the greater num-
> ber of idealistic officers with him. But in a real power struggle these Ramos
> loyalists probably will not be in a position to help Ramos. [They were scat-
> tered throughout the archipelago.] The reverse would be true of Ver and

his proteges. [Ver's men were all strategically placed in key slots.] . . .

The succession issue became a matter of considerable public and private discussion after the Mayor of Makati, Nemesio Yabut, announced on 18 March that the Makati [City Council] had voted to call upon Marcos to pronounce his wife to be his duly appointed successor. . . . Yabut is now invited to many of her functions. Yabut has also stated that he is afraid of Mrs. Marcos' brother Benjamin.

. . . Enrile said it now appears that Marcos has assented to Mrs. Marcos' wishes to have the president name her as his successor while he is still firmly in power. Under these circumstances, said Enrile, "We members of 'the group' (the Enrile group) must keep our heads down and our mouths shut. Unless we do, we will not survive." . . .

Diaz interpreted Enrile's cautionary remark to mean that Enrile will not be convening a meeting of the group for fear that Mrs. Marcos might learn of the meeting and suspect that they may be plotting against her and Marcos. Moreover, Diaz stated that he expects Enrile to make some overtures of friendship to Mrs. Marcos; and if this is what is necessary to protect oneself, then he could smile and do what is necessary to stay alive. However, Diaz said he expects a serious conflict of interest sooner or later between Marcos, on the one hand, and Mrs. Marcos and her brother on the other. When this happens, the Enrile group will definitely support Marcos. If Marcos dies before she does, and she makes her anticipated bid for the presidency, "Then as surely as night follows day, we will get rid of her, and when that day comes, General Ramos will be with us. He could not tolerate her running the country anymore than we could." . . .

. . . two members of the Enrile group stated there would be serious problems in the PI if Mrs. Marcos attempted to, or assumed, power while Marcos is still alive. They believe that elements within the military would be hesitant to move against her because of their continuing loyalty to Marcos, although these same elements are uniformly anti-Mrs. Marcos. If, on the other hand, Marcos were to die, the problem would be simplified. The military would then be united in opposing the First Lady, and she would be ordered to leave the country immediately.

Imelda had made many enemies. At any time one group or another might decide to eliminate her, or to teach her a lesson. As the intelligence report quoted General Diaz: "He expects a serious conflict of interest sooner or later between Marcos, on the one hand, and Mrs. Marcos and her brother on the other."

According to palace insiders, Ferdinand and Imelda's quarrels were becoming so fierce that they exchanged blows. The chief propagandist of the regime, Primitivo Mijares, reported that while cruising around Manila Bay in June 1972 on the presidential yacht, the First Couple began to argue about Imelda's ambitions. Words failing to make her point, Imelda scratched Ferdinand on the face and he retaliated by slugging her so hard that she fell to the deck.

In Beverly Hills, where Dovie Beams was still being visited by Marcos emissaries asking her to return her incriminating memorabilia, she said she was worried about what Imelda and Bong-Bong might do to her. One Marcos crony told her, "Don't worry about Imelda. She will be taken care of."

Five weeks later there was a horror show in Manila. On a temporary outdoor stage, the First Lady was beaming over winners of a municipal beautification contest. Out of the reception line stepped Carlito Dimahilig. Everyone else was in shirtsleeves but Dimahilig wore a dark suit. From one sleeve, he pulled a 12-inch bolo knife and lunged at Imelda. She raised her arms in defense, twisted, and fell to the stage with blood pouring from deep gashes in her arms and hands. Curiously, Ver's security men were all some distance away. Jose Aspiras, then a congressman, saved Imelda's life by grappling with the assailant as he turned to strike again. Only then did Ver's man bound through the crowd and shoot Dimahilig in the back of the head. As the assassin fell, Ver's man leaned over him and silenced Dimahilig forever with another pistol shot in the face.

Imelda told an interviewer afterward that she noticed Dimahilig as he came onto the stage because of his suit. "I saw he was trying to pull something from his sleeve, and I thought, 'Oh, he is going to do something wrong to somebody. Then he looked at me—a very fierce, deranged look, a crazy, mad look, and I thought, 'It is me!' "

Dimahilig turned his head to look away as if for a signal, then lunged. "I had no help," Imelda said. "Everyone froze. I began weaving back away from him, shielding my body with my crossed arms. . . . My arms and hands were slashed. And I was hit here [she touched her breast] so hard that I fell backwards across a table. The front of my dress was slashed open. My bra, which was white, was filled with blood. . . . I kicked at him, pushing back with my feet. I could hear shots. My aides were grappling with him, and still he lunged at me. I saw a bullet hole in his cheek. No blood. Just the hole. Then my aides stopped him." Imelda's hands and arms required seventy-five stitches.

The mysterious assassination attempt (if that is what it was) has never been explained. In the years since, it has been conjectured that the attack was intended to frighten the First Lady, not to kill her. Ver's security men claimed that they were not nearby because they were trying to stay out of camera range. As Primitivo Mijares wrote four years later, "Marcos will no longer surprise anybody, if he does away with Imelda—perhaps, in the dead of night."

Fourteen

THE ANTI-HERO

THE DEFECTION of Primitivo Mijares was the first major blow to the dictatorship. As a newspaper columnist, "Tibo" Mijares had a reputation as a man who was not too scrupulous about who paid him for what. But if you wanted to survive and prosper in Manila under martial law, you had to flatter Malacanang, and Mijares was not the only journalist doing that. His column in the government-controlled *Daily Express* was followed closely by observers of the political scene. He was one of a tiny handful of men who could walk into Ferdinand's office at almost any time without an appointment. He served as chairman of the "Media Advisory Council"—essentially as official spokesman or chief propagandist of the regime, which put him in a rare position to know what was really going on. A lawyer by training and married to a judge, Mijares was also president of the National Press Club. He was responsible for getting Arnold Zeitlin, chief of the Manila bureau of The Associated Press, thrown out of the country after a report on an army attack that leveled the Muslim community of Jolo.

At heart, Mijares was a character out of the novels of Graham Greene or Eric Ambler, a highly intelligent man of ambiguous morals whose whole life was spent on the lam. He could be as good or as bad as the occasion demanded. He left a trail of misappropriated funds, bad debts, rubber checks, and petty extortions. When Imelda turned against him, she found it easy to blacken his reputation; her courtiers spread the word that he was unable to account for funds belonging to the Press Club. Of course, neither of the Marcoses by then could account for

268

hundreds of millions of dollars in foreign aid and war reparations. So, in retrospect, Mijares emerges as something of a hero. The charges he leveled before the international press in 1974, before the U.S. Congress in 1975, and in his book *The Conjugal Dictatorship of Ferdinand and Imelda Marcos* in 1976, all of which seemed too fantastic to be believed, have since proven to be true almost without exception. To silence him, Ferdinand tried bribery, which failed. Eventually, the anger Mijares aroused in Malacanang proved fatal. As a direct consequence of the Mijares affair, at least three people were murdered.

Trouble began late in 1974 when Mijares rashly accused Kokoy Romualdez of cheating the Lopez family in a business deal involving the Manila Electric Company. Imelda's older brother was a curious character. After insisting on replacing Norberto Junior as governor of Leyte and usurping all his property, Kokoy rarely visited the island. He was its absentee governor. In Manila he was scornfully referred to (in private) as "Adobo Kokoy"—adobo is a mishmash stew of leftovers, so the nickname meant something like "pudding head." In a book of essays critical of the Marcoses, journalist Renato Constantino entitled one chapter "The Thoughts of Kokoy" and left all the pages blank. But everyone was terrified of crossing him. He was considered to be wildly irrational, vengeful, and unstable, and he had his sister's ear, which made him one of the most dangerous men in the regime. When Mijares criticized him over the Meralco deal, Romualdez told him to mind his own business, adding: "You will see what will happen to you. I will tell this to my sister."

At the time, Ferdinand was under pressure from the U.S. Congress to release some of his celebrity political prisoners to clean up his image. He freed former Senator Jose Diokno and a few others, and sent Mijares and other propagandists to the United States to invite Filipino exiles home with "full amnesty." Imelda was to follow to make a personal appeal.

Mijares planned Imelda's press campaign. To boost her image, a full-page newspaper advertisement appeared in the major Honolulu dailies headlined "Imelda, We Love You," with her picture. Underneath were eighty-three names of individuals and organizations that had apparently sponsored the ad. However, it was soon apparent that the ad had been written, designed, and paid for by the Philippine government.

By this time, Mijares had begun to fear for his life. He had reason to believe that Kokoy Romualdez was carrying out his threat. Reaching San Francisco, Mijares secretly contacted *Philippine News* editor Alex Esclamado and implied that he was preparing to defect. Esclamado told Steve Psinakis and arranged a meeting. "We planned his defection strategy," Psinakis said. They arranged a press conference for February 20, 1975, and Mijares made the following statement:

> As Malacanang reporter of the *Daily Express* (which is owned by the President's family), I became among . . . Marcos' . . . handful of trusted confidants at the onset of martial law. As a media man, it then fell on my lot to support and justify the imposition of martial law. . . .
>
> . . . I needed no convincing about the justice of Ferdinand Marcos' cause. Having covered the Philippine Congresses and Philippine presidents [since] . . . 1946, I could see what we started out to do was in the right direction. . . .
>
> But now . . . I must sever my bonds with the so-called New Society. The false facade is off. . . . Marcos has wittingly or unwittingly, consciously or unconsciously, digressed and treasonably betrayed—with full and gleeful collaboration of top associates and relatives, mostly in-laws—the avowed objectives. . . .
>
> The martial regime of Marcos was nothing but an ill-disguised plot to perpetuate himself, his wife and/or son in power by consolidating the political and economic resources of the country under his control. . . .

Three days later, there was a confidential telex from U.S. Ambassador William Sullivan to Secretary of State Kissinger saying, "Mijares' departure cannot help but be [an] acute embarrassment to Marcos. . . . [He] undoubtedly has much inside knowledge that, if made public, could cause distress to government of the Philippines."

Ferdinand first tried to discredit Mijares by circulating rumors that he had absconded with government funds, that he was paid $150,000 by the Lopezes to join the anti-Marcos exiles, and that he was staying in the United States because of a liaison with a Filipina exile. (Mijares had left his wife and family in Manila.)

Meanwhile, Mijares was playing both sides against the middle. After "defecting," he was secretly accepting money from Ferdinand's agents in exchange for information about the exiles. The FBI discovered later that Mijares had signed several vouchers for $20,000 and at least one of these signatures was authentic. The February 24, 1975, voucher bore the handwritten notation: "Sir; I received this. Tibo Mijares." True, this demonstrated the ambiguity of his ethics, but it is typical of defectors to be of two minds about what they are doing. Since Mijares was mostly afraid of Imelda and Kokoy, he might still have had some vestigial sense of loyalty or respect for "the boss" (Marcos) which he again demonstrated later. It was this irrational urge that led to his undoing.

In May 1975, a colonel in the Presidential Guard who was one of Imelda's personal favorites and often accompanied her on global junkets, Romeo Ochoco, tracked down Mijares in San Francisco and tried to persuade him to come home. "He said Marcos would talk to me about my complaints," recalled Mijares. The colonel's visit was followed by telephone calls from Trinidad Alconcel, Philippine consul general in San Francisco, who had heard that Mijares would be a star witness in Washington for the House International Relations Subcommittee in hearings on U.S.-Philippines problems. Alconcel tried to persuade Mijares not to testify and, when he refused, asked him to "pull the punches." In Manila, Ferdinand brought formal charges against Mijares and used this criminal complaint as a ruse to seek his extradition from the United States. Imelda retaliated against the *Philippine News* by having her favorite courtier, Tourism Minister Jose Aspiras, write U.S. travel agencies asking them to withdraw advertising from the paper.

Mijares flew to Washington to testify and checked into a downtown motel. He must have been under close surveillance by Ver's agents, for there, on the evening of June 16, he received a call from Manila.

"It was Marcos," Mijares said. "He started out by calling me by my nickname, Tibo. He asked me not to testify, because of what it would do to his 'New Society.' I told him it would be difficult to back out since I was already under the committee's jurisdiction. He told me his assistant would tell me something, that they had something for me."

Presidential aide Guillermo de Vega then got on the line, speaking Tagalog and Spanish to confuse wiretappers. He said $50,000 would be awaiting Mijares in San Francisco if he didn't testify. But if he went ahead with his testimony, it would be a declaration of war. The money was deposited in a San Francisco branch of Lloyds Bank in the names of Mijares and Alconcel, so Mijares could not withdraw the money until the consul counter-signed the check.

Although Nixon and Kissinger were backing the Marcos regime, congressional feeling in Washington, spurred by lobbying efforts of various exile groups, was running strongly against Ferdinand and Imelda, mainly because of the continued detention of well-known political prisoners, abuses of human rights, and torture. The U.S. Senate came close to voting to cut off military aid in December 1974, and was only dissuaded by assurances that political detainees would be released. About twelve hundred were. However, at hearings in June 1975, it was disclosed that the regime still held at least six thousand more political detainees. So the appearance of Mijares before the subcommittee caused a sensation.

"Let me trace the origin and pattern of this new tyranny in Asia," he told the panel in his opening remarks. "On Sept. 21, 1935, as established 'beyond reasonable doubt' by a Philippine court, a young man— an expert rifle marksman by his own account—felled dead with a single rifle shot a reelected congressmen." The man was Marcos, and he

> continues to entrench himself in the presidential palace in a bid to reign for life and establish an imperial dynasty. . . .
>
> . . . the reasons used by Marcos in imposing martial law were deliberately manufactured. . . . With a series of deliberately contrived crises . . . Marcos made the people lapse into a state of paralysis. . . . Then he wove a labored tale of national horror which he eventually enshrined as gospel truth in the martial law proclamation. . . . Marcos plotted to place his country under martial law as early as 1966, having decided then that he would win a reelection in 1969 "at all cost."
>
> . . . Having proclaimed martial law, he proceeded to bribe, coerce and/or intimidate the Constitutional Convention members into drafting a new charter dictated by him. . . .
>
> A dictatorial regime as it is, the martial government of Marcos has become all the more oppressive and corrupt in view of the meddling of his wife who has turned the martial regime into a conjugal dictatorship.
>
> Aside from plundering an entire nation, the conjugal dictatorship is likewise misappropriating the various items of U.S. assistance (military, economic, cultural, etc.) to the Philippines to entrench itself in power and for personal glorification.
>
> . . . Filipinos desirous of overthrowing the dictatorial yoke of Marcos are stymied by the . . . support the State Department has shown for the martial regime. . . .

After testifying, Mijares filed a formal request with the U.S. Immigration and Naturalization Service (INS) for political asylum. Immigration referred the matter to Secretary of State Kissinger. Kissinger sent a carefully worded confidential telex to the U.S. Embassy in Manila:

Department plans to reply to INS that it is possible that Mijares denouncement of the government of the Philippines might cause him problems if he returns to that country, *although we are unable to determine whether these problems could be classified as persecution* [my italics]. . . . We assume INS will then issue Mijares voluntary departure status and refer case back to department at a later date. . . . Department does not intend to discuss Mijares case with Philippine government and embassy should also avoid issue.

Ferdinand then doubled his bribe, offering Mijares through Alconcel $100,000 to recant his testimony and retire to Australia. To prove to journalists that the bribe offers were genuine, Mijares called Guillermo de Vega at Malacanang Palace while a California lawyer listened in.

De Vega verified the $100,000 bribe. Mijares asked whether Marcos would go as high as $250,000. The sum would have to be approved by Marcos personally, de Vega said.

This was enough to justify an official U.S. Justice Department investigation that President Marcos had tried to bribe a congressional witness. But before anything further could come of it, de Vega was mysteriously murdered inside Malacanang Palace. A gunman identified as Paulino Arceo was said to have entered the palace with a Smith & Wesson revolver in a mailing envelope, along with a bottle of champagne. An hour later, de Vega's body was found in his private toilet with five bullet wounds. The revolver was in the anteroom. Arceo was arrested as he tried to leave, and was charged with murder. A part-time journalist and entertainment promoter, Arceo was well enough known to palace guards to be allowed on the grounds without having his parcel inspected. Ferdinand was extremely reticent about the killing. Curiously, Arceo refused to talk to anyone except General Ver, implying that he had justification for his act that was too secret to share with anyone less than Ver. The implication was that he had been hired for the job by someone high in the regime—suspicion fixing on Imelda or Kokoy. Arceo was sentenced to death by a firing squad, but the execution was never carried out.

The publication of Mijares's book *Conjugal Dictatorship* on April 27, 1976, aroused a firestorm of outrage at Malacanang—Mijares raked up just enough of the Dovie Beams affair, torture by Ver's thugs, and the faking of the Marcos war record to cause acute embarrassment. But *Conjugal Dictatorship* was systematically plundered from every bookstore and public institution in the United States, including the Library of Congress. Eight months after his book vanished, Mijares himself disappeared.

The last anyone heard from him was a cryptic letter, postmarked Honolulu. He wrote to columnists Jack Anderson and Les Whitten that he was about to take off on "a daring sortie to the Philippines. . . . For security reasons," he cautioned, "I would request you not to breathe a word of this daring trip to anyone until I can call you by phone. Or . . . I'll send you proof from Manila, a letter with this." He drew a star with a circle around it. "Wish me luck," he added.

Mijares phoned his wife, Manila Judge Priscilla Mijares, saying he was taking a Pan American flight to Guam. According to subsequent investigations, Mijares left in the company of Querube Makalintal, a Marcos intelligence officer posing as a revenue attaché at the Philippine Consulate in San Francisco. Fabian Ver also was in San Francisco, had been in touch with Mijares, and was seen boarding the same Pan Am flight to Guam.

When her husband vanished, Judge Mijares began her own investigation. She determined that Ver and her husband flew to Guam, then boarded a Philippine Air Lines flight to Manila. Mijares and Makalintal joined Ver in the first-class section of the plane, she said. It was only after the flight landed at Manila International Airport that her husband disappeared. She said NISA agents took Mijares to Ver's headquarters at Fort Bonifacio, where he was put in a dungeon where political detainees were kept for long periods. A jailer she knew told her that he saw her husband there.

On May 30, 1977, their sixteen-year-old son Luis "Boyet" Mijares told his mother that he had received a phone call saying his father was alive and inviting the boy to come see him. He insisted on going. The boy's body was later found dumped outside Manila, his eyeballs protruding, his chest perforated with multiple stab wounds, his head bashed in, and his hands, feet, and genitals mangled. The mutilation of the body was typical of incidents where, to extract information from an uncooperative prisoner, one member of a family was grotesquely tortured in front of another. However, two university students were conveniently charged with this murder.

The U.S. Justice Department quietly closed its investigation of the Mijares case a year later, in August 1978. Justice said its investigation had confirmed that Mijares had a past history of bouncing checks and misappropriating funds, which "seriously undermined Mijares' usefulness as a key witness." They did not explain how this damaged his credibility when, in its campaign against U.S. organized crime during the same period, the Justice Department was taking great pains to record the testimony of longtime Mafia hitman Jimmy "the Weasel" Fratiano.

In 1980, Steve Psinakis arranged to have a conversation with Imelda Marcos in New York and brought up the Mijares case.

"And speaking of killings," said Psinakis, "tell me, Mrs. Marcos, has Mijares been killed?"

"How should I know?" said Imelda. "Mijares had more enemies than you can possibly imagine. He was the lowest kind of snake that ever lived." She used the past tense throughout. "Tibo was a thief, a compulsive gambler and a loser, and worst of all, a cheap extortionist. He was not a newspaperman; he was a blackmailer."

"If you knew all this about Mijares," Psinakis said, "why did your husband make him his top media man as well as the official censor of the martial law regime?" Imelda changed the subject.

Fifteen

BUSINESS AS USUAL

"THE AMERICAN BUSINESS COMMUNITY in the Philippines," *The New York Times* reported on March 11, 1972, "has greeted with relief the . . . declaration of martial law."

America was the chief beneficiary. With thirty-five thousand U.S. servicemen in the islands, American bankers managing a tenth of Manila's $2.1 billion national debt, $74 million in emergency relief, $75 million in aid, and upward of $2 billion in U.S. investments, America encouraged and condoned the new Marcos dictatorship just by continuing to do business as usual. Martial law would instill discipline, keep guns off the streets, and solve the law-and-order problem, so the temporary loss of freedom of speech, the suspension of the writ of habeas corpus and all constitutional safeguards for individual rights were not important. One telegram to President Marcos read: "The American Chamber of Commerce of the Philippines wishes you every success in your endeavors to restore peace and order, business confidence, economic growth, and the well-being of the Filipino people and nation." A State Department official commented that American corporations were "very bullish" on martial law. Since it was discovered later that Ferdinand had consulted with Nixon and Kissinger before promulgating martial law, could there have been more involved? Did he offer any concessions in return for their endorsement? Was there, in fact, more going on than met the eye? The answer is, yes.

Four weeks before martial law was declared, the Philippine Supreme Court announced that it had decided to enforce a law restricting all retail trade in the islands to Filipinos. Henceforth, American citizens and corporations could no longer purchase or own private agricultural lands, and all other economic privileges acquired under the 1946 Parity Amendment would expire on July 3, 1974. By then, American ownership must be sold off or reduced to 40 percent.

It was the old Marcos game of stick-and-carrots again. Americans saw it as an omen of worse to come. That is clearly what they were intended to fear. As Ferdinand had done to all his business rivals when he first became president, he was now threatening to beat Americans with a stick. The prospect of forfeiting these lucrative and generally trouble-free Philippine holdings was enough to cause deep anxiety in Wall Street. But the assurances that Ferdinand then gave to Nixon, Kissinger, and Byroade were a marvelous palliative. As an American oilman in Manila reported, "Marcos says, 'We'll pass the laws you need—just tell us what you want.' " Having manipulated these decisions through a Supreme Court packed with Marcos appointees, Ferdinand now was in a position to guarantee by presidential dispensation that they would not be applied so long as America showed enthusiasm for his regime. He did not scrap the court decision, but he applied it selectively—to any U.S. businessmen who refused to give him a piece of the action. "When I was there," said William Sullivan, U.S. ambassador from 1973 to 1977, "foreign investors did not come into the Philippines without distributing shares to Imelda . . . or Kokoy or some of the other cronies."

These kickbacks, bribes, inducements, and other forms of extortion were similar to armed robbery, but they were not carried out in such a blatant fashion. And the companies involved thought they were worth it, in the beginning. As Alex Melchor put it while he was still executive secretary, such deals were "cooked." Ferdinand was an expert chef, and he was always careful to grease the pan.

During the early days of martial law, the international banking community also was completely taken in by the public pretenses of the Marcos regime. Stern discipline, President Marcos professed, was necessary to transform the Philippines from a corrupt feudal society into a new era of modern technology and export-oriented industry. Until the system could be purged and modernized, martial law was imperative. This sounded reassuring to middle-class Filipinos weary of the folly and blatant corruption of the old legislature. It sounded exciting to young technocrats eager to introduce their concept of a thriving modern economy. And it was a siren song to the ears of the International Monetary Fund (IMF) and the World Bank, then headed by the aging "whiz kid" Robert McNamara. Bankers appreciate discipline. Imelda and Ferdinand Marcos were doing everything they could to woo the World Bank, for reasons that nobody outside of Malacanang fully understood at the time, except a few analysts at the CIA and the account managers of Crédit Suisse.

Eager to believe, the World Bank secretly named the Philippines a "country of concentration," which meant the amount of aid would be "higher than average for countries of similar size and income."

McNamara and his advisers were duped by a "sting" operation. The sting began with martial law, gathered momentum with a number of bold business takeovers by the regime, which gave the impression that Ferdinand really meant business, and climaxed in the staging in Manila of the International Monetary Fund–World Bank Conference of October 1976.

The Marcoses had been bidding furiously for the privilege of playing host to the conference. Late in 1974, Manila was picked, and Malacanang let it be known that no expense would be spared to assure that the international banking community found Manila a showcase of stability, prosperity, dynamism, and beauty. It was none of these things. The prospect of six thousand bankers and their guests descending upon the country for a week brought more lip-smacking in the palace than it did in the brothels, and caused a stampede to build fourteen new five-star hotels.

President Marcos, now ruling by decree, offered incentives to anyone building a hotel for the World Bank meeting, including tax holidays, deferred deduction of losses, tax exemptions, duty-free imports of equipment, and tax credits on locally purchased materials. He opened the coffers of government lending agencies—the Development Bank of the Philippines, the Government Services Insurance System, and the Philippine National Bank were directed to lend up to 75 percent of building costs. (Ultimately, they had to lend 90 percent, and in the case of Imelda's new Philippine Plaza Hotel 100 percent.) The Philippine National Bank was headed by crony Roberto Benedicto, and the Government Services Insurance System by Imelda's protégé, Jun Cruz. Imelda's favorite, Tourism Minister Jose Aspiras, approved applications to build the new hotels and other tourist facilities. Originally a Magsaysay/Lansdale man, Aspiras was an Ilocano and a tireless zealot for the Marcos 1965 presidential campaign. He had been a loyal friend of Ferdinand for many years, but his career really took off when he rescued Imelda during the 1972 "assassination attempt."

By early 1975, fourteen hotel projects were approved by Aspiras. Builders had only to promise to open in time for the World Bank meeting. Behind the rush to build was simple greed—Marcos cronies wanted to take advantage of the cheap loan money, which at 12–14 percent interest and a two-year grace period on the principal was as good as free. William Overholt, vice president for international economics at Bankers Trust Co., explained the dodge: "A Marcos crony would borrow $100 million with government guarantees to build a hotel. He'd spend only, say, $40 million on building the hotel, leaving the remaining $60 million to be stashed away in Switzerland. Of course, the hotel was undercapitalized and would go bust, so the government would have to step in and assume the obligations." This happened so often during the Marcos era that the Philippine government ended up controlling nearly four hundred corporations, mostly money losers. Losses by these firms came to $3 billion a year, roughly what it cost to run the entire government.

When all the bills were in, the fourteen new hotels cost over half a billion dollars. During the months of frenzied construction, fifty thousand workers toiled around the clock, ten thousand of them on Imelda's Philippine Plaza Hotel. Nearby, her International Convention Center (the platform for the World Bank–IMF Conference) was ready ahead of time at a staggering cost of $150 million. This should have alarmed McNamara's advisers and given them second thoughts about the pretensions to discipline of the Marcos regime, but it did not, for reasons that will become clear.

Despite the frenzy, only two of the fourteen hotels were completed in time. Imelda had been frantic to have McNamara stay at her Philippine Plaza, but it was not finished, and he wound up at the Hilton. The First Lady was not happy. Several of her contractors reportedly packed up their families and emigrated. The extra hotel capacity was not needed in any case—only three thousand of the forecasted six thousand delegates and observers showed up.

When the conference opened, delegates and their wives were wined, dined, and whisked around town in a fleet of three hundred new Mercedes-Benzes. If the bankers had been a bit more suspicious, they might have realized that what they were witnessing was one of the country's worst investment disasters. Instead, they took the spectacle of bustling Manila as a sure sign of health.

McNamara's own performance was incongruous. In statements broadcast throughout the archipelago, he called for an end to world poverty, advising impoverished Filipinos that what was required was "people who care, people who make sacrifices, people who take practical steps to see the task through. . . . We have to ask ourselves—each one of us—where we really stand."

Residents of one of the world's great slums—Manila's awesome Tondo—asked McNamara to meet with them in Tondo to see where they stood. The $32 million the World Bank had given Imelda to fix up Tondo had not trickled down. McNamara was presumably too busy implementing "people-oriented development" to respond.

Just in case any banker blundered onto Tondo, before the conference Imelda ordered sixty thousand families forcibly removed from the slum and four hundred more evicted from its edges. Their houses were quickly demolished to make it look as though the Tondo renewal project was making progress. The displaced families were carted off in garbage trucks under police guard, to isolated sites 20 miles outside Manila where they were left to put up shanties like the ones they had just left.

Unlike McNamara, the World Bank's program director for East Asia, Gregorio Votaw, was on the spot and could see what the First Lady was up to. Patiently, he explained that the Bank's concept of urban development was development in place, and this was precisely what Tondo needed—minimal relocation and dislocation. That, he said, was part of the project contract. Imelda and Ferdinand had McNamara fire him.

The flood of money to the Philippines was not exclusively the result of bureaucratic inertia and misjudgment at the IMF and World Bank. American and European private banks also were pouring great amounts of capital into the Philippine economy—with absolutely no backing except that the loans were "guaranteed" (in a manner of speaking) by the regime itself.

In 1975, American banks had $110 billion in loans outstanding overseas; by 1982, a mere seven years, the figure had risen to $451 billion. Many of these loans were made to countries like the Philippines, Brazil, Mexico, and Argentina whose balance of payments were so far in arrears already that their ability to repay no longer mattered to loan officers. A loan officer's performance is rated according to how many loans he makes. By the time the borrower defaults, the loan officer has moved to a better job at another bank. The bad loan is simply re-scheduled, to allow repayment over a longer period when still other loan officers will be stuck with the burden. Whether or not a loan ever gets paid is not as important as maintaining the interest payments that affect a bank's annual profit-and-loss statement. So long as interest is paid, a bank can have a very good year on paper, even if many of its loans are in serious trouble.

When a country or a foreign corporation defaults, international banks cannot collect the hotels, oil refineries, or earth-moving equip-ment paid for by their loans; they do not deal in collateral. International loans are secured instead by the guarantee of a third party—which may be a private commercial bank, a government-owned commercial bank, or a government itself. If the guarantee looks good on paper, little else matters. A loan will go through even if a company has borrowed much more than it can ever repay. Borrowing beyond your means is called leverage, and it is not unusual for international banks to lend great sums to companies at a leverage ratio of seven to one, especially if the loan is to be used to buy equipment or services from another customer of the bank, which makes a bad loan look decidedly better.

A case in point was S. C. Gwynne, a twenty-five-year-old American who took a bank job fresh out of college. Because he spoke French, he was promoted in less than a year to loan officer for North Africa. Six months and twenty-eight countries later, he arrived in the Philippines in 1978 to negotiate a $10 million loan for crony Rudolfo Cuenca, head of the Construction and Development Corporation of the Philippines (CDCP). Cuenca wanted the money to buy earth-moving equipment from another customer of the U.S. bank where Gwynne worked.

Gwynne was met at Manila International Airport by a genial CDCP "expediter." A red Jaguar was waiting outside, complete with a pretty girl who informed him that she and the car were at his disposal through-out his stay. Gwynne was checked into a five-star hotel, then wined and dined by Cuenca at a premier restaurant, where the finance minister of the Philippines "just happened" to drop by the table. He let Gwynne know that Cuenca was a good friend. Gwynne was then invited to fly off in the company plane to Baguio where a very nice time had been prepared for him.

Gwynne had severe reservations about authorizing the loan, but when he got back to headquarters, he began to feel pressure. The earth-moving equipment manufacturer called to make sure Gwynne took a "hard look" at the loan. The president of the bank called him to say the same thing. Said Gwynne, "He want[ed] to see this thing in loan committee, ASAP, damn the company's leverage, and damn the balance-of-payments problems in the Philippines, period."

Gwynne easily secured a partial guarantee from a large Philippine bank. (The heads of both the bank and the construction company, Gwynne knew, were "wired into the same political terminals.") Eighteen months later, Gwynne moved to another bank on the West Coast. He was no longer around when Cuenca's interest payments stopped.

In Rudi Cuenca's office, there was a framed photo showing him on the golf course with his best friend. "To Rudi," read the autograph. "Good golfing always. F. E. Marcos." A college dropout at age nineteen, Cuenca got into road construction with a loan from his father, the highway commissioner. The money was part of postwar U.S. reconstruction funds. In three years Cuenca was bankrupt, but he rescued one truck from creditors and made a comeback hauling building materials. In 1965, he was a fundraiser for Ferdinand. When the government ran out of money to finish an expressway north of Manila, Cuenca offered to do it for nothing and then collect tolls. With the encouragement of his golfing buddy, he set up the Construction and Development Corporation of the Philippines. From then on, CDCP won nearly every fat contract, including the San Juanico "Bridge of Love." Under Cuenca, in only five years road-building costs escalated ten times, from 100,000 pesos per kilometer to over 1 million pesos. Some of these projects were partly financed by the World Bank. Cuenca got a $1 billion contract to reclaim 500 hectares of Manila Bay. Through Marcos friends in the Middle East, CDCP also won more than $1 billion in Arab contracts, including $350 million to build a cross-Iraq highway. (When that project was due to be 70 percent complete, less than 4 percent of the work had been done.)

Although Cuenca's work ended up costing much more, he got most of the government's business. While Ferdinand began his congressional career as a "ten percenter," as president he demanded more. As inflated bids worked their way down the system from general contractor to subcontractor to supplier—each adding 10 percent—the total kickbacks grew to 80 percent of overall cost.

Many Filipino businessmen who were not cronies prudently turned over to Ferdinand or Imelda shares in their companies, or gave donations that amounted to protection money. Other businessmen learned the hard way. In a form of armed robbery, Ferdinand used the military and the Constabulary to seize control of businesses from people who refused to turn shares over. These takeovers were then patched together in corporate quilts to make a monopoly, squeezing out all competition. This took place in the primary industries of the islands—the sugar industry, the coconut industry, bananas, and so forth. Some of these deals were so intricate that it takes great patience to figure them out. One of the simplest was the great banana scam.

The top banana was Antonio Floirendo, who ran many of the Marcos offshore banks and corporations set up in international tax havens and frequently fronted for the First Lady. Floirendo was a banker who owned a car dealership and many other businesses in Mindanao, and was a charter member of Imelda's globetrotters.

Until martial law, the Philippine banana industry was dominated by two big international food houses, Castle & Cooke and Del Monte. Unable to win the kind of concessions he wanted from those entrenched corporations, Ferdinand decided to break their grip by bringing in United Brands. Floirendo did it for him, with the help of a prison farm.

The Davao Penal Colony in Mindanao was a Japanese POW camp during World War II, and since then had served as a prison for common criminals. Ferdinand issued a decree in 1972 giving Floirendo a lease to develop a 12,000-acre banana plantation inside the penal colony. Floirendo paid the government only $9 a year per acre to lease the rich delta land; the going rate to planters elsewhere was $30 to $50 per acre. The prisoners provided a guaranteed work force at less than 20 cents a day per man.

When the deal was offered to it, United Brands was enthusiastic. The Cincinnati company, which claims to be the world's largest producer and marketer of bananas, had been unable to enter the Philippine banana industry before. The chance to invade the territory of rivals Del Monte and Castle & Cooke was worth a lot. Loans from U.S. banks and financial assistance from United Brands flooded into Manila to pay for the development of the huge plantation. The farm's entire output, estimated at nearly seventeen million boxes of fruit a year, worth $100 million, was taken by United Brands—comprising around 10 percent of the company's $1.1 billion banana sales worldwide. Ferdinand ordered construction of a 15-mile road down to Floirendo's private dock on the

Davao Gulf, where United Brands freighters were loaded. The farm bought a $1 million private jet to fly Floirendo and his executives back and forth.

To teach them a lesson in martial law economics, Ferdinand ordered that Del Monte and Castle & Cooke had to pack a percentage of their fruit in boxes manufactured by Floirendo.

Taking over the sugar industry and the coconut industry took a bit longer. Ferdinand went after sugar with a vengeance as he forced out the Lopez clan and other old-guard sugar barons. Big money was involved—sugar amounted to 25 percent of all exports. Eventually the entire sugar and coconut businesses, from growing to harvesting, processing, and selling, became the personal monopolies of three Marcos cronies: Roberto Benedicto, Eduardo Cojuangco, Jr., and Juan Ponce Enrile.

"Bobby" Benedicto hailed from Negros, the country's sugar center. Teodoro Benedicto had founded the family fortune there at the end of the nineteenth century. With a gang of armed men, Don Teodoro burned out peasant villages, bribed local officials, and amassed an enormous property of 11,200 hectares, the largest in Negros. The Spanish Lands Department ruled that the methods Don Teodoro used were criminal and recommended that he be put on trial, but he bought off the court. Bobby inherited the fortune and the dedication. Studying law at the University of the Philippines in the thirties, he became a fraternity brother of Ferdinand Marcos. During World War II, when a submarine landed secret agent Jesus Villamor on Negros to organize an intelligence net, Villamor chose Benedicto as his local commander. Villamor said Benedicto impressed him with "his coolness, his energy . . . and his logical, analytical and cuttingly sharp mind."

Benedicto was one of the earliest Marcos backers, and chief fundraiser of his presidential campaign in 1965. Ferdinand then made him president of the Philippine National Bank. Under martial law, only his newspaper, the *Daily Express*, and his television station were allowed to stay in operation. As Ferdinand seized the assets of rivals, Benedicto was given the Lopez media chain of print, TV, and radio.

Once he had taken control of the entire sugar industry, sugar exported from the Philippines was stored in Benedicto warehouses, shipped by his tankers, insured by a company he controlled, and financed by California Overseas Bank, the Beverly Hills bank that stock certificates found in Malacanang Palace indicate Benedicto owned jointly with Ferdinand Marcos. Benedicto awarded the construction contracts on new sugar mills, receiving additional kickbacks estimated at $250 million that he shared with Malacanang.

There were many other ways Marcos and Benedicto found to squeeze the juice out of the cane—for example, by controlling local trade contracts. Friends of Marcos were given contracts to buy and sell sugar. These "paper traders" simply sold the rights to actual traders at a markup, in effect taking a cut off the top of every deal. This practice cost the industry $205 million from 1975 to 1984. In this way, the sugar industry was used to make political payoffs to anyone Ferdinand wanted to reward—politicians, military officers, relatives, and friends.

Everybody wanted in on the sugar orgy. Two U.S.-based refineries, Sucrest and Revere, were bought by Imelda and her family. Revere was purchased for $11.8 million with top banana Antonio Floirendo fronting for Imelda. Thereafter, the Marcoses could buy raw sugar from Filipino planters at whatever price they chose, have it refined by Revere and Sucrest in the United States, warehouse it till prices were good, then capture the profits overseas. The First Lady made millions by underpaying for her own country's sugar. During the period 1975–80, Revere refined and sold Philippine sugar paying 2 cents per pound below world market prices. Other U.S. refiners complained, prompting a congressional investigation. Thanks to a special deal arranged between Benedicto and Revere, the Philippine sugar industry lost $110 million by 1980. In their last ten years in power, Ferdinand and Imelda diverted more than $1.15 billion from Filipino sugar producers.

In Negros, which was now completely Benedicto country, wage disputes and labor protests were crushed by a Constabulary unit called Task Force Kanlaon. Benedicto saw to it that sugar profits purchased the Task Force's trucks and paid for their fuel and expenses. In the altar on the dashboard where Filipinos ordinarily keep a saint's image, each truck had a photo of Mr. and Mrs. Benedicto. The 431,000 sugar workers in the Philippines were already desperately poor before Marcos and Benedicto took over; cane workers were paid less than a dollar a day. The sugar barons always had been criticized for this exploitation and for salting their profits abroad, but under the Marcos-Benedicto monopoly, costs rose and profits fell, planters stopped their old-fashioned paternalism (such as it was), abolished free services, cut payrolls, and forced laborers to pay old debts. Said one grower: "If the planters are squeezed, we squeeze our labor." Real income in the canefields dropped to the lowest point since the beginning of the plantation system in the late eighteenth century. In 1986, after twenty years of Marcos rule, most Filipino sugar workers received less than 80 cents a day, in pesos that had lost their buying power by more than half, so in real terms they earned one-third their 1940 wages. On Negros alone, 750,000 children were suffering malnutrition, existing on meager rations of sweet potato and cassava, hundreds of them going blind, thousands suffering brain damage. While the world agonized over famine in Ethiopia, a worse famine was sweeping what Manila travel brochures persisted in calling Sugarlandia.

If any one rivaled Bobby Benedicto in Ferdinand's affections it was Eduardo Cojuangco, Jr. While army officers called him "Santa Claus," his critics referred to him as "Cujo." A billionaire several times over in Australia, America, and the Philippines, Cojuangco was a collector: he collected breweries in both hemispheres, he collected ponies at a $25 million stud farm in Australia, he collected other people's companies and other people's land, and he pulled together what was reputed to be the world's largest individual collection of Uzi machine guns. Nearly twenty years younger than Ferdinand, he had been an energetic supporter since the 1960s, and was the godfather of the president's son, Bong-Bong. Only two civilians ranked among the "Rolex 12"—Minister of Defense Juan Ponce Enrile and Eduardo Cojuangco, Jr.

Critics said of Cojuangco, "He does not want to run the Philippines, only to own it." Cojuangco was called "the unseen hand that everyone tends to see behind important events," "the untouchable crony," and "the second richest man in the Philippines."

Cojuangco's rise was not spectacular, because he started out on top. He was born into the powerful Cojuangco clan of Tarlac, the wealthiest Chinese family in the Philippines. It was the Cojuangcos and the rival Aquinos in the early years of this century who created the conditions in Tarlac leading to the peasant revolt of the 1920s and 1930s, eventually provoking the Huk movement. Eduardo's great-grandfather, Jose I, was a tough, pigtailed immigrant from Fukien Province who started as a building contractor in Manila in 1861, then moved to Tarlac where he invested in rice and sugar lands; he was also a moneylender, which enabled him to enlarge his landholdings rapidly through foreclosure. Nobody ever thought they were nice folks. The family acquired 16,000 hectares of prime sugar-land, a 6,500-hectare tobacco plantation, and a sugar mill. Eventually Cojuangcos also came to own the Philippine Bank of Commerce, the First United Bank, and the Philippine Long Distance Telephone Company, which in 1969 grossed $150 million. Cojuangcos took pains to be popular with American colonial officials, and after World War II their great Hacienda Luisita became a base for the CIA, a guarantee of preferential treatment.

The clan split into warring factions when Ninoy Aquino married Cory Cojuangco and campaigned for Tarlac governor in 1960. Don Jose Cojuangco, Sr. (his father-in-law), and Jose Junior (his brother-in-law) underwrote Ninoy's campaign. This aroused the wrath of other Cojuangcos, primarily Eduardo and his father, who continued to regard Aquino as an interloper from the rival clan. Eduardo accused Ninoy of consorting with the Huks. Replying to the charge, Aquino said: "It is true that I have to deal with the Huks now and then. Besides the Huks are not all bad. Without them, the rich will run amok." As to Eduardo, Ninoy added, "He thinks he can corrupt everything with his millions."

With the imposition of martial law, their situations were reversed with Aquino in jail and Cojuangco on the "Rolex 12." He acquired a seat in the Marcos rubber-stamp Congress, was the ruling party's chairman for Tarlac, governor of Tarlac, and international roving ambassador. Ferdinand put Cojuangco in charge of the horse-racing and basketball franchises, two of the biggest gambling operations in the islands. He became the director of the Manila Hilton, the owner of Filsov Shipping, the director of First Philippine Holdings (previously a Lopez firm), and eventually took over more than one hundred forty companies. Applying the full leverage of the Marcos regime, he pulled off an executive suite coup just before the downfall and became chairman of the Philippines' largest corporation, San Miguel, with branches in Hong Kong, Spain, and Mexico.

He participated in the Marcos sugar orgy, increasing his canefields with 2,000 more hectares in Negros and 5,000 in Mindanao. As a condition of purchase, he required that all workers living on the land be evicted. Cojuangco was not short of men to do his dirty work—he had a private army of five thousand mercenaries armed with M-16s, Uzis, and Galil assault rifles, which can only be purchased in bulk with Israeli government approval. Cojuangco's army was trained on Palawan by Israeli commandos, also with the approval of Tel Aviv (it would have been impossible otherwise). Cojuangco forged a godfather association with senior Filipino military officers by cultivating them and distributing financial favors discreetly, leading to his other nickname, "Santa Claus."

With a little help from Ferdinand and Juan Ponce Enrile, Cojuangco took over the entire coconut industry. They created a monopoly by controlling funding, processing, marketing, and development.

Their coconut cartel attempted to manipulate the market in America by buying up Philippine coconut oil cheap, shipping it to America, and warehousing it there till prices rose. But a sudden increase in interest rates and the Soviet grain embargo (which flooded the American market with soybean oil) caused coconut-oil prices to plummet. Cojuangco and Enrile were forced to sell their U.S. inventory at a $10 million loss. The U.S. Justice Department filed a suit charging that they had conspired to create an artificial shortage, and several U.S. firms lodged anti-trust actions, but after strings were pulled in Washington the Justice Department settled for a mild reprimand "not to do it again."

While sugar and coconut prices could be manipulated by monopoly marketing, the simplest Marcos business technique was the blunt take-over. When Ferdinand identified a choice business, he demanded a percentage of the stock. The shares could be endorsed in blank or held on Ferdinand's behalf by a dummy company, like the many set up for him by Jose Campos.

Seafront Petroleum and Mineral Resources was an oil exploration company that flowered in the mid-1970s amid reports that major oil reserves lay off Palawan Island. Early in 1976, Ferdinand demanded that the owners of Seafront turn over to him all their oil options. Grudgingly, Seafront owner Alfonso Yuchengco made the transfer to Mid-Pasig Land Development Corporation for 1 peso. Said Yuchengco, "Marcos called for me and said he wanted the options . . . I signed unwillingly." Mid-Pasig was controlled by Ferdinand's frontman, Campos. Seafront's shares were then turned over to another Marcos front, Independent Realty Corporation, controlled by Campos and another Marcos frontman, Rolando Gapud. Seafront's first well came in dry. But President Marcos announced on national television that there had been a major oil strike. This caused a stampede on the Manila stock market. Ferdinand and his cronies made at least $9.5 million and dumped all their Seafront stock. A few days later, the stock crashed by 65 percent and Ferdinand announced that he was "launching an investigation" to discover if there had been inside trading. This, said former Seafront owner Yuchengco, was "the biggest hypocrisy of all time."

Ferdinand and his cronies were masters of such manipulation. Their biggest deal was the Westinghouse nuclear power plant in Bataan, the fattest single contract ever landed in the Philippines.

The crony who engineered the deal for Ferdinand was Herminio Disini. Disini was part of the royal family, married to Inday Escolin, a first cousin of Imelda Marcos who also served as one of her physicians. Like Eduardo Cojuangco, Disini was twenty years Ferdinand's junior; like Rudi Cuenca, he was a golf partner. After martial law, Disini became president of the Wack Wack Country Club, the preserve of Manila's old money. Other players groused that Marcos and Disini cheated. Explained former golf partner M. J. Gonzales, "When Marcos played golf, he used his caddies, aides, and bodyguards to do the dirty work. You could never pin anything on him personally." Ferdinand had the lowest handicap of any chief executive in the world, which meant a lot to him.

Disini's big break came in the early 1970s, when Ferdinand used him to take over the cigarette filter business in the islands—long dominated by a British-American firm called Filtrona Philippines, Inc. Together they forced Filtrona out of business, leaving Disini's Philippine Tobacco Filters Corporation with a monopoly worth $1 million a month in profits. Disini then made a deal with Ferdinand's friend Lucio Tan, head of Fortune Tobacco, selling Tan filters so cheap that his cigarettes could undercut rivals and drive competition out of the market. In appreciation, Tan gave President Marcos $11 million in campaign contributions, plus $2.5 million a year. (In the process, Tan avoided paying some $50 million a year in taxes.)

With all the money he made in these deals, Disini created Herdis Group, Inc., a conglomerate of fifty companies with $1 billion in assets. Not wanting to tie up his own millions, he did it all with borrowed money, exploiting the Philippine government guarantees that were irresistible to foreign bankers. Disini hardly seems like the sort of man you would trust to build a nuclear power plant. There were other strange aspects to the project. The power plant sits on a jungle bluff in Bataan overlooking a stretch of the South China Sea—a site subject to tsunami tidal waves, 5 miles from a dormant volcano, and only 25 miles from three geologic faults.

It all began in 1973, when President Marcos ordered National Power to negotiate a deal to buy two 600-megawatt nuclear plants. General Electric showed interest and began negotiating with National Power. The Westinghouse district manager for the Philippines sought help from Jesus Vergara, president of Asia Industries, which handled distribution in the islands for Westinghouse. Vergara knew how things worked and advised Westinghouse that if it wanted to beat GE to the punch, it should hire a lobbyist close to Marcos, a man like Disini.

On the golf course, Vergara mentioned the job to Disini, pointing out that his commission could run into the millions. Disini arranged for Westinghouse executives to discuss their proposal in private with Ferdinand. Westinghouse offered to supply a single plant with two 620-megawatt reactors at a price of $500 million. Additional charges for fuel, power transmission lines, and so forth raised the estimated total to around $650 million.

After this private audience, Ferdinand ordered the general manager of National Power, Ramon Ravanzo, to give the business to Westinghouse. There was to be no competitive bidding.

During nine months of cultivating National Power and discussing its own proposals, GE had never gone straight to the palace. At a meeting with officials of National Power in the office of Executive Secretary Alex Melchor, GE learned to its dismay that Westinghouse had the contract sewed up.

Melchor, thinking that he still might persuade Ferdinand to drop Westinghouse if the GE proposal proved to make more sense, assembled a team of experts to compare the costs and technical details of the two proposals. Melchor's team found nearly every alternative cheaper than Westinghouse. But whatever deal Ferdinand had struck with Westinghouse pleased him so much that he was not moved by any of these arguments.

Already, the Westinghouse price was beginning to grow. When Westinghouse first got the deal, U.S. Ambassador Sullivan had told Washington that the reported cost of $500 million appeared to be low by at least 20 percent. By September, Sullivan was advising Washington that Westinghouse now said the cost would be over $1 billion. Sullivan cabled Secretary of State Kissinger: "I stressed that embassy considered great deal of American prestige riding on Westinghouse performance, and that therefore we intended to follow project closely. I pointed out that this was in effect Filipino Aswan Dam, being largest and most expensive construction project ever undertaken in this country . . .

current cost estimates are over one billion dollars."

By the time a formal contract was signed in February 1976, the deal was hardly recognizable. The power plant would now have not two but only one 626-megawatt reactor. At the prices Westinghouse was now quoting, international banks would not give Manila a loan big enough to finance the second generator. Instead of getting two reactors for $650 million, the Philippines was getting one reactor, with half the power output, for $722 million. It would cost another $387 million for interest and escalation costs, bringing the total price to $1.1 billion. Given past experience, Filipinos naturally assumed that Westinghouse had bribed the president—or, to put it the other way around, that Ferdinand had demanded a huge kickback, and that Westinghouse had agreed in order to snatch the deal away from GE. They speculated that "in the usual manner" the Marcos slice had grown larger and larger, to accommodate Disini and other cronies down the line, and as the First Lady and her family and followers queued up.

According to Vergara, who had asked Disini to intercede with Malacanang in the first place, Westinghouse paid Disini a commission of at least $50 million. Vergara said Disini gave Marcos $30 million of that, and split the rest with Vergara and Disini's business partner, Rodolfo Jacob. This meant that Ferdinand demanded and received from Disini not just 10 percent or 20 percent or 40 percent, but a whopping 60 percent. Jacob confirmed that kickbacks went to Marcos, without verifying how much. A new Disini company, Power Contractors, Inc., became chief subcontractor of civil works in the project. Another Disini outfit, Technosphere Consultants Group, provided engineering and construction management. The contract to install communications at the site was also won by a Disini-related company. And Disini's Summa Insurance Corporation was paid a $10 million premium to write a $668 million policy on the project—the largest single policy ever written in the Philippines. Disini took over Asia Industries, becoming Westinghouse's Philippine distributor.

Westinghouse denied that any money went to Marcos, and said it paid Disini only $17 million in commissions. According to the U.S. Securities and Exchange Commission, a district manager for Westinghouse in the Philippines destroyed six volumes of documents related to the project, then retired.

Once financing was finally arranged with the U.S. Export-Import Bank, Westinghouse needed a place to build the plant. The Marcos and

Romualdez families had taken over a large part of Bataan, opposite Corregidor, some of which was used to build a presidential seaside retreat, the rest turned into a tax-free industrial development zone—in which the lure of tax incentives was used to induce companies to buy sites from the royal family. Apparently Ferdinand made it a condition of the Westinghouse contract that the nuclear power plant had to be built in Bataan.

National Power, with help from the U.N.'s International Atomic Energy Agency (IAEA), picked a seaside location there, and hired Ebasco Services, a subsidiary of Enserch Corporation of Dallas, to test the safety of the site and monitor construction. Ebasco concluded that the site was vulnerable to tidal waves. National Power compromised on a nearby bluff. Westinghouse began clearing the site in March 1976, before National Power had obtained a construction permit and while Ebasco engineers were still trying to determine whether the bluff site was safe; bulldozers interfered with their seismic tests. Filipinos wondered if anyone had considered the danger of earthquakes and the dormant volcano, Mount Natib, five miles away. A team from the International Atomic Energy Agency visited the site in 1978 and recommended that construction be halted until further tests were completed. By then, Westinghouse had already spent about $200 million on the plant.

The head of the Philippine Atomic Energy Commission, Librado Ibe, said his arm was twisted by cabinet officials to let the project proceed, and that he was wined and dined and offered prostitutes by Westinghouse, with continual reminders that this was a pet project of President Marcos. Ibe gave in and issued the construction permit in April 1979, a week after the Three Mile Island accident, then took his wife and two younger children and moved to the United States. His fear for their safety seemed justified. Bankers who had questioned earlier deals by Marcos cronies had been assaulted by thugs, and were warned that their families were in danger.

Several months later, Ferdinand acted on his own experts' advice and halted construction himself, ordering an investigation (into the technical side, not the financial side). The investigators concluded that the design was unsafe, and recommended changes to incorporate new safety features after Three Mile Island. Westinghouse renegotiated the contract to meet these objections and the price rose to $1.8 billion—$55 million for added safety equipment, $645 million for higher interest costs and inflation. Eventually, the cost reached $2.2 billion. Work on the project was pushed through to completion in 1984, as if Westinghouse itself had had enough and wanted to get out. Observers wondered whether Ferdinand had really interrupted the work because of concern for safety—or because he had found yet another way to hold Westinghouse's feet to the fire.

At about the same time, Disini's business empire suddenly collapsed. He left the Philippines hastily for Austria, where he had taken the precaution of salting much of his wealth, and where he had purchased a palace outside Vienna. Fortunately, Disini had lots of friends in Austria. During his travels with Imelda, Disini and the First Lady had become good friends with Kurt Waldheim.

As former secretary of defense and head of the World Bank, McNamara surely had access to secret information about Ferdinand and Imelda. Could he have been ignorant of the dark side of the regime? Since martial law, the World Bank had poured more than $2 billion into the Philippine economy, much of it diverted by the Marcoses into Swiss banks. It was partly at the encouragement of the World Bank that private international banks and banking consortia were footing the bills for improbable ventures by Marcos cronies involving land grabs, company takeovers, gigantic kickbacks, and policies provoking widespread famine. How could the Marcos regime be a "good risk"?

It appears that the Bank was not as ignorant as it pretended to be, which became clear with the leak of the Ascher Memorandum in December 1980. This provided what one critic called "a rare glimpse of the cold rationality and lucid class consciousness that guide the actions of one of the capitalist world's most tight-lipped institutions." The Ascher Memorandum laid down guidelines by which the Bank could begin to distance itself from the Marcos regime as it headed toward disaster. That it was leaked right after Ronald Reagan was elected president revealed the concern of some people in the foreign policy community in Washington that Reagan was going to put his support behind Marcos at the very moment when Ferdinand's bubble was about to burst. What emerges from the memorandum is a simple rule of thumb: There is nothing wrong with the Bank actively supporting a brutal and unscrupulous regime so long as the Bank gets out from under before the regime collapses. The Bank can then demand payment of debt from whoever picks up the pieces. From the World Bank's point of view, a dictator's bills can be paid just as readily by his victims.

The memorandum was prepared by World Bank staff members and consultants under the direction of William Ascher, a specialist in "political risk" at Johns Hopkins University. At this time the World Bank had budgeted $3 billion for the Philippines through 1986. From 1976 to 1980, $680 million had been spent on McNamara's grand panacea: rural development. Asher's grim assessment was that these millions were completely wasted because of the tactics of Ferdinand's administration. The regime's land reform program had stopped dead and gone into reverse. Moreover, there had been a 50 percent decline in the real wages of Filipino workers between 1965 and 1975, due in part to the manipulations of men like Benedicto and Cojuangco. It was also due to the devaluation of the peso imposed by the IMF and the World Bank in 1969, before they would give Ferdinand the loans he needed to keep the economy going after he squandered the treasury to get re-elected.

Under pressure from the Bank and the IMF, Marcos had also committed himself to liberalizing Philippine industry by dismantling tariffs, withdrawing subsidies, creating incentives for foreign investors, and establishing tax-free industrial zones. The idea was to promote industry geared to produce for export rather than for domestic consumption. By 1980, the Bank could no longer ignore the failure of this policy as well. Because of the Bank's failed policies, and the extravagance of the Marcos regime, experts made the alarming projection that Manila's external debt would jump from $12.2 billion in 1980 to $19.3 billion in 1984.

Martial law had not changed the pattern of income concentration in the hands of a few. If anything, income was now even more concentrated—entirely in the hands of Ferdinand and Imelda and their inner circle instead of the traditional oligarchs.

The suspension of party politics had merely produced a "new ruling coalition" consisting of the Marcos family, its cronies and courtiers, high-level technocrats, bureaucrats, generals, and a few wealthy businessmen like the Ongpins, Zobels, and Sorianos who cohabited with the regime.

Some people in the Philippine business sector and middle class, the memo said, were now making their position clear by supporting the anti-Marcos movement and the bombing campaign. The forces of free enterprise were taking up arms against Marcos. The Bank had to adjust its policy accordingly.

The Marcos regime was being maintained artificially by the IMF and World Bank, and the Bank's principal sponsor, the United States. They were providing a diseased, brain-dead, terminally ill regime with a very expensive life-support system. To cut its losses and place itself in a better bargaining position with whatever government succeeded Marcos, the memo concluded, the Bank might have to help pull out the plug. The memo was ignored.

Sixteen

YAMASHITA'S GOLD, PART TWO

As EARLY AS 1968, Ferdinand Marcos was being called the richest man in Asia, and ten years later his personal holdings were calculated to be in excess of $5 billion, but those who made these appraisals failed to specify how he had come by such extreme wealth so quickly. Some members of this exotic, super-rich peer group had achieved their immense fortunes by fairly obvious devices, such as war profiteering and criminal racketeering, real estate speculation, domination of major economic sectors such as shipping, electronics, and oil, or had accumulated their wealth over generations by shrewd management of family, corporate, or religious funds.

To be sure, there were all the obvious sources. Among journalists, it was generally understood that some of the Marcos wealth came from the crooked sale of import licenses; from countless murky business deals; from his tobacco monopoly and other partnerships with Harry Stonehill and various international operators; from deals with Japanese and Chinese tycoons; from multinational kickbacks; from smuggling and racketeering with Chinese syndicates and Japanese Yakuza; from deals with American mobsters; and from a lion's share of Philippine gambling proceeds. A large part certainly came from the U.S. government in the form of misdirected aid funds, detoured war reparations, inflated military base rent, sidetracked World Bank and IMF millions, and secret grants made by the White House as a means of high-level bribery. Another sizable portion came from confiscating the wealth of others and seizing businesses and properties. Every journalist could tick off other examples, such as landgrabbing from hill tribes, then selling the land to multinationals, but nobody could rationalize more than $1 or $2 billion.

What was tantalizing about Ferdinand Marcos was not whether he had $10 billion or $20 billion, but that most of it could not be accounted for. This was attributed to an enormous secret hoard of gold bullion. There were persistent reports that he had vaults full of diamonds and gold; stories of a gold Buddha weighing over a ton; rumors of incredible secret bullion deals in London, Hong Kong, Sydney, and elsewhere— the clandestine sales of 10 metric tons of illicit gold bullion at a time, much greater in aggregate than the known gold reserves of the Philippines. Periodically, the London gold market, the biggest in the world, stirred with fresh rumors of secret transactions called "Marcos Black Eagle deals." The term Black Eagle originally referred to Nazi gold spirited out of the Reichsbank in Berlin just before the fall of Hitler's Third Reich. Over $2.5 billion worth of gold and currency vanished, stolen by Russians and Americans and former Nazis, some of it trickling back later into the gold market. The deals of Ferdinand Marcos were also called "Black Eagles" because they were understood to originate similarly with Axis war loot—Yamashita's Gold—and the loot was being marketed surreptitiously.

Ferdinand had first become involved in the search after the war, when he claimed that he was called in by two Filipino laborers in a dispute with two former Japanese officers over a pit full of gold bars.

Later, as part of President Quirino's Ilocano political machine, he worked closely with the Japanese-American investigator, Fukimitsu, when he interviewed Japanese sources and dug through the Imperial Army archives—only to claim that he found nothing.

The legend came back to life in 1970 when a Filipino locksmith and amateur treasure hunter, Rogelio Roxas, dug up a solid gold Buddha weighing 1 ton. Roxas, a former president of the Treasure Hunters Association of the Philippines, said he acquired a Japanese map showing a site near Baguio in abandoned shafts of Benguet mines. Armed with an old-fashioned metal detector, Roxas said he spent months systematically searching for the correct part of the tunnel. After seven months of digging, he said his party reached a cave littered with skeletons. There were no gold bars and coins, only a crate. When they pried it open they found a gold Buddha, distinctly Siamese in its features, possibly the one supposed to have been taken to Baguio by Yamashita when he moved his headquarters there. The Buddha was 28 inches tall and later was determined to weigh 2,000 pounds. The head could be removed. Inside the torso were jewels, assumed to be the crown jewels of some Siamese or Mon ruler in the Malay Peninsula. It might have been seized anywhere in Siam during the Japanese occupation; taken from a member of the Thai aristocracy or from a wealthy Chinese businessman in Bangkok, or from one of the kingdom's well-endowed temples.

The Buddha was appraised at $5 million for its gold content alone when it was discovered in 1970. By 1986, the gold content would have brought $26 million. After retrieving the piece, the excavation was said to have been abandoned because the old mine shaft started to cave in. There are speculations that this was all a cover story contrived by Roxas to protect the real site where he found the Buddha, apparently beneath a flagpole in the quadrangle of a military compound, one of the one hundred and seventy-two sites clearly marked on genuine maps. The maps were reported to contain exact instructions in code on how to dig down to the treasure and avoid booby traps.

Roxas said he received many offers for the Buddha, including one from the president's mother, Josefa. When he refused to sell, ten soldiers showed up at his house in Baguio at 2:00 A.M. one night, armed with guns and a warrant from Josefa's brother-in-law, Judge Pio Marcos. These men, agents from the National Bureau of Investigation and the Criminal Investigation Service of the Constabulary, carted the Buddha away in a truck, along with the jewels and eighteen gold bars Roxas had also recovered, each measuring 1 × 2 × 3 inches. Why Roxas had not been more discreet is beside the point. He was not expecting to be robbed by the family of the president; the leader of the raiding party was the president's brother-in-law, Marcelino Barba, the husband of Fortuna "Baby" Marcos, Ferdinand's youngest sister.

The next day, Roxas complained to Pio Marcos. Sternly, the judge warned him to be careful and keep quiet about the seizure. Roxas took the warning seriously and went into hiding.

Fourteen days later, after the story hit the Manila papers, another judge in a Baguio court ordered the military to turn over the statue. The army delayed a fortnight, while a Manila sculptor worked furiously, then delivered a Buddha made of brass, its head not detachable. The brass Buddha was kept thereafter in Ferdinand's study at Malacanang, where it was used to deflect questions about the genuine article, which was kept out of sight at his heavily guarded beach palace in Bataan. The Buddha in Ferdinand's study at Malacanang Palace was examined closely by long-time CIA resident Charles Glazer. Glazer confirmed that it was brass, that the head did not unscrew, and that it was distinctly not Siamese. The Buddha at the beach palace was later examined by a U.S. mining engineer and metallurgist, a private guest of the president, who determined that it was gold, just under 1 meter in height, weighing approximately 2,000 pounds. The head unscrewed, revealing a cavity the size of a small bean pot. Ferdinand told him frankly that it was part of Yamashita's Gold, although he did not elaborate on how it had come into his possession; presumably it was on loan from Josefa.

In May 1971, a committee of the Philippine Senate opened an investigation into the Gold Buddha affair. Ferdinand denounced the Senate inquiry as a scurrilous, politically motivated attack, and threatened a "personal vendetta." Roxas was scheduled to tell the real story of the Buddha-napping before television cameras at the Plaza Miranda rally in August 1971, when bombs and grenades were thrown by Marcos agents, killing nine people and severely injuring ninety-six, including the eight senatorial candidates present. Primitivo Mijares said palace security men told him instructions were given to the grenade throwers to "get Rogelio Roxas killed" to prevent him from talking.

Roxas was not injured, but he was prevented from telling his story. Ferdinand threatened to go after anyone who linked him and his relatives to the seizure of the Buddha. Witnesses soon began to disappear, including the Baguio police chief who had been among the night raiders, and Rogelio Roxas himself. Roxas spent the first two years of martial law in prison. On his release, he went into hiding again.

Ferdinand often answered casual inquiries about his wealth by saying that he had found Yamashita's Gold. Reporters were never sure whether he was serious. How could he be? Everyone knew that Yamashita's Gold was only a legend. On the other hand, Marcos was known to have a personal cache of bullion and diamonds. Nobody could be certain of its size or its provenance, but the *Far Eastern Economic Review* made periodic references to his "reputedly already sizeable hoard" of gold bars.

Whatever he had found earlier, in the 1950s and 1960s, the discovery of the Gold Buddha inspired Ferdinand to renew efforts to locate the remaining Japanese loot. After declaring martial law, he could dig for Yamashita's Gold with impunity. At first, his efforts were concentrated on Fort Bonifacio. He believed that the Japanese had buried much of the treasure underneath MacArthur's headquarters in the fortress. In the center of the compound, next to the officers' hall and across from MacArthur's living quarters, was a circular driveway. In its middle was the entrance to MacArthur's personal bomb shelter. When the Japanese took over the compound, they dug additional tunnels; these were deliberately blocked just before the end of the war. Ferdinand was convinced that this was a prime site of the treasure. He kept two thousand soldiers busy for years, excavating 35 miles of tunnels. In the first two years of digging he reportedly uncovered only a single gold bar. After that, however, he must have stumbled onto what he was looking for, because by 1975 he and Ver had shown several visitors specially built subterranean vaults beneath the Bataan beach palace filled with what the guests later described as staggering quantities of gold bullion, rows upon rows of gold bars. These were independent confirmations by different individuals, and their accounts are strikingly similar. Prospective brokers also were shown a large underground storeroom or warehouse near Malacanang Palace containing a similar hoard.

Next, officers of the treasure task force suggested that they start excavating Fort Santiago, under cover of a historical restoration project of the First Lady.

One of the problems encountered from the beginning was that the general location of a treasure site was inadequate. Gold takes little space. Without precise coordinates, digging in a single field could continue for months or years, missing the trove. It was a question of inches. The digging at Fort Bonifacio had gone on for nearly five years. Fort Santiago could take just as long. This was complicated by the fact that the Japanese had buried the gold deep, so it could take months of digging down to discover that you were in the wrong spot. There were clues, such as specific arrangements of certain bones at different depths, with 2,000-pound bombs waiting for those who dug straight down instead of following precise instructions coded in the engineering drawings.

To speed things up, the Marcoses invited a Swedish psychic, Olof Jonsson, living in Chicago, to visit them at Malacanang Palace. Several books had been written about Jonsson and his feats. His previous experiences in locating buried treasure were well publicized. Jonsson was also one of the world's true innocents, a modest man whose psychic gift earned more for others than it did for him. Entertaining psychics at Malacanang was something the Marcoses did from time to time for their own amusement. Both Imelda and Ferdinand were fascinated by psychic phenomena, and believed that they themselves had supernatural powers. During conversations with Jonsson, they brought up the mystery of Yamashita's Gold. Perhaps Jonsson could help.

These discussions led to other problems associated with the treasure. If it was found—thousands of tons of it—how did you dispose of it without causing world gold prices to plummet, and without revealing its origins, inviting international legal challenges? Having already recovered at least one very large cache of gold bars, and possibly others he did not mention, Ferdinand had a particular question that plagued him: all gold bars had a fingerprint in their composition, which would reveal on analysis that they came from mines in certain places. How could you disguise the gold so that nobody could discover where it came from by analyzing the composition of the bullion? You had to find a way to "launder" the gold.

Visitors to the bullion vaults under the Bataan palace reported seeing large numbers of ingots with Japanese and Chinese markings and in a variety of shapes and sizes characteristic of both countries, not the standard sizes and weights stipulated by the London gold pool, which sets international standards for bullion trading. Evidently a large portion of the loot had come from China, or from Chinese sources in Southeast Asia. The bars marked in Japanese presumably had been jewelry or coins melted down before shipment to Manila on the way home to Tokyo.

Olof Jonsson introduced the Marcoses to Norman Kirst, a smooth-talking Wisconsin wheeler-dealer. He presented himself to the Marcoses as a financier. Ferdinand told Jonsson and Kirst that one of his friends, the president of Costa Rica—José Figueroa—had told him about a man in Nevada, a mining engineer and metallurgist named Robert Curtis, who had developed two interesting processes. One enabled him to extract a slightly higher percentage of gold from any given ore, and the other process enabled him to melt down gold bars and alter the composition so the bars could be recast with any metallurgical fingerprint you wanted. With the help of this man Curtis, Yamashita's Gold could be poured into new bars to look as though it came from Benguet Consolidated or other mines in the region. Benguet was extracting around 100,000 ounces of gold per year, but the figure could be increased to cover the gradual introduction of a lot of Japanese war gold into the market. If Curtis could be persuaded to bring his equipment to Manila, it could be set up under the auspices of Benguet, so nobody would be any the wiser. The Marcoses had been buying into Benguet for years and by the mid-1970s had gained a majority ownership of the company through front men.

Kirst volunteered to get in touch with Curtis in Reno, and immediately did so on a palace telephone. He followed this up by making several trips to Nevada, where he outlined the deal to Curtis and offered to let him in on it, providing Curtis agreed to pay Kirst and Jonsson's expenses, running to several thousand a month. Ferdinand, who was addicted to codenames and Hollywood-style espionage, decided that the men involved would be called the Leber Group ("rebel" spelled backward). He would be "Charlie" and Ver "Jimmy." General Ver would coordinate operations. Imelda and Kokoy were kept informed by Kirst, evidently on the assumption that he was protecting himself, but they were not yet directly involved.

Kirst told Curtis that President Marcos had already retrieved several hundred million dollars' worth of gold bars and other valuables, including the Gold Buddha. Curtis did not believe him at first. Eventually, he became hooked by the challenge, but he remained not entirely convinced even when he flew to Manila.

Compared to most treasure hunters, Robert Curtis was a bit of a Boy Scout. He had made his living in the deserts and mountains of America's Far West as a banker and car salesman, becoming the president of several small corporations engaged in mining and processing precious metals. He was active in that fraternity of rock hounds and precious metals freaks who spend every spare moment searching for gold with metal detectors, or scheming grandly to find El Dorado and the Seven Cities of Cibola. When Kirst phoned him the first time from Malacanang Palace, Curtis had financial problems. His company, U.S. Platinum, was deep in the red because of the cost of purchasing equipment to carry out his processes. A conservative politically, Curtis had borrowed $250,000 from wealthy members of the right-wing John Birch Society and was having trouble paying it back. The prospect of solving all his financial worries by taking part in the discovery of Japanese war booty seemed like the answer to his prayers. Curtis was sincere and ingenuous and, like many engineers, single-minded about getting his work done in the most efficient manner possible. As a romantic, he was gullible about politics and business, but he understood human nature well enough to avoid becoming involved with people and projects that had a very bad smell. Since Ferdinand was the president of the Philippines, a right-wing ally of the United States, Curtis made allowances about the ethics of the situation. Engineers have to work within tolerances.

Fortunately, Curtis had a mania for accurate record keeping, and a knack for gadgetry that led him to tape-record every phone conversation he had, and even to tape face-to-face meetings with friends. Years later, when his story was challenged, he could produce thousands of pages of documentation and countless hours of tapes that took weeks to assess. Ultimately, he was able to convince stubborn unbelievers all the way up to the Pentagon, the CIA, and the White House.

Curtis worried a lot about where the gold came from, the brutal circumstances under which it was seized by the Japanese, and the horrors involved in its burial. But the practical problem confronting him was how to find it and get it out of the ground. After it was recovered, there would be plenty of time to sort out the ethics of the situation.

Characteristically, Ferdinand was not planning to pay Curtis anything for his trouble. Curtis had to ship his gold-processing equipment from Nevada to Manila at his own expense. There, space would be made available, either on a military base or at the beach palace, to set up the equipment and process the gold into new ingots. As a partner in the Leber Group, of course, Curtis was to be rewarded with a percentage of the loot. Or so it was put to him.

Curtis made two trips to the Philippines between March and July 1975. He, Olof Jonsson, and Norman Kirst first arrived in Manila together in March 1975, and were met by other members of the Leber Group, headed by Ferdinand's errand boy Amelito Mutuc. Mutuc had been President Macapagal's executive secretary, but was sacked for his ties to Harry Stonehill. He became Ferdinand's gofer, and transmitted bribes to Primitivo Mijares. Others Curtis met included Paul Jiga and Ben Balmores, who were identified as eyewitnesses to the burial of the treasure. Curtis and Jonsson were taken to over two dozen sites, the most important ones at Fort Santiago and Fort Bonifacio in Manila; at Teresa barrio 30 miles from the city; at San Agustin Church in the old walled city of Intramuros (where loot had been stashed in a deep crypt beneath the altar with the consent of the priests); at a property belonging to the wealthy Don Paco Ortigas; and at San Sebastian Church,

Christ the King Church, a railroad site, and several others. Frequently they met General Ver and a Colonel Lachica, a member of Ver's staff who headed a security force responsible for protecting the First Lady.

Curtis stayed in Malacanang Palace. He had many conversations with Ferdinand in his private chambers. At first Curtis was not absolutely convinced that the treasure existed; he did not become certain until he was overwhelmed by evidence. Ferdinand had obtained from Balmores and Jiga several of the original secret Japanese maps detailing the disposition of the treasure. In all there were 138 land locations and 34 water locations—172 sites. Japanese engineering drawings of each site indicated precisely how they had been laid out, including telltale markings at various levels, and how to avoid booby traps. Most of the maps were still in the hands of Jiga and Balmores, hidden by them for their own safety. At each site were layers of human bone—skulls, hands, arms—placed to indicate that the recoverer was proceeding correctly. It was explained to Curtis that the instructions on the maps were inscribed in a Japanese dialect that had not been in common use for one thousand years. Curtis studied modern engineering drawings of several troves, executed at Ferdinand's order by a team of Filipino engineers, geologists, architects, and cartographers. He accompanied Marcos and Ver to the beach palace at Mariveles in Bataan, to "work out all rough edges." There, Curtis was taken by General Ver to a vault in the basement. "I saw the bars stacked from floor to ceiling," he claimed. Curtis estimated that he was looking at close to $60 million in gold in that one room alone. Ver told him that this was only some of the gold from one site and that there was considerably more stored in adjacent vaults. It was at Mariveles, too, that Curtis was able to make a personal inspection of the real Gold Buddha, which was on the floor beside Ferdinand's desk. Ferdinand talked to him at length about getting the right paper records assembled and marketing the treasure to the gold pools in London and Zurich.

Curtis agreed to have two small furnaces dismantled at his plant in Reno and shipped to Manila, along with other equipment to reprocess the gold. This would be done under cover of providing mining equipment to Benguet.

Marcos and Curtis decided to concentrate first on one water site and two land sites. The water site was the wreck of the Japanese cruiser *Nachi*. The two land sites were "Teresa II" and the property of Don Paco Ortigas.

For his own confidence, Curtis wanted to begin by confirming the authenticity of the sites, the maps, and the eyewitnesses, so he spent a lot of time talking to Jiga and Balmores. When Curtis met him in 1975, Jiga gave his age as fifty-seven. He was living in Manila, employed by the Philippine Refining Company, part of an American multinational that made shampoo and toothpaste. Balmores was older and had already retired.

Curtis listened to their accounts of how they had worked as houseboys and interpreters for Japanese generals and had witnessed all the gold burials, including the sinking of the cruiser *Nachi*, then had stolen the treasure maps.

Filipinos in the Leber Group referred to Balmores and Jiga contemptuously as turncoats—dual Japanese-Filipino citizens who betrayed the Philippines to become spies, scouts, and interpreters for the Japanese high command, then betrayed their trust again when they stole the plans. They had never attempted to get the gold themselves because the Japanese had made each site too intricate for casual retrieval. They knew it would take teams of men, lots of money, and engineering skill to circumvent the booby traps and find the precise locations. Jiga and Balmores were now in thrall to Marcos. Marcos needed Balmores and Jiga, too. They had the maps, and they were intimate with the sites, having witnessed the burials. The two men were so relieved to find Curtis a sympathetic character that they turned their remaining maps over to him. Later, the older man, Balmores, blurted out to Curtis something in private that even Marcos and Ver had failed to discover— the truth that they had kept hidden for thirty years.

To find the cruiser *Nachi*, Ferdinand promised that navy PT boats and divers would be on hand to assist Olof Jonsson, once he pinpointed the exact location of the treasure with his psychic powers. As a precaution, Ferdinand then issued a presidential decree requiring his personal approval for any future salvage operations in Philippine waters. In April 1975 Jonsson, Curtis, Kirst, Balmores, and Jiga boarded a PT boat together with Ver's security men.

After Ver's divers spent hours searching fruitlessly in the place where the Japanese maps showed the wreck to be, the psychic insisted that they drop anchor several hundred yards away. Again, the divers were dispatched and within minutes surfaced to shout that Jonsson had brought them to the exact spot. Floating buoys were anchored to the bow and stern of the cruiser. When they returned to Manila, Ver was elated. But when they came back the following day, the buoys were gone. Perhaps currents had broken the ropes. It was too late in the day to relocate the vessel. On the third day, Jonsson again found the cruiser. New buoys were placed securely and Ver promised to leave a patrol boat in the area to guard against intruders. Plans were made to return in three days' time with more divers and equipment. But when they returned, the new buoys also were gone. When Curtis asked Ver about the failure of his security precautions, hinting that Ver's own men might have removed them, Ver insisted that his guard boat had been obliged to leave because it had to escort the presidential yacht on a voyage.

It was obvious to Curtis and his companions that Marcos and Ver were playing some kind of game with the wreck of the *Nachi*, so they shifted their efforts to the land site at Teresa II.

On the Japanese maps, Teresa II was described as containing 777 billion yen in treasure (1944 currency), and 777 was Ferdinand's lucky number. It was to be excavated by the Age (pronounced "ahgay") Construction Company, headed by Dr. Eduardo Escobar, Ver's personal choice for the job. Security on the site would be provided by Ver's men.

With the Japanese maps and help from Olof Jonsson's psychic powers, they located and marked the exact spot of the Teresa II site where excavation should begin. Digging started in mid-May in plain sight of nearby housing. The twenty-man work crews of the construction company were told only that they were involved in a soil test; they would be replaced by Ver's men before the treasure was reached. Digging went on around the clock, averaging 3 feet per day. On June 8, they reached the top of a concrete tunnel. When the concrete was pierced, the workers suffered headaches and nausea so severe that some were hospitalized. Balmores and Jiga said it was gas from the remains of the POWs buried alive in the tunnel—arm bones and hand bones were uncovered in curious patterns throughout the descent.

As indicated on the maps, they found a level of burned charcoal, a layer of bamboo, then a layer of crisscrossed wooden boards. Then more bones, the fender of a truck, and another piece of metal. Before they could dig further, the chief security officer vanished and came back with a truck full of heavily armed soldiers. These troops it turned out were loyal to Imelda. They took over guarding the site. When word reached Ver, his own security forces moved in, getting the drop on Imelda's troops and forcing them to put down their weapons. A marital quarrel.

Digging resumed. Curtis was lowered into the shaft and studied the two metal objects—one plainly the fender of a truck, the other a section of one of several 1,000-pound bombs guarding the treasure. This news was passed to Malacanang. It was now July 6, 1975. Digging was suddenly halted at Ferdinand's order. Primitivo Mijares had just testified before the U.S. Congress: Washington columnists Jack Anderson and Les Whitten had written a piece repeating Mijares's allegation that President Marcos was searching for Yamashita's Gold. This had alarmed Ferdinand. Although Ver had been excited about the discovery of the trucks, Ferdinand was more concerned about "leaks" in the Leber Group. He ordered Ver to question all the civilian workers. Everyone had been warned that leaks could be fatal.

That night Olof Jonsson told Curtis he was leaving Manila immediately and advised Curtis to do the same. The psychic had an intuition that they were all in grave danger. The next morning Jonsson took the first flight out. Curtis stayed long enough to see Ver and conclude arrangements for his furnaces and other processing equipment that he had gone to great expense to ship to Manila. It was too late to intercept the shipment. He was invited to spend a week on holiday in Baguio, but felt uneasy after Jonsson's warning. He claimed he had urgent business back in Reno, and boarded a flight home on July 10. Norman Kirst stayed behind, imagining that he could make a deal with President Marcos. He spent the next ten days, as he put it, "virtually entombed," until he concocted letters and cables designed to discredit Curtis. The idea was to slur Curtis so that he would not be believed if he ever revealed what the Leber Group was up to.

Curtis, meanwhile, was sitting pretty. When he had left Manila, he had taken Jiga's and Balmores's treasure maps with him. When Ferdinand discovered that the maps were gone, he made repeated attempts through intermediaries to reassure Curtis and get him back to Manila. By then Curtis had other problems. Ferdinand had double-crossed him, swindled him out of his equipment, but that was only the beginning. To pay everyone's expenses for the whole venture, Curtis once again had approached his rich moneylenders in the John Birch Society, apprised them confidentially of the Yamashita Gold deal, and had arranged to borrow another $125,000. He now owed them $375,000. The man with whom he was dealing, multi-millionaire Jay Agnew, was a member of the national council of the John Birch Society. Agnew owned a lumber company in Washington State, and his son Dan was an attorney there. Curtis claimed that they and other officials of the John Birch Society volunteered to launder his future share of the gold, which they expected to be $2 billion, and in which they now had a significant interest because of their loans to him. He said they told him the laundering would be done through an offshore company called Commonwealth Packaging Ltd., which they had set up in the Bahamas; in Nassau, the money would be deposited in a branch of the Royal Bank of Canada. Then, using various accounts controlled by senior members of the Birch Society, the money would be transferred a chunk at a time to the Royal Bank branch in Kelowna, British Columbia, where it would be credited to an account controlled by one of the key financial experts of the John Birch Society, who would retrieve it and carry it across the border. Curtis claimed that the Birchers boasted of successfully smuggling large sums into the United States through Canadian banks in this fashion.

Involved in the deal in addition to the Agnews, Curtis said, were Georgia Congressman Larry P. McDonald; former California Congressman John Schmitz, once a presidential candidate on the right-wing American party ticket; Floyd Paxton, of Yakima, Washington, who had been defeated three times in efforts to be elected to Congress; and his son Jerry Paxton of Yakima, who ran the worldwide Kwik Lok Corporation, which made the ubiquitous little plastic clips used to close bakery, produce, and frozen food bags in supermarkets. Because of his wealth, Floyd Paxton was the Birch Society's financial expert and a member of its executive committee. Curtis said Paxton would be the one who took the money out of the Royal Bank's Kelowna branch, where it would be kept in an account belonging to the Kelowna plant of Kwik Lok. Another participant, Curtis said, was Jerry Adams of Atlanta, a Bircher and head of the Great American Silver Corporation, a precious metals company being probed by the Securities and Exchange Commission. Curtis said he was told the laundering scheme had been cleared with the man then heading the Birch Society, Congressman McDonald, and Robert Welch, the millionaire candy manufacturer and founder of the Society, who once accused President Eisenhower of being a Communist.

According to Curtis, Paxton and the Agnews were very accommodating and had explained how his $2 billion share of the Japanese war booty could easily be smuggled into the United States, "without violating any laws or paying any taxes." Curtis said the Birch Society also informed General Ver that they would guarantee to launder for President Marcos the first $20 billion in gold recovered from the sites. Beyond $20 billion, the Society suggested a plan by which the gold would be offered secretly to Arab oil states in exchange for oil; Ferdinand could then sell the oil to Japan, receiving clean money.

The generosity of the Birch Society in making such an offer to Ferdinand Marcos and Fabian Ver can only be fully savored by keeping in mind that the gold in question was stolen from banks, governments, religious organizations, and private individuals throughout Asia, that the Marcoses were simultaneously swindling the U.S. government, private banks, and numerous individuals out of hundreds of millions of dollars that were salted in offshore accounts, that Ver was in direct charge of the imprisonment, torture, and murder of dissident Filipinos—and at that very moment, according to all evidence available, was getting ready to entertain kidnapped U.S. congressional witness Primitivo Mijares by having his teenage son's eyeballs plucked out of their sockets.

Now that his part in the Yamashita Gold project had collapsed and his equipment was forfeit, Curtis could not pay back the borrowed money, and he found himself facing a federal indictment on charges brought by members of the Birch Society that Curtis had obtained the funds under false pretenses. The absurdity of the Society's position was not apparent at the time to anyone but Curtis.

His back to the wall because of the Birch Society lawsuit, Curtis decided in December 1977 to take his story and his evidence (including over three hundred hours of taped phone conversations and two thousand pages of documents) to the office of Nevada Senator Paul Laxalt, then head of the Senate Intelligence Committee. This material was sent to Laxalt's aide, Robert Ashley Hall, who later became city manager of Las Vegas. Hall spent the entire New Year's weekend reviewing the materials and wrote a memo to Laxalt recommending that the evidence be turned over to the Senate Intelligence Committee. The committee reviewed it and passed the word back that nothing could be done. However, copies of the Curtis material were quietly passed to leading right-wing activists.

In desperation, Curtis decided to go public. He contacted editor Brian Greenspun of the Las Vegas *Sun,* columnist Jack Anderson, and writers for the *Philippine News* in San Francisco. They published his story in detail in 1978, such as it was known at the time.

Ferdinand responded to all the publicity by ridiculing the legend of Yamashita's Gold as a hoax, describing Curtis as a "mentally ill ex-convict," and by dispatching Fabian Ver to silence Curtis, as he had silenced Mijares. At the end of June 1978, it was reported that Fabian Ver and three unidentified Philippine colonels had secretly entered the United States to meet underworld figures in San Francisco and Chicago, and to set up murder contracts. The three colonels were recognized by Filipino exiles in San Francisco, identified as a trio believed to have engineered numerous killings. One of their targets this time was Robert Curtis.

Norman Kirst learned of the murder plot from Filipino friends and warned Olof Jonsson, with whom he was still friendly. Jonsson in turn alerted Curtis. Curtis immediately went underground, adopted a new identity, and found a new job in a new place. He has remained underground ever since.

One of the things Curtis kept completely to himself was a chilling discovery he had made on his own in Manila. Jiga and Balmores had been lying all along. Their story about being Filipino houseboys forced into service of the Japanese generals responsible for burying the treasure was a fake. After winning their confidence, Curtis had become close to the two men and Balmores apparently decided to tell him the real story. Far from being houseboys, Paul and Ben were not even Filipinos. They were Japanese. During the war, Curtis discovered, they had served in the navy, not the army, in the secret section responsible for collecting war booty and shipping it back to the Home Islands. They had risen to the rank of commander, just shy of rear admiral, and were actually the officers in charge of the marines who had buried most of the treasure. What they did not tell Curtis (and it would not have meant anything to him at the time if they had) was that they were directly responsible to two Japanese admirals. In Manila itself, they were on the staff of the man who became notorious as the "Butcher of Manila"— Rear Admiral Iwabuchi Sanji. But on a higher level they had ultimate responsibility to the man who collected the loot all over Asia and sent it back toward Japan by way of Manila—Rear Admiral Kodama Yoshio, Japan's criminal mastermind.

It was at Kodama's order that Balmores and Jiga came to bury the loot during 1943 and 1944—including the sinking of the cruiser *Nachi* by a Japanese sub before it could leave Manila Bay, an operation arranged by Rear Admiral Iwabuchi, who still had two mini-submarines at his disposal.

As naval commanders working for Kodama, a man whose power put him beyond the reach of ordinary mortals, Balmores and Jiga also were untouchables. In the Philippines, they had a free hand in burying the loot, with unlimited forced labor by POWs and all the marines they needed for security and brute force. It was not Yamashita's Gold they buried. It was Kodama's Gold. They were not helpless onlookers when thousands of POWs were hacked to pieces, drowned, or buried alive. No wonder Balmores was troubled by the memory.

Kodama was safely back in Japan by the time MacArthur invaded Luzon, but Balmores and Jiga were trapped. They made it sound as though they panicked, stole the secret maps of each site, and faded into the jungle. But, in fact, it did not happen that way.

Many months passed between MacArthur's invasion and Yamashita's surrender. Many Japanese officers did vanishing acts. Perhaps the most famous was the brilliant Colonel Tsuji. After helping Kodama loot Southeast Asia, Tsuji eluded Allied capture by disguising himself as a Buddhist monk, and wandered through Southeast Asia and China for the next three years. After the war crimes trials had ended and his friend Kodama had been freed from Sugamo Prison and could again pull strings, Tsuji returned to Japan, wrote a book about his adventures, became with Kodama a power behind the resurgence of the right wing, and was elected to the Diet.

What Jiga and Balmores did was a calculated decision. It involved not General Yamashita, but Admiral Iwabuchi. Only the basic elements are well known. Yamashita had withdrawn to the mountains and ordered all Japanese forces to leave Manila as an open city. Specifically, Yamashita instructed General Yokoyama Shizuo, the *Shimbu* Group Commander, to destroy the bridges over the Pasig River, to blow up other key installations, and then to evacuate the city. Rear Admiral Iwabuchi Sanji, who commanded the naval forces in the Manila area, was determined to fight, and General Yokoyama soon discovered that under the peculiar command and control arrangements of the Japanese army and navy, he could not force Iwabuchi to do otherwise.

Iwabuchi chose for reasons of his own to defy Yamashita's order and remain in Manila with the sixteen thousand marines and sailors under his command. As units of the First Cavalry and the 37th Division closed in on the city, Iwabuchi's forces withdrew across the Pasig River, destroying military facilities and supplies in the port area, as well as the Pasig bridges. This fulfilled the standing orders Iwabuchi had been given by naval headquarters in Tokyo not to let the Americans capture these stocks and facilities intact.

On February 3, 1945, when the first American cavalrymen entered the city, followed the next day by infantrymen, they found themselves confronted by a large Japanese force determined to fight for every inch. Iwabuchi's men had set up barbed wire and barricades, with machinegun nests and salvaged naval guns dug in at strategic intersections. At the center was Iwabuchi himself, holed up with his toughest units in the old walled city of Intramuros, behind stone walls 40 feet thick. His strong points were in government buildings heavily built of reinforced concrete. Between the Japanese and the three American divisions entering the city were seven hundred thousand Filipino civilians. MacArthur forbade air attacks in order to avoid civilian casualties. Nevertheless, civilians died in large numbers from the heavy use of artillery by both sides. Japanese fighting men added to the carnage by murdering, raping, beating, or burning hapless civilians caught within their lines. About one hundred thousand Filipino civilians died in the battle for Manila—almost six times the number of soldiers killed on both sides.

Iwabuchi's decision to stage a battle to the death has always been explained by Western military historians as a suicidal act based on the Samurai tradition of refusing to surrender. It was known that he had been ordered by his superior, Vice Admiral Okochi Denshichi, to destroy Manila's docks and other vital installations before they could fall into American hands. But nobody could figure out why Iwabuchi changed this typical military command into a suicidal showdown that resulted in some of the worst carnage of the war. It is true that he and his men were cut off from withdrawal into the mountains by MacArthur's craving to seize what he thought was an undefended city, in order to stage a triumphal procession in his own honor. That might explain a decision to fight it out to the finish, but it does not explain all the other things Iwabuchi was doing besides trying to take as many people with him as he could.

Iwabuchi hardly seemed the type to be the butcher of anywhere. He was born in 1893 in Niigato Prefecture, an impulsive but pleasant young man who impressed his fellow cadets at the Naval Academy at Etajima. He must have been bright and well connected, because at graduation he was named an imperial aide. Little is known of his career from 1915 to 1942, which seems to have been spent in the secret service, where as an imperial aide he would have been at home under the overall command of a prince, and where eventually he would have become a colleague of Kodama.

In the early spring of 1942, Iwabuchi reappeared in dispatches when he was made captain of the battleship *Kirishima* and commanded her in the Battle of Midway and at Guadalcanal. His ship was among those dispatched by Admiral Yamamoto with the mission to destroy Henderson Field on the island. The attack, led by Vice Admiral Abe aboard the flagship *Hiei*, resulted in a disastrous defeat for the Japanese, both Iwabuchi and Abe being forced to scuttle their ships. Curiously, while Abe was demoted for his part in the fiasco, Iwabuchi was promoted to rear admiral.

After this one brief appearance on regular duty at the end of 1942, Iwabuchi again became a ghost and remained one throughout 1943 and 1944, when he was suddenly appointed commander of the Manila naval district just before MacArthur's invasion of Luzon. It seems that he had returned to work as one of the naval officers seconded to Kodama, responsible for moving war loot and strategic materials to Manila for transshipment to Tokyo. It would have been natural, then, to give him the job of looking after the last-minute treasure burials in and around Manila as the Americans approached, and to make him secretly responsible for disguising the sites, disposing of the POWs and other conscripts working at the sites, and maintaining whatever defense of Manila was required until all traces of the hidden loot were gone. This would have been an awesome responsibility and it would go a long way toward explaining the murderous determination of Iwabuchi and his men, who were for a time driven quite literally insane.

Iwabuchi had a lot of civilian hostages in Intramuros, men, women, and children, and he seemed to be making heavy use of POWs inside the tunnel system beneath the old city. He also had 4,500 marines holed up in the tunnel system at Corregidor, who seemed to be remarkably busy. The end to their defense of Corregidor came spectacularly on the morning of February 26 when the Japanese defenders set off tons of ammunition and explosives stored in the tunnels. They were all killed instantly. Scores of Americans were also killed, buried in rock slides or hurled bodily off the island as Corregidor convulsed violently.

Jiga and Balmores were working directly for Iwabuchi, and it was for him, not for Yamashita, that they carried out their final excavations in the tunnel system under Fort Santiago, Fort Bonifacio, and Intramuros, and at churches, municipal buildings, bayfront and harbor sites described by Jiga and Balmores as the burial locations for the treasure. Iwabuchi controlled the only two Japanese submarines remaining in Philippine waters, one of which sank the cruiser *Nachi* with all aboard. And it was from Iwabuchi's headquarters, not Yamashita's, that Jiga and Balmores stole the treasure maps.

Eventually, the American forces besieging Iwabuchi in Manila grew tired of the slow progress they were making and brought in heavy mortars and artillery, destroying all that was left of the inner city and flattening Intramuros. Iwabuchi was thought to have held out to the last in the Finance Building, the Legislative Building, and the Bureau of Agriculture and Commerce, and was presumed to have died in the rubble of the Finance Building when it was at last silenced on March 3.

Nobody ever positively identified Iwabuchi's remains in the Finance Building. He may very well have slipped away through the tunnel system in the last stages of the battle, to survive the war in disguise. Interestingly, despite the appalling and otherwise seemingly pointless carnage and destruction, Iwabuchi was posthumously honored by the Imperial Navy with a promotion to Vice Admiral and the First Order of the Golden Kite. For what were they honoring him, really?

It is always possible that Jiga and Balmores were under orders from Kodama to make off with the maps before the end came, so that Kodama could have the sites excavated after the war by groups posing as salvage operators or construction companies. A number of Japanese salvage operators did obtain rights to work offshore in the Philippines after the war. Japanese construction companies and industrial concerns made unusually low bids to win postwar contracts in the Philippines in areas where the maps of Jiga and Balmores show locations of Yamashita's Gold. Many of the locations Ferdinand turned over to Imelda, for her bayfront landfills, excavations, and historical restorations were prime sites on the maps. After the Dovie Beams affair, Ferdinand apparently was forced to divide the treasure sites between them in return for domestic tranquility.

After stealing the maps, Balmores and Jiga went to ground, living on small stashes of treasure that they had set aside for the purpose. They could not risk being discovered by their own countrymen. If Kodama knew they had survived the flattening of Intramuros, he would find ways to regain the maps.

In the early 1950s, Jiga and Balmores ran out of money and decided it was worth the risk to make one excavation, up at an isolated site near Baguio. They hired two Filipino laborers to do the digging, recovered a mass of gold bars, and then became so excited that they refused to pay the diggers. The laborers went to Ferdinand's law office in town, and that was how he tumbled to Jiga and Balmores and his first big stash of Yamashita's Gold. Marcos reached an agreement with them in which he kept most of the gold in return for letting the two former Japanese naval officers survive, under his protection. Thus encouraged, Marcos persuaded President Quirino to strike a deal with Fukimitsu to investigate the whole story. How much was recovered as a result is not known. To protect themselves, Balmores and Jiga were obliged over the years to take ordinary jobs and live within their salaries. After being befriended by Curtis, it was again to protect themselves that they decided to turn over to him all the rest of their maps, and the aging Balmores blurted out the real story he had kept bottled up all those years.

It was probably this hunt for Yamashita's Gold that led Ferdinand Marcos to become friends with Kodama and Sasakawa during the 1950s. Kodama apparently was able to recover portions of the loot using Japanese-funded construction projects and offshore salvage operations as cover, the rights for which he must have paid Ferdinand dearly.

In 1975, when President Marcos decreed that all further offshore operations had to be approved by him personally, he bypassed Kodama and issued a salvage permit to the Korean Yakuza for the recovery of the *Nachi*. He sold the South Korean syndicate of Machii Hisayuki "coral reef exploration rights" for the entire Philippines. Machii, like many of his Japanese counterparts, had served the U.S. Counter-Intelligence Corps in South Korea after World War II by using his "Voice of the East Gang" to break up strikes and intimidate those flirting with communism. He became close to Korea's President Park Chung Hee. In 1970, Park gave Machii control of the ferry line between Pusan, South Korea, and Shimonaseki, Japan—the shortest route between the two countries. Machii became a billionaire, indulging his passion for Picassos and porcelains, all under government protection. He also enjoyed government protection in the Philippines. Apparently, the *Nachi* was completely emptied by Machii, because after that nobody showed the slightest interest in salvaging the wreck.

In 1976, after sixty-five years of unprecedented mischief, Kodama had a stroke and went into eclipse. Inevitably, there were rumors of poison. He lived another eight years, still manipulating events from behind the black curtain, finally dying in January 1984.

After declaring publicly in 1975 that the Yamashita Gold story was a hoax, Ferdinand resumed recovery efforts with renewed energy. The Teresa II site was emptied. Seven years later, in 1982, two men, one of them a full-time CIA officer, were flown in Ferdinand's helicopter to the Bataan beach palace in Mariveles, where they were taken into "the left tunnel," which was 80 feet wide, "as long as a football field," and stacked with gold bars. The gold bars were "standard size" but had "AAA" markings, and were said to have been retrieved from the Teresa II site. The two men were shown the gold vaults in 1982 because the CIA had become involved in helping Ferdinand move and market the treasure.

There were many other sites onshore and off, waiting for recovery, but without the original Japanese engineering drawings that Curtis had taken, it was little better than groping in the dark. Attempts were made to persuade Olof Jonsson to return to the Philippines to pinpoint them, but Jonsson did not need his psychic powers to know the next journey to Manila could be his last.

Seventeen

HEAVY BREATHING

THE OLD FILIPINO GAG "Four centuries in a convent, fifty years in a brothel" ceased to be a joke under the Marcoses. Behind the facade of maintaining a puritanical law-and-order regime, Ferdinand was involved with the two main components of organized crime on the Pacific rim—the Japanese and Chinese underworld. Gambling, prostitution, narcotics, and money-laundering were turned over as franchises to international syndicates, sometimes in league with American, British, and Australian organized crime figures. In the Philippines, their main interest was slavery.

Control of the media made it possible for Ferdinand to create the impression of law and order, when in fact organized crime thrived in the islands as never before. Under martial law, he was as firmly in control in Manila as the South Korean generals were in Seoul and the Chiang regime in Taipei. An American official in South Korea once remarked with surprising candor, "Between the KCIA [Korean CIA], the civil police, and military intelligence, you've got such a powerful security state here that it's impossible for organized crime to operate without official sanction. If it exists, it's state-sponsored or state-sanctioned." The same was true of Taiwan and the Philippines. The essential difference was ethnic. In Taipei and Seoul, control was kept firmly in the hands of a single ruling ethnic group, while in Manila Ferdinand parceled out franchises to Japanese, Koreans, Chinese, Australians, and Americans according to their specialties. Everybody was welcome to a piece of the pie.

317

Manila was the only major Southeast Asian city where the sex trade was run in partnership with the Japanese, with the enthusiastic cooperation of Chinese entrepreneurs and Filipino gangsters and procurers.

Ferdinand and Imelda persisted in saying that with their New Society there was no crime, no drug problem, and no prostitution. All three were officially illegal, so they did not exist. In truth, prostitution had become world class. Although Tourism Minister Jose Aspiras would certainly have denied promoting tourism through prostitution, Manila was competing internationally with Bangkok as the top destination for sex tours. In each city, it was modestly estimated that there were one hundred thousand women employed "legitimately" in what was called the "hospitality industry"—as hostesses, waitresses, go-go dancers, and massage-parlor attendants. That is, as prostitutes. These statistics included only those women employed in licensed establishments, with health permits and regular venereal disease checkups. The rule of thumb was that at least twice that number—another two hundred thousand in each metropolitan area—worked freelance, part-time, or in unlicensed establishments. With a quarter of a million women thus engaged in each place, the slow incubation of the AIDS virus could produce catastrophic consequences.

Manila and Bangkok were also rivals for the number of child prostitutes and young male prostitutes: the estimate for Manila and its satellite towns was forty thousand child prostitutes against twenty thousand in Bangkok. Thousands of young boys and girls in each country were sold into slavery each year, sent off to work without pay in brothels in Japan and South Korea, or were fed piecemeal to European and Australian gays and pederasts.

A major difference between the sex trade in Thailand and that in the Philippines was that the one thrived in a country ruled by a succession of military regimes, making it difficult to identify trends with any one leader or party, while the other boomed for twenty years under one man—Ferdinand Marcos.

There were other important differences. In Buddhist Thailand, religious tolerance and sexual tolerance had been a celebrated part of the culture since ancient times. There was little stigma attached to the sex trade. When he was asked about it, the urbane former Prime Minister Kukrit Pramoj remarked, "I think it is flattering that Westerners find us so physically attractive." In Thailand, there was no special disgrace attached to working as a bar girl or in a massage parlor, and after acquiring a wardrobe, a nest egg, and perhaps a sewing machine, a hardworking bar girl could go back to her village, marry the son of the headman, and begin life over on a better footing. In the Catholic Philippines, with its medieval obsessions and its preoccupation with female virtue, there was no such redemption.

When he was "re-elected" in 1969, President Marcos worked out a partnership or joint venture in which the sex trade was operated in collaboration with the big Yakuza gangs such as the Yamaguchi Gumi and the Inagawa Kai. According to INTERPOL, by the early 1970s more than one hundred thousand Yakuza were operating in Japan with interests throughout East Asia, making a profit of well over $5 billion a year running guns, drugs, sex rings, extortion rackets, and murder syndicates. The most notorious gang was the Sumiyoshi Rengo based in Tokyo, but the biggest was the Yamaguchi Gumi with eleven thousand members, headquartered in Kobe. They all had affiliated travel and entertainment companies. Manila editor Max Soliven said President Marcos was "in big with the Yamaguchi Gumi." Korea was the gang's primary base outside Japan, but the Philippines came second; in 1982, there were twenty-five ranking members of the gang living in and around Manila. Others ran similar operations out of Cebu. Soliven said Marcos was "very much in debt" to the Yakuza, and that their influence was strong at Malacanang Palace.

A 1987 report by the Australian National Crime Authority (NCA) said the Yakuza had over three hundred Filipino government figures on its payroll, including former top officials of the National Bureau of Investigation (NBI) and the Commission on Immigration and Deportation (CID). The NCA report said that the Yamaguchi Gumi had over four thousand operatives in Metro-Manila of whom about three thousand were local underworld contacts. The NCA claimed that the Yakuza controlled 240 businesses in Manila including massage parlors and nightclubs. Six local travel agencies acted as Yakuza fronts arranging bribes with government officials.

Prostitution became so entwined in the economic structure of the Philippines that it created powerful interest groups, especially at the palace. Under martial law, when everyone else had to get off the streets, massage parlors and saunas could stay open after midnight curfew, and the girls toiling in them were exempt. There was collusion between hotels, police, pimps, and prostitutes. Imelda's overbuilding of luxury hotels for the World Bank Conference left them desperate for guests and, with a few notable exceptions, ready to encourage any kind of occupancy. The new Manila Midtown Ramada Hotel became notorious for kickbacks from prostitution. The Ramada passed out broadsheets printed in Japanese addressed "To our Japanese guests with ladies," outlining house rules. The hotel charged a key-club fee of $10 for the right to take women into a room. According to one source, the Manila Midtown Ramada's management admitted to making 40 percent of their gross income from these fees.

The Intercontinental Hotel tried so zealously to prevent prostitution that it was threatened with a lawsuit when the management mistakenly accosted a guest with his wife. To avoid trouble, sex tour leaders usually took guests elsewhere for entertainment, then brought them back to their hotels in the morning.

The Yakuza bribed their way into lucrative, long-term relationships with many Manila businessmen, bureaucrats, and palace cronies. Senior members of Yakuza gangs opened offices in the Makati business district using import-export firms and travel agencies as fronts, all licensed by Aspiras. The Yakuza's biggest investments were made in bayfront Ermita, the tourist tenderloin. At least thirty clubs and restaurants there were run by Yakuza, using Filipino front men, and trading in women, drugs, and gunrunning.

Occasionally there were crackdowns, as Filipino gangsters and police reminded the Japanese to share their proceeds. After these crackdowns, immigration officials and bureaucrats at the Ministry of Tourism usually intervened in behalf of top-ranking Yakuza to prevent their arrests or deportation. For about 20,000 pesos (roughly $1,000), immigration men would extend the visa of an overstaying Yakuza or provide papers for a teenage Filipina on her way to a Tokyo brothel.

This all came about as a function of simple demographics: Japan provided most of the tourists arriving in the Philippines, 85 percent of them males. In their own country, prostitution was banned in 1958, forcing the sex industry to move to bath houses. For the same reason, there was an explosive growth in sex tourism providing access to women in the poorer countries of Asia, first in South Korea and Taiwan, then farther afield as living standards in those two countries improved. Because Japanese preferred to travel abroad in groups, male sex tours were easy for the Yakuza to organize, also simplifying the problem of arranging for women at the destination. With the increasing strength of the yen in the 1970s, more than a million Japanese men each year visited Taiwan, Korea, Thailand, and the Philippines exclusively for sex.

The trade also worked in the other direction. Thousands of young girls were taken to Japan each year on brief tourist visas, and then vanished into bath houses, bars, and brothels. The process began when Yakuza-backed "employment" agencies in Manila hired talent scouts to tour villages. Pretty girls in their early teens were enticed with promises of glamorous jobs. In Manila, they were taught dancing and singing, and (after passing an audition conducted by the government twice a month) officially became entertainers. The girls were then paraded before Japanese promoters. After a girl was chosen, her picture was filed in a catalogue and shown to customers, primarily bar managers. A successful promoter purchased about two hundred women a year, some for export, some for home delivery. After Ferdinand became president and the Yakuza received the franchise for Manila, the number of Filipinas shipped off to Japan and South Korea increased sharply. By 1985 it was estimated that eight thousand to ten thousand young girls were exported from Southeast Asia to Japan each year as entertainers and prostitutes, the great majority of them Filipinas. Many of the girls who went as entertainers found good jobs with decent employers and fair wages, and chose to return year after year, never being forced into prostitution. But they were the exception. Under Ferdinand and Imelda, the Philippines became the only country in the world actively exporting prostitutes. Thailand and South Korea only gave it unofficial sanction. The growing poverty in the islands under the Marcoses, especially after 1983, made women desperate to go to Japan even if it meant prostitution with next to zero earnings.

While Japan was the biggest customer, tour operators from many other countries promoted sex tours to Manila and Bangkok. The Philippines soon outdid Thailand because of economics—the standard of living in Thailand was improving dramatically while it was collapsing in the Philippines. In Ermita, instant oral sex was available for a dollar from thousands of bar girls, or from little boys and girls in the streets— some as young as four years old. In Bangkok, the price was five times higher, and child sex was only to be found in specialized emporiums.

Tourists cruising Ermita from gay dives to girl-dog shows could observe children being fondled by foreigners in doorways, alleys, parking lots, and cars parked at the curbs. Thousands of Europeans, Americans, and Australians came to Manila to find children, to photograph them performing sexual acts, or to take them home to pass around. The

Yakuza alone was estimated to earn $1.5 million *per day* from child sex. This network included Manila hotels as well as private clubs and child brothels.

In one case that was unusual only because officials actually intervened, the police raided the basement of an employment agency in Manila and found fifty-nine boys aged ten to seventeen. They were being kept prisoner so they could be used sexually by tour groups of homosexuals and pederasts.

There were large child brothels around the U.S. military bases at Subic Bay and Clark. The naval base fed brothels at Subic and Olongapo, while the airbase fed Angeles City. By both bases, children as young as fourteen months were bought, sold, and traded for the gratification of GI pedophiles. Behind the bar at Marilyn's in Olongapo, American writer P. F. Kluge discovered a barmaid who liked to show off the talents of her daughter, Valerie. The one-year-old waved, laughed, and flicked her tongue on cue, when her mother whispered, "Blow job." U.S. military authorities pointed to one lengthy court-martial as evidence that America did not condone child prostitution, but the case involved girls in their late teens and did not in any way represent the kind of prepubescent extremes typical of Seventh Fleet shore leave. Observed an Australian military attaché in Manila, with typical 'Strine aplomb, "At Subic, you're still a virgin till you've screwed a two-year-old."

Homosexual tours to Manila rivaled the heterosexual. In keeping with the First Lady's broad-mindedness and love of beauty, the Ministry of Tourism cooperated in the organization of a Miss Gay World Beauty Pageant. Pansanjan, a resort town south of Manila on Laguna de Bay, became the homosexual's Mecca. Pansanjan had less than twenty-seven thousand inhabitants, among them three thousand young male prostitutes. Their customers were primarily whites from France, New Zealand, the Netherlands, and Australia.

Many poor children were taken out of the Philippines through foster parent organizations. At the end of 1983, Australian investigators discovered a Melbourne-based syndicate called the Australian Pedophile Support Group, which assisted its members in arranging sexual relations with young Filipino boys. Nine men were arrested on pornography charges, planning to bring children to Australia to live with homosexuals. At least two of the men traveled to Manila to have sex with boys they were sponsoring through the charity World Vision. A World Vision official said that a task force set up to investigate the reports had prevented one of the two Australians from taking a boy out of the country. Officials of the Marcos regime said that the problem was under control. Child prostitution was illegal, they said, so it did not occur. In 1982, a European magazine ran a story about child prostitution in Manila featuring a little girl from Ermita. When Imelda heard about the story, she had the police track the girl down and bring her to Malacanang for a lecture. "You are dishonoring the country," the First Lady told the child. She was then released and returned to her old corner. When she did not mend her ways, she was beaten by the police and disappeared altogether.

Child sex package tours of the Philippines were especially popular in the Netherlands, West Germany, and the United States. In the leading pedophile magazine, *Spartacus,* Manila sex tours were advertised and advice was given on how to find child prostitutes when you arrived, how to negotiate payment, and how to dodge local laws. To pay travel expenses, pedophiles made videotapes, which were then sold by subscription through such magazines. The United States is the biggest importer (and producer) of films and videos portraying young children in explicit sexual acts and forms of sadomasochism. Annual turnover of the child pornography industry in America in 1980 was $1 billion. International trafficking of children was conservatively estimated as a $5 billion a year business. Under the Marcoses, Manila became the world center for its raw material.

In 1974, Sasakawa's friend and fellow billionaire President Marcos made him an honorary citizen of the Philippines. This gesture grew out of Sasakawa's interest in a little island called Lubang, 76 kilometers southwest of Manila. Lubang hit front pages all over the world in 1971 when Lieutenant Onoda Hiroo of the Japanese Imperial Army finally surrendered, twenty-six years after the end of World War II. Sasakawa gave 1 million yen (slightly more than $3,333) as a reward to the man who brought Onoda safely to the authorities. Overnight, Lubang became a popular Japanese tourist destination. Sasakawa conceived the idea of turning the island into a tourist paradise as part of his exclusive World Safari Club, which cost business tycoons nearly $2,000 to join. The club sponsored Arctic polar bear hunts and other adventures at

$30,000 for a three-week expedition. For tycoons with less energy, Sasakawa wanted to turn Lubang Island into a luxurious nudist colony for Japanese only.

With millions of dollars coming in from the Yakuza partnership in the sex trade and Manila hotels filled with sex-starved Japanese tour groups, Ferdinand was more than agreeable. Sasakawa let it be known that he was developing Lubang for tourism "at the request of Philippine President Marcos." It was at this bouyant moment that he revealed that he had been "very close to Marcos long before he became President," and considered Ferdinand and Imelda among his long-time intimates. During the 1970s, Sasakawa donated millions of dollars to Imelda's highly publicized "relief" projects. To pave over some of the residual ill-feeling about World War II in the Philippines, Sasakawa started the Japan-Philippines Friendship Society.

Lubang Island was described in World Safari Club brochures as offering wonderful opportunities to hunt exotic birds and wild boar, with after-hunting sports hosted by "private companions"—a gentle Japanese euphemism for your own personal Third World adolescent, please specify sex. To create Lubang, Sasakawa paid great sums to Malacanang through the Ministry of Tourism and spent two years on development, when the whole project collapsed over what Sasakawa called "some misunderstanding."

It was probably the same kind of misunderstanding that had spoiled President Johnson's friendship with Ferdinand. The year Ferdinand and Sasakawa had their little misunderstanding was the year Ferdinand sold all the coral reef recovery rights in the islands not to the Japanese but to the South Korean Yakuza gang of Machii Hisayuki. However, neither man let the misunderstanding interfere with the ongoing fulfillment of Japanese longings in the islands.

While they were busy gratifying the sexual cravings of Australians and Japanese, Filipinos consumed prodigious quantities of alcohol. The Ayalas and Sorianos had grown very rich producing good, cheap beer, while the Elizaldes and others became as rich distilling some of the world's cheapest rum. Although marijuana was grown for local consumption, the Philippines was not thought to be a drug center, or to play any role in the movement of heroin and morphine from the Golden Triangle to world markets. The islands had the fewest addicts in Southeast Asia. But such statistics are misleading. Under the Marcoses, the controlled press reported little drug news, and American authorities were at pains to play down the awesome quantities of heroin passing through Clark and Subic on their way from Thailand, Laos, and Vietnam to the United States. Manila was primarily a transshipment point, a dope entrepot.

The loss of the Chinese mainland to Mao in 1949 briefly disrupted the heroin trade, but it was soon up and running again when remnants of Chiang's army under General Li Mi escaped into Burma and seized control of the poppy-growing areas of the Golden Triangle, where they were supplied and supported for over thirty years by the CIA.

From then on, Chinese syndicates in Thailand and Laos—such as the *chiu chao* with its well-established ties to the KMT—controlled the refining and marketing of hard drugs supplied by General Li Mi's "opium armies" and delivered these drugs by courier to dealers in Europe and America. These same Chinese syndicates also controlled the sex trade in Thailand, Hong Kong, and Taiwan, in symbiosis with government officials.

The Chinese avoided interfering in amphetamines, which were the drugs of choice in high-strung Japan and Korea, leaving that market entirely to the Yakuza. The role of the Philippines in the drug trade was to provide couriers and a transshipment point for Chinese heroin traffickers, and to provide a secure base for the illicit manufacture and supply of amphetamines and handguns for the Yakuza in Japan and Korea.

Filipinos served as runners. With their comparatively easy access to the United States, they provided courier service for syndicates in Taiwan, Hong Kong, and Thailand.

Some Marcos diplomats were premier drug couriers, protected by diplomatic immunity. In 1971, a careless Filipino diplomat and a Bangkok merchant were arrested in New York on charges of smuggling $13 million worth of heroin. A narcotics agent acting on an informant's tip followed the two men on board a Pan American flight in Vientiane, Laos, and kept them under surveillance through Vienna and London to New York. At Kennedy International Airport, the two suspects were permitted to pass through customs without examination of their luggage. The men were Domingo S. Canieso, an attaché at the Philippine Embassy in Laos, and Tsien Sin-chou, a Chinese-born Bangkok merchant traveling on a Taiwan passport. In Manhattan, the two checked into the Lexington Hotel, where they were arrested in their rooms with more than 34 pounds of Double U-O Globe brand heroin. Canieso did not have diplomatic immunity during that particular trip because he was foolishly traveling on a tourist visa. Other diplomats were more careful, and were free to come and go without baggage inspection.

Among the busiest couriers were members of a Manila-based *chiu chao* group headed by restaurateur Lim Seng, who smuggled half a ton of No. 4 heroin into the United States during the early 1970s. A loose consortium of *chiu chao* businessmen with drug laboratories and warehouses in Thailand smuggled primarily through Malaysia and the Philippines. Lim Seng was part of their network.

Chinese of Fukienese descent in Manila were content initially to let the *chiu chao* run the heroin racket. But during the Vietnam War the demand from America sharply increased, and with it the opportunity to sell directly to GIs in the islands. Several heroin labs were set up in Manila by Fukienese, producing No. 3 heroin for local consumption. Three were in operation by 1964 when Lim Seng opened his own lab in the islands financed by an overseas Chinese insurance agency and a leading Filipino textile magnate who was a friend of President Marcos. Lim Seng brought in a *chiu chao* chemist from Hong Kong and began producing small quantities of No. 3. The sudden oversupply forced his Fukienese competitors out of business, arousing ill-feeling toward the interloper. In 1969 Lim Seng expanded to manufacturing purer No. 4 heroin for export to America. He made large buys of morphine base from the Golden Triangle through the Hoi-Sukree partnership in Malaysia and the Lim Chiong syndicate in Bangkok. The success of these operations fed Lim Seng's vanity and he invested his profits in a portfolio of securities, including stock in Benguet mines, acquired in a shady transaction with several officials of the Marcos regime. By 1971, Lim Seng was producing more than 100 kilos of No. 4 per month, protected by government officials and police.

He was exploiting Clark Air Base and Manila International Airport to export 90 percent of his annual production of 1.2 tons—10 percent of America's annual heroin supply therefore was coming from the Philippines. Much more was on its way. Late in 1971, Lim Seng ordered $1 million worth of morphine base from the Lim Chiong syndicate and paid to have a Royal Thai Navy gunboat deliver it to Manila, on the pretext of a goodwill tour. The gunboat docked at South Harbor and the morphine was handed over to Lim Seng at his suite in the Manila Hotel. Such ostentatious conduct could only be secured by elaborate payoffs to officials and security men. Given the closeness with which he watched lowly shipments of sardines, Ferdinand could hardly have been ignorant of the Manila Hotel dope transaction.

As part of America's reorganization of the Philippine armed forces and police, Ferdinand had agreed to create a Constabulary Anti-Narcotics Unit (CANU), with agents trained and equipped by Washington. This was done in part because the U.S. Congress was trying to block the Nixon administration's program of training foreign police forces in secret police skills. The White House got around Congress by shifting its training to "narcotics agents" and funding the program through the Drug Enforcement Agency. One of CANU's missions was to help U.S. narcotics agents crack down on drug traffic by GI "horse soldiers" passing through Manila. Only a few weeks after its organization, CANU operatives arrested two ex-GIs boarding a commercial flight for Okinawa with 6 ounces of No. 4. In an excess of zeal, CANU did not stop with the arrests. Based on information painfully extracted from the two Americans, CANU agents identified all the members of the Lim Seng syndicate and located two of its laboratories in Manila. The case now had gone too far for anyone in the Marcos inner circle to cover it up; too many U.S. narcotics officials knew details. Furthermore, Manila's Fukienese godfathers had been pressing Ferdinand to close Lim Seng down. Accordingly, the palace decided to sacrifice him, while in the process picking him clean. On September 28, 1972, less than a week after declaring martial law, President Marcos gave CANU permission to arrest Lim Seng and to raid his two laboratories, where they impounded over 50 kilos of No. 4.

Lim Seng offered the arresting agents a bribe of $150,000 cash, but he was turned down cold. This eagerness to buy his freedom was communicated to others in the government. When his trial opened, Lim Seng pleaded guilty, only one witness was called, and before lunch he was given the light sentence of life imprisonment. Some members of CANU objected that the trial had been rigged, and guessed that next would come an escape attempt. They posted extra surveillance. With so much public attention, Ferdinand apparently felt obliged to distance himself. He went on television to declare that he was against the very idea of drug smuggling. Whatever inducements were offered by Lim Seng's wealthy friends in Thailand and Malaysia must have fallen short. On January 7, 1973, despite the life sentence of the court, Ferdinand ordered Lim Seng's immediate execution by firing squad.

To the bitter end, Lim Seng seemed supremely confident that the execution was only a charade. His spirits were high until they put on his blindfold. Everybody else in Manila was just as surprised.

This highly publicized execution was held up as an example of how President Marcos dealt harshly with drug merchants. Many people were taken in. Ferdinand usually made a public display of arresting the most notorious criminals, then quietly released them—his stick-and-carrot game.

Meanwhile, Manila remained a major transit point for drugs. One of the most prosperous dealers was an American named Donald Stein. Stein's couriers regularly passed through Manila with huge quantities of heroin destined for the American market.

After Ferdinand's regime fell, a U.S. narcotics agent presented the Aquino government with a list of forty major drug dealers who had been convicted and jailed. He wanted to locate them in the prison system, interview them, and put the information into a narcotics data bank. Not one dealer on the list of forty could be found. They had all been released by Ferdinand after paying large bribes. Just out of curiosity, a list of forty minor drug offenders was submitted—men unable to pay big bribes—and all forty were found still in jail.

Gambling also was prohibited in the Philippines until Ferdinand legalized it in 1975, at Imelda's insistence, but like child prostitution it was always going on. In the pre-Marcos days, the Lopez clan was credited with having a large stake in illegal casinos in Manila and Ilcilo. Fernando Lopez—vice president under Garcia and Marcos—ran a chain of gambling joints in Iloilo City that had such a pernicious effect on citizens that "schools were abandoned, regular occupations neglected." Lopez was said to have kept his casinos open during the occupation by sharing his profits with Japanese officers.

But it was only when American and British casino operators entered the picture that gambling in the Philippines rose to international standards, with ties to Las Vegas, Miami, the Bahamas, Macao, and Monaco earning hundreds of millions of dollars.

The most successful speakeasy casino in Manila in the 1920s was the Tiro Al Blanco in Santa Mesa, which offered roulette, chemin de fer, dice, blackjack, and poker. It was protected by wealthy patrons, among them mayors of Manila such as Miguel Romualdez. By the 1930s, there were three establishments considered "respectable"—the Club Filipino, the Carambola Club, and the Philippine Columbian. They posed as dinner clubs, but were casinos where wealthy Filipinos and foreign guests could lose fortunes at monte or poker. During the war, the big action was run inside the POW camps by Ted Lewin. More than six thousand Americans, Britons, and other nationals including women and children were interned at two large camps at Santo Tomas University in Manila and at the University of the Philippines College of Agriculture in rural Los Banos. Both camps were administered by the internees themselves. Lewin was a King Rat. He organized games and so impressed Japanese officers with his skill that they asked him to run a casino for them. With Liberation, Lewin opened a private club in the Manila suburb of Pasay City, catering to wealthy Filipinos and American soldiers, and including a bar and casino. Manila was wide open. Harry Stonehill was hustling U.S. Army trucks, Ferdinand Marcos was selling import permits and fake war service records, and the atmosphere at the club reeked of Bogart and *Casablanca.* Ted Lewin did so well that he moved into the bayfront, starting the Club Cairo. There were two roulette tables, two crap tables, ten blackjack tables, and anything else you wanted.

Lewin had mob ties in America and operated under cover of being a sports promoter, occasionally arranging a prizefight or a visit of the Harlem Globetrotters. When the daughter-in-law of Fernando Lopez left her husband and fled to the States with her child, Lewin was said to have arranged to have the infant kidnapped and returned to Manila. He also ran a string of crooked Filipinos with PX privileges acquired on the basis of their alleged guerrilla service during the war, and sold the goods on the black market.

According to Primitivo Mijares, Lewin once gave President Magsaysay a campaign contribution, then asked for a favor. Magsaysay was slow to realize there were strings attached. Mijares quoted him as remarking, plaintively, "But he gave me that money for the cause of good government; how can I now accede to this request which would lead to bad government? Tell him, 'No.' I can't do it."

In the 1950s, Lewin had a penthouse in Manila at the Shellburne Hotel across from the U.S. Embassy. Because he was an American citizen with criminal connections, the CIA assisted the FBI by bugging Lewin's penthouse. Tapes were read by the CIA station for leads on backstage political deals that might be arranged with Lewin's help. Lewin at this point was having an affair with the wife of a major in the U.S. Counter-Intelligence Corps. More than sex was involved: Lewin's group was counterfeiting U.S. military scrip to buy goods from the PX for the black market. Periodically, the army would cancel old scrip and issue new without advance notice to catch the counterfeiters. The CIC major's wife kept Lewin informed of these impending changes in scrip, and not one of his ring was caught.

Lewin was part of the Marcos and Stonehill network. During the climax of the Stonehill scandal in 1962, he was among the men deported from the islands by Justice Minister Jose Diokno. When Ferdinand became president in 1965, Lewin was allowed to come back, picking up where he had left off. Until the early 1970s, Lewin remained the key man in Manila gambling, with the protection of President Marcos and Ver's NISA. But having an understanding with Ferdinand sometimes was not enough. One also had to have an understanding with the First Lady. The happy days of the Club Cairo came to an end when Lewin ran afoul of Kokoy Romualdez.

Kokoy had been running up large tabs at the club. One night, Lewin had his bouncers throw him out in the street. Kokoy ran to his sister. The moment martial law was declared, Romualdez came back to the Club Cairo with a flying squad of NISA thugs and watched while they beat Lewin's club operators. Even that was not enough to settle the score, and Romualdez continued to harbor a grudge. "He has never felt himself fully satisfied," said Mijares. "Kokoy feels he can never fully avenge himself on Lewin's hirelings. . . ." Shortly after that Lewin was said to have died of a sudden heart attack.

In competition with Lewin's casinos, several Filipino CIA alumni, among them Lansdale's friend Terry Adevoso, set up a multi-million-dollar corporation and in October 1966 bought a luxurious double-decker ship from a Hong Kong builder for $700,000. It was described as a floating restaurant, but was really an offshore casino. Kokoy did just as badly there. In 1975, a second floating casino appeared on the waterfront, a ship bought for $4 million by the Peninsula Tourist and Shipping Company, with Alfredo and Benjamin Romualdez among the owners, fronting for the First Lady. In honor of Imelda's involvement, Ferdinand decreed that gambling was now legal. Press photos at the gala opening showed Imelda taking the first roll of dice, while Gina Lollobrigida looked on with Macao gambling wizard Stanley Ho.

Filipinos thought Stanley Ho was "very mysterious," and perhaps even a bit sinister. A British citizen, resident in Hong Kong, he was the acknowledged master of gambling operations in the Far East. His net worth was conservatively estimated at around U.S. $600 million.

The Ho legend was unusual. His grandfather was a compradore or "fixer" for the Jardines-Mathieson commercial empire, one of the most powerful and lucrative jobs a Chinese could have. His grand-uncle was on the Jardines board, became the wealthiest property owner in Hong Kong, and was knighted by King George V for his generosity, becoming Sir Robert Hotung. Stanley Ho's own father, the compradore of one of the other great fortunes of Hong Kong and Shanghai, the Sassoons, lost his fortune through insider trading in Jardines shares and was ruined financially in the ensuing scandal. He fled to Saigon before World War II to escape the effects of the scandal, leaving Stanley and his mother in Hong Kong to fend for themselves.

For the time being, the scandal made family connections meaningless. Stanley and his mother were shunned, and life as an outcast was difficult. Just before the Japanese arrived, his grand-uncle Sir Robert Hotung prudently left for neutral Macao to sit out the war, and a great many other Hong Kong citizens followed.

At the age of twenty, Stanley Ho was among them, a dropout from college at the end of his third year. Although still a social outcast in polite society because of his father, he had inherited phenomenal connections through his grand-uncle and grandfather that were greatly appreciated by impolite society. A Chinese friend offered him a job as a junior secretary in a company set up to arrange barter deals between the Macao government and the Japanese military authorities. Huge profits were to be made. Stanley learned Japanese. He said he also learned it was possible in Macao to make a million dollars a week.

By the war's end he was himself a millionaire, or close to it, and he started his own export-import business in Macao and Hong Kong, profiting enormously on trade during the Korean War. He put his profits into Hong Kong real estate, and by the late 1950s was one of the wealthiest young men in the Crown Colony.

While Hong Kong boomed, Macao was dead. Its harbor was unusable because of tons of Pearl River silt. Its hotels were moldering Portuguese colonial buildings lacking modern conveniences, and gambling was limited to mah-jongg and one decrepit casino. It took four hours to get there by slow ferry from Hong Kong, and the few tourists who came did not want to stay overnight. Stanley Ho was about to change all that.

The twenty-five-year gambling concession for Macao was up for renewal. The idea was to wrest it away from its previous holders, the

Fu clan. He formed a group with a number of influential Chinese associates, and made a bid the Portuguese government could not resist. In addition to building new casinos, new hotels, and new tourist attractions, they offered to dredge the harbor, opening Macao to international shipping and to new high-speed tourist ferries. To clinch the deal, Ho offered to resettle the tens of thousands of squatters on the Macao waterfront and completely renovate the area. After a bitter struggle with the Fu clan, owners of Hong Kong's Furama Hotel, Ho and his partners won the Macao casino operating license.

Ho's new hotels and casinos transformed Macao. Residents of Hong Kong, unable to gamble legally except on horse racing, began going to Macao for weekends. To move visitors faster, Ho put together the world's biggest commercial fleet of jet hydrofoils, delivering twenty-one thousand passengers a day.

By the 1980s Stanley Ho was contributing more than 50 percent of Macao's entire annual revenue, and began investing in hotel casinos in Australia, Pakistan, Indonesia, the Philippines, Malaysia, Spain, and Portugal. As one of the Orient's richest and most powerful men, Ho generally received good press. He gave a lot of money to charities. But his line of work inevitably raised eyebrows. He was a frequent visitor to San Francisco and Las Vegas, where he reportedly had interests in Caesar's Palace. Hong Kong sources pointed out that there was never any evidence linking Ho personally to criminal activities of any kind, but this was not the case with his longtime business partner, Yip Hon.

For years, Yip Hon was the brain behind Ho's gaming tables, a professional gambler who had previously worked as a croupier for the Fu clan. In 1980, San Francisco narcotics investigators alleged that Yip Hon was a top official in the Luen Kung Lok Triad, and was "the source of supply for a major New York Chinatown heroin dealer." According to an Organized Crime Strike Force, Yip and his son were among the owners of an eleven-story building on Mott Street in New York's Chinatown that was considered by the Drug Enforcement Agency to be "a center for narcotics and gambling operations." However, no charges or indictments resulted from these allegations.

On one occasion, it is said, Yip wrote Caesar's Palace a check for $800,000. This drew the attention of the U.S. Customs Service currency investigations division. They knew that Yip was a close associate of Hong Kong millionaire Lee Wai-man, a target of U.S. criminal investigators because of allegations that he was involved in the transfer of large amounts of currency between the United States and the Far East narcotic and gambling empires. However, again, no charges or indictments resulted.

After two decades of close collaboration, relations between Stanley Ho and Yip Hon soured, and he bought Yip out. Twenty years of running Macao's casinos had made all the partners billionaires, but not impervious to triad rivalries. In the summer of 1987, Thomas Chung, Ho's right-hand man, was fatally stabbed in Macao's Victoria Park as he walked to his car after a game of tennis.

In February 1988, the U.S. Justice Department published a Report on Asian Organized Crime in which both Yip Hon and Stanley Ho were featured, but the entire section on Ho was deleted just prior to printing. Embarrassingly, they neglected to remove his name from the glossary at the back.

When gambling was legalized in the Philippines, Stanley Ho got the franchise. Imelda's gambling ship was crewed by Roberto Benedicto's company, Northern Lines, but Ho's men ran the tables. Profits were undisclosed, but Malacanang was guaranteed two thirds of the net take, with one third going to the owners—which meant that Ferdinand took two thirds and Imelda and her brothers one third. Operating costs included paying a hefty fee to Stanley Ho.

From gambling revenues, some 1.2 billion pesos were said to have been siphoned off by Imelda's family. The Ministry of Finance disputed this, claiming that the money was spent on the First Lady's new Kidney Center and construction of Imelda's new University of Life.

The floating casino, originally known as Manila Bay Enterprises, was always considered a Romualdez operation. One of Kokoy's most trusted subordinates sat on the board, the volume for the day was always turned over to him, and Kokoy would divvy it out. Alfredo "Bejo" Romualdez, Imelda's younger brother and former navy reserve commander, commanded the floating casino as his rubber duck. In one of the periodic trade-offs between the president and the First Lady, Ferdinand gave Alfredo control over all organized casino gambling in the Philippines. Alfredo wasted no time opening casinos throughout the islands.

A tug-of-war continued over who got to keep the profits, Ferdinand or Imelda. In 1977, Ferdinand set up the Philippine Amusement and Gaming Corporation (PAGCOR). This shifted control of gambling back into his hands. He made it all sound rather grand. PAGCOR was exempt from income taxes, import duties, and audit. It would centralize and integrate the operation of all games into one corporate entity. All profits would be used for civic and social projects to promote welfare. This would boost tourism and eliminate corruption in the operation of gambling, he said, without the direct involvement of the government. But this was just soft soap.

PAGCOR was 60 percent government-owned (with the voting power vested in Ferdinand) and 40 percent private (in Romualdez hands). This allowed Ferdinand to determine the disposition of the casino funds personally, instead of leaving that to Imelda's brothers. As it was exempt from public audit, there was no way to determine how much was earned, but a Marcos decree of December 1982 revealed that PAGCOR by then had generated nearly 1.7 billion pesos in revenues and passed on nearly 1 billion of it to the government. This "public" share of the earnings was deposited in Roberto Benedicto's Traders Royal Bank. Once in the bank, it vanished.

By February 1978, the Romualdez family's floating casino had forced the CIA's floating casino out of business. There was only one left on the bayfront. But the following year, Imelda's ship was torched by the Light-a-Fire Movement. Gambling operations had to be moved to the handsome Philippine Village Hotel next to the airport. Stanley Ho was said to have put up his own money to get the airport casino running, in return for 30 percent of the take. Edward Marcelo (who had wanted the rights to salvage the *Nachi*) was the chairman and president of PAGCOR, fronting for Imelda, and the casino paid him rent at six times the going commercial rate. Ho had equal say with Marcelo in all decisions on how the casinos were run, and Ho's boys directly supervised every detail of operations. But Filipino gambling sources said Marcos routinely double-crossed Ho, so that Ho never got his fair share of profits.

Ferdinand's ties to the American Mafia traced back to two of his old friends, Harry Stonehill and Ted Lewin. A native of Chicago, Stonehill was said to have gotten his start in the postwar Philippines with the help of Chicago Mafia godfather Tony Accardo. It was Accardo—a former bodyguard and enforcer for Al Capone—who took over the Capone mob and outlasted rival Sam Giancana to become the elder statesman of organized crime from Chicago to the West Coast. Accardo is said to have arranged for Stonehill to acquire his original cigarette manufacturing machines and packaging for a brand called "Puppies," which had failed in America, and the Mafia don was then the major source of the stolen American cigarettes smuggled into the Philippines by the Marcos-Ver-Crisologo syndicate. Ferdinand did make a number of unexplained trips to Chicago in the 1950s, and to Miami, and the Bahamas, where he became involved in business deals with millionaire ex-convict Wallace Groves and gambling and black-money interests tied to Meyer Lansky. Sources at the U.S. Justice Department said Ferdinand apparently was able to get favors from Accardo over the years, including Mafia assistance for Ver's NISA agents when they wanted to make trouble for Filipino exiles. Ver kept a resident agent in Chicago, one of whose missions was said to be maintaining a liaison with the mob.

Cigarette smuggling in the Philippines was worth millions to the Mafia over the years, but it was only part of the cake. Lim Seng was providing one-tenth of the heroin supplied to the United States, and his American customers were a mixture of Mafia families and Chinese tongs. The development of world-class gambling casinos in the islands provided another outlet for money-laundering and the movement of black money. One way black money moved between America and the Far East was for Asian gamblers to visit Las Vegas, Reno, and Lake Tahoe, where they spent a few nights at the tables and signed IOUs to cover their "losses." These IOUs were then sold to West Coast banks that redeemed them through banks in Hong Kong. Everyone involved made money through commissions, and in the process large sums were transferred across the Pacific that experts in organized crime insist were in payment of narcotics shipments and other illegal transactions. The money that was repatriated moved around the world in the form of computer bytes and pixels in "tested telex" transfers through the international banking system, laundering the funds electronically. So much money was to be made in this sort of currency exchange that separate bids were made to acquire that franchise in every casino.*

During the years of the Marcos regime, a number of Mafia figures and people with ties to the Mafia visited the islands to gamble, vacation, and do business.

In the 1970s, millionaire ex-convict Wallace Groves visited the Philippines. Groves had gained ownership of Grand Bahama Island 60 miles across the Gulf Stream from Palm Beach through an elaborate

*In 1987, the Aquino government was shaken by an allegation that Ting-Ting Cojuangco, President Aquino's sister-in-law, had accepted a million-dollar bribe from an Australian to assure him of the money-exchange franchise in Philippine casinos.

conspiracy with Nassau's Bay Street Boys, ending in a scandal that toppled the white government of the Bahamas. His casinos in Nassau and Freeport, Grand Bahama, had been run for him by people who had associations with the Mafia's Meyer Lansky, and Groves himself was busy at the time laundering millions of dollars for the CIA through banks and casinos in the Bahamas.

One of the three principle owners of Groves's Grand Bahama Port Authority was the Wall Street house, Allen & Co., run by Charlie Allen and his brother Herbert. The Allens also owned a big chunk of Benguet mines in the Philippines and Herbert was a golfing partner of President Marcos. One of the Allens once said, "We trade every day with hustlers, deal makers, shysters, con men. . . . That's the way businesses get started. That's the way this country was built."

Groves must have realized what an asset it would be for him to own a piece of a major gold mine on the opposite side of the planet, especially one being traded on the New York Stock Exchange. In the casino business there was always the need for a lucrative legitimate enterprise through which profits could be laundered.

In a complex deal, Groves and the Allens were able to parlay their Grand Bahama holdings into nearly complete control of Benguet mines. President Marcos allowed the deal to go through, but only after he personally "investigated" its "legal proprieties"—a well-publicized procedure that caused Benguet stock to go up and down in wild swings, earning Marcos cronies huge profits through insider trading. Ferdinand Marcos, Wallace Groves, and the Allens thus all had an interest in the Benguet mines and Grand Bahama Island. This lasted until 1973, when the deadline was approaching for all foreign-owned businesses to turn over at least 60 percent ownership to Filipinos. Ferdinand used this to exert pressure on Groves and the Allens to cut a new deal, in which he became the majority owner of Benguet. As their part in the deal, the Allens continued to control the management of the mines, and they and Groves kept Benguet's foreign operations and took back Marcos's interest in Grand Bahama. Like a Monopoly game.

Although Ferdinand had planned to keep his part of Benguet all to himself, the Dovie Beams scandal gave Imelda the upper hand, and she insisted that he turn over the company to her. Ferdinand dutifully arranged for the shares to be transferred to one of Kokoy's front men.

The idea of owning a big private island seemed to be very popular among underworld figures. New York Mafia boss Joey Gallo was an occasional guest at Malacanang Palace and was taken to the Marcos retreat on Fuga Island, the smuggling stronghold off the northern tip of Luzon. Fuga was easily accessible from Taiwan, Hong Kong, and Macao, and had been used by Ferdinand for years as a private hideaway. According to a former member of Ver's Presidential Security Command, Gallo came back to Manila later to make Ferdinand a business deal. The Mafia had decided to take over Fuga Island to create their own version of Macao, with gambling, resort hotels, money-laundering, and drugs, a development plan reminiscent of that proposed by Sasakawa for Lubang. He said Gallo delivered two cashier's checks in partial payment for three islands, including Fuga and neighboring Barit and Mabay. But when Gallo got back to New York, he was gunned down by rivals. The palace security man said, "President Marcos naturally kept the money."

Eighteen

BLACK GOLD

FERDINAND DID NOT ABANDON the search for Yamashita's Gold after Robert Curtis and Olof Jonsson fled his "Leber Group" in 1975. Far from it. Instead, he went into partnership with various Yakuza bosses and the CIA, helping it finance intrigues from Australia to Iran in return for CIA help airlifting out the contents of his vaults. Hence the mysterious "AAA" markings on many of the ingots, and the continuing involvement of wealthy right-wing Australian brokers in Marcos gold deals for years afterward.

In 1982, when the CIA was forced to back away from a decade of meddling in Australian politics, and to abandon its Nugan-Hand Bank conduit for black money, Ferdinand had to find other ways to dispose of his gold. He seemed to be in a particular hurry in 1983, for there was a flurry of huge gold deals being offered outside CIA channels that year, with total sums so large that they strain credibility to the breaking point.

How could anybody have 500 metric tons of World War II gold tucked away in his basement? And 1,000 tons more in his beach cottage, and 500 tons more in the basement of a warehouse down the street? Plus still more on four levels beneath a nearby bank? In the end it does not matter really whether the gold ever existed. It only matters that a lot of responsible people believed it did, and acted accordingly, including senior officers of the CIA, and of the National Security Council, and a chairman of the Joint Chiefs of Staff. Believing in gold is like believing in God: the belief is the reality. And once you begin to believe any of it, you are committed to believe it all. Still, it is better to begin by taking a small step at a time.

Massive secret gold shipments did take place from the Philippines during the twenty years Ferdinand was president. Of that, many sober people now are satisfied. This gold did not originate in the Central Bank or from mines like Benguet, although it was often presented as such. To be sure, gold was stolen regularly from Benguet by its own employees. The original mines, situated in the crater of an extinct volcano, were plagued by theft. Miners called "high graders" smuggled out the best ore, removing 16 percent of gold production each year (half a ton of gold) and selling it to a Chinese syndicate. The same occurred at other mining companies in the islands.

By contrast, the secret gold shipments identified with President Marcos involved thousands of metric tons, much of it in bars of exotic sizes marked with peculiar symbols not normally used in the international gold trade, including Japanese and Chinese markings, and the recurring "AAA." A lot of people thought the reports of secret Marcos gold deals were nonsense or lies. But if the bullion was imaginary, another of Ferdinand's lifelong fabrications, he would hardly have invented the many shapes and sizes, and the odd but consistent markings (which, in any case, unconnected people saw and remarked upon), and he could not have imagined the difficulty he encountered in recasting the ingots so they could be sold without raising too many questions about their origins.

The quantities involved were far in excess of the Philippine government's known bullion reserves. I say "known" because governments, like misers, have taken pains to keep the true size of their reserves hidden. Most of the Marcos gold seems to have been sold through Australian, American, Japanese, and European intermediaries to oil-rich Middle Eastern syndicates, using devious methods designed to avoid agitating world gold prices. Other secret deals were made directly to the gold pools in Zurich and London, where they were referred to as "Marcos Black Eagle deals." Still other contracts appear to have been arranged through the scandal-ridden Vatican Bank, headed by American Bishop Paul Marcinckus. If these reports were true (and the documentation is persuasive when seen all together), the only possible explanation was that Ferdinand Marcos indeed had found Yamashita's Gold.

People had been searching for it since 1945, without the public disclosure of any absolute confirmation that it existed. Or was there?

The most frequent reports made by CIA agents in Manila over the years, it turns out, involved secret gold deals by President Marcos. The CIA was keeping a close watch. In some instances the Agency was not just watching, but helping. CIA sources stated that the Agency set up a conduit for the transfer of very large sums of black money out of the Philippines to Honolulu, in gold as well as currency, and was using this to obligate Ferdinand and to keep an eye on his financial transactions. This was confirmed publicly during sworn testimony in a Honolulu court case, and privately by one of the men directly involved. According to the testimony, the Honolulu conduit was set up for the CIA by the American Ron Rewald, with the help of Filipino billionaire banker Enrique Zobel, a close friend of the Marcoses and of the sultan of Brunei. Rewald got to know Zobel because he ran a polo club in Hawaii, and Zobel was a world-class polo player. Rewald testified that Zobel was (like him) a CIA collaborator, and that through such joint ventures as Ayala-Hawaii, they and the CIA were to "shelter monies of highly placed foreign diplomats and businessmen who wished to 'export' cash to the United States, where it would be available to them in the event of an emergency." During the same period, we now know that the sultan of Brunei (another ardent polo player) was lending millions to the Agency as part of the secret Iran-Contra arms deal of Lieutenant Colonel Oliver North, but his money went astray when the CIA mistakenly gave him the wrong numbers for a Swiss bank account. That the CIA's "secret team" was obtaining millions privately from the sultan reinforces allegations that it was obtaining millions similarly from President Marcos. Might this explain why the White House felt so obligated to Ferdinand that President Reagan did everything short of intervention to keep him in power?

A little background helps to set the stage: The total amount of "white gold" thought to have been mined "legitimately" throughout recorded history is estimated rather ingenuously at 90,000 tons. This does not take into account so-called black gold mined clandestinely, stolen, or acquired in narcotics and other criminal activities, or accumulated in the Soviet Union, or in areas of the world such as Asia where public records have not been kept, which could add up to two or three times as much, or more. There is no way, for example, that anyone could guess how much gold had been accumulated privately in imperial China over the last two or three thousand years, but we can be certain that more of it changed ownership during the first half of the twentieth century than at any other time since Kublai Khan seven centuries earlier. Yamashita's Gold would have been derived from both types—"white gold" and "black gold."

The world's annual legitimate gold production is controlled at 1,400 tons per year, in line with market demand. Prices are set by the five-member London gold pool, which is not eager to lose this privilege to the Swiss gold pool in Zurich. The "London Five" were Moccata & Gold-smid, Sharps Pixley, Johnson Matthey,* Rothschild's, and Samuel Montagu, known by their critics as "the cartel." Officially, less than 200 tons of gold was produced in the Philippines during the 1970s. Only a third of that was refined there, the rest being exported in unrefined copper ore. The gold extracted from the copper ore then was sold back to the Philippine Central Bank (on paper), but remained physically in the gold pools of London, Zurich, New York, and Tokyo, credited to the Philippines. This procedure was customary because transporting bullion was costly and buyers were reluctant to buy gold if they would have to ship it from the Philippines to international financial centers. Better to keep the bullion in a gold pool and only transfer the ownership. For our purposes, gold was selling for $10 million per metric ton in 1983.

The temptation for a dictator to abscond with his government's gold reserves is always great. Ernie Maceda, who worked for him for many years, said President Marcos was in a position to steal as much gold as he wanted without anyone knowing. During the first full year of martial law, 1973, Manila's gold reserves dropped by 45 percent, or 25 tons, then worth $250 million. A U.S. official said he was "extremely suspicious" because this could not be explained by market forces. For the next several years the reserves stayed at 33 tons, which the same official called statistically impossible.

But there was a limit to how much anyone could steal from the Central Bank. One official said that even the thousands of commemorative gold coins minted for the celebration of Ferdinand's sixtieth birthday, bearing the likenesses of Imelda and Ferdinand, found in Malacanang after they fled, could not have come from the reserves. He speculated that Ferdinand must have acquired the gold in the coins "outside the Central Bank system."

In 1978, the international monetary authorities decided to allow

---

*Outside Great Britain, this organization was usually referred to by the generic name "Johnson Matthey" – without distinguishing between its many divisions, ranging from chemicals to jewelry stores. Except where I have indicated otherwise, I am referring exclusively to its banking division and bullion operations.

government central banks to buy gold directly from private sources. This gave Ferdinand a discreet way to convert some of his hoard of ingots into cash. He issued a decree placing the entire gold procedure in the islands in the hands of the government. Thereafter, all gold mined in the Philippines had to be sold directly to the Central Bank. This made it possible for him to sell some of his own gold to the Central Bank through a variety of intermediaries, and the bank could then send the gold to financial centers without attracting attention. Cracked a Filipino journalist at the time, "The Leber Group must be busy now making plans with key people in the Central Bank to buy gold bullion from 'private sources.'"

How much gold Ferdinand sold to the Central Bank in this way naturally was not recorded for posterity. Most of his gold was already refined, and once in the Central Bank could be moved directly into the international market—if a way could be found to disguise it from the inevitable statisticians, a question of complicating the paper chase. The way was found when Jaime Ongpin, then the head of Benguet, had a long talk with Dr. Henry Jarecki of Mocatta Metals, which was intimately related to Mocatta & Goldsmid of the gold cartel. At the time, it was costing Benguet more to mine gold than the company could earn from selling its ore to the government, which would only pay world market prices. Jarecki told Ongpin that to earn income from gold, well-known banks will lease quantities of dormant bullion from central banks, paying the owner a set fee for the right to use the gold in transactions over a specified period of time. They then invest the gold in creative ways and turn a tidy profit.

Ongpin took the hint. In 1979, Benguet began borrowing 55,000 ounces a year from the Philippine Central Bank (or so it was claimed). This was equal to half the mine's annual production. Benguet immediately sold the borrowed gold and invested the proceeds in the volatile money market. The earnings from these investments were good enough to subsidize gold production at the mines. Ongpin said he knew in advance that he would have more than enough new bullion from the mines to cover his borrowings. It is also possible that he acquired this gold not from the Central Bank but from President Marcos, for whom the Ongpin brothers did many things, and who in due course gained control of Benguet—only to forfeit it to the First Lady.

Following Ongpin's lead, in November 1981 the Philippine Monetary Board (Ferdinand Marcos) announced that it would place what it called "excess locally derived gold reserves" on the international market. During the next three months some 300,000 ounces of "excess" gold were shipped to Hong Kong, New York, London, and Zurich for the sort of commodity leasing Dr. Jarecki had described. The Central Bank entered into such contracts with banks in the United States, Canada, Great Britain, and West Germany for leasing periods of three or six months. These banks first had to undertake to move the bullion from Manila to banking centers. Then, for a fee of up to 1 percent a year, the depository banks could "play" with the gold. Throughout the process, the Central Bank retained ownership. This provided a discreet way for Ferdinand to get some of his black gold physically out of the islands. Once in the international trading centers, its ownership could be transferred by President Marcos easily to any Marcos front.

In addition, a former Filipino diplomat said Ferdinand's personal plane often ferried gold bullion to a Zurich bank. Commercial airlines also were used, as evidenced by their waybills. Twelve secret shipments of gold in all were said to have taken place by commercial airlines including KLM, PAL, Air France, and Sabena. On September 16, 1983, for example, a KLM flight to Zurich carried a cargo of 7 tons of bullion. At the same time, another 3,000 kilos were shipped by air to London.

Another former Philippine diplomat, Ferdinand's errand boy Amelito Mutuc, who was involved in the Leber Group with Robert Curtis, said that Ferdinand recovered $14 billion worth of Yamashita's Gold just from the digs pinpointed by Olof Jonsson in 1975, mostly from the Teresa II site. This bullion, he said, was stored in the underground vaults of the special warehouse near Malacanang Palace, and in the basement vaults of the Bataan beach palace. In 1978, the year Ferdinand put all gold marketing in the archipelago under his direct control, it was reported that he sold 2,200 tons of Japanese war loot in a single deal and was attempting to sell more. In 1979, Professor Belinda Aquino of the University of Hawaii observed that President Marcos had been wooing the military with "Japanese war booty."

When Curtis left in 1975, taking most of the original Japanese treasure maps with him, he had to abandon the equipment he had shipped to Manila to reprocess the gold into sizes and specifications that would be acceptable on the world market. This camouflage was important. Ferdinand explained to his intimates once that his government would be toppled if his plans for cashing in the treasure became public. He was quoted as saying that disclosure could bring "another world war" because of the outrage of the governments of countries whose national treasures he planned to sell.

The choice available to Ferdinand was to recast some of the loot in the standard 12.5-kilo bars recognized by the London gold market (known as "Good London Delivery"), and to recast the rest in nonstandard ingots that would seem to originate from a place such as New Guinea or Australia where there were many gold mines, and where odd shapes, sizes, and markings were not a particular novelty. Although Hong Kong gold traders were initially mystified by reports that much of the Marcos gold was marked "AAA," a good deal of gold originating in Australia in years past had been poured into ingots shaped like a book, many of them stamped "AAA"—a hallmark peculiar to the market Down Under and familiar to expert London traders. Also common in Australia were ingots transferred there for safekeeping from the Dutch East Indies at the start of World War II. Many of these were stamped "Sumatra Lloyd" and later were sold to wealthy Australian buyers. It would not attract unwholesome attention if Ferdinand recast some of his hoard so that it could be sold through rich friends in Australia, in small rectangular ingots marked either "AAA" or "Sumatra Lloyd."

An Australian official confirmed that to his knowledge, during 1981–83 Ferdinand was trying to have 450 metric tons of gold reprocessed, melted down, and made into smaller bars with an Australian stamp to hide its source.

As far back as 1975 Ferdinand had struck a deal with the gold bullion trader Johnson Matthey, one of the five members of the London gold pool, to build a gold-processing plant in the Philippines. When Robert Curtis first arrived in Manila that year, to discuss shipping out his own equipment, he saw newspaper reports that President Marcos was negotiating with Johnson Matthey to build a precious metals refinery. General Ver told Curtis not to be alarmed by the stories or by the presence of Johnson Matthey people in Manila. He insisted that when President Marcos promised Curtis no member of the cartel would be allowed to establish a refinery in the islands, his word was good. Ver explained that Ferdinand had to entertain Johnson Matthey people when they were in town "because the company has been handling the sales of Philippine gold for a long time." As Curtis was leaving Manila several months later, he realized how good Ferdinand's word was when he read a news story saying that Malacanang had reached an agreement with Johnson Matthey, and that the new refinery would be built in Quezon City.

Once the refinery was completed in 1978, it became possible to cast much of the gold in Ferdinand's vaults to standard 12.5-kilo ingots. This factory also may have been used to produce the odd-shaped "AAA" ingots, but it is possible that those were recast, for reasons of discretion, on the equipment forfeited by Curtis. Ferdinand doubtless knew that Johnson Matthey also minted its own tiny gold bars of 3¾ ounces which were common currency in India and the Arabian Gulf, so he may have cast some of his gold in bars for sale in India.

It is worth noting that of the London Five, Johnson Matthey had a reputation among its peers for being rather sly. According to Stephen Fay—editor of the British magazine *Business,* and for many years with the *Sunday Times*—Johnson Matthey's banking division "encouraged and fostered speculation, concentrated loans in a few large hands, dealt with rascals, failed to dismiss officers who lived beyond their means, became involved in 'splendid financiering' and pursued a course that entirely ignored straightforward, upright, legitimate banking business." Although extreme secrecy was maintained about the bank's parent bullion trader, as in all things having to do with the London Five, this malignant cancer may have permeated the entire body of Johnson Matthey, making it susceptible to a role in whatever undertaking President Marcos cared to engineer.

While he was casting ingots at Johnson Matthey's factory in Quezon City, Ferdinand also devised a scheme to float large loans using as collateral gold bullion that he was as yet unable to get out of the Philippines. This scheme was discovered in November 1983 when U.S. Customs examined a pouchful of documents carried into America by one of Ver's agents. The documents described four floors of gold bullion stored beneath a privately owned bank in Manila (Benedicto's bank). The deal was to be made through an accountant who appeared to have CIA connections in Alexandria, Virginia. The accountant refused to talk, telling Customs the deal involved "national security."

Buddy Gomez, then billionaire Enrique Zobel's right-hand man, said he was asked by Zobel in 1979 to set up a meeting in Hong Kong to arrange the transfer of gold out of the Philippines on behalf of Elizabeth Marcos Rocka, the sister of the president. Most of her gold eventually was moved through branches of the Nugan-Hand Bank in Hong Kong and Sydney with CIA help and the participation of a number of wealthy Australians. Her husband, Ludwig Rocka, helped Nugan-Hand set up a Manila branch that same year, 1979, in the Magsaysay Building, which included among its occupants a number of CIA fronts.

Rocka then shared the office suite with the bank and with a senior American military/intelligence officer who headed that branch. Elizabeth still had $3.5 million in cash on deposit in Sydney when the Nugan-Hand Bank collapsed in 1982. Of her precious metals account, no record survived the shredder.

Ferdinand Marcos obviously was not the only member of the family with gold bullion overseas. An Australian broker said he was told by Andrew Tan, a close friend of Bong-Bong, that Bong-Bong had "tons of 12.5-kilo gold bars" stashed in Hong Kong, London, the United States, Singapore, Switzerland, Panama, and the Netherlands Antilles. Since Ferdinand clearly intended Bong-Bong to be his heir, it would seem logical for him to make provisions for his son to gain access to the principal deposits, or to hold them in common. So it would be a reasonable assumption that the bulk of Ferdinand's holdings were in the same locations.

In 1985, Norberto Romualdez III, Imelda's nephew, was mistakenly approached by emissaries of Arab oil sheiks who said they were aware of a particular precious metals account in Europe containing 5 metric tons of gold controlled by the Romualdez family, in this instance apparently meaning less prominent members of Imelda's immediate family. Norberto was from the other branch of the clan and knew nothing. An American in San Jose, California, said he was asked to help move another 5 metric tons of gold out of the Philippines for the Romualdez family in the fall of 1985—this time a deal involving the husbands of two of Imelda's nieces, one living in Canada and the other in West Germany. It follows that if the husbands of the First Lady's nieces had at least 5 metric tons, each of Imelda's sisters and brothers probably had much more. Given the number in the family, this would represent a total well in excess of 50 tons. Kokoy and his brother Alfredo, being almost as acquisitive as their eldest sister, doubtless had a great deal more than Alita or Conchita.

Nugan-Hand collapsed after the mysterious shooting death of one of its principals, Frank Nugan, and a scandal in which the CIA was accused of meddling in Australian internal affairs to topple the Labor government of Gough Whitlam. According to one source, the CIA helped Ferdinand move gold through Australia, partly to pay off the wealthy conservative middlemen who were at the sharp end of its campaign against a "takeover" by leftists Down Under. Some gold was reported to have been flown directly from Clark Air Base to U.S. Air Force facilities in Australia, specifically the deep black security base at Pine Gap, where it could go in and out without anyone being the wiser, and leave Pine Gap by truck in various disguises. After the bank collapsed, Ferdinand continued to make deals through these same wealthy Australian connections, but without the convenience of the Nugan-Hand channel. Apparently, he also continued to receive help from the CIA in airlifting gold out to Hong Kong and elsewhere, and returned the favor for over a decade by conspiring with the Agency and the White House to make up false end-user certificates to mislead Congress and the Pentagon about the real destination of American arms shipments.

Inevitably, using channels other than Nugan-Hand resulted in a number of leaks and embarrassing disclosures, but these described such large sums that ordinary people, unaccustomed to the bizarre extremes of black-money transactions, regarded them as unbelievable.

In one deal, Tony Grant, a British solicitor with Denton, Hall, Burgin & Warren in Hong Kong—a firm that numbered among its clients some of the wealthiest people in the Far East, including Singapore's Ng family—approached Tokyo-based businessman Michael Young about buying eighty-five gold bars, each weighing 50 kilos. The bars were owned, he told Young, by "older generation people," and were marked "AAA" or "Sumatra Lloyd." The deal fell through when the sellers refused to allow inspection without a letter of intent to purchase. (Providing a letter of intent can be dangerous if you are not certain of delivery and quality.)

In 1982, General Ramon Cannu of Ver's Presidential Security Command was put in charge of shipping out 50 tons of gold, according to a retired American soldier of fortune in the Federal Witness Protection Program who used the pseudonym Ron Lusk. Lusk said he was sent to Manila by Bankers Trust-Zurich to help charter two Boeing 747s to fly the gold to Switzerland. Lusk said the gold was stored under a warehouse near Malacanang. He was shown bullion properly stored in copper boxes, including bars with Japanese and Chinese markings. The deal collapsed at the last minute, according to Lusk, because the principals could not agree on how to split the profit.

At least three shipments of gold and silver bullion were documented in a still secret U.S. Treasury report, originating from U.S. Navy intelligence sources. One shipment of 8 tons of silver bullion was loaded by Ver's security men aboard the American President Lines ship *President Kennedy,* and delivered to Los Angeles, where it went on in trucks belonging to Alba Forwarding Service to Drexel, Burnham, Lambert Trading in New York. Drexel confirmed the shipment, but saw nothing out of the ordinary in view of the fact that the proceeds were deposited by Drexel, Burnham in the Philippine Central Bank's account at the Federal Reserve Bank. However, the money then was wired at President Marcos's instruction to various European accounts identified only by number, including some in Switzerland. According to European banking sources, in late 1983, a single one of Ferdinand's Crédit Suisse accounts—one in the name "Avertina Foundation C.A.R."—contained 922 pounds of gold bullion worth $5,277,100.

Brian Lendrum, the head of American Express Private Bank in Hong Kong in 1983, was approached by a group of Filipino colonels, closely identified with President Marcos, who said they had "a very large amount of gold for sale." The shipment was said to be "imminent." Lendrum later received a letter in flowery prose stating that the deal was approved by "the highest person in the land." For some reason, the gold failed to materialize. According to a Chinese gold dealer in Hong Kong, the colonels approached a number of banks in addition to American Express, and eventually concluded a better deal elsewhere; he said he knew this because he saw some of the paperwork. The amounts involved were huge, he said, more than 50 tons, $500 million worth of gold in all.

R. B. Wilson, of Australia's Kerr & Associates, said he was contacted by C. Troncoso in California with an offer to deliver 60 metric tons of Marcos gold per week for a five-year period, in a deal connected to the Mitsubishi Bank in Las Vegas, part of the Japanese giant. Wilson became angry and talked about the deal when the participants bypassed him and he lost his commission. He said he understood that a total of 4,000 metric tons was involved, worth roughly $40 billion.

The people who bypassed Wilson may have been the same ones who then brought in Norman Lester "Tony" Dacus of Las Vegas, because the amounts involved were similar. Dacus was married to a Filipina whose uncle was in the Presidential Security Command, working for Ver at Malacanang. After the Marcoses fled into exile, Dacus disclosed he had contracts to broker a number of gold deals, and produced a lot of documentation to back it up. Viewed in isolation, the Dacus claims might have seemed a bit bizarre, but to anyone acquainted with the background they fit together like shoes and socks. He said he brokered Marcos gold to a consortium from Australia, England, and America. He produced telexes, correspondence, and contracts representing billions of dollars, including nine contracts approved by the Hong Kong-Shanghai Bank. One of these transactions referred to the purchase of 15,600 metric tons of gold over two years at $400 per ounce, delivery to be made weekly in 60-ton quantities (as in the Wilson deal). At $10 million per metric ton, this would have been worth $150 billion on the open market, perhaps somewhat less as it was being offered under the table.

There are people and syndicates aside from Arab oil tycoons who have such sums, among them drug merchants—in recent years cocaine syndicates and their bankers—who no longer can be bothered to count their cash receipts, finding it sufficient to weigh them. They are anxious to get rid of currency in favor of precious metals and gems. Organized crime in America, for example, with an estimated annual revenue of $150 billion, would find gold an excellent way to launder dollars that are rapidly diminishing in value.

The seller's bank, Dacus said, was the Hang Lung Bank, Hong Kong; the buyer's bank was the Heritage Bank & Trust, Salt Lake City. The corresponding bank was the Mitsubishi Bank's Hong Kong branch. (In R. B. Wilson's case, it was the Mitsubishi Bank in Las Vegas.) Dacus claimed that six other banks were involved: Swiss American Bank, Antigua; Hong Kong–Shanghai Bank, Hong Kong; Bank of America, San Francisco; Chartered Bank, Hong Kong; Chase Manhattan, Nassau; and Owner's Bank, Hong Kong. Dacus said he was promised $100 million in commissions on this deal if he brokered it all. He claimed that when the deal went through, 60 tons of gold each week were trucked to Clark, where it was flown by U.S. Air Force planes and CIA pilots to Hong Kong between May and August of 1983, when the shipments from Clark suddenly halted with the Aquino assassination. Dacus said frankly that he was certain at least two of the 60-ton gold shipments took place, because he was paid commissions on them.

Dacus claimed that the Hang Lung Bank later went bankrupt because of the interruption of the gold deal and that the Mitsubishi Bank lost several hundred thousand dollars. According to Dacus, Pedro Laurel and Domingo Clemente, the Marcos men arranging the deal in Manila, were locked up in the Black Room at Malacanang Palace because they were causing problems and knew too much about the deals. Dacus said Ferdinand was angry because Clemente attracted too much attention; he rented a top floor of Manila's Ramada Inn and was "spending money like crazy." Dacus said President Marcos had Laurel and

Clemente murdered in the Black Room. He knew this, Dacus said, because the job in the Presidential Security Command held by the uncle of his Filipino wife was as one of Ver's jailers in the Black Room.

Although Dacus had a lot of documentation to back up his claims, other people that he said were involved denied they knew anything about it. This comes as no surprise. When the Robert Curtis story about Yamashita's Gold was first reported in the American press in the late 1970s, Ferdinand exerted his influence on other people involved to get them to deny or recant statements they had made about the gold, and even resorted to bribery and hitmen. The detail that the CIA airlift was terminated abruptly because of the Aquino assassination is persuasive because Washington was very anxious at that moment to demonstrate its displeasure, particularly with General Ver.

In May 1983, just before the CIA airlift described by Dacus, an employee of one of the leading international banks in Luxembourg turned over to the CIA station there photocopies he had made of an extraordinary sales agreement that was passing through his hands. His bank was acting as the corresponding bank in a deal that had been negotiated between President Marcos and a consortium of foreign buyers. The deal specified a total of 4.2 million ingots of gold, each weighing 12.5 kilos, hallmarked from the Central Bank of the Philippines. This represented a total of 1,682,855,200 ounces. It was to be a graduated deal, involving sales of different quantities (called tranches) at various stages. The first tranche, which had been approved, was for 716,045 units of 12.5 kilos each that were still in the Philippines; the sale price for this alone was described as $124 billion. Among the terms of the deal was a stipulation that no mention of the sale was to be made to any Philippine embassy or consulate, and in particular that under no circumstance should Imelda and Ferdinand Marcos be identified with it in any way.

The cover letter set out how payment was to be transferred through the Luxembourg bank to the Philippine Central Bank. It was signed by a number of attorneys representing the buyers, who were identified as the members of the London gold pool. Ferdinand appeared to be selling to members of the London pool gold bullion that was largely in their physical possession already. All of this was to be accompanied by a letter of immunity from seizure, investigation, or arrest, signed by President Marcos.

These documents, including memoranda of agreement on presidential letterhead signed by Ferdinand's executive assistant, Konsehala Candelarin V. Santiago, were carefully examined by the U.S. Embassy and were certified authentic with a stamp and seal by the vice consul. The existence of these documents has never been revealed. In 1986 the *Philippines Free Press* obtained a copy of the insurance agreement covering the first tranche of this same deal, but the newspaper apparently was unaware of the more detailed documents given the CIA in Luxembourg. The insurance document was from Manila's Mercantile Insurance Company, owned by the Unson family, sugar oligarchs close to Ferdinand Marcos. Crony Bobby Benedicto was a major stockholder. Written on Mercantile's letterhead and signed by its vice president for finance, the letter described a "Memorandum of Agreement to purchase gold bars" numbering 716,045 pieces (the first tranche of the Luxembourg documents), the shipment of which was to be insured by Mercantile. The letter, dated February 4, 1983, was addressed to "Foreign Buyers" through "The Engineering Construction Company Ltd." on Shirley Street in Nassau. The attorney representing the foreign buyers was identified as Daniel W. Swihart and the broker was identified as John Ramsingh, representing the funding banks.

The Dacus story and the Luxembourg papers apparently describe the same mammoth sale. They are amplified further by a document evidently drawn up by Ferdinand himself on May 27, 1983, for what may have been the remaining tranches of this same gold deal. A copy of this contract was provided by an entirely different and uninvolved source. During a party given at the Washington home of the commandant of the U.S. Marine Corps, P. X. Kelley, in the first week of July 1985, a well-known journalist with a reputation for accuracy said he met a prominent American business executive, once a vice president of one of the big defense contractors. The executive took the reporter aside and told him of his involvement in a contract to sell Marcos gold. The executive claimed he became involved through a friend of his, a retired air force colonel. The colonel, the executive said, had made many flights to Manila over the years, and had become friendly with a number of senior Filipino military officers. At the colonel's suggestion, the executive said he traveled to Manila where he was informed privately that President Marcos had tons of gold that he was trying to sell through frontmen, for an amount between $240 billion and $790 billion. (The figures vary because once again it was a graduated deal, in which the total could be increased once the initial transaction terms were fulfilled.) The executive was shown a large vault containing some of the gold bars, which were properly sized and hallmarked for international trading. This was a preliminary tranche of 100 metric tons still in Manila that Ferdinand wanted to sell immediately. A Hong Kong bank was to be the intermediary. The executive gave the reporter a copy of the contract, which is in my files.

According to the contract, much of the rest of the gold was already outside the Philippines, in the gold pools. This included gold that had been transmitted to London in a multiplicity of ways over the years between 1970 and 1983. Since then it had been sitting under Threadneedle Street at the Bank of England and in other bullion vaults at Rothschild's, Johnson Matthey, Mocatta & Goldsmid, and other members of the cartel. The Marcoses were on very familiar terms with the cartel. While their children were attending school in England, they made use of an otherwise unused Rothschild mansion in London as if they owned it.

Specifically, 38,000 metric tons worth $380 billion was said to be in "good London delivery" 12.5-kilo bars, and another 37,000 metric tons in bigger ingots weighing 75 kilos. Taken together, these 75,000 tons would be nearly equal to all the gold estimated to have been mined legitimately throughout history. The U.S. executive said an Australian syndicate headed by a wealthy friend of President Marcos was brokering the deal, along with two Americans and a group in Europe.

Initially, Ferdinand wanted to arrange the deal in a curious way. Instead of the buyers purchasing the gold itself in the form of gold certificates, he would sell them Philippine Central Bank treasury notes in U.S. dollar denominations, which they could then cash in for gold certificates. (On this transaction, he insisted upon receiving 1 percent himself as a commission.) The buyers were immediately suspicious and refused to proceed on these terms because of the possibility that he was attempting some form of ingenious fraud. At the very least he was trying to complicate the paper chase so that he could claim, if it ever became necessary, to have received the billions of dollars as foreign loans in exchange for Philippine Central Bank notes. He may have had other reasons for handling the sale in this manner, but after months of dickering Ferdinand dropped the intermediate stage of treasury notes and offered to sell the bullion directly. The contract was signed, witnessed, and notarized on November 6, 1984.

The American executive said he closely examined the original contract, which included the names of the Australian and two Americans acting for President Marcos. Then he drew some interesting conclusions:

"Marcos wished to sell this gold," he said. "I don't know who the gold belonged to. I don't know whether it was his stock of gold—I've always assumed that it belonged to somebody other than him. He was in the position of selling it. Whether he held title to it or not, I don't know.

"I was told that most, if not all the gold, was outside the Philippines. Most interested buyers were aware that there was this much gold available, but they did not want to go and do any negotiating within the country [the Philippines] itself. Almost without exception, people said, 'We want nothing to do with going into the country.'

"I remember being told at one time that there were twelve other nations who were part of this same pool [of owners], and that these nations had asked many times to have their gold returned. . . ."

How do you find buyers with this much money?

"Well," the executive said, "you don't find them all in one place. You find people who are interested in buying in much smaller tranches. . . . Most of the buyers are from the Middle East. Great pockets of Middle Easterners are interested in precious metals. They look upon gold and diamonds as the ideal way of holding wealth."

The executive eventually walked away from the deal.

The most surprising revelation here was that the executive understood all along that the gold bullion did not belong to Ferdinand Marcos, although Marcos controlled it. The gold belonged to twelve other countries that were trying to get it back. Nobody ever really thought the gold did belong to Ferdinand, except in the sense that he found it and recovered it. On this basis, theoretically at least, he was entitled to the usual finder's fee of 50 percent or whatever. And if he secretly attempted to keep the whole lot, well, he would not be the first successful treasure hunter to do so.

On the other hand, while people wrote of it as "Yamashita's Gold," or "Marcos gold," surprisingly little concern was ever expressed in magazines or newspapers for its true owners, the individual citizens and governments overrun by the Japanese, then methodically looted by Kodama and his cohort in the name of the chrysanthemum.

Nowhere in all the other material associated with Ferdinand Marcos is there the slightest clue that what he was up to so furtively had been discovered by Kodama's victims, or that they were taking action against him singly or jointly. Yet the American executive plainly asserted that he was not sure whose gold it was, but certainly not Ferdinand's, and that President Marcos was trying urgently to sell it in 1983 under increasing pressure from its rightful owners—owners who were not pressing him individually but as a bloc of twelve countries, being aided in some way by a group of one hundred generals.

First, the executive drew attention to the fact that the contract mentioned a group of generals and "the VIPs."

"The VIPs," he said "—you'll see one reference there, 'GRLS'—were the Generals. They were always referred to [during discussions in Manila] never as the VIPs, always as the Generals. Plural. And when I said, 'Who?' they said, 'There's a group of about one hundred of them.' "

He was given to understand that the Hundred Generals were connected in some manner to the true owners of the gold, or were somehow representatives of the twelve countries that were pressing Ferdinand Marcos to sell the gold and turn the proceeds over to them, or to return the gold itself to them. The executive gathered that this pressure had been under way for some years, and that by 1983 the pressure had increased to the point that Marcos was trying desperately to sell off huge quantities that he had already squirreled away in the gold pools.

A number of obvious questions immediately crowd forward: Who were these twelve countries? How did they discover Ferdinand was secretly recovering and selling off treasure looted from them? How did they come to band together, despite inevitable differences in political systems, to bring pressure on him? Who were the VIPs or Generals? Were they the senior military officers and political leaders of the twelve countries in question, or were they not necessarily from those countries, but acting for them in some manner—perhaps as paladins, or as brokers?

The twelve nations might be taken to mean the current political incarnations of the countries conquered by the Japanese: South Korea, China, Taiwan, Thailand, Burma, Malaysia, Indonesia, Singapore, Laos, Cambodia, Vietnam, and either Brunei or Hong Kong. The thirteenth, the Philippines, would not be included because its ruler was the one in possession or control of the treasure.

One item in the contract answers one of the questions immediately: While Ferdinand was to receive 1 percent for his role in brokering the deal, the Generals or VIPs were to receive 2 percent. Although his take was only 1 percent, it was fifty times more than that of any of the individual Generals.

This meant that the Generals were involved in brokering the deal, or needed to be compensated for the trouble they had been put to as intermediaries. Indeed, there are references to "Intermediaries/ Beneficiaries" (implicitly the Generals) who "shall be paid individually and separately . . . to their respective Accounts with their designated Bank/s."

In addition to the 1 percent for Ferdinand and 2 percent to the Generals as intermediaries, there would be the customary fees, commissions, and incentives to other brokers and banks involved, adding up to about $80 billion in all.

The bulk of the proceeds evidently were then to be turned over to the twelve nations as the rightful owners of the treasure. If the full $790 billion sale was concluded, this would represent something on the order of $700 billion net to be split twelve ways, or a bit less than $60 billion for each country. As a parlor game, Yamashita's Gold could displace Monopoly.

Given these staggering sums, one might well wonder whether this transaction had anything to do with the sudden acute strain placed on the London gold pool in the months that followed. By 1984, the commercial banking division of Johnson Matthey was in deep trouble due to improper loans and procedures. This much was admitted eventually as the scandal hit the press and brought rude questions in Parliament. But there may have been a good deal more to it than simply impropriety in the banking division. If the banking division alone was in trouble, it could have been rescued by the parent gold bullion trader. But for reasons that were never disclosed, the parent was in no position to rescue its progeny. Although extreme secrecy was maintained by the Bank of England and the other members of the Five, the crisis went so deep that it endangered the entire London pool and risked forfeiting British domination of the world gold trade to the gnomes of Zurich.

Secretly, the Bank of England and the four remaining members of the cartel were obliged to intervene over a tense weekend in September 1984 to nip the scandal in the bud before the international gold markets reopened on Monday Hong Kong time. All of Johnson Matthey was taken over abruptly and curtly by the Bank of England. Senior executives of Johnson Matthey were purged and sent packing as if to get them out of sight urgently, the way the establishment customarily handles the discovery in its midst of Soviet moles.

The Bank of England and the British government continue to insist that the bullion side of Johnson Matthey had nothing to do with the crisis. However, since Johnson Matthey Bankers (JMB) handled 15 percent of the London bullion trade, or 7.5 percent of the annual world market, scandal in its commercial bank division might make people worried about the bullion division and start a run on gold. Such a run could cost the London pool dearly and leave the London Five a hundred tons short. What the Bank of England was fighting, according to Deputy Governor Kit McMahon, was a "potential systemic threat."

Some members of Parliament were not convinced. Two of the most suspicious were Dr. David Owen, leader of the Social Democrats, and the Labour party's Brian Sedgemore. Shortly after the JMB rescue, Owen wrote privately to the Bank of England to say that his economic advisers had shown him that JMB's bullion operations also were not sound, that there had been "sizable losses." The governor of the Bank, Robin Leigh-Pemberton, replied that Owen's sources were misinformed and that "The problems which gave rise to the rescue operation for JMB . . . do not arise in relation to its bullion and other dealing operations. . . ." In July 1985, Chancellor of the Exchequer Nigel Lawson gave Parliament an update on the JMB investigation: "Although, strictly speaking, [the investigators] have not so far established prima facie evidence of fraud, they have revealed serious and unexplained gaps in the records of Johnson Matthey Bankers, including . . . missing documents relating to substantial past transactions. . . ."

In February 1986, Dr. Owen resumed his attack, telling Commons: "Customs and Excise believe that something like 7.25 million [pounds sterling] worth of gold bullion may have been smuggled into this country since April last year [1985] until 11 days ago [February 16, 1986]." Owen went on:

> The House has been attempting to discuss the problem of Johnson Matthey Bankers since October 1984 and there has never been a specific debate on that issue. It has many ramifications. It involves the Prime Minister because of her refusal to establish a public tribunal of inquiry. . . . It involves the Chancellor of the Exchequer because of his repeated assurances over the Governor of the Bank of England's claim that the bullion trading of JMB was sound and, of course, it involves the judgment of the Governor of the Bank of England.

It is my submission that it is urgent because today we have seen JMB's headquarters raided by Customs and Excise under a warrant, to look at the transactions in the gold bullion market. We know that around thirty other premises in the country have also been similarly raided. . . . I understand that there have been twelve arrests. . . .

. . . There is reason to believe that the smuggling and purchase of gold at below market price by JMB has been continuing for a considerable time.

He then confronted the prime minister, saying, "Since the Governor of the Bank of England has repeatedly said that the banking and gold bullion business of Johnson Matthey Bankers is sound, will the Prime Minister now set up a tribunal of inquiry?"

Prime Minister Thatcher replied, simply: "No, sir."

Six days later, Brian Sedgemore again took up the cry, asking the Chancellor of the Exchequer to set up an inquiry "into the operation of the gold bullion market . . . and bullion frauds since 1980." The Exchequer responded, "No, since the Government has full confidence that the existing investigations into bullion-related fraud will be effective."

One aspect of the transaction concerned nonpayment of the Value Added Tax, a form of technical smuggling. JMB purchased gold bullion from people who brought the gold to England from Switzerland and other unidentified locations. When JMB purchased the gold, they paid the market price and the 15 percent tax to the sellers. By customary practice it was then up to the sellers to turn over the 15 percent excise to British Customs, but instead they skipped with the extra money as a special commission. British tax laws were changed to close the loophole.

Sedgemore and Owen charged in the House of Commons that millions of dollars' worth of gold had been brought into England, without payment of taxes, from April of 1985 until February of 1986. Although neither Sedgemore nor Owen drew attention to this, these activities ended only days before Marcos fled the Philippines.

The JMB-parent bullion corporation was sold in mid-April of 1986 (appropriately enough) to the biggest Australian banking, mining, and bullion syndicate, Mase-Westpac.

Could Johnson Matthey (which General Ver said had been "handling Philippine gold for years") have become the principal overseas repository of Marcos gold—of Yamashita's Gold—only to be crippled when too much was attempted? Were there any old friends of Ferdinand Marcos among the wealthy tycoons behind Mase-Westpac—the richest banking syndicate Down Under?

It may be wrong to read too much into these coincidences, but the Thatcher government seemed determined to block any scrutiny by Parliament of the way Johnson Matthey handled its bullion business. One is reminded of the time President Macapagal abruptly announced that he was calling off the Stonehill investigation as "an act of national self-preservation."

In the end, I could not avoid the conclusion that Ferdinand Marcos had found some of Yamashita's Gold, enough of it to explain the large quantities of gold bullion observed over the years by various people whose separate descriptions bore persuasive similarities. I was also inclined to believe the many reports of secret gold shipments of a few thousand tons here and there between 1975 and 1983. If Marcos could seize billions of dollars in legitimate assets from wealthy Filipino oligarchs, and abscond with billions in foreign aid, it was at least *possible* for him to have seized tens of billions in bootleg black gold, conceivably as much as $50 or even $100 billion. What I found difficult to believe were the galactic sums mentioned in the big secret Marcos gold contracts of 1983–84, all of which were related, when for urgent medical and political reasons he seemed to be trying frantically to dispose of everything that he had built up in overseas vaults since the early 1950s. Just the first tranches alone boggle the mind. If these sums had totalled around $100 or $150 billion, there might have been some way to stretch the mind around them by thinking in terms of cocaine proceeds. I asked myself, why couldn't Marcos have as much salted away as the Medellin dope cartel, especially if it had been stolen originally by the Japanese army and secret service during a great world war? But upward of $700 billion?

The overlord of the Japanese secret service, the prince for whom Kodama worked, was said to have estimated after the war that the treasure buried around Manila as a whole was worth $50 billion (1950 dollars) and would take a century to uncover. Okay. Even allowing for inflation, could this have increased in value to $700 billion? Compare this to the 1988 assets of America's largest bank, Citicorp ($204 billion), and Japan's largest securities firm, Nomura ($374 billion). Until more concrete evidence emerges, which presupposes a willingness of governments to make public investigations, the contracts must speak for themselves. They are signed by numerous attorneys and brokers for buyers as well as sellers, representing some of the world's leading banking institutions. They would not all have put their names to paper if they were not reasonably certain that the gold existed. Only time will tell.

Not one of the twelve countries looted by Japan ever made any statement or announcement to the effect that it had recovered a portion of national treasure making up Yamashita's Gold. There would be no reason to disclose it—many reasons to keep silent, and deny all.

By his own admission, we know that Ferdinand was quietly paying off a number of political leaders and senior military officers in neighboring countries. In 1976, when he confiscated the offshore oil options of Seafront Petroleum, he explained to Seafront's owner Alfonso Yuchengco why he was doing so. Because Seafront's concessions "were outside the Philippines' territorial waters," he said (meaning in international waters off the coast of Palawan), he had to "give some shares to the political and military officers of the countries surrounding the Philippines so they wouldn't cause any problems."

Whether or not that was his real reason for paying them off, he was nevertheless paying them off. Could he have been doing so because they were pressing him to return some of the gold he was recovering from Teresa II and other sites? "Their" gold?

As to the Hundred Generals, there was no difficulty figuring out who they might be, once you knew where to look.

Over the years, clandestinely, thousands of tons of gold had been moved for Ferdinand Marcos with the cooperation and participation of a number of generals and secret agents who, therefore, knew how much gold was moved and where it went. Completely aside from their professional affiliations with the U.S. government and its allies, most of these men were interlocked through a global network of ultraconservative, anti-Communist clubs, lobbying groups, consultancies, and professional organizations. Hard, concrete evidence shows them to have become directly involved in the hunt for Yamashita's Gold while Ferdinand Marcos was in power, and then taking up the recovery effort again for themselves after he fled into exile. Since they considered themselves to be paladins in other respects, could they have turned on Ferdinand in 1983 and held his feet to the fire?

Nineteen

CLOAK AND DAGGER

WHETHER FERDINAND FIRST APPROACHED the CIA about Yamashita's Gold, or the CIA approached him, is not important, for he had been involved with the Agency intermittently since the early 1950s. Where the gold was concerned, the group he dealt with was a veritable Who's Who of American clandestine operations. Among them were some of the same men fleetingly exposed in the Iran-Contra scandal—a quasi-private military intelligence cell calling itself "The Enterprise" and engaged in worldwide intrigues for the White House involving huge black-bag payoffs. Marcos and Ver themselves were implicated in the Iran-Contra scandal for providing the false end-user certificates that allowed the secret team to divert arms wherever it wished.

Hundreds of millions of dollars were involved in the Iran-Contra arms deals, with collusion among the United States, Israel, the Philippines, and other countries, including all the cloak-and-dagger paraphernalia of Swiss numbered accounts, dummy companies, and clandestine ships and planes. But as one of The Enterprise testified, "This is pipsqueak stuff."

Reading between the lines of Lieutenant Colonel North's testimony, it is clear that CIA director William Casey was proud of having an "off the shelf" team of private operators funded by unofficial sources. This enabled Casey to avoid the kind of interference from Congress that had been blocking the Reagan administration's initiatives to topple the Sandinista government in Nicaragua. But Casey's gambit was not entirely new. The members of The Enterprise were all larger-than-life characters who had worked together for many years, a first generation of colorful old OSS hands, and a second generation of hard-nosed covert action types who cut their milk teeth at the Bay of Pigs. Some of their names have since become familiar: John Singlaub, Richard Secord, Ray Cline, Theodore Shackley, Thomas Clines, and others.

But no longer around is the man who, in a way, started it all going: the CIA's original overseas paymaster and Mister Black Bag. His name was Paul Helliwell.

Helliwell was America's chief of intelligence in China during World War II, part of the same overall operation as Captain (later Rear Admiral) Milton "Mary" Miles, who supported the charming but ruthless Nationalist Chinese secret police boss, Tai Li, until Tai Li's death in a booby-trapped plane soon after the end of World War II. As China desk officer for the OSS, Helliwell became the man who controlled the pipeline of covert funds for secret operations throughout East Asia after the war. This was virgin territory. A lawyer by training, he evolved a system of handling black money from a multitude of sources, many of them extra-legal, laundering it, and moving it around in a shell game through banks he set up like walnuts for that purpose, using artful dodgers as couriers and financial sleight of hand. Often, he ended up with more money than he began, because of the way black funds have of growing when freed of legal restraints, and thanks to the violent death in war and revolution of so many of his depositors, leaving their inheritance to be spent as the Agency wished.

Thanks to the CIA's part in rescuing the regime of Generalissimo Chiang in 1949, Helliwell had access to its black resources. In 1949 Helliwell and a handful of other CIA agents salvaged Claire Chennault's Civil Air Transport (CAT) and other American and Chinese aircraft from the mainland, and transferred them by ship to Taiwan.

He spent the years immediately following Mao's victory reorganizing the U.S. line of defense around Red China. With war-surplus Victory ships and Liberty ships, and some of Chennault's planes, he set up Sea Supply Corporation and Air America, using the Philippines and Thailand as staging bases for secret operations throughout Southeast Asia. As a means of harassing Red China from the rear, and gathering intelligence, Sea Supply ferried materiel to Thailand to support the KMT opium armies in Burma and the rebellious Champa tribesmen in eastern Tibet. CAT and Air America flew these supplies from Thailand into the Golden Triangle poppy fields and across upper Burma to the Himalayas, and flew supplies from the Philippines for the beleaguered French at Dienbienphu.

It was an expensive business. The KMT and the CIA paid off General Phao, the commander of the Thai police, who obligingly transshipped heroin from the opium armies down to Bangkok for export. They also paid the KMT's General Li Mi what it took to keep his army of ten thousand going, which Li Mi was not about to do with his share of the opium proceeds. All this took a lot of gold bullion, but Helliwell rose to the occasion. He and other Agency financial experts in the field followed basic rules laid down by the original CIA director of covert operations, Frank Wisner. First get the rich people on your side, including the rich gangsters, then set up channels for black money so you can provide funds across borders to the people who need them to get the job done. Kim Philby said Wisner once told him, "It is essential to secure the overt cooperation of people with conspicuous access to wealth in their own right." The cooperation of rich people hid the transfer of black money.

On the other side of the world in Europe, a program similar to Helliwell's was set up by a Hungarian-born OSS officer, Nicolas Deak. Eventually, this matured into the legitimate money trader Deak & Company, a glossy firm with fifty-nine international offices. Deak's services were used by the CIA's Kim Roosevelt to finance the 1953 coup against Mohammed Mossadeq in Iran, which involved paying massive bribes to undermine Mossadeq in favor of the young Shah.

At the end of the Pacific War, most of the money in Asia was in the hands of relatively few people: those who had managed to hold onto what they had before the war, and those who had taken advantage of the war to help themselves to the wealth of others. Both groups contributed to Helliwell's operations for the same reason, dread of communism. Helliwell supported right-wing groups all over Asia by drawing on the coffers of the Chiangs, the Korean generals, and the *kuromaku* of Japan, foremost among them Kodama.

Half of Kodama's personal wartime hoard of $200 million was turned over to the Counter-Intelligence Corps (CIC) in 1948, as part of the complex deal worked out between MacArthur and Chiang for Kodama's freedom and that of his powerful cellmates. The $100 million that the CIC got, shy of what it had to split with the generalissimo (perhaps fifty-fifty), became seed money and fertilizer for Helliwell's money tree. The CIC used Kodama first to pay off pro-American politicians in Japan, Korea, Thailand, and Indonesia. After ten years literally as an employee of G-2, Kodama was officially put on the CIA payroll in 1958. That same year, he became the Lockheed agent in Japan, receiving $6.3 million in bribes either from Lockheed or from the CIA through Lockheed during the years from 1966 to 1972. Kodama preferred cash, so Lockheed delivered it to him via Deak & Company couriers. The Lockheed affair climaxed in 1976 with the arrest of Prime Minister Tanaka for bribery, of which he was later convicted.

The Counter-Intelligence Corps and its successor agency, the CIA, naturally never revealed exactly how they spent the $100 million provided by Kodama, but a number of new anti-Communist organizations soon came into existence and established cells throughout the Far East. One of these was the religious cult of the Moonies, founded by the South Korean Sun Myung Moon, with help from the CIA and its South Korean stepchild, the KCIA. Another was the Asian Peoples' Anti-Communist League (APACL), founded by South Korea's Syngman Rhee, Taiwan's Chiang Kai-shek, and the CIA. Kodama's old friend Sasakawa Ryiochi became the champion of the Moonies in Japan, and one of the prime movers behind the Japanese branch of APACL. In 1970, Sasakawa organized the World Anti-Communist League as the successor to APACL. According to one version, the Reverend Moon and Sasakawa jawboned with prominent Japanese rightists at one of Sasakawa's speedboat racing courses at the foot of Mount Fuji and laid their plans to spread the League worldwide. During its early years, WACL was widely reported to have been financed largely from Sasakawa's huge fortune.

Among other covert operations, Helliwell's black-money channels were used to underwrite Lansdale's anti-Huk campaign in the Philippines, the election of President Magsaysay, and subsequent Filipino political contests. From the Philippines, it was used to pay the Indonesians fighting Sukarno. When America became entangled in Vietnam, Helliwell's financial magic was used to keep the Saigon generals happy and to set up overseas accounts for Laotian princelings and druglords.

Glamorous as they were in cloak-and-dagger terms, the CIA operations in Tibet, Burma, and Indonesia were military failures and intelligence failures as well, although many of the technical people—pilots and individual agents—performed heroic feats under hazardous conditions. They failed not for want of daring and ingenuity in the field, but because of bad judgment, questionable motives, and evasion of responsibility at policy levels in Washington. One of the KMT opium generals, General Lee, told me that his troops got such a bad reception from villagers on the Chinese side of the border that they stopped making forays, and thereafter provided the CIA with intelligence that was invented to suit the occasion.

Helliwell's financial methods, on the other hand, were seen as a great success, with application worldwide. What could not be achieved by killing people often could be done by buying allies and paying off enemies, something Asians and Europeans had learned to do centuries earlier. In 1960—following Castro's victory in Cuba the previous year—CIA covert operations director Richard Bissell brought Helliwell back from the Far East to set up a Western Hemisphere version of Sea Supply and Air America out of Miami called Southern Air Transport, and a new chain of black-money banks to pay for the Bay of Pigs operation that Bissell was planning.

Among Helliwell's creations were Castle Bank and Mercantile Bank & Trust in the Bahamas. One of his associates was Wallace Groves, who was involved with Ferdinand in the Benguet mines. Like Kodama, Groves was taken on as a CIA adviser.

Helliwell thereby became the paymaster for the Bay of Pigs. He did not scrap his Asian networks, he just extended them around the world, his string of banks eventually stretching from Florida and the Bahamas to the Caymans, the Netherlands Antilles, Panama, Honolulu, Hong Kong, Manila, Bangkok, Singapore, Sydney, Beirut, and Teheran. No one will ever know how much flight capital flowed through the murky streams between these banks. One by one, the banks collapsed in scandal, lasting only as long as they were needed, to be replaced somewhere else by their clones. One of these clones was the Nugan-Hand Bank, which became a pipeline for the Marcos gold deals.

Working for Paul Helliwell in China near the end of the Pacific War were two young intelligence officers, Ray Cline and John Singlaub, one a brilliant analyst, the other a paramilitary expert.

Singlaub was a legitimate American hero. As a young OSS agent, he parachuted behind German lines in France in 1944 to help the Resistance prepare for D-Day. According to legend, during the liberation of Singapore it was Singlaub who parachuted in to unlock the gates of Changi Prison. Near the end of the war, he was dropped into China to train KMT guerrillas, in the process developing an inflexible anti-Communist bond with the Chiang regime. When the Japanese surrendered, he was appointed chief of the U.S. military mission in Mukden, Manchuria, attempting from there to influence the outcome of the Chinese civil war. With Mao's victory, Singlaub succeeded Paul Helliwell as China desk officer for the CIA. As a paramilitary expert, he helped organize the Ranger Training Center at Fort Benning, Georgia, to prepare army commandos for CIA missions, and directed many of the agent drops in China, most of whom vanished without a trace. During the Korean War he became CIA deputy chief in South Korea, rising to the rank of general.

Understandably, Singlaub the centurion came to be regarded with awe by a whole generation of American military men and intelligence officers, many of whom shared his conservative views about the way things should be in Asia. Around him grew a following that developed into an infrastructure at the Pentagon and CIA.

When Singlaub took over the China desk from Paul Helliwell, one of his top agents was Ray Cline. After the Chiang regime fled to Taiwan, Cline became a key operative in Taipei because of his close friendship with the generalissimo's son and heir, Chiang Ching-kuo ("CCK"). They engaged in heroic all-night drinking bouts that became a legend in the Agency. Cline also was the conduit through which CIA funds flowed to set up the Asian People's Anti-Communist League (APACL) in Taiwan and South Korea in 1955–56, which soon had its own agents operating throughout the Far East. One of the chief fundraisers for Cline's creation was Kodama's fellow *kuromaku* Sasakawa. At Sasakawa's initiative, the APACL eventually became the World Anti-Communist League, and was headed for many years by Chiang Kai-shek's henchman, Ku Cheng-kang.

Cline's drinking buddy, the generalissimo's son, rose to be security chief, defense minister, and ultimately president of Taiwan. From 1958 to 1962, Cline served as CIA station chief in Taipei, and had extraordinary influence. Cline and CCK worked in harness to carry out black operations throughout Asia, including the struggle to dominate the overseas Chinese communities in the Philippines and Indonesia. Together they set up the Political Warfare Cadres Academy in Peitou, outside Taipei. An exceptionally clever and intelligent man, Cline went back to Washington at the end of 1962 to become the CIA's deputy director for intelligence worldwide. In this position he continued to work closely with Paul Helliwell, John Singlaub, and CCK, and would have been kept well informed on Marcos gold deals by agents in Manila, since these deals were an item of great interest.

The decision of President Eisenhower to begin planning an invasion of Cuba, and to explore options for assassinating Fidel Castro, led the CIA to strike a bargain with Mafia don Santo Trafficante, whose casinos and brothels in Havana had been closed down by Castro, and anti-Castro operations became a joint venture with the Mafia. The Kennedys intensified the effort, bringing new players into the forefront of the CIA's covert action group. Two of this new generation were Theodore Shackley and Thomas Clines. For the next three decades, Clines and Shackley moved back and forth from Asia to the Caribbean leaving in their path all manner of invasions, military coups, political assassinations, and what one member of The Enterprise boasted were "the biggest black-bag operations of all time."

Shackley and Clines were among those given the job of organizing the Bay of Pigs invasion. Its embarrassing failure cost Allen Dulles his job as head of the CIA and Richard Bissell his as director of covert operations. But Shackley and Clines were moved on to the next urgent task at hand: helping to arrange the assassination of Fidel Castro, his brother Raul, Che Guevara, and others in Operation Mongoose.

It was the decision of the Kennedy brothers to bring General Edward Lansdale back from Manila and Saigon to plan Operation Mongoose. They, like so many others, had allowed themselves to be convinced that Lansdale's Huk campaign and the election of Magsaysay had been an unqualified success. It took many months for the realization to sink in that Lansdale lived in a covert version of Disneyland. This became apparent within the Agency when word spread that the general was planning a triumphal victory parade through Havana: it would be accomplished by having a submarine surface one night off the Malecon to fire star shells into the sky, which Catholic Cubans would take to be the Second Coming.

On assuming the presidency, Lyndon Johnson turned his attention away from Cuba to Vietnam, and Shackley and Clines were sent off to apply their peculiar specialty in Indochina. Operation Mongoose was turned into Operation Phoenix, a monthly bounty hunt to destroy America's enemies at the village level by assassinating them. Phoenix resulted in the killing (often with silenced pistols in the middle of the night) of more than twenty thousand Vietnamese, some said fifty thousand—mostly civilians—reaching an estimated total of seventy-five thousand people throughout Indochina, including women and children. The overall coordination of Phoenix was attributed to William Colby, but General John Singlaub ran the cutting edge in Vietnam (called SOG, or Special Operations Group), while Shackley and Clines ran the parallel program in Laos. The chief of secret air operations throughout was General Heinie Aderholt, an amiable, immensely likeable technical wizard and old OSS hand who earlier had run air operations in Indonesia and Tibet for Paul Helliwell. His deputy air wing commander for Singlaub's SOG was air force Lieutenant Colonel Richard Secord. It was in this way that many of the key elements of The Enterprise first came together.

While Operation Phoenix failed to have any decisive effect on the outcome of the Indochina War, considerable success was being achieved simply by buying the loyalty of military officers and politicians. Businessmen, drug merchants, and statesmen like Ferdinand Marcos gladly cooperated with the CIA in return for help in moving their hidden funds to overseas banks, where the Agency felt free to dip into them to achieve its own ends.

Because buying was demonstrably more effective than killing, Paul Helliwell's black-money network bore down and gave birth to Nugan-Hand, with its head office in Sydney and branches in Manila, Hong Kong, Bangkok, Singapore, Honolulu, and Washington, D.C. One of Nugan-Hand's covert associates described the bank as a convenience provided "for people out of Southeast Asia during the Vietnam War . . . they needed to buy property and they needed to buy gold and they needed to put their money on deposit and they couldn't have it up in Thailand or Laos or Cambodia or Vietnam. . . ." (Or stuck in bank vaults in the Philippines.)

Sprinkled through Nugan-Hand were a number of Ray Cline's and John Singlaub's closest associates in the military intelligence community: In Washington, Walter McDonald, the CIA's deputy director for economic research, arranged for former CIA director William Colby to become legal counsel to Nugan-Hand. The Honolulu office was headed by retired General Edwin F. Black, for many years a top aide of CIA director Allen Dulles, a member of the NSC staff, and chief of the U.S. military in Thailand during the Vietnam War. The Washington branch was headed by retired Rear Admiral Earl P. Yates, former chief-of-staff for plans and policy of the U.S. Pacific Command, in charge of all strategic planning as far as the Arabian Gulf. The Manila branch was headed by General Leroy Manor, former special assistant to the Joint Chiefs of Staff for counterinsurgency and covert operations, who was said to have retired from active duty to undertake secret missions, including negotiating the 1979 military base rental agreement in the Philippines. Manor spent seven months negotiating the base agreement, concluding with the payment to Ferdinand of $500 million. The general then immediately accepted the post as head of the Manila branch of Nugan-Hand.

Among the questions raised is whether it was entirely proper for General Manor, as chief negotiator of the $500 million base agreement, to head a bank doing business with President Marcos and his family—and in the process accept delivery of a duty-free Ferrari. What this revealed about Manor's own judgment is less important than what it revealed about Washington's involvement with Ferdinand. The Pentagon said Manor had retired from active duty to undertake assignments too secret to discuss, including "special liaison" with President Marcos; Nugan-Hand's business in Manila was reported to include secret CIA airlifts of tons of black gold. Did "special liaison" mean shepherding Yamashita's Gold out through the Agency's black-money channels? Manor told a journalist that he was sent out to run the Manila office "to learn"—sent out by whom, to learn what?

By the 1970s, this hard core of the CIA's covert action group was acquiring positions of exceptional leverage. In 1966, Ray Cline had left his post as the CIA's deputy director of intelligence after repeated clashes with the new CIA director, Admiral Raborn. Cline made a lateral move, becoming station chief in Frankfurt, West Germany, then landed on his feet when he returned to Washington to take over the State Department's Bureau of Intelligence and Research. In this position, he was in a much better slot to influence foreign policy.

General John Singlaub became a deputy assistant secretary of defense from 1971 to 1973, then commander-in-chief of all U.S. forces in South Korea.

Shackley and Clines became station chief and deputy respectively in Saigon during the bone-crushing period 1968–72, then directed Operation Phoenix from CIA headquarters in Virginia from 1973 to 1975. As Saigon station chief, Shackley was a primary instrument for Henry Kissinger's grim initiatives throughout Indochina. The interruption in his tenure at Saigon in 1972 came when he and Clines were brought back long enough to mastermind the violent overthrow of Chile's popularly elected Marxist president, Salvador Allende, during which Allende was murdered. By the time Watergate removed Nixon from the Oval Office, Shackley was the CIA's deputy director for operations, in charge of covert action worldwide.

The fall of Saigon shifted the focus of covert action to other capitals. Richard Secord went to Iran, where he commanded the U.S. military mission. In Washington, Shackley and Clines became as alarmed by the rise of Gough Whitlam and the Labor party in Australia as they had been by the election of Salvador Allende in Chile. It is not unusual for CIA field officers to become overinvolved in local passions, but the Agency's senior executives are expected to remain aloof, serving only as instruments of the president. The Agency's worst setbacks were experienced when its senior executives became obsessed with particular missions, as when Bissell became relentless in his commitment to the Bay of Pigs invasion. Shackley now showed similar signs. Men who worked with him said he was "paranoid" about Whitlam and his Labor party, considering it to be under the control or influence of Communists.

For some time, the CIA had been running a variety of covert operations in Australia, involving Nugan-Hand and strange comings and goings at the big U.S. technical intelligence base called Pine Gap, near Alice Springs in the Outback. Many of these intrigues were carried on with the knowing collaboration of the Australian Security Intelligence Organization, ASIO, headed by Brigadier Sir Charles Spry, who had close personal ties to the CIA going back to Allen Dulles and the OSS. Colonel Secord, who had become Singlaub and Shackley's primary air operations man in Indochina, was identified with these Australian operations during the Vietnam War, and apparently continued to serve as a link afterwards for the movement of black money and weapons from the Philippines and Australia to Iran.

When he testified before Congress during the Iran-Contra hearings, it was Secord who said: "This is pipsqueak stuff. When I was in Southeast Asia, we used to pay our people in cash and gold bullion. I've been involved in some of the biggest black-bag operations of all time."

By moving Ferdinand's illicit gold out through Nugan-Hand, the Agency would be able to do financial favors for its wealthy friends in Australia, allowing them to collect fat commissions in offshore accounts or to provide them temporarily with the spot financing they might need to make a leveraged hostile takeover. Those favors could then be called in whenever the Agency wished.

Many of the CIA's Australian initiatives were directed at keeping the Labor party out of office. When, despite them, Whitlam became Australia's new prime minister, he began doing what any new chief of state would, moving to bring Canberra's intelligence service under his own control. As time passed Whitlam found alarming indications that the ASIO might actually be conspiring with the CIA to bring his government down, including leaking information designed to embarrass members of his cabinet in order to force their resignation. Whitlam began sacking people at ASIO that he felt were responsible, including some of the CIA's best friends Down Under.

From Washington, Shackley counterattacked. He informed the ASIO's Sir Charles Spry that what Whitlam was doing was causing the CIA "grave concern," and unless something was done urgently the Agency would have to break off its "mutually beneficial relationships" with the ASIO. Apparently Shackley also appealed to MI6 in London to do something urgently. Three days later the Australian governor-general, a largely ceremonial post appointed by the queen, exercised an obscure point of law that had never before seen the light of day and removed Whitlam from office. Since then, there have been questions raised in the House of Commons about whether MI6 might have been responsible.

The downfall of Gough Whitlam endeared the CIA to a whole generation of Australian tycoons horrified by what the British Labour party had done to their counterparts in England, and who felt that their own liberties were jeopardized by Whitlam's rise. For that reason alone, the Agency enjoyed unprecedented freedom to operate in and through Australia from 1975 to 1982.

Nugan-Hand with headquarters in Sydney became a black hole for hot money from all over Asia. During the fall of Saigon, a member of the secret team told me, "On separate occasions, I was offered one million dollars in cash by individual businessmen, mostly Chinese, to fly them and their families out to the Philippines or Central America. One association of Chinese businessmen offered me $100 million (a million per head) to get them all out at once to Costa Rica. I'm sorry I didn't do it. I could have done it easily, but I just didn't have any time. They must have gone elsewhere."

For the next decade Iran provided a useful laundering facility and opportunities for the sort of arms deals that secret agents like to engineer on the side. These included the resale of weapons stockpiles left over in Thailand. So while Marcos gold and Chinese flight capital moved through Australia to Teheran and Beirut, some of the proceeds helped grease the way for new business arrangements. Nugan-Hand served as an intermediary in the sale of at least one spy ship to the Shah of Iran. In Teheran Richard Secord was the chief Pentagon representative in these deals. Everything was sold—from jet fighters and radar-transparent patrol boats (made of carbon fiber and exotic plastics) to espionage equipment, AWACS spy planes, and missile systems. Clines established a company called the Egyptian-American Transport and Services Corporation (EATSCO), and began looking for other outlets for weapons.

Ferdinand's role in many of these CIA weapons deals was to provide false end-user certificates in order to mask the real destination. The procedure was simple. As the world's largest weapons dealer, when America sold armaments to another country, Congress required guarantees that the weapons would not be resold to a third country without authorization. This guarantee was provided in the form of certificates that specified exactly to whom the weapons were going. The certificates had to be approved individually by the State Department and the Pentagon. Fabian Ver, as chief of staff of the Philippine armed forces, signed end-user certificates stating, for example, that the weapons were being resold by Israel to the Philippines. That was enough to satisfy Congress and the Pentagon, who knew that anything involving the Philippines would be hopeless to trace. Instead, the weapons would go to countries that were blacklisted.

For reasons of their own, members of the secret team were showing increasing signs of operating independently of the CIA establishment. Some of this was inevitable, due to the multiplication of CIA proprietaries, bogus banks, and laundering operations.

That came to an abrupt halt when Jimmy Carter became president, decided to clean house, and immediately ran head-on into this right-wing cabal.

One of Carter's cost-cutting moves was a decision to reduce the size of American forces in South Korea. This was an unpardonable error of judgment from the point of view of General Singlaub, who had spent the better part of his life building up the Korean generals as a solid rock of anti-communism in the Far East, a praetorian guard. As chief-of-staff of the United Nations command in Seoul, Singlaub publicly denounced the decision of his commander-in-chief. President Carter immediately fired him, and Singlaub was forced to resign from the army.

Carter also had his new CIA director, Admiral Stansfield Turner, sack Shackley and Clines. EATSCO, the arms broker set up by Thomas Clines, later pleaded guilty to defrauding the U.S. government of some $8 million by overbilling customers. Richard Secord, who had risen to major general and deputy assistant secretary of defense for Africa, the Middle East and Central Asia, eventually was embarrassed by the disclosures of the EATSCO affair, and retired from the air force after being accused by the Justice Department of illegally using his Pentagon post to intercede for Clines's company.

To add to their woes, the overthrow of the Shah canceled Iran as a place of remuneration for covert CIA agents. As part of his campaign for human rights, Carter also invoked the Harkin Amendment to cut off U.S. military aid to dictator Anastasio Somoza, which put a kink in the CIA hose leading to Central America.

While the Shah was still in power, Nugan-Hand was said to have laundered "billions" for him. After his expulsion, the bank set to work moving the Shah's assets to safer places. Soon afterward, Frank Nugan's body was found outside Sydney slumped behind the wheel of his Mercedes, a bullet hole in his head and a rifle beside him. His partner Michael Hand (long identified with the CIA) vanished off the face of the earth. Nugan-Hand Bank collapsed in scandal, and all its generals and admirals sought employment elsewhere.

For a moment it seemed as though the warlocks had been put to flight. But they had only been driven underground. In a series of stunning reversals, President Carter was embarrassed by a parade of misfortunes, including the humiliating failure of his attempt to rescue American hostages in Iran—a military fiasco that seemed to have been produced by Mack Sennett, directed by Harold Lloyd, and carried out by the Keystone Cops.

That there was a systematic campaign to unhorse President Carter has never been in doubt, although its dimensions remain unmeasured. Ferdinand Marcos must have been pleased with Carter's defeat and the election of Ronald Reagan, because it brought on a new era of U.S.-Philippine relations.

After Reagan's election and the appointment of his friend William

Casey as the new director of the CIA, the old secret team of Singlaub, Shackley, and the others was reorganized into a privately funded, seemingly random group of civilian consultancies, but with interlocking membership. The Enterprise became a shadow CIA, modeled on England's Special Operations Executive in World War II, an elite group that was the despair of the regular Secret Intelligence Service. When an initiative could not be undertaken by Casey's CIA for reasons of political sensitivity, the private consultants were brought in.

Secord described how this came about: "One of the problems with the CIA is that they don't have experienced people running the show. You have shoe clerks running the railroad. The Carter Administration eviscerated the CIA; it was just wrecked, and the Clandestine branch, which was very small, was finished. I think Casey was trying to do a good job, but he was too old to really be effective." Secord and The Enterprise stepped into the breach.

As a civilian, John Singlaub became more active than ever in right-wing causes and anti-Communist movements. Under Reagan he regained the influence he had lost under Carter. He served as chairman of the World Anti-Communist League, and headed its American chapter, the Council for World Freedom. In 1981 he attended a WACL meeting in Taipei, where he was reported to have been given nearly $20,000 by Ray Cline's old friend, President Chiang Ching-kuo, to set up the American chapter. Lieutenant General Daniel O. Graham, the former director of the Defense Intelligence Agency, became its vice-chairman.

The League's rosters included U.S. congressmen and senators, British Members of Parliament, Nazi collaborators, notorious terrorists, death squad leaders from Latin America, assorted right-wing strongmen, and underworld figures. Among its Asian sponsors were the Chiangs, Park Chung Hee, Sasakawa Ryiochi, Kodama Yoshio, and the Reverend Moon. During his twenty years of dictatorship, President Marcos regularly attended WACL annual meetings, as did Ray Cline, John Singlaub, Kodama, and Sasakawa.

Under pressure from the Reagan White House in 1982, Singlaub's U.S. chapter of the League was granted tax-exempt status by the IRS. Ronald Reagan himself regularly sent messages to WACL conferences, asserting that "Our combined efforts are moving the tide of history toward world freedom."

Many of the organizations lobbying for conservative causes in Washington, such as the Conservative Caucus, had interlocking directorships with WACL. Tracing the interlocks could lead to interesting discoveries. For example, Western Goals, established to keep track of subversives in America, was headed by Singlaub's friend Congressman Larry McDonald, whose financial backers included Nelson Bunker Hunt, who had tried to corner the silver market. McDonald was also head of the John Birch Society when Bob Curtis said it had offered to launder over $20 billion in Yamashita's Gold. It may be only coincidence that the biggest corporation in McDonald's constituency in Georgia was Lockheed, which had paid millions to Japanese officials through Kodama, the man most responsible for gathering Yamashita's Gold and hiding it in the Philippines. Congressman McDonald was one of the passengers aboard Korean Air Lines flight 007 shot down when it intruded into Soviet airspace in 1983.

Singlaub exerted direct personal influence within the National Security Council through the military staff of generals and colonels in the Executive Office Building. When he was not in Washington his contact with the NSC was carried out for him by the Washington-based conservative lobbyist, Andrew Messing. Singlaub's access to the NSC came in part through his close friendship with Major General Robert L. Schweitzer, formerly with the Pentagon's Strategy, Plans and Policy Office, and through General John W. Vessey, chairman of the Joint Chiefs of Staff. Schweitzer also was chairman of the Inter-American Defense Board, responsible for Nicaragua, El Salvador, and Honduras. In 1986, just as the Iran-Contra scandal was breaking, Schweitzer retired and joined Singlaub and The Enterprise in the civilian world, taking a post as adviser with Singlaub in a Washington consulting firm called GeoMiliTech Corporation. Similarly, when Ted Shackley had retired under pressure from the CIA, he had joined a consulting firm in Houston started by Thomas Clines.

In these new positions, they became especially useful to President Reagan when Congress passed the Boland Amendment, ordering the White House and the CIA to cease paying the Contras to overthrow Nicaragua's Sandinista government. To get around the Boland Amendment, the NSC's Lieutenant Colonel North struck a deal with the CIA's Casey to bring in Secord, Hakim, Shackley, and Clines—and later their associates Singlaub, Aderholt, and Schweitzer—to run guns to the Contras privately, once again turning to Ferdinand Marcos for the false end-user certificates. The whole secret team network had again come full circle, back to Manila.

By this point Ferdinand had been supplying these fake certificates to the CIA for more than a decade. This was no small deceit. More than $8 million in weapons was involved in a single shipment, totalling $100 million in 1983 alone. A Filipino arms dealer associated with General Ver received a 5 percent commission on the proceeds of these sales; so, in that year, the dealer who was handling just the paperwork in Manila made $5 million. It is a tribute to the ingenuity of Fabian Ver that he was not content merely to sign the certificates. He went one step further and billed his own army for the cost of the shipments, then pocketed the money. Documents show that Ver, in collaboration with Israeli generals and U.S. businessmen, charged the Philippine armed forces hundreds of millions of dollars for armaments that never arrived.*

In November 1984, Ted Shackley was said to have been contacted by former members of the Shah's SAVAK now working for the Ayatollah Khomeini, and informed that President Reagan could regain Iran by supporting moderates in the regime with secret arms shipments. The key figures in this latest intrigue turned out to be Iranian arms merchant Manucher Ghorbanifar and the CIA's old friend Adnan Khashoggi, Ferdinand's pal and Imelda's disco partner, fellow Lockheed agent and business associate of Kodama. In this manner, they suggested that Reagan could ransom American hostages being held by Palestinians backed by the Ayatollah. Shackley reportedly passed this suggestion on to Colonel North, and the Iran side of the Iran-Contra conspiracy was set into motion.

At Colonel North's urging, The Enterprise engineered both the Iranian and the Contra arms deals through a number of private fronts, buying American equipment cheap, selling it dear, and salting the difference in Swiss accounts—$6 million in one alone. For his part, John Singlaub was asked by North to solicit funds from foreign countries, and was believed to have done so from South Korea, Taiwan, and the Philippines. Singlaub also brokered a $5.3 million arms deal for the Contras,

*Apparently he was still at it in 1986, long after escaping to his villa in the United States. In October 1986, a cargo vessel was seized off Negros by Philippine customs officials carrying war materials bound for Iran. The shipment, traced to Ver, was stopping at a private pier owned jointly by Geronimo Velasco (a business associate of Ferdinand Marcos and Harry Stonehill) and Juan Ponce Enrile. Enrile retorted that he knew nothing about the weapons, and they were doubtless being sent to the Communist guerrillas of the New People's Army.

including thousands of AK-47 assault rifles, apparently obtained cheap from his old adversary the People's Republic.

When the Iran-Contra mess burst like a boil in 1986, Singlaub and his friends were already busy elsewhere, armed with picks and shovels, taking up where Ferdinand Marcos had left off in the hunt for what was left of Yamashita's Gold.

Twenty

THE CROWN PRINCE

THE END WAS A LONG TIME in coming, but when it came, hardly a shot was fired. Because of its unrestrained greed, the Marcos dynasty had no substance. Everything was a sham. Like Imelda's Film Center, the contractors had cheated on materials everywhere; the edifice went up without internal reinforcement, and at the first serious tremor it collapsed.

Signs of stress first appeared in 1981 with the defection of a figure of little significance on the outer fringes of the crony network—Chinese businessman Dewey Dee. Although he was a minor character, Dewey Dee's defection revealed the hollowness of the regime and the fragility of its financial structure. So much of the money borrowed by the Philippines from foreign banks over the years had been embezzled and salted away elsewhere by Imelda, Ferdinand, and their respective followers that nothing was left in the till for emergencies. Most of the money in Manila existed only on paper that was kited endlessly by cronies until the sky was full of waltzing IOUs.

At age forty-two, Dewey Dee was well connected. He came from the influential Dee clan, which had prospered during the first half of the twentieth century from a profitable friendship between President Quezon and Dee Chuan, head of the prewar Chinese chambers of commerce. Dewey's branch of the Dee clan was in the textile industry, weaving fabrics and manufacturing garments with underpaid Filipino labor. Dee employed nearly fifty thousand people, directly and indirectly, in various companies. His keystone was Continental Manufacturing Corporation, a joint venture 40 percent owned by the Japanese giants Mitsubishi and Marubeni. Dee was president of five Continental subsidiaries, ran a stockbrokerage and a bank. With all these credentials, he was able to get loans whenever he wished.

Dewey was an aggressive businessman, a risk taker, and one of the Manila stock market's big speculators. An amendment to Continental's corporate by-laws gave him complete freedom to obtain loans up to 94 million pesos on behalf of the company. Dewey was clever enough to borrow seven times that amount. Using the company as collateral, he approached different banks and lending institutions, and took out loan after loan till he had accumulated a debt of over $90 million. Under President Marcos, banking laws were relaxed, to favor cronies. No central records were kept that would tip off a lender that Dee had over-mortgaged his companies.

He was salting this borrowed money in the United States, Canada, and Latin America, using discreet channels in the Chinese money market. After another trip to America, he returned to the Philippines on December 30, 1980, for a family business meeting. One week after that, he reportedly slipped another $1 million out of the country, double-crossing several black-money operators in the process.

A few days later, Dee skipped, leaving personal and corporate debts exceeding $90 million. His forty-five creditors included the government-controlled Development Bank of the Philippines (DBP), Citibank, Banque Nationale de Paris, sixteen commercial banks, eleven investment houses, three offshore banking units, and fourteen other private institutions. Among the Filipino creditors he burned were three of the most influential palace cronies: Disini, Cuenca, and Silverio. They were wheeling and dealing on a scale far greater than Dewey Dee, kiting commercial paper in imperial style. As they were intimates of President Marcos, they could take financial risks that others would not dare. But they were unprepared for Dewey Dee's vanishing act.

His sudden disappearance left scores of banks and loan companies holding worthless notes. To cover themselves, they pressed other loan customers to pay up. Many were short of cash and could not pay. Panic spread through the financial community. Depositors rushed to withdraw savings. Some of the weaker banks, loan companies, and corporations went bankrupt. To avert a total collapse, Ferdinand had to authorize a government bailout package of several hundred million dollars. Some of the bailout money came from tax revenues and Central Bank certificate sales, but the bulk came from U.S. bank loans, which greatly enlarged the Philippines' foreign debt.

Ironically, the firms that needed the most help were the big crony companies: Rudi Cuenca's Construction and Development Corporation of the Philippines, Herminio Disini's Herdis Group, and Roberto Silverio's Delta Motors. The Herdis empire of thirty-two companies crumbled because Dee had borrowed heavily from Disini's International Corporate Bank and Atrium Capital Corporation. They were also hard hit by panic pullouts of money market fund placements. Disini needed more than a billion pesos to cover his financial embarrassment. Too much of his personal wealth was salted away in Vienna and elsewhere. Silverio's Philippine Underwriters Finance Corporation also foundered.

Ferdinand acted as if the problems besetting his cronies were all the fault of Dewey Dee. He ordered his justice minister to prepare a case against Dee and to cooperate with international organizations in seeking his return. By this time, Dee was safe and sound in Costa Rica.

One of those worst hit by the Dee scandal was Ramon Lee of Alfa Integrated Textile Mills. Lee's debts were said to be nearly 800 million pesos, and to avoid bankruptcy he needed urgent help from the Development Bank. Under orders from President Marcos, the Development Bank bought up Lee's equity, leaving him with only minimal holding in Alfa. If this had happened just once or twice, Ferdinand might have been able to limit the damage. But crony capitalism was at fault, not Dewey Dee. Some of the biggest crony empires had to be taken over by government banks. Eventually, they were resold to other cronies at fire-sale prices. By then the country's meager financial reserves had been depleted.

After Dewey Dee, other wealthy businessmen fled, leaving heaps of bad paper that cost Philippine banks between $600 and $950 million. Most of the two dozen luxury hotels built for the 1976 World Bank Conference went into receivership. Official disbursements to relieve the crony corporations totaled $1.5 billion. Only two cronies survived with undiminished power: billionaires Eduardo Cojuangco and Roberto Benedicto. The whole edifice was tottering.

The first to flee from the inner circle was Herminio Disini, who ran off to Switzerland and then Austria, leaving $657 million in debts. U.S. Ambassador Stephen Bosworth told Manila reporters later that, to his knowledge, wealthy Philippine entrepreneurs had salted at least $10 billion abroad by 1984, and if only half that sum was returned, the country would not need any additional loans from the World Bank. Another crony to hit the road was Manuel Elizalde of the rum distilling family, who also fled to Costa Rica. He had become famous for exploiting the discovery of the Stone Age Tasaday on the island of Mindanao, which was prominently featured in *National Geographic* and *Life* magazine. Only a few international celebrities were ever allowed to see the Tasaday. The whole thing was subsequently alleged to be a hoax, with Elizalde dolling up primitive tribespeople to act stone-age.

After two years hiding in Central America and the Caribbean, Dewey Dee surfaced at Vancouver in December 1982, bearing a Costa Rican passport. He told the Canadian government he had been merely a front man for Marcos, and now feared for his life. He was given sanctuary as a refugee. No official request was made for his extradition. The Dee affair, like the Stonehill scandal, was so murky, and involved so many people close to Ferdinand, that a serious investigation would only have caused more trouble. There was also speculation that Dee and Elizalde had been feeding inside information to the CIA and had fled in the face of exposure.

Ferdinand had a lot to hide because he was desperately ill. The disease lupus, which had afflicted him for many years without being identified, had finally taken its toll on his kidneys and had been diagnosed correctly. He urgently needed a transplant of his right kidney, but it was delayed repeatedly because of the pressure of events.

Ferdinand had been suffering unexplained ailments since August 1942, when he spent five months bedridden in a guerrilla camp with a mysterious fever and stomach pains. But for thirty years his doctors did not recognize the disease—they always thought it was something else. Before he married Imelda, Ferdinand had his appendix removed because of the chronic severe pain around his right kidney. When he was elected president in 1965, he still suffered acute pain, but told people that shrapnel had lodged near his liver. Then, he became convinced that the pain came from gallstones. An American doctor refused to agree with that diagnosis, but was ignored. In 1971, the correct diagnosis finally was made, and kept secret. Ferdinand would not give up the presidency, so he did not want his enemies to know he had an incurable disease that might prove fatal. Secretly, he began seeing kidney specialists. A doctor from the Philippines who mentioned this to a colleague in America in 1973 predicted even then that President

Marcos would not live more than a year or two.

By 1978, visitors to Malacanang noticed that the president found it difficult to rise from his chair without help. In 1979, his ill health became obvious even to TV viewers. Lupus gets its name from a rash that looks like the skin damage when humans are attacked by wolves. Ferdinand's rash was explained as an allergy; his puffy face and arthritic fingers were not acknowledged. He alternated between alertness and intense fatigue. Bouts of slurred speech and paranoia made it necessary periodically for him to go into seclusion. During a severe attack, he was unable to handle affairs of state. He had always been a cunning and skillful politician; the illness made him heavy-handed and sullen.

The effects came and went. When the disease was in remission, Ferdinand put on a display of good health, had videotapes made and photos taken, though he was undergoing kidney dialysis every four days. Across front pages and TV screens his press aides splashed pictures of him engaged in rigorous physical activity. He posed naked from the waist up, jogging or water-skiing.

By 1980, his disease was common knowledge to the palace staff and began leaking to the press. Two American specialists were brought to Malacanang to confirm the diagnosis, and they recommended an immediate transplant no later than February 1980.

When Ferdinand told U.S. Ambassador Richard Murphy confidentially about his need for surgery, the Department of State arranged for a room at Stanford Medical Research Center with an open date, bypassing the long waiting list most people had to endure for a donor organ. Because of the pressure of events, Ferdinand kept postponing the surgery. In 1981, he "lifted" martial law to create a favorable atmosphere for a forthcoming election, although he had no intention of losing. He also restored the writ of habeas corpus, but only after he had signed two secret decrees in September 1980 and January 1981 called the Public Safety Act and the National Security Act, which empowered him to order arrests, shut down the media, and suspend habeas corpus any time he wished. These decrees also granted him, his cabinet, and certain other public officials immunity from prosecution for any official acts performed during the martial law period. During the election Ferdinand was highly visible on television, taking advantage of videotapes made when he felt good. He let Imelda do most of the campaigning. As expected, he won.

But his right kidney was giving out. In the summer of 1982 there was a medical crisis and he was hospitalized. A state visit to the United States, planned for mid-September, nearly was canceled. He was able to proceed only when two dialysis machines were installed in the Philippine Embassy in Washington. During the visit, Ferdinand disappeared frequently, leaving Imelda in charge of matters of state. Among his friends there was speculation that he might die at any moment, and a power struggle began for the succession.

The Reagan White House and the State Department helped maintain the ruse that nothing was wrong. Certain American journalists cooperated, deriding the lupus reports as mere gossip. But in August 1983 Ferdinand again went into deep seclusion. People who saw him then said his deterioration was dramatic. The disease was affecting his brain. Subordinates began making more of the decisions.

He underwent the first transplant that August at the Kidney Center in Manila. It was a failure—his immune system rejected the new organ. Ferdinand's recovery was in grave doubt.

At this extremely delicate point, Ninoy Aquino returned from exile. This was the moment that Aquino and anti-Marcos factions in the CIA and State Department had been waiting for. Ferdinand was so sick that he was in no condition to orchestrate countermeasures. Nobody knew how his subordinates or Imelda would respond in Ferdinand's absence—there was a possibility that they would be immobilized. The risks in not acting were even greater. President Marcos might die at any moment, leaving the palace to Ver and Imelda. If Aquino was back in the islands, he could provide a popular centrist rallying point for the opposition.

There were essentially two factions in Washington: a conservative group that had regained leverage with the election of President Reagan, and pockets of liberals remaining from the presidency of Jimmy Carter who held influential positions in the State Department, Pentagon, and CIA. They were not arrayed against each other like rugby teams, but as time passed, it became apparent that officials in Washington were first influencing events one way, then the other.

As early as July 1983, General Ver, who was on intimate terms with William Casey's shadowy right-wing Enterprise, became suspicious that others in the Agency wanted Ferdinand out, and particularly wanted to get rid of Ver. Cynically or not, they planned to use Ninoy Aquino as a means to speed the process. It was not unusual for the Agency to have seemingly contradictory conspiracies under way simultaneously.

In fact, it is the norm, just as the Agency may slip money to all contenders in a political campaign. Whatever the outcome, the CIA can claim credit for its prescience. According to Colonel Balbino Diego, head of the legal division of Ver's Presidential Security Command, the CIA initiative against Ver began in the summer of 1983. It was arranged that he would be invited to a Washington conference of allied security leaders from right-wing governments. The Agency had gone so far as to have Ver's air ticket booked for Friday, August 19, two days before Aquino's return. (Nobody was certain when Aquino would arrive, but Ver was keeping close track of the exiled leader's movements, and if the CIA wanted Ver to leave Manila on August 19, that was a clear signal that Aquino would arrive soon afterward.) Ver suspected that they wanted him out of the way so that if Ferdinand suffered further postoperative complications, Aquino would be in a position to shoulder Imelda aside and assume power. So the threat he posed to Imelda was greater than to Ver.

Aquino had decided months earlier, in the spring of 1983, to return to the islands. A new election was scheduled for the rubber-stamp national assembly and he planned (even if it was from a prison cell) to help rally the opposition. The First Lady was on a shopping trip to New York City in May 1983, and Aquino went to see her. Afterward Imelda said Aquino told her his Harvard University grant was about to expire and his heart bypass was clogging up. She quoted him as saying, "My days are numbered. My time is up. I want to go home."

She warned him not to return. "We have many loyal followers," she said. "They might think that if they killed you, they'd be doing us a favor." Later, Aquino was also warned by Defense Minister Juan Ponce Enrile that he should delay his return because Enrile could not guarantee his safety.

These were ominous portents, but when he learned that Ferdinand had undergone the first transplant and was in critical condition, Aquino decided to take the gamble, and began the long journey home. To obscure his exact plans, he flew first to Tokyo, then to Hong Kong and Singapore. His passport had expired, but he had obtained a blank one (he claimed it came from a sympathetic Philippine Embassy official in Washington). From Singapore, he crossed the causeway to the state of Johore in Malaysia to visit a friend, and spent a night in Kuala Lumpur. There, to throw Ver off, Filipino Muslim dissidents gave him a false passport in another name, and on Friday, August 19, Aquino flew out for Taipei on the last leg. Transitting Hong Kong's Kai Tak Airport, he switched to his new Filipino passport, with the name Marcial Bonifacio. ("Marcial" a pun for martial law, "Bonifacio" the prison where he spent so many years.)

A group of journalists assembled in Taipei to escort Aquino home. One was Ken Kashiwahara, Aquino's brother-in-law, a veteran TV reporter based in San Francisco. The night before boarding their plane to Manila, Aquino and Kashiwahara were talking in a room at the Grand Hotel overlooking Taipei. Aquino said, "I just got a report from Manila. I may get hit at the airport when I land, and then they will hit the hit man. That's why I'm going to wear this"—he held up a bulletproof vest. "But you know," he went on, "if they get me in the head, I'm a goner."

Aquino and ten journalists, plus two Japanese television crews, boarded China Airlines Flight 811 at Chiang Kai-shek Airport. He spent the flight talking with the reporters, putting on his bulletproof vest, and saying his rosary as the plane began its descent to Manila. Aquino had planned the Sunday arrival (the twelfth anniversary of the Plaza Miranda bombings) so that more people could come to the airport to greet him. The plane landed at 1:05 P.M. In the terminal there was a welcoming crowd of ten thousand, complete with a band playing "Tie a Yellow Ribbon."

Other people were waiting for him as well. By the previous day, all of them knew when he was arriving, and on which aircraft. Tourism Minister Jose Aspiras, one of the men closest to Imelda, had exchanged cables with the China Airlines office in Taipei and knew every detail. Certain people in the regime seemed to make it a point to absent themselves. Imelda Marcos was having a very long and highly visible lunch with friends at the Via Mare seafood restaurant near the Cultural Center. Fabian Ver was out of sight at secret police headquarters in Fort Bonifacio. Defense Minister Enrile was playing golf at Wack Wack. With President Marcos recovering from surgery, Enrile at the links, and Imelda out to lunch, the levers of government were being worked by Fabian Ver, Tourism Minister Aspiras, Information Minister Gregorio Cendana, and top crony Eduardo Cojuangco, plus the generals loyal to Ver who were commanding the main security forces. Since around 6:00 A.M., Cendana and Aspiras had been at the airport, waiting. Cojuangco hovered nearby.

Something peculiar was going on. U.S. Air Force radar operators at two air-defense installations on Luzon were abruptly replaced by a full battle staff of Filipinos. When an American sergeant asked what was happening, the Filipino officer in charge told him, "Blow off—it's none of your business." This involved internal affairs, he added. Two fully armed Filipino F-5 jet fighters were scrambled to find Aquino's airliner and force it down at Basa Air Base, 35 miles north of Manila, but it was cloudy and they could not find it. The Filipino ground radar operators took over the hunt. A second flight of F-5 fighters was scrambled to try again. They also failed. The fifth ranking officer in the Philippine Air Force, Colonel Umberto Capawan, was in charge of the main control room at Villamor Air Base next to Manila International Airport. He was a member of Fabian Ver's inner circle. At Wallace Air Station north of Manila, a U.S. Air Force major asked his American superior what was happening. The superior answered, "We think we know what's going on." He did not elaborate.

When the China Airlines flight landed at Manila International and rolled up to the landing bay at Gate 8, one thousand soldiers from the Metropolitan Command (METROCOM) were in positions around the airport and on the tarmac. A blue van from the Aviation Security Command (AVSECOM) drew up and disgorged another group of soldiers, who took up positions around the front part of the CAL plane. When its left front door was opened and joined to the accordian chute feeding into Gate 8, three uniformed security men in shirtsleeves climbed aboard—two from AVSECOM and one from METROCOM. They took Aquino by the arms, felt to see if he wore body armor, then hustled him off the plane, preventing any journalists from accompanying them.

Instead of proceeding straight down the tunnel to the terminal, where other journalists were waiting, the three security men steered Aquino through a side door and down metal stairs leading to the tarmac. A government press aide working for Cendana immediately blocked the doorway so the journalists scrambling off the plane could not see down the ladder. Before Aquino's feet could touch Philippine soil, a shot rang out. One of the three security men escorting Aquino down the steps had shot him in the back of the head at point-blank range. Inside the blue van, other security men quickly picked up the dead body of Rolando Galman and threw it onto the tarmac next to Aquino's still form. These soldiers immediately began firing bullets into Galman, as if they were just now killing him. Galman had been dead quite a while. He was now lying on his stomach, but there was dried blood from earlier bullet holes running the opposite direction, uphill, indicating that he had been lying on his back when he was actually killed. The Marcos government would announce that Galman had appeared at the aircraft from nowhere and had murdered Aquino as part of a Communist conspiracy, and only then had Galman been slain by the security men "protecting" Aquino.

Immediately after the murder, Aspiras and Cendana were said to have driven straight to the Via Mare seafood restaurant by the Cultural Center to inform Imelda. Joined by Fabian Ver, Eduardo Cojuangco, and others, they all proceeded to the room where Ferdinand Marcos was recuperating from his surgery. According to one of those present, when he was told what had been done, Ferdinand exploded in anger, seized a small dish from the bedside table, and threw it at Ver, saying: "You fools, they will all blame me."

Many people immediately recognized that the Aquino murder did not have the hallmarks of a Marcos operation. If Ferdinand had been running things, the theory goes, Aquino would have been taken into custody at Manila Airport and escorted to Ver's headquarters at Fort Bonifacio. Whether he would have had Aquino killed then is a subject for conjecture. But if he had decided to dispose of his rival, it would have been more in character to announce that Aquino had suffered a heart attack because his clogged bypass could not handle the excitement of coming home, and he died on the way to a hospital. President Marcos, many argued, was much too clever to have Aquino shot in broad daylight as he stepped off a plane full of journalists. There was something hysterical about the way it had been done. (A source in MI6 chose the word "barmy.") Ferdinand might be many things, but he was neither an hysteric nor a fool.

Thirty hours after the Aquino assassination, the president appeared on television, looking frail and ill. He called the killing a "barbaric act" and said he had "practically begged Aquino not to come home." He said Aquino ignored these warnings "on the advice of some of his more influential persons [sic] and on his own judgment." Ferdinand asserted rather lamely that no government officials, military men, or soldiers were involved in the shooting, and that the assassin was a lone gunman (Galman), hired either by the Communists or someone acting out of revenge. He ridiculed the widespread suggestions that Imelda had played a role. (Manila street gossip had it that she had insisted upon Aquino being slain before his feet touched the ground. Some theorists claimed that was the only way to comprehend the peculiar timing.) The bitter joke immediately swept Manila that, according to President Marcos, Aquino had shot Galman, then committed suicide.

There were eyewitnesses, photographs, tape recordings, and videotapes which, taken together, would prove beyond reasonable doubt that the man who shot Aquino was one of his three military escorts. Ueda Katsuo of Kyodo News Service watched from a plane window. "I heard a pop and saw Aquino fall down on the runway. . . . Then I looked up and saw a man who had appeared from the side of the truck." The man stood in front of Aquino, not behind, and his hands were empty. Aquino had been shot from behind and above, on the ladder, a position occupied only by his military escorts. The bullet entered behind his ear at a downward angle. Another Japanese journalist, Wakamiya Kiyoshi, flatly accused the Marcos government of killing Aquino. His evidence consisted of film footage, released a week later as part of a documentary analyzing videotape, film, and stills from the China Airlines flight. When Cardinal Jaime Sin saw the documentary, he said, "It is very clear. I think the commission [appointed by Ferdinand to investigate the murder] should see this and make some conclusions. Immediately you can see who was the culprit, the bullet did not come from somewhere, it came from above. So how many people were able to go up [the stairway]? Very few; maybe three including Aquino's military escorts. . . . And the assassin will be there. I don't know, but it is clear on the video. So what more [investigation is needed]?"

There were two eyewitnesses to the shooting who had yet to come forward because of fear for their own safety. One was the so-called Crying Lady, Rebecca Quijano, who later testified that she saw from her aircraft window a security man behind Aquino shooting him in the back of the head. During the Marcos-orchestrated trial, the judges pronounced her testimony "dubious." One problem with her testimony was that the aircraft's soundproofing prevented her from hearing the shot, and her reliability as a witness could be attacked because of her fragile emotional state—a result of shock and terror. In January 1988, the other eyewitness came forward: airport cargo handler Jesse Barcelona, who was driving a baggage cart to the plane when he, too, saw (and heard) the pistol fired into the nape of Aquino's neck.

In the months that followed, Ferdinand organized a complete whitewash, including a laborious investigation and rigged court proceedings against Ver and twenty-five other men, members of METRO-COM and AVSECOM. Meanwhile, Imelda had Gate 8 at Manila International remodeled, perhaps coincidentally, making it impossible for investigators to reconstruct the crime at the site. During the trial, Ferdinand made the gesture of suspending Ver temporarily from his posts as security chief and armed forces chief-of-staff. The United States tried repeatedly to persuade him to dump Ver permanently, to conduct the trial fairly, or at least not to reinstate Ver whatever the outcome of the trial. It is one of the fascinating aspects of America's love affair with Ferdinand Marcos that Washington was able to isolate Ver as an ogre, and Imelda as an eccentric, while refusing to acknowledge Ferdinand's ultimate responsibility in shaping their behavior.

Washington also failed to assign degrees of culpability to others in the inner circle such as Eduardo Cojuangco. More effort was made to muddle the situation than to clarify it. Various attempts were made by Washington to bring pressure to bear on the court, including the disclosure of affidavits from U.S. Air Force personnel revealing that the two flights of F-5 jet fighters had been scrambled to force Aquino's plane down at one of the bases controlled by Ver. That it took nearly two years for the Department of State to release these affidavits indicates the intensity of the factional conflict going on in Washington. The Reagan White House was doing everything it could to block any revelations that might damage Ferdinand's position.

All else aside, the Aquino murder proved beyond doubt that Ferdinand Marcos was no longer fully in command. Whether he died in office or retired to make way for a chosen successor, the palace was about to change hands, and prospects for the future were not good. A Manila businessman who was a close friend of the president, management consultant David Sycip, told Ferdinand, "It's not the assassination that's causing trouble, but the perception that it would not have happened if you weren't sick and losing control."

If Washington thought it was going to be easy to defang General Ver, they miscalculated. So long as he was both de facto army chief-of-staff and secret police boss, he was backed by a long string of Ilocano generals, colonels, and majors personally loyal to him and to President Marcos, and it would be difficult to force the outcome of the succession struggle without neutralizing them.

Just before his fatal trip to Manila in 1983, Ninoy Aquino had made some predictions. He gave two succession scenarios when he testified before the Committee on Foreign Affairs in the House of Representatives in June 1983. The first scenario predicted that Marcos wanted a collective leadership to succeed him, with Bong-Bong as heir apparent and Imelda as regent.

He said Ferdinand was preparing to establish a dynasty along the Somoza model, and this was the reason he had recalled his son from the University of Pennsylvania, before graduation, and made him governor of Ilocos Norte. The incumbent governor, Bong-Bong's aunt Elizabeth, had to retire because of Alzheimer's disease.

During the reign of Imelda and Bong-Bong, there would be a support structure of technocrats and military dominated by General Ver. In time, a second scenario would unfold, and Imelda would be "retired" for her own good, accompanied by a full military takeover attributed to the Communist menace. With Bong-Bong as figurehead, Ver would promise to hold elections "when order has been restored."

The star of the first scenario was Imelda. But she had been getting increasingly bad reviews. She had been a popular campaigner during Ferdinand's rise to power. But with martial law, and her more astonishing spending sprees, her increasingly bizarre private life and public statements, Imelda's popularity had declined sharply and she had come to be regarded as "the madwoman of Malacanang." Image was for her a matter of obsessive concern. In 1979, the Manila *Bulletin* Sunday magazine, *Panorama,* ran a poll on who was the most admired citizen in the country. Before the results could be trucked to newsstands, Malacanang ordered distribution halted. President Marcos had placed first, but Imelda was furious. She came in behind Jesus Christ, Ninoy Aquino, and Jose Maria Sison, the imprisoned chairman of the Communist party of the Philippines.

Talk of Imelda ruling as regent gained momentum after Ferdinand told an American television interviewer that his wife would not succeed him, but "the person who does succeed me will need her support— otherwise he will not succeed." Filipinos interpreted the remark to mean that Bong-Bong would rule with his mother as regent, the power behind the throne. Imelda had once said, "I would be a hypocrite if I said I did not wish [Bong-Bong] would someday be president. Every mother has a legitimate right to wish success for her children." She elaborated: "I try to keep Bong-Bong close to his father, so he will learn much. He went with his father to the opening of the Chamber of Agriculture and rode on a tractor. He went with his father to Fort Magsaysay and rode on a helicopter. He's learning judo now, and swimming, and horseback riding." He was learning to reign if not to rule.

Ferdinand Romualdez "Bong-Bong" Marcos was at the time of the Aquino murder trial twenty-five years old. By all accounts a spoiled child, he was packed off to school first in England and later in the United States. One of Imelda's Filipino biographers wrote, "His every whim and wish was granted, despite warnings from a stern, candid English headmaster who wrote that he would be ill-equipped for the rigors of serious academic work if he never learned the meaning of the word 'no.'" Imelda liked to imply that Bong-Bong finished at Oxford, but he did not finish at the University of Pennsylvania either. He was a perennial adolescent who liked guns, girls, and hanging out with General Ver's son, Irwin, who was his frequent companion and bodyguard. During a trip to America, Bong-Bong was stopped for speeding in New Jersey and state troopers discovered a loaded gun lying on the passenger seat. Charges were dropped because Bong-Bong had diplomatic immunity.

To enhance his prestige as heir apparent, Bong-Bong was named chairman of the telecommunications corporation Philcomsat, and was liberal in using its money. During the last three months of the Marcos regime, he withdrew $500,000 in corporate funds. The high point of Bong-Bong's career as crown prince was when President Nixon promised that he would be the first Filipino on the moon.

Of his two sisters, only Imee, the eldest, had a flair for public life. There was speculation that if Bong-Bong needed more than ten years of Imelda's regency to mature, Imee might succeed her mother. Apparently a bright student, she attended Princeton University during the 1970s. Her parents provided a luxurious estate off campus. Under the guise of protecting Imee, General Ver was able to send a number of agents to America to keep an eye on anti-Marcos exiles. Her college expenses were paid from public funds through the Philippine National Bank. Imee was given a portfolio of investments through the Marcos Foundation. For political exposure, she "won" a seat in the puppet national assembly. To gain administrative experience, she headed a youth group that deified the Marcos family with Nazi-style midnight ceremonies. To prove she was her own person, she led anti-U.S. demonstrations outside the embassy.

Imelda cherished hopes of marrying Imee to Prince Charles. As an alternative, she tried to marry her to the son of banana king Antonio Floirendo, but this dream soured when the boy married someone else. Imee took matters into her own hands and eloped with Tomas

"Tommy" Manotoc, an amateur golfer and professional basketball coach, who had divorced his first wife six weeks earlier after ten years of marriage and two children. His divorce occurred in the Dominican Republic, and was not legal in the Philippines. He and Imee were married on December 4, 1981, in a civil ceremony at Arlington, Virginia. When the couple reappeared in Manila, Imelda was beside herself with rage. Aside from his divorce, Tommy's maternal aunts were married to none other than Raul Manglapus and Eugenio Lopez, both hated adversaries of the Marcos regime. Tommy's older brother had married the daughter of another adversary, conservative opposition leader Eva Kalaw.

Ferdinand seemed reconciled to the event. But according to Manotoc, Imelda went "berserk"—he said he had never been abused so violently. Because she refused to recognize the marriage, the couple temporarily was obliged to live apart. On December 29, Tommy disappeared. The next day, palace officials telephoned the Manotoc family to reassure them that the armed forces were in on the search. Lieutenant General Fidel Ramos told the press that a ransom note had been delivered. The Manotocs themselves pointed the finger at Malacanang. Six weeks later, Tommy reappeared. At a press conference presided over by Enrile and attended by Ver, Tommy said he had been kidnapped by Communists and held in a mountain hideout until he was rescued by the army. He insisted there was nothing to allegations that he had been kidnapped on orders from Imelda. Eventually, Imelda resigned herself to the match.

Irene, the youngest, was the most docile of the children, the chubby baby of the family. She studied music and kept a low profile. When she traveled abroad, General Ver's son Rexan was her regular bodyguard. In June 1983, Irene married Gregorio Araneta III, the stepson of Napoleon Valeriano. Imelda reportedly spent $20 million in government funds to create a royal wedding in Grandmother Josefa's hometown of Sarrat. The little town was turned upside down. She transformed the local church into a cathedral, laid on twenty-four additional Philippine Airline flights, and ferried the eighty-six-piece Philippine Philharmonic Orchestra to Sarrat. With help from Kurt Waldheim of Austria and King Hassan of Morocco, she imported a silver carriage from Vienna and seven white Arab stallions from Rabat for the bride's ride to the church.

Two months later an earthquake hit the Ilocos, killing twenty and demolishing the church. Local people took it as an omen.

After the wedding, Greggie Araneta was set up in business, including a corporation in San Francisco called Saddle Trading, with fat contracts from the Philippine government. The firm made handsome profits by selling everything to Manila at a 25 percent markup.

There was another member of the Marcos dynasty, a child named Aimee, variously identified as a grandchild or a niece. Family portraits include Aimee along with Imelda, Bong-Bong, Irene, and Imee. Her exact origin was never disclosed, but she was to play the role of ingenue in the last act.

Twenty-one

PEOPLE POWER

AS ANXIETY GREW about Ferdinand's ability to control the outcome, American officials and unofficials came to Manila thick and fast. Indiana Senator Richard Lugar, head of the Committee on Foreign Relations, sent a member of his staff, Frederick Brown, to Manila during the first two weeks of August 1985 to evaluate the deteriorating situation. Brown had separate audiences with Ferdinand and Imelda, Lieutenant General Fidel Ramos, Cardinal Sin, and Eduardo Cojuangco. He reported that Imelda and Ferdinand seemed to be

> living in a fantasy world where the president has full possession of his physical powers and enjoys the overwhelming support of his people. . . . There appeared to be a conviction that nothing more than the tactical, manipulative style of the past two decades is needed to meet the challenges of the present. . . . There was an aura of permanence of power, which seemed bizarre. . . . Marcos believes that he enjoys the support of the highest levels of the Executive branch of the U.S. government. Congress may huff and puff, Assistant Secretaries may harass him. . . . But in the end, he believes the U.S. will not pull its support.

Brown concluded that one of the few promising developments in Manila was the emergence of RAM, the Reform the Army Movement.

Over the years, Ferdinand had larded the officer corps with thousands of his own henchmen, and had corrupted the rank-and-file by using them to rig elections, to beat up or intimidate honest opponents, and to arrest, torture, and execute dissidents of all persuasions. Stubborn defenders of the army insisted that only the Muslims and the Communist-led NPA committed atrocities; the army itself could do no wrong. Critics of the army pointed out numerous examples of atrocities, not only during field operations but during elections, and not only among particular units like Cojuangco's paramilitary Monkees or the Constabulary's 5th CSU that specialized in torture. Although the size of the NPA was greatly inflated, and the immediate danger of a Communist takeover was grossly exaggerated, a civil war was going on with revolutionary extremes, and both sides committed atrocities. The basic problem was that the very large and comparatively well-equipped Filipino Army had become so inept militarily that it could not make an impact without resorting to Lansdale-style terrorist tactics. Sadistic extremes and psychopathic behavior had been a part of the Filipino landscape for generations, but they were encouraged by the Marcos government as a means to frighten opposition. Until the time came when a protracted nationwide campaign or violent upheaval established a new ethic, these abuses would continue.

Despite the universal acceptance of brutality as normal, there were still many officers and men in the armed forces who had a conscience, commanders who endured the Marcos years grudgingly. After the declaration of martial law, a few of these men had met secretly. Most of them were professional soldiers, graduates of the Philippine Military Academy, with further training in America or Europe. They called themselves the Reform the Army Movement, RAM. It was this group that the Pentagon and CIA had fixed upon, and was covertly encouraging.

A secret strategy conference was held in Washington in October 1985 to decide what to do next. Among those who attended was retired General Edward G. Lansdale. When I asked Lansdale about the meeting, he passed it off as simply a discussion of RAM, but others who attended were more forthcoming. Discussion ranged over the whole picture of American security interests in the Far East and the Pacific, and it all boiled down to two elementary questions: Should the United States keep its military bases in the Philippines and risk becoming involved in "another Vietnam," or create alternative bases in Guam and the Yap Islands? If the U.S. bases were going to remain in the Philippines, how could control of the Filipino armed forces be shifted from General Ver and his loyalists to the Reform the Army Movement?

In any succession scenario, the Philippine military could play a decisive role. Whoever controlled the army would determine the outcome. Ver would have to be eased out, and his faction neutralized. This would be RAM's job, manipulated by the CIA through assets in and around RAM ranks.

The key military figure in the RAM scenario was Lieutenant General Fidel Ramos, head of the Constabulary and the Integrated National Police, and also vice chief-of-staff of the armed forces, who was considered a good officer, reliably pro-American.

The chief political figure in RAM was Juan Ponce Enrile, an intimate ally of President Marcos, but a vain man with political ambitions who many at the conference contended could be compromised and manipulated.

As a result of the Washington conference, the United States set into motion initiatives intended to bring new pressure on Ferdinand to dump Ver in favor of Ramos, and to quietly build RAM's numbers and prestige. Other strategies were developed to increase the visibility of Ramos, to build his reputation as an honest commander and most promising chief-of-staff, to cultivate Enrile and encourage him to take a stand.

If events could be engineered so that Enrile acted in harness with Ramos, the general could provide the spine while Enrile provided the flash.

RAM was outraged by the handling of Aquino's return, and the disgrace his murder brought to the military. Enrile's American friends began telling him that it was a pity he could not take over. With his brains, his charm, and his popularity with the armed forces, he could restore the government of the Philippines to a state of grace, win renewed confidence and backing from the United States, and regain the trust of the IMF and World Bank. Sweet talk.

If Enrile had presidential ambitions before 1984, he hid them. But in that year he began to admit in public that he would like to be president some time in the future, after Ferdinand Marcos was no longer interested in the job. The seed of an idea had been planted, and Enrile's "boys" in RAM were not going to let him forget.

From 1984 on, the search for the remainder of Yamashita's Gold was overseen by a Manila company called Nippon Star, virtually the same group of men who had run the Leber Group ten years earlier. Nippon Star was set up originally by ordinary gold seekers who failed to find anything significant. Their company was taken over by the CIA, in keeping with the Agency's practice of turning existing companies into fronts and inserting their own people.

After that, the Manila end of Nippon Star was run by Cesar Lehran of the old Leber Group, a Filipino whose allegiance was owed to Fabian Ver. The company was listed as wholly owned by Phoenix Exploration Services, Ltd., 90 Chancery Lane, London. That company, in turn, was wholly owned by Helmut Trading (apparently a play on words), registered in Liberia under a bearer stock, so its true ownership could never be traced. Associated with Nippon Star, though, was a group calling itself the Phoenix Overseas Project, understood to be one of the fronts of General Singlaub, whose American base was in Phoenix, Arizona. Whatever the case, Singlaub made use of the Nippon Star offices whenever he was in Manila. Another affiliate of Nippon Star was the Delta International Group, headed by Vernon R. Twyman of Tulsa, Oklahoma, a leader of the Praise The Lord Church and its PTL religious broadcasting network. Twyman once told Nippon Star stockholders that they had a "joint venture" arrangement with Sultan Omar Dinalan's Sod Research & Recovery of the Philippines, a friend of President Marcos and one of those involved in excavating for Yamashita's Gold since 1975 or earlier. Thus both Singlaub and Twyman were involved as private citizens with Ferdinand's gold recovery effort at least as early as 1984.

The fact that big guns of the PTL were busy in the same areas as General Singlaub and his military-intelligence associates is hardly surprising. Many American conservative activists were quite naturally also members of PTL and other fundamentalist crusades such as Moral Majority, the Reverend Moon's CAUSA, and so forth. So it is hardly surprising that activists in some of these religious groups were drawn into the search for Yamashita's Gold.

Jerry Falwell, Jimmy Swaggart, and Pat Robertson were becoming well known to Filipinos, along with the Campus Crusade for Christ, the Church of the Four Square Gospel, and others that evangelized aggressively with the direct encouragement of President Marcos. These individuals turned a blind eye to the brutality of the regime. During the Reagan administration, right-wing religious leaders were sometimes approached directly by Colonel North to participate in CIA covert operations, including funding the Contras. It was perhaps fitting that conservative religious groups were involved in the great Christian crusade for Yamashita's Gold.

While career officers in Washington were maneuvering to oust Ver, and to brace Enrile and Ramos to remove Ferdinand, a counterplot was being pursued energetically by the White House. It was the fruit of a romance Ferdinand had been conducting with American conservatives since President Carter attempted to force him to end human rights abuses and to permit the political opposition to function. On a personal level, President Reagan had a deep and abiding commitment to President Marcos that was not entirely rational.

Speaking about prospects for elections, on February 11, 1985, Reagan told *The New York Times:* "The Philippines and the U.S. certainly have a close relationship and alliance over the years, and we've had a good relationship with President Marcos. Now, we realize there is an opposition party that we believe is also pledged to democracy.... What we're hopeful of is that the democratic processes will take place, and even if there is a change of party there, it would be that opposition faction which is still democratic in its principles."

It was a curious statement. There had never been anything remotely democratic about the Marcos regime, and the relationship between Ferdinand and the U.S. government had not been "good" since President Johnson bribed him in 1966. That is, it had been neither wholesome nor constructive, neither friendly nor amiable. But in terms of covert operations such as fake end-user certificates and secret disbursements of gold, it had been useful. As for Marcos's political opposition, Reagan seemed to regard them with the same visceral loathing that General MacArthur had evinced.

On August 13, 1985, those same democratic opposition leaders of whom Reagan spoke formally tried to impeach President Marcos. As the basis for impeachment, they cited reports that he had made huge, secret investments overseas. These charges were not dreamed up in Manila, but stemmed from discoveries then being made by congressional investigators in America, under the auspices of New York Congressman Stephen Solarz and others. But the impeachment effort was premature and failed. The CIA had been reporting to the White House for seventeen years—at least since 1968—that Ferdinand was looting his country of billions, much of it from various forms of U.S. aid. President Carter had been informed of this, but Reagan seemed wholly ignorant. In his own defense, Reagan once remarked that when he went to Manila the first time, as governor of California, to attend the opening of Imelda's Cultural Center, he had been told that Marcos made his millions before he became president.

While the 1985 impeachment campaign failed, the CIA effort to inspire Juan Ponce Enrile at last showed signs of succeeding. Enrile and RAM were actively plotting to seize power. Ferdinand was deteriorating so rapidly that there were long periods when he posed no serious impediment to a coup. So long as he remained an invalid, Ver had to seek his approval for all major decisions. The target date for the RAM coup was set for 2:00 A.M. Christmas morning, 1985, or alternatively a week later at 2:00 A.M. New Year's Day, 1986. The scenario called for four hundred RAM commandos to slip up the Pasig River to storm Malacanang from the rear, overcoming the Presidential Security Command. Other RAM units would take the main radio and TV stations. It was expected that General Fidel Ramos would join them, bringing with him other units of the armed forces for a showdown with Ver.

Enrile had been building the nucleus of his own private army in his home territory of Cagayan Valley. New recruits were trained on an island off Cagayan that Enrile used as a private retreat. They could be rushed to Manila by helicopter to join any operation RAM started.

According to this scenario, a RAM junta would form a new government, with Enrile as its political leader and Ramos heading the armed forces. Elections would be held two to five years later. Enrile then would be the junta's candidate for president.

The RAM plot was actively encouraged by U.S. intelligence officers, but it was almost stymied by President Reagan's stubborn conviction that Ferdinand Marcos must remain in power. Assistant secretaries of defense including Richard Armitage and Richard Perle warned Congress that the New People's Army was going through a period of explosive growth, putting it in a position to seize power, jeopardizing U.S. bases and other interests in the islands. This was simply not true, but it served to alarm conservative leaders about the urgent need to make changes of some kind in Manila. If Ferdinand Marcos was no longer competent, and his chosen successors were either sinister or eccentric, something had to be done. President Reagan seemed to agree in principle, but by all accounts was adamant that Ferdinand himself must remain.

On October 10, 1985, Senator Paul Laxalt was sent to Manila as Reagan's personal emissary to talk with Marcos. His visit was the culmination of a series of discreet White House warnings. Laxalt cautioned Ferdinand directly against fully reinstating Ver and warned him about what the Reagan White House liked to refer to ominously as "the growing Communist insurgency"—meaning, essentially, the growing middle-class opposition to Ferdinand. Laxalt eventually published an account of this trip, using the murky language politicians resort to when they are amending history:

> My mission . . . was to communicate President Reagan's concerns about the future of the Philippines. The President was concerned about the general political instability . . . and whether President Marcos still enjoyed the support of the people. . . . These concerns had already been expressed to President Marcos through repeated contacts by our State Department people and others. But President Marcos apparently believed that they were just the musings of the bureaucracy, and not really the views of President Reagan. So the President decided to send me as a personal emissary. I delivered President Marcos a handwritten letter from President Reagan.

It may be true, as Laxalt claimed, that Reagan was asking Ferdinand to compromise on the replacement of Ver as army chief-of-staff, but Reagan was certainly not demanding Ver's complete removal from power, nor did he do so even at the crunch six months later. Reagan's views, as we shall see, remained to the bitter end firmly in favor of a deal with Ferdinand. Laxalt's version therefore smacks of historical revision. Nancy and Ronald Reagan were both personal friends of Imelda and Ferdinand, and spoke often on the telephone, a friendship that the Marcoses cultivated assiduously.

The next day, Laxalt and Ambassador Bosworth met Marcos again, this time with General Ramos in attendance. Laxalt later stated that it was at this meeting that he first broached the idea of Ferdinand calling a snap presidential election, earlier than the one scheduled routinely for 1987, to demonstrate that he still had the popular support he claimed. However, CIA director William Casey was the first to suggest this to Ferdinand, not Laxalt. One interpretation since given to the snap election proposal is that it was a cunning trick to lure Ferdinand into a confrontation, in which his domestic and foreign enemies could embarrass him and jerk the rug from under his feet. This may have been the hope of some elements in the State Department and CIA, but there is no real evidence that Reagan, Laxalt, or Casey had that in mind. Rather, what the Reagan inner circle was proposing was that Ferdinand disarm his liberal critics in America by staging another sham election. (After all, weren't sham elections how the democratic process worked in the Philippines?) In the event, both Marcos and Reagan were dumbfounded by the consequences.

On November 3, 1985, after brooding about the proposal, Ferdinand agreed and announced the snap election, fully confident that he would win—as was the White House. The election date was set for three months hence, February 7, 1986. This would settle the preposterous claim that his government was inept, corrupt, and unpopular.

His announcement took everyone by surprise. Enrile and RAM decided to put their coup plot on the back burner until they saw the outcome.

Nine days later, the Moral Majority's Reverend Jerry Falwell arrived in Manila. It was portrayed as an informal visit, but Falwell was accorded unusually heavy coverage by the U.S. press. This was not the first time President Reagan made use of unofficial emissaries to pat Ferdinand on the back. With Falwell was a delegation of twelve conservative American business and political leaders, including Thomas Boatwright, a former U.S. ambassador; former Congressman John Mackie; retired U.S. Air Force General Tom Meredith; and international lawyer Hans Nathan who, curiously enough, was one of the defense attorneys in the ongoing multi-million-dollar tax suit that the Internal Revenue Service brought against Harry Stonehill. (Depositions had been taken over the years from scores of Marcos intimates in the Philippines and Taiwan, and the case was still in litigation in America twenty-five years after Stonehill was deported from the islands and subsequently disappeared.)

Falwell's stay was spent in the close company of Ferdinand and Imelda. He was escorted everywhere by Ver's security men. Falwell told Manila reporters that it was time for American policymakers (Congress and the State Department) to stop "bellyaching." He criticized the U.S. press for its "unfair" treatment of Ferdinand, and for giving the impression that Manila was some kind of "war zone." He added, "Sure, there are troublemakers here. We have them in the United States too. It's unreal that tourism has almost dried up here because of that kind of fear, when in fact this is a paradise." Parroting what he had been told by Imelda and Ferdinand, Falwell said that if the Philippines fell to the Communists, "forget it—there will never be another election and neither the United States nor anybody else will ever, ever, liberate the country." He added that he "felt a lot safer in Manila than New York or Washington."

Falwell might have regretted his words if he had known that a few days earlier Dr. Potenciano Baccay, one of President Marcos's kidney doctors, had been brutally murdered, evidently by the same people who were showing Falwell's group such a good time—Ver's men. Ferdinand's first transplant operation in August 1983, the time of the Aquino murder, had been a failure, and by Christmas of that year, surviving on one diseased kidney, he was desperate enough to consult a faith healer. In mid-November 1984, Ferdinand once again disappeared from sight. Rumors spread that he had been hospitalized secretly to replace the failed transplanted kidney. Information Minister Cendana labeled the stories "simply preposterous." It was also rumored that, to reduce the danger of the transplant being rejected, Ferdinand insisted that the organ donor be his sister, Elizabeth, who was dying of Alzheimer's disease. According to medical scuttlebutt in Manila, Elizabeth was in no position to disagree.

When Ferdinand later learned from Ver that someone in his own circle had leaked absolute confirmation of the second transplant to the CIA, he ordered Ver to find the leak and silence it. There were only a few people who could have provided such confirmation. Ver already knew that there had been no leak to the CIA, only to an American reporter. But he was waging a single-minded campaign to inflame Ferdinand toward the Agency.

He knew that one month before Falwell's visit, in October 1985, Dr. Baccay and Dr. Enrique Ona, director of transplantation at Manila's National Kidney Center, had been indiscreet during a conversation with a reporter from *The Pittsburgh Press*. They told the reporter that President Marcos had undergone two kidney transplants at the Kidney Center in Manila, the first in August 1983, the second in November 1984. "Mike" Baccay, a nephrologist at the Kidney Center, added that the surgeon who did the first transplant was Dr. G. Baird Helfrich, director of Renal Transplants at Georgetown Medical Center. When that transplant had been rejected, a second transplant had been performed by Dr. Barry Kahan, director of transplantation for Herrmann Hospital in Houston, with the help of a new drug to suppress the body's resistance to an alien organ.

In the first week of November 1985, Ver's men struck. Mike Baccay was abducted from his home in full view of his family, by men lying in wait for his return. The doctor was found a short time later in his blood-soaked van, with nearly a hundred stab wounds. The "Death of a Thousand Cuts"—an East Asian specialty—is administered first to the extremities, working up to the torso and the vital organs, to maximize pain and extract information. Brigadier General Alfredo Yson, district police chief of Muntinglupa, the suburb where Dr. Baccay lived, and one of Ver's inner circle, announced that the physician was a victim of "a gang robbery," as evidenced by some valuables and household items left in the van. Other police sources disputed this, asking, if it was a robbery, why were the stolen articles abandoned, and why had the thieves waited for Baccay, abducted, and tortured him?

On December 2, 1985, the Aquino trial formally ended in the acquittal of General Ver and all twenty-five other defendants; the court found that Galman, working alone, slipped through a cordon of more than one thousand soldiers to shoot Aquino as he came down the ramp. Evidence that Galman had been killed some time earlier was ignored. Ferdinand immediately reinstated Ver as army chief-of-staff. Protest demonstrations began throughout Manila. The verdict was condemned by Cardinal Sin and other prominent Filipinos. In a carefully minced statement reflecting its two minds, the Reagan administration said it was very difficult to reconcile the verdict with the finding of a separate citizens' panel, which had blamed Ver and others. Members of the U.S. Congress condemned the trial as a mockery of justice.

The following day, Aquino's widow, Corazon, announced her candidacy for president. Opposition parties united under her banner. As the campaign warmed up, Doy Laurel put aside his own presidential ambitions to be her running mate, uniting the opposition. Ferdinand announced that his running mate would be Senator Arturo Tolentino. A one-time reformer, in recent years Tolentino had lost his spark and was given the cruel and doubtless unfair nickname "Jukebox"—"Put a few coins in," the joke went, "and he'll play any tune you want."

Liberals in Washington struck a blow in December when a congressional committee began hearings into allegations that Imelda and Ferdinand had accumulated major real estate holdings in America.

Except for brief appearances in which his features were puffy and jaundiced, and he had to be carried onto the stage seated in his throne chair, Ferdinand left the campaigning to Tolentino. Since his second kidney transplant, he had lost control of his bladder and had to suffer the humiliation of wearing diapers. (His favorite brand: Pampers.) Even with the diapers, there were accidents. During televised news conferences from his offices at Malacanang, in the closing weeks before the snap election, he was carefully rigged behind an ornate desk, with only the upper part of his body showing on camera. These news conferences were attended by diplomatic observers from various embassies. A military attaché told me he found the spectacle excruciating: "There the poor bastard was, lying into the camera, all the time trying desperately not to pee into his own shoes."

When Ver was reinstated as chief-of-staff and security boss, he began working on Ferdinand with renewed vigor, doctoring intelligence reports to convince his boss that the CIA had penetrated even his cabinet. Ver retouched a wire service story, which quoted Senator John Stennis saying that some U.S. congressmen thought the CIA should have Marcos assassinated. Before sending it to Ferdinand, Ver rephrased it to say that Stennis, a Reagan supporter, was urging that Marcos be assassinated.

As February 1986 approached, and the fifty-seven-day campaign neared its end, Cory Aquino held a rally of 1 million people in Manila. Senior Marcos supporters acknowledged for the first time that he might be defeated. The same realization occurred to Ferdinand. He reversed his earlier public assurances that the armed forces would remain in their barracks during the voting, and now said the army would guard polling places and municipal and provincial points where tallies would be transmitted. In retaliation, NAMFREL announced plans to post monitors at all polling places to check tampering. Senator Richard Lugar and foreign observers representing many countries arrived in Manila to act as watchdogs. Cardinal Sin let it be known that he thought Mrs. Aquino would make a good president.

On February 7, there was a heavy turnout of the nation's 26 million voters. Poll watchers reported extraordinary harassment and intimidation, the theft of voter lists and ballot boxes, and the flying of voters from district to district to cast multiple ballots. Most foreign observers saw and heard about widespread fraud, vote tampering, and violence by Ferdinand's followers. One of my colleagues spent a night in an army "safe house" in one of the outlying provinces, and found it stacked from wall to wall with fake ballot boxes loaded with bogus ballots, waiting for army distribution on election day.

General Ramos later acknowledged publicly that Ver supplied guns to thugs directed by Roberto Benedicto, Eduardo Cojuangco, and Kokoy Romualdez. Enrile, playing his usual game of mixed doubles, provided 350,000 bogus ballots for President Marcos from his stronghold of Cagayan Valley.

Returns were monitored by the official government Committee on Elections, COMELEC, but women who were punching the results into computers said the tallies were being modified electronically by Marcos programmers. To counter this, nuns guarded the ballot boxes at each poll, clutching them in their arms, defying soldiers in full battle dress, and initial counts at each poll were phoned to Manila and broadcast on Church Radio, before they could be altered. Something of a landslide was taking place, but not for Ferdinand Marcos. The opposition was jubilant.

"The people and I have won!" declared Cory Aquino the following day. Both sides claimed to be leading in the formal tally, which would take a week to complete. But Mrs. Aquino demanded that President Marcos concede. In the gloom of Malacanang, he hinted sourly that he might issue a decree invalidating the entire vote.

Many foreign journalists were having their first glimpse of Ferdinand and Imelda in the flesh. P. J. O'Rourke joined the mob at a press conference in Malacanang, covering for *Rolling Stone.* After marveling at the bad taste evident everywhere in Imelda's garish interior decorating, he found a chair and watched Ferdinand perform. His face was "puffy and opaque. There was something of Nixon to his look, but not quite as nervous, and something of Mao but not quite as dead. . . . I dozed in my fake-bamboo chair and was startled awake when Marcos said, 'When you see a nun touch a ballot box, that's an illegal act.' "

Ferdinand had spent $430 million to buy votes. This forced the Central Bank to raise interest rates by 50 percent. Nearly half a billion dollars failed to buy him the election, even when backed by 200,000 soldiers, 1 million bogus ballots, and subverted computers.

Four days later, President Reagan reassured the world during a televised news conference that there had been "fraud on both sides" of the Philippine election. Reagan seemed to be endorsing Marcos as the victor, causing consternation among many of his own White House aides. Only hours earlier, Senator Lugar, the official head of Reagan's observer team, had told the president that a fair vote count would show Aquino the winner. At the news conference, Reagan hemmed and hawed: "Whether there is enough evidence that you can really keep on pointing the finger or not, I don't know. I'm sure even elections in our own country—there are some evidences of fraud in places and areas. And I don't know the extent of this over there—but also do we have any evidence that it's all been one-sided, or has this been sort of the election tactics that have been followed there?"

As if to put matters to rest, Reagan announced that he was dispatching diplomatic troubleshooter Philip Habib to look into the allegations of fraud. Habib had served as assistant secretary of state for East Asia and the Pacific from 1974 to 1976, and knew the Philippines. He arrived in Manila on February 14, two hours before the puppet national assembly proclaimed Ferdinand Marcos the winner by 1.5 million votes.

Cory Aquino called for a nonviolent campaign of strikes and boycotts. Cardinal Sin urged Catholics to join. Ferdinand responded by blaming priests and nuns for all the election violence, fraud, and intimidation.

A reporter who went to the palace expecting to see a riot saw "just Bong-Bong and a BMW full of 'junior cronies' driving none too steadily out of the palace gate after a private victory party."

Habib went straight from the airport to Malacanang. Trade and Industry Minister Roberto Ongpin was chosen to lead negotiations for the regime. According to Ongpin, Habib put Marcos under severe pressure, not to give up office but to revise his cabinet as a gesture to placate his enemies in America. Most important was the immediate replacement of Ver by Ramos. These, Ongpin said, were Reagan's conditions for continued White House support. Reagan and Habib were *not* demanding that President Marcos step down. To the contrary, if Ferdinand made these changes, Reagan would back him to remain in Malacanang as president of the Philippines at least until he served out his current term in 1987.

Ferdinand flatly refused. He knew when his adversaries were uncertain, and Reagan obviously was not on firm ground. Ongpin said the sticking point always was Ver, who kept telling Ferdinand that he was putting his head in a noose. Ferdinand finally agreed to replace Ver with Ramos as chief-of-staff, but only if Ver remained as secret police boss, which was just switching nameplates. To this Ongpin said Habib agreed, but only on the conditions that Roberto Ongpin would go to Washington to replace Kokoy Romualdez as ambassador, and other cabinet changes would be made, presumably the purging of Tourism Minister Aspiras and Information Minister Cendana, who were popularly linked to the Aquino slaying because they had been at the scene.

Realizing that he had won, Ferdinand concurred. It was a major victory for him. Nothing would really change. It was up to Habib to persuade Cory Aquino to agree.

After their meeting, Ferdinand made a public announcement that he was retiring Ver as army chief-of-staff, but hedged by not announcing the effective date. He said Ver would remain in place at least until March 1, after which he would still be chief of the secret police and a top military adviser.

Because President Reagan's earlier statement on the election had laid an egg, the next day (February 15) the White House grudgingly acknowledged that the election had been, well, a bad show. Reagan admitted that "It has become evident, sadly, that the elections were marred by widespread fraud and violence perpetrated largely by the ruling party. It was so extreme that the election's credibility has been called into question both within the Philippines and in the U.S."

What Reagan did *not* say was that he was abandoning Ferdinand Marcos. Instead, he became unctuous and suggested, in what was not the high point of his political career, that the opposition stop making such a clamor and cut a deal with his old friend at Malacanang: "At this difficult juncture it is imperative that all responsible Filipinos seek peaceful ways and to avoid violence, which would benefit only those who wish to see an end to democracy." Declared Congressman Lee Hamilton a bit more candidly, "The election was rigged."

February 16 was a big day in Manila. One million angry citizens turned out for an Aquino rally in which she declared her own victory in the election and vowed to expel Marcos through civil disobedience. Cardinal Sin and the Philippine bishops issued a pastoral letter denouncing Marcos, saying that he had lost the moral foundation to rule, and should step down.

The next day, February 17, Habib met again with Ferdinand for two hours, working out details of the Reagan compromise, then he saw Cory Aquino for fifty-five minutes to spell out the deal to her. Aquino bluntly refused, and told him she would accept nothing less than the removal of Ferdinand from office. Habib also visited Cardinal Sin, who said seraphically, "We talked about angels." And Habib met privately with Ramos and Enrile.

On the 19th the U.S. Senate, by a vote of 85 to 9, passed a resolution condemning the election. Said Senator Edward Kennedy, "Corazon Aquino won that election lock, stock and barrel." The foreign affairs subcommittee of the House of Representatives voted unanimously to put military aid in escrow while Ferdinand remained in power and to channel future aid through private and church organizations until legitimate government was established.

Denouncing these actions as foreign intervention, Ferdinand warned that Filipinos would not submit to dictates from abroad. He said he might press charges of sedition and rebellion against his opponents if they resorted to civil disobedience.

That Friday, February 21, Habib made a last, vain attempt to talk Cory Aquino into a compromise with Ferdinand. Again she refused. She was preparing to leave Manila for Cebu, where she planned another huge rally. On Saturday, something happened backstage that forced Habib to leave the Philippines abruptly three days ahead of schedule, his official agenda a failure. Nobody was quite sure how he had concluded matters, except that President Marcos was still in Malacanang where President Reagan wanted him. In the face of Aquino's refusal to compromise, Reagan actually had begun to waver. He was under intense pressure from the State Department, Congress, and the intelligence community to stand aside and let the natural forces at play in Manila have their chance to work. Among these "natural forces" were some that were distinctly unnatural.

There was a hidden agenda. It had been debated by the country team at the U.S. Embassy and in Washington for many months— whether or not to give the green light to RAM's coup plot. The indications are that a very preliminary American signal was given to Enrile and RAM on Thursday, February 20, two days before Habib left, because on that day RAM committed itself tentatively to going ahead with its long-awaited assault on Malacanang from the Pasig River, the time set for 2:00 A.M. Sunday morning. The signal would not have been given unless some CIA officers in Manila had reached the conclusion that the Reagan compromise was doomed, and that more direct measures had to be taken. Their decision appears to have been reached independently, without seeking approval from CIA director Casey. Theoretically, but only theoretically, a final signal would have to await a decision, or "finding," by President Reagan, in consultation with the National Security Council on Habib's return to Washington. A widespread feeling had grown among intelligence officers over the years that President Reagan did not comprehend or care about the subtleties and nuances at play on the fields of the Lord. So, if a coup could be encouraged to happen a few hours before Reagan was obliged to make such a decision, all the better. When Habib reached Washington on Sunday, he could present Reagan with a situation in Manila that had developed its own momentum.

It is important to keep in mind that the green light was "preliminary." This achieved two mischievous purposes: By being provisional, it avoided the need for confirmation from Washington. And it stopped short of obliging Enrile to make a firm commitment to proceed, which he was characteristically determined to avoid. RAM was put on alert, but its officers did not bring in the troops needed to carry out the coup. Forty-eight hours before the assault was to begin, its leaders were still holding coffee klatches, and Enrile's private army was still sitting around in the barracks in Cagayan smoking cigarettes.

But it did start the ball rolling, obliging Enrile to make some very preliminary moves. And, most important, it put his American friends in a position to increase psychological pressure enormously, hoping to reach a point where Enrile and RAM would stampede and initiate the coup on their own, sucking Washington in and taking the decision out of President Reagan's hands.

Accordingly, on Friday, while Habib was paying his final call on Cory Aquino, Juan Ponce Enrile was busy writing a letter of resignation, which he let people know he was planning to deliver to Malacanang on Monday. Ferdinand planned to stage his own inauguration on Tuesday. The Enrile letter of resignation was a decoy. If the defense minister was intending to go through the ritual of a formal resignation on Monday, it would seem that nothing was planned before then. By Friday night, journalists had been tipped about the pending resignation, and Enrile spoke to them openly about it on the phone, arranging to meet the reporters for coffee the following morning at the Atrium Mall in Makati to explain his decision.

Fabian Ver also had a hidden agenda. He had now selected his targets as traitors in the Marcos cabinet: Trade and Industry Minister

Roberto Ongpin, Prime Minister Cesar Virata, and Defense Minister Enrile, backed by General Fidel Ramos. Virata was an economist, an apolitical technocrat who had been boosted into his position by pressure on President Marcos from the IMF and World Bank, which thought highly of Virata's administrative ability. Ver was suspicious of Virata because he was admired by the foreign community. To neutralize him, Ver assigned a team of his own security agents to be Virata's bodyguards around the clock. According to close friends, Virata said he was "scared shitless."

Next, Ver offered a similar team of thugs as bodyguards for Roberto Ongpin. His blood turning cold, Ongpin thanked him but politely declined. He then went straight to Enrile and asked for and received a full bodyguard of RAM officers to protect him from Ver.

As leading members of the Philippine Chinese banking community, Roberto and Jaime Ongpin had become a nuisance to Ver—a nuisance that he was unable to overcome by intimidation. For years, Ver had been trying to take over the gray money market in Manila's Chinatown and the Ermita tourist district, and had failed. Repeated clashes had occurred between Ver's thugs and the Chinese syndicates that moved money in and out of the Philippines and owed their allegiance to the Ongpins. At least one elderly Chinese broker had died of a "heart attack" in Ver's hands, and others had been beaten by Ver's men on the streets, in broad daylight.

By Friday, February 21, Ver thought he had everything figured out. He told Ferdinand that at Habib's instigation, Ongpin, Enrile, and Ramos had all joined in a CIA plot to have RAM officers assassinate Marcos. There were reports of several American navy ships taking up positions offshore. Ver had drafted fresh intelligence reports on secret RAM meetings and conspiracies under way during Habib's stay, including Habib's meetings with Enrile and Ramos. Ver said that Roberto Ongpin was using his position as lead negotiator to conspire against Marcos. As evidence, Ver explained that he had offered Ongpin a team of bodyguards, but Ongpin had got them from Enrile instead, which proved that they were all part of the same conspiracy. These bodyguards, Ver said, were actually trained RAM assassins, working for Enrile and Ramos, who would gain access to Malacanang by coming in with Ongpin, and then murder President Marcos.

Ferdinand ordered Ver to arrest Ongpin's bodyguards at once. Ver waited till late that Friday night, then had them arrested and taken to

Malacanang for interrogation. They were to be displayed during a televised news conference when their assassination plot would be revealed to the world. During their interrogation, however, Ver learned of the real RAM plot, prepared six months earlier, in which commandos would storm Malacanang from the Pasig River—set for 2:00 A.M. Sunday morning.

The initiative was now in Ver's hands, and the pace quickened.

Over the years, the CIA and the National Security Agency had established in the Philippines America's largest telecommunications and technical intelligence base in the Far East, capable of monitoring radio and microwave phone transmissions all over Asia, linked to surveillance satellites that could discern something as small as the numbers on an automobile license plate. Although these were generally directed outward, to cover the Pacific and the Asian mainland, they were also capable of keeping close watch within the Philippines. They could easily monitor all of Fabian Ver's secret communications throughout the archipelago. The Pentagon and the CIA had helped Ver acquire the telecommunications net used by NISA and the Presidential Security Command. In the early 1980s, more than $10 million had been spent to upgrade Ver's telecom system with new computerized electronics from Stromberg-Carlson. Not only could the CIA and NSA monitor the entire system, but they could patch into it at will to interrupt messages, or to substitute false messages. When Ver's transmissions were scrambled, they could be instantly unscrambled.

A twenty-four-hour vigil was being maintained by U.S. technicians on all of Ver's communications, particularly his scrambled transmissions to field units around Metro-Manila. On Tuesday, February 18, while Habib was still trying to work out the Reagan compromise between Marcos and Aquino, Enrile's American friends tipped him that Ver was about to stage a countermove against RAM, possibly with simultaneous strikes against Ramos, Enrile, and Roberto Ongpin.

On Wednesday, Enrile's friends contacted him again to warn that Ver had placed the Presidential Security Command on red alert. They would keep him advised of any new developments.

On Thursday, Enrile's friends listened in as Ver's forces repositioned themselves around Metro-Manila. If Ver was allowed to proceed, many of the embassy's top assets in the regime soon would be neutralized. Philip Habib was still negotiating, but someone at the CIA station (nobody is sure who) gave RAM the nod. Plans for the Sunday morning coup went into high gear. The embassy was then falsely informed that RAM had taken the initiative on its own, and its plan was now irreversible.

On Friday, Enrile's friends informed him that Ver had ordered his men to prepare for a series of arrests.

Saturday morning, Enrile was driven to the Atrium Mall in Makati for coffee at the 365 Club with the journalists who wanted to hear about his forthcoming letter of resignation. While they were chatting, Enrile received a phone call telling him that during the night Ver had arrested the RAM team guarding Roberto Ongpin. A few minutes later, a call came from Ongpin himself, confirming the arrests, and warning Enrile to be careful.

The defense minister cut short his press conference and went straight home "for lunch." There, with his wife Cristina, he found RAM leaders Colonel Gregorio Honasan and Colonel Eduardo Kapunan, with other members of RAM and Enrile's closest aides from the ministry. They had reliable information that Ver had designated teams to round up everyone in RAM. Honasan told Enrile, "If they issue arrest orders against me and the others, it may eventually implicate you; they might arrest you also."

Another urgent message came from Enrile's American friends: they had just intercepted a transmission from Ver ordering his men to proceed with the arrest of Enrile, Ramos, Ongpin, and the others. The coup plot for Sunday had been blown. If Enrile was going to do anything, he would have to act now. Philip Habib was cutting short his stay by three days and leaving immediately. It would not do for President Reagan's negotiator to be in Manila if all hell was going to break loose. It might seem as if he was involved, or responsible.

In his study, Enrile told his "boys" that they had two choices—either disperse or fight. The RAM officers wanted to disperse immediately throughout the islands, to hide, then regroup and fight. They asked Enrile what he preferred. He hesitated for a moment, partly because his knees were knocking so hard that he was not certain he could stand up. It might be possible for RAM to vanish into the undergrowth, but Enrile had no such option. He pushed himself up from his chair, walked jerkily up a short flight of steps to a cabinet holding his prized fishing rods and guns, reached inside, and started handing out Uzis. He took out a flak jacket and put it on. His legs were still shaking uncontrollably. Back at his desk, he picked up the phone and called Fidel Ramos at

Camp Crame. He briefed Ramos on what was happening. Ramos already knew. He also had friends in low places. They agreed to meet at Camp Aguinaldo, across the street from Camp Crame.

By 3:00 P.M. Saturday afternoon, Enrile, Honasan, and Kapunan were at the Defense Ministry in Camp Aguinaldo. Enrile had his Uzi slung around his flak jacket. His aides were rounding up RAM loyalists while he made phone calls. He reached Cardinal Sin and told him what was happening. Sin pledged to help. Then Enrile called Ambassador Bosworth and the Japanese ambassador. Later, Enrile explained, "I did this so the world would know in case we would be annihilated."

At 6:30 P.M. Enrile called a press conference. Inside the Defense Ministry, an undistinguished glass-and-concrete structure facing a broad, green parade ground, Enrile now had two hundred armed supporters and another two hundred on the way. This was the force that had been intended to assault Malacanang, and it was assembling with something less than blinding speed. Under the circumstances, it is surprising that everything happened so slowly. If Ver had chosen to strike, there was little RAM could have done. Enrile signaled his units in Cagayan Valley, and they were preparing to move, coming down by airlift through Clark where the Americans were expecting them. As yet, there were not enough men to stage a serious defense. Ranged against them were ten thousand men in Ver's Presidential Security Command, plus thousands of soldiers commanded by Ilocanos that Ver could call in from METROCOM, AVSECOM, and the army. Enrile's only chance was General Ramos.

Fidel Ramos was also calling in his most trusted troops. As chief of the Constabulary and combined police forces, and vice chief-of-staff of the armed forces, Ramos could count on thousands of soldiers and Constabulary, but they were scattered throughout the islands. Ramos and Enrile both were telephoning field commanders, asking for their support. A few were responding; others were too far away to offer anything but their blessing.

In the meantime, Ver inexplicably failed to strike. Had he grown so accustomed to Gestapo methods that he never learned the basic rudiments of military command? He had forfeited the advantage of surprise; he had let hours pass while Enrile and the RAM commanders came to a decision, and allowed them to make their way unchallenged across sprawling Metro-Manila to Camp Aguinaldo, a trip that can take over an hour. Even there, Ver failed to pounce while evening came and the revolt became public knowledge. Could the CIA agents have been exaggerating the imminent danger of arrest in order to frighten Enrile and provoke him into action? Ver's troops were nowhere to be seen.

In fact, Ver was completely unaware of what was transpiring. Although the previous days had been filled with tension and conspiracy, Ver had personal commitments that Saturday which kept him occupied through the afternoon and early evening. He and Imelda Marcos were the official sponsors at the wedding of Major General Vicente Piccio's son at Villamor Air Base chapel. Ver's men were so terrified of him that they did not dare break into the ceremonies. It was a long wedding. When the service finally ended and the guests prepared to dash through the chicken soup heat to the wedding reception, Ver's men at last interrupted to tell him the bad news. Ver and Imelda immediately excused themselves from the reception and rushed anxiously back to Malacanang. A wedding had cost them the throne.

Fidel Ramos joined Enrile for the six-thirty press conference at the Defense Ministry. Together, they announced that they were resigning their posts, effective immediately, and throwing their support to Cory Aquino. They accused Ferdinand Marcos of stealing the election, and of abusing his powers for years. Both men were in good positions to know. They demanded that he resign. "We will have to make a stand here," Enrile said, "and if we have to go down, we will go down." Then, for two hours, while Enrile chain-smoked, the two men described to reporters exactly how Marcos had stolen the election, and to some extent how he had robbed the public treasury. Enrile admitted that he had personally added 350,000 bogus pro-Marcos ballots to the box. But he had now seen the light. Ramos charged that Ferdinand had perverted the armed forces in the conduct of the election and had allowed "acts of political terrorism and fraud" to be carried out by Roberto Benedicto, Eduardo Cojuangco, and Kokoy Romualdez.

While Enrile and Ramos made a clean breast of things, Cardinal Sin spoke over Radio Veritas, asking everyone, including priests and nuns, to descend into the streets to protect the rebels.

In Cebu, Cory Aquino was informed of these developments. She was uncertain of Enrile's motives, but she phoned the Defense Ministry to offer him her prayers. The American Embassy contacted her next, and asked if she would allow a helicopter to pick her up and take her to safety on a U.S. Navy vessel steaming conveniently nearby, which would transport her to any place she chose. She refused, and went into hiding with her own people, in case Ver had plans for her as well.

Responding to Cardinal Sin's appeal, thousands of civilians surrounded the Defense Ministry and tens of thousands more formed a sea of bodies around the main entrances to Camp Aguinaldo and Camp Crame, which face each other across an eight-lane boulevard. The sheer mass of people provided a human shield.

In Washington, the White House issued a statement shifting its position toward the Aquino camp, endorsing the statements by Enrile and Ramos that the Marcos regime no longer had the mandate of the people.

After their long news conference, Enrile and Ramos split up. Ramos returned to Camp Crame.

Just before 10:00 P.M., Enrile received two messages that President Marcos wanted to talk with him. He refused. He was asked to contact Ver. When Ver came on the line, he asked Enrile to promise that RAM's forces would not attack Malacanang.

At 10:30 P.M., Ferdinand told a palace press conference that he would annihilate the rebels with heavy artillery and tanks. Just how he proposed to do so, with nearly a hundred thousand civilians blocking the way, was not clear. During the night, Enrile was joined by Brigadier General Ramon Farolan, the commissioner of customs, who had defected to the rebels. Radio Veritas broadcast reports that many military units in the Metro-Manila area had joined the rebels, and units on other islands had pledged their support. These reports were false, calculated to demoralize Ver's forces, put positive pressure on the undecided, and add to the confidence of the people in the streets—who did not go home to sleep. The broadcasts were concocted by CIA agents who had set up shop in a back office of the Defense Ministry, where they could stay in close contact with Enrile. They kept Ramos and Enrile informed of everything Ver did, and passed on all communications coming out of Malacanang. Enrile stayed in frequent contact with Ambassador Bosworth through the CIA link in the back room.

In Washington that Sunday, Reagan met for eighty-five minutes with national security advisers to hear Philip Habib's report and to discuss the options. The conclusion was simple: Ferdinand was finished, medically and politically. Following the meeting, Reagan sent a private message to Malacanang, asking Ferdinand "what his thoughts were about transitioning to a new government." Bowing to the overwhelming popular support for the rebellion and for Aquino's obvious victory,

Reagan took his first positive step in a fortnight and declared himself tentatively on the side of the angels. A White House statement was issued saying America would cut off all aid to the Marcos government if violence ensued. "Any attempt to resolve this situation by force will surely result in bloodshed and casualties, further polarize Philippine society and cause untold damage to the relationship between our governments. . . . We cannot continue our existing military assistance if the government uses that aid against other elements of the Philippine military which enjoy substantial popular backing. The president urges in the strongest possible terms that violence be avoided. . . ."

By noon Sunday, February 23, nearly 125,000 people were packed around the gates of the two camps. These were not the only entrances to Camp Aguinaldo or to Camp Crame, but they were the focus of all attention. Word came that Ver was at last preparing an attack. Enrile decided to move in with Ramos at Camp Crame, to concentrate their small force.

At 3:00 P.M., under orders from Ver, a contingent of marines rumbled toward Camp Crame in Armored Personnel Carriers. They were stopped more than a mile from the entrance by a mass of humans who linked arms and refused to budge. Most people thought the APCs were tanks, but the result was the same. Nuns knelt before them to say their rosaries. Girls gave the marines bouquets and asked them to climb down and join the crowd. Ver's APCs went no further. Out of this confrontation, ordinary street Filipinos, Tondo people and faceless, joined with the middle class, and both discovered a kind of spontaneous collective will that they had never exerted before, and a common bond they had never nurtured. It electrified them. Tears streamed down faces. Some began to sing. "People Power" was born.

Unsure what kind of attack was planned, or perhaps already under way, Enrile called Ambassador Bosworth Sunday evening. He then phoned Ver and told him that many of those who had once been faithful to Ferdinand would die in whatever showdown took place. Through the night, Ramos and Enrile continued to launch publicity assaults on Radio Veritas. Finally, Enrile agreed to speak on the phone with Ferdinand. The president was warm and friendly. All was forgiven, he said. Let's call the whole thing off. Enrile said it was too late for that.

No attack came Saturday night because Ferdinand was busy hedging his bets. He ordered a barge towed up the Pasig River in the dark to the palace quay, where it was loaded with three hundred packed crates, most of them extraordinarily heavy. The downtown vaults under the bank and under the warehouse were emptied separately. Yamashita's Gold was taking a trip. The barge was towed down the Pasig in the dark late Sunday night, out to Manila Bay and over to the Philippine naval headquarters. There its cargo was transferred to another vessel, the presidential yacht *Ang Pangulo (The President).* The yacht sailed immediately and eventually reached Hong Kong. Nobody was quite certain what happened to the cargo—everyone connected with the yacht denied knowledge. During this same period, the vaults beneath the Bataan beach palace also were emptied of whatever was in them.

All day Monday, Enrile and Ramos waited for an attack. Ver had moved in some artillery, placing it in Camp Aguinaldo facing Camp Crame. Tension built, and Ramos and some aides went jogging to work it off.

At 11:00 A.M. that same Monday morning, Ferdinand called a press conference to declare a state of emergency. The whole Marcos family assembled in the anteroom, rather than the main hall, because only a few journalists and cameramen showed up. What was happening in the streets was more newsworthy. Ferdinand, his face swollen like a melon, his eyes rheumy, seemed to be in a drugged state, talking in his sleep. He was a very sick man. More than once, among themselves, the journalists had asked each other why, with all the billions he had salted away, Ferdinand simply did not step down gracefully, retire to his palace in Bataan or to one of his palaces in the Ilocos, where he would be safe among his own people, and spend his twilight as an elder statesman.

He seemed to be disoriented. For twenty years, he had been running the whole show, making all the decisions, so long that nobody dared interrupt him even now if his utterance did not make sense. It became obvious why Ver had not seriously attacked the rebels. Ferdinand was locked in some vague internal struggle with history. If he let Ver loose and Ver caused a bloodbath, how would Ferdinand be remembered? Perhaps Habib or Bosworth or somebody else had raised the idea of history to him during the past week, perhaps Ronald Reagan during one of their personal phone calls.

Fabian Ver, in full dress uniform, was extremely tense, like a Doberman lunging on the end of his leash. Struggling to maintain his composure, he bent over the ornate desk to ask Ferdinand—perhaps for the thousandth time—for permission to bomb Camp Crame. Ferdinand said no. Ver pleaded with him. "My order is 'no.' " The television cameras recorded the exchange mutely. Ver was desperate. "Our negotiations and our prior dialogue have not succeeded, Mr. President . . . we cannot withdraw all the time. . . ." Ver finally realized that nothing he said penetrated. He saluted, stepped backward, and left with the other officers. Ferdinand ignored them and told the television cameras that he was going ahead with his inauguration on Tuesday. In the midst of the news conference, Ramos and Enrile seized Channel 4 and cut their old friend off in mid-sentence.

Ver tried to get around the prohibition against bombing Camp Crame by sending in a helicopter assault team. The team landed inside the perimeter of Camp Crame and defected. A detachment of jet fighter pilots also defected, followed by navy units.

As the crisis came to a head, President Reagan was awakened at 5:00 A.M. Monday morning in Washington to approve a blunt statement that, in effect, at last urged Ferdinand to resign. It was then 6:00 P.M. Monday, Manila time. The White House statement, transmitted to Malacanang by Ambassador Bosworth, said the Reagan administration believed attempts to prolong "the life of the present regime by violence are futile."

Ferdinand still planned to go ahead with his inauguration. He had brought to the palace Supreme Court Chief Justice Ramon Aquino (no relation to Cory Aquino), to have dinner and spend the night, so the justice could swear him in the next morning. The chief justice was entertained at dinner by Bong-Bong, Imee, Irene, and their husbands. All the food at the palace was being catered during the crisis by the Via Mare restaurant, where Imelda had lunched while Ninoy Aquino died. Meals were served by uniformed waiters from the restaurant. The Marcos children stayed up all night with their father, who wanted to talk with them.

During the long night, Ferdinand placed a call to Senator Paul Laxalt at his Capitol Hill office. It was nearly 1:00 A.M. in Manila, nearly 2:00 P.M. Washington time. They talked for twenty minutes. Ferdinand had an idea—perhaps inspired by Bong-Bong or Imee—that U.S. helicopters could rescue them from Malacanang and take them to Clark, where they could change to aircraft that would fly them north to the Ilocos. There they could rally loyal troops and retake the country.

Senator Laxalt agreed to discuss it personally with President Reagan and phone back. He was driven up Pennsylvania Avenue to the White House, where he explained Ferdinand's plan. Reagan said the matter was now settled, it was all over, but that Ferdinand would be guaranteed his peace, his safety, and his dignity. Laxalt returned to the Hill and called back at 5:30 A.M. Manila time, Tuesday, repeating what Reagan had said. Ferdinand asked, "What do you think I should do?" Laxalt answered, "You should cut and cut cleanly. I think the time has come."

There was a long silence, then Ferdinand said, "I am so very, very disappointed." He could not believe that Reagan had let him down.

Imelda phoned Nancy Reagan, asking her to intercede with her husband. A short while later, Mrs. Reagan called back, and told Imelda that they would be welcome in the United States.

Still unable to accept the finality of it, Ferdinand called his labor minister, Blas Ople, an old ally, who was in Washington. Ople confirmed the overwhelmingly negative attitude there. As gently as he could, Ople asked why they did not simply leave. Ferdinand said it was Imelda's idea—she was reluctant to go. "She is here beside me. She does not want to leave." There it was.

He went back on television, this time on Channel 9, a network controlled by his daughter Imee. "We have no intention of going abroad. We will defend the republic until the last breath of our life and to the last drop of blood."

Just before 9:30 A.M., Ferdinand phoned Enrile again, offering to set up a provisional government in which Enrile and Cory would rule with him as a triumvirate. Enrile did not want to have any part of it. He was angry because the phone call made him late for the inauguration of Cory Aquino, set for 10:00 A.M. at Wack Wack.

Two hours later, Ferdinand had himself inaugurated at Malacanang. Midway through the ceremonies, Imee's Channel 9 was taken off the air by the rebels.

Long ago, Imelda had ordered seven elaborate outfits and gowns for the inaugural festivities. Instead, she wore a simple white, puff-sleeved terno, the Filipino national dress. She wept throughout while Imee, Irene, and Bong-Bong (dressed in custom-tailored fatigues) looked on. About five thousand loyalists came to the palace to watch. The Marcoses provided box lunches. Imelda and Ferdinand stood together on the platform and sang "Because of You." It was a peculiar scene, like watching a rerun of Nelson Eddy and Jeannette MacDonald. Some people in the throng found it very touching, and wept. The other Mrs. Marcos, Carmen Ortega, was not among the invited guests. She was on the other side of town, with all the other Marcos children.

Late Tuesday afternoon, somebody fired random shots at Malacanang Palace. Ferdinand phoned Enrile, asking him to send RAM security men to the palace to stop whoever was doing the shooting. He told Enrile that he planned to leave Malacanang soon, and he was asking Ambassador Bosworth to provide U.S. helicopters.

Four choppers arrived at 8:30 P.M. Before boarding, Ferdinand was taken by launch across the Pasig to the palace park, where some of the U.S. helicopters were boarding members of the presidential party on the larger landing pad. He had come for a last talk with Enrile, who was waiting in the shadows, covered by his own RAM guard. The two men had worked together closely for nearly thirty years, enriching each other beyond most men's fantasies. They knew things about each other that nobody else knew. According to witnesses, the meeting ended with words of conciliation and a long embrace between the two men.

At 9:00 P.M., Ferdinand and his family and closest friends got aboard the last chopper on the palace pad and left for Clark Air Base. A few of the regime's top officials left with them. A U.S. Navy boat took another group down the Pasig to Subic Bay Naval Base. Some strays had to rush to board the final helicopters on the far side of the Pasig; aide Jolly Benitez missed the last boat to cross and had to suffer the indignity of renting a dugout to ferry him over. On the palace side, Ver climbed aboard Ferdinand's helicopter with an Uzi slung around his neck. An American crewman asked him to unload the Uzi for safety reasons. Ver snarled, "Don't fuck with me."

Bong-Bong was the last to board. The pilot of the helicopter was about to lift off when someone in very expensive combat fatigues ran up and signaled wildly to open the door. The flight engineer stuck his head out and said they already had a full load. Bong-Bong stuck a gun in his face and pushed his way in, snapping, "I'm his goddam son!" As the choppers left, Ver's security forces hastily abandoned the palace and began thinking about their own survival. Within hours, the un-locked palace administration building had been looted. Portraits of Imelda and Ferdinand were torn down, slashed, and stomped. A few youths gained entrance to the locked palace, where they rummaged through the private chambers. Little serious damage was done. In Imelda's suite they found photographs strewn all over the floor, and condoms in her bathroom. There were twelve hundred pairs of shoes, five hundred brassieres, most of them black, and a large stock of girdles size 42. In the basement was her bulletproof brassiere. In his separate suite filled with medical equipment and kidney dialysis machines, the last meal of President Marcos lay half-eaten on his table.

The presidential party stayed at Clark Air Base until 5:00 A.M.

Wednesday. During the night, there was a bitter exchange between Ferdinand and American officials. He demanded to be flown to his home in the Ilocos. They had orders from President Reagan and the joint chiefs-of-staff to fly him to America. At 4:00 A.M., Ferdinand stopped arguing and the sleepy and sullen group began boarding jet transports for Guam and Hawaii.

In Washington, Secretary of State George Shultz released a statement: "We praise the decision of President Marcos. Reason and compassion have prevailed in ways that best serve the Filipino nation and people. In his long term as president, Ferdinand Marcos showed himself to be a staunch friend of the United States. We are gratified that his departure from office has come peacefully, characterized by the dignity and strength that have marked his many years of leadership."

The dynasty had fallen, before it could really get started.

When the aircraft carrying the Marcoses and their entourage landed in Honolulu, nobody was in the mood for speeches. Along with their personal effects and papers, the planes carried jewels and gold valued at $10 million. Petty cash. Elsewhere in the world, in those deep, dark vaults where flight capital grows like truffles, the Marcoses had so many billions in gold bullion and hard currency that the numbers are meaningless.

But there was never enough. As they stumbled wearily off the plane and made their way across the tarmac, Ferdinand and Imelda were trailed by the remainder of their dynasty—Imee, Irene, Bong-Bong, and pretty little Aimee, her tiny arms sweetly hugging that ubiquitous symbol of infancy, a box of diapers. Pampers, actually. They were not for her, of course. She had been toilet-trained for a long time. They were for her dad, the president. Underneath the top Pampers was something Aimee was carrying through customs for her mom: a very large stash of pearls—48 square feet of pearls, to be exact, when they were spread out.

Mere bagatelles.

Epilogue

PARADISE LOST

THE REGIME LASTED for twenty years only because Filipinos allowed themselves to be convinced that the dictator was in firm control, that his secret police were everywhere, that his army was overwhelmingly powerful, and that Ferdinand Marcos himself was supernaturally endowed. These things were true up to a point. Beyond that, the impression of power and omniscience was exaggerated by showmanship and grotesque extremes of cruelty. Ordinary people were psyched out. It was the logical outcome of Edward Lansdale's shallow insight into human nature, which failed in Vietnam but worked in the Philippines. Inexperienced at resistance, and unaccustomed to armed struggle, when they finally took to the streets of Manila in exasperation and the Marcoses fled without a struggle, nobody was more astounded than Filipinos themselves, who coined the term "People Power" with refreshing innocence.

After the sudden departure of Ferdinand and Imelda, many Filipinos thought everything was going to change. But in fact little changed. The country had been so thoroughly looted that it had serious problems just feeding itself. Famine continued on Negros and other islands, and in Manila the number of street beggars was up sharply. Washington was more interested in returning the Philippines to status quo than in promoting dramatic reforms. The status quo meant getting back to strongman rule as quickly as possible, while paying elaborate homage to democratic principles. The talk about encouraging a healthy opposition, and about correcting the feudal serfdom of the vast majority of

Filipinos, was just talk. The norm established in the islands under American suzerainty was the rule of the elite, enforced by death squads, the democracy of the Ku Klux Klan. Cory Aquino, while apparently genuinely committed to land reform and correction of other long-standing abuses, was confronted by so many entrenched enemies of reform that she was forced to defer action indefinitely in order to concentrate on mere survival. So long as there was no genuine reform, whatever money was produced in the islands would continue to flee to safer places. Beautiful as it was, the Philippines was a place to rob, not a place to live.

After a honeymoon with the people, and the ratification of a new constitution, the Aquino government was obliged to purge itself of its reformers and to permit the reintroduction of some of the worst aspects of the Marcos regime. Negotiations with the NPA were broken off and a state of civil war resumed. Vigilante gangs identical to those under Marcos were reinstated and legitimized by Aquino's military staff to fight the "Communist menace."

In March 1987, President Reagan approved a "finding" which cast a pall over all prospects for improvement, providing $10 million for two years of increased CIA involvement in the Philippine government's counterinsurgency campaign. This included technical assistance, helping the Philippine military with intelligence gathering, providing computers, computer training, and so on. It authorized the Agency to hire Filipinos to spy on each other. CIA agents in the islands would increase by 10 percent, and they would have freedom to deal directly with Filipino soldiers at all ranks, rather than only at the chief-of-staff level.

It was a decision on a par with the meddling of MacArthur, with Truman and Eisenhower giving Lansdale a license to kill Huks and to fake the election of Magsaysay, with Johnson bribing Marcos to become involved in the Vietnam War, and with Nixon and Kissinger endorsing the Marcos seizure of dictatorial power.

The proper atmosphere for this decision was created in the same manner as the Tonkin Gulf Incident, by a rash of dubious reports of secret Soviet arms shipments to the NPA, and the alleged presence of Soviet advisers in NPA training camps. Marcos had done the same thing in his long buildup toward martial law, as Enrile had faked the attack on his car.

The head of one of the largest of the new post-Marcos vigilante groups, "Rising Masses," was Jun Porras Pala, a radio announcer and public crusader in Davao City, who created a right-wing reign of terror in Mindanao. Identifying villages known to be sympathetic to the NPA, Pala issued ultimatums on his radio station telling the villagers to join his group, or they would become targets. Thousands of villagers either joined or fled. When civil officials and religious activists opposed Pala, he broadcast death threats against them. The Aquino government did not put him in jail or in a mental hospital. Instead, Pala's group was encouraged by Davao's military police commander. The new defense minister, West Point graduate Rafael Ileto, and Local Governments Secretary Jaime Ferrer (both old Lansdale men) publicly endorsed the vigilantes. General Fidel Ramos, the hero of the Marcos overthrow, praised vigilantes as "civilian organizations dedicated to the defense of their community."

The vigilante phenomenon in the countryside coincided with the rebirth of anti-Communist anxiety in the cities. Once again the middle class was being told that a Communist takeover was imminent, and once again it was easily convinced. The right wing, failing repeatedly in its efforts to topple Aquino with inept military plots, reverted to terrorist tactics. Leaders of the left and right were brutally slain, including Jaime Ferrer on the right and Leandro Alejandro on the left. Ernie Maceda dusted off the old Marcos bromide and suggested that Alejandro had been killed by his own people to cast suspicion on the right.

Christian fundamentalist sects like Joy of the Lord Jesus, the Word of Life International, and Heaven's Magic preached rabid anti-Communist doctrines fomenting fear and hatred in the barrios. Most aggressive of the Christian groups was CAUSA International, the political arm of the Reverend Moon's Unification Church, which had aided U.S. efforts to support the Contras in Nicaragua. The chairman of CAUSA, Bo Hik Pak, acknowledged CIA funding. In August and October 1986, CAUSA held conferences on national security in Manila, bringing together people like General John Singlaub and Ray Cline with top Philippine strongmen such as Fidel Ramos and Juan Ponce Enrile. In March 1987, CAUSA organized a Philippine national conference of vigilante groups, with the raving right-wing terrorist from Davao, Jun Porras Pala, as the keynote speaker. At the conclusion of the conference, participants agreed to organize nine regional CAUSA chapters throughout the Philippines.

The rise of right-wing death squads and the Philippine operations of John Singlaub were not mere coincidence. Singlaub had direct ties to at least one of the Filipino vigilante groups. Alberto Maguigad, alias "Jake Madigan," boasted that his Counter-Insurgency Command, based in Cagayan de Oro, was funded by Singlaub. Maguigad bragged that two Green Berets were training his men in counterinsurgency tactics.

A senior Philippine military officer said Singlaub was traveling the country meeting right-wing groups to create the right psychological atmosphere for a new Operation Phoenix. We might well wonder whose names would be on the list for extermination. Singlaub also was said to be bringing Special Forces veterans to the islands to train selected units of the Philippine armed forces—at least thirty-seven American mercenaries being imported by Singlaub for that purpose. Chief-of-Staff Fidel Ramos ridiculed the allegation: "I would like you to know that the new armed forces of the Philippines has nothing to do with General Singlaub, he had nothing to do with us before, he has nothing to do with us now, and he will have nothing to do with us in the future. This is a lot of baloney. We don't want him and we don't need him."

Ramos had been acquainted with Singlaub for many years, from Korea and Vietnam. In July 1986, Singlaub came to see Ramos in Manila. Four months later, in November 1986, Singlaub returned to the Philippines with Ray Cline and Major General Robert Schweitzer, recently retired from Reagan's NSC staff. Singlaub and Cline apparently were the two secret envoys Reagan sent to Manila that November to warn Defense Minister Enrile not to attempt a coup against Mrs. Aquino. But while they were there, they held a few other meetings, including one with Enrile, Fidel Ramos, and Brigadier General Felix Brawner. These meetings were so secret that some of the men who attended entered the Philippines under false names. Cory Aquino's brother, Jose Cojuangco, was present at two of the meetings, which were held at the Aquino sugar plantation in Tarlac Province, although Cojuangco later denied he was there. It was soon after this meeting that Reagan approved his "finding" to expand CIA operations in the islands.

What were Singlaub and his secret team really up to in the Philippines—and why the right-wing feeding frenzy?

Funding secret right-wing "initiatives" had not become any cheaper since the fall of Ferdinand Marcos. There was always the rest of Yamashita's Gold, another $100 billion or so—the real reason why John Singlaub was back in the Philippines.

In September 1985, five months before Marcos fell, Singlaub came to Manila personally to get permission to dig. A senior Philippine government official said that Ambassador Bosworth, acting on White House orders, accompanied Singlaub to a meeting that September with Finance Minister Jaime Ongpin. The source said that Singlaub also asked for security protection, or approval to employ private guards. One of Singlaub's high-level official contacts was retired Brigadier General Luis Villareal, who directed the National Intelligence Coordinating Agency, and served as president of the Philippine Anti-Communist League.

Shortly after Singlaub's visit, Vernon Twyman's Delta International Group in Tulsa, Oklahoma, got in touch with a Georgia engineer, Al Meyers, who had developed a laser device to find buried gold. A testing laboratory had tested and accepted the device, which reacted when its beam encountered heavy metals of certain densities. The rest was high school trigonometry. Meyers had already been approached by a Houston group, Great Southern & Salvage, which specialized in offshore recovery. They all went to the Philippines to pinpoint Yamashita's Gold at several sites. After having problems with Twyman, Meyers broke off and went to work on his own at a reef in Calatagan Bay, 70 miles south-southwest of Manila. He was helped by Paul Jiga, who told Meyers he had watched a Japanese general's men bury the gold at the reef with the slave labor of Allied POWs, booby-trap it, and cork the hole with a huge slab of concrete, after which they machine-gunned the POWs and left their bodies to be devoured by sharks. Ben Balmores, who had retired more than ten years earlier, was in hiding from the treasure hunters and was reported to be in failing mental health.

Initially, Meyers dealt with Cesar Loran and Alfonso Adeva at Nippon Star, but after Ferdinand and Imelda fled, Meyers was taken to see President Aquino. Among the seven others attending the meeting were Mrs. Aquino's uncle, Congressman Francisco Sumulong, the person she designated to deal with people attempting to recover the gold. The standard arrangement offered Meyers by Sumulong was 75 percent of any treasure to the government of the Philippines, the remainder to the finder.

Meyers said he promised Aquino that his efforts would not cost her government a peso, but he needed coast guard protection in the form of an armed government launch to protect his crew from marauders— Filipinos and Americans connected to other groups that were also searching for the gold at various sites. Meyers told Aquino he expected to recover about 800 tons of gold at the one site. Mrs. Aquino was said to have exclaimed, "My God, it is the second miracle!"

Meanwhile, the PTL-affiliated Tulsans associated with General Singlaub's Phoenix Overseas Project obtained permission to work a different site with Nippon Star. Singlaub's people actually began digging at one site three months before the fall of Ferdinand Marcos, and apparently uncovered some 110-pound gold bars, which renewed their determination. They seem to have had difficulty dealing with Marcos and Ver, so by all accounts Singlaub himself was happy to see Marcos go, and was soon making fresh arrangements with the new government. Cory Aquino's speech writer, Teodoro Locsin, apparently assisted Singlaub in obtaining the necessary new permits. Cory's brother, Jose Cojuangco, reportedly offered to support Singlaub's recovery effort financially, and to guarantee security by providing Constabulary troops at their prime site in Batangas Province, the Laurel stronghold south of Manila.

Juan Ponce Enrile also assured Singlaub of military support, if necessary with his own private army. But just to be sure, Singlaub brought in his own U.S. Special Forces. It was the arrival of these men, thirty-seven in all, which inspired the rumors that Singlaub was training the Philippine armed forces in counterinsurgency, the rumors denied by Fidel Ramos.

Actually finding the gold was another matter. Locations of some land sites were known, as the reefs were known, but the tricky problem remained to pinpoint the exact position and find the way to reach it without setting off booby traps. This was what had stymied Ferdinand until he brought in Olof Jonsson. While Meyers was working his reef site in Calatagan Bay, for example, he found it impossible to approach the treasure directly, because—aside from the explosives planted in the reef—the access tunnel had been designed to cave in on anyone excavating along the obvious approach. To reach the treasure from any other direction required knowing its exact location and the precise situation of 2,000-pound bombs. The original Japanese detail maps had gone with Robert Curtis, and Curtis had vanished.

In the autumn of 1986, according to well-informed sources in Manila, two men representing Singlaub went to work tracking Curtis down. Before the year was out, they had found him, living in a new town, with a new job and new name. They identified themselves as representatives of Nippon Star. Curtis already knew all about Nippon

Star—he had kept a wary eye on developments from a distance. The two men pleaded with him to become involved once again in the search. They desperately needed his maps and his knowledge of the sites. Curtis refused.

A few days later, Curtis was contacted by someone closer to Singlaub. Someone who also had ties to Jay Agnew and his associates at the John Birch Society, who Curtis said had offered to launder up to $20 billion in gold for Ferdinand Marcos. He was extremely anxious to meet Curtis personally, to discuss the Nippon Star project. Curtis again said he did not want anything to do with those people.

The contact man admitted, reluctantly, that General Singlaub was involved, and pleaded with Curtis not to go to the press. Nippon Star had received too much publicity, so it was being shut down and everything would be handled from then on through offshore corporations set up in Panama and Nigeria. He said they needed Curtis badly. In the weeks to follow, he called Curtis again and again, and eventually came to see him.

What John Singlaub was after, he said, was to set up an endowment to fund anti-Communist activities around the world that the U.S. Congress refused to support. They would uncover the gold, give a big cut to the Philippines, and keep the rest for the endowment, which would dispense the funds as needed. They knew generally where to dig, but they needed the detail maps and engineering drawings from Curtis to do the excavating more precisely. Without the maps, it would take much longer and the gold might be missed by inches. They were trying to recruit Olof Jonsson also.

Curtis still refused to become involved.

His phone rang again. This time it was General Robert Schweitzer at the Pentagon. Although he had retired from the army and the National Security Council to work with Singlaub, Schweitzer still had the use of a Pentagon office.

General Schweitzer said he was calling about General John Singlaub's search for Yamashita's Gold. Curtis took the precaution of phoning his caller back on the main Pentagon switchboard, to make sure he was who he said he was.

Schweitzer's message was simple: Curtis *must* help Singlaub get Yamashita's Gold—to help in the fight against communism in Nicaragua and elsewhere.

"It is your patriotic duty," he told Curtis.

Soon afterward, Curtis was on his way to Hong Kong. He spent three days discussing the proposition with General Singlaub, General Schweitzer, and others. According to reliable sources in Hong Kong and Manila, Singlaub and his group were well prepared for the meeting. They had detailed CIA dossiers on Curtis, knew all about him and his history, and they knew how to play him.

Curtis was offered a seat on the board of Singlaub's new endowment, which would administer the recovery operation and determine the disposition of all the gold found. He would be one of a small group of its directors, among them General Singlaub and six other active or retired U.S. generals. Associated with them would be several leading Filipinos, including Cory's brother Jose Cojuangco and his uncle, Congressman Sumulong. Schweitzer was not among the directors listed, nor were two others whom Schweitzer wanted to bring in on the project—Ray Cline and General John Vessey, the former chairman of the Joint Chiefs of Staff. Singlaub reportedly was afraid that they would attract unwanted publicity. Although there had been many stories in the Filipino press, up to this point there had been only a few in America because the whole idea of Yamashita's Gold sounded so preposterous. Singlaub was worried that the involvement of Cline and particularly of Vessey would finally alert American journalists to the fact that there was more going on than just, as one foreign correspondent in Manila put it indelicately, "a harebrained treasure hunt by a bunch of wacko right-wing dildos." Billions of dollars were at stake.

No matter what anyone else thought, Singlaub and his circle of American generals were absolutely convinced of the reality of Yamashita's Gold, enough to risk becoming targets of ridicule while they searched for it. Many of them had been in the CIA hierarchy since World War II, involved in shaping the postwar governments of Japan, South Korea, Taiwan, and the Philippines. In doing so they had employed the patrons of the Yakuza, and had become friends and fellow conspirators of the *Kuromaku,* Sasakawa and Kodama. Nobody was in a better position than these men to know about the loot Kodama had hidden. They had access to top-secret Japanese military archives, CIA archives, Pentagon archives, all of them beyond the reach of ordinary people, and the inside track on papers Ferdinand Marcos had left behind when he fled. For twenty years, they had used CIA assets to keep close track of Ferdinand's secret gold deals. At some point in the early

1970s, the CIA had become involved in those gold deals through Paul Helliwell's black-money conduits and the branches of Nugan-Hand Bank.

If the CIA did fly tons of gold out of Clark for President Marcos, some of these men were well informed and might even have approved the flights. If Marcos bullion was slipped out through Australia with the help of wealthy tycoons there, using Nugan-Hand channels, some of these men might have been among those at the CIA who authorized its movement. If the huge Marcos gold transactions of 1983 and 1984 were real, and were concluded, some of these men were in a position to know about it, and may have been the ones holding his feet to the fire as he got ready for his first kidney transplant. Singlaub had even been in touch with Dovie Beams's old adversary, Potenciano Ilusorio, now (thanks to President Marcos) a major stockholder in Benguet Exploration, a unit of Benguet Consolidated Mines. Singlaub was said to be helping a group of American executives who wanted to acquire Benguet. In New York, business reporters speculated among themselves that the acquisition was of interest to Allen & Company, who had a history of involvement with Benguet.

If none of these reports was true, why were a platoon of America's top generals back in the Philippines digging for Yamashita's Gold?

Curtis decided to throw his lot in with them—but his decision was short-lived. In the Philippines, newspapers soon were full of stories about Singlaub's searches. His men were excavating ten sites simultaneously, with extremely tight security provided by the Philippine military and the U.S. Special Forces. With the assistance of Curtis in pinpointing exact locations, they expected to hit the first major deposit of treasure "at any time." Many of the remaining sites were in areas controlled by the NPA, and contingency plans were in place, in case of a military confrontation. Nobody wanted the gold to fall into the wrong hands.

Despite all their preoccupation with tight security, Curtis became alarmed at the way General Singlaub himself attracted attention, alarmed at the very high profile of what was supposed to be an extremely secret operation. He was also a bit disturbed by some of the disclosures of the Iran-Contra hearings, which revealed a high incidence of bungling, dishonesty, and venality. In addition, he had discovered that his old enemies in the John Birch Society were sitting on the sidelines, waiting to turn Kodama's blood-soaked booty into a new holy war. Alarmed and disgusted, Curtis took his priceless maps and threatened to vanish once again, unless Singlaub and the other brass hats withdrew and left the excavation to the specialists.

Ferdinand Marcos also had not forgotten Yamashita's Gold. Far away in Honolulu, where he continued to plot his eventual return to power, he held long telephone conversations with men in the Virginia suburbs of Washington who claimed to be arms dealers. They taped the conversations and turned them over to Congress and the press. During the phone calls, Ferdinand said he would pay for the tanks and rockets he needed with thousands of tons of gold still hidden in the Philippines. How many tons, asked the phony arms dealer. Ferdinand whispered hoarsely, "Thousands." Why, in one place alone, he added, he had 4,000 tons of bullion stashed, worth over $40 billion.

Nobody knew where his bullion had gone. Before fleeing from Malacanang, Ferdinand had taken the trouble to have a barge haul away the gold he had stashed in the palace, and trucks haul away the bullion in the vaults beneath the warehouse and the bank. Nobody knew where the presidential yacht had taken its cargo—to Hong Kong, or to some intermediate point like Lubang or Fuga. As to the bullion hidden beneath the Bataan beach palace, some people suspected that it had been taken hurriedly across to Corregidor and hidden among the maze of tunnels on the island. Just as a precaution, permission was obtained from the government of Cory Aquino to "renovate" the war memorial at Corregidor.

Although Marcos was obliged to live quietly under public scrutiny in Honolulu, there were other brief glimpses of hidden treasure; in mid-1988, frustrated by his exile, he was reported to have offered President Aquino $5 billion in cash to let him come home. As an opening ante it showed promise, but it fell far short of a serious bid.

Curtis got his wish. Singlaub and the other celebrity generals withdrew to let him dig away in secret beneath Fort Santiago. Hiding his real identity as much as possible, keeping to himself and shunning publicity, and working with a team of diggers provided by Cory Aquino, Curtis made gradual progress toward what he thought would be one of the big deposits of bullion hidden under the fort by Admirals Kodama and Iwabuchi. In March 1988, nearing their objective, the diggers hit a Japanese sand trap. Two workmen died. Curtis said the trap was one of those put in place to discourage recovery. The deaths brought the flare-up of publicity that Curtis had been trying to avoid, but after a few days it subsided as most people contented themselves with a snigger.

As Curtis and his excavators returned to work, they were joined by Olof Jonsson, back in the Philippines for the first time since 1975 to help Curtis pinpoint the trove.

In the national assembly, old supporters of Ferdinand Marcos threatened a complete investigation, and grumbled that Curtis was "destroying a national monument"—to what, they did not say.

Imelda and Ferdinand were gone, but in paradise lost, you could still hear the serpent slither.

ACKNOWLEDGMENTS

This book—like *The Soong Dynasty*—is the result of a collaboration with Peggy Sawyer Seagrave, and continues a path of inquiry that we began years ago.

Many sources in the Philippines agreed to cooperate only on strict conditions of anonymity. Because of the vindictive nature of so many characters described in the book, and the history of grisly murders for retribution in the islands, and in America, I believe their concern is more than justified.

I enlisted the help of a number of established investigative reporters in Washington, San Francisco, Honolulu, Hong Kong, and Manila. Some were well known, such as Washington columnists Dale Van Atta, Jack Anderson, and Joseph Spear. I was helped particularly by Washington investigative journalist Donald Goldberg, whose contribution to the book on the subject of Yamashita's Gold especially has been considerable, and by David Kaplan of the Center for Investigative Reporting in San Francisco, a co-author with Alex Dubro of the recent book *Yakuza*. Both Kaplan and Goldberg also kindly offered to review the manuscript and suggest corrections. In San Francisco, Jerome Garchik was a limitless source of background. And when it came to rationalizing the astronomical sums in the secret Marcos gold deals, Peter Fuhrman of the London bureau of *Forbes* was a classic of serene contemplation.

Van Atta and Goldberg also undertook investigations for me overseas, including trips to London, Manila, Hong Kong, and Honolulu, during which they conducted many vital interviews. Goldberg also interviewed sources in Las Vegas, New York, San Francisco, Los Angeles, and elsewhere. Also in Washington, I had the assistance of Bob Malone, Lucette Lagnado, Mike Binstein, Corky Johnson, Jane Winebrenner, Stu Harris, Opal Ginn, and Robin Reynolds.

In Honolulu, Hong Kong, and Manila, correspondent Tom Marks was a major asset. A contributor from Asia to *The Wall Street Journal*, Marks had the exceptional value of being a graduate of West Point, a former analyst for the Defense Intelligence Agency, and an instructor and doctoral candidate at the University of Hawaii, specializing in the Philippines and counterinsurgency. He made trips for me to Manila and elsewhere in the islands, including field maneuvers with the Philippine Army, and often disagreed with my conclusions. The University of Hawaii has a large collection of materials on the Philippines, and Tom Marks arranged for me to have the help of a number of students in assembling archives and chasing down obscure documentary evidence. My thanks to them all.

Among those who helped anonymously in Manila were researchers who conducted lengthy tape-recorded interviews with the Romualdez family, and various people closely associated with General Lansdale and the CIA.

Also in Manila, I had the help of Guy Sacerdoti, for years the correspondent there of the *Far Eastern Economic Review,* who covered the fall of the Marcos regime and now publishes an economic newsletter on the Philippines. Sacerdoti was able to provide independent confirmation of a number of controversial points through his own sources in the financial community.

In Hong Kong, I had the help of Kevin Sinclair, columnist of the *South China Morning Post,* and some guidance, encouragement, and background materials from the Reverend Edward Kelly.

To amass the necessary documentation, I relied heavily on professional researchers in England and the United States. In America, this included the invaluable assistance of Edward Leslie, who had worked with me on *The Soong Dynasty* and *Yellow Rain,* and who has since published his own first book, *Desperate Journeys, Abandoned Souls.* He was assisted by Mary Anne Vitto, Elaine Wittig, Maxine Demchak, and Eric Klein. In London, Elizabeth Murray helped to solve a number of riddles particularly regarding the role of Admiral Iwabuchi, and the puzzling affair of Johnson Matthey. At Harvard, author Carl Nagin was a great help, and he also pursued inquiries for me in Hong Kong and Taiwan.

The mass of material was collated and fed into two computers with the aid of Ineke van den Winkel. Special thanks also to Koko and Pip, who will be sorely missed.

Other field reporting, interviews, and research in Europe, East Asia, Australia, and the Philippines was carried out directly by Peggy Sawyer or by me. All of this produced twenty-seven crates of documents, and resulted in a revealing computer-generated Marcos chronology nearly a thousand pages long.

NOTES

It seemed only fair to spare the reader the burden of the nearly four thousand annotations that originally accompanied this book to the publisher. Instead, a few highlights from each chapter follow, with some general comments on my sources.

Prologue: A DISEASE OF THE HEART

The falsification of the Marcos legend has been appreciated for years, but nobody was quite certain what the real story was. See, for example, the comments on Hartzell Spence in Raymond Bonner, *Waltzing with a Dictator,* pp. 10–11. Former Senator Raul Manglapus, foreign minister of the Aquino government and the composer of the "Magsaysay Mambo," once charged (see Canoy, *The Counterfeit Revolution,* p. 37) that Marcos "paid an American a huge sum of money to write in 1964 . . . that infamous book [*For Every Tear a Victory*] in an attempt to disguise with false hyperbole the fake character of [his] political career." Similar criticisms have been made about Benjamin Gray's biography of Marcos.

My quote from an American soldier shooting Filipinos a hundred years ago is from the newspaper *Ang Katipunan,* June 1985, but many similar comments can be found in Miller's *Benevolent Assimilation.*

One: MURDER MOST FOUL

For the early history of Ferdinand Marcos, there were essentially two categories of information: (1) the official version sponsored by Marcos; and (2) sources contradicting it, including Filipino and American government archives. Since the question of authenticity is approached head-on in the chapter, and the reader is directly involved in examining the contradictions, it is not necessary to go into detail here.

The official biographies are revealing when closely compared because the discrepancies jump out at you; also, Marcos cannot resist screwing up his face and winking to make himself look clever, in the process disclosing more than he intends. What he boasts about in one version is different from what he boasts about in another. There are many magazine articles and collections of World War II anecdotes, and affidavits, which provide still other versions from Marcos. He is often several places at once. Simply by comparing these sources, a different version of his life emerges. It is then possible to cross-check specific details by going to U.S. government records, including the National Archives, and Filipino archives in Manila, to check names, dates, and assertions; some of the contradictions became visible only when they were sorted by a computer program. We followed up with interviews to confirm the alternative versions.

These records are not complete; many of the Marcos materials are missing from American archives, including the Library of Congress. In Manila, for example, the historical records of the Benguet mines donated to the U.S. Embassy obviously have been laundered or artfully looted of potentially revealing material.

In one particular instance, I found the Gray biography refreshingly accurate: his account of the Nalundasan murder case. Gray was a clever man and a capable writer. Although he reportedly wrote the book to order, his stealthy reconstruction of the court case can be read two ways, and leaves an indelible impression of Marcos as a young bounder, and of his chief accuser, tiny Calixto Aguinaldo, as a decent if pitiable fellow fallen among scoundrels.

Although many Filipinos knew quite a bit about Marcos and his real origins, they did not publish this information because of justifiable fear of retribution. However, rumors became widespread and were repeated from time to time in the American press. After Marcos fled, Filipino journalists such as editor Max Solivan, whose family had been well acquainted with the Marcoses in Ilocos Norte for the better part of this century, verified the details.

Marcos was outspoken about his wealthy patron, whom he referred to as Judge Quaioit, but these references were meaningless until we determined that his name was not Quaioit but Chua, primarily a difference in romanization. The pronunciation is the same, but the spelling throws you off the track. Various well-informed and independent sources in Manila, including two who were cabinet-level associates of President Marcos, confirmed that Judge Chua, who died in 1983, was the putative father.

I have drawn a lot of material for this and other chapters from the outstanding Manila magazine *Graphic,* which was a crusading but fairly typical Filipino journal published in the 1950s and 1960s, the golden age of muckraking, until it was closed down by Marcos under martial law and its editors jailed.

Readers interested in more background might sample the books by Nituda, Canoy, and Mijares. The official Marcos biography of his mother, Josefa, written by Cesar Mella and J. S. Vinluan, is also revealing. The best studies of the Chinese community in the Ilocos were written by the missionary scholars Mr. and Mrs. Reynolds, whose books are complementary. And the most engaging study of the wily President Quezon is by John Gunther. For general background, surprisingly the best overview is the Foreign Area Studies of the Department of State's *The Philippines: A Country Study.*

Pacifico Marcos, Ferdinand's brother, remained in Manila after the fall, in business with Ferdinand's putative half brother Julian Chua, keeping an extremely low profile.

Two: THE ROSE OF TACLOBAN

There are a number of sources on the Romualdez family history, of varying quality, including an authorized biography by the Manila society-page journalist and friend of Imelda, Kerima Polotan, which I found useful for some quotes and details. Only two sources are of any great significance or real merit. Foremost is Loreto Romualdez Ramos, Imelda's first cousin, about fifteen years older than Imelda, a frequent visitor to Imelda's homes in Manila and Leyte during her childhood, and in the early days of the Marcos administration a not infrequent guest at Malacanang Palace. Loreto is generally acknowledged to be the historian of the Romualdez clan, and a woman of great dignity and charm, although her branch fell on hard times thanks to Imelda and her vindictive brothers.

The other excellent source is Filipino author Carmen Pedrosa, who wrote the only serious or critical biography of Imelda in existence, a small and obscure work published many years ago in Manila—obscure because it was suppressed. One of Pedrosa's chief sources was Loreto Romualdez Ramos. When the first edition of her book appeared in Manila, Pedrosa was forced to flee the country, even before martial law was declared.

Pedrosa had done her homework, tracked down authentic sources including the family servants, and generally assembled an extremely valuable compendium of family lore. Anyone writing about Imelda must be indebted to her. Unfortunately, the book suffers from a perplexing organizational flaw: it has no precise chronology. Excellent material is arranged in such a way that it is all but impossible to see cause-and-effect. An updated version was published in London in 1987, adding some interesting new material after the downfall.

To understand Imelda and her brothers, I felt that it was imperative to resolve the chronology and discover the cause-and-effect. We conducted lengthy interviews with Loreto Romualdez Ramos in Manila, during which all the known details of Imelda's life were reviewed, the chronology was carefully re-examined, and a special effort was made to resolve how one thing led to another. In this way we were able both to reconfirm and to clarify much of what Pedrosa had written, in the process reassembling events in their proper order, supplemented with much original material from Loreto. More important, we discovered how the eccentric personalities of the Romualdez clan were what caused the tragedies that shaped Imelda and her siblings, and eventually came full circle like the sting of a scorpion's tail. Revenge was the driving force for Imelda, Kokoy, and Alfredo. And from revenge grew greed.

I visited many of the places associated with Imelda's life, interviewed townsfolk, villagers, and had many amusing hours with museum curators in Tacloban responsible for Imelda's memorabilia at the Santo Nino Shrine. I found Leytenos universally good-natured, and the island itself superb.

Orestes, Imelda's father, died of cancer in the 1950s. Pedrosa conducted lengthy interviews with the maid who slept on the next plank in his garage, and the maid said Orestes came out to the garage and forced himself upon the unwilling Medy repeatedly. This was also confirmed by the maid's husband, who was a servant in the house and also witnessed these nocturnal assaults and their consequences. Cousin Loreto confirmed this during our taped interviews, referring to Orestes as being sexually "incandescent hot."

Three: THE LOST COMMAND

Ferdinand's bogus heroism during World War II has been treated in several Filipino books and journals such as *We Forum,* a journal that was shut down as a consequence, and more recently by Jeff Gerth and Joel Brinkley writing in *The New York Times* and John Sharkey in *The Washington Post,* whose articles were based on the emergence of U.S. Army files on Marcos that had been hidden away by the Pentagon for decades. John Sharkey had been pursuing these records for years, urged on by a Filipino physician who knew the legend was a hoax. Sharkey had been writing repeatedly to army historians and government bureaucrats who continually stonewalled. Similarly, scholar and author Alfred McCoy was on their trail, and it was McCoy who, while looking for other material in the National Archives, discovered that the missing Marcos war records had miraculously reappeared and drew this to the attention of the *Times.* Subsequent congressional investigation determined that the Pentagon, after mischievously burying the records for decades in a Midwestern vault, had just as mischievously slipped them back into the archives where they belonged, to await McCoy's serendipitous discovery. These records established beyond reasonable doubt that Marcos was lying in instance after instance, and that his claims to many medals were false. But unfortunately they did not immediately resolve what Marcos actually was doing during the period in question. This would have required a close study of the Japanese occupation and the wartime guerrilla movement—a study none of the journalists apparently was in a position to undertake.

Several Filipino authors were well-known guerrilla leaders during the war but had little knowledge of areas beyond their immediate control, so they knew Marcos was lying but could not say exactly what he was doing. There was no way to avoid making such a study, so I went back to square one and started over. Working with charts, computer programs, and unit histories, we tracked all the contradictory Marcos claims, comparing them to each other and to actual events. Specific details were drawn from the U.S. National Archives, from individual intelligence reports, and from depositions made by U.S. military officers during the war and army special investigators immediately afterward, when they were given the job of checking the Marcos claims. Other material was drawn from the MacArthur Library in Norfolk, Virginia.

Among the most comic accounts of Marcos heroism is the Filipino anthology of heroic tales, Ongpauco's *They Refused to Die.*

Nobody can savor the bogus heroism of Ferdinand Marcos properly without grasping the equally bogus heroism of General Douglas MacArthur, who had a large team of flacks engaged exclusively in the job of falsifying his public image with the people back home. It is only recently that scholars have cut through the sludge and started to reveal the MacArthur legend for what it really is. So far the major works are historian Carol M. Petillo's *Douglas MacArthur: The Philippine Years,* and the excellent military history of the Pacific War by Ronald H. Spector, *Eagle Against the Sun.* Both quote as well from previously unknown diaries by Dwight Eisenhower, which reveal that Ike (who knew him well) considered MacArthur to be a poseur and a coward.

My description of the Quirino brothers is how the Department of State and the CIA summed them up for President Truman. Laurel's work for the Japanese is documented by David Joel Steinberg in *Philippine Collaboration in World War II.* Since Laurel's responsibilities as interior minister included liaison with the Kempeitei, it follows that people like Marcos who worked for Laurel had an implicit association with the Kempeitei. The Villamor quote comes from Willoughby's *The Guerrilla Resistance Movement in the Philippines: 1941–1945.* Quotes from Captain Hunt come from National Archive documents. The source for the radio message ordering Ferdinand's execution is Gray, *Rendezvous with Destiny,* which was sprinkled with accuracies.

Four: YAMASHITA'S GOLD

All the chapters having to do with Yamashita's Gold are drawn from related materials, so comments about sources for one chapter can be taken to apply to the others.

The Ben and Paul story is in several parts, chronologically. The first part is the basic story, covering the period up to 1945, and appears in Chapter Four. The second part, in Chapter Sixteen, resumes their story and covers the period up to 1975; this was made public by Bob Curtis after his return from Manila, and was widely published, including a long series of articles in the Las Vegas *Sun* and another in *The Philippine News* of San Francisco, with parallel articles appearing simultaneously in Jack Anderson's syndicated column.

Ben and Paul have never disclosed their real Japanese names and live a shadowy and pseudonymous existence. Now in his seventies, Ben is no longer able to remember details. It was Bob Curtis who told us he discovered from Ben and Paul that they had been lying all along—that they had been Japanese naval officers, not Filipino houseboys, and by their own admission had been participants (not mere spectators) in the mass murder and live burial of Allied POWs.

What was really going on in Manila, and which Ben and Paul were a party to, is detailed in Chapter Five, and the reader is referred to the notes there.

After articles began to appear saying that Marcos was not a legitimate war hero, Marcos launched a counterattack through his press office. He produced a blizzard of affidavits from Filipinos and Americans who "confirmed" that Marcos really was a legitimate hero. The two Americans primarily involved in signing these affidavits were Lieutenant Jamison and Sergeant Guzman, whose accounts were contradicted by the long-missing U.S. Army records. Both Guzman and Jamison were guests at Malacanang Palace, and were given prominent play as heroes themselves in the official Marcos biographies. Once the Marcos records reappeared, it became clear that U.S. Army investigators concluded all the Marcos claims were false.

The Lino Patajo and Duque stories were related by Marcos himself.

When I say that Defense Secretary Weinberger had "knowledge," I mean that material had been originated by the Defense Department and tucked away by the Pentagon in its own archives, where the Pentagon made dogged efforts to keep it out of the hands of journalists. Whether his many assistants at the Pentagon had direct knowledge and failed to inform him is another matter, although I have shown that President Johnson was specifically said by his own advisers to be "aware" of the issue. The U.S. Army, which Weinberger nominally headed, itself had investigated Marcos and thoroughly discredited his claims, as had the Veterans Administration, and a subsequent congressional investigation into the disposition of these records showed that the Weinberger Pentagon chose consciously and deliberately to keep the records submerged despite honest efforts to obtain them under the Freedom of Information and Privacy Act. Many articles had been published directly challenging the authenticity of the Marcos war claims *before* Weinberger presented Marcos with the case of medals, and the CIA and DIA had been filing routinely on the bogus heroism issue for many years. For Weinberger not to have been apprised of the falsity of the Marcos claims would be tantamount to neglect of duty on the part of his Pentagon staff.

My account of the killing of Mariano Marcos came from Charlie Glazer, a CIA officer who was attached after World War II to Malacanang Palace as its liaison officer with the U.S. government. Glazer served in this position for many years, and eventually retired to live out his years in Manila. In the mid-1980s, I became friends with Glazer and with Dorothy Bohannon, the widow of General Lansdale's executive officer, Colonel "Bo" Bohannon, also a lifelong Manila resident plugged into the CIA circuit. Glazer died of cancer of the throat in 1987; Dorothy Bohannon, a woman of great charm, died of a heart attack soon afterward. Many of my insights into CIA "initiatives" in Manila came from Charlie, and it was Dorothy who made possible the taped interviews with Loreto Romualdez Ramos.

General Lansdale told me he remembered Marcos after the war only as "another ambitious young guy pushing for recognition." Glazer remembered Marcos quite differently, suggesting that Lansdale was being typically evasive. Lansdale died just before Glazer.

It is all the more interesting, therefore, that Charlie Glazer's account of the murder of Mariano Marcos came from Lansdale's special assistant for many years, Helen Jones. A Filipino-American, Helen had been an outstanding guerrilla during World War II, and had firsthand knowledge of Mariano's execution at the hands of guerrillas under the command of her colleague, Major Barnett. Being drawn and quartered by carabao is not unusual. In the 1950s, a close friend of Colonel Valeriano was executed in that fashion by anti-government guerrillas enraged by his conduct of paramilitary operations against them.

Five: UNNATURAL ACTS

Sasakawa's prison record and his involvement with Kodama and others in money raising through the fear of political denunciation has been written about extensively, and he speaks openly of it himself in interviews. For Sasakawa and Kodama, see Dubro and Kaplan's "Soft-Core Fascism: The Rehabilitation of Ryoichi Sasakawa," *Village Voice,* October 4, 1983, and also Kaplan and Dubro's bedrock book, *Yakuza,* which describes the evolution of the Japanese underworld. See also the *Japan-Asia Quarterly Review* (Winter 1974), and the business monthly *Insight* (April 1978). Details of Kodama's career can be gleaned from Toland's *Rising Sun* and Manchester's *American Caesar.* Other bits and pieces come from accounts of the Japanese conquest of Korea, Manchuria, North China, and Southeast Asia. The role of Chiang Kai-shek and the Green Gang, Big-eared Tu, and the Ku brothers is described in *The Soong Dynasty.* Iwabuchi's mysterious career was reconstructed by me from the tiny fragments available in Japanese records. Experts on Japanese military history find Iwabuchi's scanty records extremely strange. My explanation of what he was really doing in Manila, and the real reason for his slaughter of a hundred thousand civilians, is in keeping with the picture that is only now gradually emerging of the conspiracy of the Japanese *kurumaku* in looting East and Southeast Asia as part of a power struggle over the Chrysanthemum throne.

For MacArthur's role in returning Fascists to power after the war in Tokyo, Manila, and elsewhere, see Steinberg's *Philippine Collaboration in World War II,* and sections in Toland, Manchester, Petillo, and Spector dealing with the conduct of the war crimes trials.

Willoughby, Whitney, Parsons, and Soriano are all dead, but the record is clear on their political views. Their own books and the biographies of MacArthur give ample evidence. Willoughby's and Soriano's involvements with the Spanish Fascists were notorious.

My main source on the Huks is the classic by Kerkvliet, *The Huk Rebellion,* and of course Lansdale's own book, *In the Midst of Wars.*

Floro Crisologo was murdered by his friends, appropriately, at the confessional. Sources on his thuggery include McCoy's *Priests on Trial* and many editions of the excellent *Far Eastern Economic Review,* edited spiritedly by my old friend Derek Davies and now owned by Dow-Jones.

The Avelino quote is from Art Zich's "The Marcos Era," in *The Wilson Quarterly,* vol. 10, no. 3 (Summer 1986).

Fernando Lopez is dead, but for his games with the Japanese, see Alfred McCoy's *Southeast Asia Under Japanese Occupation.*

Heinie Aderholt is one of my folk heroes from the days of aerial derring-do in World War II and Dragonlady days in Indochina, and we have many close mutual friends who played leading roles in black operations throughout Asia. Many of them appear in my first book, a history of mercenary pilots called *Soldiers of Fortune,* which included a chapter on Heinie's secret air operations in the Far East. What General Aderholt and his colleagues in the field were doing, they often did brilliantly, and condemnation should be redirected to the White House, the Pentagon, and Langley, where the decisions to interfere there were made.

Valeriano is dead. My sources on him included interviews with his widow conducted for me by Tom Marks, and with Valeriano's old cronies in Manila.

The Stonehill case continues unresolved in U.S. courts decades after he was expelled from the Philippines, and meanwhile the IRS has attached handsome trust funds Stonehill set up for his children. Sources on the Stonehill connection include pieces written by Robert Shaplen for *The New Yorker* listed in my bibliography, and extensive coverage in the U.S. press (*Time, Newsweek,* etc.) from that period. Also see Pool and Vanzi's *Revolution in the Philippines* and McCoy's *Priests on Trial.* The Philippine press covered the case exhaustively. Ed Leslie also tracked down the U.S. court records on the Stonehill case, and many interviews were conducted in the Philippines linking Stonehill, Lim, Marcos, and others. See *United States of America v. Harry Stonehill et al.,* Civ. No. 65-127-GSJ, U.S. District Court, Central District of California, July 23, 1976.

The Tinio quote was from *Life* Magazine, November 26, 1965. The Campos quote was in the Los Angeles *Times,* March 26, 1985. The Duque and Fukimitsu material was from the Los Angeles *Times,* May 28, 1978.

Six: COWBOYS IN THE PALACE

Among the materials I had access to were ten thousand pages of top-secret CIA documents. These included a full year of intelligence summaries to the president, in which I examined closely the sections dealing with the Philippines. Although this included a great deal of sensitive material, I have only used very brief extracts directly related to the purpose of this book, showing readers how policy decisions were made or influenced by the kind of information being passed on to the president. This has special relevance to Chapters Five, Six, and Thirteen. Documents cited in other chapters came separately from the State Department and the CIA. The depressing conclusion to be reached is that America intervened too often, and that no matter whether the president of the United States was well informed or poorly informed, he usually made (in some cases was encouraged to make) bad decisions that brought bad people into positions of power. These decisions were sometimes affected, as in the case of General Lansdale, by the distorted (not to say lunatic) perceptions of the senior agent in the field. However, in the eyes of much of the world, venality and insincerity have become hallmarks of American foreign policy.

I corresponded with General Lansdale shortly before his death. Aside from a few useful details, his letters and books revealed a lifelong characteristic of evasion and distortion. It reminded me of suggestions in recent years that van Gogh's artistic perceptions were altered by drugs used to combat his psychic distress. Lansdale was an extremely charming man, which was his great asset. He was a snake-oil salesman from the early America of Andrew Jackson, who became addicted to his own product. At some point early in World War II he became bemused by his own fantasy world, and never regained a self-critical faculty. As I point out in a later chapter, even the CIA eventually began to suspect that Lansdale was nuts, as described by Thomas Powers in his book *The Man Who Kept the Secrets.*

The role of Gabe Kaplan was drawn from many sources, including Lansdale and Joseph Smith's *Portrait of a Cold Warrior.*

Jose Crisol is described as a secret policeman in Rosenberg's *Marcos and Martial Law in the Philippines.* See also Pool and Vanzi, and Bello and Rivera's *Logistics of Repression* (p. 35), which discusses Crisol's relationship to the CIA. See discussions of Crisol's work with Lansdale in the Abueva biography, *Ramon Magsaysay.*

The murder plot of Lovett and Spruance is told in Smith's *Portrait of a Cold Warrior*. Admiral Spruance and General Lovett were grizzled heroes of World War II, and Lovett was CIA station chief while Spruance was ambassador. Smith worked for them and gives a delightful insight into how the CIA fights dirty.

Seven: A MESS OF POTAGE

This chapter was based primarily on published sources in the Philippines, supplemented by interviews with insiders such as Loreto Romualdez Ramos, who was still intimate with Imelda at the time. But all the published versions conflicted. The long relationship between Ferdinand and Carmen Ortega, for example, was familiar to politically aware Filipinos for many years, but it was not something that could be discussed openly, and no journalist who heard about it was in a position to verify the rumors. It was only when we developed a computerized chronology that we were able to resolve the dates and determine cause-and-effect. Everything was then rechecked with Loreto to be certain we had it right.

This is as good a place as any to point out that we made repeated efforts to arrange interviews with the Marcoses, especially with Imelda, and were blocked each time. Our letters were delivered by hand to their Honolulu residences, and culminated in writing to the primary Marcos attorney in Honolulu. This letter was delivered personally by Tom Marks to the receptionist in the lawyer's office, and Marks waited to observe the attorney pick up the letter and ask the secretary, "What's this?" No response was made by the attorney or by the Marcoses.

It may be pertinent that the attorney in question had just been reported to have advised the Marcoses not to grant any more interviews because of the universally bad press they were receiving. While interviews with the principals may be regarded as essential in some biographies, they are impossible in others, and in cases where the principals can be shown to be creatures of their own invention, interviews are of dubious significance. Characteristically, Marcos would only deny everything, invent a fanciful rationalization, or refuse to talk and end the interview. But the effort had to be made in any case.

The first to publish a mention of Carmen Ortega was Primitivo Mijares.

Ted Lewin's life in Manila gambling is described by Joseph Smith in his book *Portrait of a Cold Warrior* and by Fidel Ongpauco in *They Refused to Die*. Extensive interviews about Lewin were conducted by us with Manila sources.

About the Stonehill payment of $5 million: it had long been rumored that Stonehill had paid huge bribes to Philippine government officials, but no figures were mentioned and no evidence was published. All our attempts to obtain copies of original documents in the legal proceedings in American courts were stonewalled at the IRS and other government agencies in Washington and in California. Don Goldberg nearly obtained six cubic feet of documents relating to the case over the last thirteen years, but was blocked by the IRS at the last moment apparently to avoid disclosure of the political considerations. Many of the people directly involved in the Stonehill affair (who now occupy major positions in the Aquino administration) continue to refuse to talk about it. Ed Leslie was finally able to obtain legal summaries of the proceedings, which revealed that Stonehill had paid a bribe (to high officials in the Philippine government) totaling $5 million in cash. See *United States of America* v. *Harry Stonehill et al.,* Civ. No. 65-127-GSJ, U.S. District Court, Central District of California, July 23, 1976.

The men deported from the Philippines in the Stonehill affair were *accused,* and had not been tried by Filipino courts. President Macapagal, in fact, said he was deporting them and avoiding court trials as "an act of national preservation." Upon examining the U.S. court records from California Central District, I found that the records do not refer to these matters as allegations but as statements of fact.

Lino Bocalan was a convicted criminal, convicted and sentenced to prison by Filipino courts, and later released from prison when Marcos became president. Bocalan also was part of the smuggling net set up by the CIA with Kodama, Sasakawa, and Marcos to provide logistical support to the Sumatran colonels fighting Sukarno—a matter about which Sasakawa boasted. See, for example, *Life* Magazine, November 26, 1965, and materials cited earlier for Kodama and Sasakawa.

The possibility that Ver is Marcos's half brother has been repeated in many published sources, including *The New York Times.*

Eight: THE HIDDEN AGENDA

This chapter was assembled from published newspaper accounts mingled with recently declassified State Department files and embassy cable traffic. Seen together, they are very revealing. Most of the time they are not seen together.

The U.S. government has taken pains to obscure many of its dealings with Marcos, so there is a limit to how much we are able to uncover, even under the Freedom of Information/Privacy Act. For example, when investigative reporter Don Goldberg repeatedly asked the Department of State to release its files on Yamashita's Gold, the Department told him he had no justification for asking. State then reclassified the entire Yamashita Gold file to block further Freedom of Information attempts.

In the same manner, all the material and documents relating to the "special arrangement" between Marcos and LBJ continues to be tightly classified more than two decades later, as is the result of the congressional hearings into those special arrangements. Washington is afraid of the embarrassment it would suffer if LBJ's deals with Marcos were ever to see the light of day.

For the role of the Chinese in Manila, see Blaker's *The Chinese in the Philippines: A Study of Power and Change,* and McBeath's *Political Integration of the Philippine Chinese* (p. 246). In addition, see Scott Anderson and Jon Lee Anderson, *Inside the League,* pp. 46, 60, 61–63, 65, 68–70, and 129.

Nine: LADY BOUNTIFUL

My object in this chapter is only to reveal ironies. Imelda was always perfectly capable of dramatizing her own persona and never needed help to make her case. I have taken just a few of the many vignettes and quotations that writers customarily have used to assassinate her character, and I have tried to remain as neutral or deadpan as possible. This has not been easy, but the effort has been made conscientiously. There were times early in her career when it was only possible to feel compassion and sympathy for her, but this compulsion gradually wears off.

The subject of the "Black Room" in Malacanang comes up repeatedly, and I cite statements made by people who worked there as guards, and various incidents in which people were taken there and never reappeared. (Interviews in Manila also confirmed the story of the Black Room.) I have tried to handle the subject with restraint, because the murders that reportedly took place were so bizarre and involved such horrible atrocities that the effect on readers' sensibilities might be counterproductive.

Jaime Ferrer was interviewed for this book by Don Goldberg and Dale Van Atta in Manila, on the condition of strict anonymity. However, Ferrer was assassinated shortly afterward in the summer of 1987, and I consider that thereafter the need for anonymity ceased.

Jose Campos turned state's evidence and provided the Aquino government with details of what he had done for Marcos.

Jonathan Kwitny's *The Crimes of Patriots* deals at length with the Nugan-Hand scandal.

On the question of Walton helping Marcos set up his new secret police state, see Plate and Darvi's *Secret Police* and Bello and Rivera's *The Logistics of Repression*. For the Taiwan connection, see S. and J. L. Anderson's *Inside the League* and Boorman's profile of Chiang Ching-kuo in his *Biographical Dictionary of Republican China*. Links between Ver and Crisologo can be seen in McCoy's *Priests on Trial* and Mijares's *The Conjugal Dictatorship of Ferdinand and Imelda Marcos*. Ver and AMWORLD are described in the December 14, 1986, San Francisco *Examiner;* the January 10, 1987, Honolulu *Advertiser;* the April 7, 1986, Los Angeles *Times;* the January–February 1987 *Ang Katipunan;* the December 17, 1987, *Philippine News;* and the *Herald-Examiner* of January 11, 1987.

The account of Maceda and Salas working against Doy Laurel is from Nick Joaquin's *Doy Laurel in Profile*.

Ten: THE CASTING COUCH

My Dovie Beams material comes from a variety of sources, including California's *Asian-American News* (interviews with Dovie Beams) and the Rotea book titled *Marcos' Lovie Dovie.* Dovie was said to have undertaken the book with the encouragement of the Lopez clan; it was widely reported that the Lopezes were encouraging Dovie, and Rotea had been a reporter on Lopez newspapers. Charges were leveled in the pro-Marcos magazine *Republic Weekly* that "she was used as the tool of a certain oligarch who wanted to even the score with President Marcos." The dossier prepared on Dovie for Imelda, which was among the documents seized from the Marcoses on their arrival in Hawaii, raises the question, saying, "What truth was there that she was being used by certain local politicians and the American CIA?"

Marcos had just rigged the 1969 presidential election, and the opposition was afraid that he was going to arrange to stay in power permanently by declaring martial law or by putting Imelda in office. The device of embarrassing Marcos in public, or creating domestic strife between Ferdinand and Imelda, was a natural weapon for the opposition to choose. That is why there were many rumors that the Lopez clan was backing Dovie. Eugenio Lopez, Jr., was the director for communications for the Movement for a Free Philippines in the United States, according to Rodriguez, *The Marcos Regime* (p. 232).

It is apparent that Rotea was to ghost-write the book, because Dovie provided him with her reminiscences on tape and gave him many photographs which she autographed with affectionate remarks. These are published in the book, along with direct quotations from the tapes. Generally, Rotea presents Dovie in a sympathetic manner, but in an apparent attempt to be objective he goes on to include negative material from a propaganda effort by Ferdinand and Imelda to discredit Dovie that includes nude photos of her. These are the photos reportedly taken by Ferdinand Marcos during their trysts, and are generally acknowledged by knowledgeable sources in Manila to be authentic. Nobody has ever seriously believed otherwise. But the inclusion of this negative material in the Rotea book offended Dovie.

Somehow, Dovie ended up with many millions of dollars in real estate in Beverly Hills and Pasadena, obtained through progressively larger property loans from California banks. In 1987, Dovie and her new husband, Sergio Villagran, were indicted by a federal grand jury in California on charges involving $18 million in fraudulent loans, including forty-two counts of bank fraud, bankruptcy fraud, and making false statements on loan applications. In Manila, it was conjectured that Marcos might have made Dovie a settlement through the Beverly Hills bank he owned with Roberto Benedicto, and that Dovie gradually parlayed her position at this bank into leverage at other banks, but this is only conjecture. It was likely to be some time before the case was resolved. If found guilty, Dovie faced a total of 141 years in jail and a fine of $10.5 million; her husband faced 136 years in prison and a fine of $10.25 million.

The statements made by Dovie to other interviewers over the years actually bear out what Rotea put in his book. The main problem with the book is that it was hastily written. The tape-recorded conversations are so ludicrous that I have avoided using them except for very brief extracts.

I became acquainted with Ambassador Byroade in 1965 while he was posted to Rangoon, and Dovie's account of Byroade's involvement in Imelda's attempts to get her out of Manila does not clash jarringly with my impressions.

The affection of Ferdinand Marcos for Gretchen Cojuangco is described by Mijares and was mentioned also in *Parade* Magazine, December 17, 1978.

Diosdado Bote is dead. Dovie's account of his visit to her was related in the *Asian-American News* interviews.

For a good summary of how Marcos turned the electoral system to his own purposes, see *Manipulated Elections*.

Delfin Cueto is dead. He was killed in a gun battle with the bodyguards of the mayor of Makati.

The story about Imelda taking a swing at Carmen Soriano is from Mijares. In his book, the singer is identified only as C.S., but Filipino sources confirm this was

Carmen Soriano. (Photographs of Imelda which appeared in *Vanity Affair* in August 1986 show her posing in look-alike costume and make-up. Filipino friends immediately identified the woman in the picture as Carmen Soriano and were startled when they read the caption identifying the woman as Imelda.)

Eleven: IRON BUTTERFLY

Some CIA extracts in this chapter came from the NID or National Intelligence Digest, a summary prepared every day of the week for the president; others came from individual field agent reports or the files of CIA analysts. Since these all concern a dictatorship that has since collapsed, the only material really still sensitive was the identification of the CIA's sources and names of agents and analysts, all of which I have deleted.

Sources in New York and California who mingled with Imelda's twilight groupies asserted that she was a lesbian, and that her friendship with Cristina Ford had been "very serious." One New York gay source even called her "the world's leading lesbian—certainly the richest." I remain unconvinced. There was not enough hard evidence to dispel lingering doubts.

Cristina Ford stories appeared in the recent biography by Lacey, and the lesbian rumors were repeated in *Newsweek,* March 24, 1986, and *Vanity Fair* for August 1986. The Ford stockholders' suit also was widely reported. Phil Bronstein, who has done some of the best reporting on the Philippines, described his encounter with Imelda to Don Goldberg. Ziballa's love affair with Imelda is described in Chapter Two, and was related on tape by cousin Loreto. See also Pedrosa.

The Cruz affair was described in detail by Barbara Gonzales in the magazine *West* of April 13, 1986. Imelda's affection for Cliburn, Fonteyn, Nureyev, and others has been widely reported, for example, in Pool and Vanzi; the grand pianos were described in *The New York Times.* Armand Hammer's dealings with Imelda Marcos and the fact that some galleries raised prices when dealing with Imelda were reported in *The New York Times,* April 27, 1986, and *Arts & Antiques* Magazine (summer 1986).

The Lopez quote is from Tom Buckley, *Harper's* (February 1972).

The story about the one-way mirror came to me originally from former *Time* correspondent Art Zich, now contributing to a number of leading magazines, who has spent many years in Asia and the Pacific. Corky Johnson of Jack Anderson's staff corroborated it with Ruben Cusipag, a friend of Ninoy Aquino, who told us that Aquino carried the snapshot of Imelda on the john around in his wallet for years thereafter. Corky then reconfirmed the verification with acting Philippine Ambassador to Canada Boyani Mangibin.

I explain in the text that Mijares discussed the Plaza Miranda bombing with Ver's security men while Mijares still was chief propagandist of the dictatorship. This is generally accepted in Manila as the truth. It was further supported by a victim of the bombing, the senator and former justice minister Jose Diokno, quoted in *The New York Times,* September 7, 1971.

The Karagatan affair was summarized in *Graphic,* July 26, 1972. But see also Canoy, *The Counterfeit Revolution* (p. 3).

Eduardo Cojuangco's feud with other members of his clan and with the Aquinos is famous in the Philippines.

The endorsement of martial law in the Philippines by Nixon, Kissinger, and Byroade was first published by Mijares in *The Conjugal Dictatorship of Ferdinand and Imelda Marcos,* and ten years later was reconfirmed by Ray Bonner in his book *Waltzing with a Dictator.* For further discussion of Kissinger and Mijares, see Psinakis, *Two Terrorists Meet.* The real significance of these charges is that Marcos was not simply asking endorsement of a plan to declare martial law for a brief period to see him through a crisis, but that Marcos was using it to stay in power beyond the constitutional limit of two terms. Therefore, Washington was endorsing implicitly a violation of the Philippine constitution.

Twelve: SALVAGING DEMOCRACY

This chapter is only the tip of the iceberg. There is a very large literature on human rights abuses in the Philippines, and among the authorities is the scholar and bestselling author Alfred McCoy, who is married to a Filipino and now teaches at a university in Australia.

Records of Aguinaldo's role in the treatment of political prisoners were maintained by the Catholic Church. Most of my biographical data on Aguinaldo came from a publication called *Pumipiglas,* produced in 1980 by the Catholic-dominated Association of Major Religious Superiors in the Philippines with the cooperation of Task Force Detainees, a Catholic watchdog force working to document cases of human rights abuse. Both the Association and the Task Force were highly regarded for their accuracy. Not surprisingly, Aguinaldo has never been prosecuted. He was very close to former Defense Minister Enrile, to Chiefs-of-Staff Fidel Ramos and Rocky Ileto (both West Pointers), and to RAM leaders such as Colonel Greg Honasan, who were all close to the CIA station. Knowledgeable sources claimed that Aguinaldo knew too many embarrassing things about too many people ever to be prosecuted. Early in 1988, having avoided all these charges, Aguinaldo was elected governor of Enrile's home province.

The Aquino government eventually brought homicide charges against Colonel Honasan and other members of his RAM military clique (Enrile's "my boys") for the appallingly grisly murder in 1987 of the young labor leader Olalia, but Honasan and his comrades escaped from a prison ship in Manila Bay. It is asserted in Manila legal circles that if they are recaptured and brought to trial, they may be charged additionally with the murders of Dr. Mike Baccay and the son of Primitivo Mijares, who apparently were slain with identical pathology signatures. Honasan once boasted rather sadistically that if RAM had succeeded in storming Malacanang Palace, his plan for President Marcos was to "separate him from his dialysis machine and watch him go" (quoted by Lewis Simons in *Worth Dying For*). See also *Far Eastern Economic Review,* July 2, 1973; *Commonweal,* January 12, 1973; *Philippines Repression and Resistance* (pp. 135–137); and Bello and Rivera, *Logistics of Repression.*

The torture and killing of Purificacion Pedro is from *Pumipiglas,* as well as the Philippine *Liberation Courier* of February 1977, and McCoy's *Priests on Trial.*

The floating casino and the role of Psinakis are described in Pool and Vanzi. See also Psinakis's own account in *Two Terrorists Meet* and *Far Eastern Economic Review,* January 18, 1980, September 19, 1980, and October 14, 1977. Sources on Burns include *Far Eastern Economic Review,* March 5, 1982, and *Mother Jones* (June 1983).

Al Haig's comments on fighting terrorism were in *The Nation,* March 20, 1982. For the arrest of Doris Nueval, Corky Johnson interviewed her friend Tess Malolos. I was provided with documentation from the lawyers involved in the Seattle murder case. See also Jack Anderson's syndicated column, September 11, 1982.

Thirteen: FILIPINO ROULETTE

Because he continues to occupy a position in the Philippine government, I have constructed Enrile's story largely from previously published sources, supplemented by some CIA material and interviews. Although he played the Cesar Romero role in the Marcos tyranny and turned on his old friend in the crunch, his charm and opportunism were not unusual in the Philippines. Nearly everything known about Enrile has appeared at one time or another in *Far Eastern Economic Review.*

Fourteen: THE ANTI-HERO

Among informed observers in Manila, including American and other foreign diplomats, there does not seem to be any question that Mijares was taken to the Black Room at Malacanang (rather than to Ver's military headquarters), and was tortured there before being murdered, and that his son was brought to the Black Room and tortured in front of him, grotesquely mutilated, and then killed. The unresolved question is whether President Marcos ever participated or was a spectator in activities in the Black Room, or whether these activities were carried out only by Ver's specialists. The only likely reason for having the Black Room at Malacanang (instead of torturing people elsewhere) was as a convenience to the occupants of the palace.

That his peers identified Marcos with murder is illustrated by an exchange early in 1988 in Kuala Lumpur, Malaysia, reported in *Far Eastern Economic Review.* Prime Minister Dato Seri Mahathir Mohammed was using increasingly draconian measures to clamp down on dissent and political opposition. Accused of being "another Ferdinand Marcos," Mahathir retorted: "How many men have I killed?"

Fifteen: BUSINESS AS USUAL

There are many, many sources running to thousands of pages on how Marcos took over various Philippine businesses. For basic overviews, see Canoy, *The Counterfeit Revolution,* and Rosenberg, *Marcos and Martial Law in the Philippines.* Much of my material on the takeover of the sugar, coconut, and banana industries came from astute intelligence reporting by the U.S. Department of Agriculture, which maintained close watch through the Manila Embassy.

While the Marcos cronies are now thoroughly discredited, Eduardo Cojuangco and Roberto Benedicto (both billionaires) have remained invisible and have avoided any serious embarrassment. They fled when Marcos fell and have not returned to the islands since. It has been asserted repeatedly in Manila that if Cojuangco returned, he would be charged immediately with, among other things, involvement in plotting the Aquino assassination, because he was hovering nearby and because one of his hired guns, a member of his Monkees Team trained by Israeli commandos on Bugsuc Island off Palawan, was among the men accompanying Ninoy at the time he was shot. He was not the man who pulled the trigger, but was identified as the one on the tape recordings who had the exchange with the killer that ran: "I'll do it." "No, I'll do it." That Cojuangco was temporarily in uniform directing bomb attacks by the Monkees is attested to by Canoy (p. 19) and in Stauffer, *The Marcos Regime* (p. 52). That Cojuangco had ambitions to succeed Marcos as dictator, in partnership with Fabian Ver, is clear from reports of a Cojuangco-Ver coup plot recounted by Lewis Simons in his recent book *Worth Dying For.*

Since the downfall, many of Eduardo Cojuangco's questionably acquired properties were sequestered by his cousin, Mrs. Aquino, and some private agreement is alleged to have been reached between branches of the clan for Eduardo not to return. On the basis of his U.S. investments alone, many of them in breweries, he was still regarded as a billionaire several times over, second in wealth only to Marcos and one notch ahead of Enrile. It was also asserted that while in America he continued to meddle in plots and conspiracies to overthrow Mrs. Aquino, but the U.S. government, which was not disposed to prosecute, allowed Cojuangco to enter and leave the country freely and to conduct business as usual.

While it was permissive toward Eduardo Cojuangco, Washington tightened the screws on Steve Psinakis in 1987–88 and began prosecuting him, primarily on the basis of ten-year-old charges that a length of detonator cord had been found (or planted) in his trash barrel in an alley behind his San Francisco home, by an FBI baglady. See *The Washington Post,* March 10, 1986.

It is instructive to compare the U.S. Justice Department's treatment of Mijares and Psinakis with its special treatment of the Mafia hitman Jimmy "The Weasel" Fratiano, reported in *The Last Mafioso* by Ovid Demaris.

In the case of the Westinghouse nuclear plant, where legal controversy may continue for some time, I found the most balanced reporting to have been done by *Fortune* Magazine (September 1986), so I adhered to its formula in presenting the various arguments. I supplemented my account with recently declassified State Department documents.

One of the unsettled issues is whether there is anything intrinsically wrong with paying multi-million-dollar commissions to government officials or lobbyists, so long as they are seen as commissions rather than bribes. In the Lockheed scandal, Japanese courts concluded that Prime Minister Tanaka should go to jail. The payment Quezon made to General MacArthur, and Kodama made to General Willoughby, come to mind. Coffeeshop sophists contend that cumshaw is a way of life in Asia, and that nothing would get done if Westerners did not profer tea money wherever possible. My opinion is that the Westinghouse nuclear plant story so far is not shocking so much as it is hilarious.

The World Bank story, on the other hand, is depressing. For more details, see Bello et al., *Development Debacle: The World Bank in the Philippines.*

Banker S. C. Gywnne was also a gifted writer, and his full account of this extraordinary adventure is worth reading in *Harper's* (September 1983).

The Sullivan cable is from recently declassified State Department documents. "Wild Bill" Sullivan had close ties to the CIA and was U.S. ambassador to Laos during the height of the secret war, and later to Iran at the height of its crisis.

Sixteen: YAMASHITA'S GOLD, PART TWO

This chapter is a continuation of Chapter Four. The major new element is the involvement of mining engineer Robert Curtis, through Norman Kirst and Olof Jonsson, and the discovery that "houseboys" Ben and Paul were lying. Three years after Curtis fled Manila, he told much of his story to the Las Vegas *Sun* and *The Philippine News* of San Francisco, and to columnists Jack Anderson and Les Whitten. It was in their published versions of the Curtis story that his charges were made about members of the John Birch Society offering to launder the gold bullion. The point is that Curtis borrowed a great deal of money from the Birchers to underwrite the cost of shipping his equipment to Manila, and according to Curtis the loan was made against proceeds to be gained from laundering his share of the treasure recovered. These points were not challenged when they were so widely published, but suit was brought against Curtis for nonpayment. At the time these stories appeared (1978), many people thought Curtis was a nut and that the whole Yamashita Gold story was too weird to be true.

The Las Vegas *Sun* is a good paper, run by an editor, Bryan Greenspun, highly respected in the profession. Greenspun is a close friend of columnist Jack Anderson, and Anderson in turn was personally acquainted with Ferdinand and Imelda, having written many columns flattering to the Marcoses before he learned more and soured on them. Anderson then became a severe critic, and he and Whitten wrote extensively about Primitivo Mijares in an effort to draw attention to the folly of American policy supporting the Marcos regime.

Rather than rely on any of these published versions, we tracked Curtis down ourselves. Don Goldberg found him under his new identity, and examined hundreds of hours of tape recordings and thousands of pages of documents—including receipts, contracts, waybills, letters, and so forth—which backed up what Curtis said. I mention this only because, in the end, we concluded that Curtis was telling the truth all along.

Later, I sent Goldberg to Manila to conduct interviews with many others, including close associates of President Marcos, members of Ver's forces responsible for the security of the president and the First Lady, second-echelon cronies, members of the Manila underworld, and wealthy oligarchs who owned property on which there were said to be Yamashita Gold sites. These included Don Paco Ortigas, who had several major sites on his property. These people were all involved in one way or another in the Marcos gold hunt, and through them we were able to confirm details of the story as related by Curtis. In due course, we cultivated a string of informants in Manila, Hong Kong, and Washington who informed me of inside developments on the gold story, and it was in this way that I already had a front row seat when General Singlaub and his associates came on stage.

Curtis knew surprisingly few details about the origins of the gold during World War II, and nothing at all about Kodama and Iwabuchi. His attention was fixed on technical matters. He knew all about the Japanese enlarging the tunnel system under Manila and hiding much of the treasure in the tunnels, but not about the personalities and politics involved. Those discoveries all came about as a consequence of research Peggy and I began over a decade earlier into Kodama, Generalissimo Chiang, and the Green Gang, for *The Soong Dynasty* and another book in progress.

For general background on the conspiracy of the Japanese ultra right, see the World War II histories, including the best short history, Spector's *Eagle Against the Sun;* also Toland's *Rising Sun;* Manchester's *American Caesar,* supplemented by Deacon's *Kempei Tai;* Kaplan and Dubro's *Yakuza;* and McCoy's *Southeast Asia Under Japanese Occupation.* In his book *The Last Emperor,* Edward Behr provides a graphic glimpse of how the Japanese went about looting Manchuria and North China; the methods applied elsewhere were similar. See also Michael Montgomery's excellent *Imperialist Japan: The Yen to Dominate* (London: Christopher Helm, 1987).

Seventeen: HEAVY BREATHING

Readers who would like to learn more about what is being done to end child abuse internationally might contact Defense for Children International in Washington, D.C. I obtained files on child prostitution also from U.S. congressional hearings. Kaplan and Dubro have surveyed the subject well in *Yakuza.*

Jonathan Kwitny of the *Wall Street Journal* examined the CIA's involvement with Asian organized crime in his books *Endless Enemies* and *The Crimes of Patriots.* McCoy's *The Politics of Heroin in Southeast Asia* is the definitive book on international narcotics, and I am indebted to him for material drawn from this and other books he has written. For my own background, I grew up in the Golden Triangle and have been acquainted all my adult life with the major and minor opium warlords—including Kachin rebel leaders, Shan princes, and KMT generals—many of whom have been genial family friends. Inevitably, perhaps, I have come to regard Washington's position on narcotics to be immensely and consistently hypocritical. True, Shan hill people grow opium poppies, but heroin was invented by Bayer pharmaceutical, and absolutely none of the proceeds from international narcotics trafficking ever re-enters the Shan state. The opium poppy is one plant that will never be destroyed by attacking its roots.

The story of Lewin and the major's wife is from Smith, *Portrait of a Cold Warrior.* Lewin's attachment to Stonehill is documented in the U.S. court records cited above.

The gambling roles of Alfredo and Kokoy were well known in Manila. Dale Van Atta interviewed the current official head of Philippine gambling for me and reconfirmed that Kokoy was the boss for Imelda.

The story of Wallace Groves will be familiar to readers of the *Wall Street Journal* and *The New York Times;* readers without access to the *Times* index in libraries or its electronic database may see Kwitny's *Patriots* or David McClintock's *Indecent Exposure.*

The story of the Mafia's interest in buying Fuga Island was related to Don Goldberg in Manila by a member of the Malacanang Palace security guard.

Eighteen: BLACK GOLD

The Marcos gold deals sound bizarre because of the fantastic sums mentioned in the contracts. But I am not urging the reader to give them credence uncritically; I am simply reporting the growing evidence that much of this *may* be true, indeed probably is. Marcos may have been lying about a great many things, but he was not lying about everything. He did all he could to keep the gold deals secret. Evidence of the involvement with him of so many American generals and covert operatives raises questions that properly should be addressed in congressional hearings, but there is little reason to hope that hearings will occur, or that they would change anything.

It may be that we should disregard the overall figures in each contract and take seriously only the amount mentioned as the first tranche, which was the amount Marcos was immediately anxious to ship. Marcos could have hugely inflated the total ultimately available, the way he cheated at golf, to make gold buyers think he had endless resources. But even if we believe only the first tranche, we are still talking about astronomical sums, normal only for Pentagon contracts or cocaine druglords. For that matter, Marcos was after a fashion a Pentagon contractor and an underworld czar, and the amounts confronting us represent criminal proceeds from Japanese military conquests—much of it stolen from the Asian underworld. Considering all this, are the figures really so strange? The answer is no.

Dale Van Atta interviewed Zobel's chief aide Buddy Gomez, who had been appointed Mrs. Aquino's consul in Hawaii. I have portions of Ron Rewald's court testimony in Honolulu, obtained originally by investigators at the U.S. Congress, and then passed on to me. In these sworn affidavits, Rewald describes the relationship that he and Zobel had with the CIA.

The CIA's misinforming the sultan of Brunei came out during the Iran-Contra hearings.

Jaime Ongpin committed suicide on December 7, 1987. I took the story about Jarecki from *Fortune,* June 2, 1980.

Johnson Matthey executives are still being investigated by Crown prosecutors. What they knew or did not know about Marcos gold deals remains an official secret, and thus not likely to be revealed for at least a generation. For an overview of the crisis, see Fay's *Portrait of an Old Lady: Turmoil at the Bank of England.* See also *The Financial Times, The Times* (London), and *The Economist* coverage, and Hansard's, the record of proceedings in Parliament.

Dacus and other Marcos gold brokers were interviewed by the Center for Constitutional Rights of New York City, which was working with the Aquino government commission trying to track down the missing Marcos loot. Their findings were perused for me by Don Goldberg and Mike Binstein. The information on Lusk and still other brokers came to me from investigative journalist Bob Malone.

I have copies of many of the gold sales documents, including the contract mentioning the hundred generals, which was passed by the American executive at the Marine Corps commandant's party. We have examined the contracts Xeroxed and passed to the CIA by the banker in Luxembourg, as well as the supporting insurance papers for the same transaction. Dale Van Atta had discussions with London and Hong Kong gold merchants. The names of attorneys and brokers that I mention as being listed in the documents were taken directly from the contracts.

Nineteen: CLOAK AND DAGGER

There has been a flurry of books and articles recently examining one aspect or another of The Enterprise, for the role of current or former CIA agents in the Iran-Contra scandal, or the Nugan-Hand scandal. Most of these books (like Bob Woodward's *Veil*) deal only with one or two facets of The Enterprise. But if a reader patiently works his way through all of them, the pieces begin to fit together to produce the picture of a fraternity linked in its membership and undertakings since World War II. Aside from Woodward, these include books by Armstrong, Kwitny, Powers, Marchetti, and Maas. See also *The Chronology*, by the National Security Archive in Washington.

General Li Mi, General Phao, and Nicholas Deak are all dead, but details of their activities are in McCoy's *The Politics of Heroin in Southeast Asia*, Anthony Sampson's *The Arms Bazaar*, and Kwitny's *Endless Enemies* and *Crimes of Patriots*.

For the Mafia's role in Havana and its relationship with the CIA, see Powers's *The Man Who Kept the Secrets*.

General Secord talked about the overcharging in a *Playboy* interview.

The connection between Lockheed and Kodama has been covered extensively in the international press, but see, for instance, Kaplan and Dubro.

Twenty: THE CROWN PRINCE

We had many telephone interviews with Dewey Dee's lawyer in Vancouver, but Dee himself remained Delphic because of the restraints imposed by his appeal for Canadian asylum. Elizalde took refuge in Costa Rica, where he had a big estate with a large mansion staffed by pretty girls, until the Costa Rican government suddenly expelled him in 1987 as an undesirable. Whether his Stone Age Tasaday tribe was real or a hoax has yet to be fully resolved; the allegation was that Elizalde contrived the Tasaday hoax using a handful of primitives from ordinary hill tribes, training them to pose naked and repeat cryptic stories about their origins. His exact motive, other than self-aggrandizement, is unclear. This sort of thing apparently was being done by members of the Marcos group as a form of amusement. At one point Ferdinand began importing African game to stock a tiny Filipino island, to have an exotic place to take cronies and lovelies. Bong-Bong is said to have enjoyed several helicopter hunting trips there, but the project collapsed when the South Africans providing the rare game learned what was being done to the animals.

The story of Imee and Tommy Manotoc was heavily covered in the world press at the time. After the downfall, they did not linger in America, soon turning up in Morocco. What little information I was able to glean on Aimee Marcos came from custodians of the Santo Nino Shrine (the Imelda Shrine) in her home town of Tacloban.

Twenty-one: PEOPLE POWER

Armitage and Perle were both quoted in *The New York Times* and *The Washington Post* as making these inflammatory statements before congressional committees.

Enrile told interviewers shortly after Marcos fled that his knees were knocking so badly he could hardly stand, and the statement was published in a number of Manila papers. It is evident that this and other revealing disclosures were blurted out in an excess of excitement during the Marcos downfall. Not much had been known about Enrile, Fidel Ramos, and others before the People Power coup, but in the enthusiasm of the moment Enrile in particular opened up, as did the much younger leaders of the RAM movement. Filipino journalists, suffocated for years by the Marcos regime, seized the opportunity and published every scrap, some of it picked up and repeated by the international press. Enrile boasted to foreign interviewers about his role in the plots leading up to the overthrow, letting slip in the process many previously unknown bits and pieces about his own personal life. At the time, all the Manila papers called him "Rambo," which must have done wonders for his self-esteem. According to Lewis Simons, Enrile seriously hoped to emerge as the new leader of the Philippines.

U.S. Customs stopped Aimee Marcos, discovered and confiscated the pearls.

Epilogue: PARADISE LOST

Even before Marcos fled, General Singlaub and his group (many of whom I knew personally) came in from stage right. The Singlaub group invited Curtis to Hong Kong to become a member of the board of directors of the foundation that would make use of the gold recovered. I stayed informed primarily through personal contacts in Manila and Washington, including the Pentagon and Capitol Hill, and in this way came to know who was involved in the new gold hunt, what other generals were associated with Singlaub in his anti-Communist foundation, and what their objectives were.

Curtis continued to possess the original Japanese maps and keep them deeply hidden, which was why he remained a pivotal player. He told people who became too inquisitive that he burned the maps.

Many stories about John Singlaub and his treasure hunt appeared in the Manila press, a few in the international press, tending to expose him to ridicule because of the widespread assumption that the gold was a hoax. Yamashita's Gold has been a subject of great interest to many people, so there is nothing odd or peculiar about the interest of General Singlaub, who is a very serious man. While he may be controversial, and is portrayed by his critics as a champion of the lunatic fringe, I found him remarkably personable and a man of extraordinary conviction. His involvement with Yamashita's Gold therefore strikes me as fascinating rather than ridiculous. There is nothing at all ridiculous about John Singlaub.

Mrs. Aquino eventually pushed through a land reform program, but it had no more teeth than previous efforts. For example, all oligarchs were given several months in which to transfer ownership of their estates to corporations, which were exempt from land reform measures. It was sadly obvious that nobody in power was prepared to enact the draconian measures necessary to correct the basic defect in Philippine society, from which most of its other evils grow. Despite the brief excitement of People Power and the sweet interlude of Cory Aquino, the real revolution, the real regurgitation, has yet to come.

BIBLIOGRAPHY

Abaya, Hernando J. *Betrayal in the Philippines.* New York: A. A. Wyn, 1946.

Abinales, P. N. *Militarization: Philippines.* Paper delivered at the Workshop on "Militarization and Society" sponsored by the Asian Peace Research Association, April 3–6, 1982, International House of Japan, Tokyo.

Abueva, Jose V. "The Philippines: Tradition and Change." *Asian Studies* (January 1970).

———. *Ramon Magsaysay: A Political Biography.* Manila: Solidaridad Publishing House, 1971.

Adkins, John H. "Philippines 1971: Events of a Year, Trends of the Future." *Asian Studies* (December 1972).

———. "Philippines 1972: We'll Wait and See." *Asian Studies* (February 1973).

Agoncillo, Teodore A. *A Short History of the Philippines.* New York: Mentor Books, 1975.

———. *The Burden of Proof.* Manila: University of the Philippines Press for the U. P. Jorge B. Vargas Filipiniana Research Center, 1984.

Aguirre, Col. Alexander P. *A People's Revolution of Our Time.* Quezon City: Pan-Service Master Consultants, 1986.

Alexander, Garth. *The Invisible China: The Overseas Chinese and the Politics of Southeast Asia.* New York: The Macmillan Company, 1973.

Alip, Eufronio M. *The Philippine Presidents.* Manila: Alip & Sons, 1958.

Amnesty International. *Report of an Amnesty International Mission to the Republic of the Philippines, 22 November–5 December 1975.* London: AI Publications, 1977.

AMPO Japan-Asia Quarterly Review. *Free Trade Zones and Industrialization of Asia.* Tokyo: Pacific-Asia Resources Center, 1977.

———. "Profile: Sasagawa [sic] Ryoichi—Impresario of the Japanese Right." *AMPO Japan-Asia Quarterly Review* (Winter 1974).

Anderson, Scott, and Anderson, Jon Lee. *Inside the League.* New York: Dodd, Mead, 1986.

Anti-Slavery Society. *The Philippines.* London: Anti-Slavery Society, 1983.

Aquino, Belinda A. "Political Violence in the Philippines, Aftermath of the Aquino Assassination." *Southeast Asian Affairs.* Singapore: Institute of Southeast Asian Studies, 1984.

Arillo, Cecilio T. *Breakaway: The Inside Story of the Four-Day Revolution in the Philippines.* Manila: Kyodo Printing Company, 1986.

Association of Major Religious Superiors in the Philippines. *Political Detainees in the Philippines.* Manila: Association of Major Religious Superiors in the Philippines, 1976.

Bain, David Haward. *Sitting in Darkness.* Boston: Houghton Mifflin, 1984.

Baron, Cynthia S., and Suazo, Melba M. *Nine Letters.* Quezon City: Gerardo P. Baron, 1986.

Behr, Edward. *The Last Emperor.* New York: Bantam Books, 1987.

Bello, Walden. "Edging Toward the Quagmire: The United States and the Philippine Crisis." *World Policy Journal* (Winter 1985–86).

——. "From the Ashes: The Rebirth of the Philippine Revolution." *Third World Quarterly* (January 1986).

——, Kinley, David, and Elinson, Elaine. *Development Debacle: The World Bank in the Philippines.* San Francisco: Institute for Food and Development Policy, 1982.

——, and Rivera, Severina, eds. *The Logistics of Repression.* Washington, D.C.: Friends of the Filipino People, 1977.

Blaker, James Ronald. *The Chinese in the Philippines: A Study of Power and Change.* Ph.D., 1970. Columbus, Ohio: Ohio State University, University Microfilms.

Bonner, Raymond. *Waltzing with a Dictator.* New York: Times Books, 1987.

Boorman, Howard L., ed. *Biographical Dictionary of Republican China.* Vols. 1–5. New York: Columbia University Press, 1967.

Box, Steven. *Power, Crime, and Mystification.* London: Tavistock Publications, 1983.

Bresnan, John. *Crisis in the Philippines.* Princeton, N.J.: Princeton University Press, 1986.

Broyles, J. Allen. *The John Birch Society: Anatomy of a Protest.* Boston: Beacon Press, 1964.

Bunge, F. M., ed. *Philippines: A Country Study.* 3rd edn. Washington, D.C.: Government Printing Office, 1983.

Burrows, William E. *Deep Black: Space Espionage and National Security.* New York: Random House, 1986.

Buss, Claude. "Waking from a Dream." *The Wilson Quarterly,* vol. 10, no. 3 (Summer 1986).

Butwell, Richard. "The Philippines: Changing of the Guard." *Asian Studies* (January 1966).

——. "The Philippines: Prelude to Elections." *Asian Studies* (January 1965).

——. *Southeast Asia Today and Tomorrow.* 4th edn. New York: Frederick A. Praeger, 1985.

Canoy, Reuben R. *The Counterfeit Revolution.* Manila: Philippines Editions, 1981.

Carbonell-Catilo, Ma. Aurora, de Leon, Josie H., and Nicolas, Eleanor E. *Manipulated Elections.* Manila: Privately printed, 1985.

Center for Democracy. *The Presidential Election Process in the Philippines.* Washington, D.C.: Government Printing Office, 1986.

Chu, Wong Kwok. "The Jones Bills 1912–16." *Journal of Southeast Asian Studies* (September 1982).

Corpuz, Onofre Dizon. "Western Colonisation and the Filipino Response." *Journal of Southeast Asian Studies* (March 1962).

Corsino, MacArthur F. "The Philippines in 1980: At the Crossroads." *Southeast Asian Affairs,* 1981.

Costa, H. de la. *Readings in Philippine History.* Manila: Bookmark, Inc., 1965.

Crisostomo, Isabelo T. *The Challenge of Leadership.* Quezon City: J. Kriz Publishing Enterprises, 1969.

———. *Imelda Romualdez Marcos: Heart of the Revolution.* Quezon City: J. Kriz Publishing Enterprises, 1980.

———. *Marcos the Revolutionary.* Quezon City: J. Kriz Publishing Enterprises, 1973.

Crisostomo, Juan. "Marcos and the Philippines." *AMPO Japan-Asia Quarterly Review,* vol. 8, no. 2 (April–September 1976).

Dallin, Alexander. *Black Box: KAL 007 and the Superpowers.* Berkeley: University of California Press, 1985.

Day, Beth. *The Philippines: Shattered Showcase of Democracy in Asia.* New York: M. Evans and Co., 1974.

Deacon, Richard. *Kempei Tai.* New York: Berkley Books, 1983.

Demaris, Ovid. *The Last Mafioso.* New York: Bantam Books, 1981.

Dobrin, Arthur, Dobrin, Lyn, and Liotti, Thomas F. *Convictions: Political Prisoners, Their Stories.* Maryknoll, N.Y.: Orbis Books, 1981.

Dodd, Joseph W. "The Consequences of the Legislature in Developing Societies: The Case of the Philippines." *Asian Profile,* vol. 6, no. 1 (February 1978).

Doherty, John F., S.J. *Cronies and Enemies: The Current Philippine Scene.* Philippine Studies Occasional Papers, No. 5, Center for Asian and Pacific Studies, University of Hawaii, August 1982.

Doronila, Amando. "The Transformation of Patron-Client Relations and Its Political Consequences in Postwar Philippines." *Journal of Southeast Asian Studies* (March 1985).

Dubro, Alec, and Kaplan, David E. "Soft-Core Fascism: The Rehabilitation of Ryoichi Sasakawa." *Village Voice,* Oct. 4, 1983.

Dumaine, Brian. "The $2.2 Billion Nuclear Fiasco." *Fortune,* Sept. 1, 1986.

Emery, Robert F. "The Successful Philippine Decontrol and Devaluation." *Asian Survey* (June 1963).

Evans, Derek. *The Light and the Burning.* Winfield, B.C., Canada: Wood Lake Books, 1982.

Far Eastern Economic Review Ltd. *All-Asia Guide*. Hong Kong, 1982.

Fay, Stephen. *Portrait of an Old Lady: Turmoil at the Bank of England*. Harmondsworth, Middlesex: Penguin Books, 1987.

Feder, Ernest. *Perverse Development*. Quezon City: Foundation for Nationalist Studies, 1983.

Feliciano, Gloria D., and Inban, Crispulo J., Jr. *Philippine Mass Media in Perspective*. Quezon City: Capitol Publishing House, 1967.

Fenton, James. *The Snap Revolution*. Harmondsworth, Middlesex: Penguin Books, 1986.

Fernandez, Emmanuel O. "Relocation—Marcos Style." *AMPO Japan-Asia Quarterly Review*, vol. 8, no. 1 (March 1976).

Fifield, Russell H. "The Challenge to Magsaysay." *Foreign Affairs*, vol. 33, no. 149 (October 1954).

"Filipino Political Prisoners Resist by Hunger Strike." *AMPO Japan-Asia Quarterly Review*, vol. 8, no. 1 (March 1976).

First Quarter Storm of 1970. Manila: Silangan Publishers, 1970.

Foreign Affairs and National Defense Division, Congressional Research Service, Library of Congress. *Insurgency and Counterinsurgency in the Philippines*. Washington, D.C.: Government Printing Office, 1985.

General Accounting Office. *Briefing Report to Senator Edward M. Kennedy: The Philippines, Accountability and Control of U.S. Economic Assistance*. Washington, D.C.: GAO, May 1986.

Gleeck, Lewis E., Jr. *The American Governors-General and High Commissioners in the Philippines*. Quezon City: New Day Publishers, 1986.

Gray, Benjamin A. *Rendezvous with Destiny*. Manila: McCullough Printing Company, 1968.

Green, Timothy. *The New World of Gold: The Inside Story of the Mines, the Markets, the Politics, the Investors*. New York: Walker and Company, 1981.

Gregor, A. James. *Crisis in the Philippines*. Washington, D.C.: Ethics and Public Policy Center, 1984.

————. "Succession in the Philippines: The Prevailing Alternatives and American Interests." *Global Affairs* (July 1986).

————, and Chang, Maria Hsai. *The Iron Triangle: A U.S. Security Policy for Northeast Asia*. Stanford, Calif.: Hoover Institution Press, 1984.

Grossholtz, Jean. "Philippines 1973: Whither Marcos?" *Asian Survey* (January 1974).

Guidebook to Malacanang. Quezon City: Kayumanggi Press, 1986.

Guilatco, Linda. "Japan in the Philippines: 1974–1977." *AMPO Japan-Asian Quarterly Review*, vol. 9, no. 3 (July–November 1977).

Gunther, John. *Inside Asia*. New York: Harper & Brothers, 1942.

Hall, D. G. E. *A History of South-East Asia*. 4th edn. Houndmills, England: Macmillan Education Ltd., 1981.

Harries, Meirion, and Harries, Susie. *Sheathing the Sword: The Demilitarisation of Japan*. London: Hamish Hamilton, 1987.

Hart, Donn V. *Compadrinazgo.* DeKalb, Ill.: Northern Illinois University Press, 1977.

————. "Guerrilla Warfare and the Filipino Resistance on Negros Island in the Bisayas [sic], 1942–1945." *Journal of Southeast Asian History,* vol. 5, no. 1.

Haruhi, Rono. "The Japanese Sex Industry." *AMPO Japan-Asia Quarterly Review,* vol. 18, nos. 2–3.

Hearing Before the Committee on Foreign Relations, U.S. Senate. *The President's Trip to Asia.* Washington, D.C.: Government Printing Office, 1983.

Hearings Before the Subcommittee on Asian and Pacific Affairs of the Committee on Foreign Affairs, House of Representatives. *United States-Philippines Relations and the Base Aid Agreement.* Washington, D.C.: Government Printing Office, 1983.

Hearing and Markup Before the Committee on Foreign Affairs and Its Subcommittee on Asia and Pacific Affairs, House of Representatives. *The Consequences of the Aquino Assassination.* Washington, D.C.: Government Printing Office, 1984.

Hearing Before the Committee on Foreign Relations, U.S. Senate. *Nomination of Hon. Michael H. Armacost.* Washington, D.C.: Government Printing Office, 1984.

Hearing Before the Committee on Foreign Relations, U.S. Senate. *Practice of Torture by Foreign Governments and U.S. Efforts to Oppose Its Use.* Washington, D.C.: Government Printing Office, 1984.

Hearing Before the Subcommittee on East Asian and Pacific Affairs of the Committee on Foreign Relations, U.S. Senate. *Situation in the Philippines and Implications for U.S. Policy.* Washington, D.C.: Government Printing Office, 1984.

Hearings and Markup Before the Subcommittee on Asian and Pacific Affairs of the Committee on Foreign Affairs, House of Representatives. *Foreign Assistance Legislation for Fiscal Year 1985.* Washington, D.C.: Government Printing Office, 1984.

Hearings and Markup Before the Committee on Foreign Affairs and Its Subcommittee on Asian and Pacific Affairs, House of Representatives. *Recent Events in the Philippines Fall 1985.* Washington, D.C.: Government Printing Office, 1985.

Hearings Before the Subcommittees on Asian and Pacific Affairs and on International Economic Policy and Trade of the Committee on Foreign Affairs, House of Representatives. *United States-Japan Trade Relations.* Washington, D.C.: Government Printing Office, 1985.

Hearing and Markup Before the Subcommittee on Asian and Pacific Affairs of the Committee on Foreign Affairs, House of Representatives. *The Philippine Election and the Implications for U.S. Policy.* Washington, D.C.: Government Printing Office, 1986.

Hearing Before the Committee on Foreign Relations, U.S. Senate. *The Philippine Presidential Election.* Washington, D.C.: Government Printing Office, 1986.

Hearings Before the Subcommittee on International Economic Policy, Oceans and Environment of the Committee on Foreign Relations, U.S. Senate. *U.S. Economic Growth and the Third World Debt.* Washington, D.C.: Government Printing Office, 1986.

Heidhues, Mary F. Somers. *Southeast Asia's Chinese Minorities.* Hawthorne, Australia: Longman Australia Pty, 1974.

Higgott, R., and Robison, R., eds. *Southeast Asia. Essays in the Political Economy of Structural Change.* London: Routledge & Kegan Paul, 1985.

Hill, Gerald N., and Hill, Kathleen Thompson. *The Aquino Assassination.* Sonoma, Calif.: Hilltop Publishing Company, 1983.

Hutchinson, Joseph F., Jr. "Quezon's Rule in Philippine Independence," in Norman G. Owen, ed., *Compadre Colonials: Studies on the Philippines Under American Rule.* Michigan Papers on South and Southeast Asia, No. 3, 1971.

International Commission of Jurists. *The Philippines: Human Rights After Martial Law.* Geneva: International Commission of Jurists, 1984.

James, D. Clayton. *The Years of MacArthur: Vol. I, 1880–1941.* Boston: Houghton Mifflin, 1970.

———. *The Years of MacArthur: Vol. II, 1941–1945.* Boston: Houghton Mifflin, 1975.

———. *The Years of MacArthur: Vol. III, 1945–1964.* Boston: Houghton Mifflin, 1985.

Jensen, Irene. *The Chinese in the Philippines During the American Regime: 1898–1946.* San Francisco: R. and E. Research Associates, 1975.

Joaquin, Nick. *The Aquinos of Tarlac.* Metro Manila: Cacho Hermanos, 1983.

———. *Doy Laurel in Profile.* Makati Metro Manila: Lahi, 1985.

———. *Manila: Sin City? and Other Chronicles.* Metro Manila: National Book Store, 1980.

———. *A Question of Heroes.* Metro Manila: Asia Book Corporation of America, 1977.

Jocano, F. Landa. *Myths and Legends of the Early Filipinos.* Quezon City: no publisher, 1971.

Johnson, R. W. *Shootdown: Flight 007 and the American Connection.* New York: Viking Penguin, 1986.

Kann, Peter R. "The Philippines Without Democracy." *Foreign Affairs,* vol. 52 (April 1974).

Kaplan, David, and Dubro, Alec. *Yakuza.* Reading, Mass.: Addison-Wesley, 1986.

Karnow, Stanley. *Vietnam.* New York: Viking Press, 1983.

Kerkvliet, Benedict J. *The Huk Rebellion.* Berkeley: University of California Press, 1977.

Kitazawa, Yoko. "Japan-Indonesia Corruption." *AMPO Japan-Asia Quarterly Review,* vol. 8, no. 1 (March 1976).

Kluge, P. F. "Why They *Love* Us in the Philippines." *Playboy* (September 1986).

Knightly, Phillip. *The First Casualty*. New York: Harcourt Brace Jovanovich, 1975.

Kolko, Gabriel. "The Philippines: Another Vietnam?" *Commonweal*, vol. 97, no. 14 (Jan. 12, 1973).

Krinks, Peter. "Old Wine in a New Bottle: Land Settlement and Agrarian Problems in the Philippines." *Journal of Southeast Asian Studies* (March 1974).

Kroef, Justus M. van der. "Communism and Reform in the Philippines." *Pacific Affairs* (Spring 1976).

KSP editorial team. *In the Face of Adversity*. Rome: KSP Komite ng. Sambayanang Filipino, n.d.

Kwitney, Jonathan. *The Crimes of Patriots*. New York: W. W. Norton, 1987.

———. *Endless Enemies*. New York: Viking Penguin, 1984.

Lacey, Robert. *Ford*. Boston: Little, Brown, 1986.

Lande, Carl H. "Authoritarian Rule in the Philippines: Some Critical Views." *Pacific Affairs* (October 1981).

———. "Parties and Politics in the Philippines." *Asian Studies* (September 1968).

———, and Cigler, Allan J. "Competition and Turnover in Philippine Congressional Elections, 1907–1969." *Asian Studies* (October 1979).

———, and Hooley, Richard. "Aquino Takes Charge." *Foreign Affairs* (July 1986).

Lansdale, Edward Geary. *In the Midst of Wars*. New York: Harper & Row, 1972.

Lawson, Don. *Marcos and the Philippines*. New York: Franklin Watts, 1984.

Lawyers Committee for Human Rights. *"Salvaging" Democracy: Human Rights in the Philippines*. New York: Lawyers Committee for Human Rights, 1985.

Lear, Elmer. *The Japanese Occupation of the Philippines, Leyte, 1941–1945*. Data paper No. 42, Southeast Asia Program, Department of Far Eastern Studies, Cornell University, Ithaca, New York, June 1961.

Leary, Virginia. *The Philippines: Human Rights After Martial Law*. Mansfield: Philippines Research Center, 1984.

Lethbridge, H. J. *Hard Graft in Hong Kong*. Hong Kong: Oxford University Press, 1985.

Lind, John E. *Philippine Debt to Foreign Banks*. San Francisco: California/Nevada Interfaith Committee on Corporate Responsibility, 1984.

Lomax, David. *The Money Makers*. London: BBC Publications, 1986.

Lopez-Gonzaga, Violeta B. *Crisis and Poverty in Sugarlandia: The Case of Bacolod*. Bacolod: La Salle Social Research Center, 1985.

Lupdag, Anselmo D. *In Search of Filipino Leadership*. Quezon City: New Day Publishers, 1984.

Maas, Peter. *Man Hunt*. London: Grafton Books, 1987.

Macapagal, Diosdado. *Democracy in the Philippines*. Downsview, Ontario: Ruben J. Cusipag, 1976.

Machado, K. G. "Changing Aspects of Factionalism in Philippine Local Politics." *Asian Survey* (December 1971).
———. "From Traditional Faction to Machine: Changing Patterns of Political Leadership and Organization in the Rural Philippines." *Journal of Asian Studies*, vol. 33, no. 4 (August 1974).
Mamot, Patricio R. *People Power*. Quezon City: New Day Publishers, 1986.
Manchester, William. *American Caesar*. New York: Dell, 1978.
Manglapus, Raul S. *A Pen for Democracy*. Washington, D.C.: Movement for a Free Philippines, 1983.
Manila, Quijano de. *The Quartet of the Tiger Moon*. Manila: Book Stop, Inc., 1986.
———. *Reportage on the Marcoses*. Rizal: National Book Store, 1979.
Manning, Robert A. "The Philippines in Crisis." *Foreign Affairs*, vol. 63, no. 2 (Winter 1984–85).
Maramag, Ileana. *Imelda Romualdez Marcos*. Manila: Office of Media Affairs, 1982.
———. *The Second Marcos Inaugural*. Tokyo: Toppan Printing Company, 1970.
Maramba, Asuncion David. *Ninoy Aquino: The Man and the Legend*. Metro Manila: Cacho Hermanos, 1984.
Marchetti, Victor, and Marks, John D. *The CIA and the Cult of Intelligence*. New York: Dell, 1984.
Marcos, Ferdinand E. *Today's Revolution: Democracy*. Manila: no publisher, 1971.
———. *Notes on the New Society of the Philippines*. Manila: no publisher, 1973.
———. *The Democratic Revolution in the Philippines*. No city, no publisher, 1977.
———. *Human Rights*. Quezon City: University of the Philippines, 1977.
———. *An Introduction to the Politics of Transition*. Manila: no publisher, 1978.
———. *Progress and Martial Law*. Manila: no publisher, 1981.
———. *The New Philippine Republic*. Manila: no publisher, 1982.
———. *The Filipino Ideology*. Manila: no publisher, 1983.
———. *The Third World in an Age of Crisis*. Manila. No publisher.
Marcos, Mrs. Imelda Romualdez. *Golden Quotations of Our First Lady*. Caloocan City: Philippine Graphic Arts, 1978.
The Marcos Administration. Manila: National Media Production Center, 1981.
Marley, Ross. "Is Ferdinand Marcos a Political Genius?" *Filipinas*, no. 5 (Fall 1985).
Mauricio, Luis R. *Renato Constantino and the Marcos Watch*. Quezon City: Karrel, Inc., 1972.
May, R. J., and Nemenzo, Francisco, eds. *The Philippines After Marcos*. London: Croom Helm, 1985.
McBeath, Gerald Alan. *Political Integration of the Philippine Chinese*. Ph.D., 1970. Berkeley: University of California, University Microfilms.

——. *Political Integration of the Philippine Chinese.* Berkeley: Center for South and Southeast Asia Studies, University of California, Research Monograph No. 8, February 1973.

McClintock, David. *Indecent Exposure.* New York: Dell, 1982.

McCoy, Alfred W. *Narcotics and Organized Crime in Australia.* Artarmon, Australia: Harper & Row, 1980.

——. *The Politics of Heroin in Southeast Asia.* New York: Harper & Row, 1972.

——. *Priests on Trial.* Victoria: Penguin Books, 1984.

——. *Southeast Asia Under Japanese Occupation.* New Haven: Yale University Southeast Asia Studies, 1980.

——, and Jesus, Ed C. de, eds. *Philippine Social History.* Manila: Ateneo de Manila University Press, 1982.

McHale, Thomas R. "American Colonial Policy Towards the Philippines." *Journal of Southeast Asian Studies* (March 1962).

Meadows, Martin. "Challenge to the 'New Era' in Philippine Politics." *Pacific Affairs* (Fall 1964).

——. "Colonialism, Social Structure and Nationalism: The Philippine Case." *Pacific Affairs* (Fall 1971).

——. "Philippine Political Parties and the 1961 Elections." *Pacific Affairs* (Fall 1962).

——. "Recent Developments in Philippine-American Relations: A Case Study in Emergent Nationalism." *Asian Survey* (June 1965).

Mella, Cesar T. *Marcos, the War Years.* Quezon City: President's Center for Special Studies, 1981.

——, and Vinluan, Joaquin Sison. *The President's Mother.* Manila: United Publishing Company, 1984.

Mercado, Monina Allearey, ed. *People Power.* Manila: The James B. Reuter, S.J., Foundation, 1986.

Mijares, Primitivo. *The Conjugal Dictatorship of Ferdinand and Imelda Marcos.* San Francisco: Union Square Publications, 1986.

Miller, Stuart Creighton. *Benevolent Assimilation.* New Haven: Yale University Press, 1982.

——. "Compadre Colonialism." *The Wilson Quarterly,* vol. 10, no. 3 (Summer 1986).

Milne, R. S. "The New Administration and the New Economic Program in the Philippines." *Asian Survey* (September 1963).

——. "Political Finance in Southeast Asia with Particular Reference to the Philippines and Malaysia." *Pacific Affairs* (Winter 1968–69).

Mr. & Mrs. Publishing Co. *Reports of the Fact-finding Board on the Assassination of Senator Benigno S. Aquino Jr.* Manila: Mr. & Mrs. Publishing Company, 1984.

Muego, Benjamin Navarro. "The Executive Committee in the Philippines." *Asian Survey* (November 1983).

———. "The New Society Five Years Later: The State of Oppression." *Southeast Asian Affairs*, 1978.

———. *The "New Society" of the Philippines: A Case Study of a Developmental Movement Regime*. Ph.D., 1976. Ann Arbor, Mich.: Southern Illinois University, University Microfilms.

———. "The Philippines: From Martial Law to 'Crisis Government.'" *Southeast Asian Affairs*, 1979.

The National Security Archives. *The Chronology: The Documented Day-by-Day Account of the Secret Military Assistance to Iran and the Contras.* New York: Warner Books, 1987.

Neher, Clark. "The Philippines 1979: Cracks in the Fortress." *Asian Survey* (February 1980).

Nelson, Raymond. *The Philippines.* New York: Walker and Company, 1968.

Newton, Agnes Keith. *Bare Feet in the Palace.* Boston: Little, Brown, 1955.

Nituda, Victor G. *The Young Marcos.* Manila: Foresight International, 1979.

Nollendo, Jose N. *The Life of Ferdinand Edralin Marcos: An Analysis.* Quezon City: Filipino Publishing Company, 1966.

Ocampo, Estaban A. de. "Dr. Jose Rizal, Father of Filipino Nationalism." *Journal of Southeast Asian Studies* (March 1962).

Oglesby, Carl, and Shaull, Richard. *Containment and Change.* New York: The Macmillan Company, 1967.

Omohundro, John T. *Chinese Merchant Families in Iloilo.* Manila: Ateneo de Manila University Press, 1981.

Ongpauco, Lt. Col. Fidel L. *They Refused to Die.* Quebec: Levesque Publications, 1982.

Overholt, William H. "Land Reform in the Philippines." *Asian Studies* (May 1976).

Pedrosa, Carmen Navarro. *Imelda Marcos.* New York: St. Martin's Press, 1987.

———. *The Untold Story of Imelda Marcos.* Rizal: Tandem Publishing Company, 1969.

Peralta, Laverne Y. *Who Is Who: Philippine Guerrilla Movement 1942–1945.* No city, no publisher, 1972.

Permanent Peoples' Tribunal Session on the Philippines. *Philippines Repression and Resistance.* London: KSP Komite ng. Sambayanang, 1980.

Peters, Edward. *Torture.* New York: Basil Blackwell, 1985.

Peters, Jens. *The Philippines: A Travel Survival Kit.* Victoria: Lonely Planet Publications, 1981.

Petillo, Carol M. *Douglas MacArthur: The Philippine Years.* Bloomington, Ind.: Indiana University Press, 1981.

Philippines: The Silenced Democracy. Maryknoll, N.Y.: Orbis Books, 1976.

Plate, Thomas, and Darvi, Andrea. *Secret Police.* London: Sphere Books, 1981.

Polotan, Kerima. *Imelda Romualdez Marcos.* Rizal: no publisher, 1970.

Pomeroy, William J. *An American-Made Tragedy.* New York: International Publishers, 1974.

Pool, Fred, and Vanzi, Max. *Revolution in the Philippines.* New York: McGraw-Hill, 1984.

Powers, Thomas. *The Man Who Kept the Secrets: Richard Helms and the CIA.* New York: Pocket Books, 1979.

Prados, John. *Presidents' Secret Wars: CIA and Pentagon Covert Operations Since World War II.* New York: William Morrow, 1986.

Project 28 Days. *Bayan Ko.* Hong Kong: Toppan Printing Company, 1986.

Psinakis, Steve. *Two Terrorists Meet.* San Francisco: Alchemy Books, 1981.

Quirino, Carlos. *Chick Parsons.* Quezon City: New Day Publishers, 1984.

———. *Eminent Filipinos.* Manila: Philippine Textbook Publishers, 1965.

Rajaretnam, M. "The Philippines in 1979: Towards Political Change." *Southeast Asian Affairs,* 1980.

———. "The Philippines: A Survey for 1976." *Southeast Asian Affairs,* 1977.

———. "The Philippines: A Question of Earnest Intentions." *Southeast Asian Affairs,* 1976.

Report of the Readiness Subcommittee of the Committee on Armed Services, House of Representatives. Ninety-ninth Congress, Second Session. *Investigation of the Costs Involved in Moving Former President Marcos and His Party from Manila to Hawaii.* Washington, D.C.: Government Printing Office, 1986.

Reynolds, Harriet R. *Continuity and Change in the Chinese Family in the Ilocos Provinces, Philippines.* Ph.D., 1964. The Hartford Seminary Foundation, University Microfilms.

Reynolds, Ira. *Chinese Acculturation in Ilocos: Economic Political, Religions.* Ph.D., 1964. The Hartford Seminary Foundation, University Microfilms.

Richter, Linda Kay. *Land Reform and Tourism Development: Policy-Making in Martial Law Philippines.* Ph.D., 1980. University of Kansas, University Microfilms.

Rigos, Cirilo A. "The Posture of the Church in the Philippines Under Martial Law." *Southeast Asian Affairs,* 1975.

Rizal, Jose. *El Filibusterismo.* Rizal: National Book Store, 1971.

———. *Noli me Tangere.* London: Longman Group, 1961.

Roberts, John G. "The Lockheed–Japan–Watergate Connection." *AMPO Japan-Asia Quarterly Review,* vol. 8, no. 1 (March 1976).

Rodriguez, Filemon C. *The Marcos Regime: The Rape of the Nation.* New York: Vantage Press, 1985.

Rosenberg, David A., ed. *Marcos and Martial Law in the Philippines.* Ithaca, N.Y.: Cornell University Press, 1979.

Rotea, Hermie. *Marcos' Lovey Dovie.* Los Angeles: Liberty Publishing, 1983.

Rowan, Roy. "The High-Flying First Lady of the Philippines." *Fortune,* July 2, 1979.

Sampson, Anthony. *The Arms Bazaar.* London: Hodder & Stoughton, 1977.

———. *Black and Gold.* London: Hodder & Stoughton, 1987.

Santiago, Miriam Defensor. *The 1972 Constitution.* Quezon City: New Day Publishers, 1973.

Sayer, Tan, and Botting, Douglas. *Nazi Gold.* London: Grafton Books, 1985.

Schirmer, Daniel B. "Those Philippine Bases." *Monthly Review* (March 1986).

Schott, Joseph L. *The Ordeal of Samar.* Indianapolis: Howard W. Sams, 1964.

Shalom, Stephen R. "Counter-Insurgency in the Philippines." *Journal of Contemporary Asia.*

Shaplen, Robert. "Letters from Manila." *The New Yorker Magazine.* Jan. 15, 1966, vol. 41; Dec. 20, 1969, vol. 45; March 26, 1979, vol. 55; and May 3, 1976, vol. 52, Feb. 4, 1985, vol. 60.

———. "A Reporter at Large: From Marcos to Aquino." *The New Yorker Magazine,* Aug. 15, 1986.

Silliman, G. Sidney. "The Philippines in 1983: Authoritarianism Beleaguered." *Asian Survey* (February 1984).

Simoniya, N. A. *Overseas Chinese in Southeast Asia—A Russian Study.* Data Paper No. 45, Southeast Asia Program, Department of Far Eastern Studies, Cornell University, Ithaca, New York, December 1961.

Smith, Joseph B. *Portrait of a Cold Warrior.* New York: Ballantine Books, 1976.

Sodusta, Jesucita L. G. "Land Reform in the Philippines Past and Present." *Southeast Asian Affairs,* 1981.

———, and Palongpalong, Artemio. "The Philippines in 1981: Normalization and Instability." *Southeast Asian Affairs,* 1982.

Some Are Smarter Than Others. Manila: Privately printed, 1979.

Spector, Ronald H. *Eagle Against the Sun.* London: Penguin Books, 1987.

Spence, Hartzell. *For Every Tear a Victory.* New York: McGraw-Hill, 1964.

Starner, Frances. "Philippine Economic Development and the Two Party System." *Asian Survey* (July 1962).

———. "The Philippines: Politics of the 'New Era.'" *Asian Studies* (January 1963).

Stauffer, Robert B. "The Manila-Washington Connection." *Philippine Social Sciences & Humanities Review,* vol. 47, nos. 1–4 (January–December 1983).

———. *The Marcos Regime: Failure of Transnational Developmentalism and Hegemony-Building from Above and Outside.* Honolulu: University of Hawaii, August, 1985.

———. "Philippine Authoritarianism: Framework for Peripheral 'Development.'" *Pacific Affairs* (Fall 1977).

Steinberg, David Joel. "An Ambiguous Legacy: Years at War in the Philippines." *Pacific Affairs* (Summer 1972).

———. *Philippine Collaboration in World War II.* Manila: Solidaridad Publishing House in cooperation with Michigan University Press, 1967.

———. *The Philippines: A Singular and a Plural Place.* Boulder, Colo.: Westview Press, 1982.

———, ed. *In Search of Southeast Asia.* Honolulu: University of Hawaii Press, 1985.

Sturtevant, David R. "Sakdalism and Philippine Radicalism." *The Journal of Asian Studies* (February 1962).

Suhrke, Astri. "Political Rituals in Developing Nations: The Case of the Philippines." *Journal of Southeast Asian Studies* (September 1971).

Task Force Detainees Philippines. *Pumipiglas.* Manila: Association of Major Religious Superiors in the Philippines, 1980.

Tatad, Francisco S. *Marcos of the Philippines.* Manila: Department of Public Information, 1975.

Tesoro, Benjamin D. *The Rise and Fall of the Marcos Mafia.* Manila: Maprecious Enterprises Philippines, 1986.

Third World Studies Center. "The Control of the Philippine Banaba [sic] Industry." *AMPO Japan-Asia Quarterly Review,* vol. 13, no. 3 (1981).

Thompson, Jr., James C., Stanley, Peter W., and Perry, John Curtis. *Sentimental Imperialists.* New York: Harper & Row, 1981.

Tilman, Robert O. "The Philippines in 1970: A Difficult Decade Begins." *Asian Survey* (February 1971).

Toland, John. *The Rising Sun.* New York: Random House, 1971.

The Tower Commission Report. New York: Bantam Books and Time Books, 1987.

Trinidad, Corky. *Marcos: The Rise and Fall of a Regime. A Cartoon Biography.* Honolulu: Arthouse Books, 1986.

Valeriano, Napoleon D., and Bohannan, Charles T. R. *Counter-Guerrilla Operations: The Philippine Experience.* New York: Frederick A. Praeger, 1962.

Vega, Guillermo C. de. *An Epic.* Republic of the Philippines: no publisher, 1974.

Vellut, J. L. "Foreign Relations of the Second Republic of the Philippines, 1943–1945." *Journal of Southeast Asian History,* vol. 5, no. 1 (March 1964).

———. "Japanese Reparations to the Philippines." *Asian Studies* (October 1963).

Vicker, Ray. *The Realms of Gold.* New York: Charles Scribner's Sons, 1975.

Weatherbee, Donald E., ed. *Southeast Asia Divided: The ASEAN-Indochina Crisis.* Boulder, Colo.: Westview Press, 1985.

Wechsberg, Joseph. *The Merchant Bankers.* New York: Pocket Books, 1966.

Weightman, George H. "The Philippine-Chinese Image of the Filipino." *Pacific Affairs* (Fall–Winter 1967–68).

West, Nigel. *M.I.5. 1945–72.* London: Hodder & Stoughton, 1983.

Wickberg, Edgar. "The Chinese Mestizo in Philippine History." *Journal of Southeast Asian History,* vol. 5, no. 1 (March 1964).

———. "Early Chinese Economic Influence in the Philippines." *Pacific Affairs* (Fall 1962).

Wideman, Bernard. "The Philippines: Five Years of Martial Law." *AMPO Japan-Asia Quarterly Review,* vol. 9, no. 3 (July–November 1977).

Willoughby, Charles A., comp. *The Guerrilla Resistance Movement in the Philippines: 1941–1945.* New York: Vantage Press, 1972.

Woodward, Bob. *Veil: The Secret Wars of the CIA, 1981–1987.* New York: Simon & Schuster, 1987.

Wurfel, David. "The Aquino Legacy and the Emerging Succession Struggle in the Philippines, 1984." *Southeast Asian Affairs,* 1985.

——. "Elites of Wealth and Elites of Power, the Changing Dynamic." *Southeast Asian Affairs,* 1979.

——. "Martial Law in the Philippines: The Methods of Regime Survival." *Pacific Affairs* (Spring 1977).

Wyatt, David K., and Woodside, Alexander. *Moral Order and the Question of Change.* New Haven: Yale University Southeast Asia Studies, 1982.

Yamakawa, Akio. "The Lockheed Scandal: What Do the People Make of It?" *AMPO Japan-Asia Quarterly Review,* vol. 8, no. 2 (April–September 1976).

Yengoyan, Aram A., and Makil, Perla. *Philippine Society and the Individual.* Mich.: Center for South and Southeast Asian Studies, 1984.

Youngblood, Robert L. "Church Opposition of Martial Law in the Philippines." *Asian Survey* (May 1978).

——. "The Philippines in 1982: Marcos Gets Tough with Domestic Critics." *Asian Survey* (February 1983).

Zich, Arthur. "The Marcos Era." *The Wilson Quarterly,* vol. 10, no. 3 (Summer 1986).

Zwick, Jim. *Militarism: Repression in the Philippines.* Montreal: Center for Developing Area Studies, McGill University, 1982.

INDEX

471